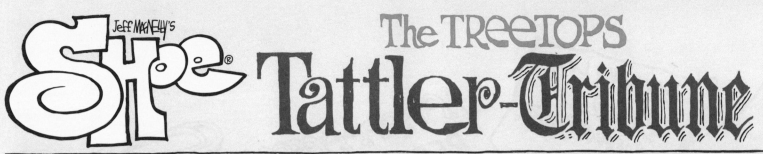

Jeff MacNelly's Shoe®

The Treetops Tattler-Tribune

Foreword by DAVE BARRY
Backward by MIKE PETERS

THE FIRST 27 YEARS! - EDITED BY CHRIS CASSATT & SUSIE MACNELLY

WORLD ENDS AT 10, DETAILS AT 11

PRESS
HOMELAND INSECURITY

HOMELAND INSECURITY DIRECTOR SHOCKS THE WORLD WITH ANNOUNCEMENT

(Treetops, VA) At a press conference earlier today Senator Batson D. Belfry, Director of Homeland Insecurity, a little-known agency buried deep in the bowels of the capitol, made a shocking announcement declaring the end of the world as we know it. A handful of media personalities were on hand and gawked in disbelief but were comforted by the fact that Senator Belfry has a long track record of misrepresenting the truth. Although Belfry failed to supply any facts to support his outrageous claim, members of several cable news networks didn't hesitate to broadcast his speech live. Panic spread quickly throughout Washington and the nation. The stock market crashed, riots broke out in all major cities, and the world as we know it ended at 10 PM. (Details at 11)

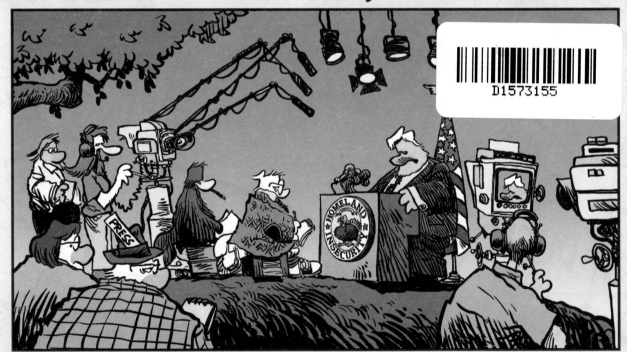

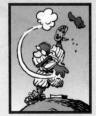

YOUTH PITCHES YES-HITTER

(AP) 12-year-old slowballing right-hander Skyler Fishhawk stunned the preadolescent baseball world yesterday when he hurled the first recorded yes-hitter in history. A yes-hitter, as everyone knows is (Please see Page 34)

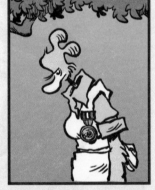

MEDAL AWARDED TO DINER OWNER

Roz, owner of Roz's Diner in Treetops, East Virginia, was awarded a medal for "bravery under grease fire" during a brief ceremony at the firehouse. Roz, whose quick thinking saved the lives of all her patrons, is also credited with rescuing twenty-three pounds of fried onion rings, a toy poodle named Bubba, and a half-eaten bologna sandwich. (Related story on page 97)

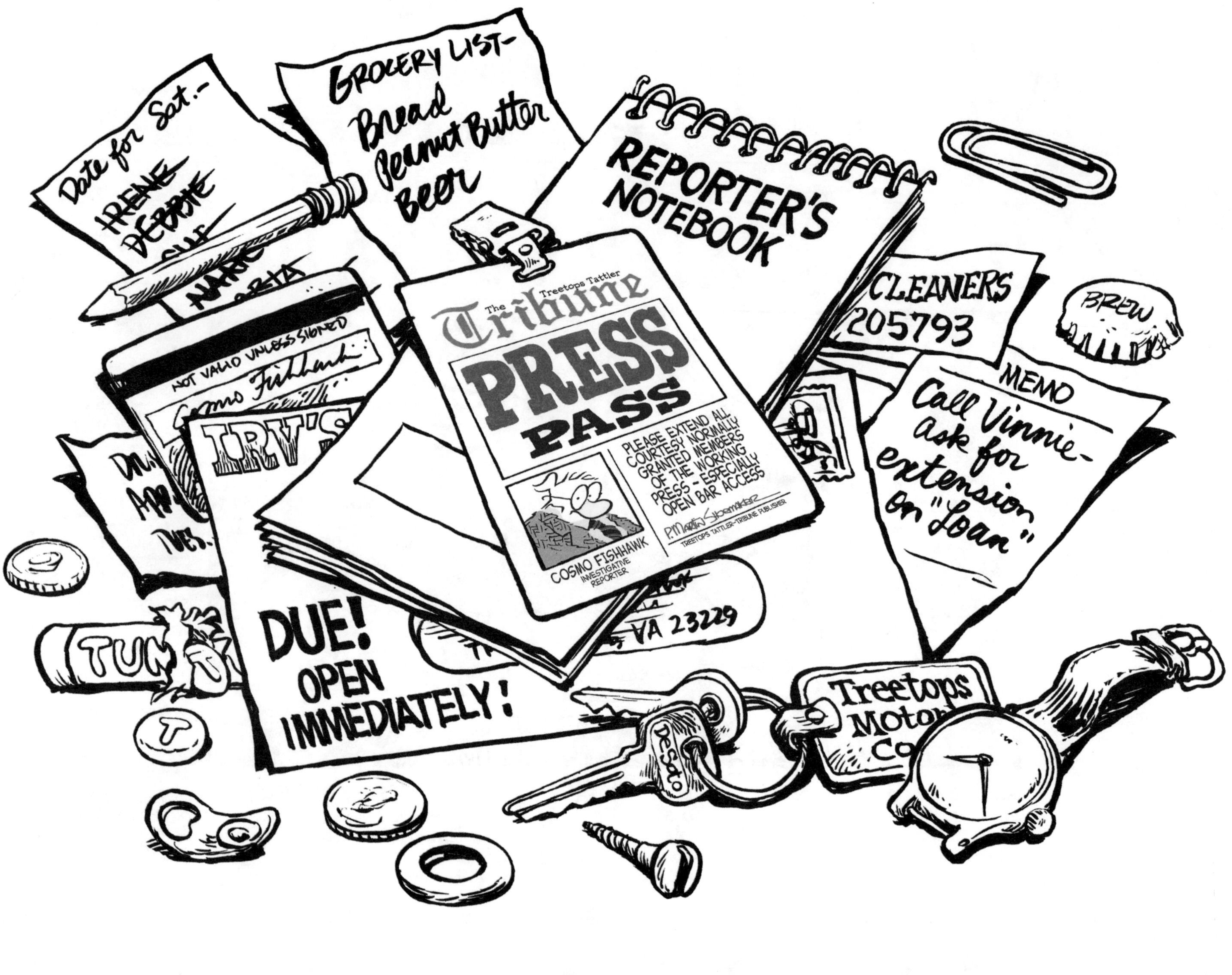

Date for Sat.-
IRENE
DEBBIE
GROCERY LIST-
Bread
Peanut Butter
Beer
REPORTER'S NOTEBOOK
CLEANERS
205793
BREW
NOT VALID UNLESS SIGNED
Cosmo Fishhawk
IRV'S
The Treetops Tattler Tribune
PRESS PASS
PLEASE EXTEND ALL COURTESY NORMALLY GRANTED MEMBERS OF THE WORKING PRESS - ESPECIALLY OPEN BAR ACCESS
TREETOPS TATTLER-TRIBUNE PUBLISHER
COSMO FISHHAWK
INVESTIGATIVE REPORTER
MEMO
Call Vinnie-
ask for
extension
on "Loan"
VA 23229
DUE!
OPEN
IMMEDIATELY!
TUN
DeSoto
Treetops

JEFF MACNELLY
OUTSTANDING CARTOONIST OF THE YEAR
1978
PRESENTED BY
NATIONAL CARTOONISTS SOCIETY

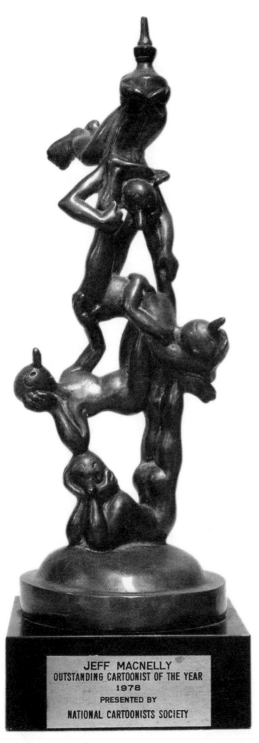

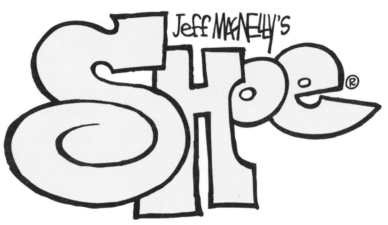

27 Years of

Jeff MacNelly's Shoe®

Edited by
Chris Cassatt
and Susie MacNelly

JEFF MacNELLY
OUTSTANDING CARTOONIST OF THE YEAR
1979
PRESENTED BY
THE NATIONAL CARTOONISTS SOCIETY

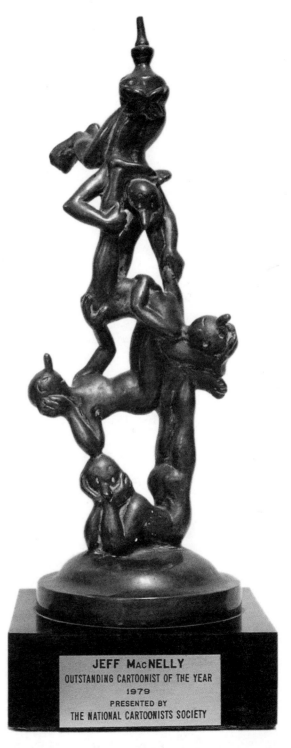

The photos sprinkled through this book, in no particular order, are the contents of a large drawer in Jeff's studio.

Many thanks to everyone who helped fill that drawer over the years, especially Rita MacNelly, David Burnett, and David Kennerly.

With Jeff's *Shoe* team in place he finally had the time to paint and sculpt. Jeff's genius encompassed multiple mediums—oils, acrylics, sculpture, and fine art reproductions. Visit Jeff's fine art Web site at Jeff-MacNelly.com and the Gallery on Greene in Key West, Florida. For the official *Shoe* Web site go to MacNelly.com.

Shoe is syndicated internationally by Tribune Media Services, Inc.

04 05 06 07 08 DUB 10 9 8 7 6 5 4 3 2 1

ISBN: 0-7407-4666-9

Library of Congress Control Number: 2004103564

ATTENTION: SCHOOLS AND BUSINESSES

Andrews McMeel books are available at quantity discounts with bulk purchase for educational, business, or sales promotional use. For information, please write to: Special Sales Department, Andrews McMeel Publishing, 4520 Main Street, Kansas City, Missouri 64111.

Dedicated to the MacNelly boys: Danny, Matt, Jeff, and Jake

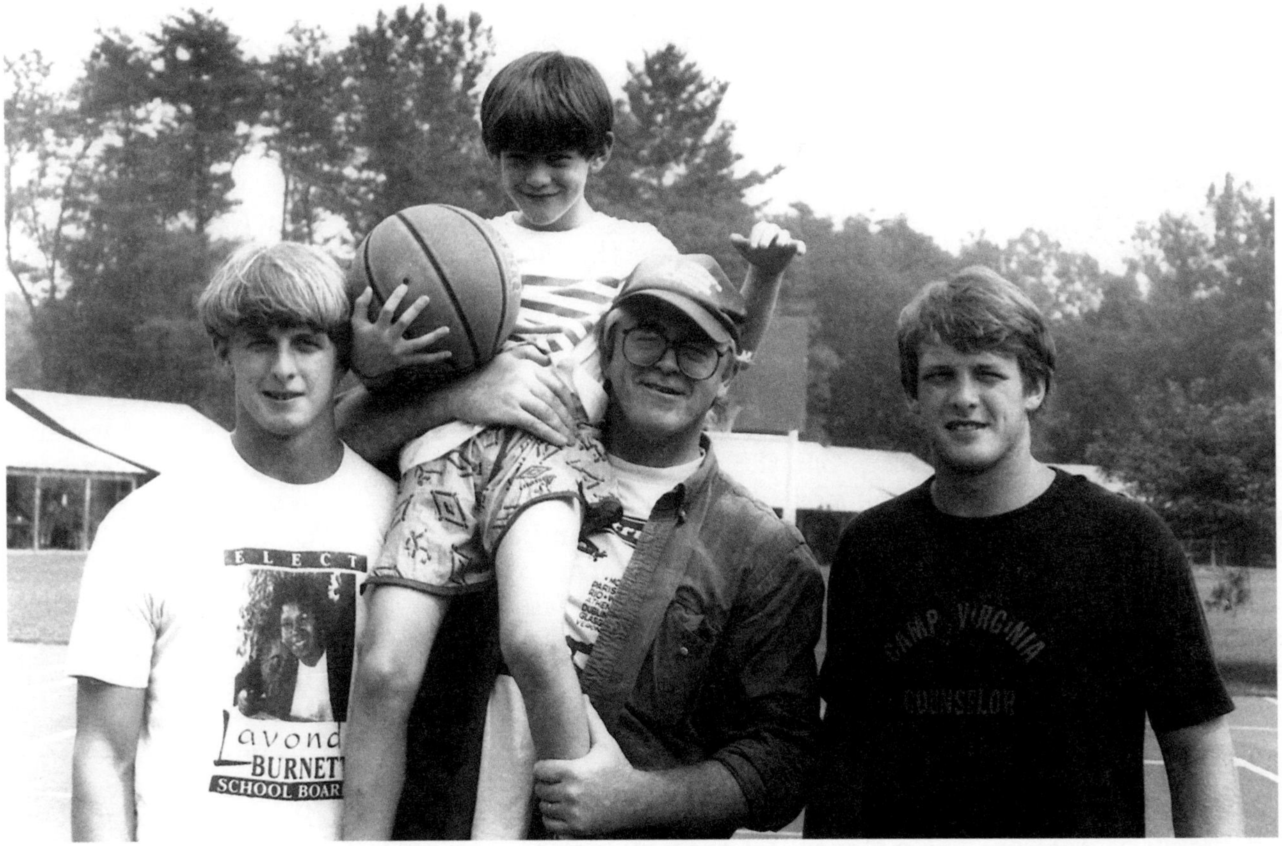
E L E C T
Lavond
BURNETT
SCHOOL BOAR
CAMP VIRGINIA
COUNSELOR

Foreword by Dave Barry

Jeff MacNelly's funeral was the funniest funeral I ever attended. And I've attended some funny funerals, including one that culminated in the mourners setting off fireworks.

But Jeff's was the funniest. The church was packed to overflowing, and the service consisted mainly of Jeff's pals getting up and telling stories about him. And even though we were devastated and weepy, the more Jeff stories we heard, the more that church shook with laughter.

That tells you two of the most important things to know about Jeff MacNelly

— A lot of people loved him.

— He was funny as hell.

He was even funny about his own demise. When I found out he was sick, I called him, and he simply would not allow us to have a depressing conversation. I can still hear his voice, booming from the phone: People keep telling me, Jeff, if you have to get cancer, lymphoma is the best kind to get, he said. So really, I should feel great!

Jeff could see the humor in anything, which is one reason why he was a wonderful cartoonist. Another one is that he was a superb artist; he could easily have made a living as a serious painter or sculptor.

But the characteristic that I think most distinguished him was that, despite his vast talent, and all the success and honors it brought him, he was a regular guy. He won three Pulitzer Prizes — think about that: three Pulitzer Prizes — and he'd have been a welcome guest at any power salon in Washington.

But he wasn't interested in the pursuit of status, or any other activity that entailed the wearing of a suit. He was far happier living on a farm with some dogs and various old vehicles in various stages of operability. His choice of companions was based not on who was important, but who was fun to hang out with, and as a result he had an astonishing range of friends, from mechanics to moguls. He treated them all the same. He was a regular guy, who happened to be a genius.

Those two aspects of Jeff — the regular guy, and the genius — found a perfect partnership in *Shoe*. It's a comic strip about regular people — Okay, regular birds — who act out, and comment on, the pretensions, ironies, foibles, weirdnesses, and lunacies of the world, as perceived by the brilliant MacNelly mind.

Some years ago, Jeff and his wife, Susie, were staying at my house in Miami. Jeff had some drawing to do — he always had some drawing to do — and he was working at the kitchen table. As it happened, he was drawing a *Shoe* strip, and I noticed that, as he worked, he grinned. He was a great grinner: He had a jaw the size of a lawn tractor.

Anyway, that's how I remember him: drawing and grinning, creating the world of *Shoe*. Jeff is gone, but that world is still here, captured in his pen strokes, in the book you're holding.

Read it, and grin.

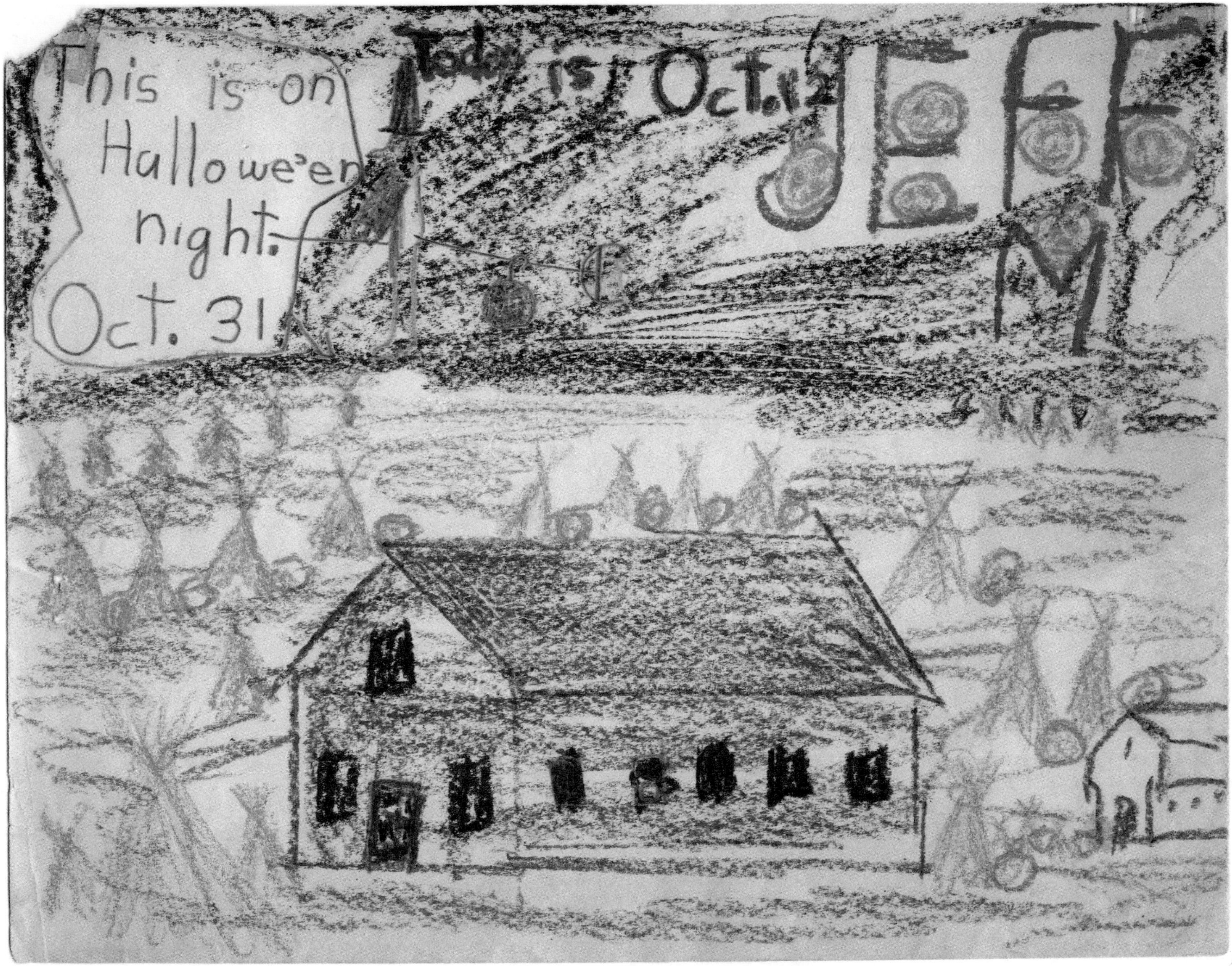
This is on Hallowe'en night. Oct. 31
Today is Oct. 12
JEFF M

Jeff's first cartoon, age four

PHILLIPS ACADEMY
Counselor's Report

Name ___Jeffrey K. MacNelly___ Class __1965__ Date __February 23, 1964__

Because of Jeff's mid-term failure in English, his poor grade in mathematics, his at best questionable effort in both courses, and the clear evidence about the dormitory of his lack of concern for his academic situation, I have felt is advisable to request of the faculty that Jeff be placed on the No Excuse list. This will work some hardship on Jeff's social life for the remainder of the term, but it is hoped that it will bring his grades up enough so that the danger of failure and more serious restriction becomes less imminent. Jeff's English teacher, Mr. Fersch, has summed it up well. "Jeff can do the work, but he has not been applying himself. He must begin working or he will fail."

Actual notes from several of Jeff's teachers . . . As Dave Barry would say, "We're not making this up!"

In the dormitory Jeff, though not a leader in dormitory hacks, is too easily led into trouble. He has a tendency when a guest in our apartment to make others, except his circle of admirers, feel uncomfortable because of his frequent noisy and banal asides on the current conversation. His politeness often seems to be an unwelcome duty and to lack sincerity.

Jeff's ability and energy put forth for the school in the area of art are highly praiseworthy. The fine prom decorations are a tribute to his talent. Equally so was the smooth and efficient way in which he got the job done. It is hoped that Jeff will with a little maturity be able to bring other areas of his life better into focus and achieve for himself a more well-rounded attitude.

The Very First Shoe

RRING!
TRASH
HELLO. THIS IS P. MARTIN SHOEMAKER SPEAKING...
MACNELLY
WHILE I AM OUT OF THE OFFICE MY CALLS ARE BEING HANDLED BY AN AUTOMATIC ANSWERING DEVICE. IF YOU WANT TO LEAVE A MESSAGE, START SPEAKING AT THE SOUND OF THE CLICK.
CLICK.

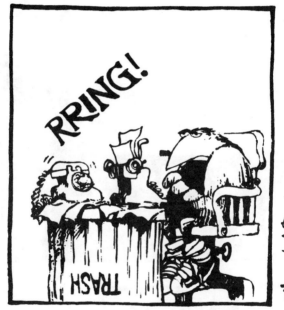

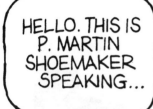

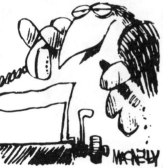

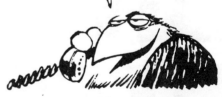

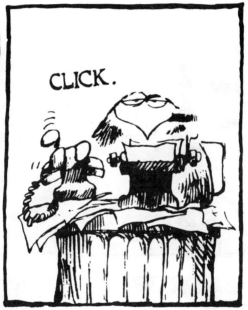

September 13, 1977

The First Sunday

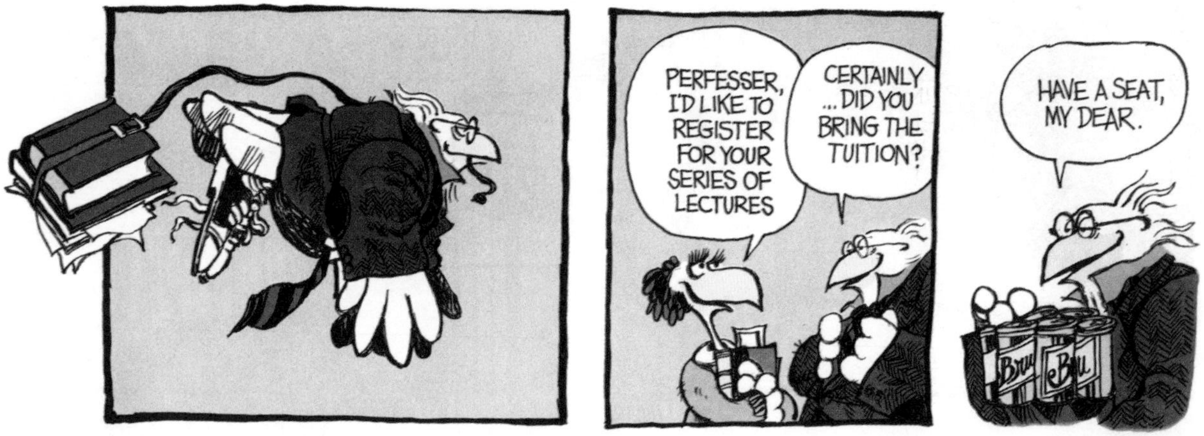
PERFESSER, I'D LIKE TO REGISTER FOR YOUR SERIES OF LECTURES
CERTAINLY ...DID YOU BRING THE TUITION?
HAVE A SEAT, MY DEAR.

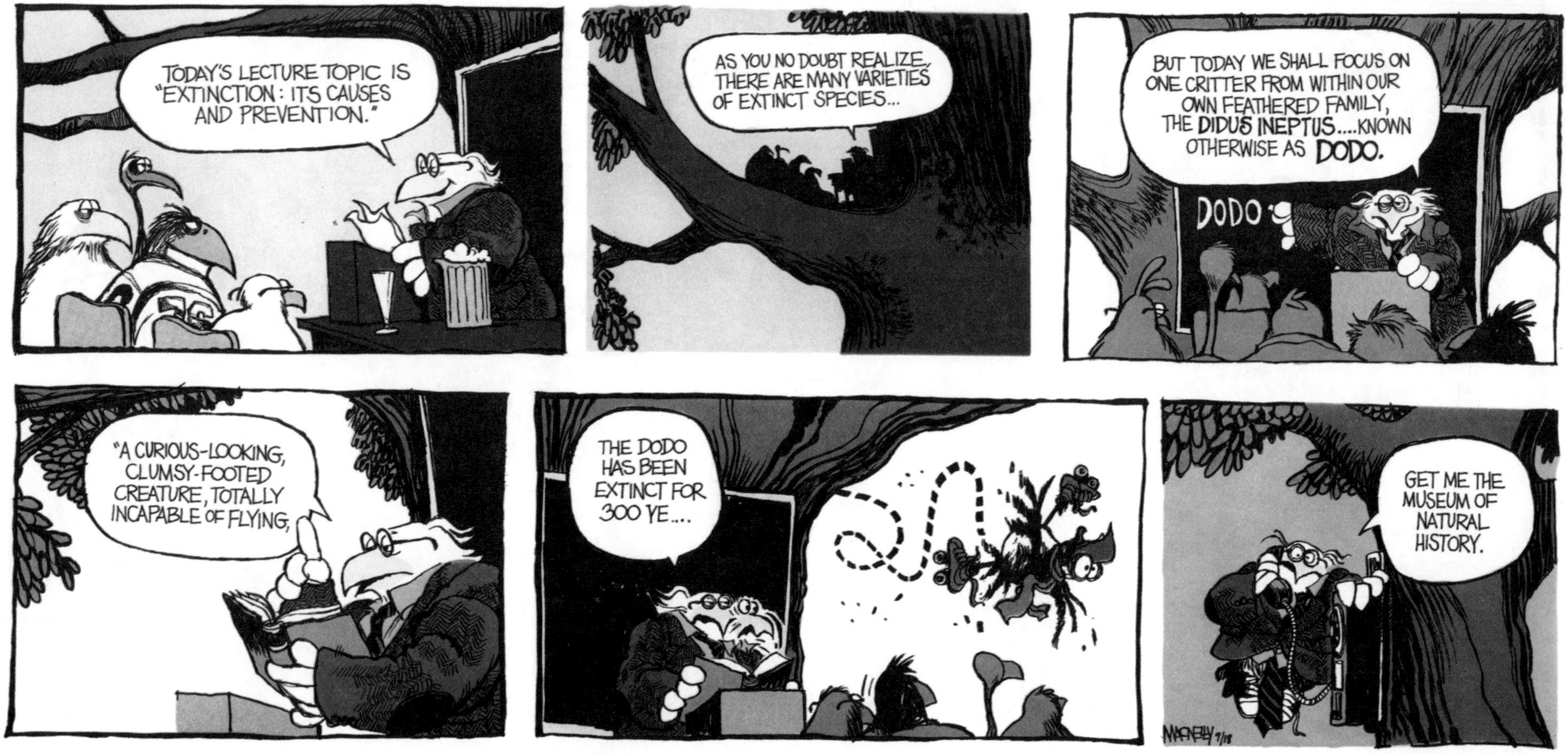
TODAY'S LECTURE TOPIC IS "EXTINCTION: ITS CAUSES AND PREVENTION."
AS YOU NO DOUBT REALIZE, THERE ARE MANY VARIETIES OF EXTINCT SPECIES...
BUT TODAY WE SHALL FOCUS ON ONE CRITTER FROM WITHIN OUR OWN FEATHERED FAMILY, THE DIDUS INEPTUS....KNOWN OTHERWISE AS DODO.
DODO:
"A CURIOUS-LOOKING, CLUMSY-FOOTED CREATURE, TOTALLY INCAPABLE OF FLYING,
THE DODO HAS BEEN EXTINCT FOR 300 YE....
GET ME THE MUSEUM OF NATURAL HISTORY.

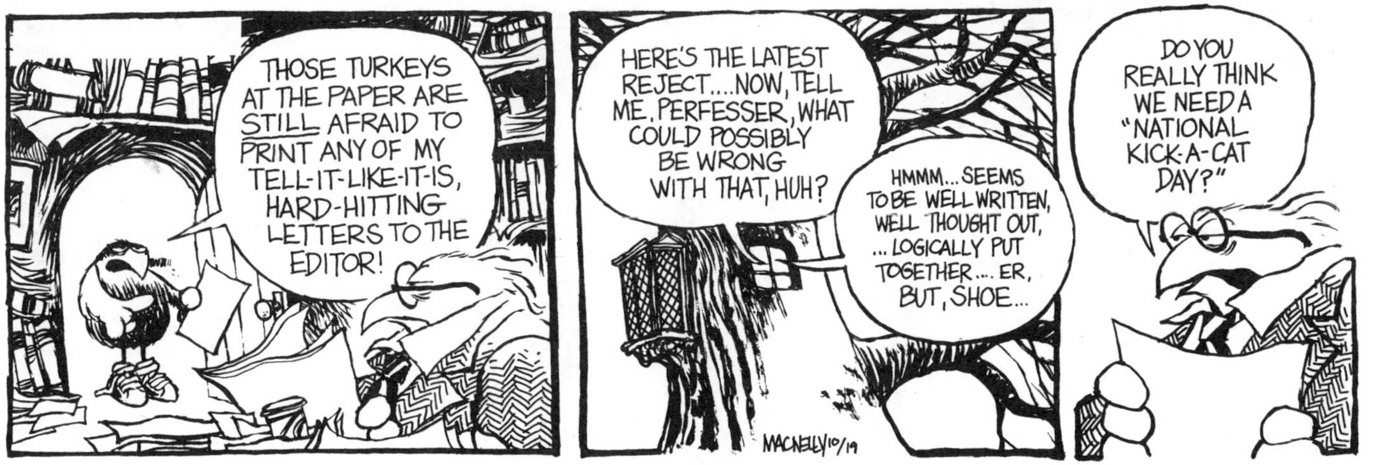
THOSE TURKEYS AT THE PAPER ARE STILL AFRAID TO PRINT ANY OF MY TELL-IT-LIKE-IT-IS, HARD-HITTING LETTERS TO THE EDITOR!
HERE'S THE LATEST REJECT....NOW, TELL ME, PERFESSER, WHAT COULD POSSIBLY BE WRONG WITH THAT, HUH?
HMMM... SEEMS TO BE WELL WRITTEN, WELL THOUGHT OUT, ... LOGICALLY PUT TOGETHER.... ER, BUT, SHOE...
MACNELLY 10/19
DO YOU REALLY THINK WE NEED A "NATIONAL KICK-A-CAT DAY?"

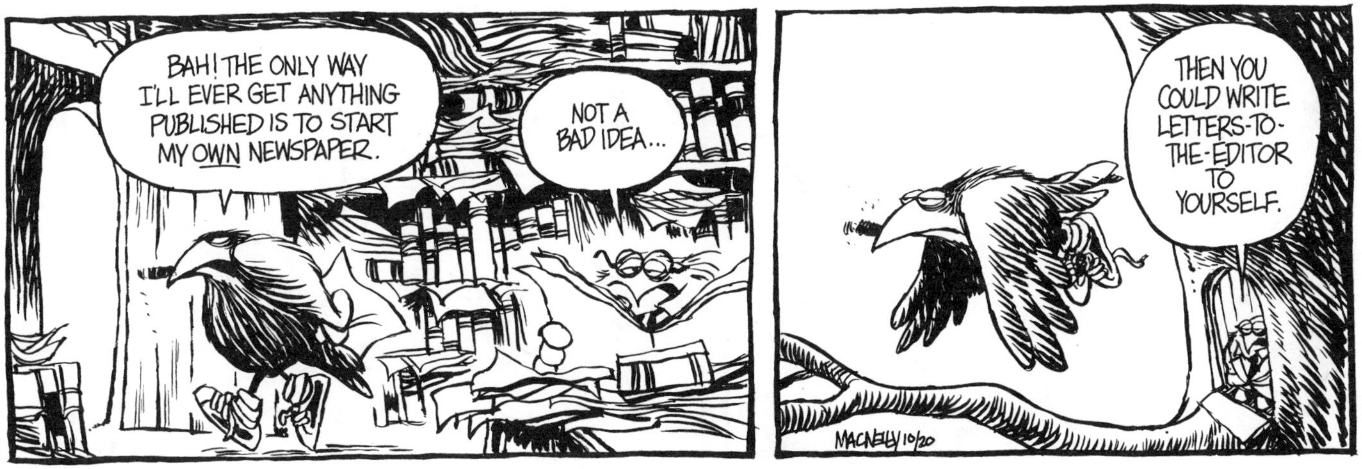
BAH! THE ONLY WAY I'LL EVER GET ANYTHING PUBLISHED IS TO START MY OWN NEWSPAPER.
NOT A BAD IDEA...
THEN YOU COULD WRITE LETTERS-TO-THE-EDITOR TO YOURSELF.
MACNELLY 10/20

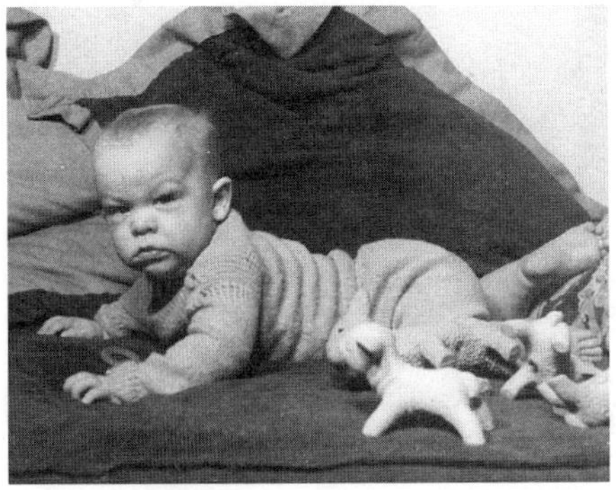

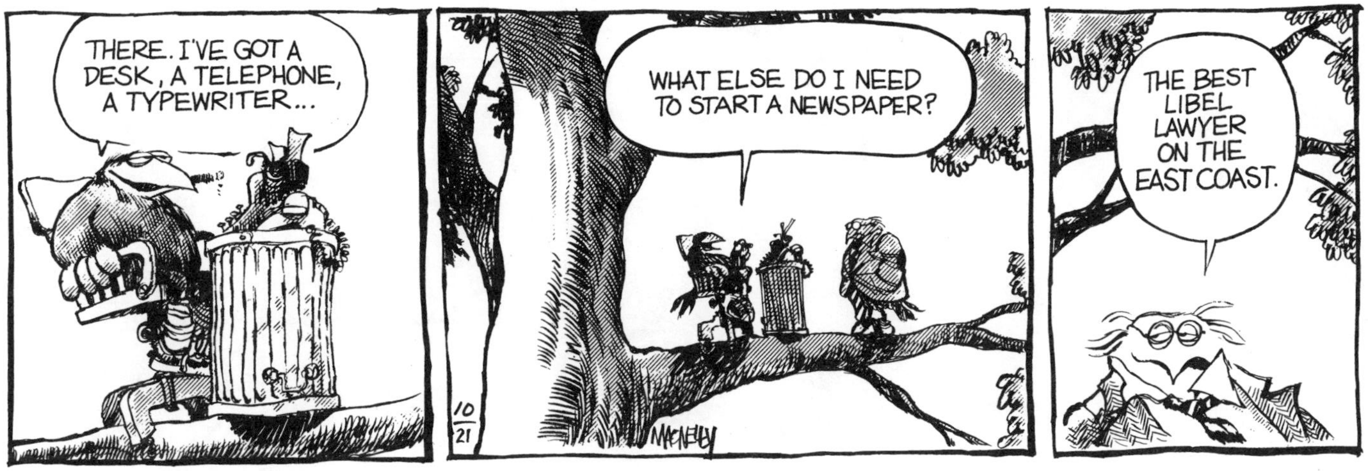
THERE. I'VE GOT A DESK, A TELEPHONE, A TYPEWRITER...
WHAT ELSE DO I NEED TO START A NEWSPAPER?
10/21
MACNELLY
THE BEST LIBEL LAWYER ON THE EAST COAST.

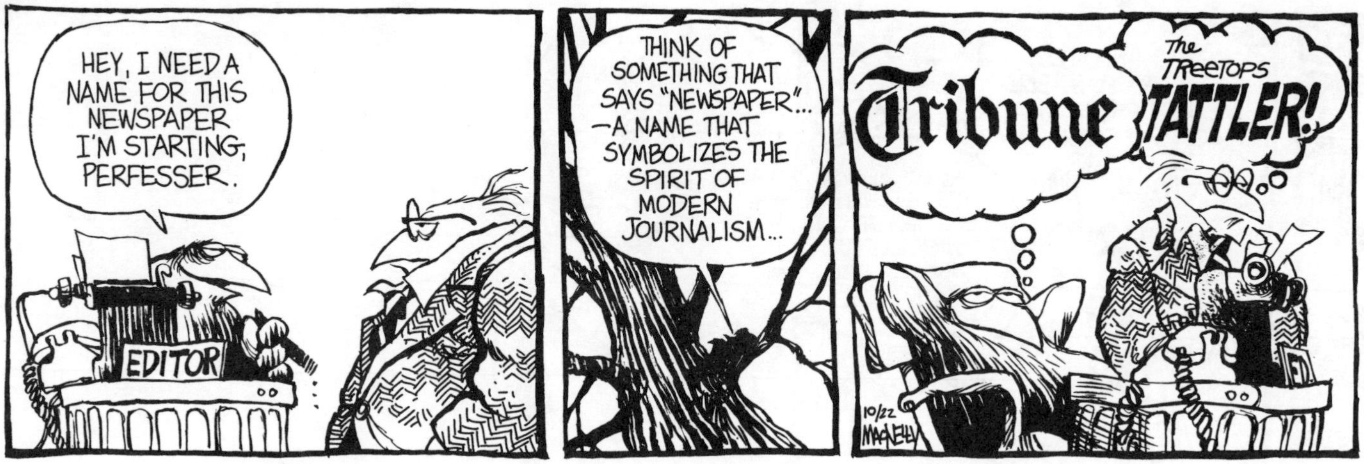
HEY, I NEED A NAME FOR THIS NEWSPAPER I'M STARTING, PERFESSER.
EDITOR
THINK OF SOMETHING THAT SAYS "NEWSPAPER"... —A NAME THAT SYMBOLIZES THE SPIRIT OF MODERN JOURNALISM...
Tribune
The TREETOPS TATTLER!
10/22
MACNELLY

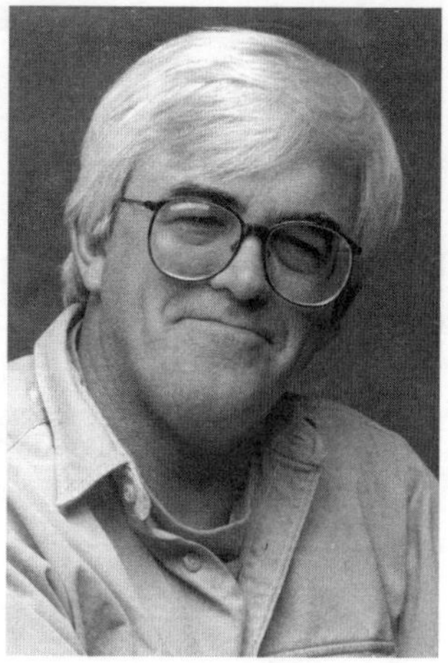

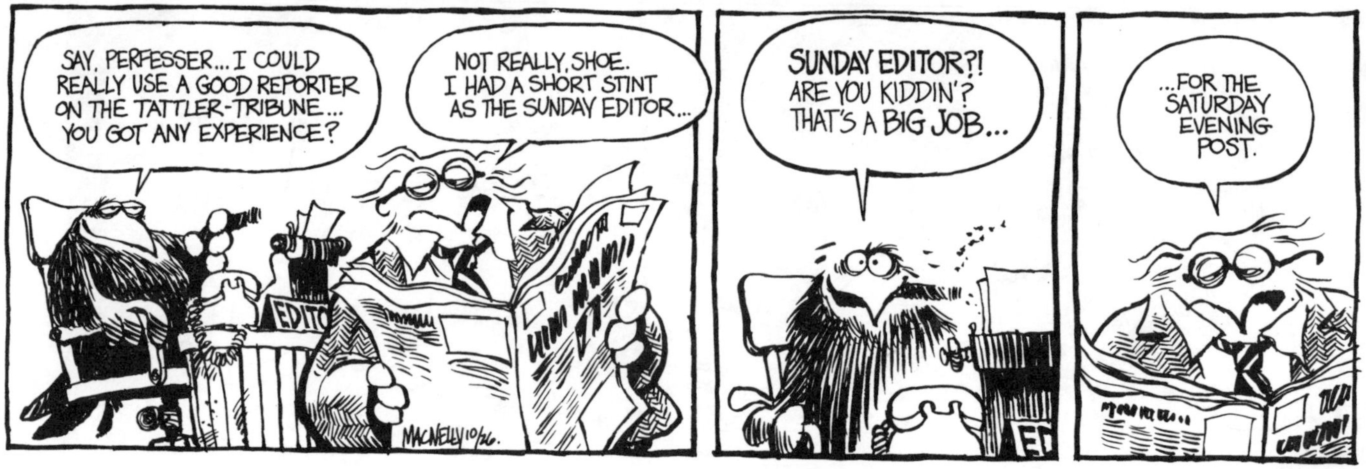
SAY, PERFESSER... I COULD REALLY USE A GOOD REPORTER ON THE TATTLER-TRIBUNE... YOU GOT ANY EXPERIENCE?
NOT REALLY, SHOE. I HAD A SHORT STINT AS THE SUNDAY EDITOR...
MACNELLY 10/26.
SUNDAY EDITOR?! ARE YOU KIDDIN'? THAT'S A BIG JOB...
...FOR THE SATURDAY EVENING POST.

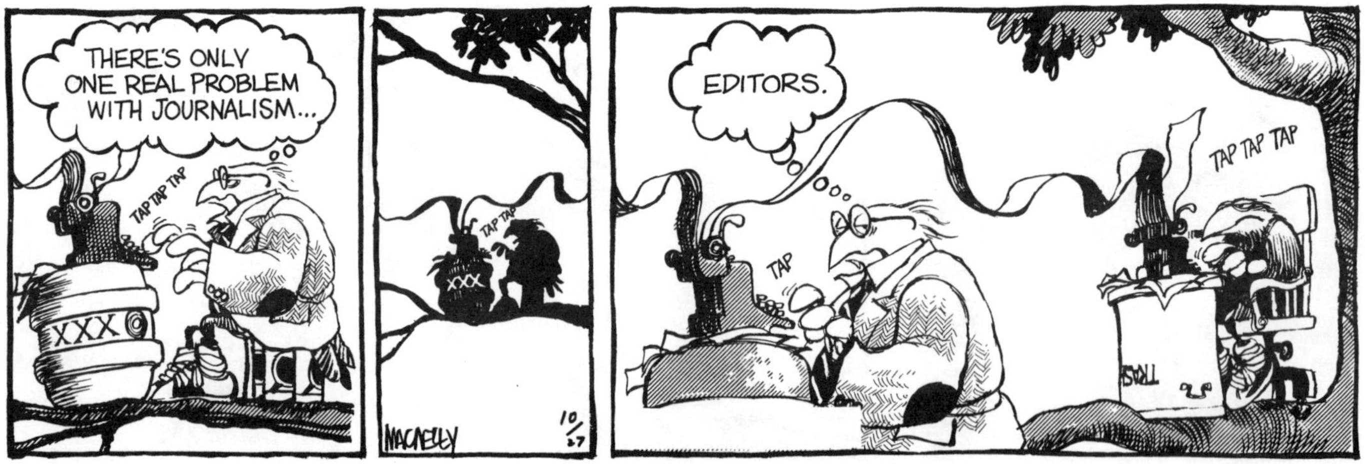
THERE'S ONLY ONE REAL PROBLEM WITH JOURNALISM...
TAP TAP TAP
XXX
TAP TAP
MACNELLY
10/27
EDITORS.
TAP
TAP TAP TAP
TRASH

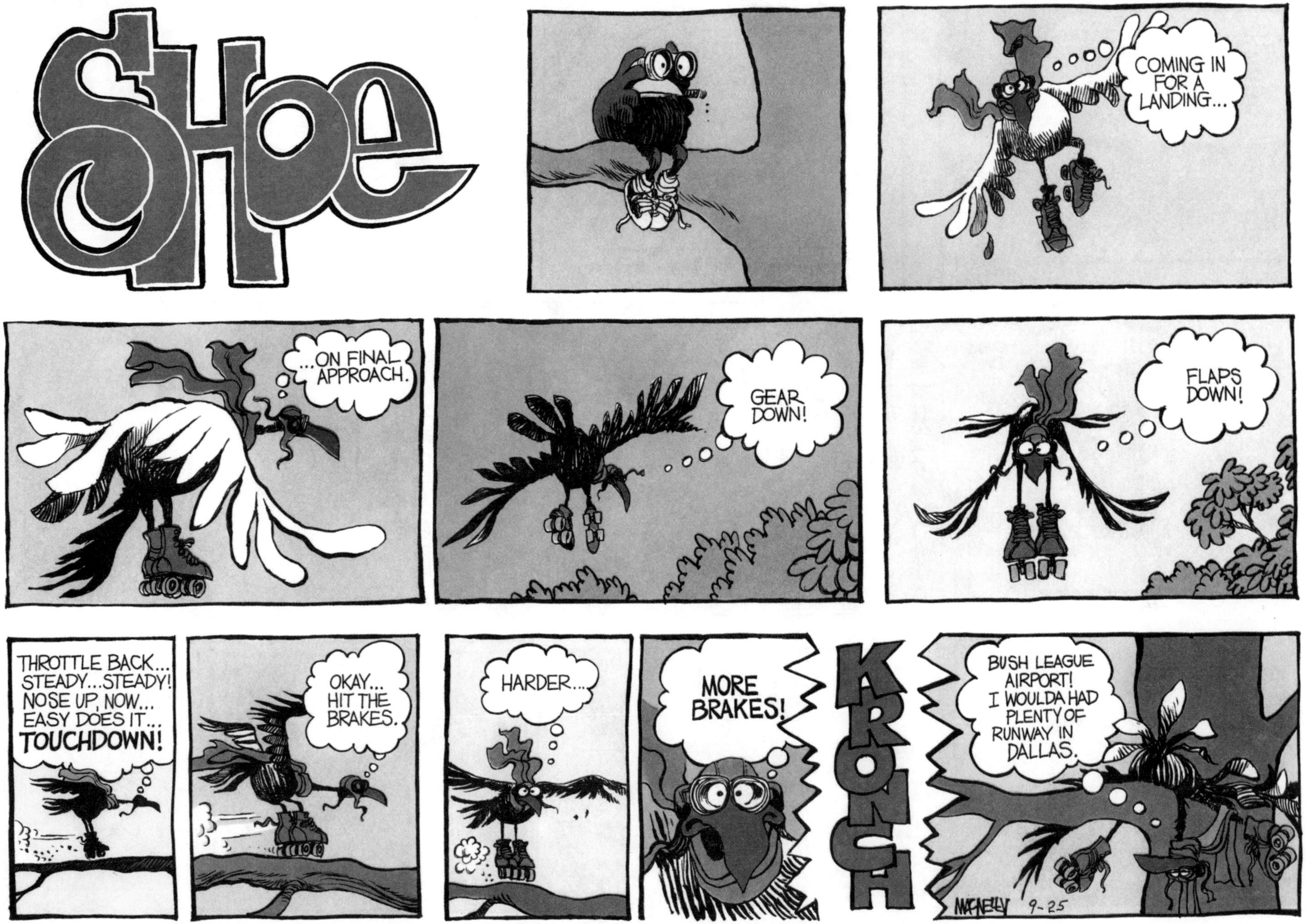
SHOE
COMING IN FOR A LANDING...
...ON FINAL APPROACH.
GEAR DOWN!
FLAPS DOWN!
THROTTLE BACK... STEADY...STEADY! NOSE UP, NOW... EASY DOES IT... TOUCHDOWN!
OKAY... HIT THE BRAKES.
HARDER...
MORE BRAKES!
KRONCH
BUSH LEAGUE AIRPORT! I WOULDA HAD PLENTY OF RUNWAY IN DALLAS.
MACNELLY 9-25

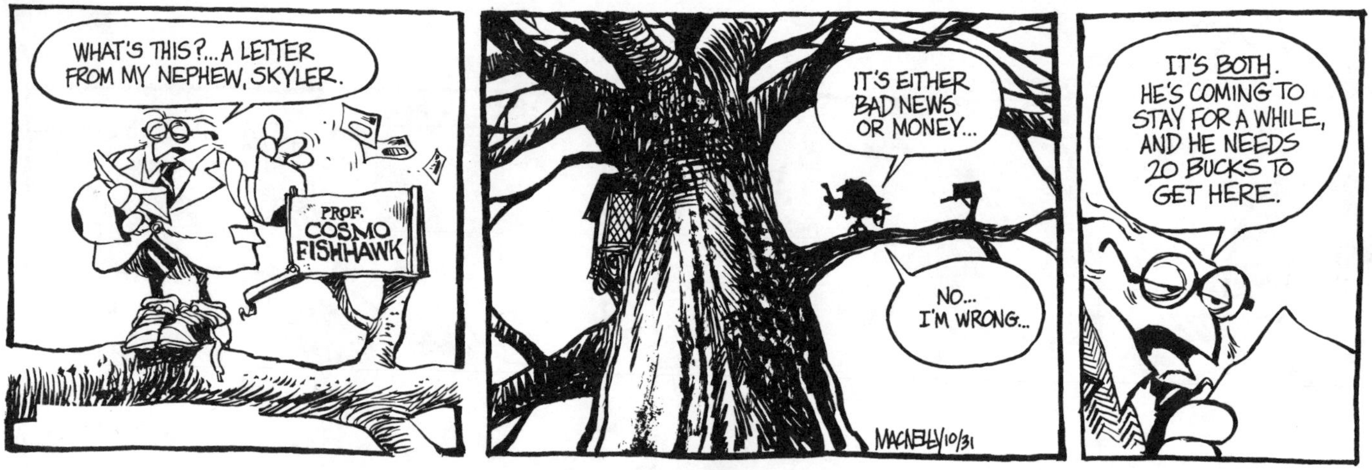
WHAT'S THIS?...A LETTER FROM MY NEPHEW, SKYLER.
PROF. COSMO FISHHAWK
IT'S EITHER BAD NEWS OR MONEY...
NO... I'M WRONG...
MACNELLY 10/31
IT'S BOTH. HE'S COMING TO STAY FOR A WHILE, AND HE NEEDS 20 BUCKS TO GET HERE.

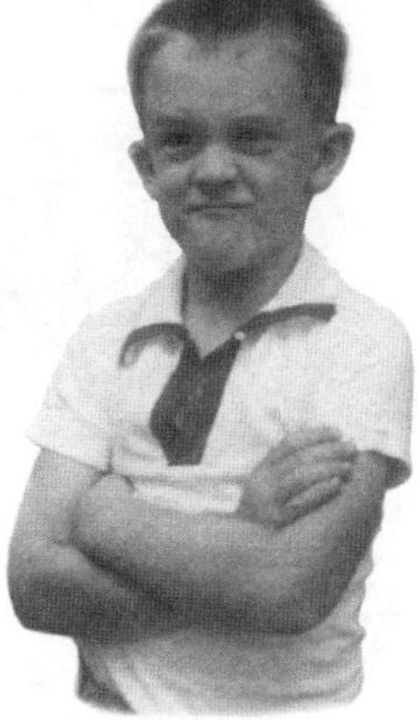

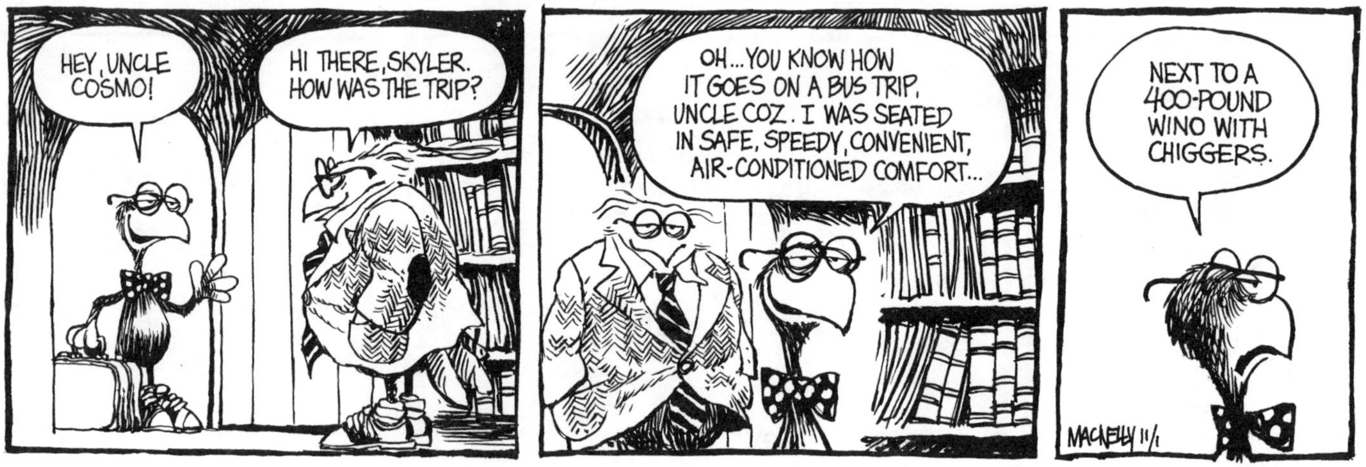
HEY, UNCLE COSMO!
HI THERE, SKYLER. HOW WAS THE TRIP?
OH...YOU KNOW HOW IT GOES ON A BUS TRIP, UNCLE COZ. I WAS SEATED IN SAFE, SPEEDY, CONVENIENT, AIR-CONDITIONED COMFORT...
NEXT TO A 400-POUND WINO WITH CHIGGERS.
MACNELLY 11/1

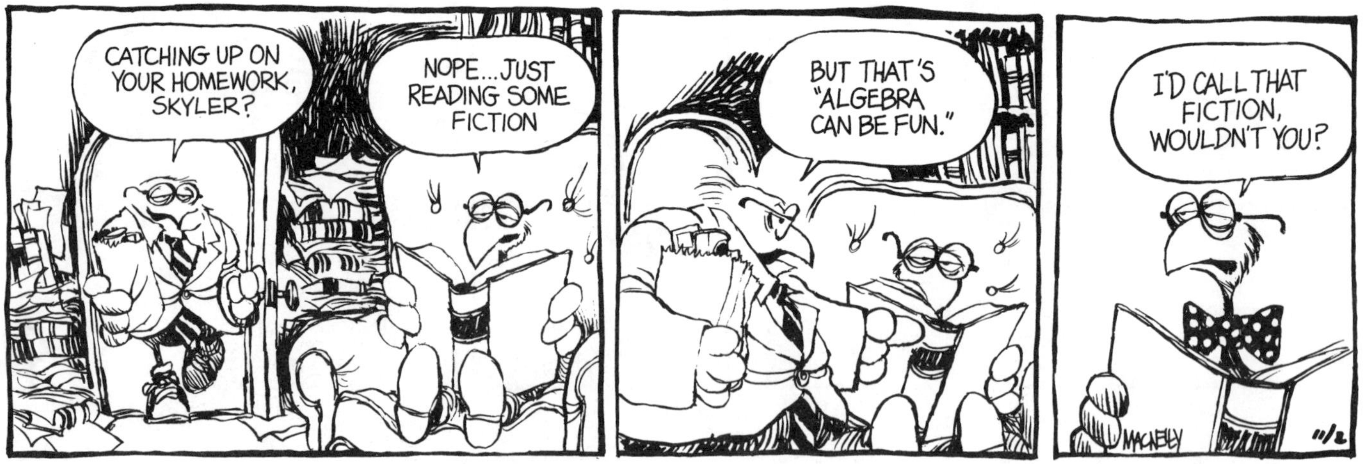
CATCHING UP ON YOUR HOMEWORK, SKYLER?
NOPE...JUST READING SOME FICTION
BUT THAT'S "ALGEBRA CAN BE FUN."
I'D CALL THAT FICTION, WOULDN'T YOU?
MACNELLY
11/2

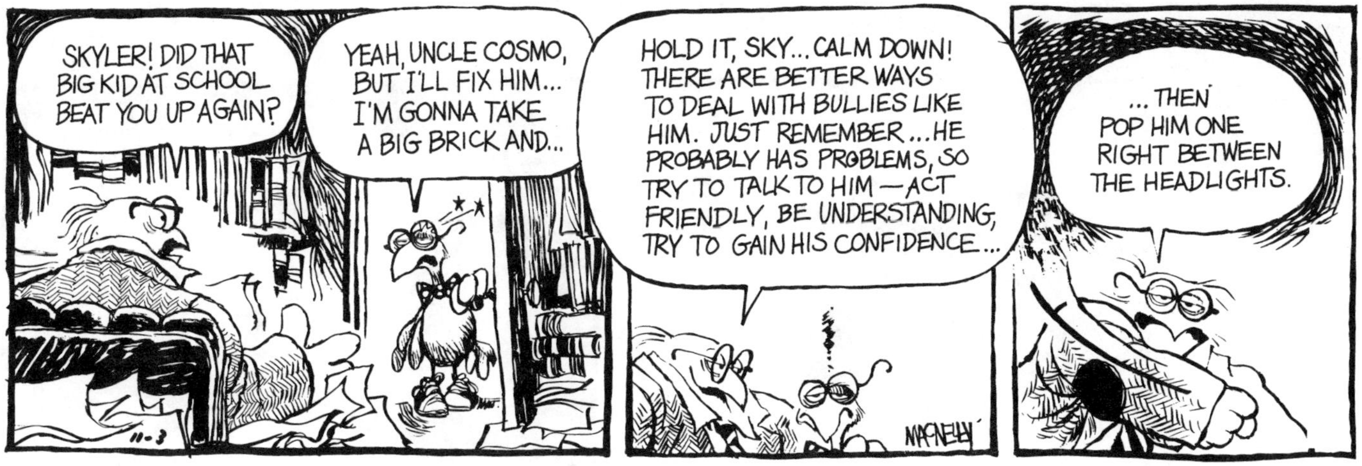
SKYLER! DID THAT BIG KID AT SCHOOL BEAT YOU UP AGAIN?
YEAH, UNCLE COSMO, BUT I'LL FIX HIM... I'M GONNA TAKE A BIG BRICK AND...
HOLD IT, SKY... CALM DOWN! THERE ARE BETTER WAYS TO DEAL WITH BULLIES LIKE HIM. JUST REMEMBER... HE PROBABLY HAS PROBLEMS, SO TRY TO TALK TO HIM—ACT FRIENDLY, BE UNDERSTANDING, TRY TO GAIN HIS CONFIDENCE...
...THEN POP HIM ONE RIGHT BETWEEN THE HEADLIGHTS.
11-3
MACNELLY

Jeff's first summer adventure to Central America, age fourteen. That's him in the upper right of the photo.

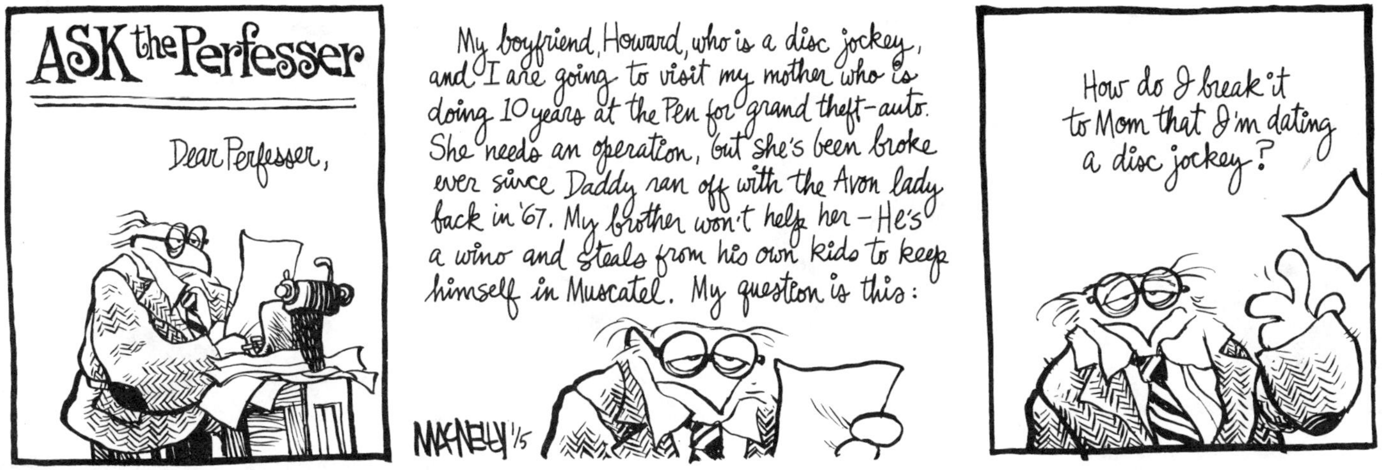
ASK the Perfesser
Dear Perfesser,
My boyfriend, Howard, who is a disc jockey, and I are going to visit my mother who is doing 10 years at the Pen for grand theft-auto. She needs an operation, but she's been broke ever since Daddy ran off with the Avon lady back in '67. My brother won't help her—He's a wino and steals from his own kids to keep himself in Muscatel. My question is this:
How do I break it to Mom that I'm dating a disc jockey?
MACNELLY 1/5

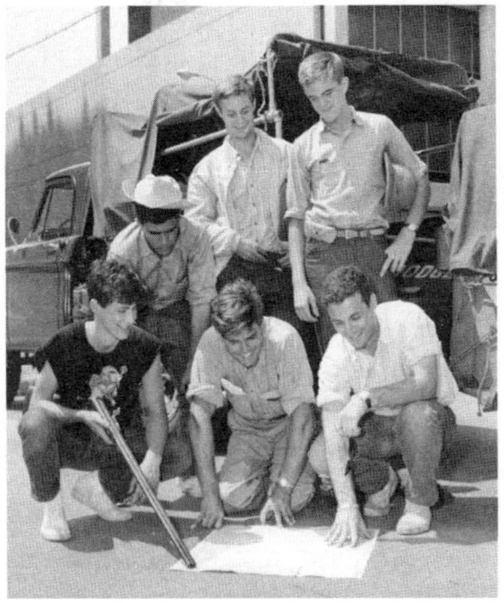

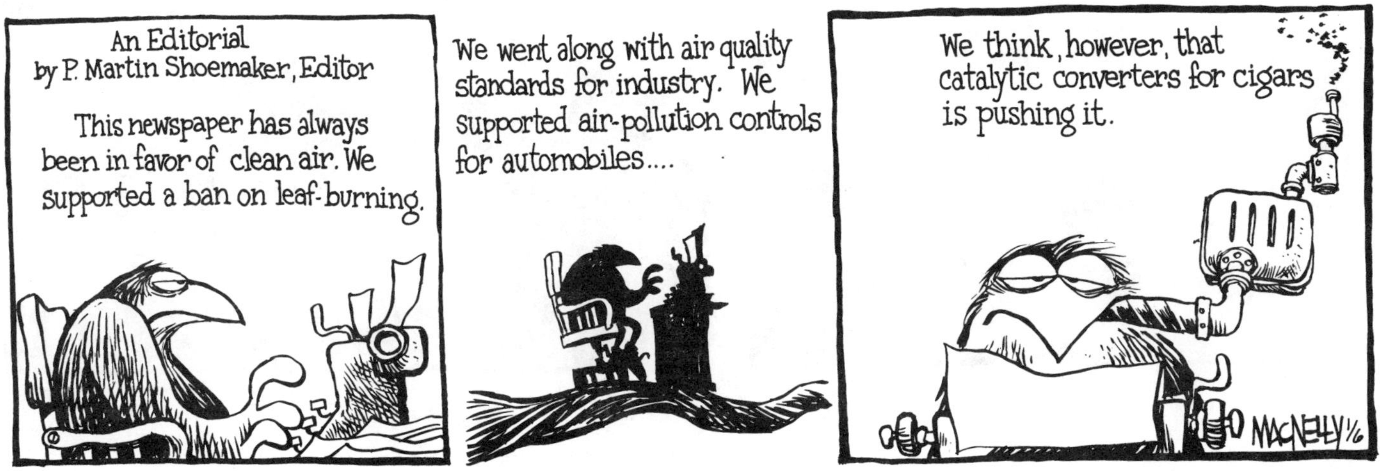
An Editorial
by P. Martin Shoemaker, Editor
This newspaper has always been in favor of clean air. We supported a ban on leaf-burning.
We went along with air quality standards for industry. We supported air-pollution controls for automobiles....
We think, however, that catalytic converters for cigars is pushing it.
MACNELLY 1/6

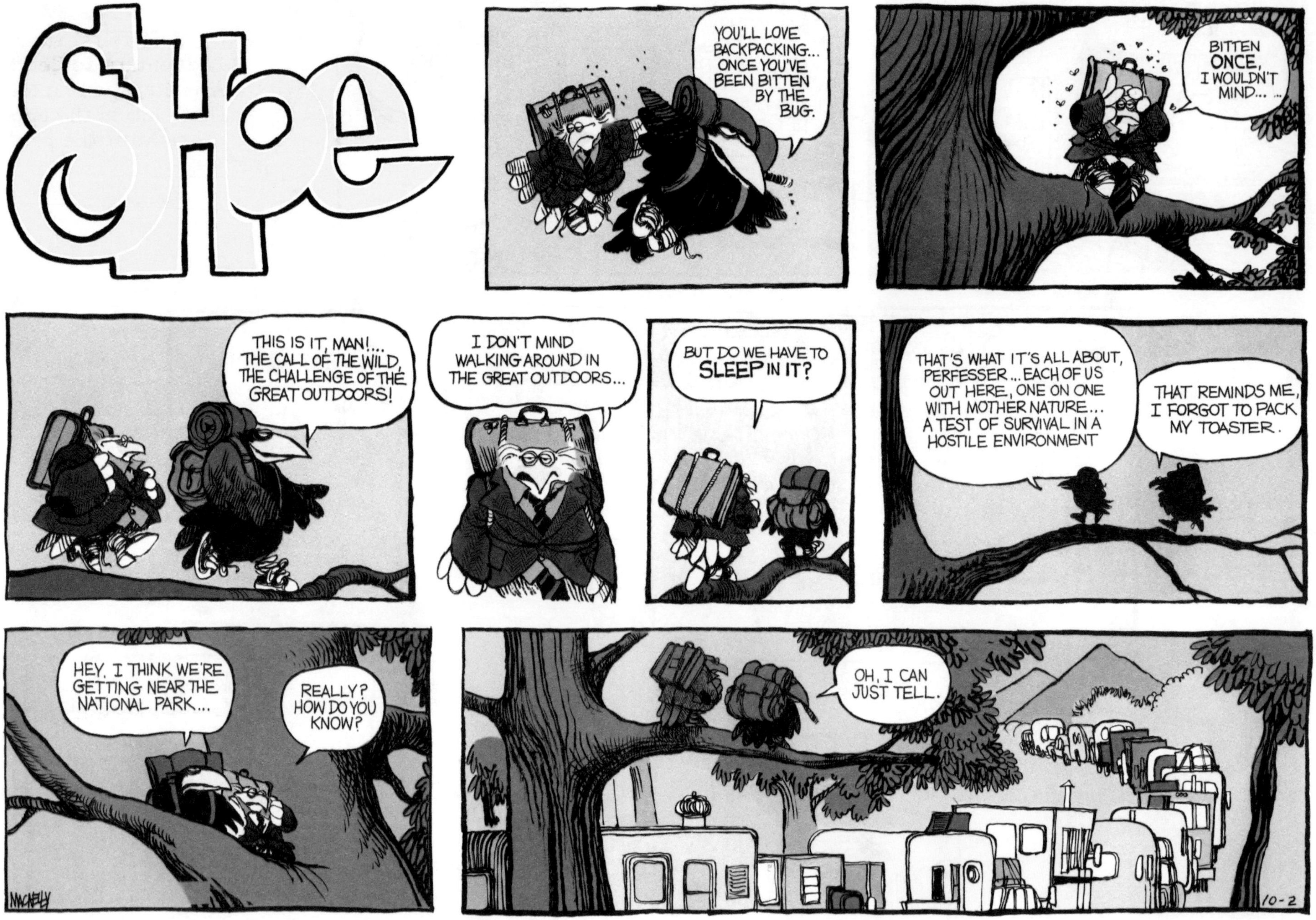
Shoe
YOU'LL LOVE BACKPACKING... ONCE YOU'VE BEEN BITTEN BY THE BUG.
BITTEN ONCE, I WOULDN'T MIND... ...
THIS IS IT, MAN!... THE CALL OF THE WILD, THE CHALLENGE OF THE GREAT OUTDOORS!
I DON'T MIND WALKING AROUND IN THE GREAT OUTDOORS...
BUT DO WE HAVE TO SLEEP IN IT?
THAT'S WHAT IT'S ALL ABOUT, PERFESSER... EACH OF US OUT HERE, ONE ON ONE WITH MOTHER NATURE... A TEST OF SURVIVAL IN A HOSTILE ENVIRONMENT
THAT REMINDS ME, I FORGOT TO PACK MY TOASTER.
HEY, I THINK WE'RE GETTING NEAR THE NATIONAL PARK...
REALLY? HOW DO YOU KNOW?
OH, I CAN JUST TELL.
MACNELLY
10-2

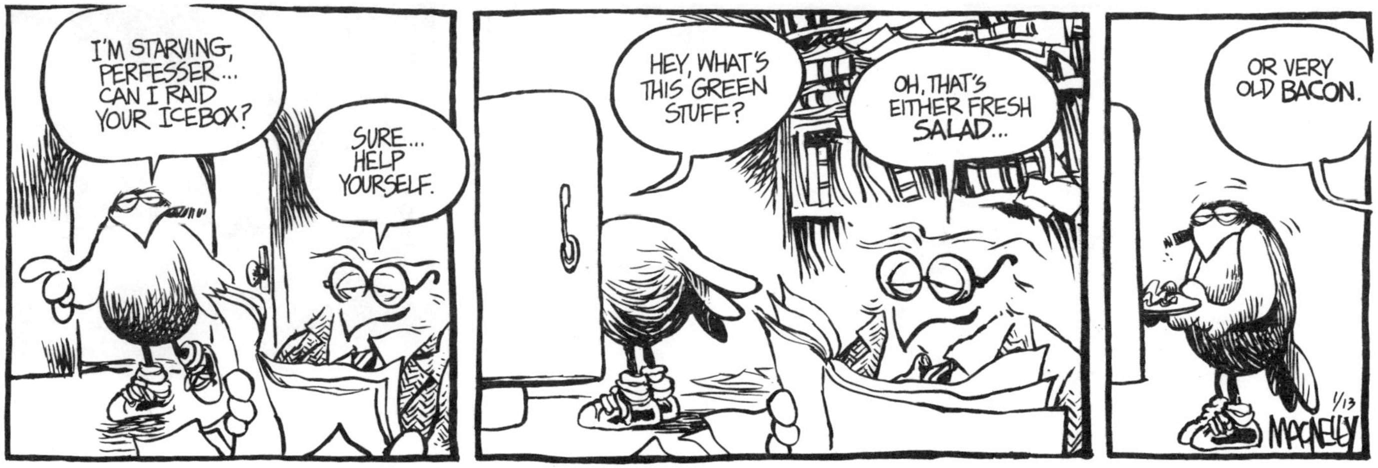
I'M STARVING, PERFESSER... CAN I RAID YOUR ICEBOX?
SURE... HELP YOURSELF.
HEY, WHAT'S THIS GREEN STUFF?
OH, THAT'S EITHER FRESH SALAD...
OR VERY OLD BACON.
1/13
MACNELLY

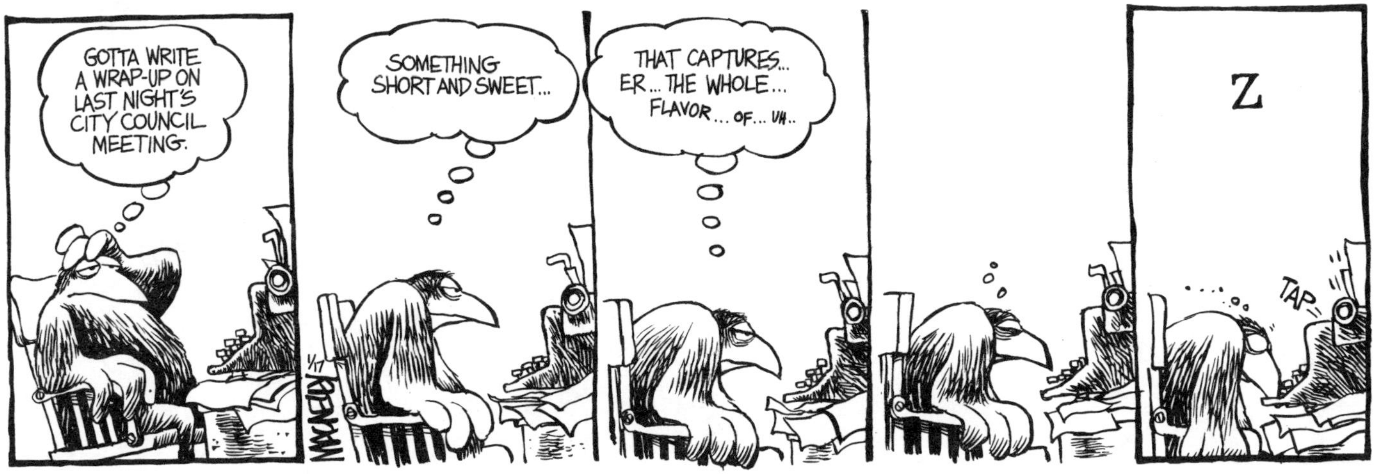
GOTTA WRITE A WRAP-UP ON LAST NIGHT'S CITY COUNCIL MEETING.
1/17
MACNELLY
SOMETHING SHORT AND SWEET...
THAT CAPTURES... ER... THE WHOLE... FLAVOR... OF... UH..
Z
TAP

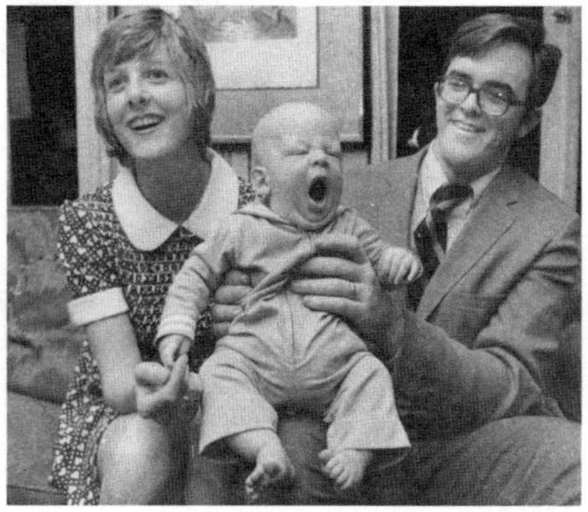

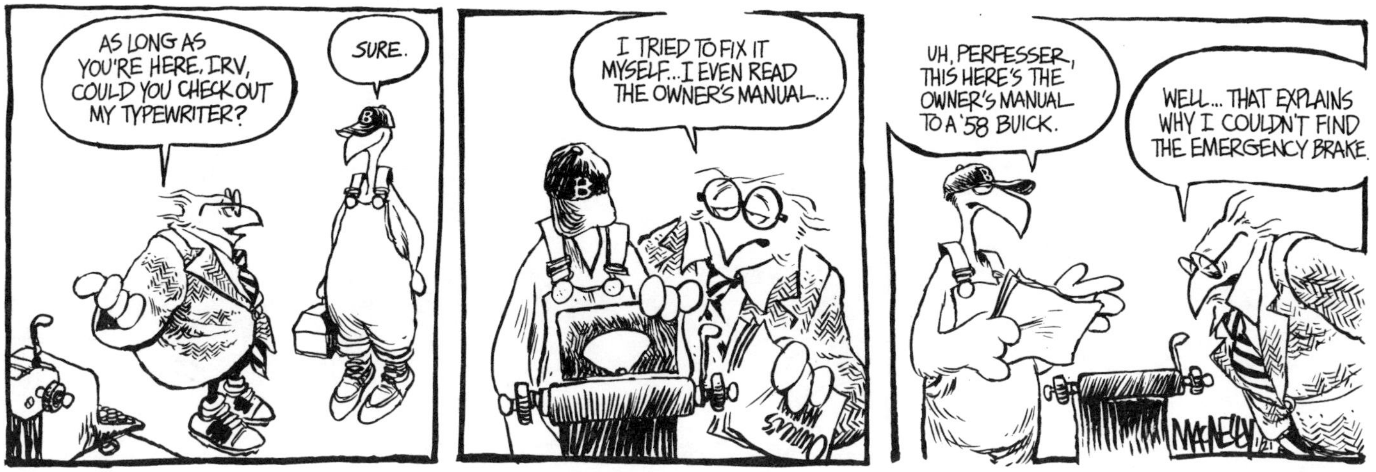
AS LONG AS YOU'RE HERE, IRV, COULD YOU CHECK OUT MY TYPEWRITER?
SURE.
I TRIED TO FIX IT MYSELF... I EVEN READ THE OWNER'S MANUAL...
UH, PERFESSER, THIS HERE'S THE OWNER'S MANUAL TO A '58 BUICK.
WELL... THAT EXPLAINS WHY I COULDN'T FIND THE EMERGENCY BRAKE.
MACNELLY

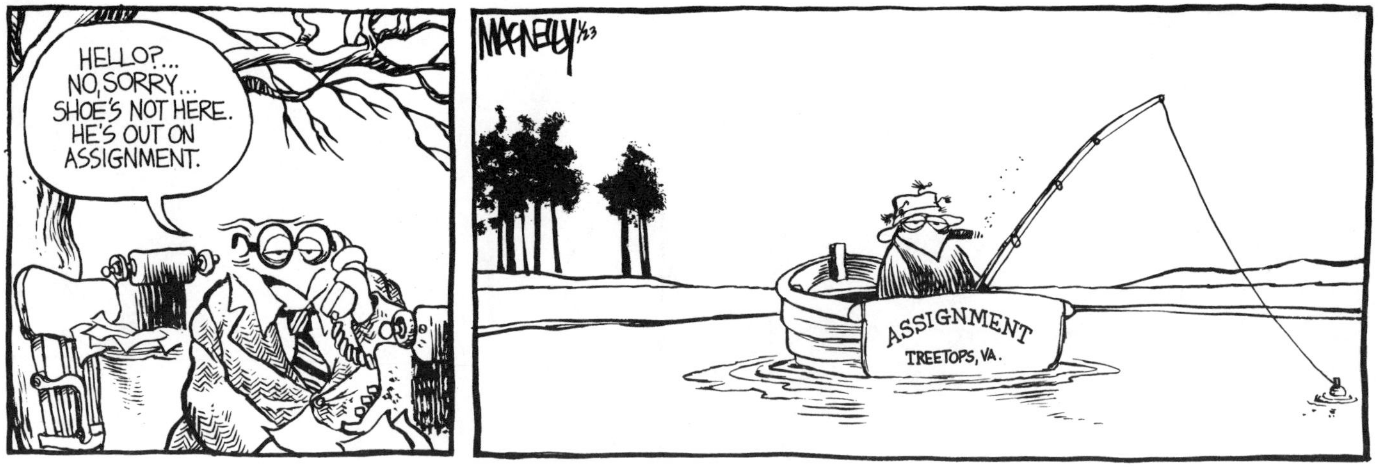
HELLO?... NO, SORRY... SHOE'S NOT HERE. HE'S OUT ON ASSIGNMENT.
ASSIGNMENT
TREETOPS, VA.

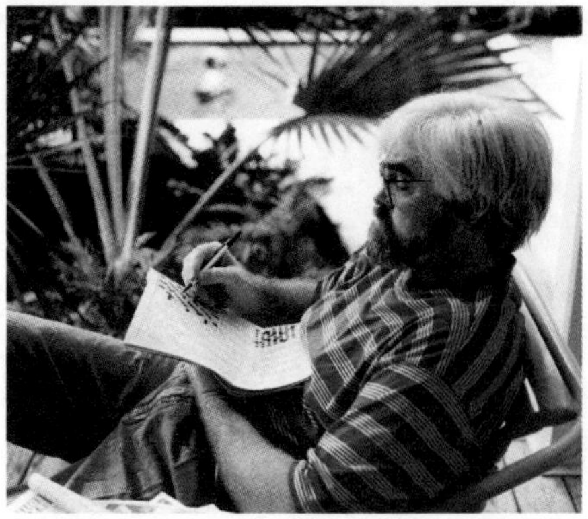

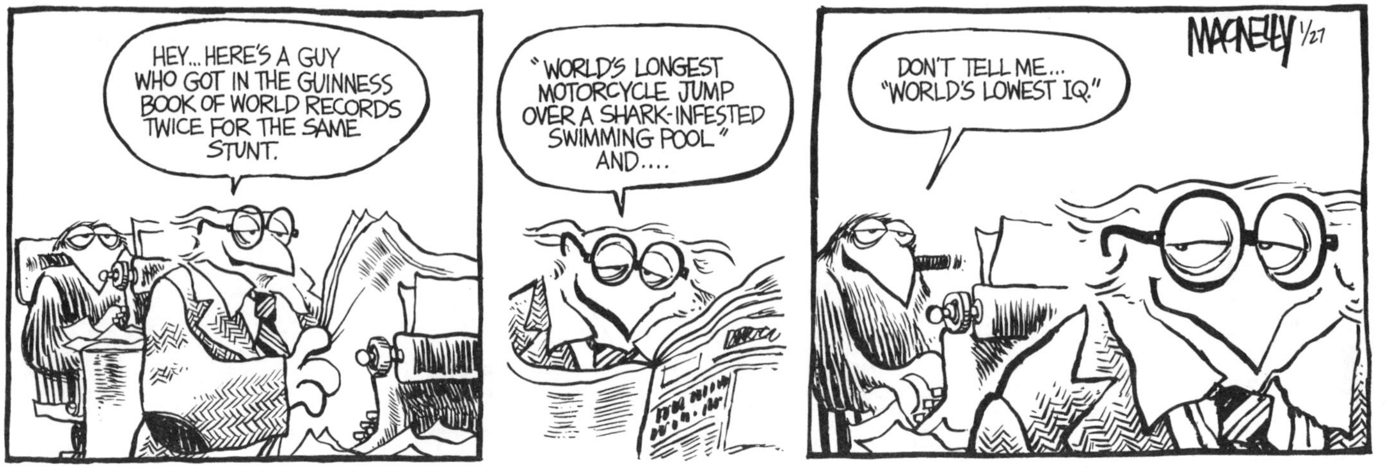
HEY... HERE'S A GUY WHO GOT IN THE GUINNESS BOOK OF WORLD RECORDS TWICE FOR THE SAME STUNT.
"WORLD'S LONGEST MOTORCYCLE JUMP OVER A SHARK-INFESTED SWIMMING POOL" AND....
DON'T TELL ME... "WORLD'S LOWEST IQ."

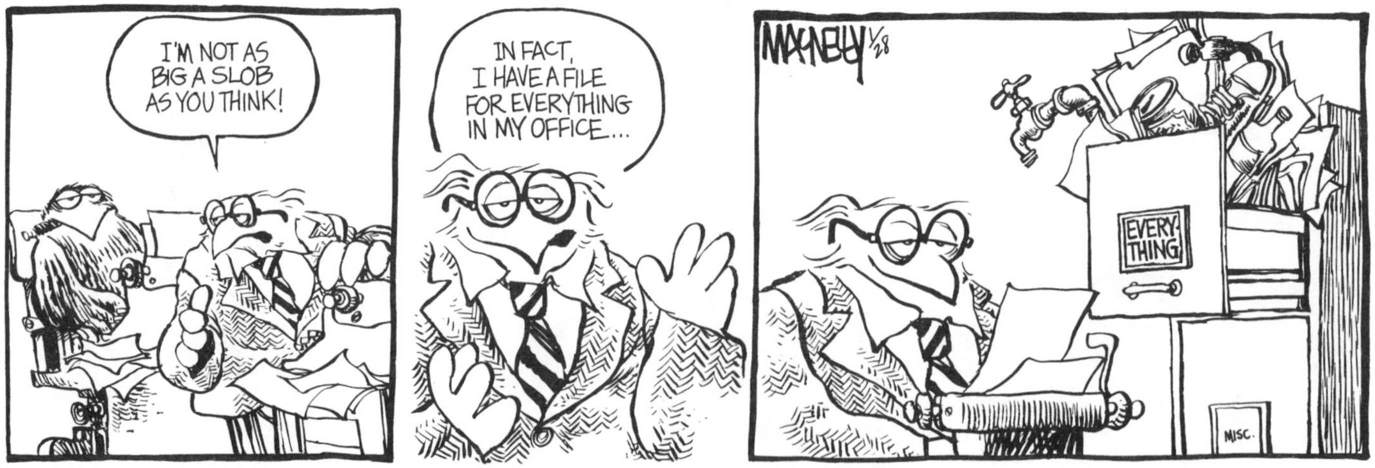
I'M NOT AS BIG A SLOB AS YOU THINK!
IN FACT, I HAVE A FILE FOR EVERYTHING IN MY OFFICE...
EVERY-THING
MISC.

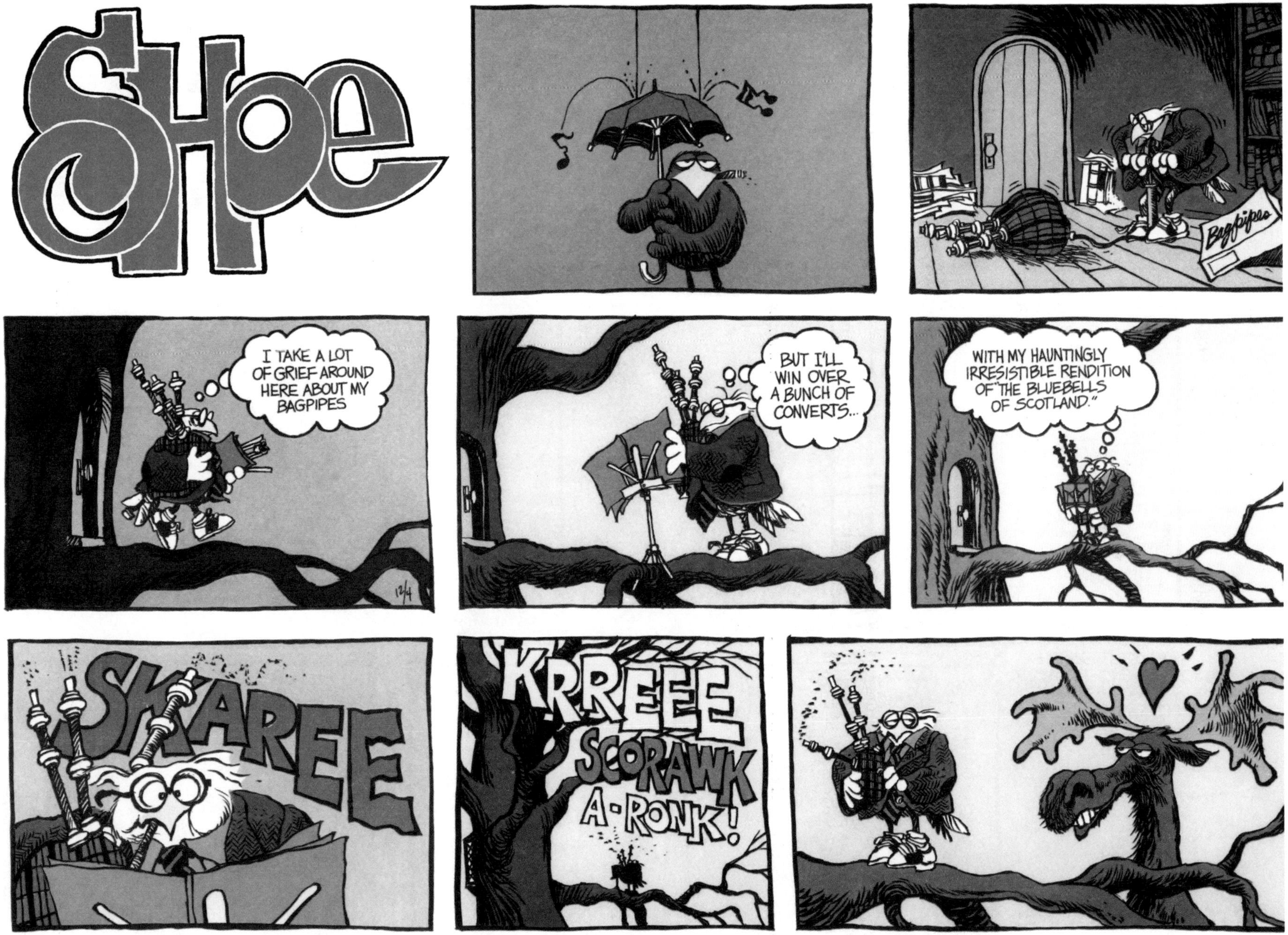
SHOE
I TAKE A LOT OF GRIEF AROUND HERE ABOUT MY BAGPIPES
BUT I'LL WIN OVER A BUNCH OF CONVERTS...
WITH MY HAUNTINGLY IRRESISTIBLE RENDITION OF "THE BLUEBELLS OF SCOTLAND."
SKAREE
KRREEE
SCORAWK
A-RONK!

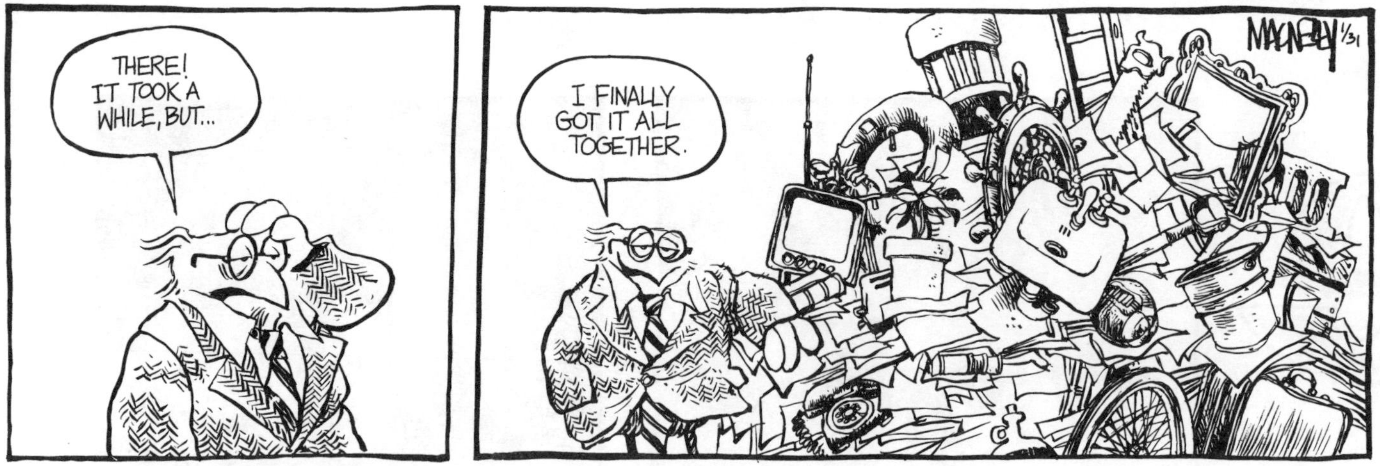
THERE! IT TOOK A WHILE, BUT...
I FINALLY GOT IT ALL TOGETHER.
MACNELLY 1/31

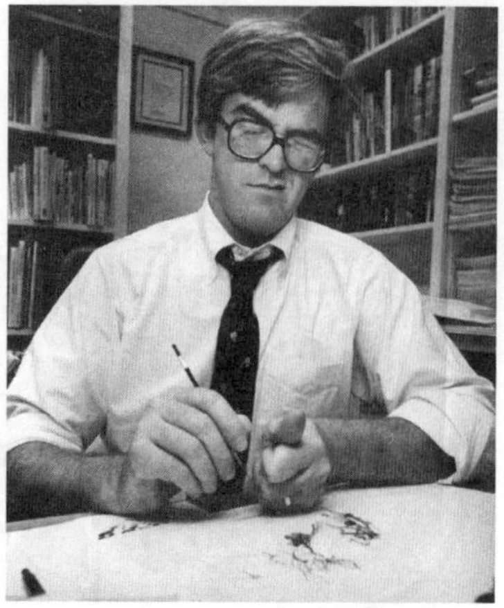

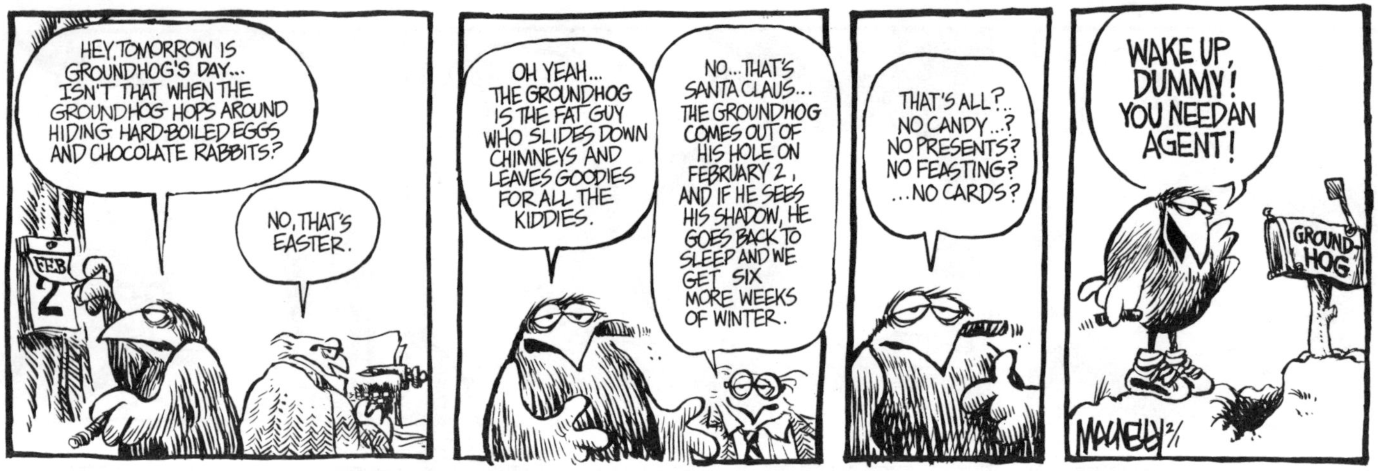
HEY, TOMORROW IS GROUNDHOG'S DAY... ISN'T THAT WHEN THE GROUNDHOG HOPS AROUND HIDING HARD-BOILED EGGS AND CHOCOLATE RABBITS?
NO, THAT'S EASTER.
FEB 2
OH YEAH... THE GROUNDHOG IS THE FAT GUY WHO SLIDES DOWN CHIMNEYS AND LEAVES GOODIES FOR ALL THE KIDDIES.
NO... THAT'S SANTA CLAUS... THE GROUNDHOG COMES OUT OF HIS HOLE ON FEBRUARY 2, AND IF HE SEES HIS SHADOW, HE GOES BACK TO SLEEP AND WE GET SIX MORE WEEKS OF WINTER.
THAT'S ALL?... NO CANDY...? NO PRESENTS? NO FEASTING? ...NO CARDS?
WAKE UP, DUMMY! YOU NEED AN AGENT!
GROUND-HOG
MACNELLY 2/1

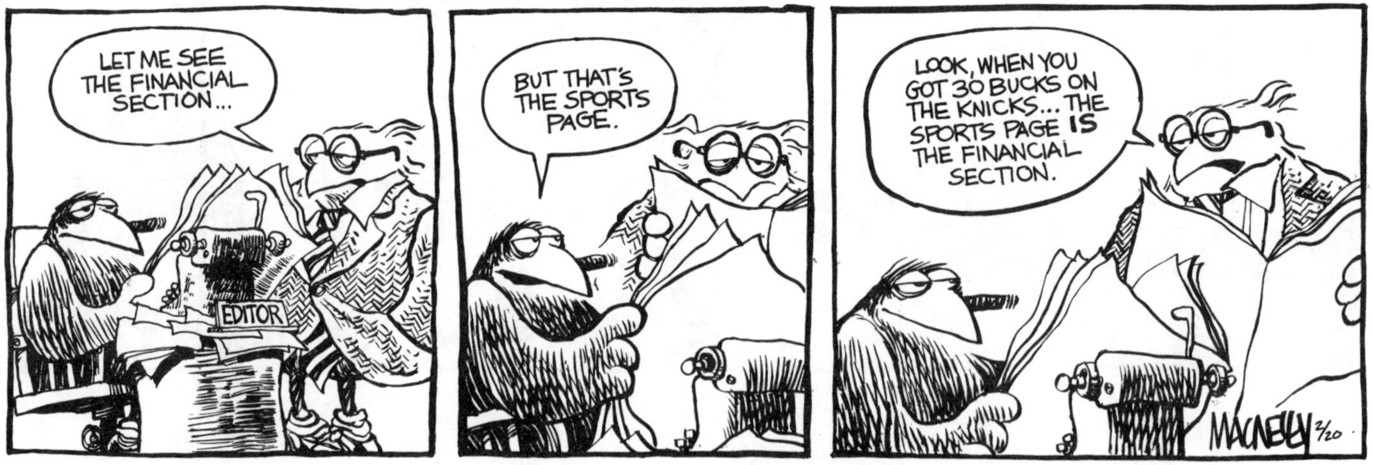
LET ME SEE THE FINANCIAL SECTION...
EDITOR
BUT THAT'S THE SPORTS PAGE.
LOOK, WHEN YOU GOT 30 BUCKS ON THE KNICKS... THE SPORTS PAGE IS THE FINANCIAL SECTION.
MACNELLY 2/20

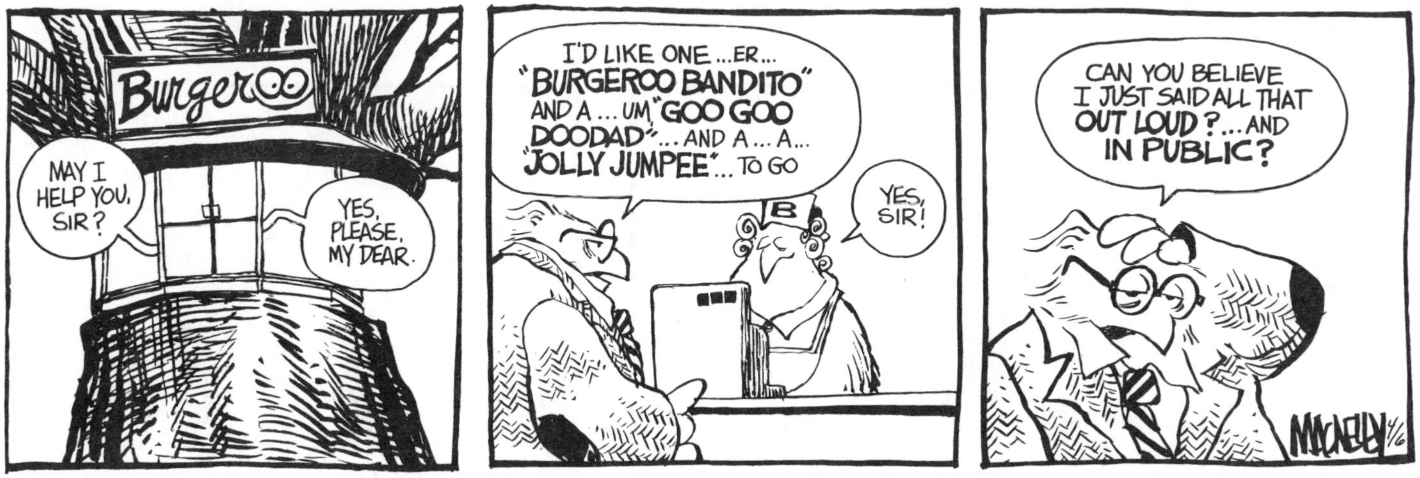
Burgeroo
MAY I HELP YOU, SIR?
YES, PLEASE, MY DEAR.
I'D LIKE ONE ...ER... "BURGEROO BANDITO" AND A ... UM, "GOO GOO DOODAD"... AND A ... A... "JOLLY JUMPEE"... TO GO
YES, SIR!
CAN YOU BELIEVE I JUST SAID ALL THAT OUT LOUD ?... AND IN PUBLIC?
MACNELLY

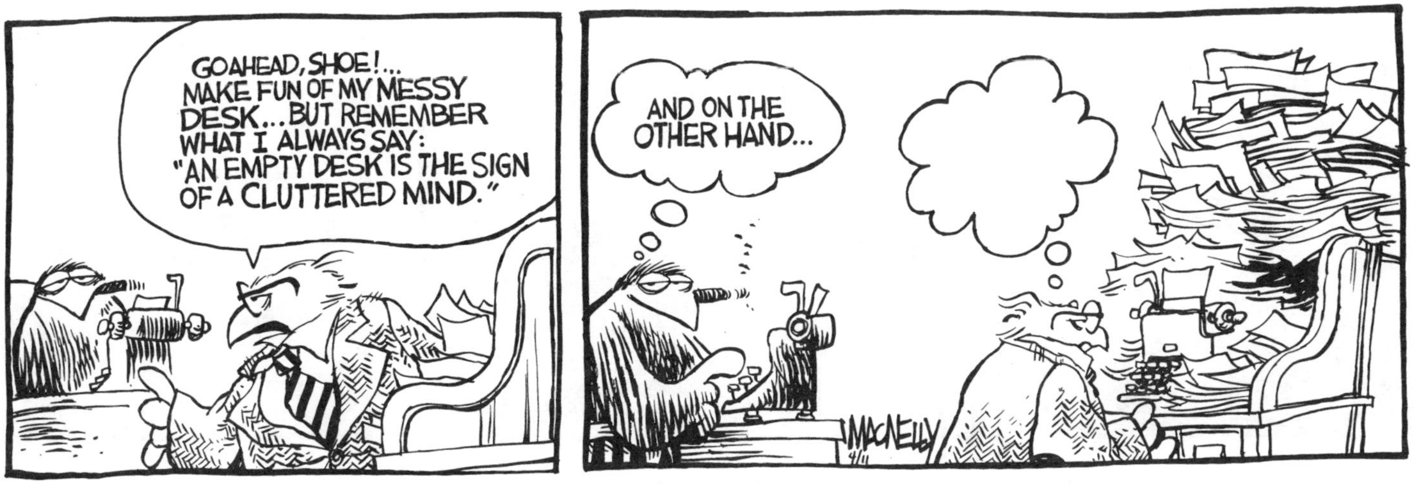
GO AHEAD, SHOE!... MAKE FUN OF MY MESSY DESK... BUT REMEMBER WHAT I ALWAYS SAY: "AN EMPTY DESK IS THE SIGN OF A CLUTTERED MIND."
AND ON THE OTHER HAND...
MACNELLY

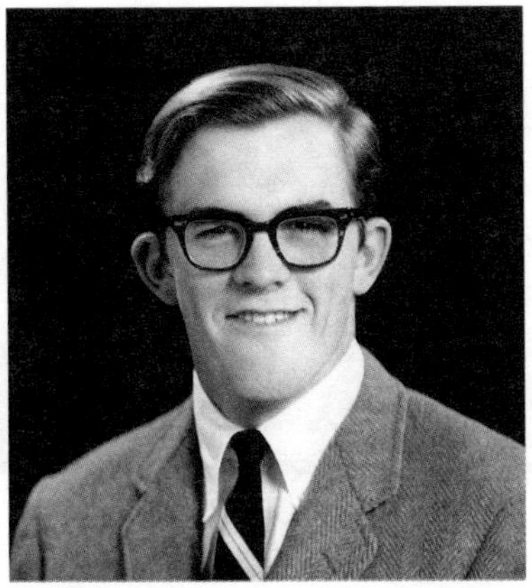

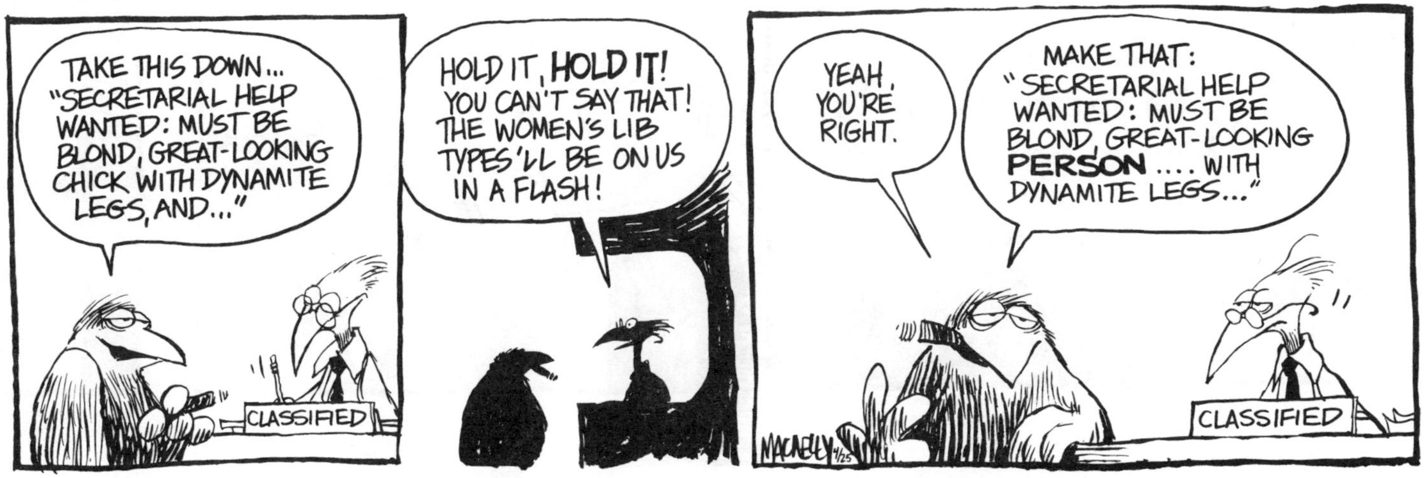
TAKE THIS DOWN... "SECRETARIAL HELP WANTED: MUST BE BLOND, GREAT-LOOKING CHICK WITH DYNAMITE LEGS, AND..."
CLASSIFIED
HOLD IT, HOLD IT! YOU CAN'T SAY THAT! THE WOMEN'S LIB TYPES'LL BE ON US IN A FLASH!
YEAH, YOU'RE RIGHT.
MAKE THAT: "SECRETARIAL HELP WANTED: MUST BE BLOND, GREAT-LOOKING PERSON .... WITH DYNAMITE LEGS..."
CLASSIFIED
MACNELLY

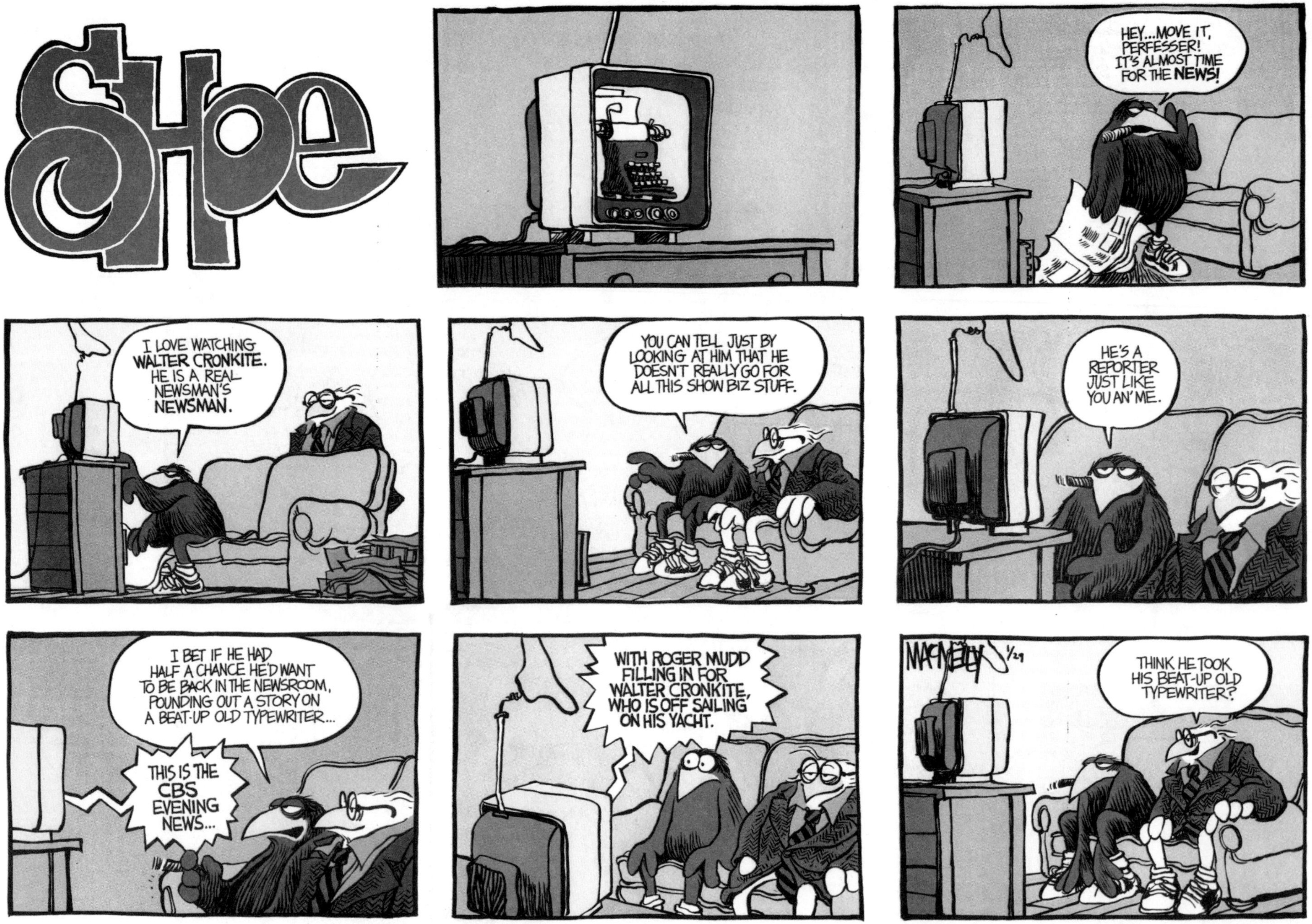
SHOE
HEY...MOVE IT, PERFESSER! IT'S ALMOST TIME FOR THE NEWS!
I LOVE WATCHING WALTER CRONKITE. HE IS A REAL NEWSMAN'S NEWSMAN.
YOU CAN TELL JUST BY LOOKING AT HIM THAT HE DOESN'T REALLY GO FOR ALL THIS SHOW BIZ STUFF.
HE'S A REPORTER JUST LIKE YOU AN' ME.
I BET IF HE HAD HALF A CHANCE HE'D WANT TO BE BACK IN THE NEWSROOM, POUNDING OUT A STORY ON A BEAT-UP OLD TYPEWRITER...
THIS IS THE CBS EVENING NEWS...
WITH ROGER MUDD FILLING IN FOR WALTER CRONKITE, WHO IS OFF SAILING ON HIS YACHT.
MACNELLY 1/29
THINK HE TOOK HIS BEAT-UP OLD TYPEWRITER?

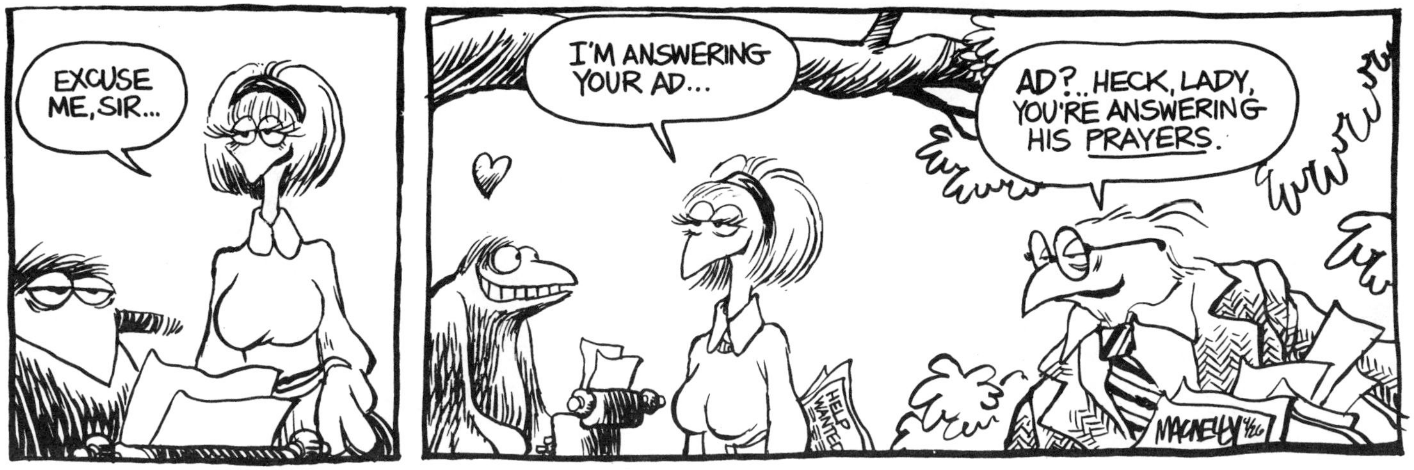
EXCUSE ME, SIR...
I'M ANSWERING YOUR AD...
AD?.. HECK, LADY, YOU'RE ANSWERING HIS PRAYERS.
MACNELLY 4/26

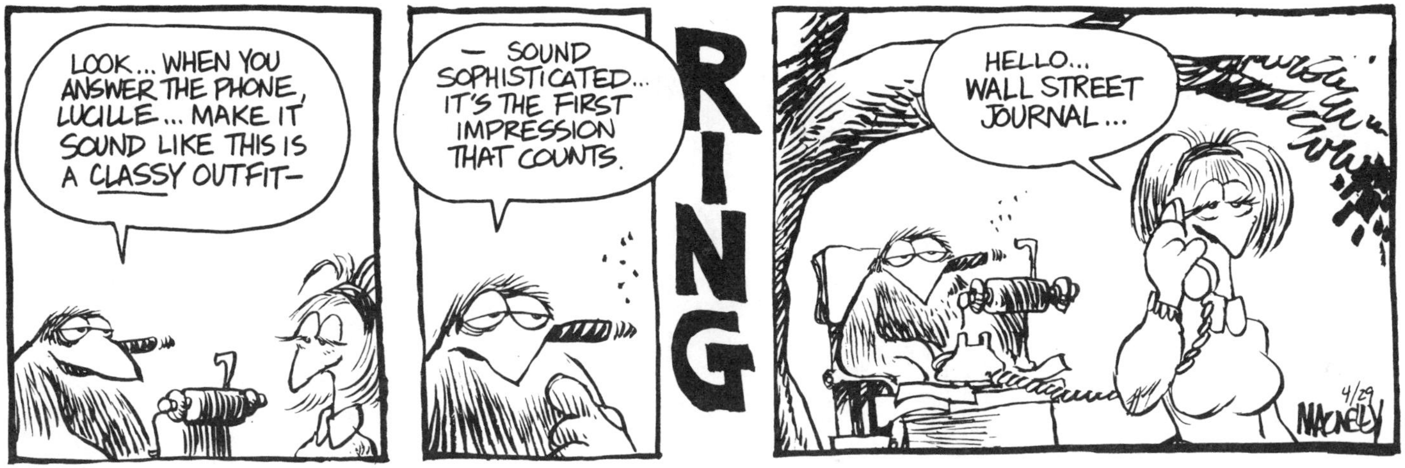
LOOK... WHEN YOU ANSWER THE PHONE, LUCILLE... MAKE IT SOUND LIKE THIS IS A CLASSY OUTFIT—
— SOUND SOPHISTICATED... IT'S THE FIRST IMPRESSION THAT COUNTS.
RING
HELLO... WALL STREET JOURNAL...
4/29 MACNELLY

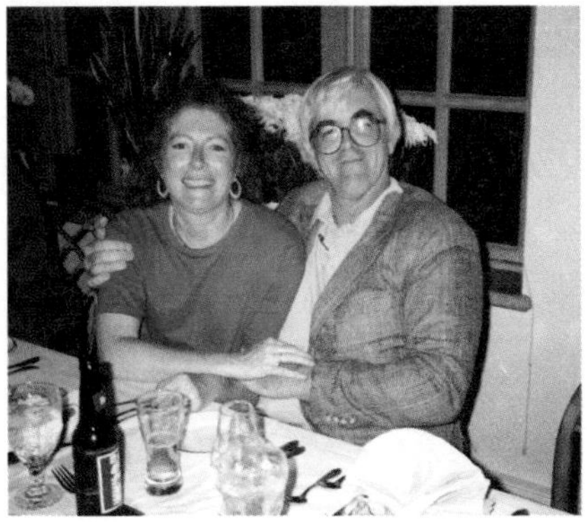

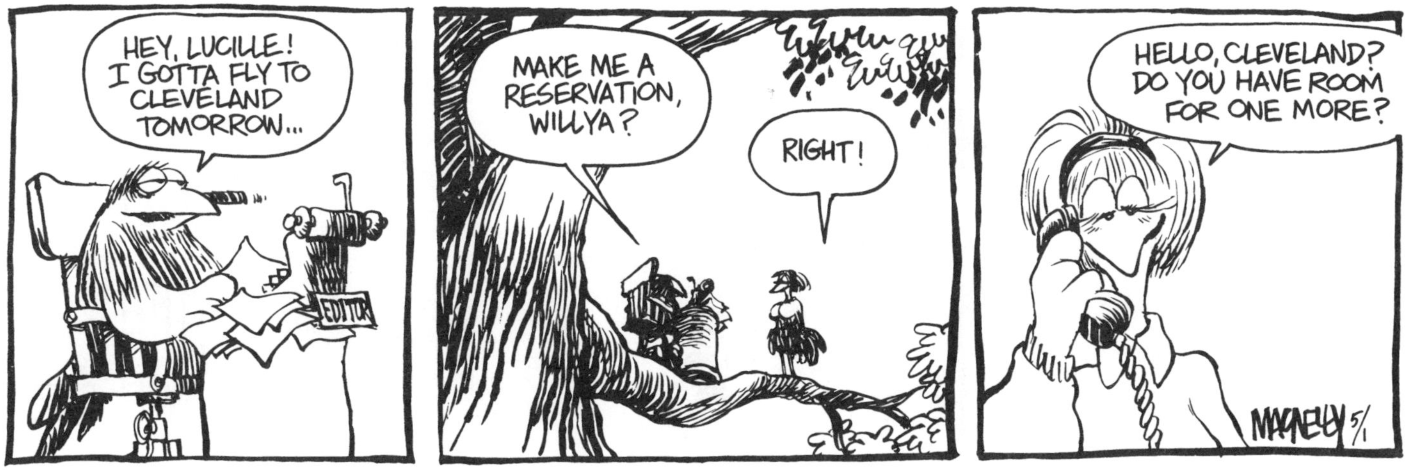
HEY, LUCILLE! I GOTTA FLY TO CLEVELAND TOMORROW...
EDITOR
MAKE ME A RESERVATION, WILLYA?
RIGHT!
HELLO, CLEVELAND? DO YOU HAVE ROOM FOR ONE MORE?
MACNELLY 5/1

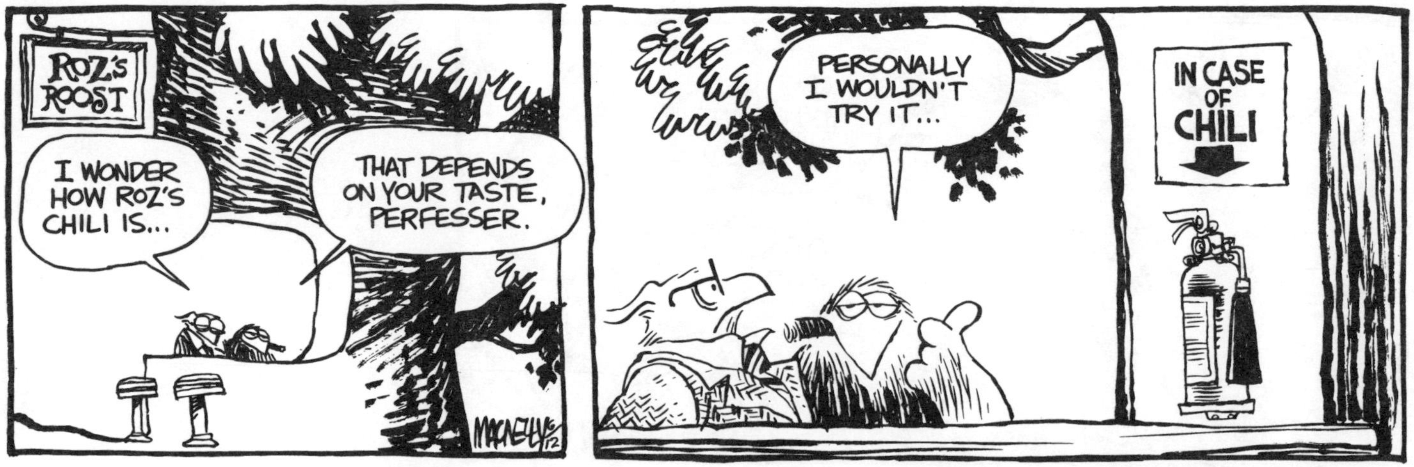
ROZ'S ROOST
I WONDER HOW ROZ'S CHILI IS...
THAT DEPENDS ON YOUR TASTE, PERFESSER.
PERSONALLY I WOULDN'T TRY IT...
IN CASE OF CHILI

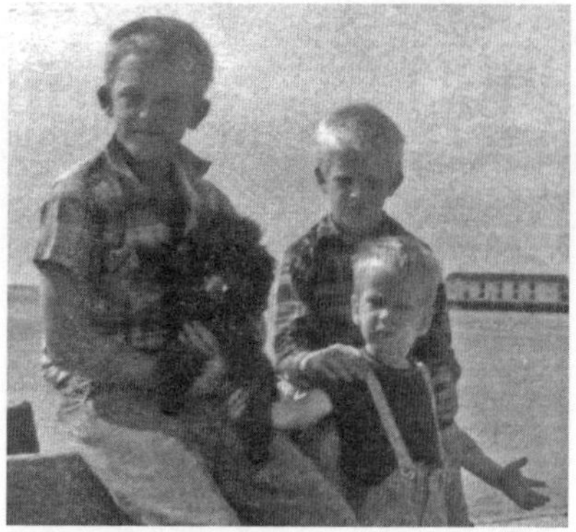

Jeff with brothers Bruce and Jocko

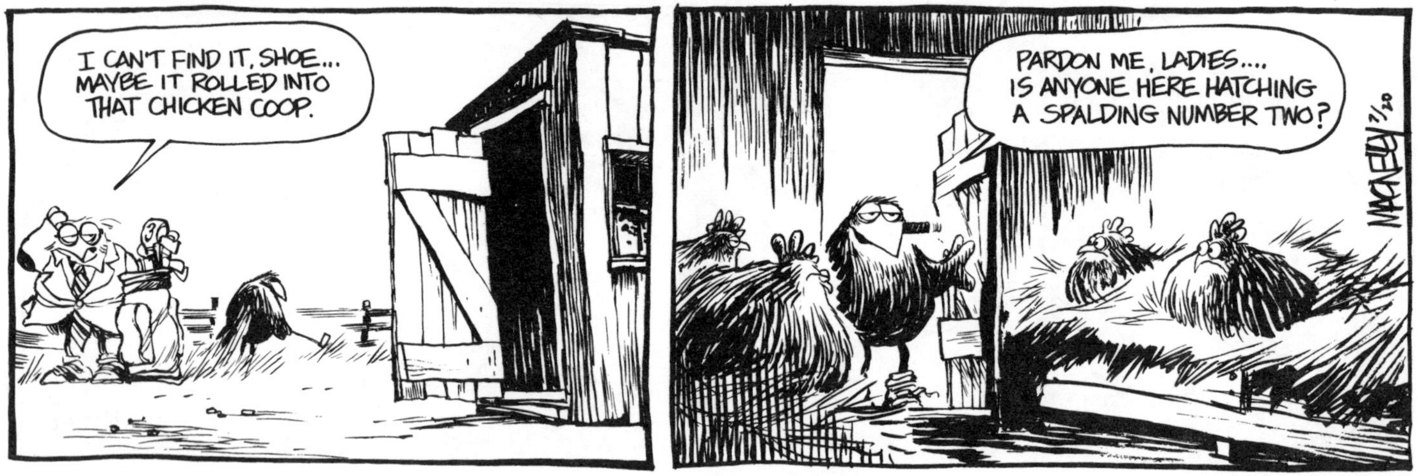
I CAN'T FIND IT, SHOE... MAYBE IT ROLLED INTO THAT CHICKEN COOP.
PARDON ME, LADIES.... IS ANYONE HERE HATCHING A SPALDING NUMBER TWO?
MACNELLY 7/20

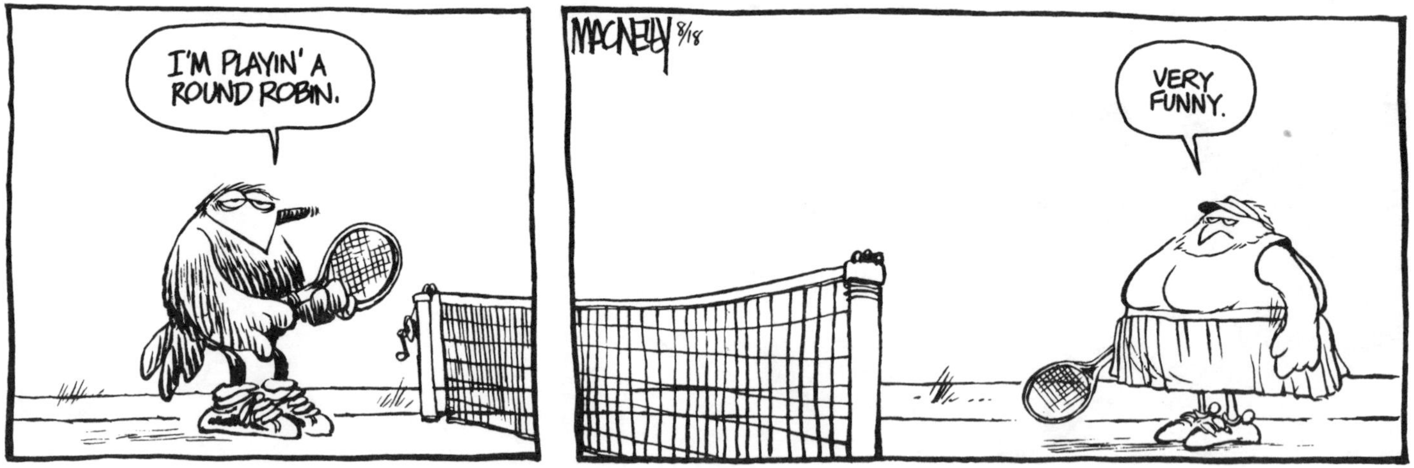
I'M PLAYIN' A ROUND ROBIN.
MACNELLY 8/18
VERY FUNNY.

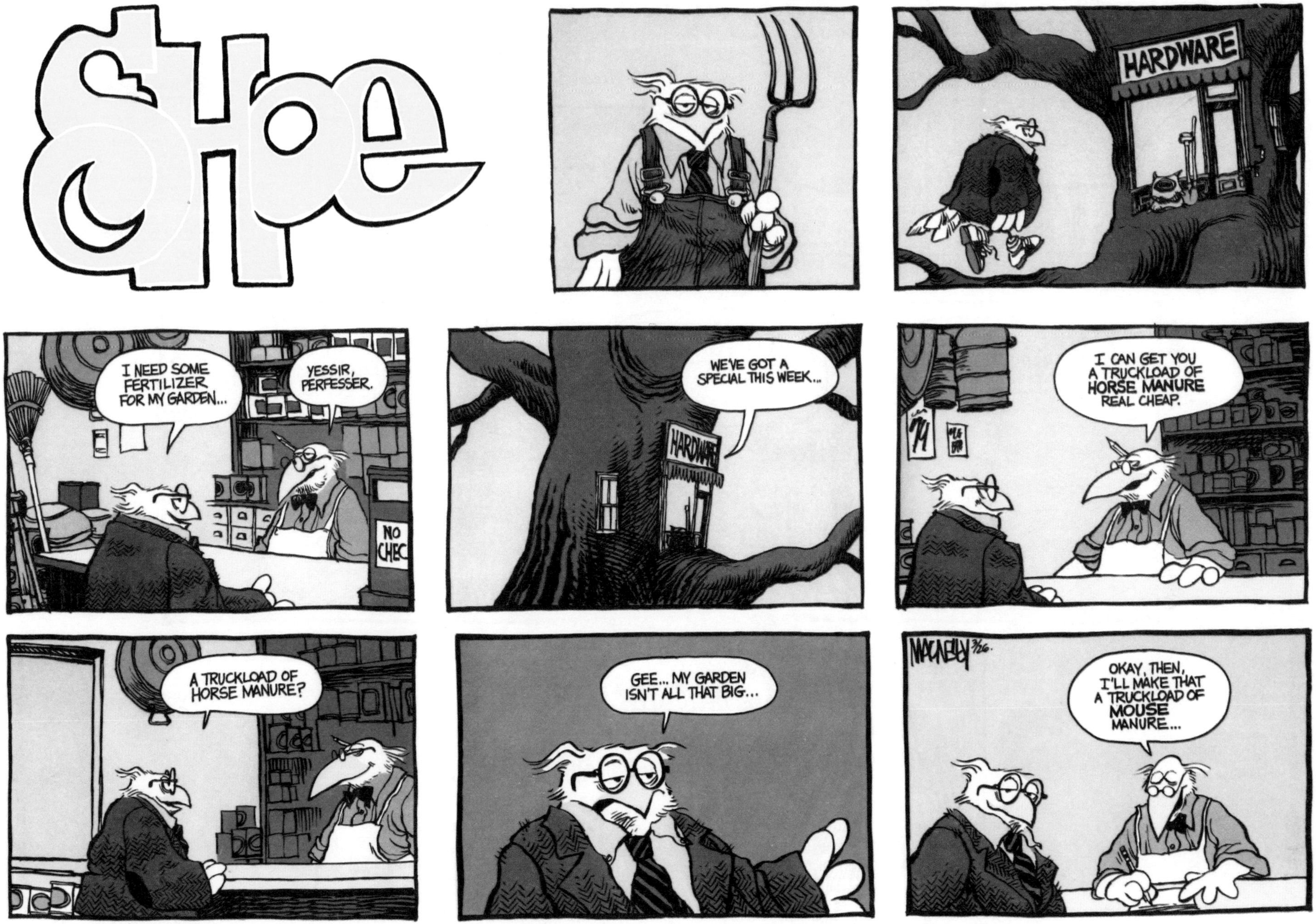
SHOE
HARDWARE
I NEED SOME FERTILIZER FOR MY GARDEN...
YESSIR, PERFESSER.
NO CHEC
WE'VE GOT A SPECIAL THIS WEEK...
HARDWARE
I CAN GET YOU A TRUCKLOAD OF HORSE MANURE REAL CHEAP.
A TRUCKLOAD OF HORSE MANURE?
GEE... MY GARDEN ISN'T ALL THAT BIG...
MACNELLY
OKAY, THEN, I'LL MAKE THAT A TRUCKLOAD OF MOUSE MANURE...

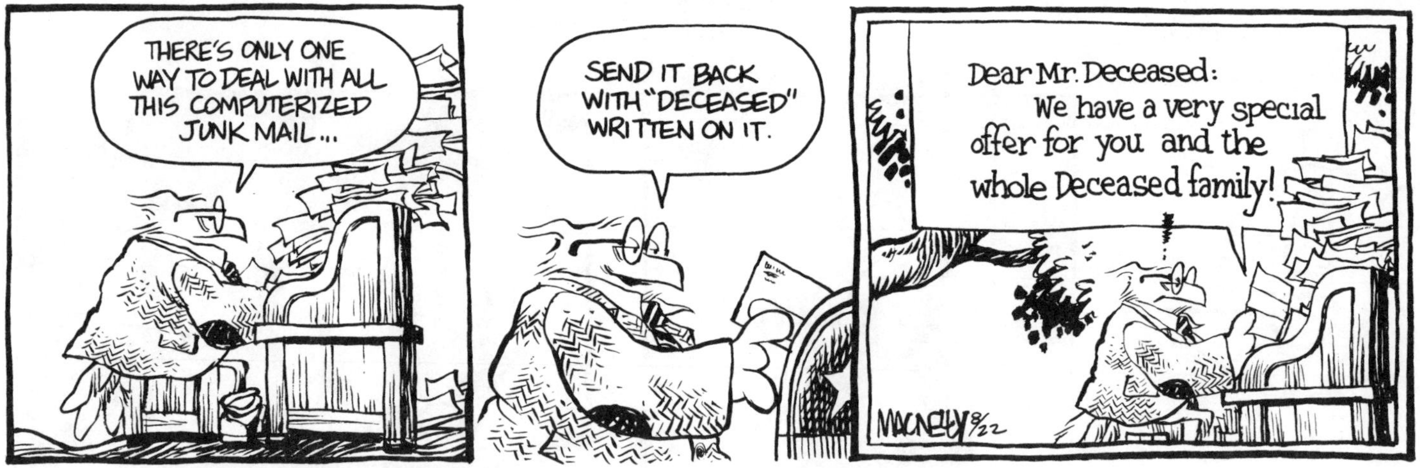
THERE'S ONLY ONE WAY TO DEAL WITH ALL THIS COMPUTERIZED JUNK MAIL...
SEND IT BACK WITH "DECEASED" WRITTEN ON IT.
Dear Mr. Deceased:
We have a very special offer for you and the whole Deceased family!
MACNELLY 8/22

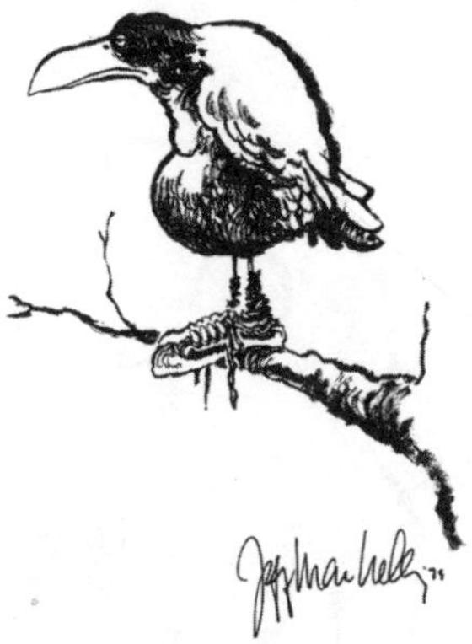

The very first known drawing of Shoe

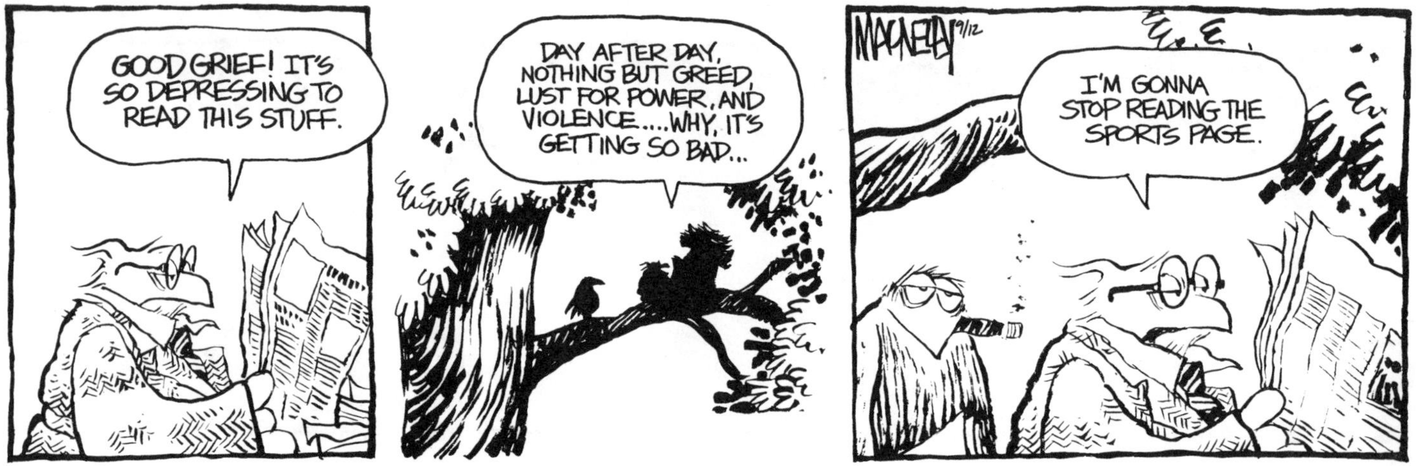
GOOD GRIEF! IT'S SO DEPRESSING TO READ THIS STUFF.
DAY AFTER DAY, NOTHING BUT GREED, LUST FOR POWER, AND VIOLENCE....WHY, IT'S GETTING SO BAD...
MACNELLY 9/12
I'M GONNA STOP READING THE SPORTS PAGE.

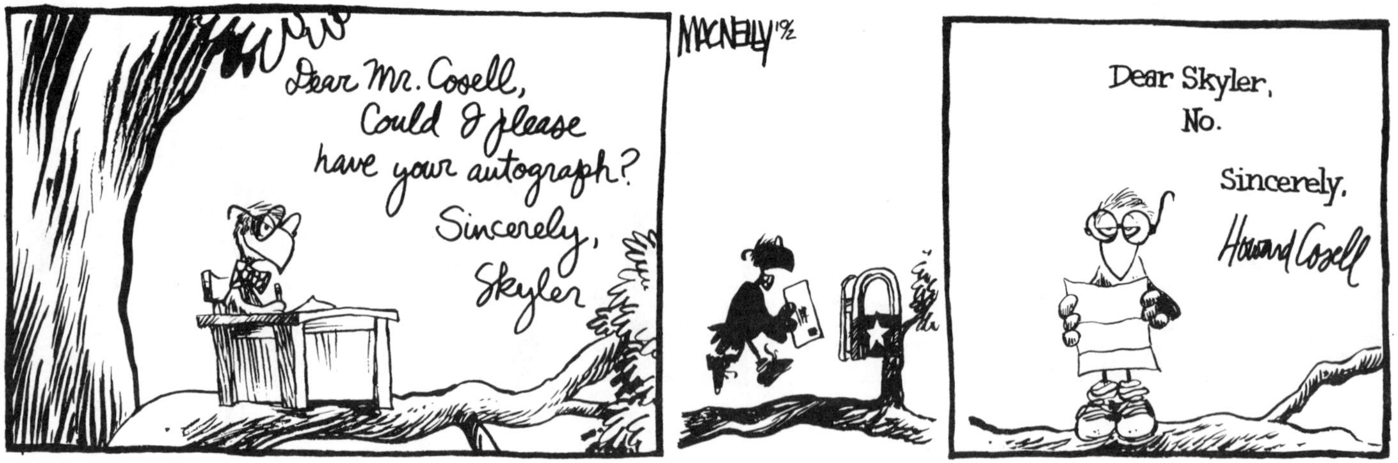
Dear Mr. Cosell,
Could I please have your autograph?
Sincerely,
Skyler
MACNELLY 10/2
Dear Skyler,
No.
Sincerely,
Howard Cosell

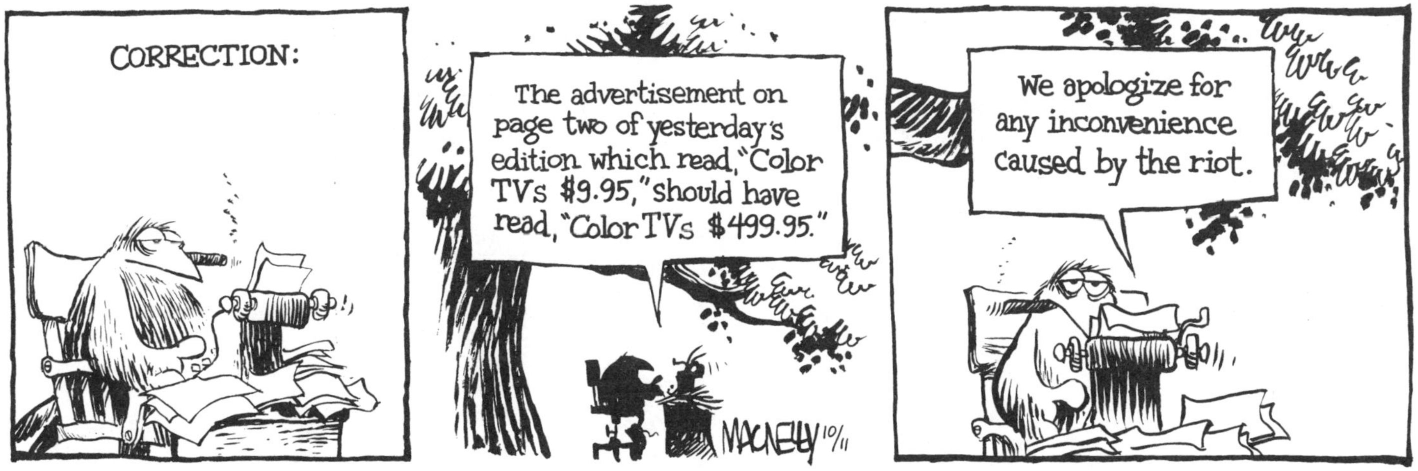
CORRECTION:
The advertisement on page two of yesterday's edition which read, "Color TVs $9.95," should have read, "Color TVs $499.95."
We apologize for any inconvenience caused by the riot.
MACNELLY 10/11

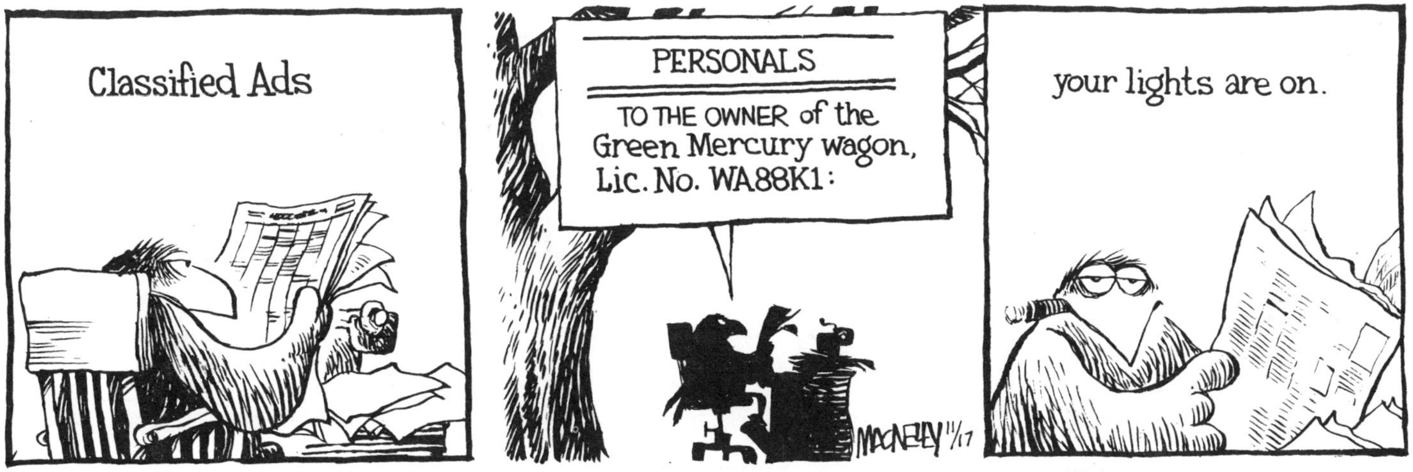
Classified Ads
PERSONALS
TO THE OWNER of the Green Mercury wagon, Lic. No. WA88K1:
your lights are on.
MACNELLY 11/17

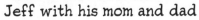

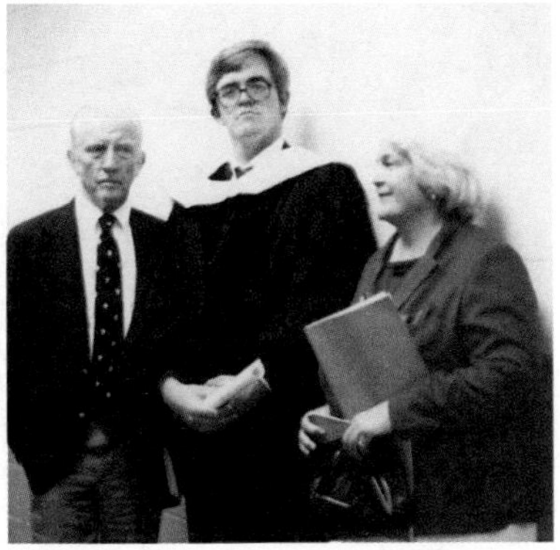
Jeff with his mom and dad

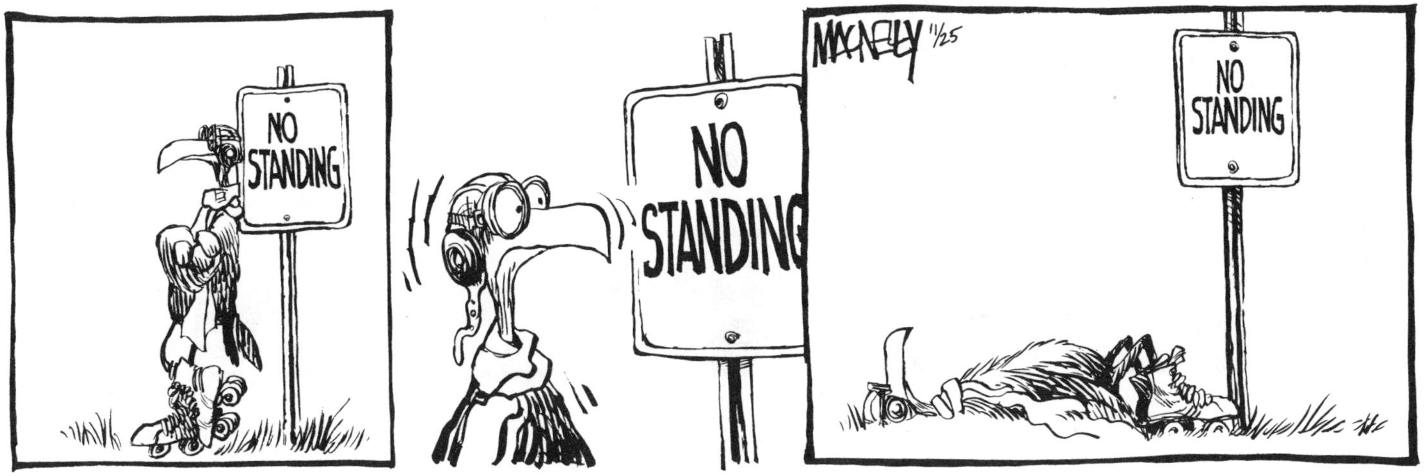
NO STANDING
NO STANDING
MACNELLY 11/25
NO STANDING

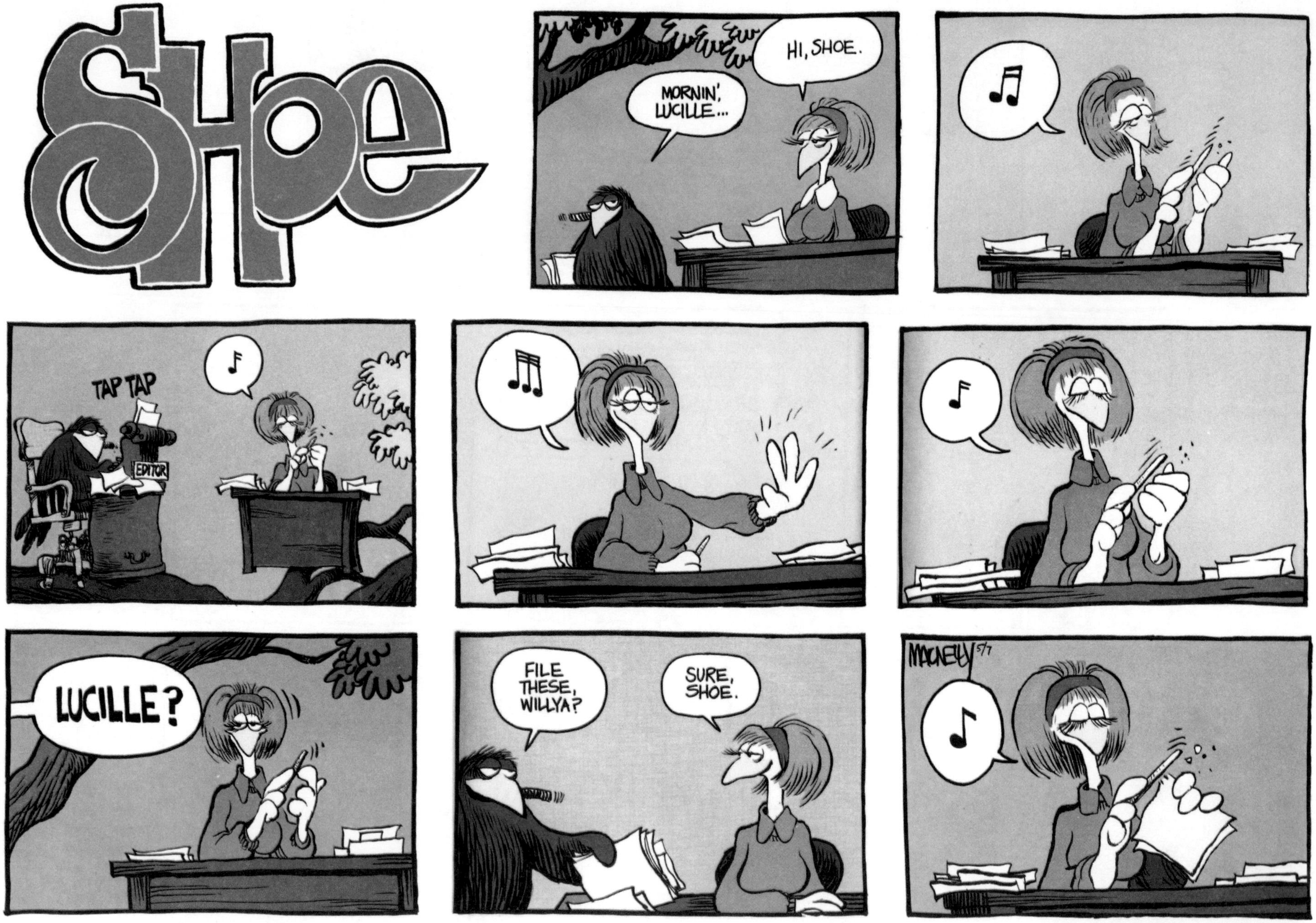
SHOE
MORNIN', LUCILLE...
HI, SHOE.
TAP TAP
EDITOR
LUCILLE?
FILE THESE, WILLYA?
SURE, SHOE.
MACNELLY

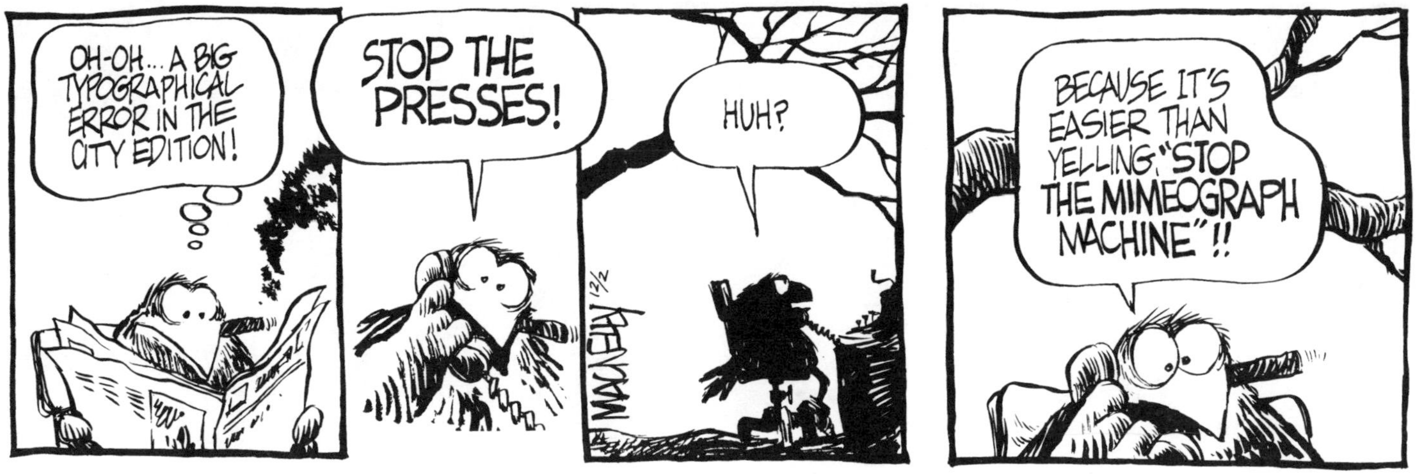
OH-OH... A BIG TYPOGRAPHICAL ERROR IN THE CITY EDITION!
STOP THE PRESSES!
HUH?
MACNELLY 12/2
BECAUSE IT'S EASIER THAN YELLING, "STOP THE MIMEOGRAPH MACHINE"!!

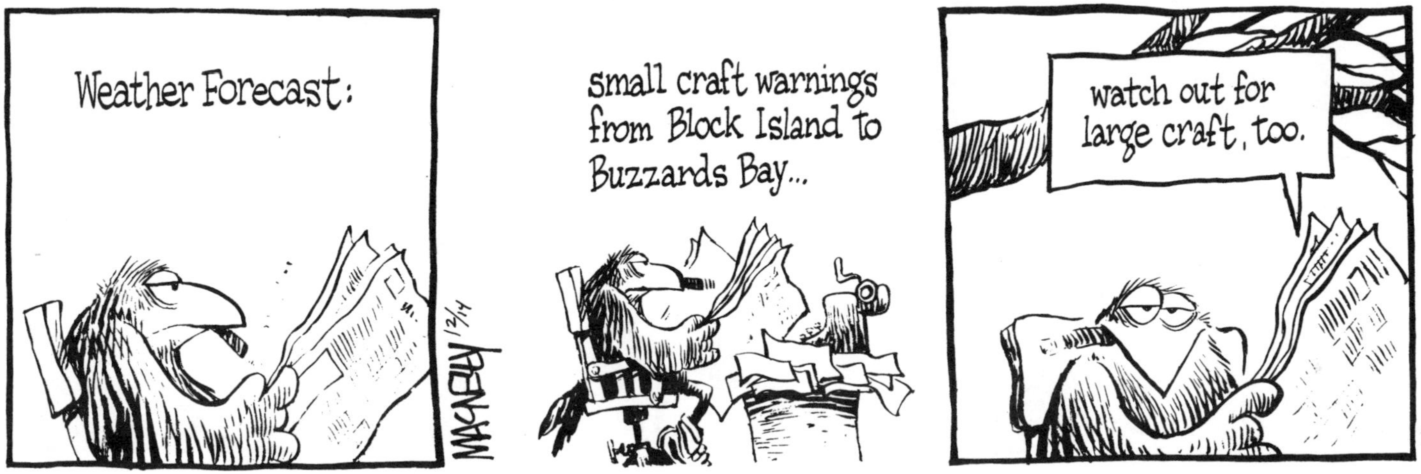
Weather Forecast:
MACNELLY 12/4
small craft warnings from Block Island to Buzzards Bay...
watch out for large craft, too.

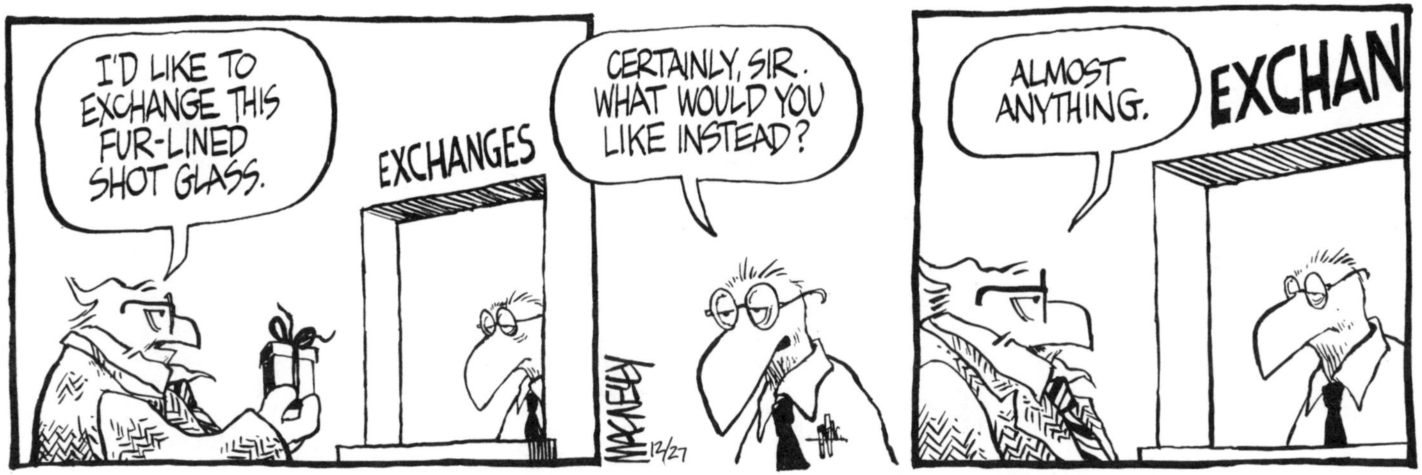
I'D LIKE TO EXCHANGE THIS FUR-LINED SHOT GLASS.
EXCHANGES
CERTAINLY, SIR. WHAT WOULD YOU LIKE INSTEAD?
MACNELLY 12/27
ALMOST ANYTHING.
EXCHAN

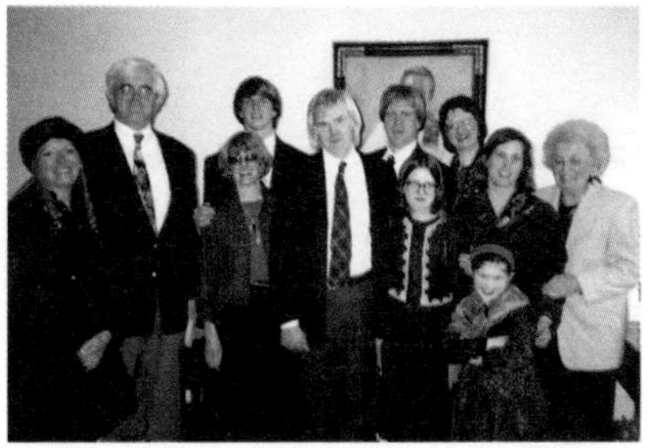

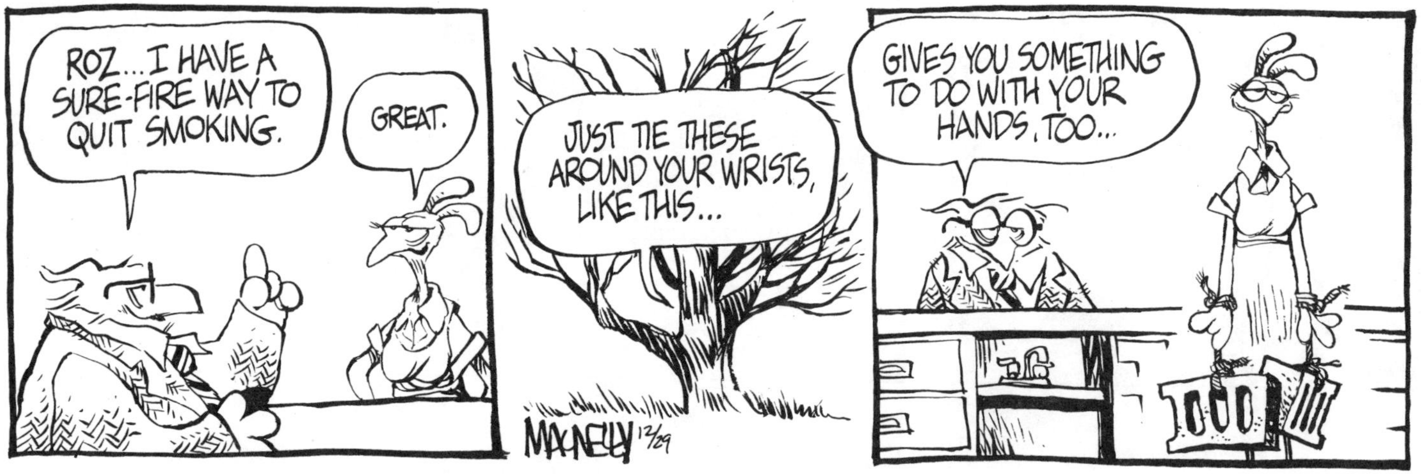
ROZ... I HAVE A SURE-FIRE WAY TO QUIT SMOKING.
GREAT.
JUST TIE THESE AROUND YOUR WRISTS, LIKE THIS...
GIVES YOU SOMETHING TO DO WITH YOUR HANDS, TOO...
MACNELLY 12/29

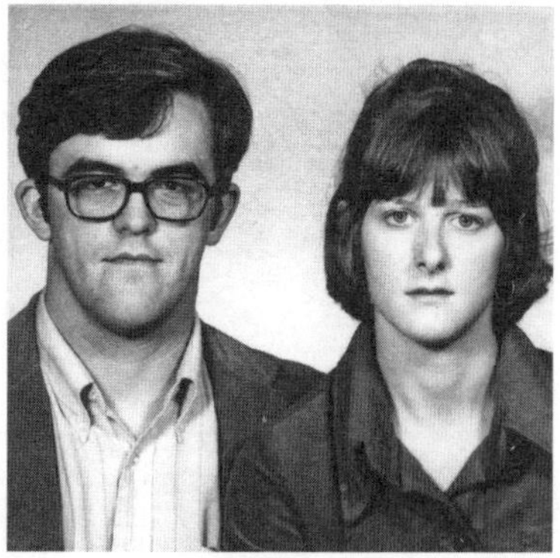

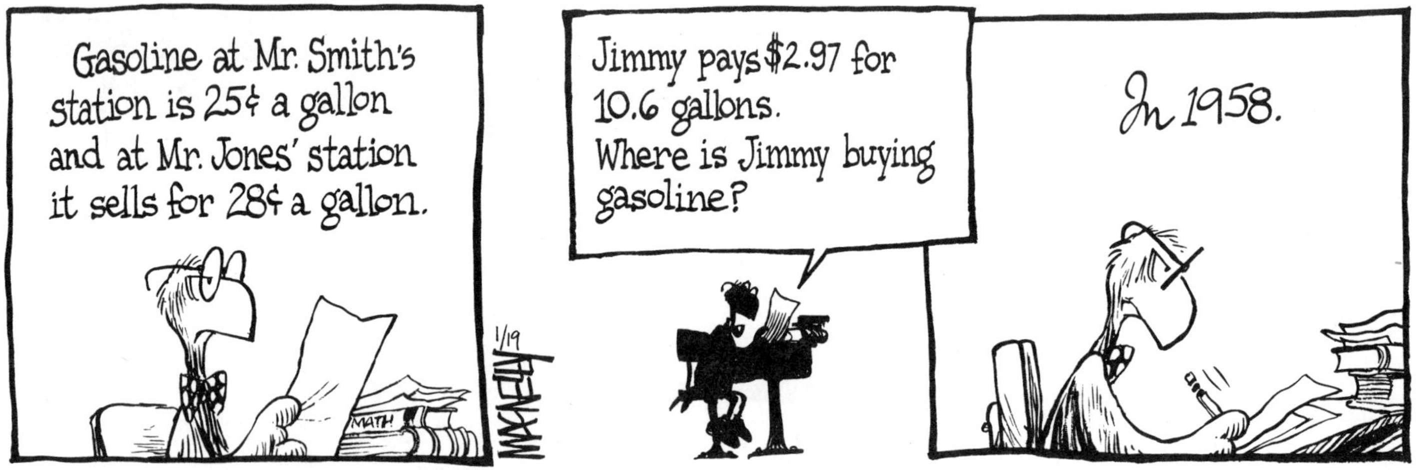
Gasoline at Mr. Smith's station is 25¢ a gallon and at Mr. Jones' station it sells for 28¢ a gallon.
MATH
MACNELLY 1/19
Jimmy pays $2.97 for 10.6 gallons. Where is Jimmy buying gasoline?
In 1958.

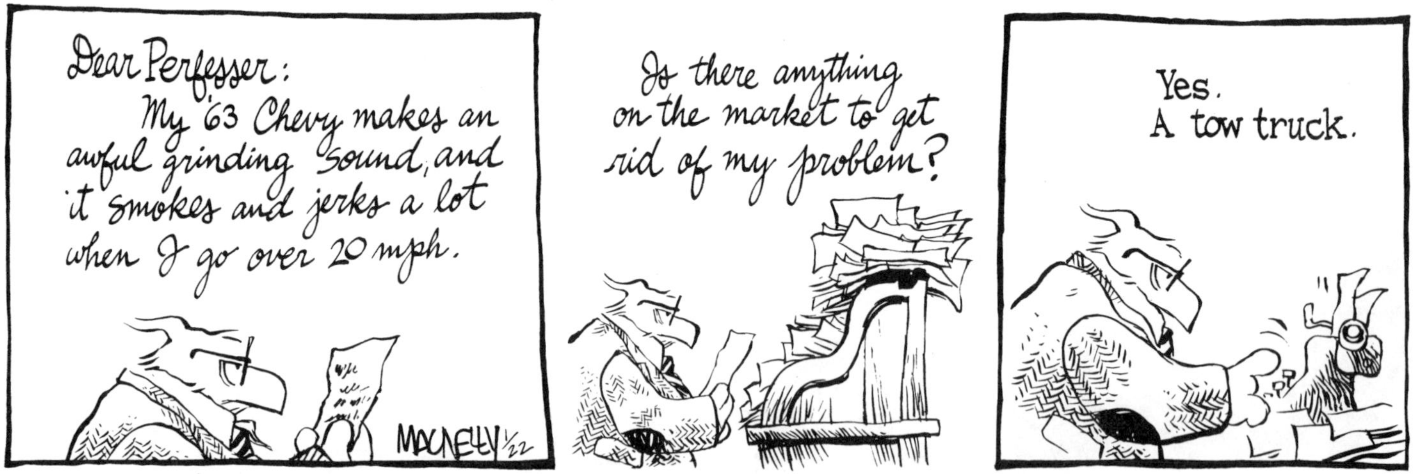
Dear Perfesser: My '63 Chevy makes an awful grinding sound, and it smokes and jerks a lot when I go over 20 mph.
MACNELLY 1/22
Is there anything on the market to get rid of my problem?
Yes. A tow truck.

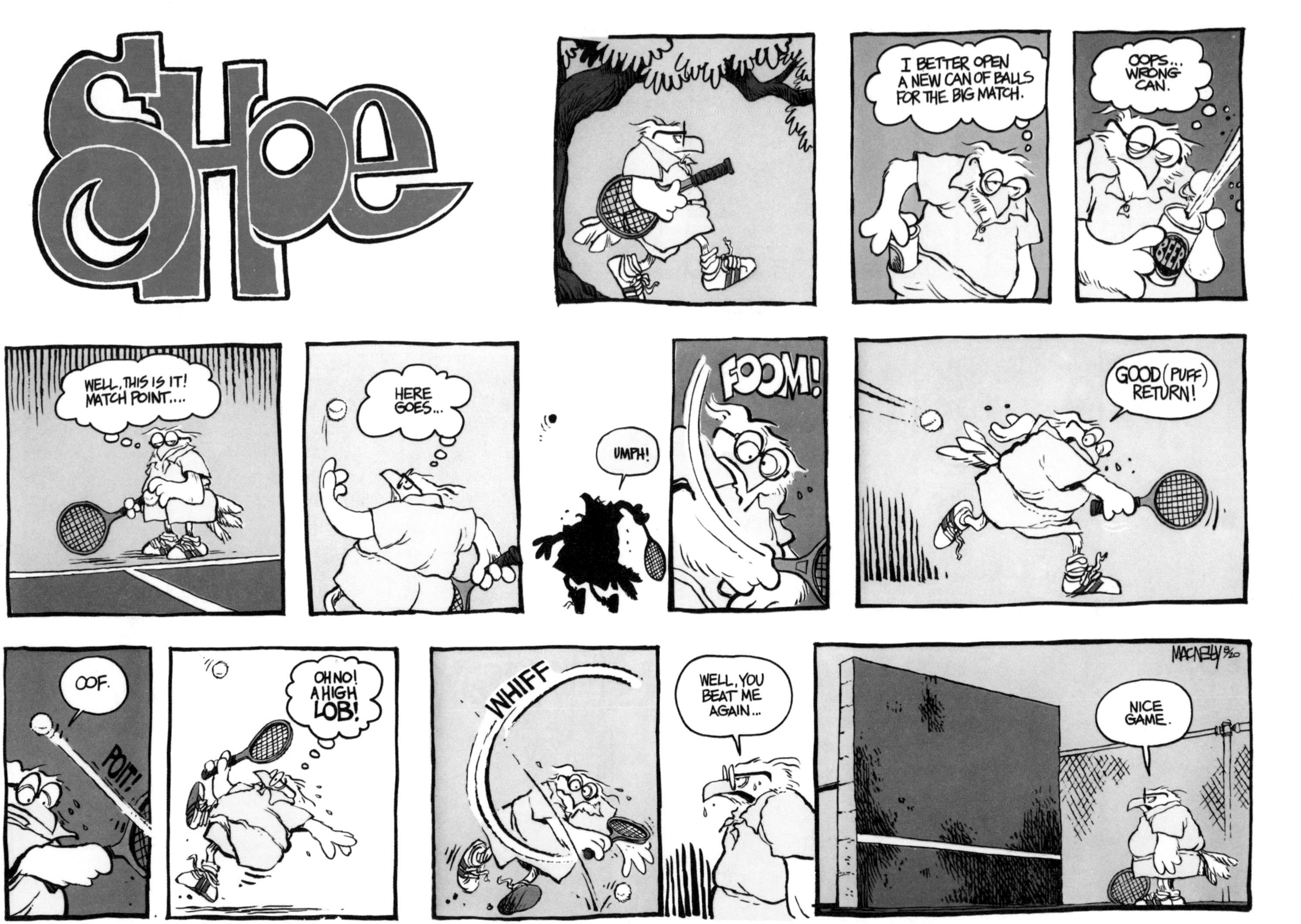

SHOE
I BETTER OPEN A NEW CAN OF BALLS FOR THE BIG MATCH.
OOPS... WRONG CAN.
BEER
WELL, THIS IS IT! MATCH POINT....
HERE GOES...
UMPH!
FOOM!
GOOD (PUFF) RETURN!
OOF.
POIT!
OH NO! A HIGH LOB!
WHIFF
WELL, YOU BEAT ME AGAIN...
NICE GAME.
MACNELLY

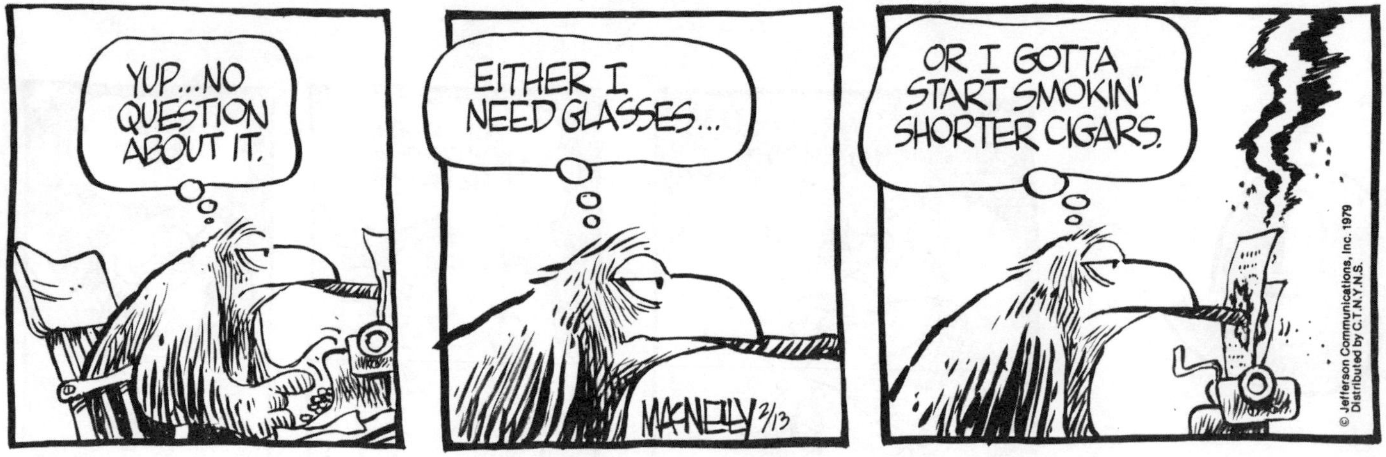
YUP...NO QUESTION ABOUT IT.
EITHER I NEED GLASSES...
OR I GOTTA START SMOKIN' SHORTER CIGARS.
MACNELLY 2/13
© Jefferson Communications, Inc. 1979 Distributed by C.T.N.Y.N.S.

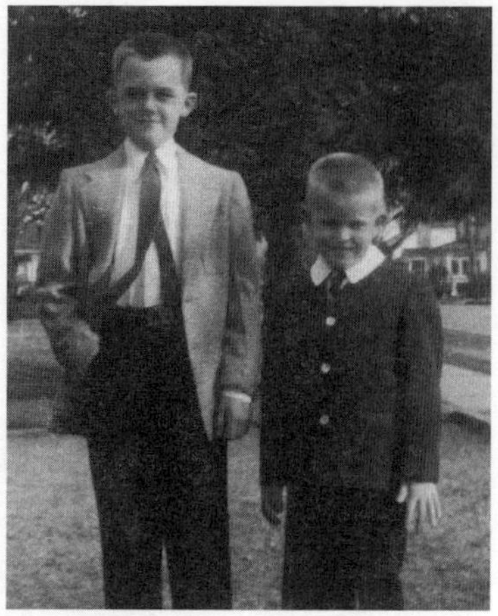

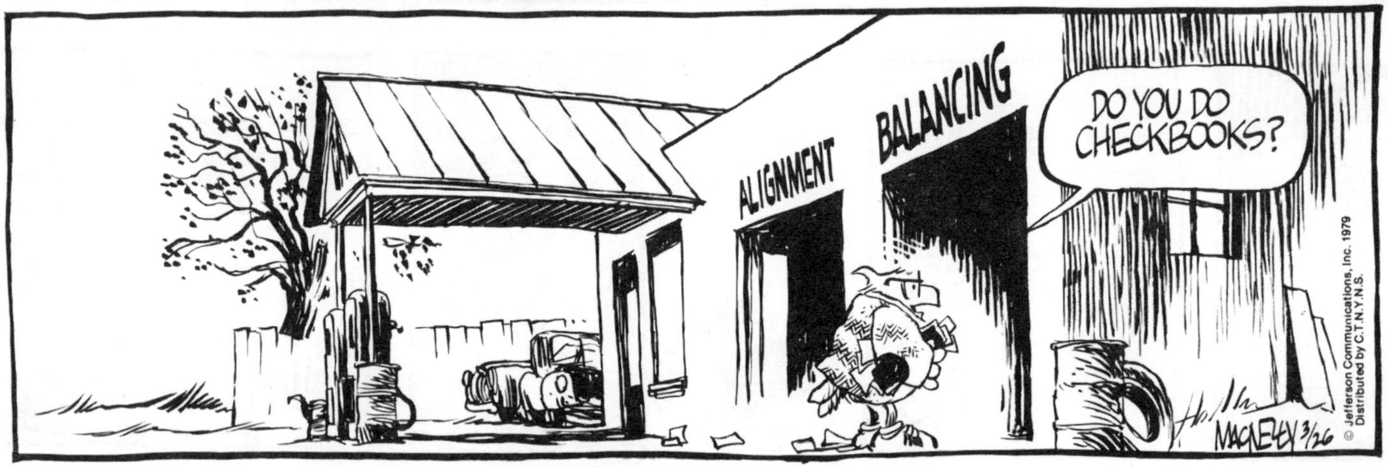
ALIGNMENT
BALANCING
DO YOU DO CHECKBOOKS?
MACNELLY 3/26
© Jefferson Communications, Inc. 1979 Distributed by C.T.N.Y.N.S.

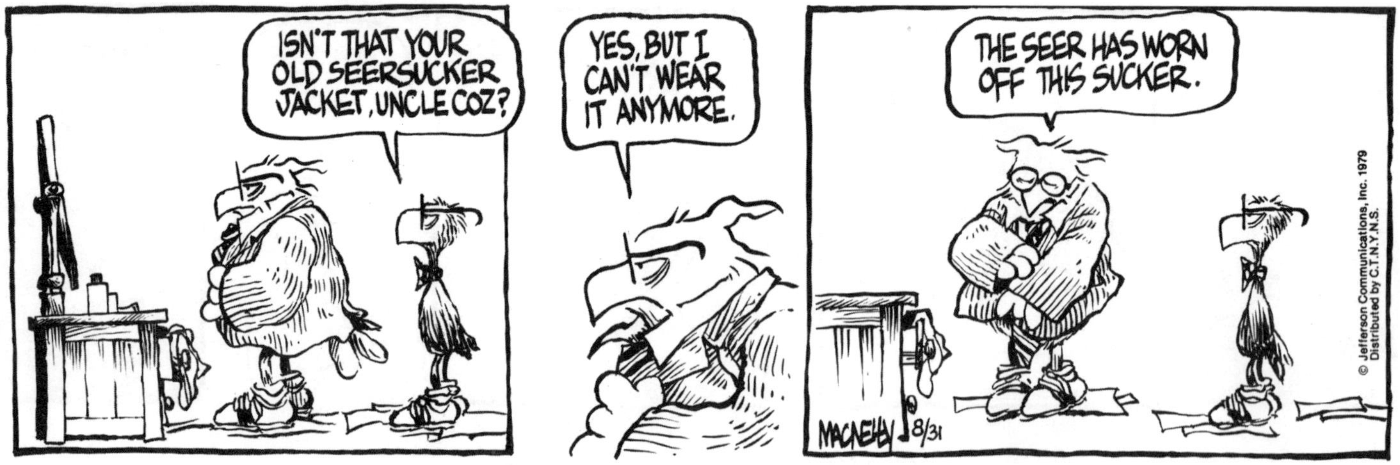
ISN'T THAT YOUR OLD SEERSUCKER JACKET, UNCLE COZ?
YES, BUT I CAN'T WEAR IT ANYMORE.
THE SEER HAS WORN OFF THIS SUCKER.
MACNELLY 8/31
© Jefferson Communications, Inc. 1979 Distributed by C.T.N.Y.N.S.

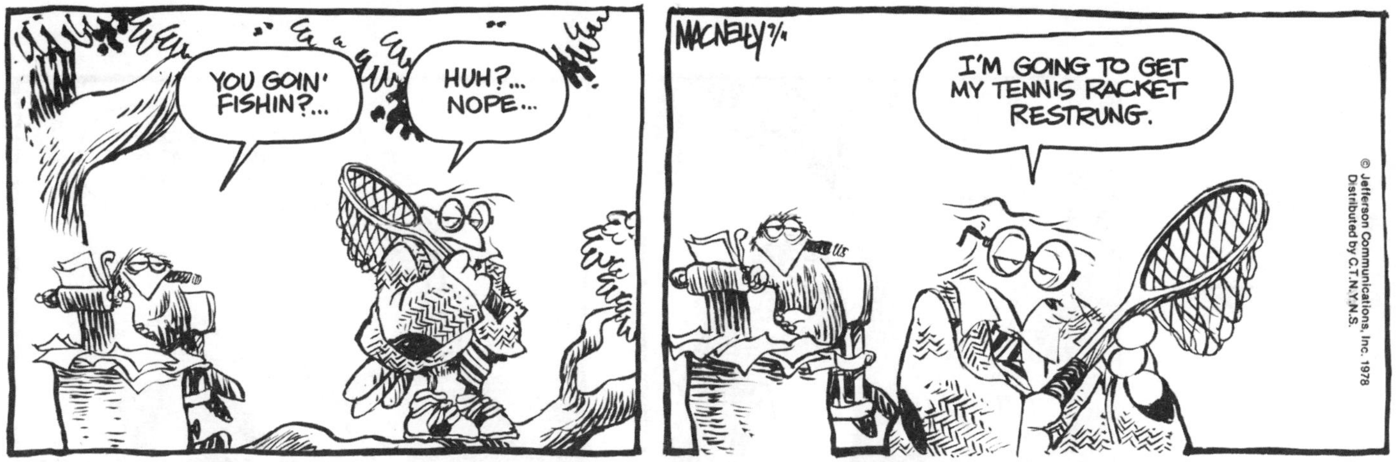
YOU GOIN' FISHIN?...
HUH?... NOPE...
MACNELLY 9/4
I'M GOING TO GET MY TENNIS RACKET RESTRUNG.
© Jefferson Communications, Inc. 1978
Distributed by C.T.N.Y.N.S.

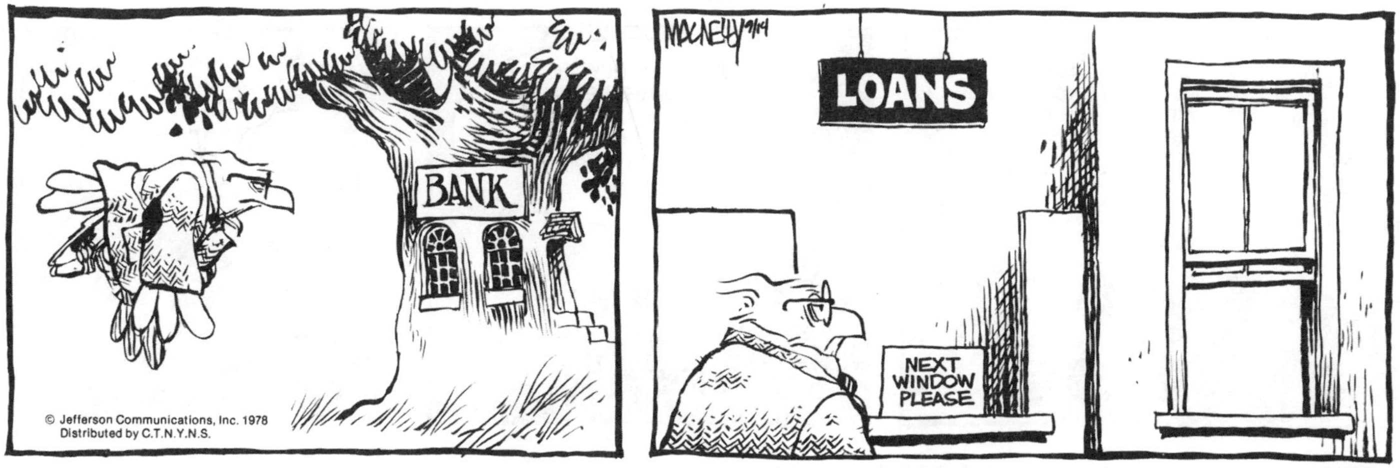
BANK
© Jefferson Communications, Inc. 1978
Distributed by C.T.N.Y.N.S.
LOANS
NEXT WINDOW PLEASE

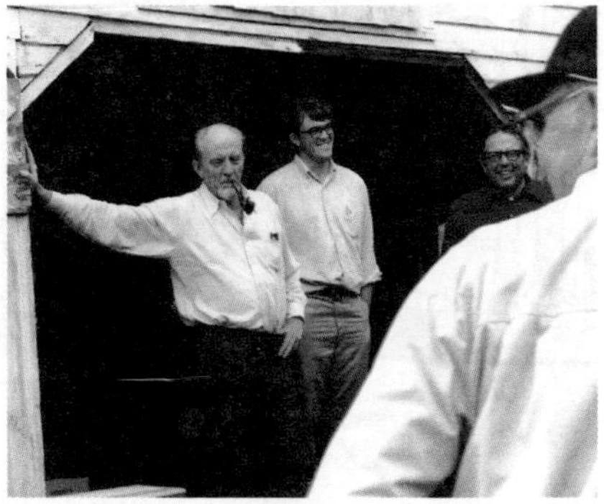

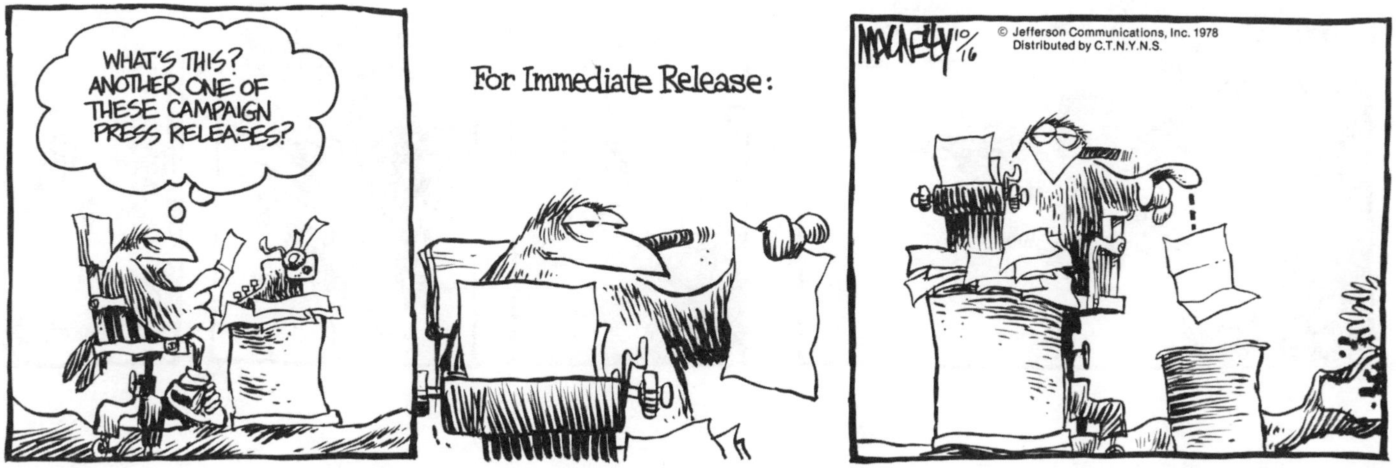
WHAT'S THIS? ANOTHER ONE OF THESE CAMPAIGN PRESS RELEASES?
For Immediate Release:
© Jefferson Communications, Inc. 1978
Distributed by C.T.N.Y.N.S.

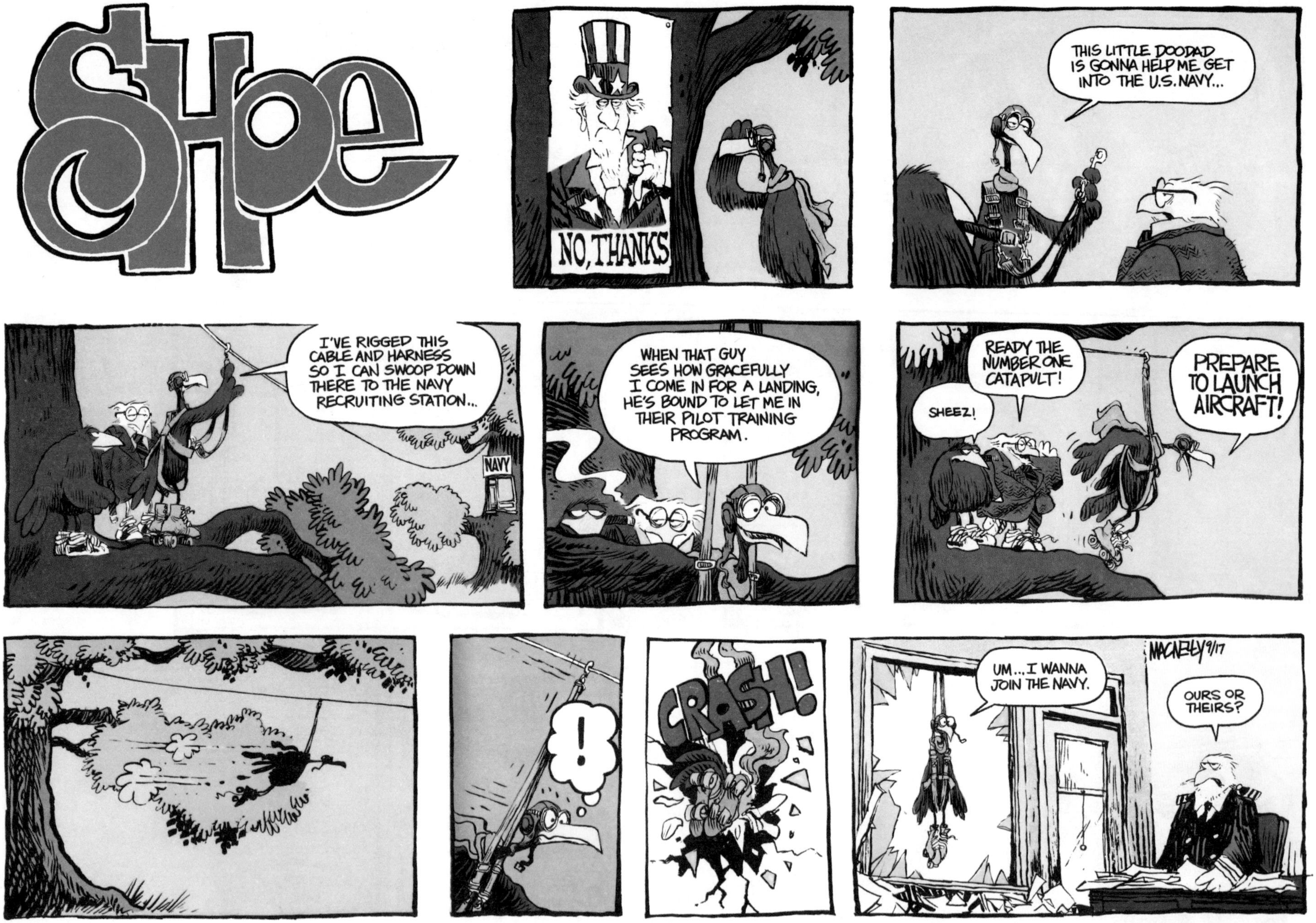
SHOE
NO, THANKS
THIS LITTLE DOODAD IS GONNA HELP ME GET INTO THE U.S. NAVY...
I'VE RIGGED THIS CABLE AND HARNESS SO I CAN SWOOP DOWN THERE TO THE NAVY RECRUITING STATION...
NAVY
WHEN THAT GUY SEES HOW GRACEFULLY I COME IN FOR A LANDING, HE'S BOUND TO LET ME IN THEIR PILOT TRAINING PROGRAM.
SHEEZ!
READY THE NUMBER ONE CATAPULT!
PREPARE TO LAUNCH AIRCRAFT!
!
CRASH!
MACNELLY 9/17
UM... I WANNA JOIN THE NAVY.
OURS OR THEIRS?

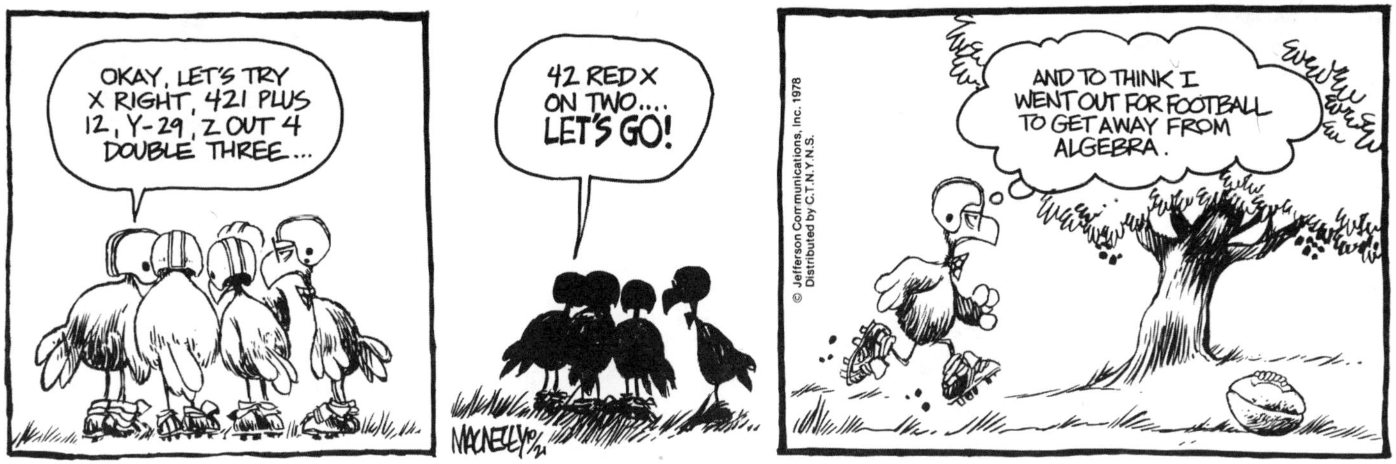
OKAY, LET'S TRY X RIGHT, 421 PLUS 12, Y-29, Z OUT 4 DOUBLE THREE...
42 RED X ON TWO.... LET'S GO!
© Jefferson Communications, Inc. 1978
Distributed by C.T.N.Y.N.S.
AND TO THINK I WENT OUT FOR FOOTBALL TO GET AWAY FROM ALGEBRA.

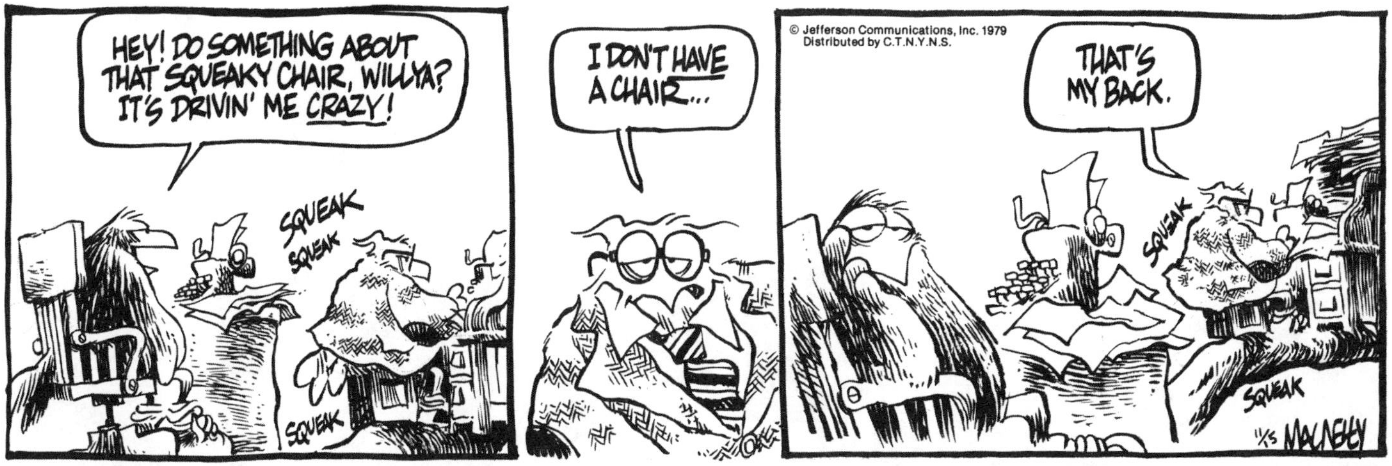
HEY! DO SOMETHING ABOUT THAT SQUEAKY CHAIR, WILLYA? IT'S DRIVIN' ME CRAZY!
SQUEAK
SQUEAK
SQUEAK
I DON'T HAVE A CHAIR...
© Jefferson Communications, Inc. 1979
Distributed by C.T.N.Y.N.S.
THAT'S MY BACK.
SQUEAK
SQUEAK
MACNELLY

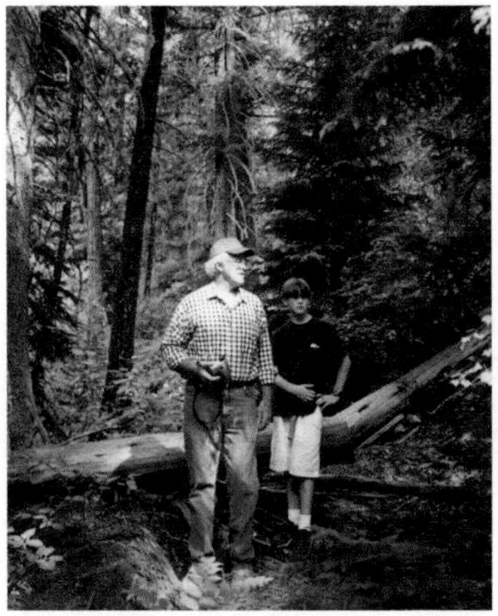

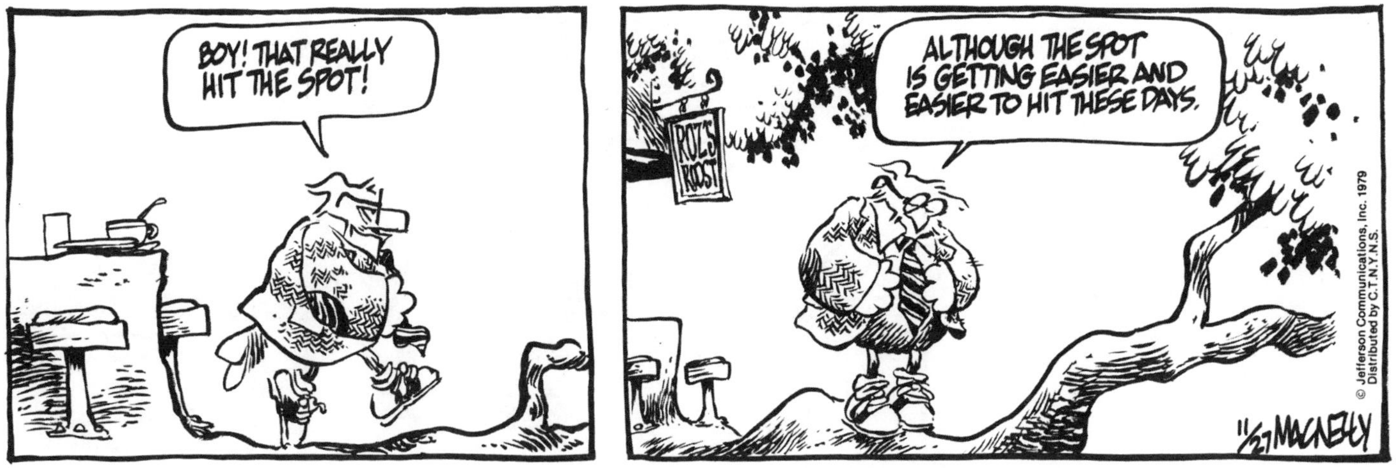
BOY! THAT REALLY HIT THE SPOT!
ROZ'S ROOST
ALTHOUGH THE SPOT IS GETTING EASIER AND EASIER TO HIT THESE DAYS.
© Jefferson Communications, Inc. 1979
Distributed by C.T.N.Y.N.S.
MACNELLY

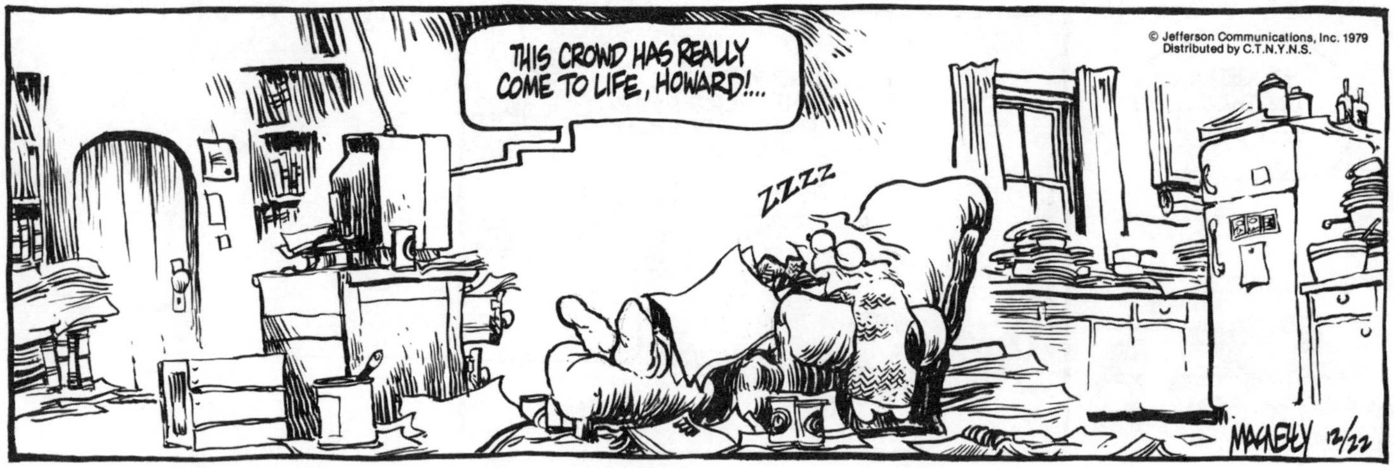
THIS CROWD HAS REALLY COME TO LIFE, HOWARD!...
ZZZZ
© Jefferson Communications, Inc. 1979 Distributed by C.T.N.Y.N.S.
MACNELLY 12/22

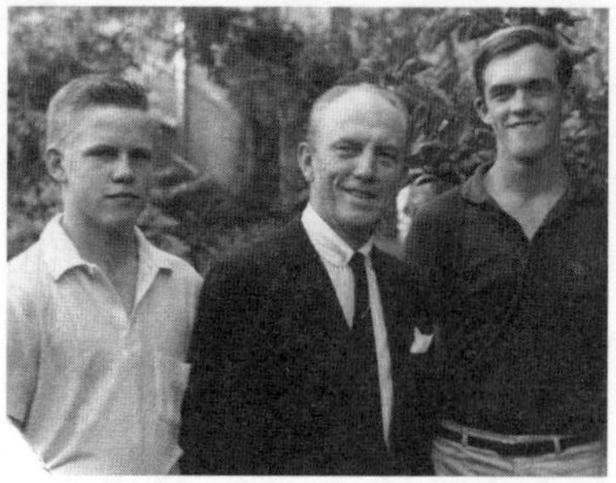

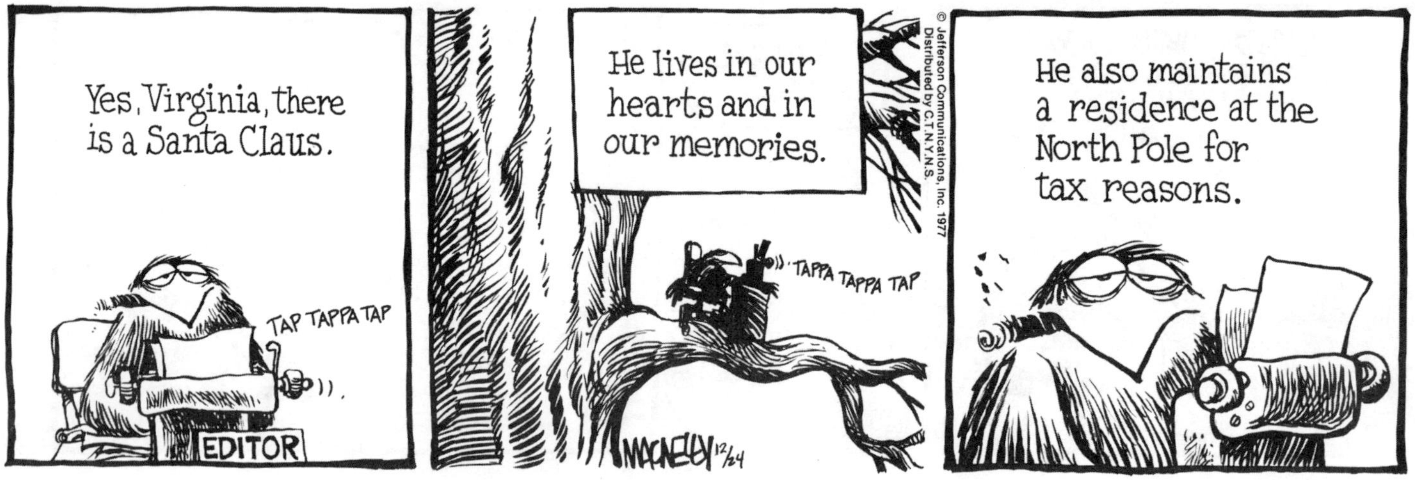
Yes, Virginia, there is a Santa Claus.
TAP TAPPA TAP
EDITOR
He lives in our hearts and in our memories.
TAPPA TAPPA TAP
MACNELLY 12/24
© Jefferson Communications, Inc. 1977 Distributed by C.T.N.Y.N.S.
He also maintains a residence at the North Pole for tax reasons.

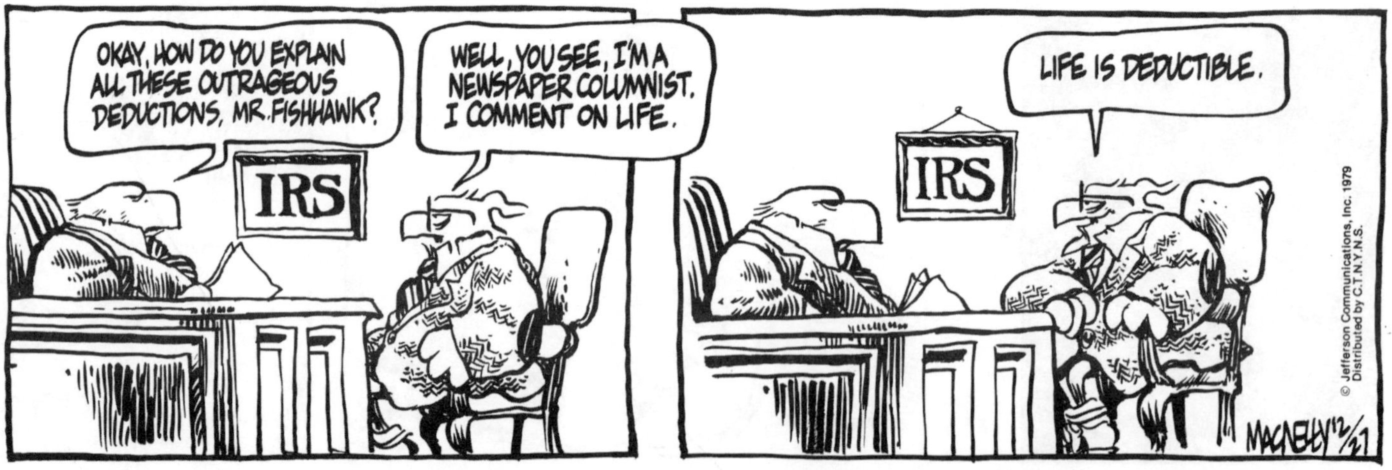
OKAY, HOW DO YOU EXPLAIN ALL THESE OUTRAGEOUS DEDUCTIONS, MR. FISHHAWK?
IRS
WELL, YOU SEE, I'M A NEWSPAPER COLUMNIST. I COMMENT ON LIFE.
IRS
LIFE IS DEDUCTIBLE.
© Jefferson Communications, Inc. 1979 Distributed by C.T.N.Y.N.S.
MACNELLY 12/27

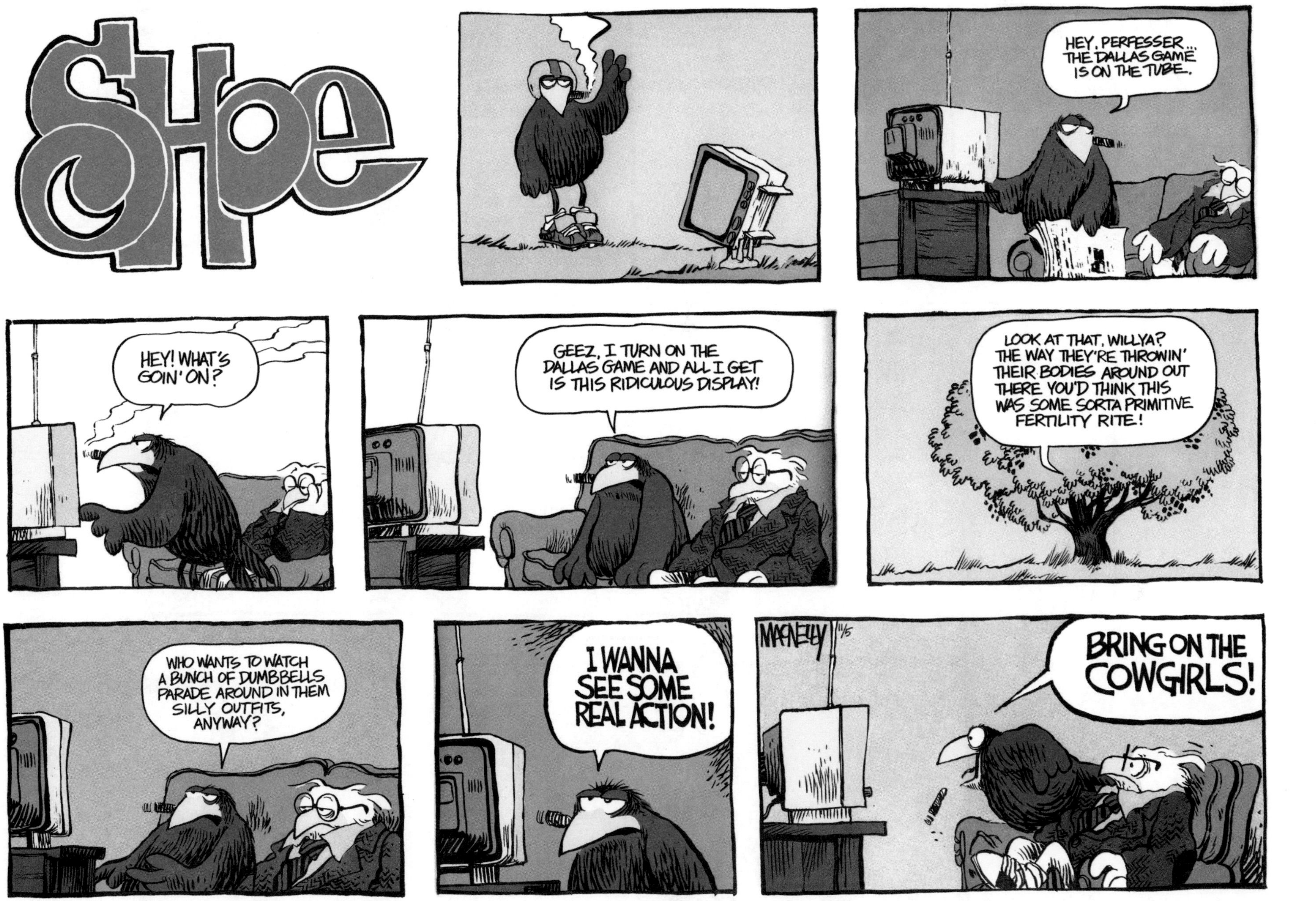
SHOE
HEY, PERFESSER... THE DALLAS GAME IS ON THE TUBE.
HEY! WHAT'S GOIN' ON?
GEEZ, I TURN ON THE DALLAS GAME AND ALL I GET IS THIS RIDICULOUS DISPLAY!
LOOK AT THAT, WILLYA? THE WAY THEY'RE THROWIN' THEIR BODIES AROUND OUT THERE YOU'D THINK THIS WAS SOME SORTA PRIMITIVE FERTILITY RITE!
WHO WANTS TO WATCH A BUNCH OF DUMBBELLS PARADE AROUND IN THEM SILLY OUTFITS, ANYWAY?
I WANNA SEE SOME REAL ACTION!
MACNELLY 11/5
BRING ON THE COWGIRLS!

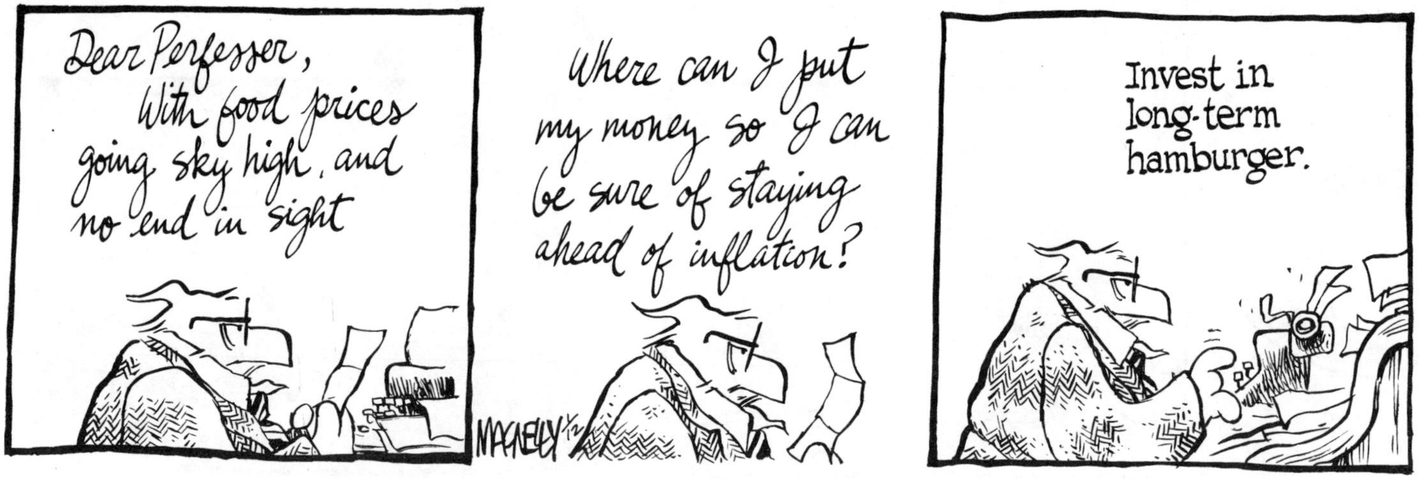
Dear Perfesser,
With food prices going sky high, and no end in sight
Where can I put my money so I can be sure of staying ahead of inflation?
Invest in long-term hamburger.

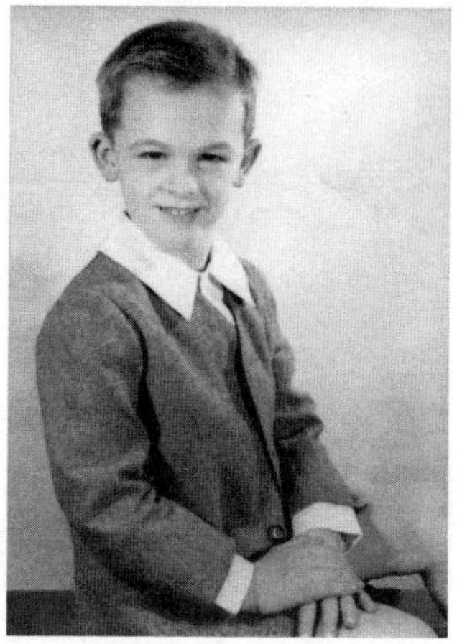

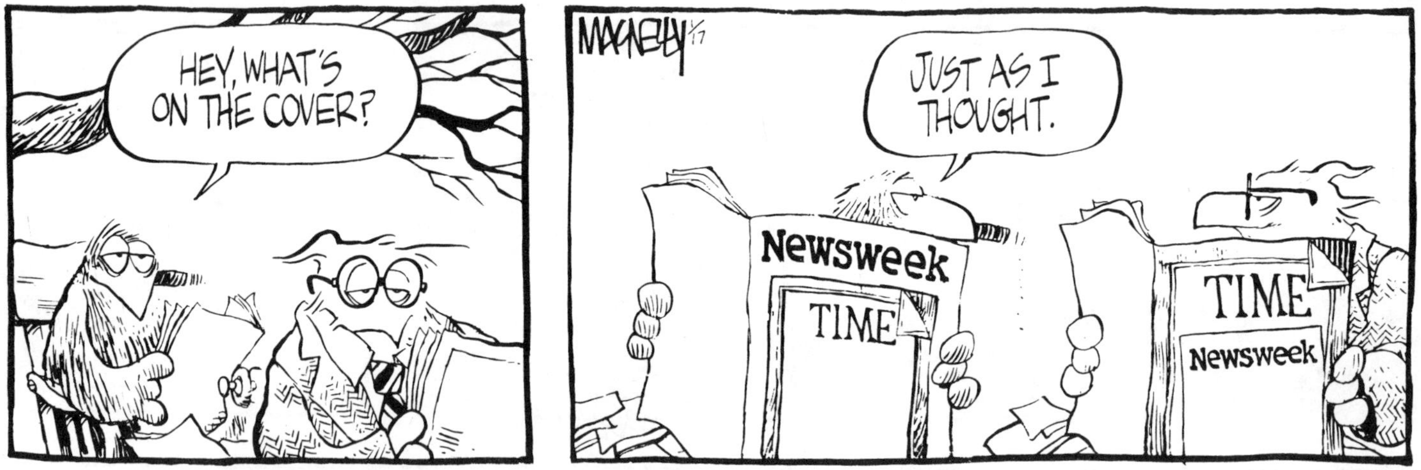
HEY, WHAT'S ON THE COVER?
JUST AS I THOUGHT.
Newsweek
TIME
TIME
Newsweek

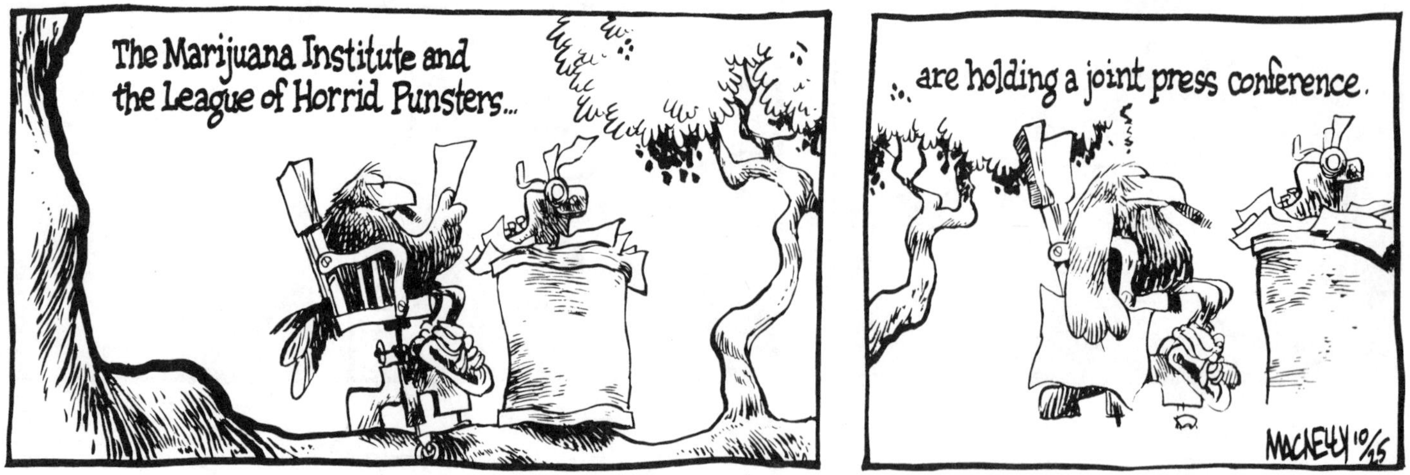
The Marijuana Institute and the League of Horrid Punsters...
.. are holding a joint press conference.

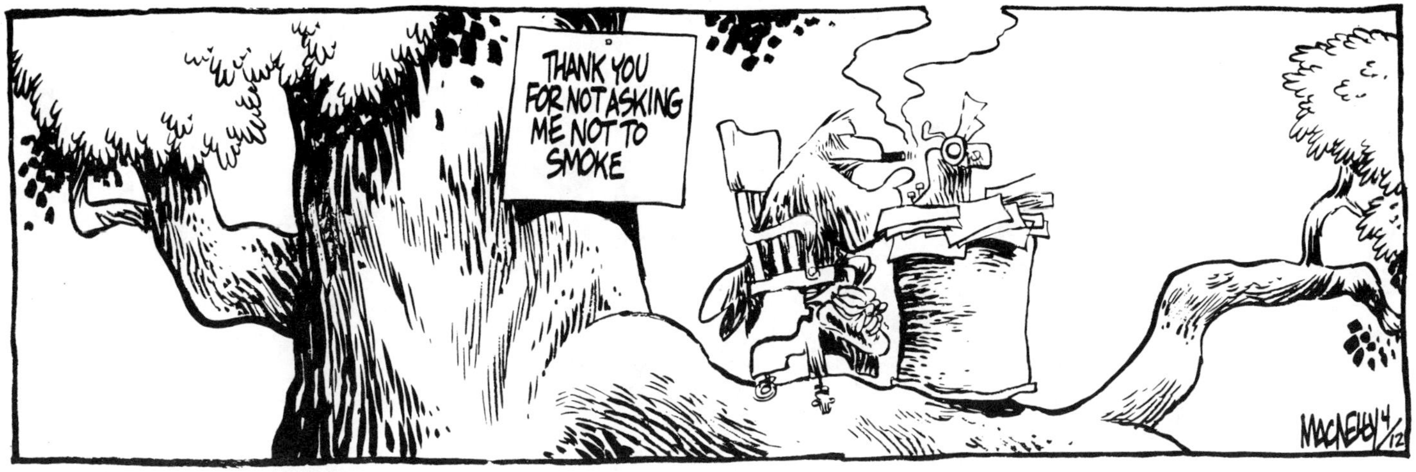
THANK YOU FOR NOT ASKING ME NOT TO SMOKE
MACNELLY 4/12

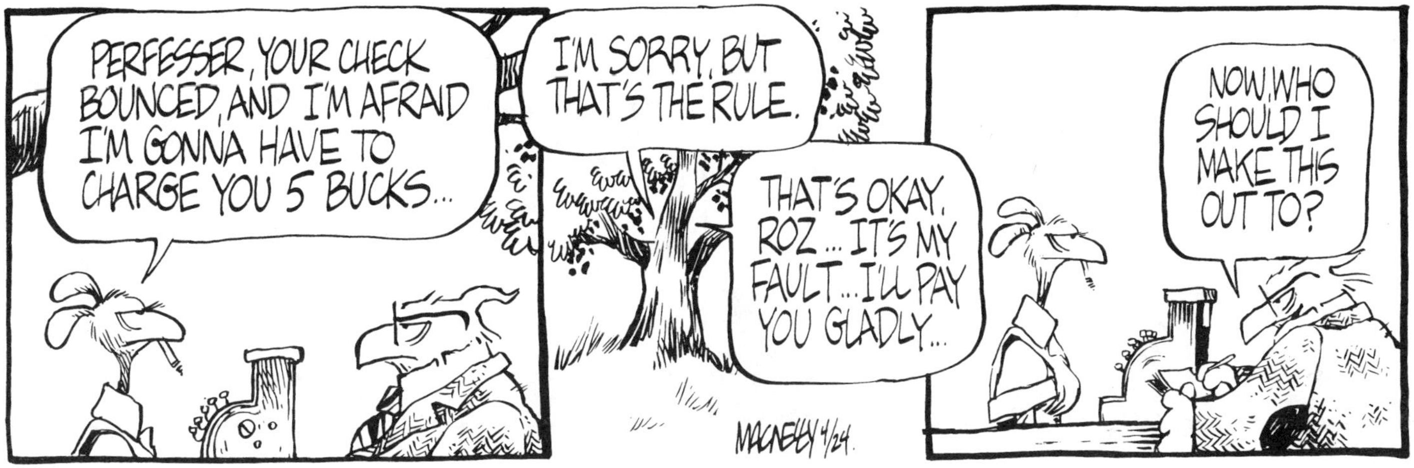
PERFESSER, YOUR CHECK BOUNCED, AND I'M AFRAID I'M GONNA HAVE TO CHARGE YOU 5 BUCKS...
I'M SORRY, BUT THAT'S THE RULE.
THAT'S OKAY, ROZ... IT'S MY FAULT... I'LL PAY YOU GLADLY...
MACNELLY 4/24
NOW, WHO SHOULD I MAKE THIS OUT TO?

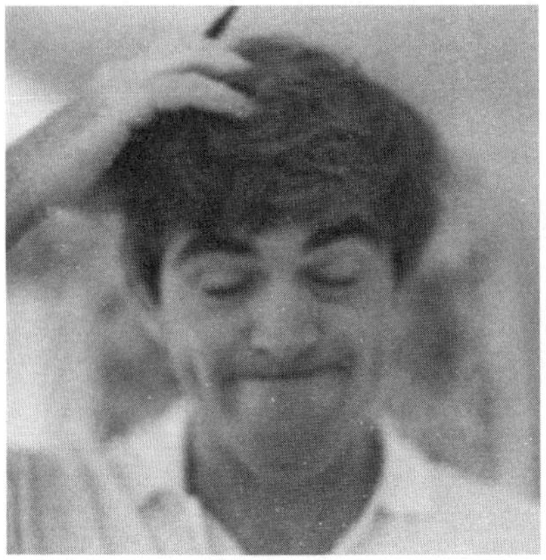

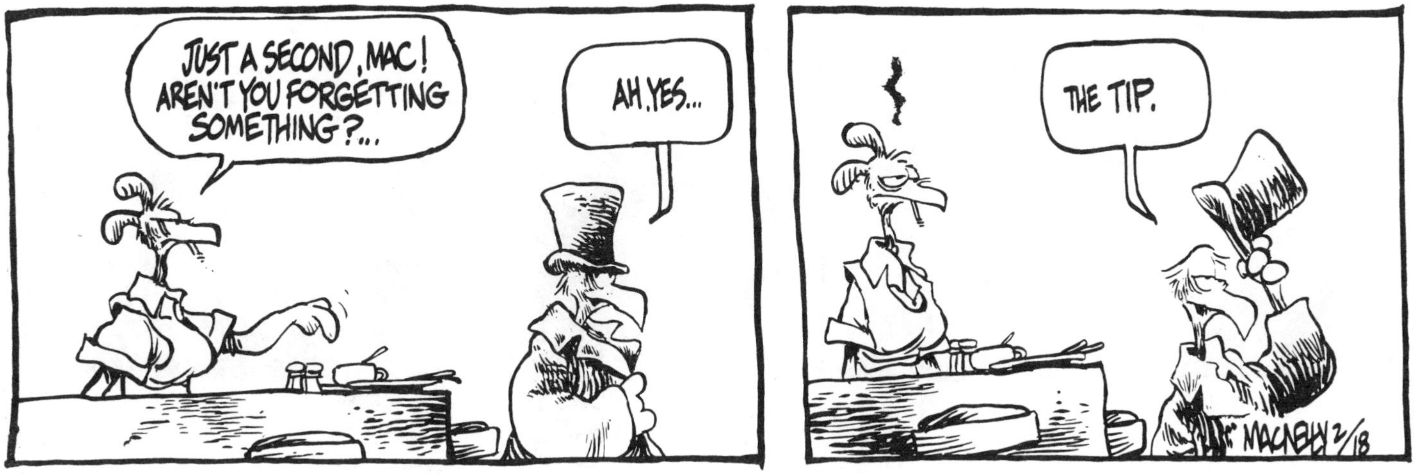
JUST A SECOND, MAC! AREN'T YOU FORGETTING SOMETHING?...
AH, YES...
THE TIP.
MACNELLY 2/18

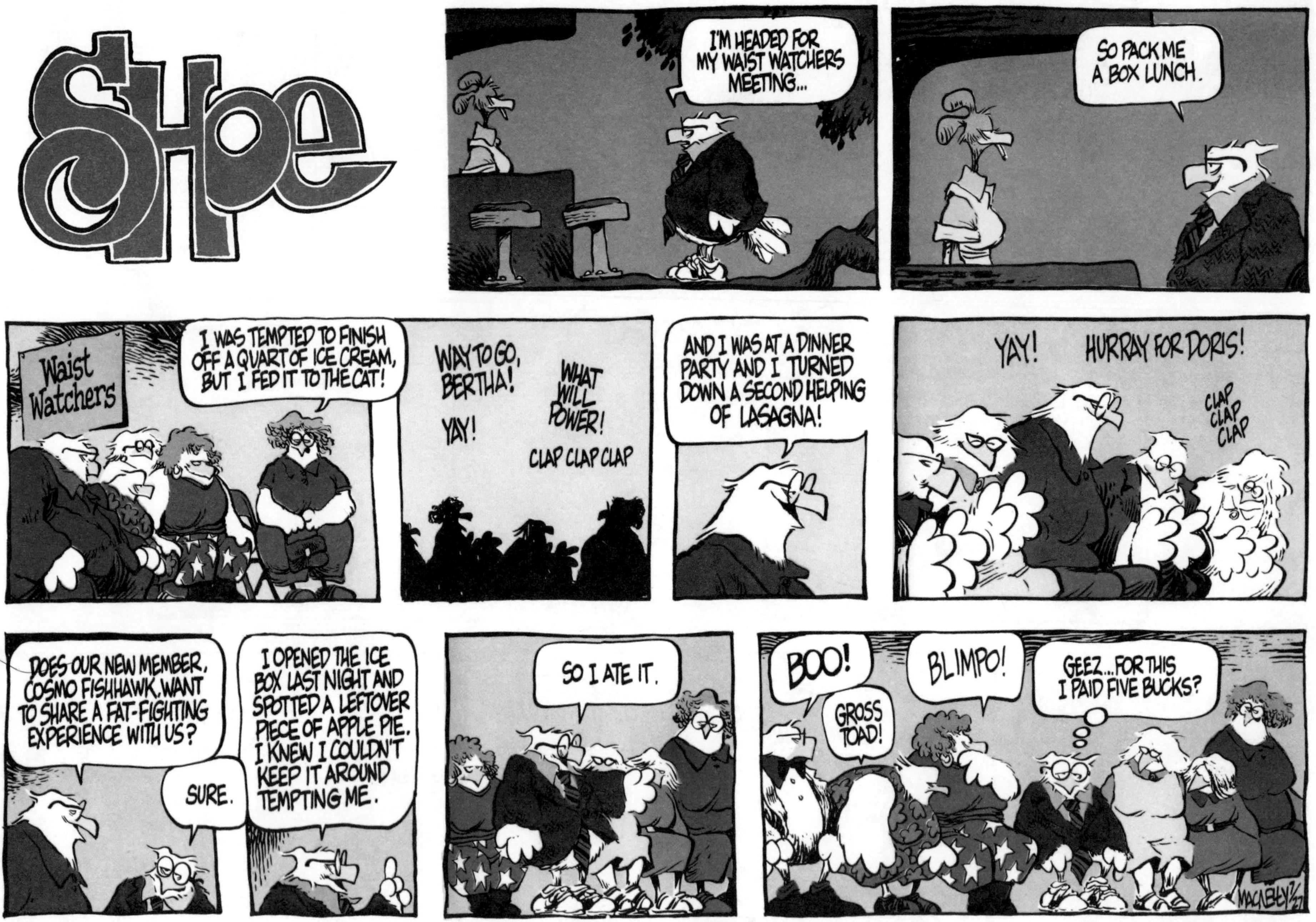
Shoe
I'M HEADED FOR MY WAIST WATCHERS MEETING...
SO PACK ME A BOX LUNCH.
Waist Watchers
I WAS TEMPTED TO FINISH OFF A QUART OF ICE CREAM, BUT I FED IT TO THE CAT!
WAY TO GO, BERTHA!
WHAT WILL POWER!
YAY!
CLAP CLAP CLAP
AND I WAS AT A DINNER PARTY AND I TURNED DOWN A SECOND HELPING OF LASAGNA!
YAY!
HURRAY FOR DORIS!
CLAP CLAP CLAP
DOES OUR NEW MEMBER, COSMO FISHHAWK, WANT TO SHARE A FAT-FIGHTING EXPERIENCE WITH US?
SURE.
I OPENED THE ICE BOX LAST NIGHT AND SPOTTED A LEFTOVER PIECE OF APPLE PIE. I KNEW I COULDN'T KEEP IT AROUND TEMPTING ME.
SO I ATE IT.
BOO!
GROSS TOAD!
BLIMPO!
GEEZ...FOR THIS I PAID FIVE BUCKS?
MACNELLY

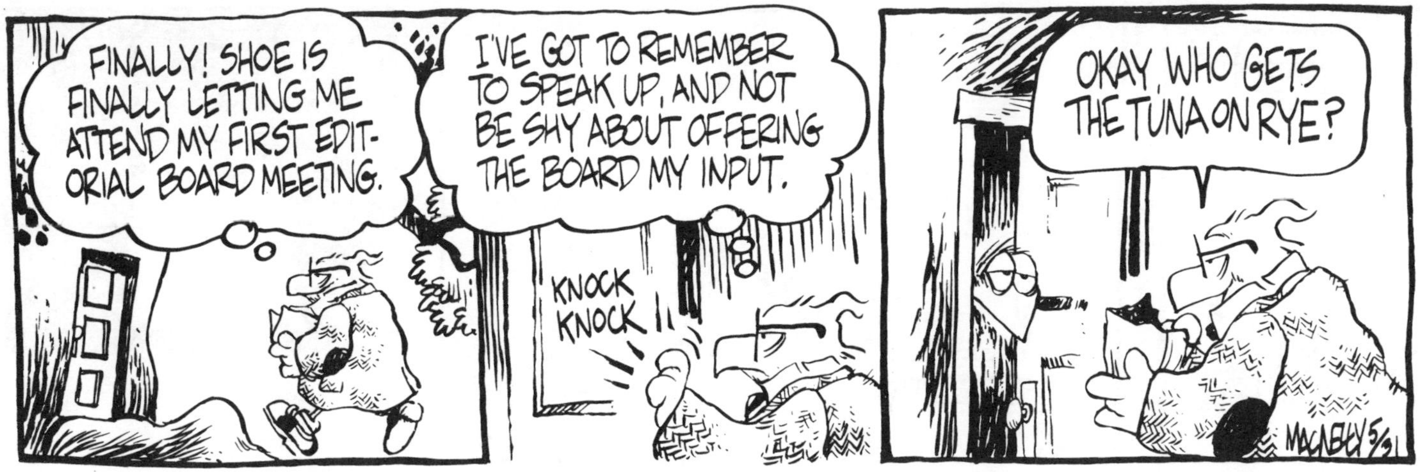
FINALLY! SHOE IS FINALLY LETTING ME ATTEND MY FIRST EDITORIAL BOARD MEETING.
I'VE GOT TO REMEMBER TO SPEAK UP, AND NOT BE SHY ABOUT OFFERING THE BOARD MY INPUT.
KNOCK KNOCK
OKAY, WHO GETS THE TUNA ON RYE?
MACNELLY

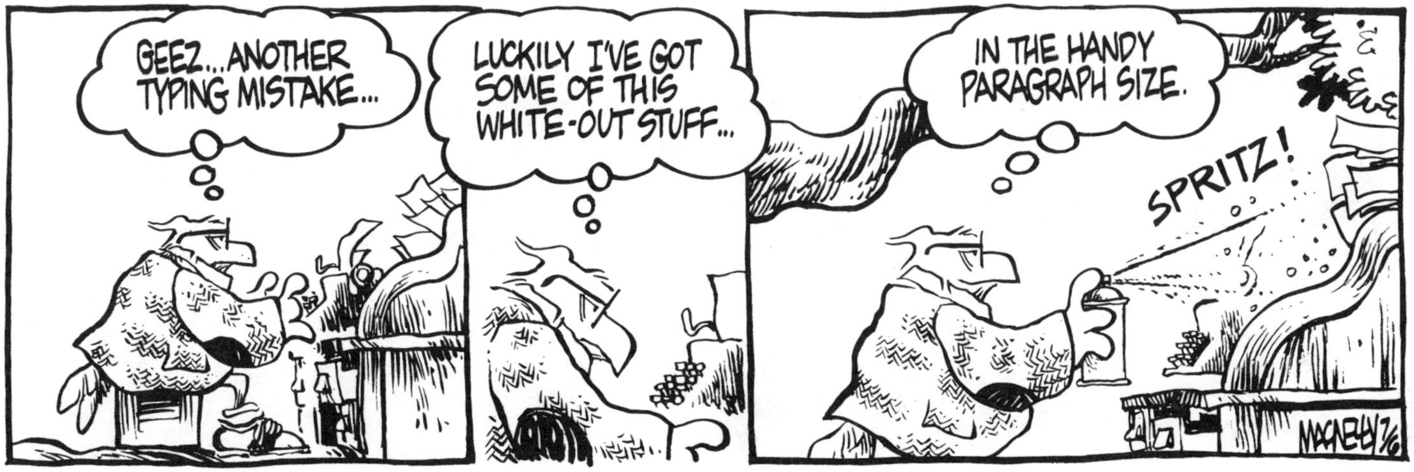
GEEZ...ANOTHER TYPING MISTAKE...
LUCKILY I'VE GOT SOME OF THIS WHITE-OUT STUFF...
IN THE HANDY PARAGRAPH SIZE.
SPRITZ!
MACNELLY

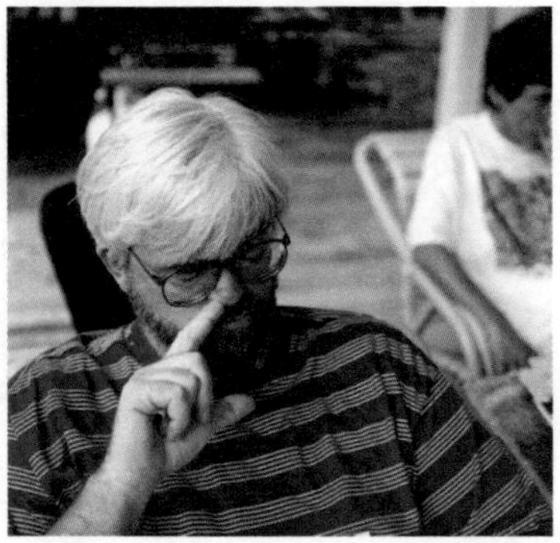

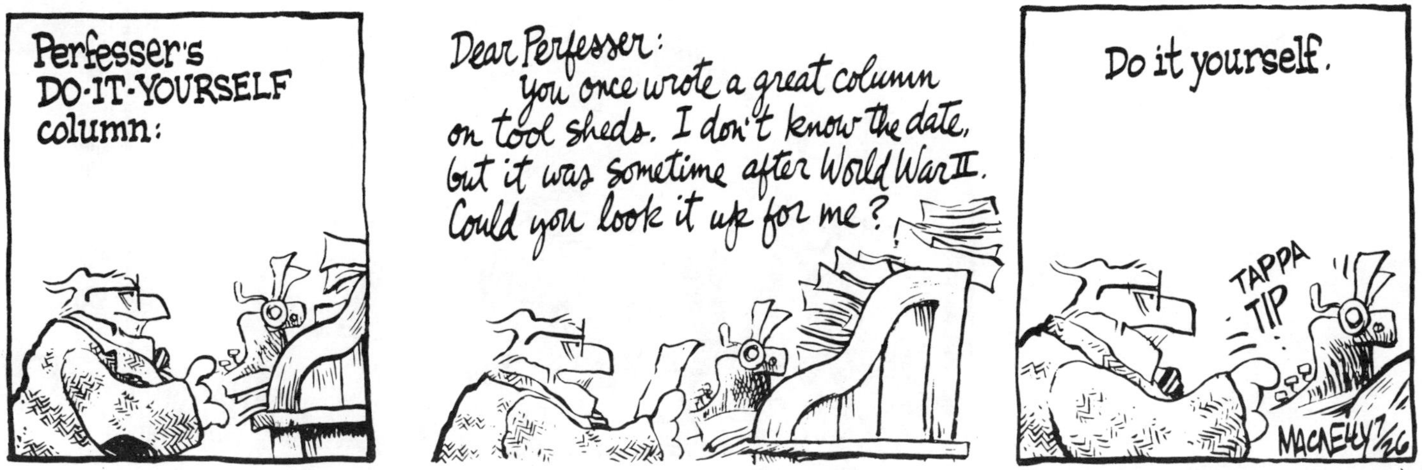
Perfesser's DO-IT-YOURSELF column:
Dear Perfesser:
You once wrote a great column on tool sheds. I don't know the date, but it was sometime after World War II. Could you look it up for me?
Do it yourself.
TAPPA TIP
MACNELLY

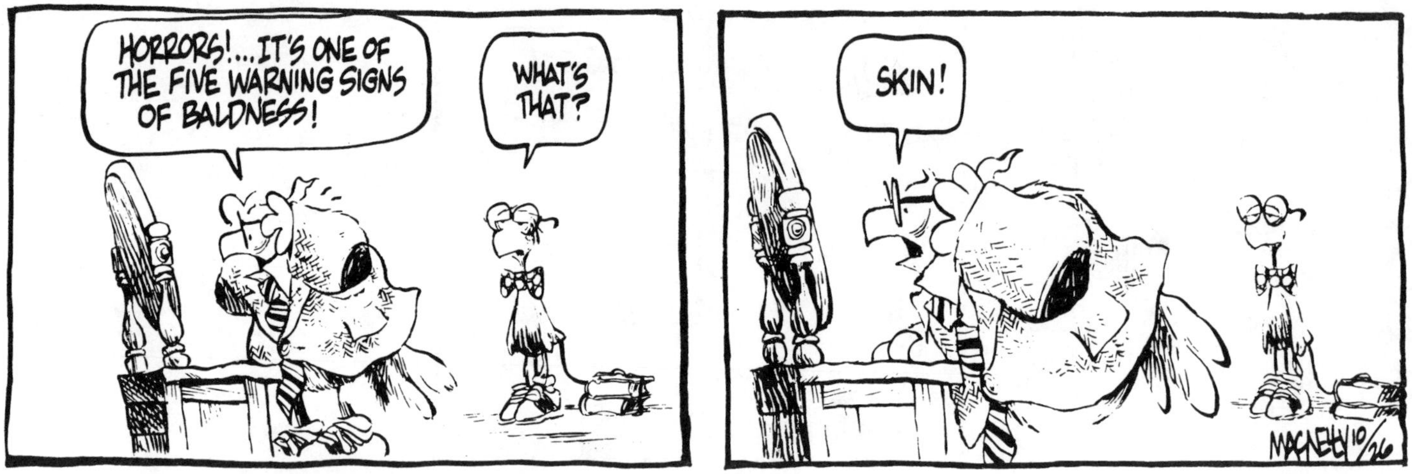
HORRORS!...IT'S ONE OF THE FIVE WARNING SIGNS OF BALDNESS!
WHAT'S THAT?
SKIN!
MACNELLY 10/26

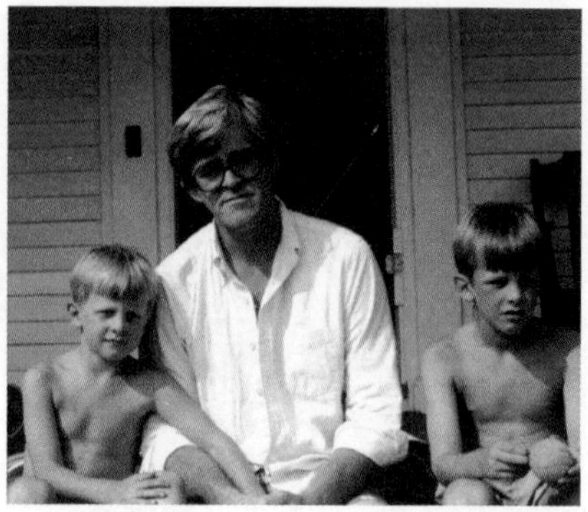

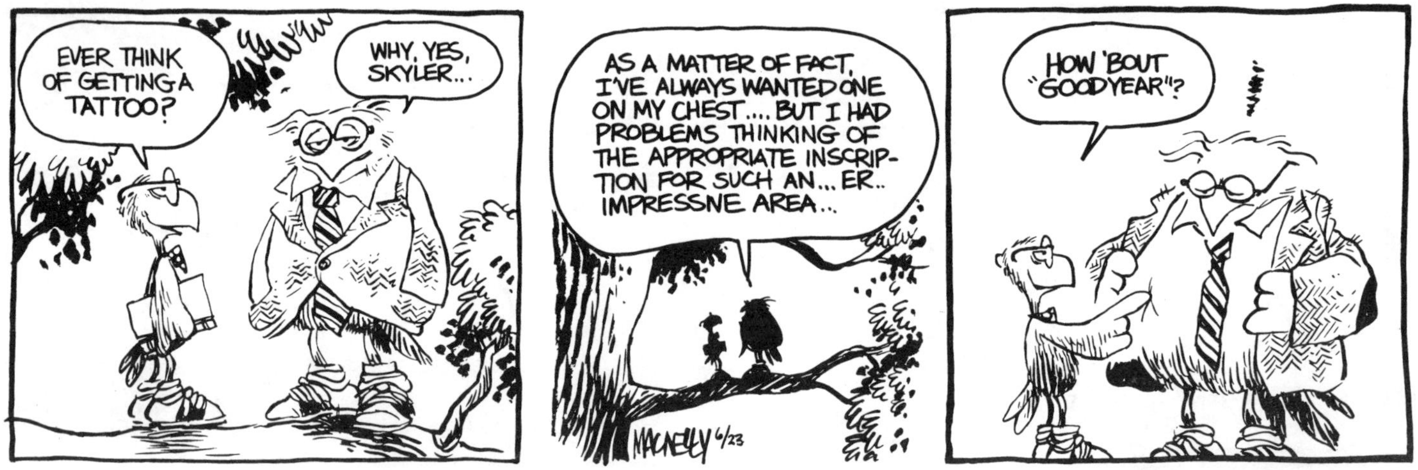
EVER THINK OF GETTING A TATTOO?
WHY, YES, SKYLER...
AS A MATTER OF FACT, I'VE ALWAYS WANTED ONE ON MY CHEST.... BUT I HAD PROBLEMS THINKING OF THE APPROPRIATE INSCRIPTION FOR SUCH AN... ER.. IMPRESSIVE AREA...
MACNELLY 6/23
HOW 'BOUT "GOODYEAR"?

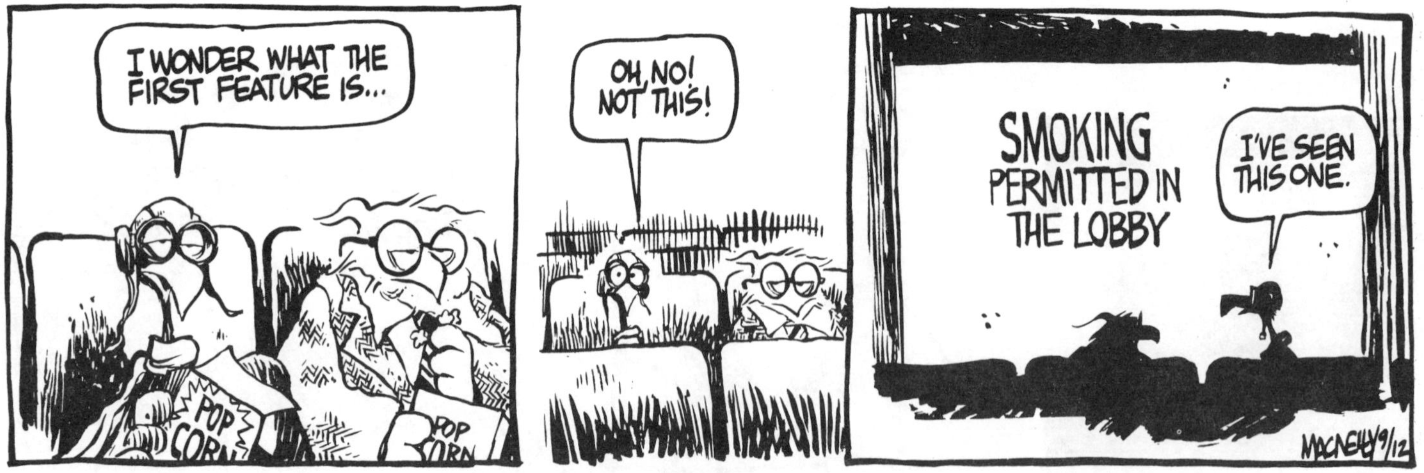
I WONDER WHAT THE FIRST FEATURE IS...
POP CORN
POP CORN
OH, NO! NOT THIS!
SMOKING PERMITTED IN THE LOBBY
I'VE SEEN THIS ONE.
MACNELLY 9/12

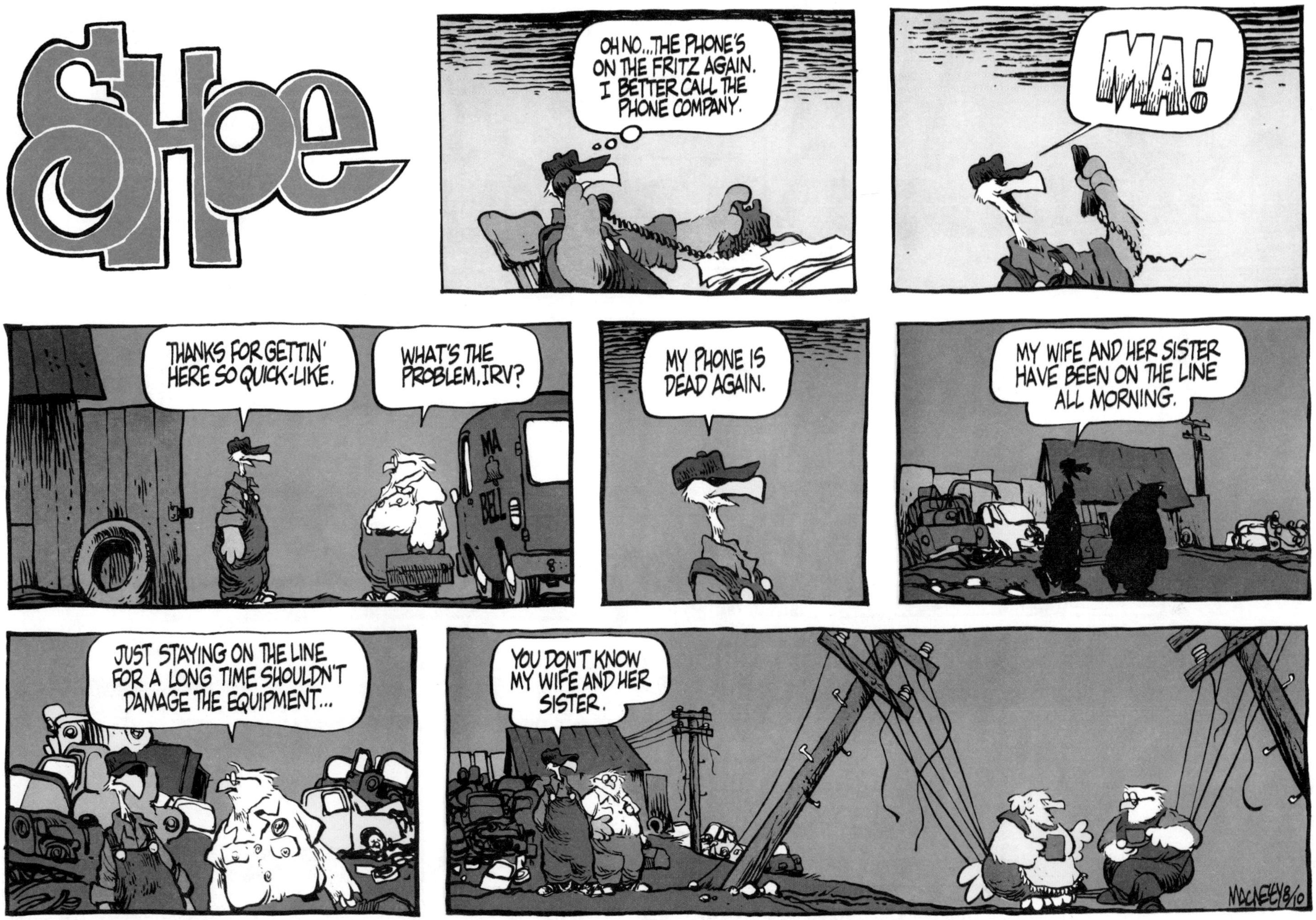
SHOE
OH NO...THE PHONE'S ON THE FRITZ AGAIN. I BETTER CALL THE PHONE COMPANY.
MA!
THANKS FOR GETTIN' HERE SO QUICK-LIKE.
WHAT'S THE PROBLEM, IRV?
MA BELL
MY PHONE IS DEAD AGAIN.
MY WIFE AND HER SISTER HAVE BEEN ON THE LINE ALL MORNING.
JUST STAYING ON THE LINE FOR A LONG TIME SHOULDN'T DAMAGE THE EQUIPMENT...
YOU DON'T KNOW MY WIFE AND HER SISTER.

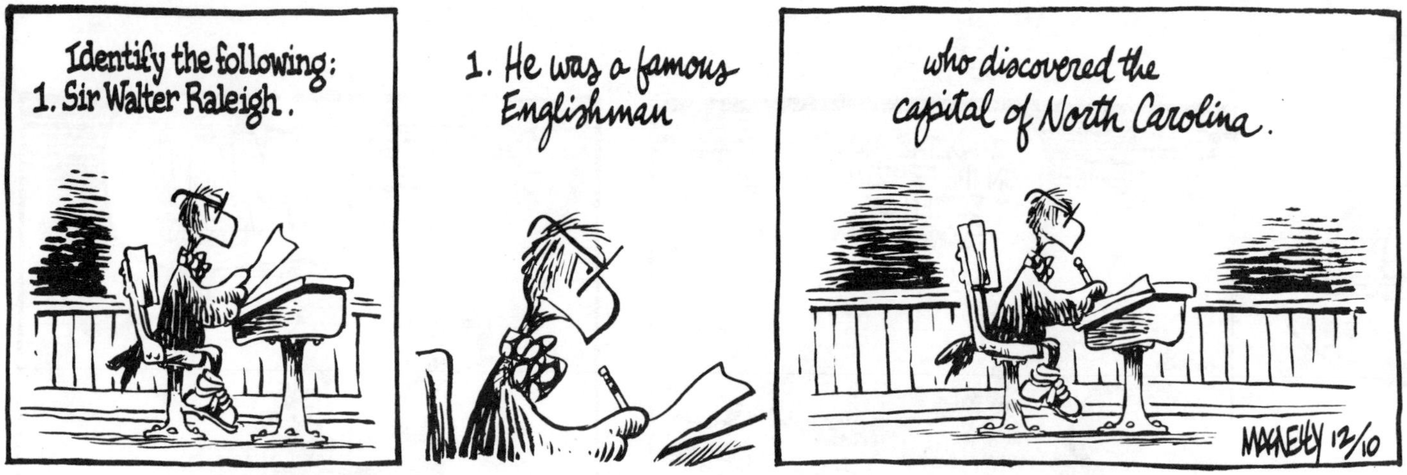
Identify the following:
1. Sir Walter Raleigh.
1. He was a famous Englishman
who discovered the capital of North Carolina.
MACNELLY 12/10

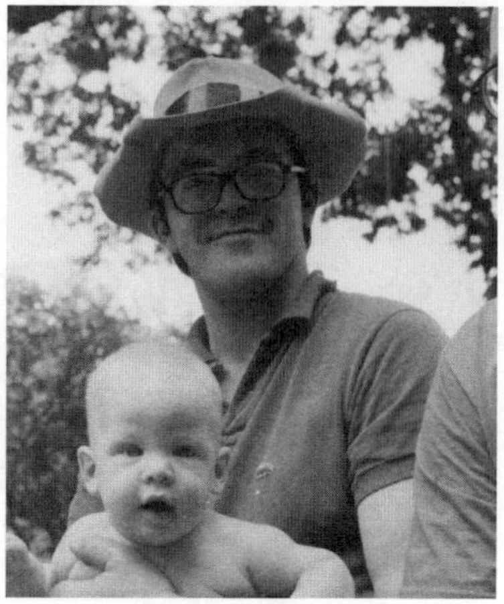

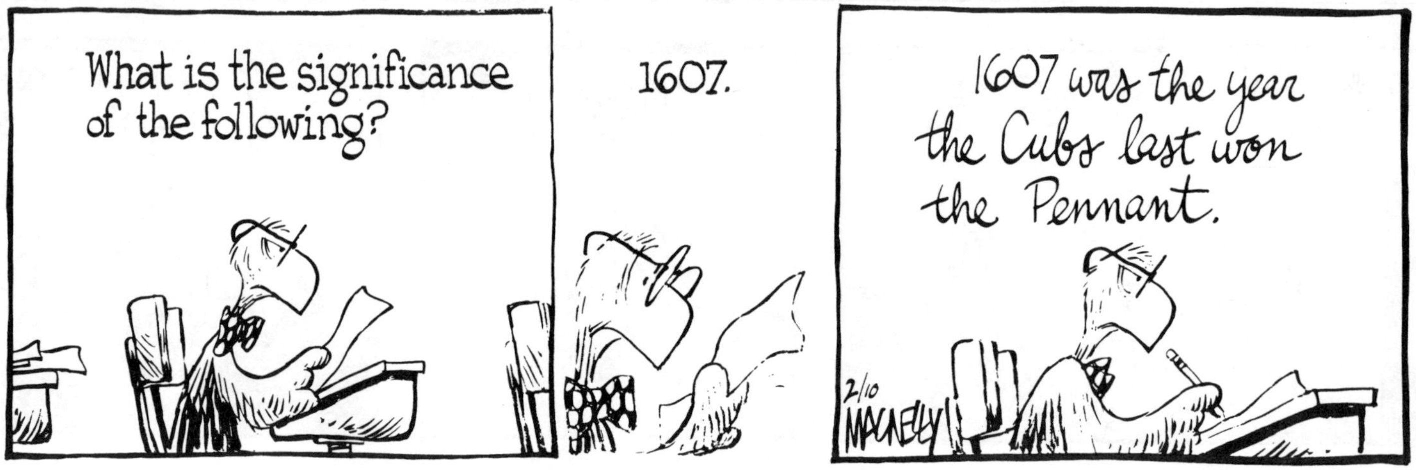
What is the significance of the following?
1607.
1607 was the year the Cubs last won the Pennant.
2/10 MACNELLY

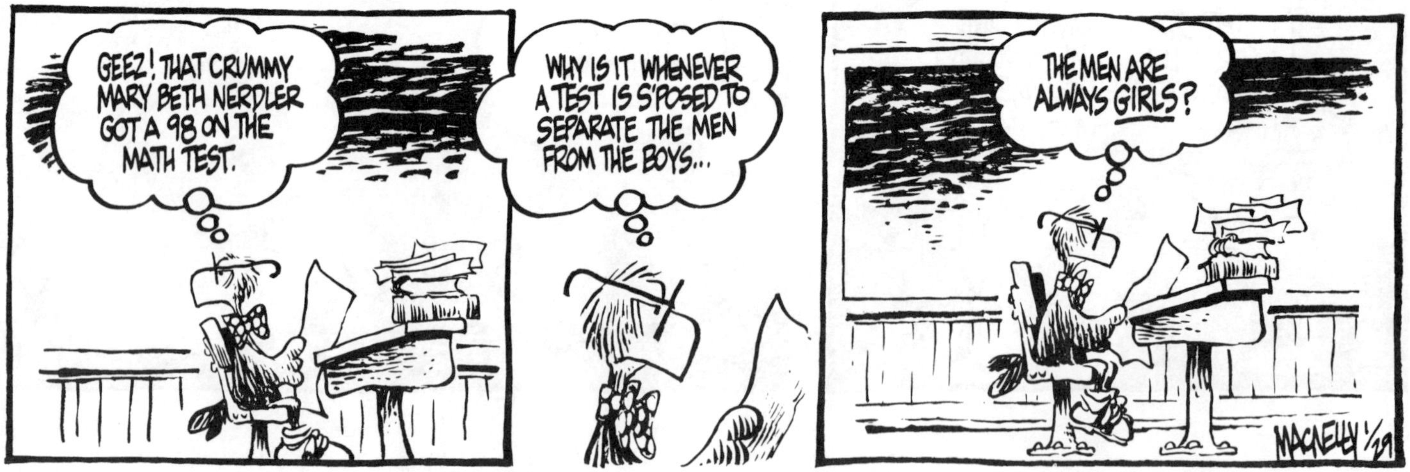
GEEZ! THAT CRUMMY MARY BETH NERDLER GOT A 98 ON THE MATH TEST.
WHY IS IT WHENEVER A TEST IS S'POSED TO SEPARATE THE MEN FROM THE BOYS...
THE MEN ARE ALWAYS GIRLS?
MACNELLY 1/29

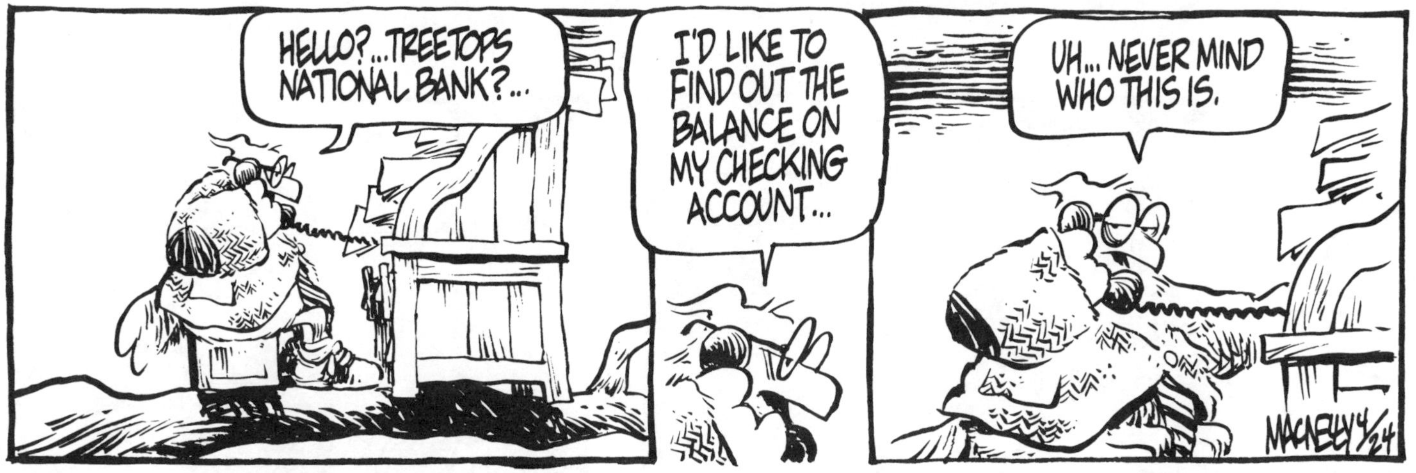
HELLO?...TREETOPS NATIONAL BANK?...
I'D LIKE TO FIND OUT THE BALANCE ON MY CHECKING ACCOUNT...
UH... NEVER MIND WHO THIS IS.
MACNELLY 4/24

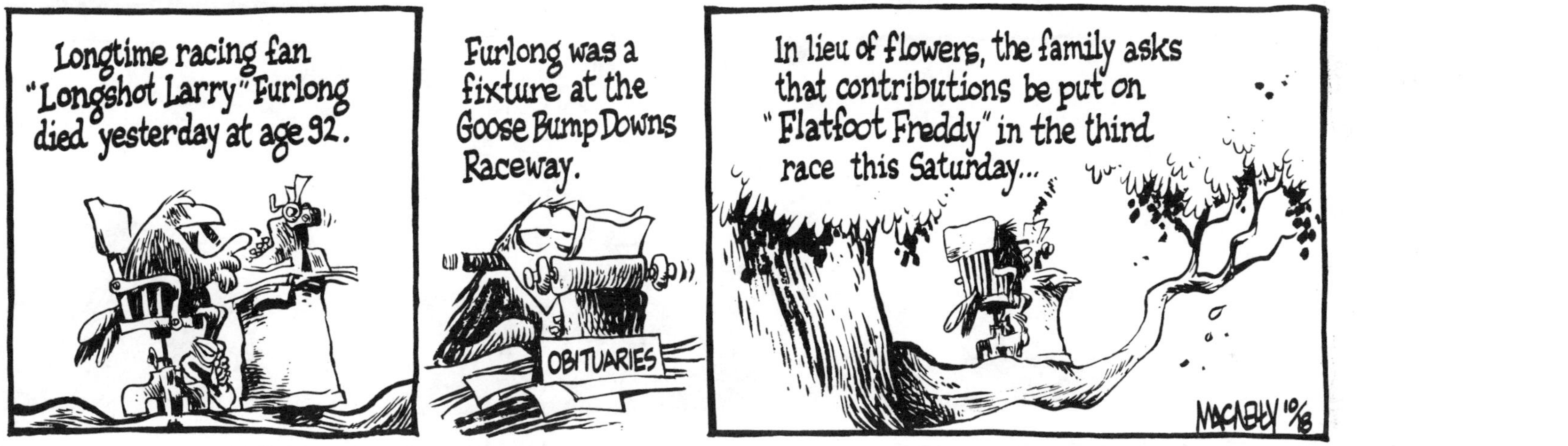
Longtime racing fan "Longshot Larry" Furlong died yesterday at age 92.
Furlong was a fixture at the Goose Bump Downs Raceway.
OBITUARIES
In lieu of flowers, the family asks that contributions be put on "Flatfoot Freddy" in the third race this Saturday...
MACNELLY 10/18

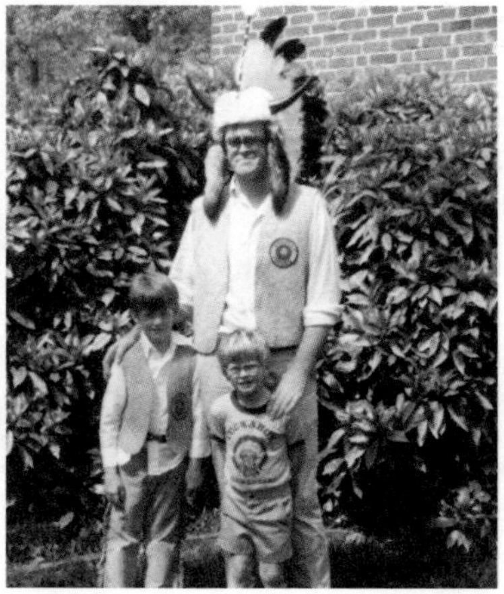

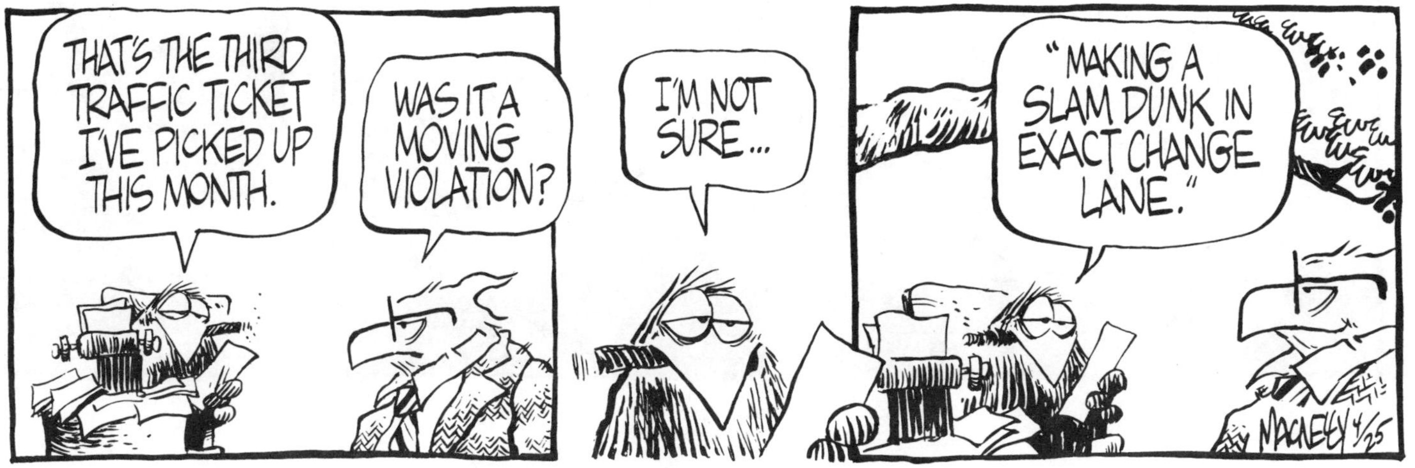
THAT'S THE THIRD TRAFFIC TICKET I'VE PICKED UP THIS MONTH.
WAS IT A MOVING VIOLATION?
I'M NOT SURE...
"MAKING A SLAM DUNK IN EXACT CHANGE LANE."
MACNELLY 4/25

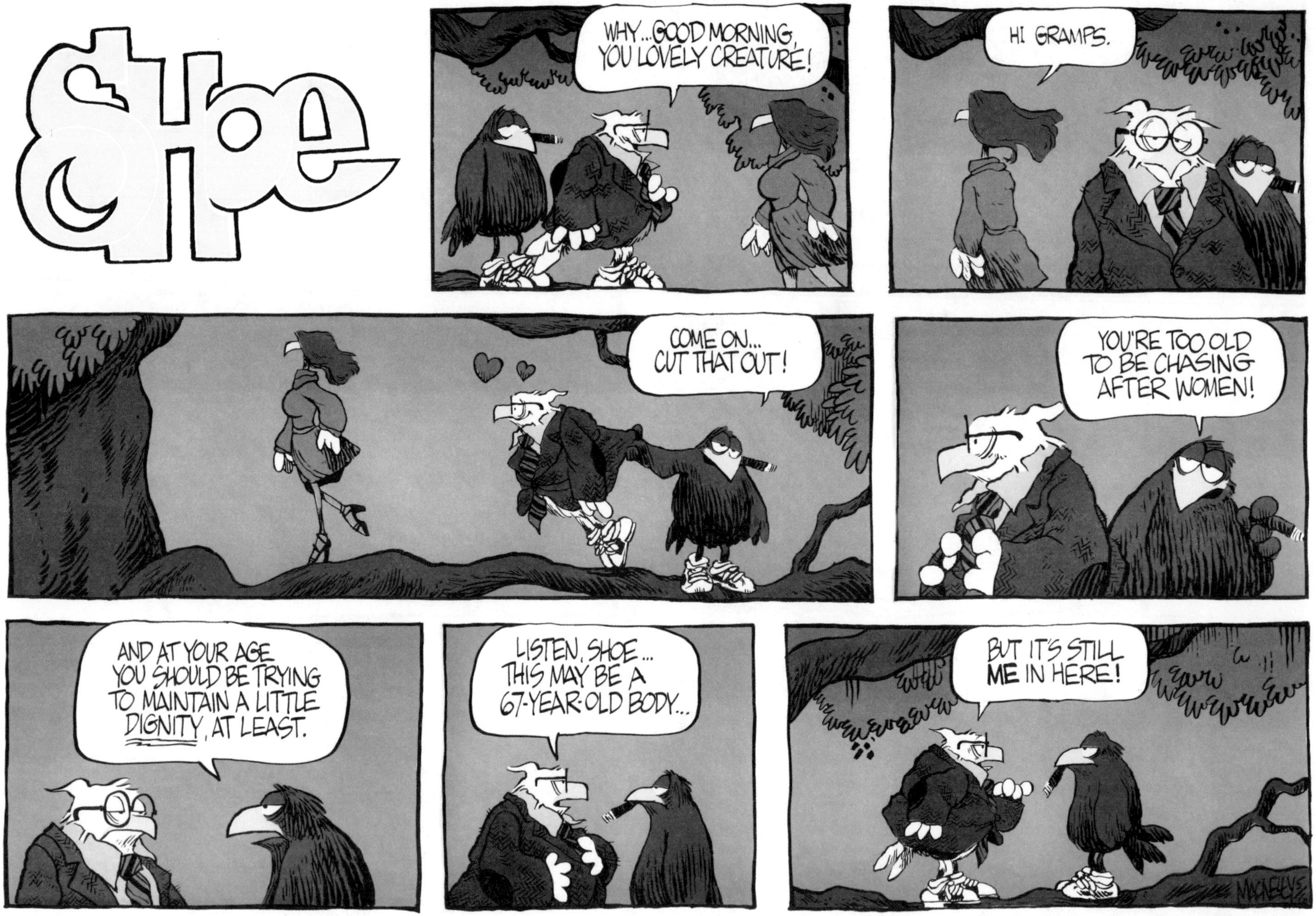
Shoe
WHY...GOOD MORNING, YOU LOVELY CREATURE!
HI GRAMPS.
COME ON... CUT THAT OUT!
YOU'RE TOO OLD TO BE CHASING AFTER WOMEN!
AND AT YOUR AGE YOU SHOULD BE TRYING TO MAINTAIN A LITTLE DIGNITY, AT LEAST.
LISTEN, SHOE... THIS MAY BE A 67-YEAR-OLD BODY...
BUT IT'S STILL ME IN HERE!
MACNELLY

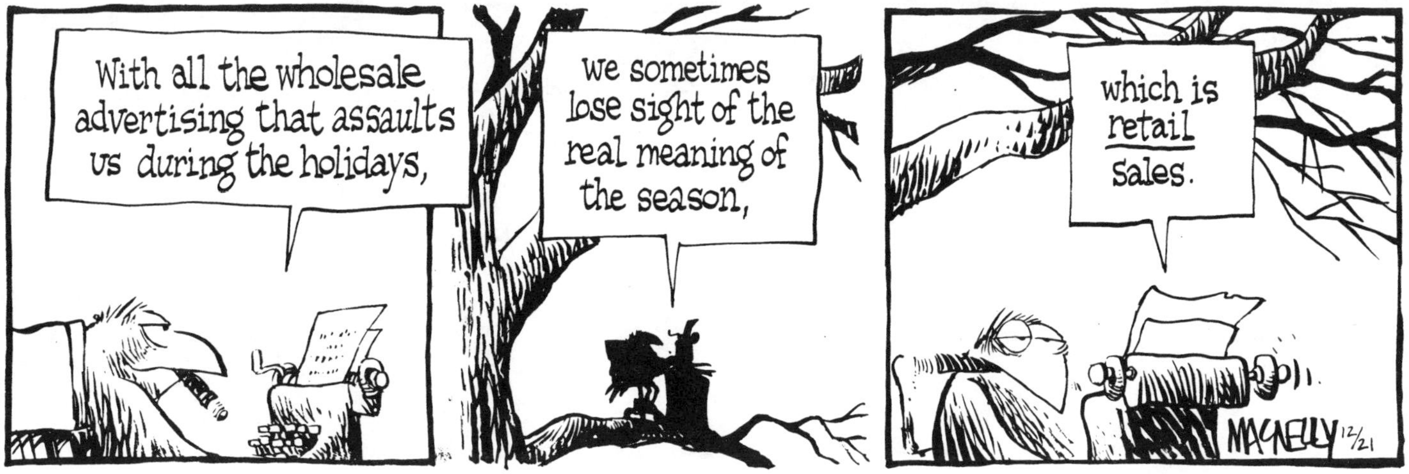
With all the wholesale advertising that assaults us during the holidays,
we sometimes lose sight of the real meaning of the season,
which is retail sales.
MACNELLY 12/21

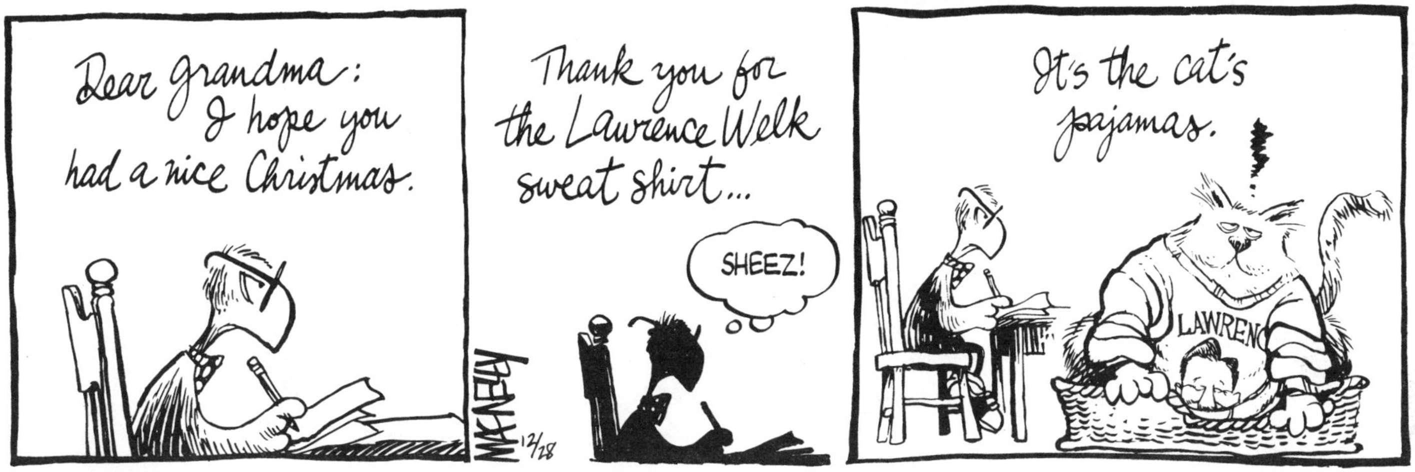
Dear Grandma: I hope you had a nice Christmas.
MACNELLY 12/28
Thank you for the Lawrence Welk sweat shirt...
SHEEZ!
It's the cat's pajamas.
LAWRENC

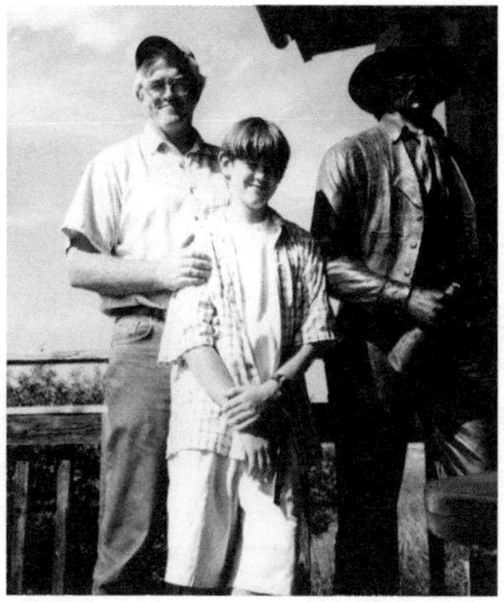

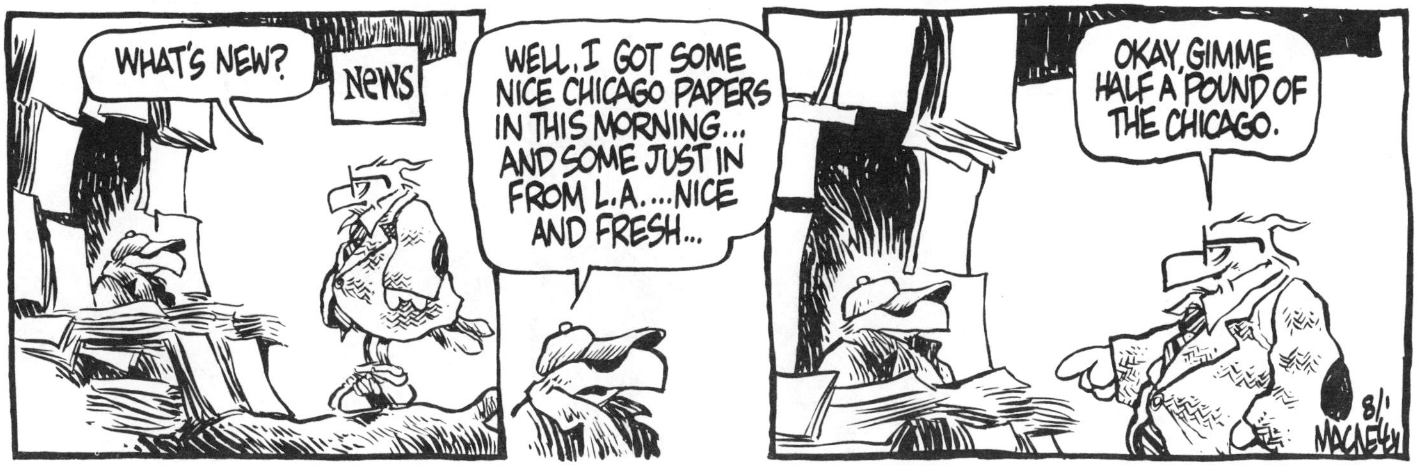
WHAT'S NEW?
NEWS
WELL, I GOT SOME NICE CHICAGO PAPERS IN THIS MORNING... AND SOME JUST IN FROM L.A....NICE AND FRESH...
OKAY, GIMME HALF A POUND OF THE CHICAGO.
8/1 MACNELLY

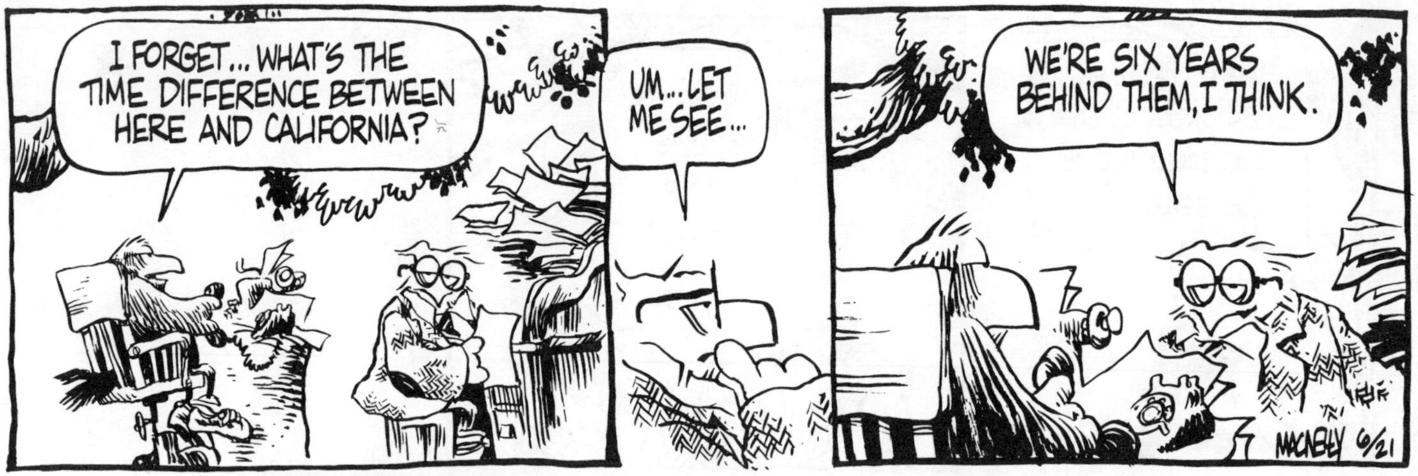
I FORGET... WHAT'S THE TIME DIFFERENCE BETWEEN HERE AND CALIFORNIA?
UM... LET ME SEE...
WE'RE SIX YEARS BEHIND THEM, I THINK.
MACNELLY 6/21

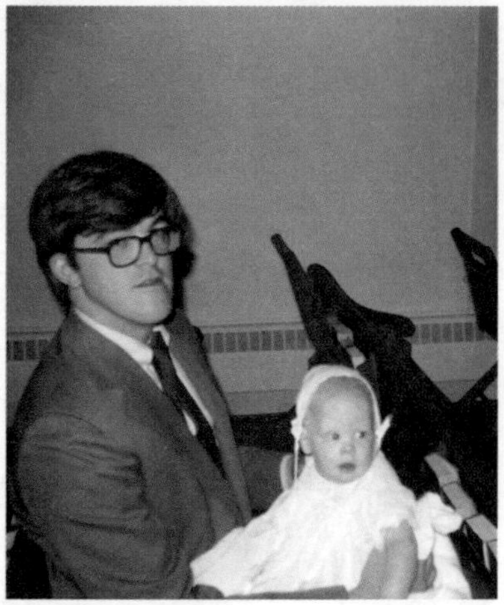

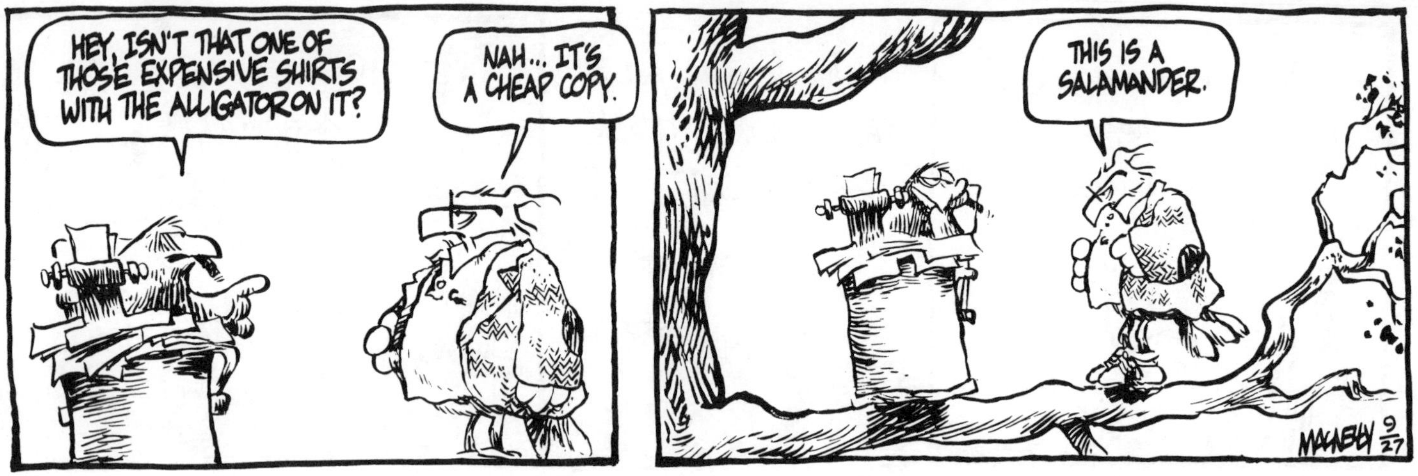
HEY, ISN'T THAT ONE OF THOSE EXPENSIVE SHIRTS WITH THE ALLIGATOR ON IT?
NAH... IT'S A CHEAP COPY.
THIS IS A SALAMANDER.
MACNELLY 9/27

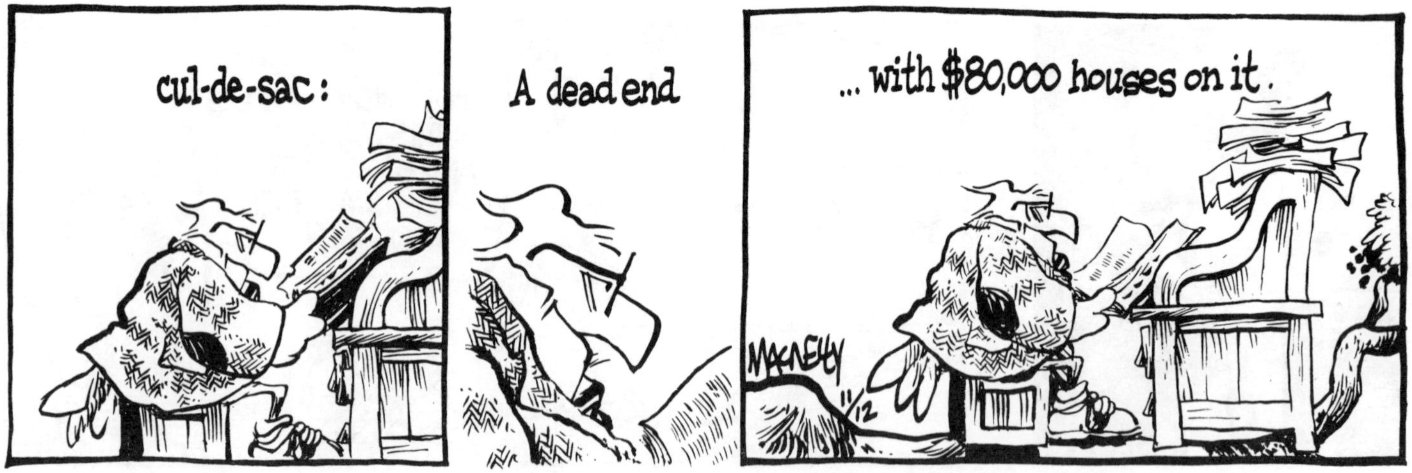
cul-de-sac:
A dead end
... with $80,000 houses on it.
MACNELLY 11/12

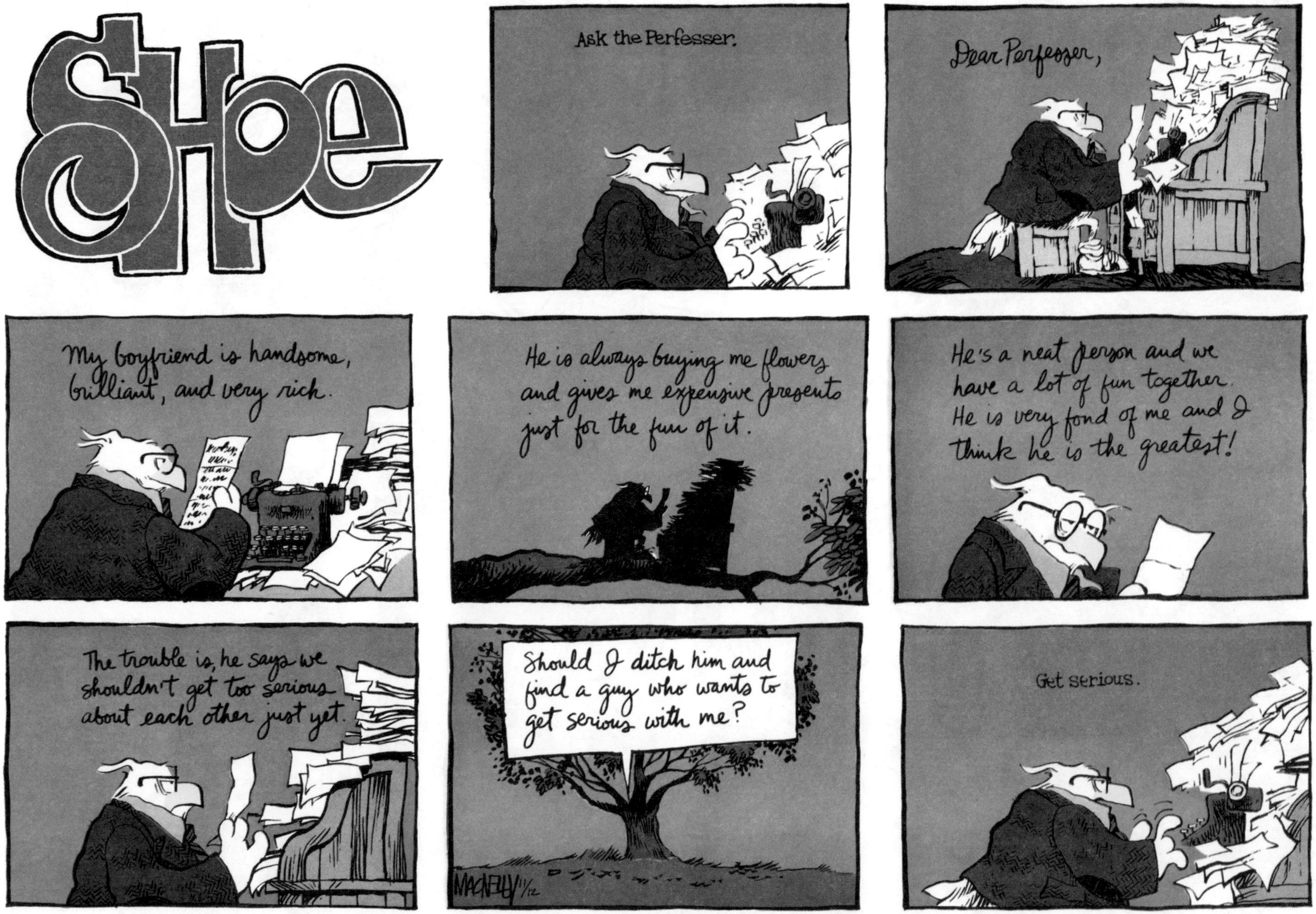
SHOE
Ask the Perfesser.
Dear Perfesser,
My boyfriend is handsome, brilliant, and very rich.
He is always buying me flowers and gives me expensive presents just for the fun of it.
He's a neat person and we have a lot of fun together. He is very fond of me and I think he is the greatest!
The trouble is, he says we shouldn't get too serious about each other just yet.
Should I ditch him and find a guy who wants to get serious with me?
MACNELLY 11/12
Get serious.

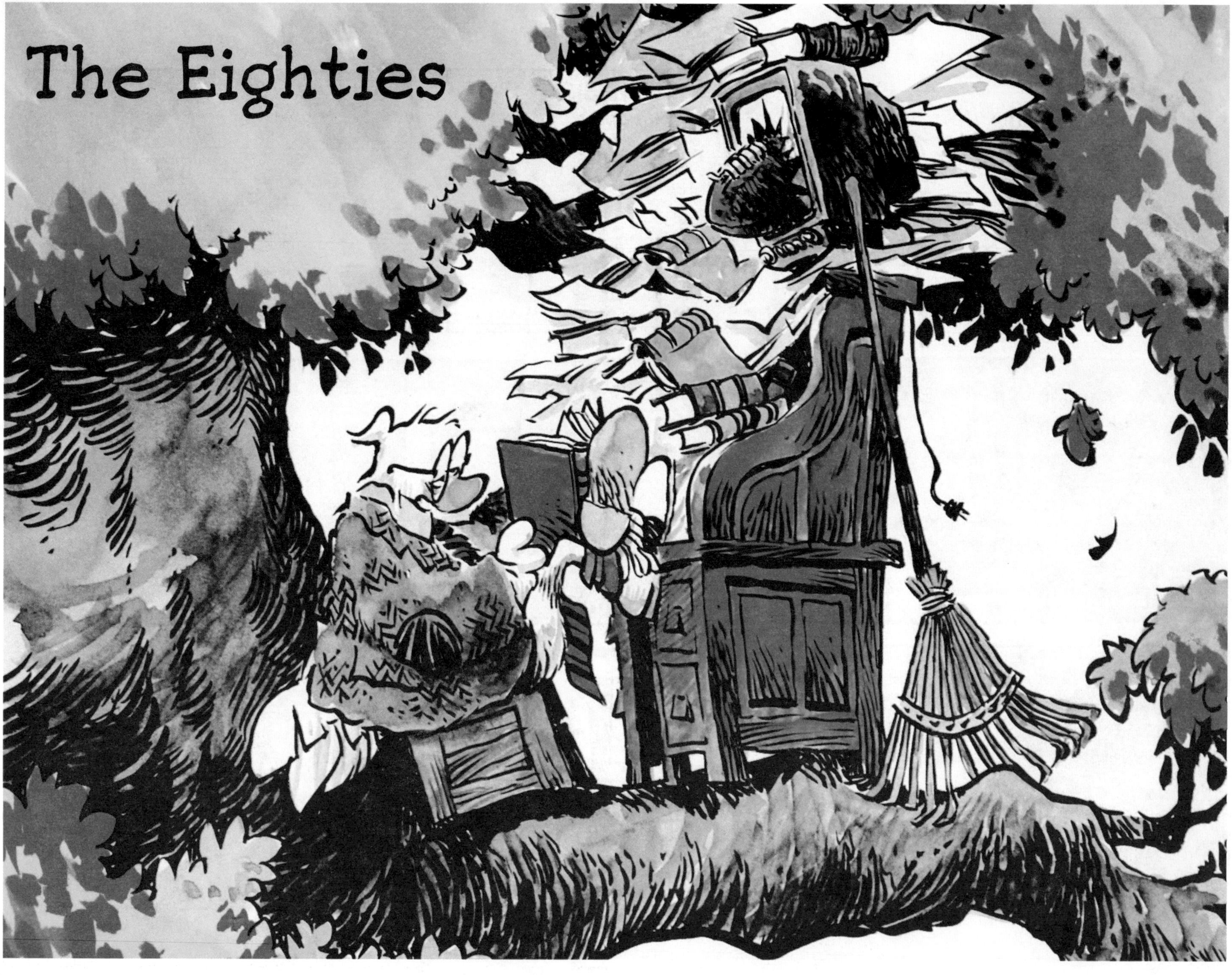
The Eighties

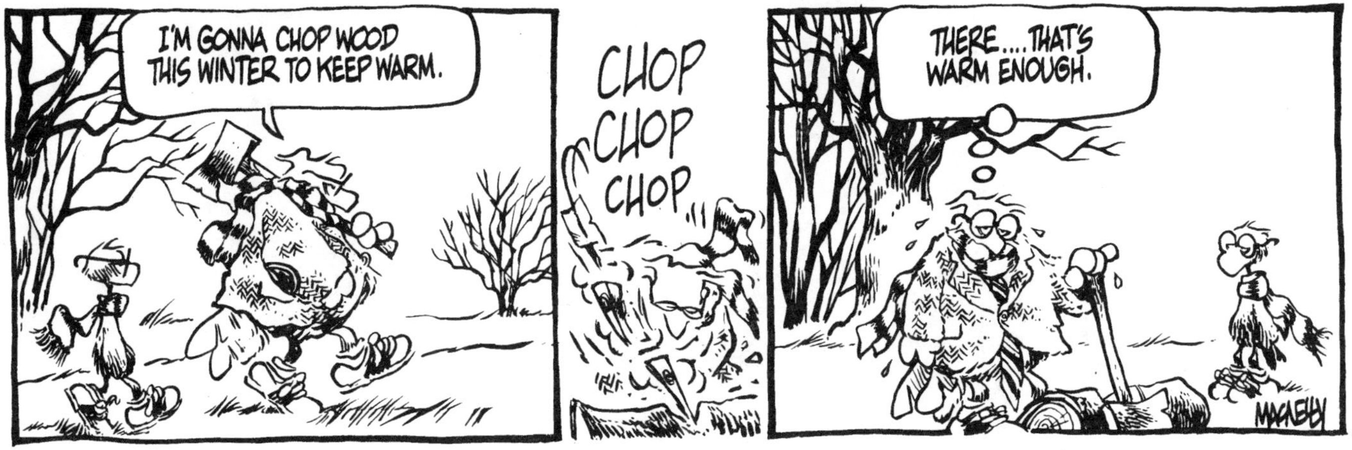
I'M GONNA CHOP WOOD THIS WINTER TO KEEP WARM.
CHOP CHOP CHOP
THERE.... THAT'S WARM ENOUGH.
MACNELLY

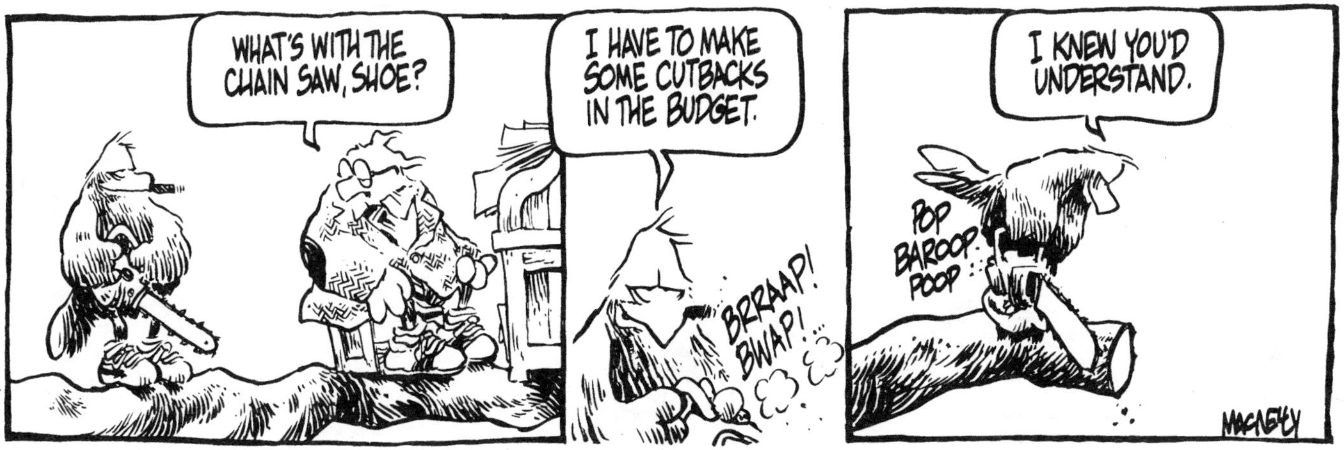
WHAT'S WITH THE CHAIN SAW, SHOE?
I HAVE TO MAKE SOME CUTBACKS IN THE BUDGET.
BRRAAP! BWAP!
I KNEW YOU'D UNDERSTAND.
POP BAROOP POOP
MACNELLY

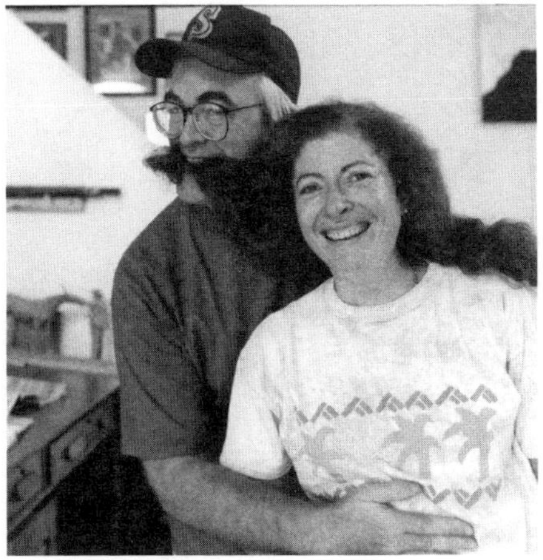

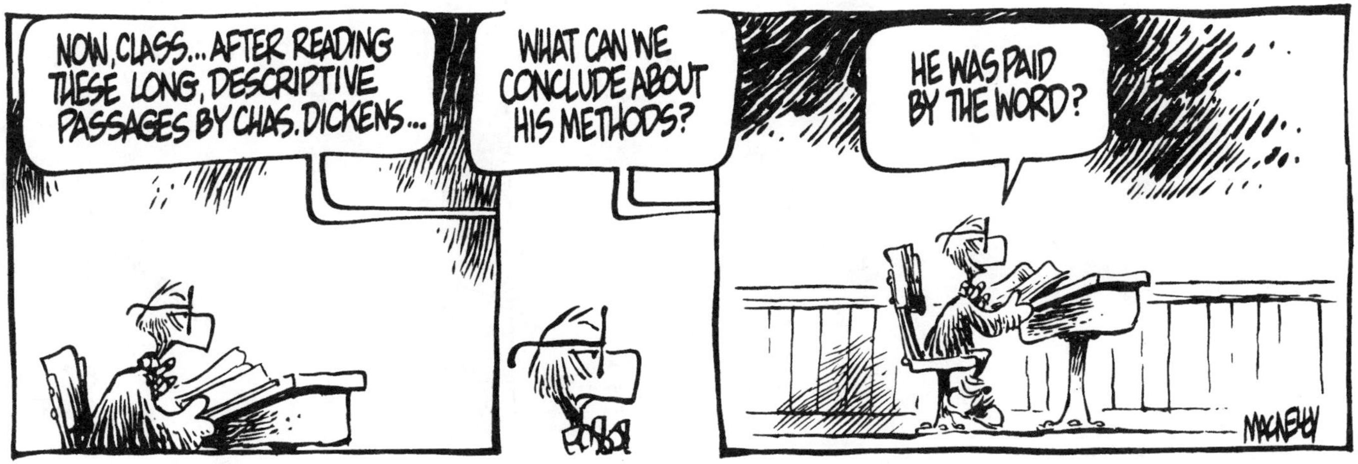
NOW, CLASS... AFTER READING THESE LONG, DESCRIPTIVE PASSAGES BY CHAS. DICKENS...
WHAT CAN WE CONCLUDE ABOUT HIS METHODS?
HE WAS PAID BY THE WORD?
MACNELLY

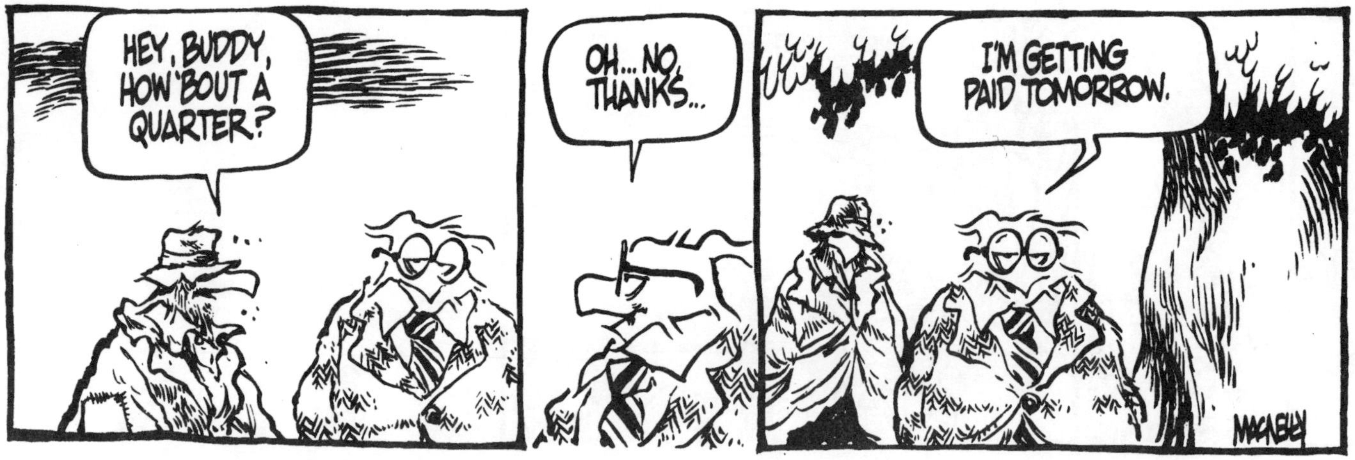
HEY, BUDDY, HOW 'BOUT A QUARTER?
OH... NO, THANKS...
I'M GETTING PAID TOMORROW.
MACNELLY

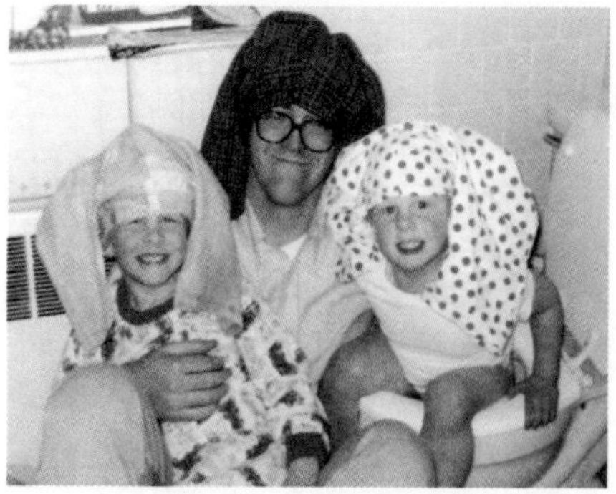

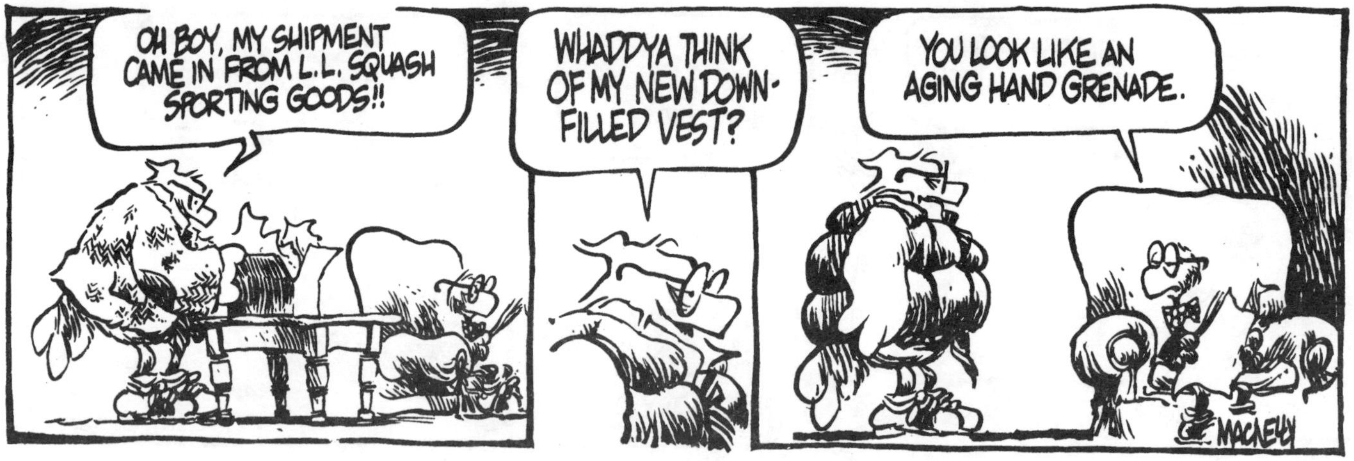
OH BOY, MY SHIPMENT CAME IN FROM L.L. SQUASH SPORTING GOODS!!
WHADDYA THINK OF MY NEW DOWN-FILLED VEST?
YOU LOOK LIKE AN AGING HAND GRENADE.
MACNELLY

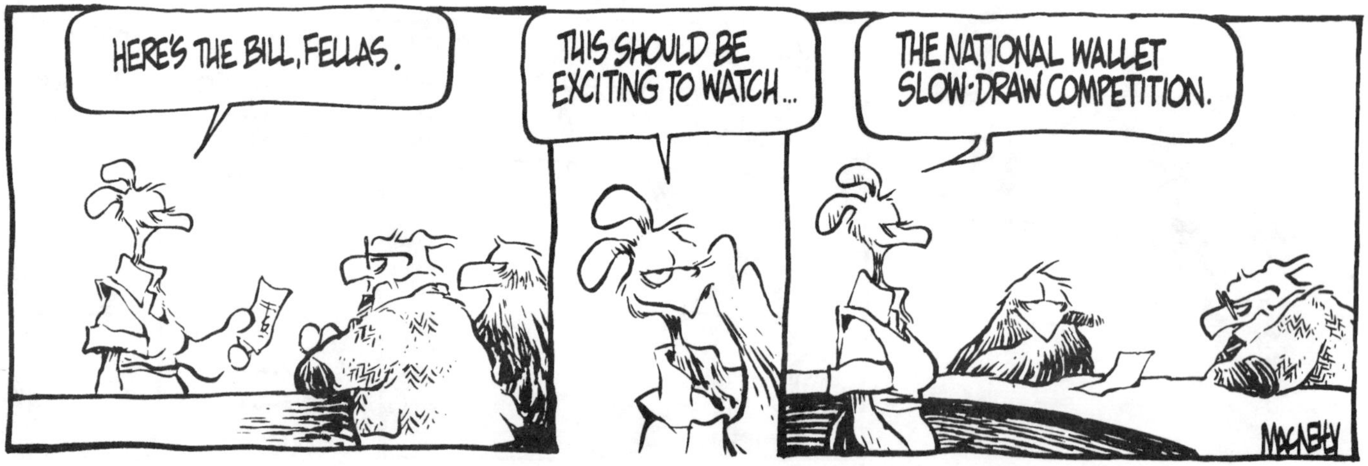
HERE'S THE BILL, FELLAS.
THIS SHOULD BE EXCITING TO WATCH...
THE NATIONAL WALLET SLOW-DRAW COMPETITION.
MACNELLY

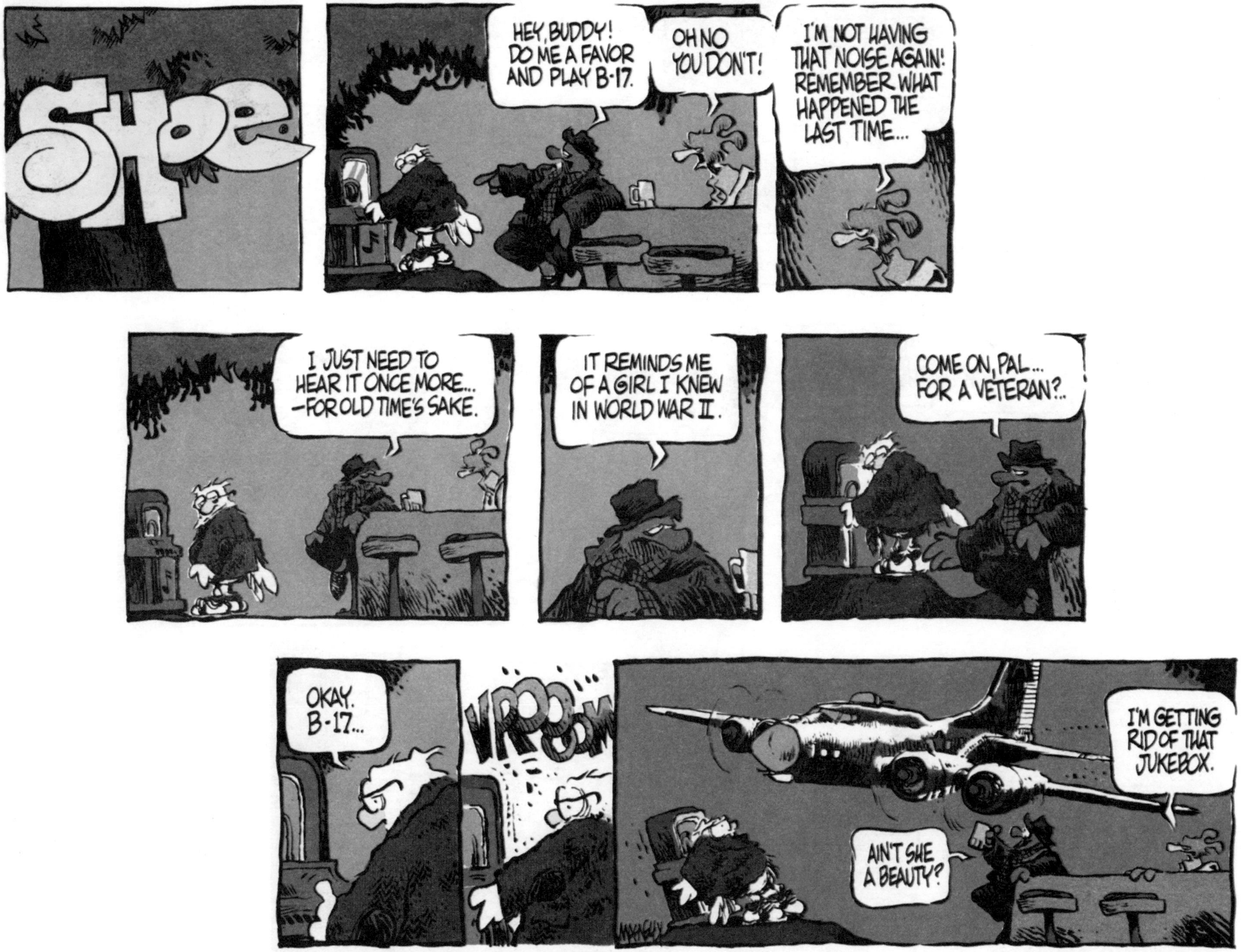
SHOE
HEY, BUDDY! DO ME A FAVOR AND PLAY B-17.
OH NO YOU DON'T!
I'M NOT HAVING THAT NOISE AGAIN! REMEMBER WHAT HAPPENED THE LAST TIME...
I JUST NEED TO HEAR IT ONCE MORE... —FOR OLD TIME'S SAKE.
IT REMINDS ME OF A GIRL I KNEW IN WORLD WAR II.
COME ON, PAL... FOR A VETERAN?..
OKAY. B-17...
VROOOOM
I'M GETTING RID OF THAT JUKEBOX.
AIN'T SHE A BEAUTY?
MACNELLY

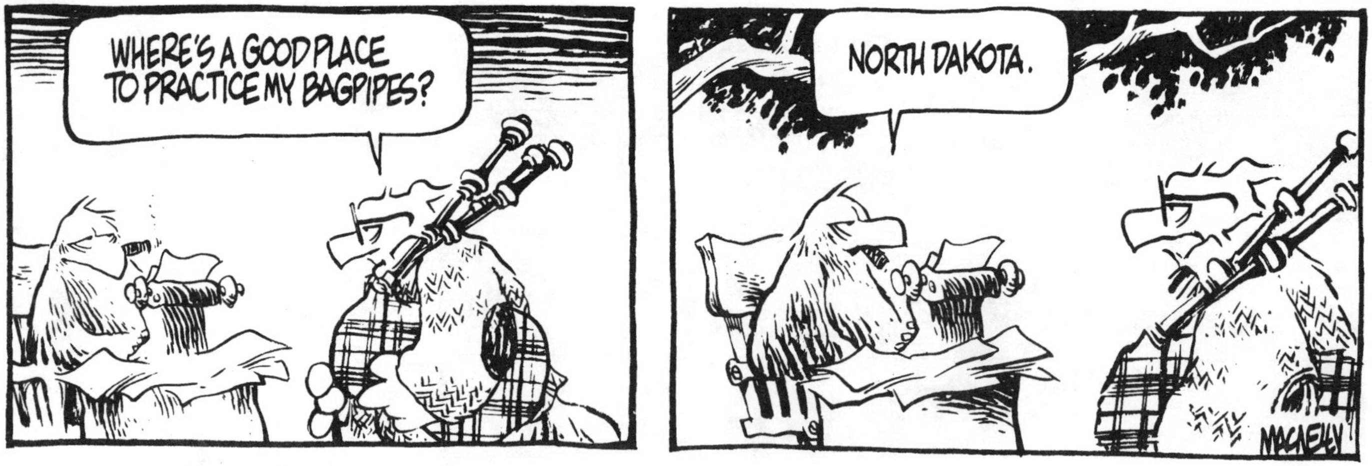
WHERE'S A GOOD PLACE TO PRACTICE MY BAGPIPES?
NORTH DAKOTA.
MACNELLY

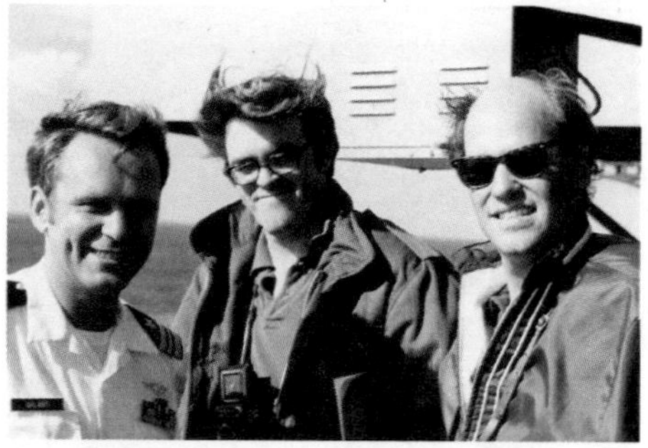

Paul Galanti, Jeff, and Ross Mackenzie

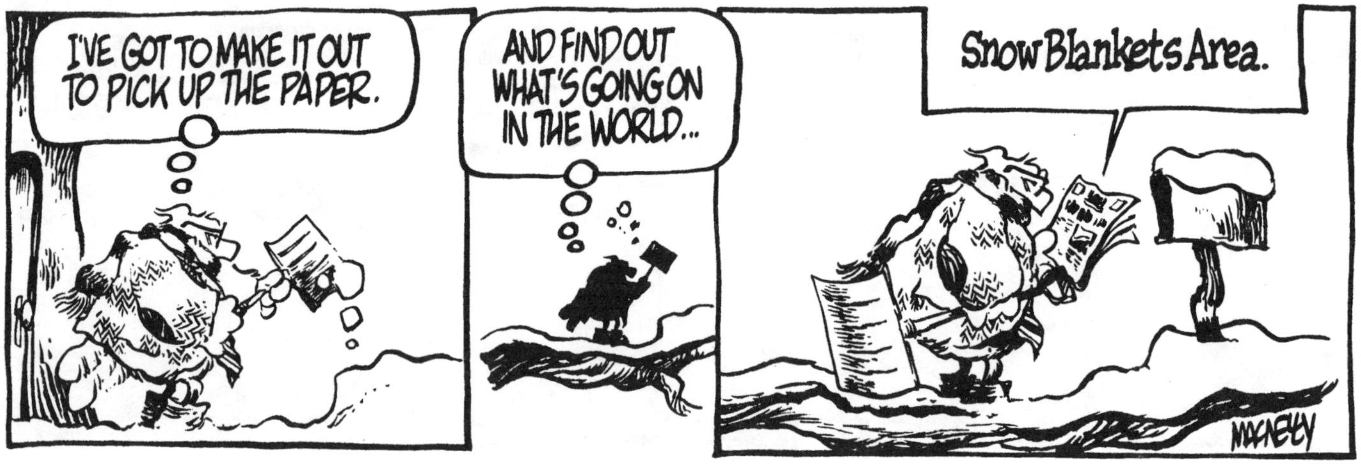
I'VE GOT TO MAKE IT OUT TO PICK UP THE PAPER.
AND FIND OUT WHAT'S GOING ON IN THE WORLD...
Snow Blankets Area.
MACNELLY

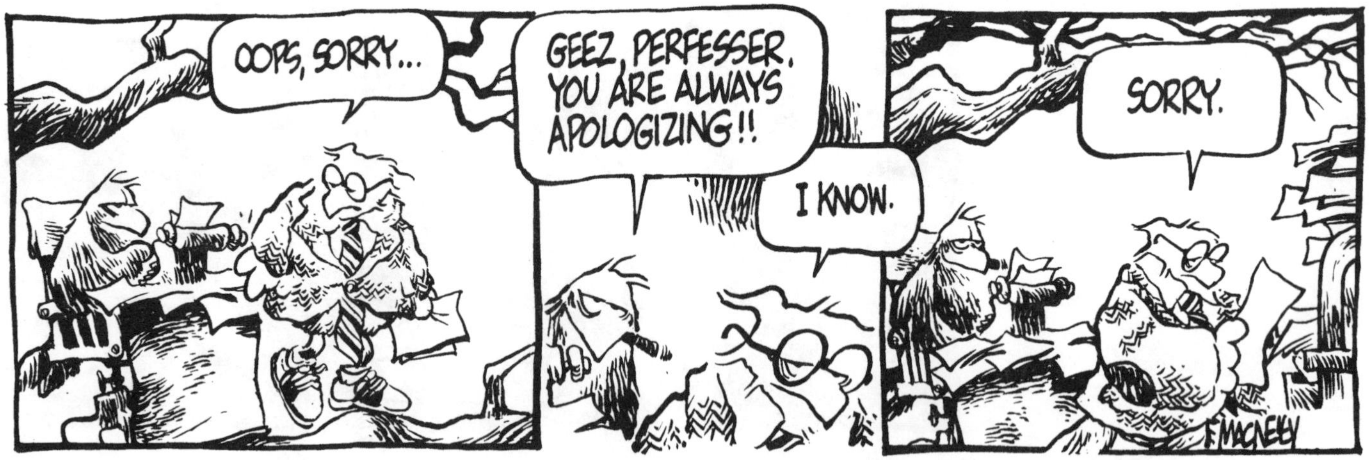
OOPS, SORRY...
GEEZ, PERFESSER, YOU ARE ALWAYS APOLOGIZING!!
I KNOW.
SORRY.
MACNELLY

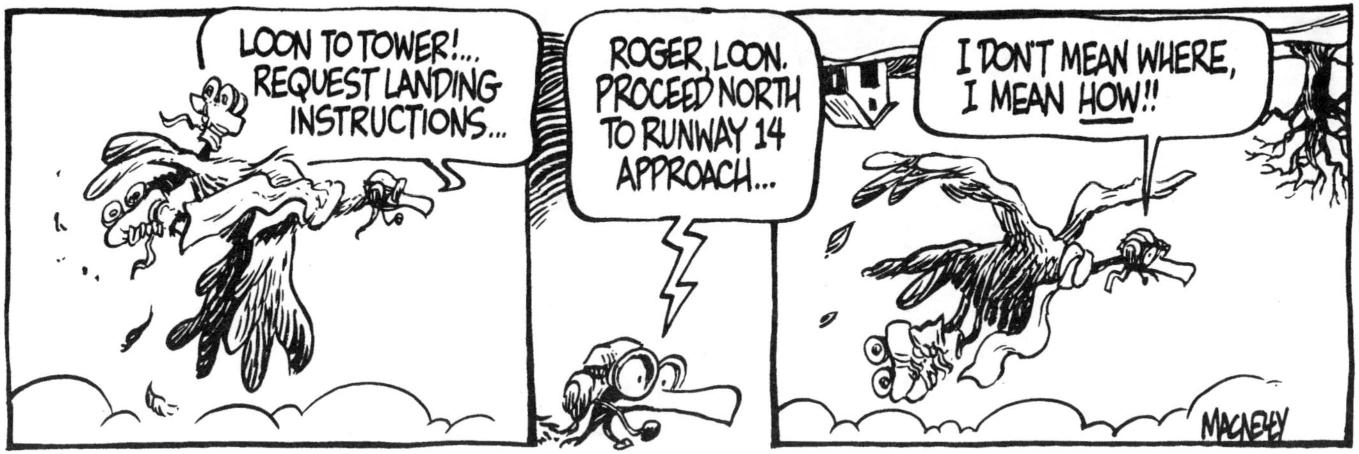
LOON TO TOWER!... REQUEST LANDING INSTRUCTIONS...
ROGER, LOON. PROCEED NORTH TO RUNWAY 14 APPROACH...
I DON'T MEAN WHERE, I MEAN HOW!!
MACNELLY

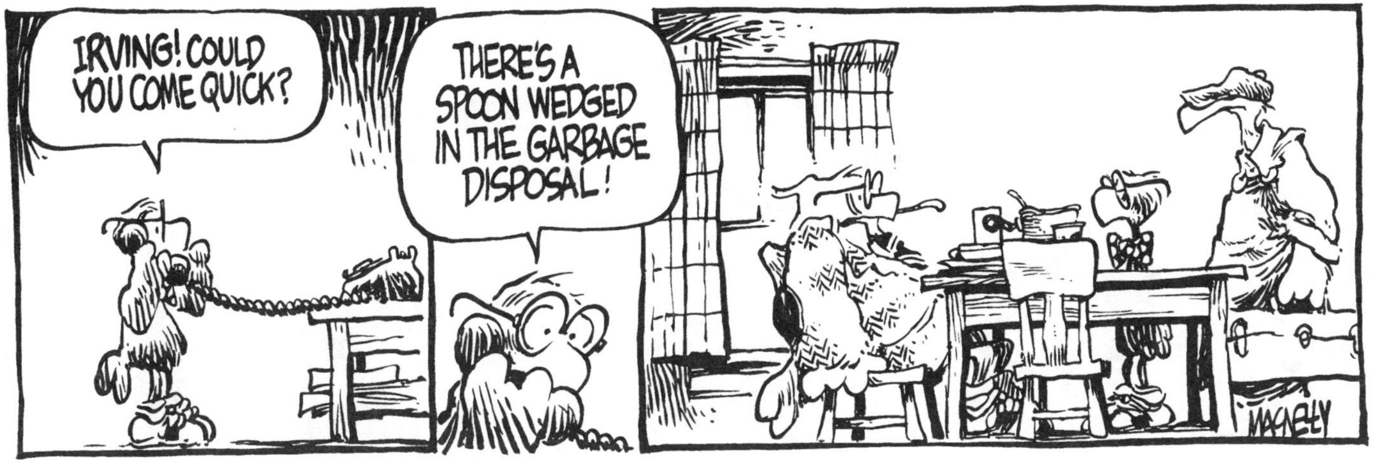
IRVING! COULD YOU COME QUICK?
THERE'S A SPOON WEDGED IN THE GARBAGE DISPOSAL!
MACNELLY

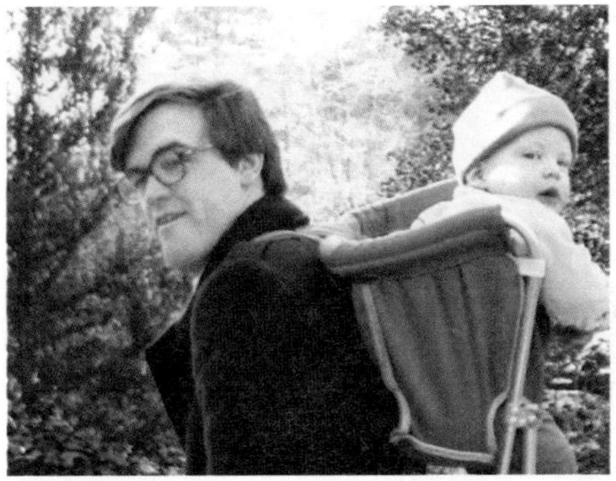

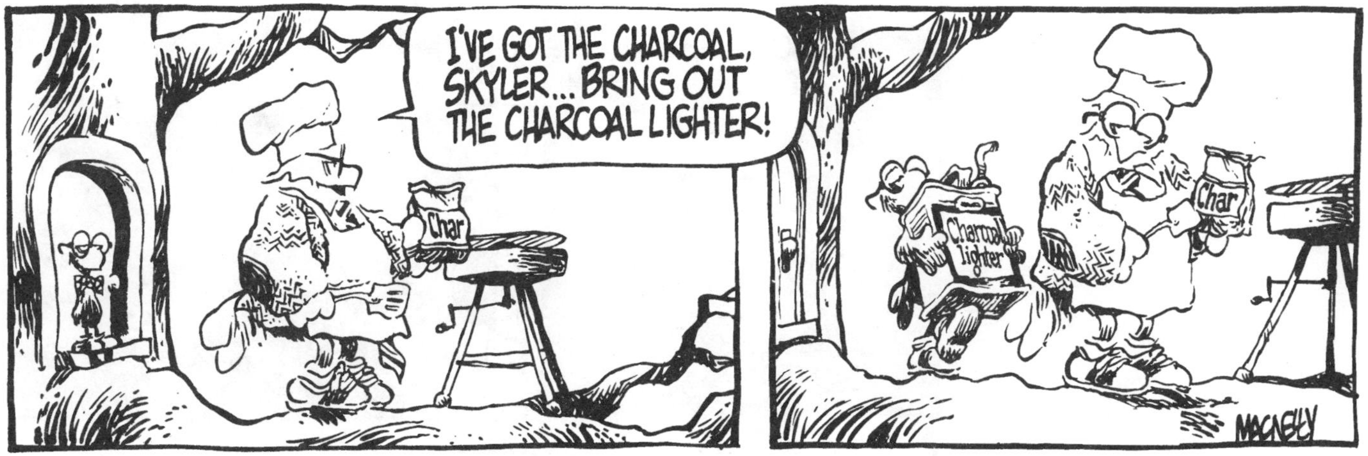
I'VE GOT THE CHARCOAL, SKYLER... BRING OUT THE CHARCOAL LIGHTER!
Char
Charcoal lighter
Char
MACNELLY

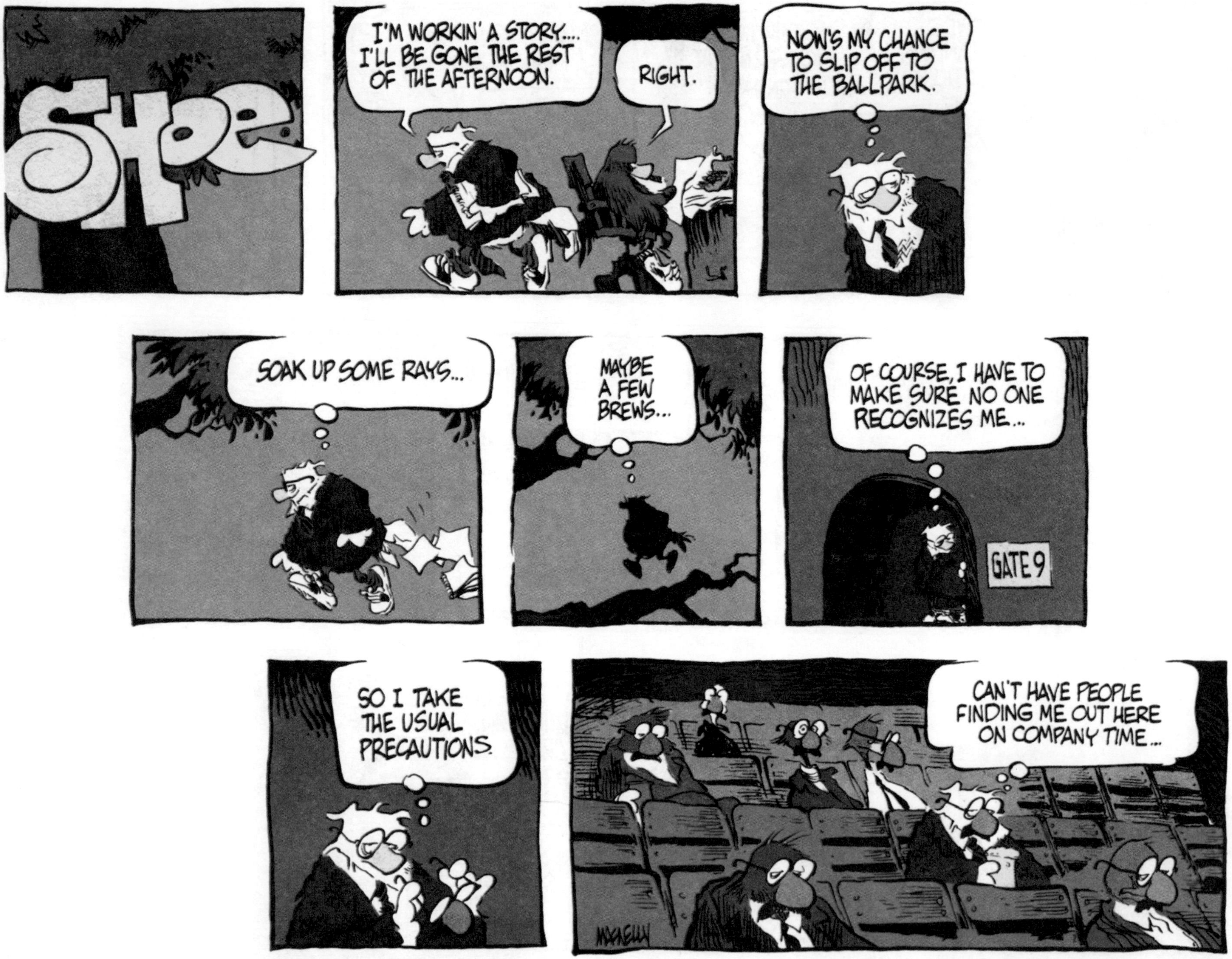
SHOE
I'M WORKIN' A STORY.... I'LL BE GONE THE REST OF THE AFTERNOON.
RIGHT.
NOW'S MY CHANCE TO SLIP OFF TO THE BALLPARK.
SOAK UP SOME RAYS...
MAYBE A FEW BREWS...
OF COURSE, I HAVE TO MAKE SURE NO ONE RECOGNIZES ME...
GATE 9
SO I TAKE THE USUAL PRECAUTIONS.
CAN'T HAVE PEOPLE FINDING ME OUT HERE ON COMPANY TIME...
MACNELLY

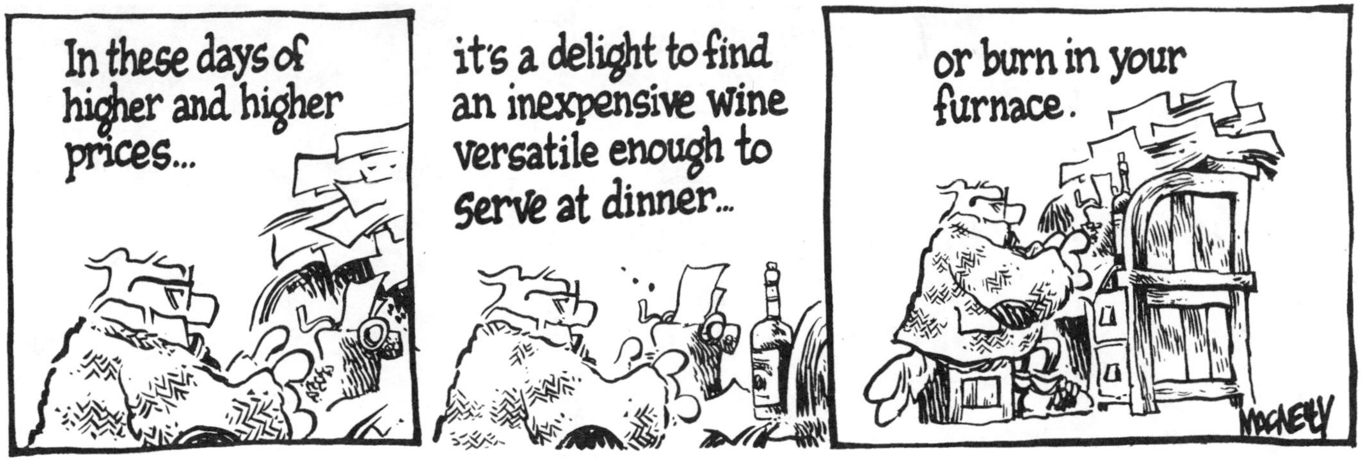
In these days of higher and higher prices...
it's a delight to find an inexpensive wine versatile enough to serve at dinner...
or burn in your furnace.
MACNELLY

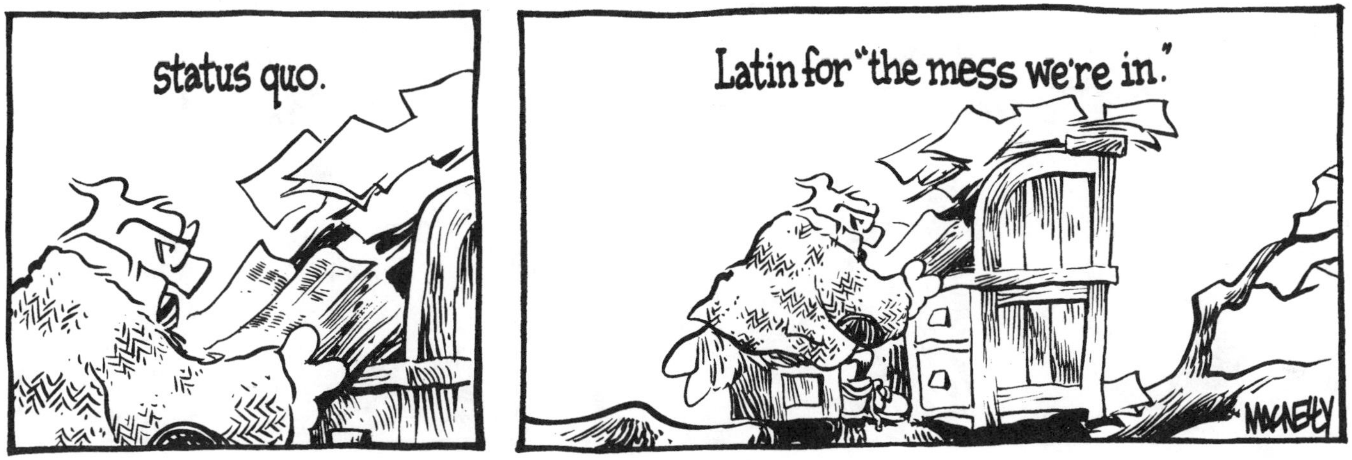
status quo.
Latin for "the mess we're in."
MACNELLY

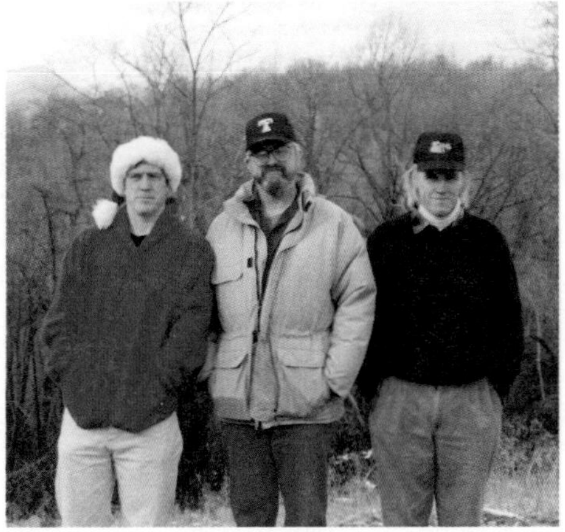

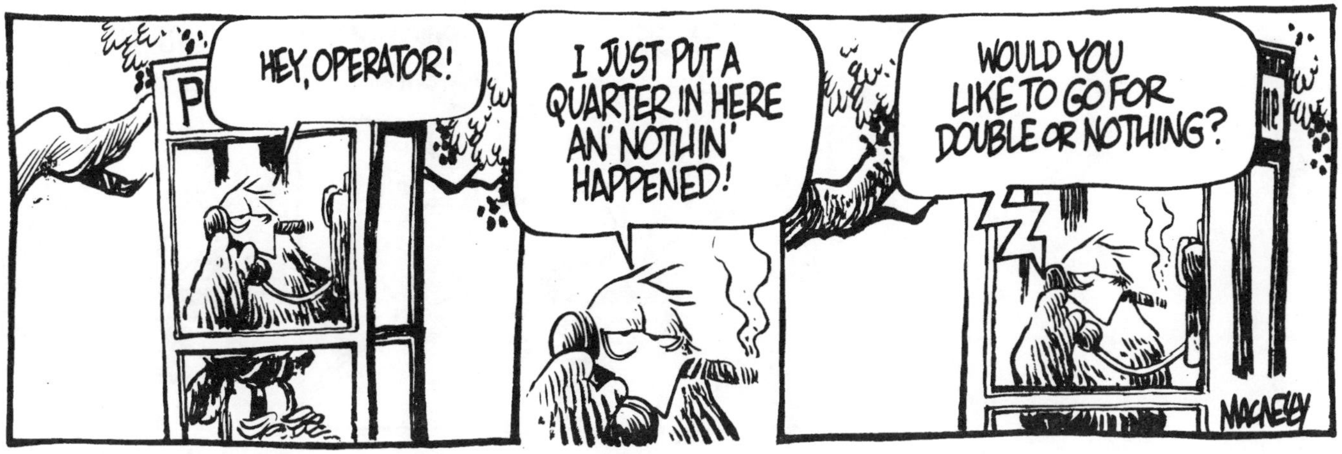
HEY, OPERATOR!
I JUST PUT A QUARTER IN HERE AN' NOTHIN' HAPPENED!
WOULD YOU LIKE TO GO FOR DOUBLE OR NOTHING?
MACNELLY

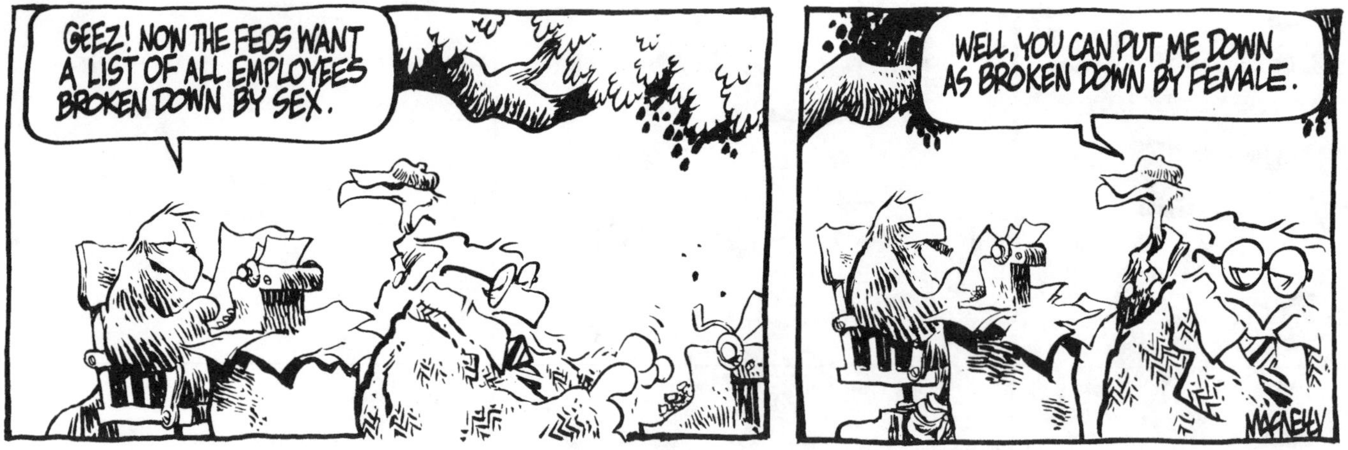
GEEZ! NOW THE FEDS WANT A LIST OF ALL EMPLOYEES BROKEN DOWN BY SEX.
WELL, YOU CAN PUT ME DOWN AS BROKEN DOWN BY FEMALE.
MACNELLY

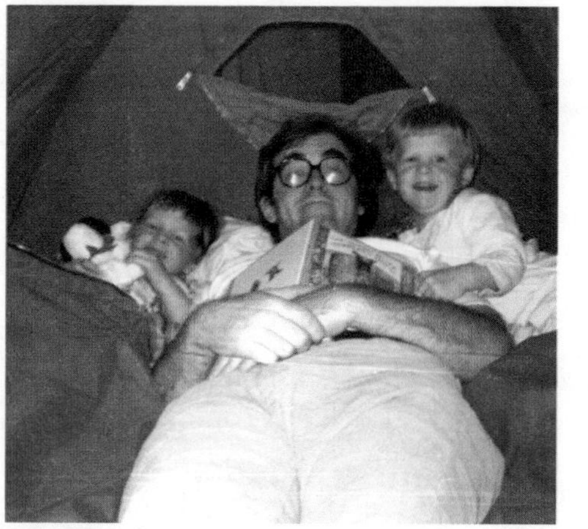

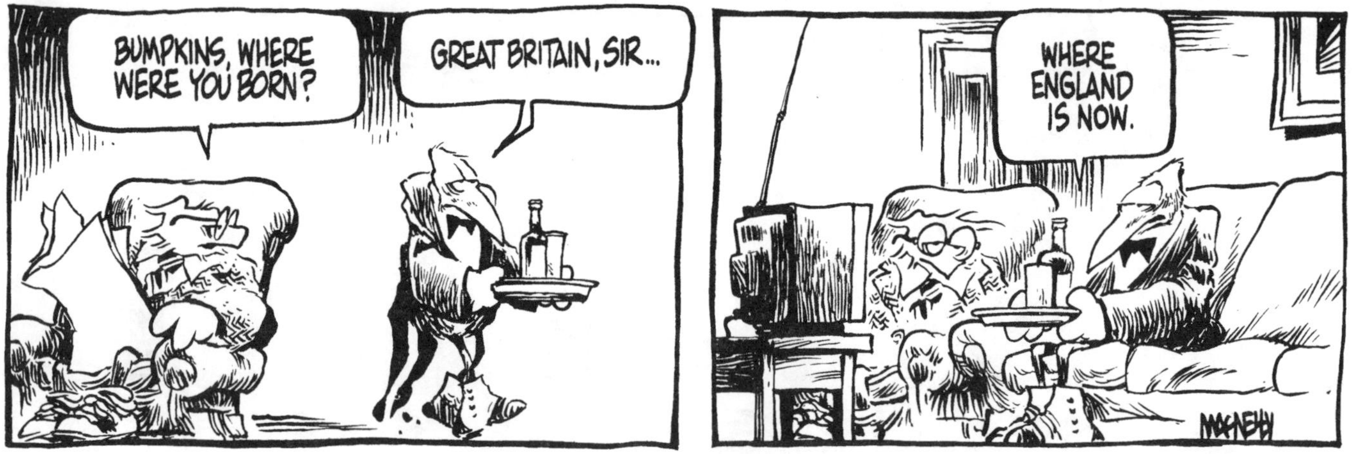
BUMPKINS, WHERE WERE YOU BORN?
GREAT BRITAIN, SIR...
WHERE ENGLAND IS NOW.
MACNELLY

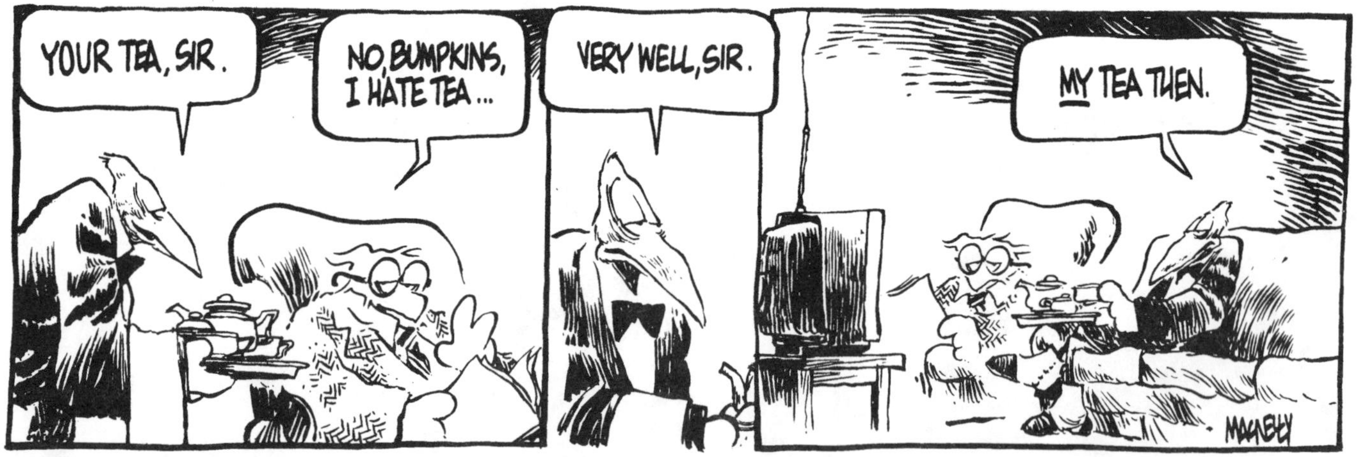
YOUR TEA, SIR.
NO, BUMPKINS, I HATE TEA...
VERY WELL, SIR.
MY TEA THEN.
MACNELLY

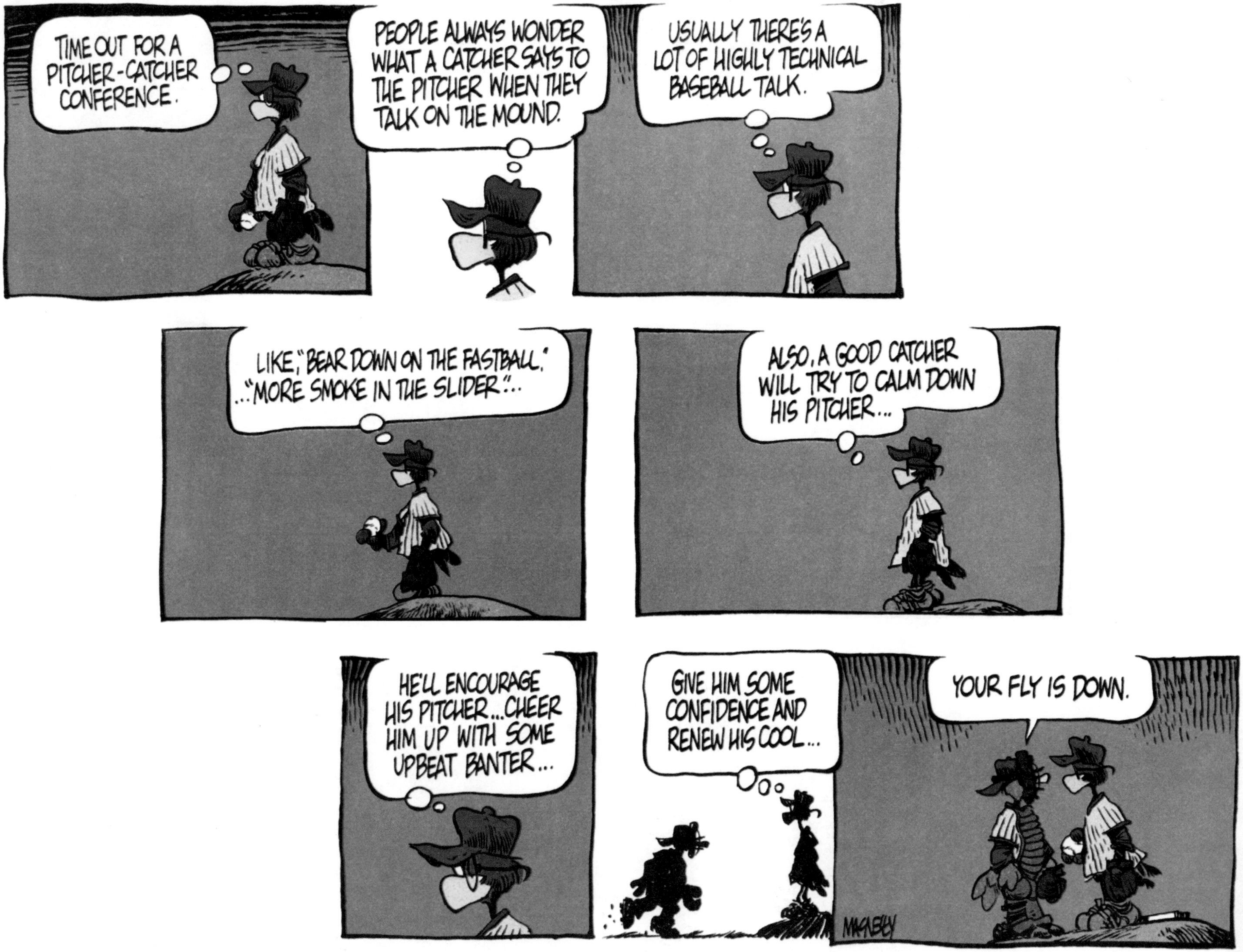
TIME OUT FOR A PITCHER-CATCHER CONFERENCE.
PEOPLE ALWAYS WONDER WHAT A CATCHER SAYS TO THE PITCHER WHEN THEY TALK ON THE MOUND.
USUALLY THERE'S A LOT OF HIGHLY TECHNICAL BASEBALL TALK.
LIKE, "BEAR DOWN ON THE FASTBALL." ..."MORE SMOKE IN THE SLIDER."...
ALSO, A GOOD CATCHER WILL TRY TO CALM DOWN HIS PITCHER...
HE'LL ENCOURAGE HIS PITCHER...CHEER HIM UP WITH SOME UPBEAT BANTER...
GIVE HIM SOME CONFIDENCE AND RENEW HIS COOL...
YOUR FLY IS DOWN.
MACNELLY

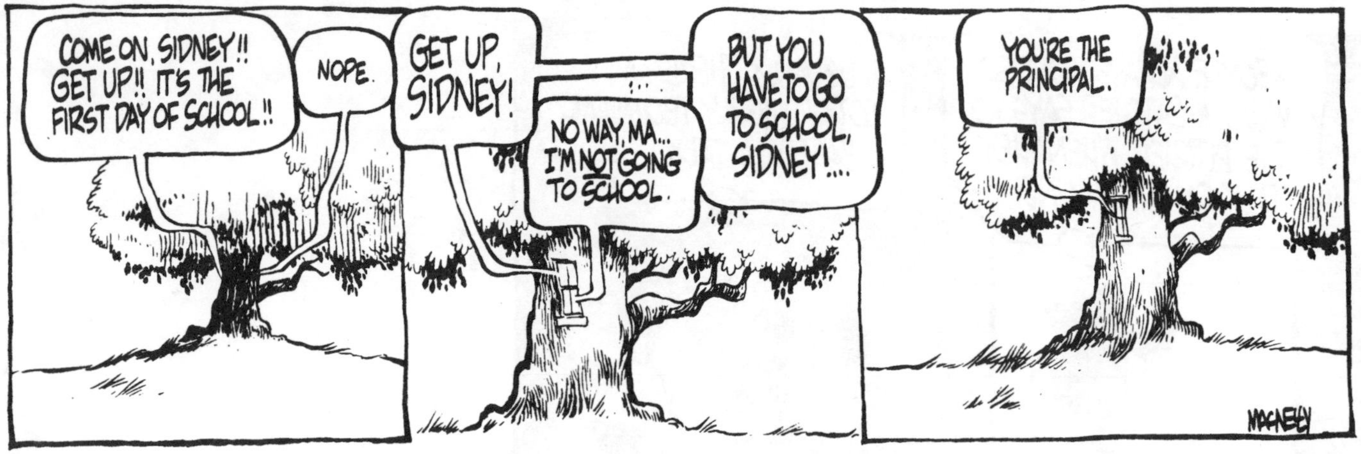
COME ON, SIDNEY!! GET UP!! IT'S THE FIRST DAY OF SCHOOL!!
NOPE.
GET UP, SIDNEY!
NO WAY, MA... I'M NOT GOING TO SCHOOL.
BUT YOU HAVE TO GO TO SCHOOL, SIDNEY!...
YOU'RE THE PRINCIPAL.
MACNELLY

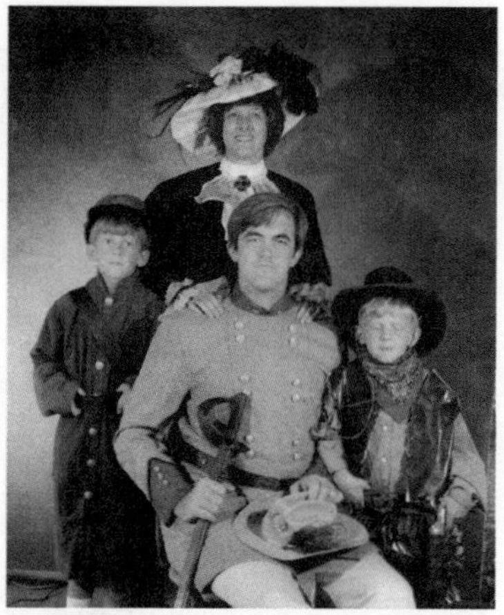

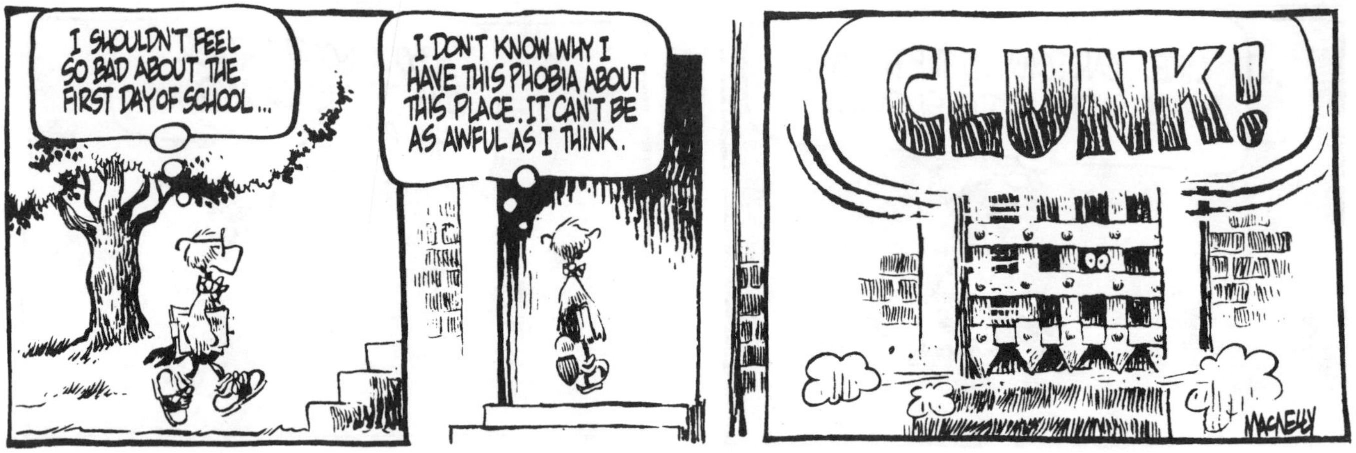
I SHOULDN'T FEEL SO BAD ABOUT THE FIRST DAY OF SCHOOL...
I DON'T KNOW WHY I HAVE THIS PHOBIA ABOUT THIS PLACE. IT CAN'T BE AS AWFUL AS I THINK.
CLUNK!
MACNELLY

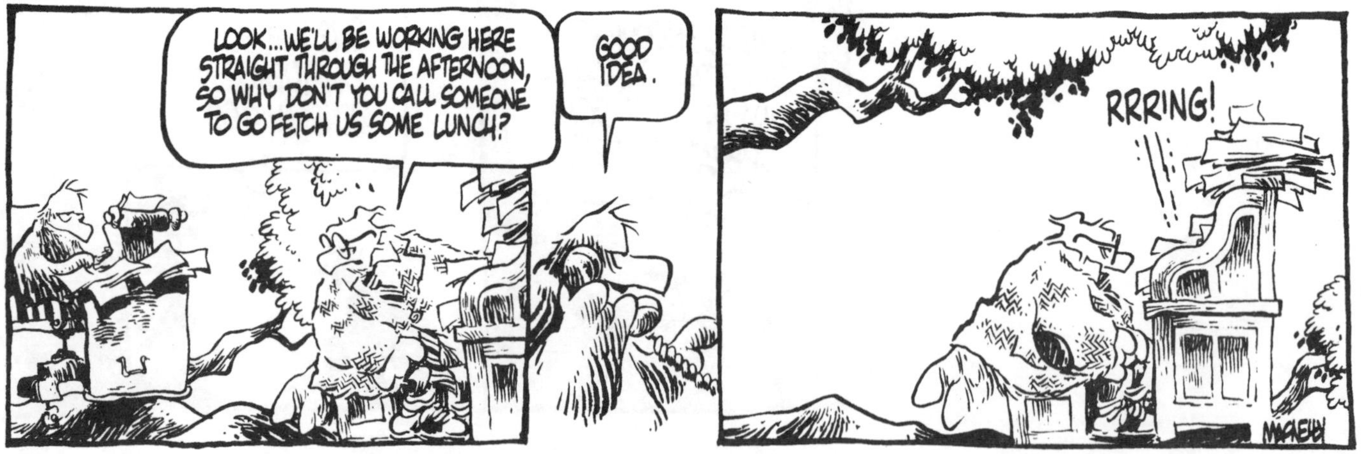
LOOK...WE'LL BE WORKING HERE STRAIGHT THROUGH THE AFTERNOON, SO WHY DON'T YOU CALL SOMEONE TO GO FETCH US SOME LUNCH?
GOOD IDEA.
RRRING!
MACNELLY

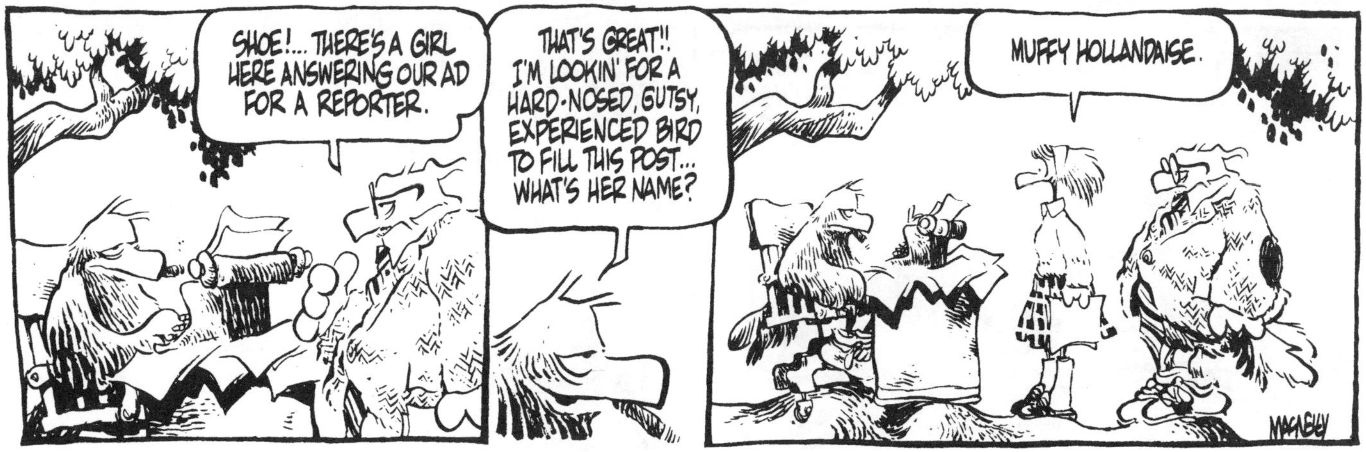
SHOE!... THERE'S A GIRL HERE ANSWERING OUR AD FOR A REPORTER.
THAT'S GREAT!! I'M LOOKIN' FOR A HARD-NOSED, GUTSY, EXPERIENCED BIRD TO FILL THIS POST... WHAT'S HER NAME?
MUFFY HOLLANDAISE.
MACNELLY

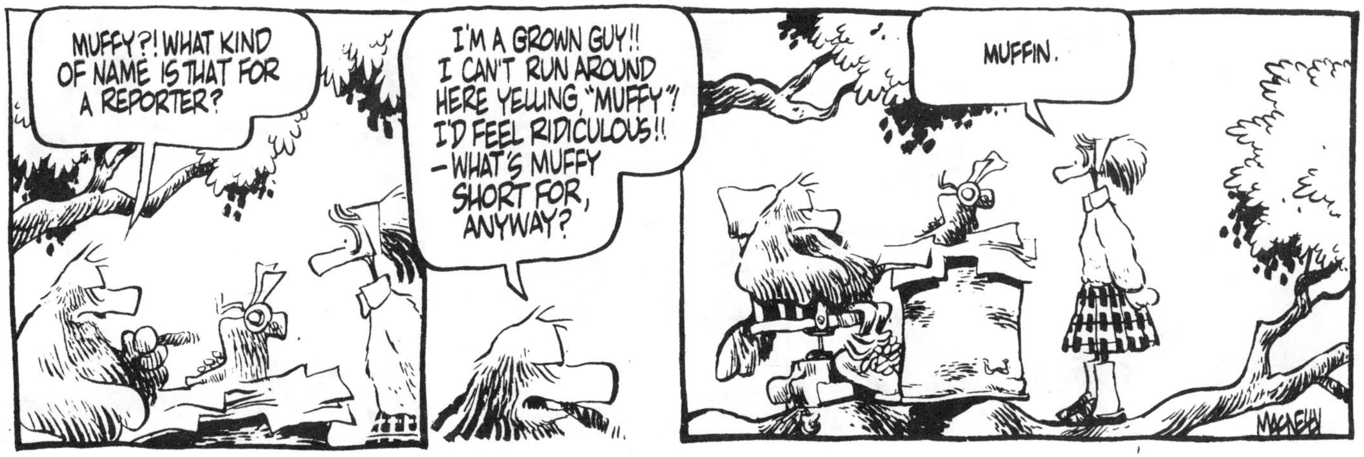
MUFFY?! WHAT KIND OF NAME IS THAT FOR A REPORTER?
I'M A GROWN GUY!! I CAN'T RUN AROUND HERE YELLING, "MUFFY"! I'D FEEL RIDICULOUS!! — WHAT'S MUFFY SHORT FOR, ANYWAY?
MUFFIN.
MACNELLY

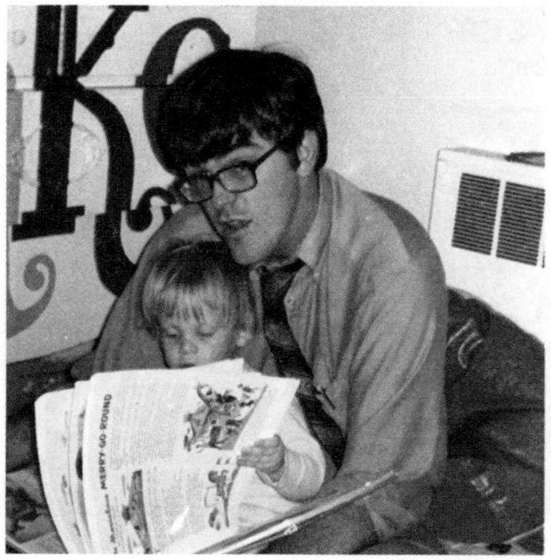

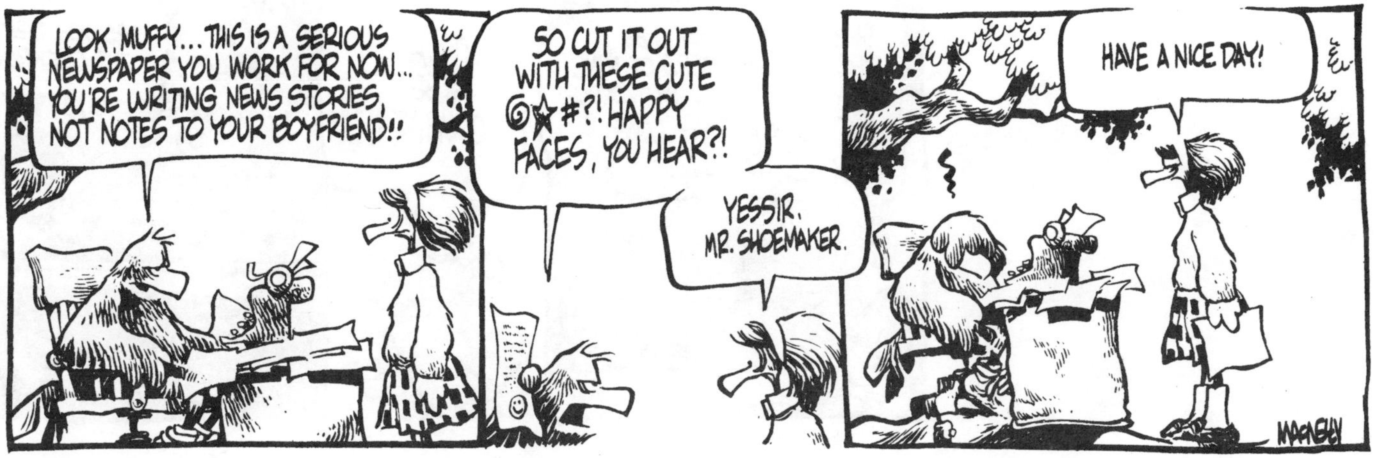
LOOK, MUFFY... THIS IS A SERIOUS NEWSPAPER YOU WORK FOR NOW... YOU'RE WRITING NEWS STORIES, NOT NOTES TO YOUR BOYFRIEND!!
SO CUT IT OUT WITH THESE CUTE @☆#?! HAPPY FACES, YOU HEAR?!
YESSIR, MR. SHOEMAKER.
HAVE A NICE DAY!
MACNELLY

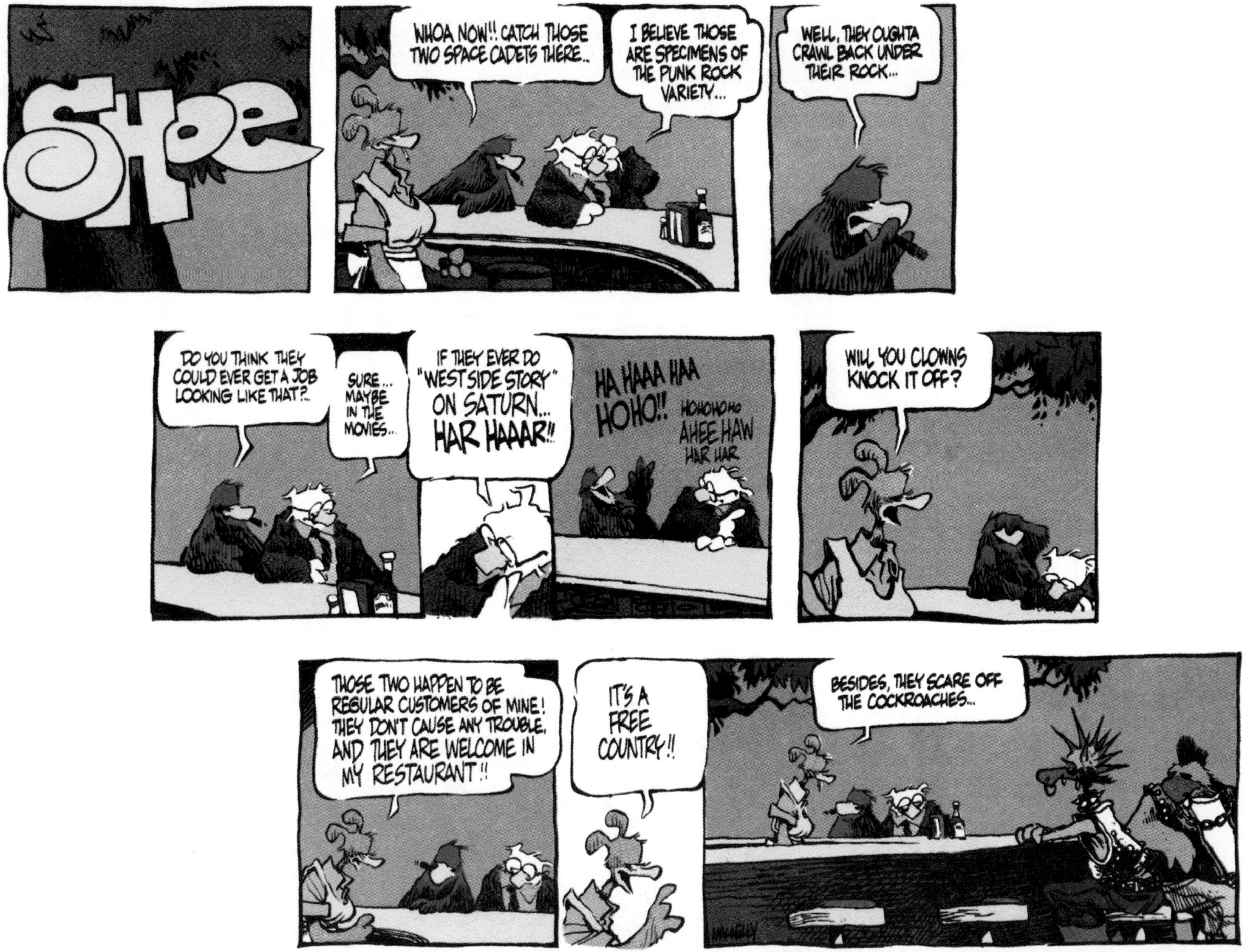
SHOE
WHOA NOW!! CATCH THOSE TWO SPACE CADETS THERE..
I BELIEVE THOSE ARE SPECIMENS OF THE PUNK ROCK VARIETY...
WELL, THEY OUGHTA CRAWL BACK UNDER THEIR ROCK...
DO YOU THINK THEY COULD EVER GET A JOB LOOKING LIKE THAT?..
SURE... MAYBE IN THE MOVIES...
IF THEY EVER DO "WEST SIDE STORY" ON SATURN... HAR HAAAR!!
HA HAAA HAA HOHO!!
HOHOHOHO AHEE HAW HAR HAR
WILL YOU CLOWNS KNOCK IT OFF?
THOSE TWO HAPPEN TO BE REGULAR CUSTOMERS OF MINE! THEY DON'T CAUSE ANY TROUBLE, AND THEY ARE WELCOME IN MY RESTAURANT!!
IT'S A FREE COUNTRY!!
BESIDES, THEY SCARE OFF THE COCKROACHES...

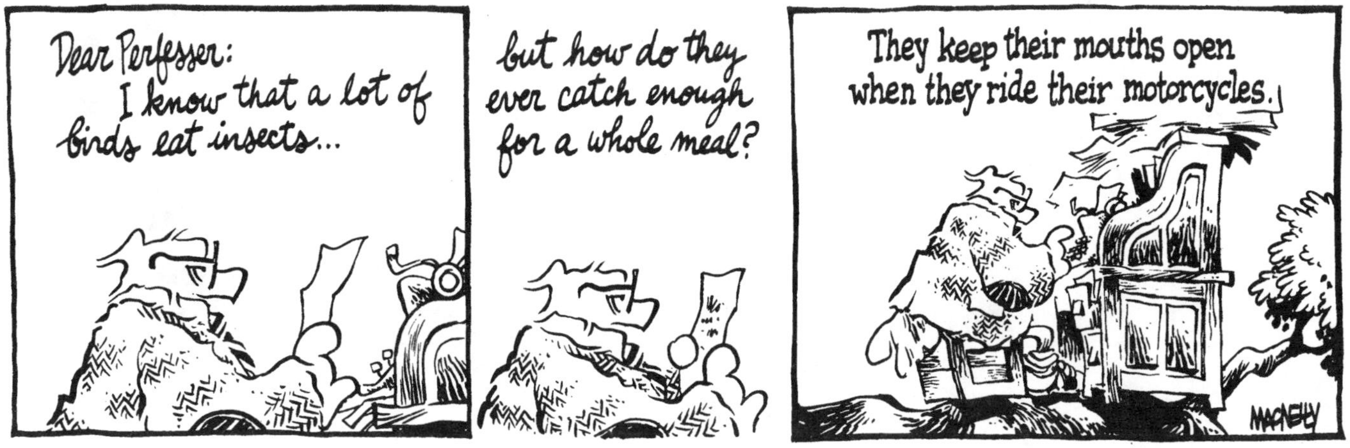
Dear Perfesser:
I know that a lot of birds eat insects...
but how do they ever catch enough for a whole meal?
They keep their mouths open when they ride their motorcycles.
MACNELLY

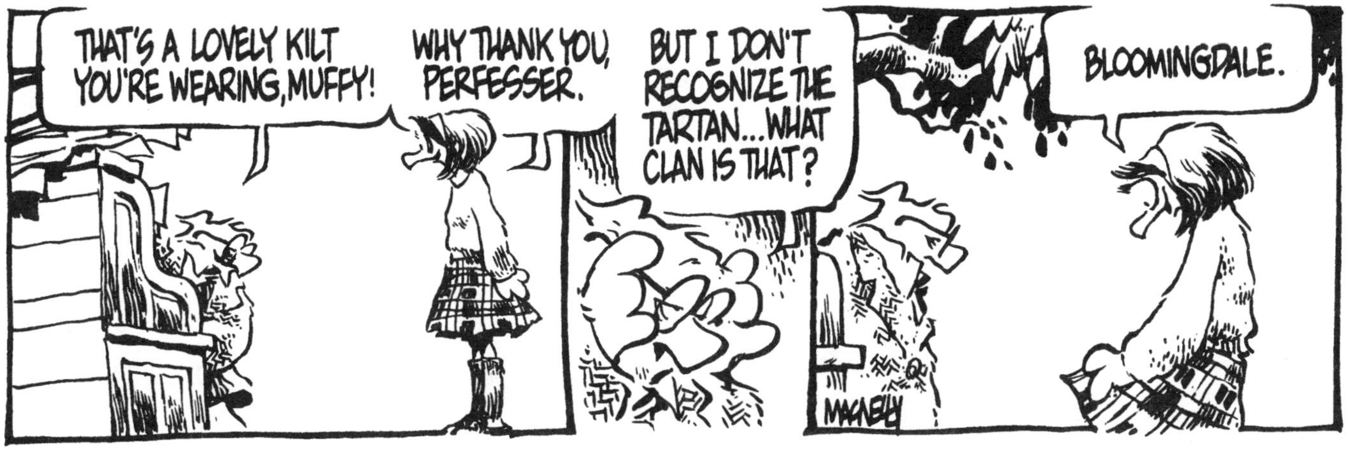
THAT'S A LOVELY KILT YOU'RE WEARING, MUFFY!
WHY THANK YOU, PERFESSER.
BUT I DON'T RECOGNIZE THE TARTAN... WHAT CLAN IS THAT?
BLOOMINGDALE.
MACNELLY

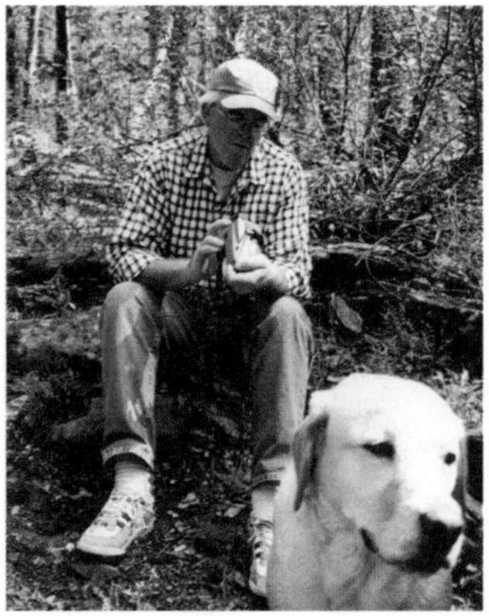

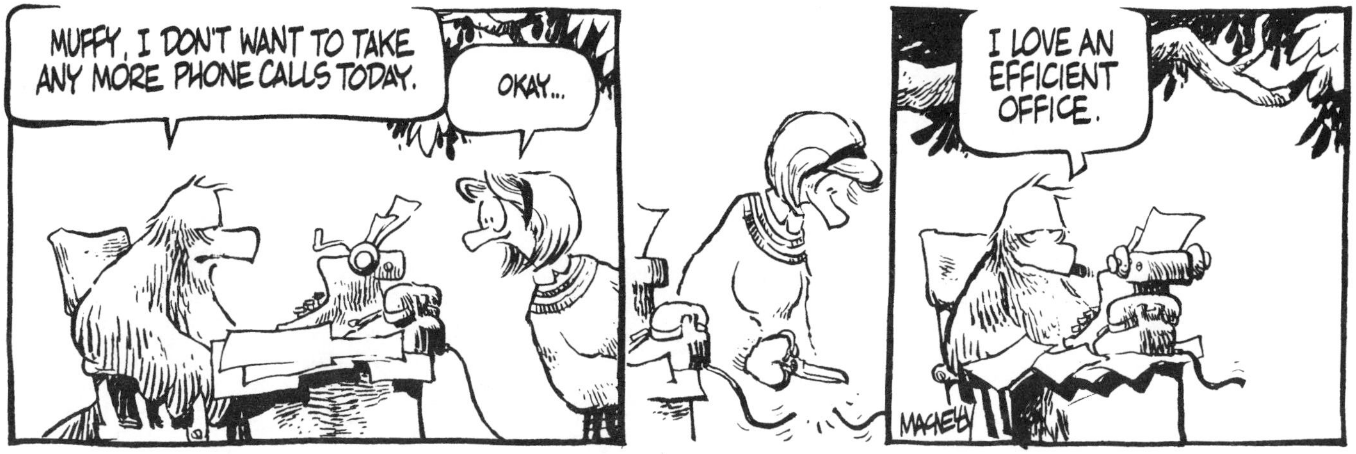
MUFFY, I DON'T WANT TO TAKE ANY MORE PHONE CALLS TODAY.
OKAY...
I LOVE AN EFFICIENT OFFICE.
MACNELLY

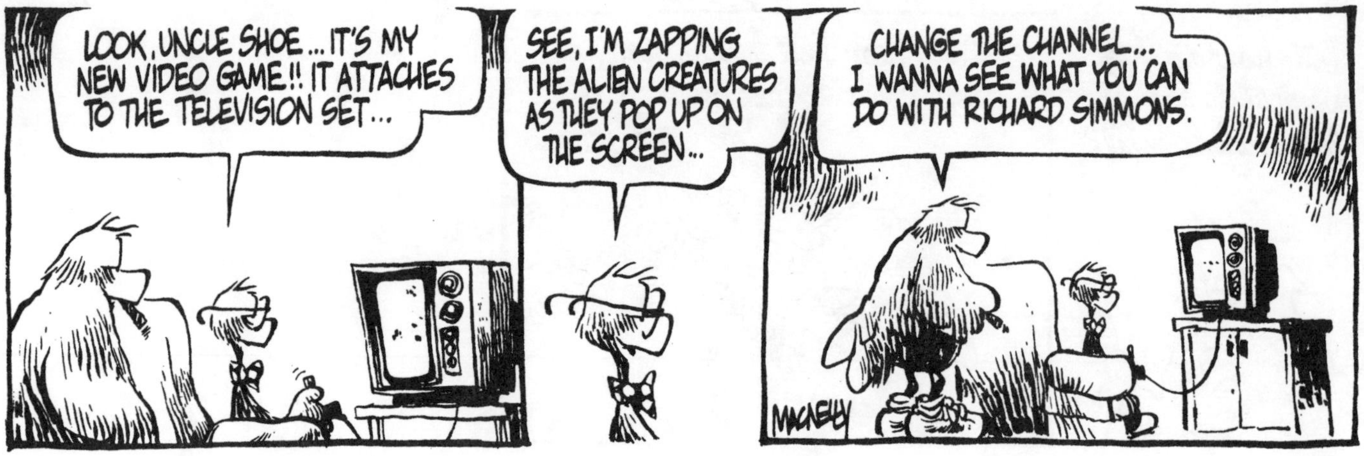
LOOK, UNCLE SHOE... IT'S MY NEW VIDEO GAME!! IT ATTACHES TO THE TELEVISION SET...
SEE, I'M ZAPPING THE ALIEN CREATURES AS THEY POP UP ON THE SCREEN...
CHANGE THE CHANNEL... I WANNA SEE WHAT YOU CAN DO WITH RICHARD SIMMONS.
MACNELLY

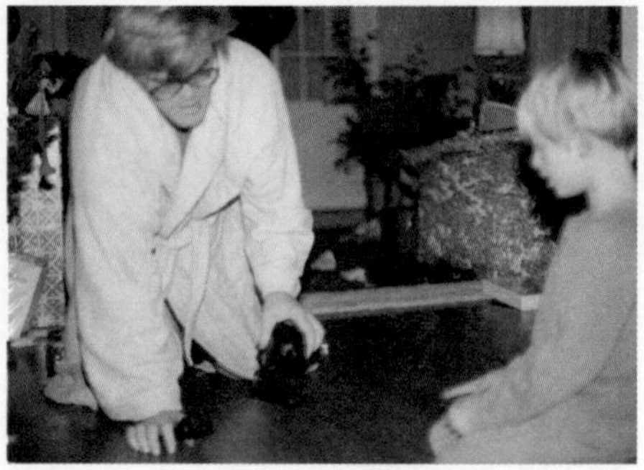

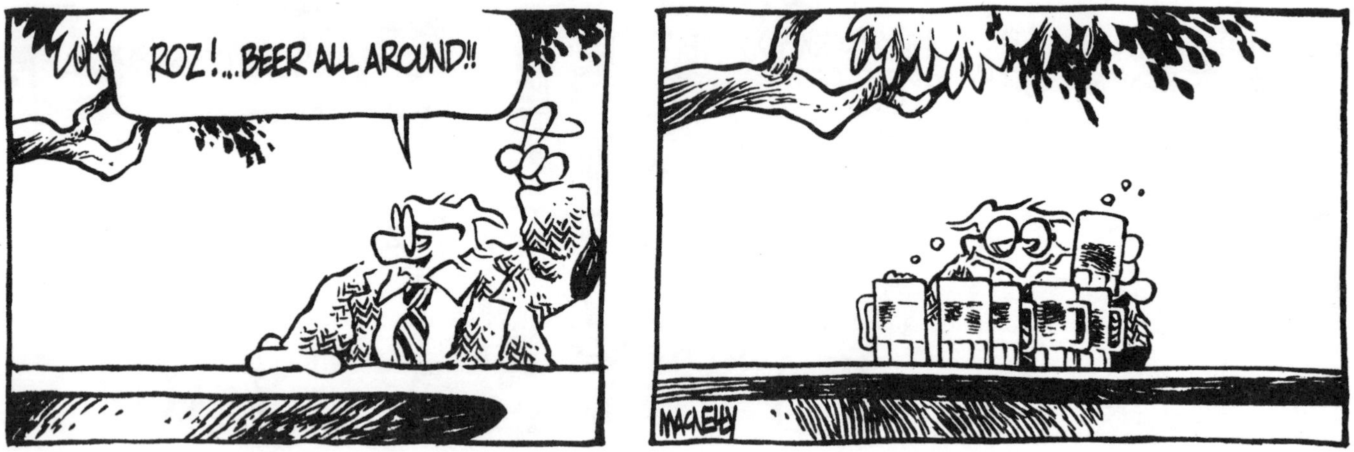
ROZ!...BEER ALL AROUND!!
MACNELLY

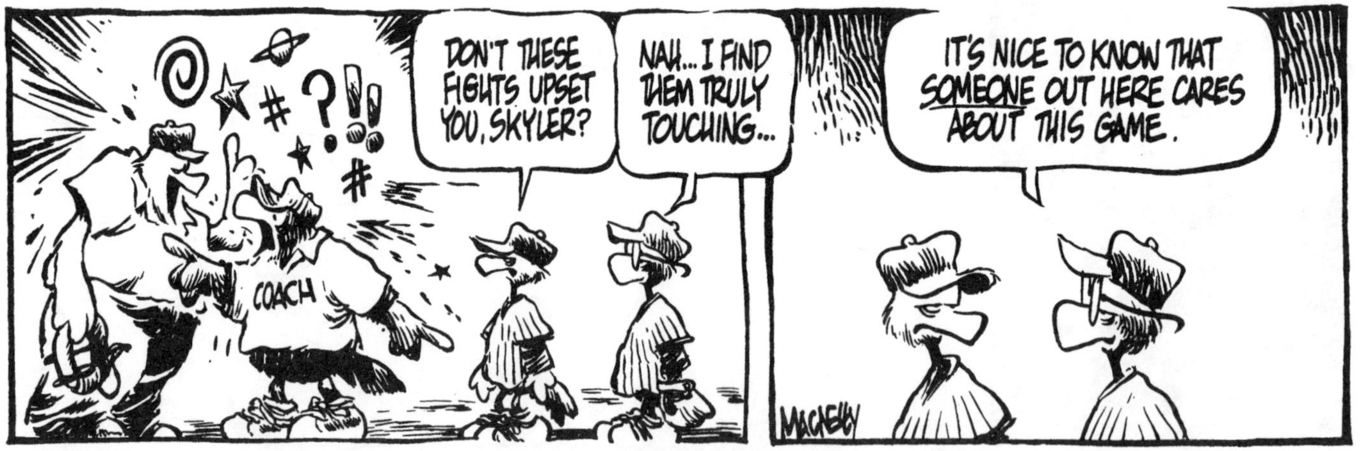
COACH
DON'T THESE FIGHTS UPSET YOU, SKYLER?
NAH... I FIND THEM TRULY TOUCHING...
IT'S NICE TO KNOW THAT SOMEONE OUT HERE CARES ABOUT THIS GAME.
MACNELLY

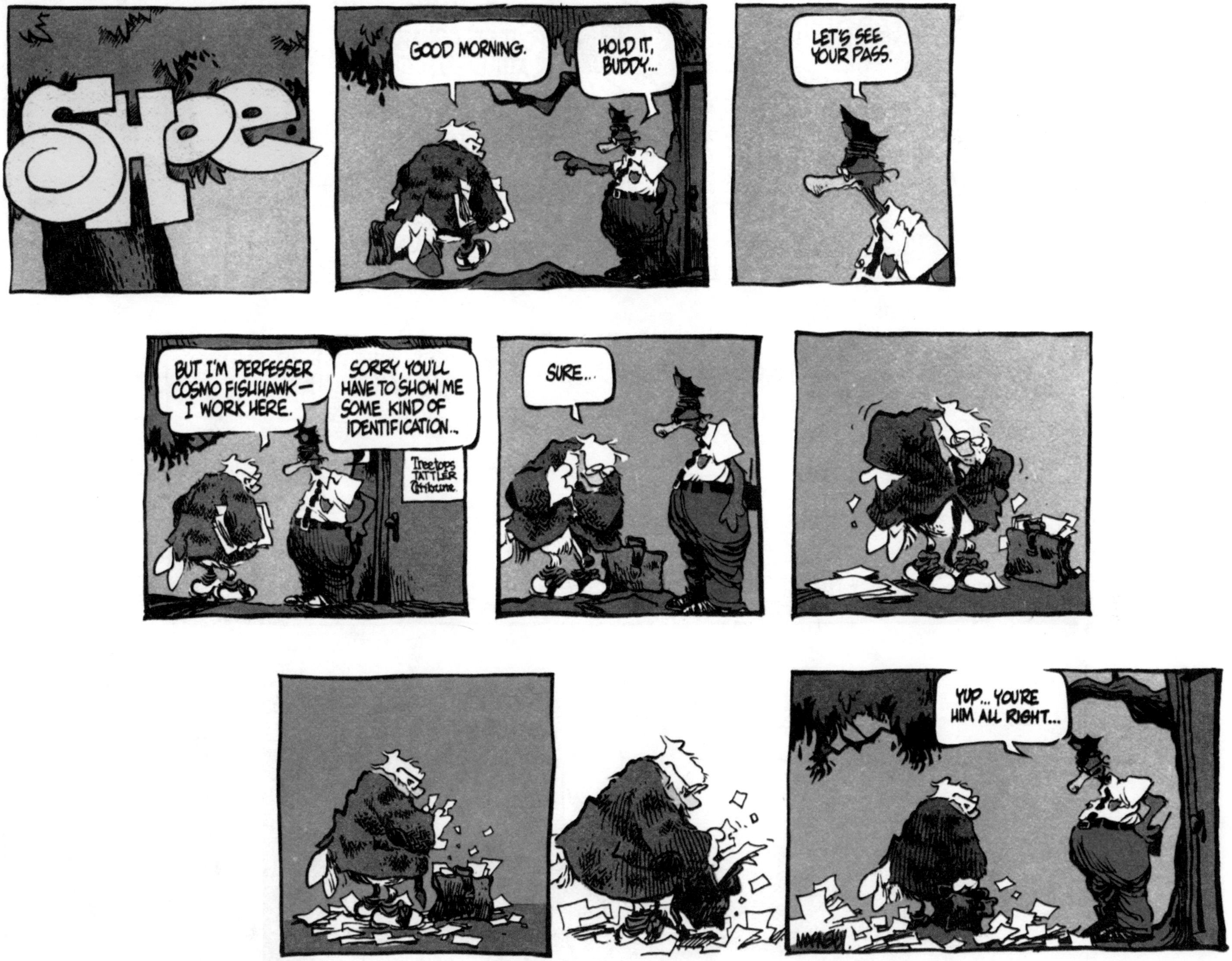
SHOE
GOOD MORNING.
HOLD IT, BUDDY...
LET'S SEE YOUR PASS.
BUT I'M PERFESSER COSMO FISHHAWK— I WORK HERE.
SORRY, YOU'LL HAVE TO SHOW ME SOME KIND OF IDENTIFICATION..
Treetops TATTLER Tribune
SURE...
YUP... YOU'RE HIM ALL RIGHT...
MACNELLY

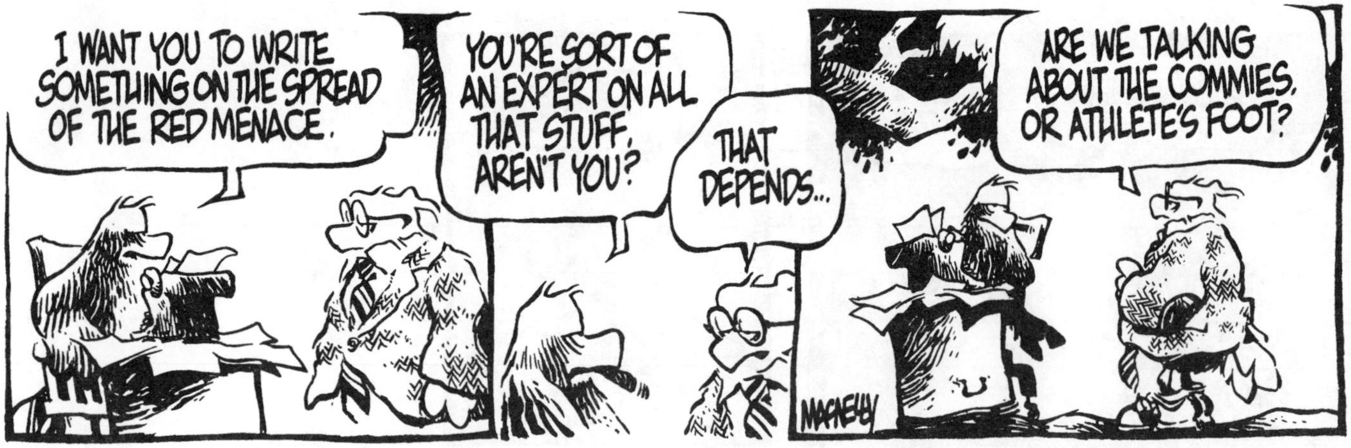
I WANT YOU TO WRITE SOMETHING ON THE SPREAD OF THE RED MENACE.
YOU'RE SORT OF AN EXPERT ON ALL THAT STUFF, AREN'T YOU?
THAT DEPENDS...
ARE WE TALKING ABOUT THE COMMIES, OR ATHLETE'S FOOT?
MACNELLY

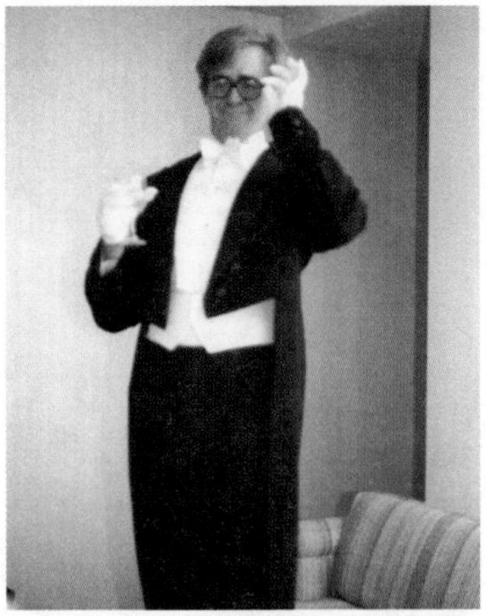

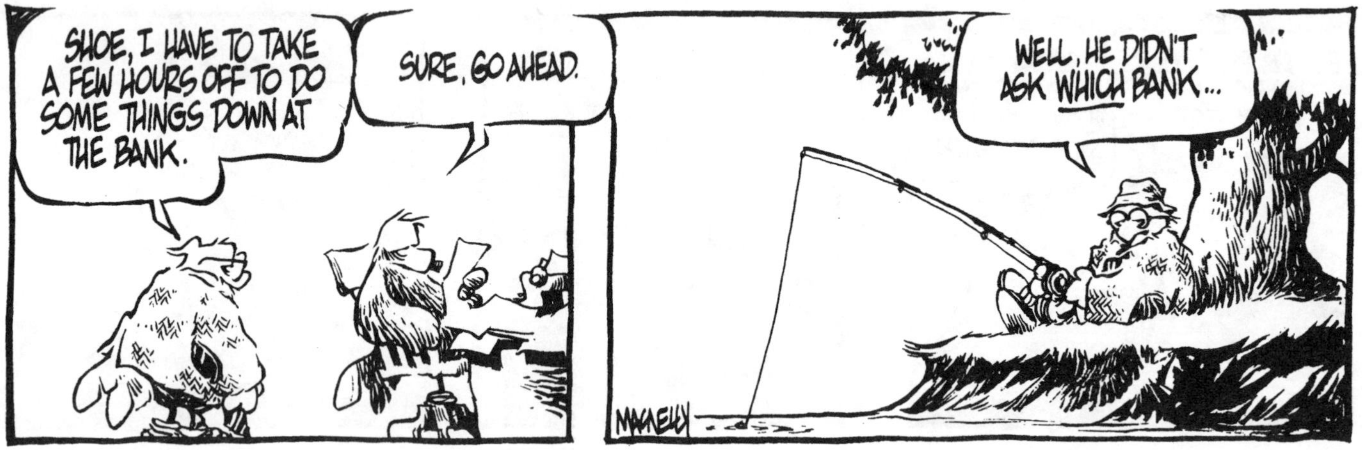
SHOE, I HAVE TO TAKE A FEW HOURS OFF TO DO SOME THINGS DOWN AT THE BANK.
SURE, GO AHEAD.
WELL, HE DIDN'T ASK WHICH BANK...
MACNELLY

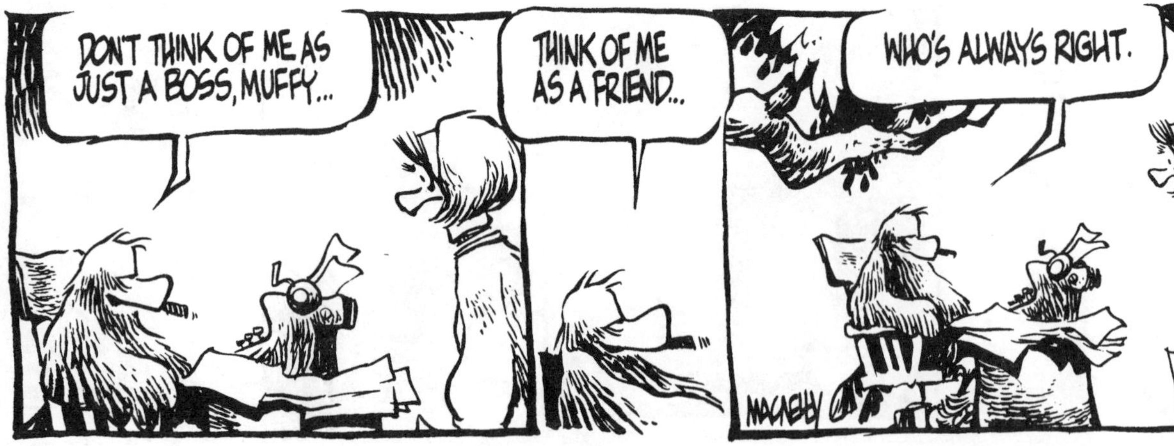
DON'T THINK OF ME AS JUST A BOSS, MUFFY...
THINK OF ME AS A FRIEND...
WHO'S ALWAYS RIGHT.
MACNELLY

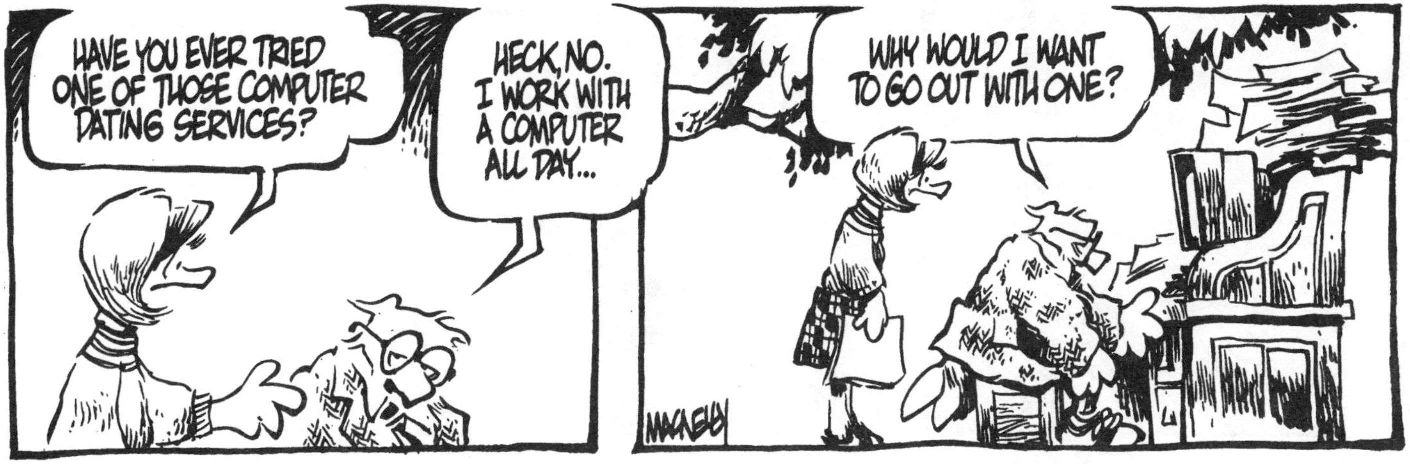
HAVE YOU EVER TRIED ONE OF THOSE COMPUTER DATING SERVICES?
HECK, NO. I WORK WITH A COMPUTER ALL DAY...
WHY WOULD I WANT TO GO OUT WITH ONE?
MACNELLY

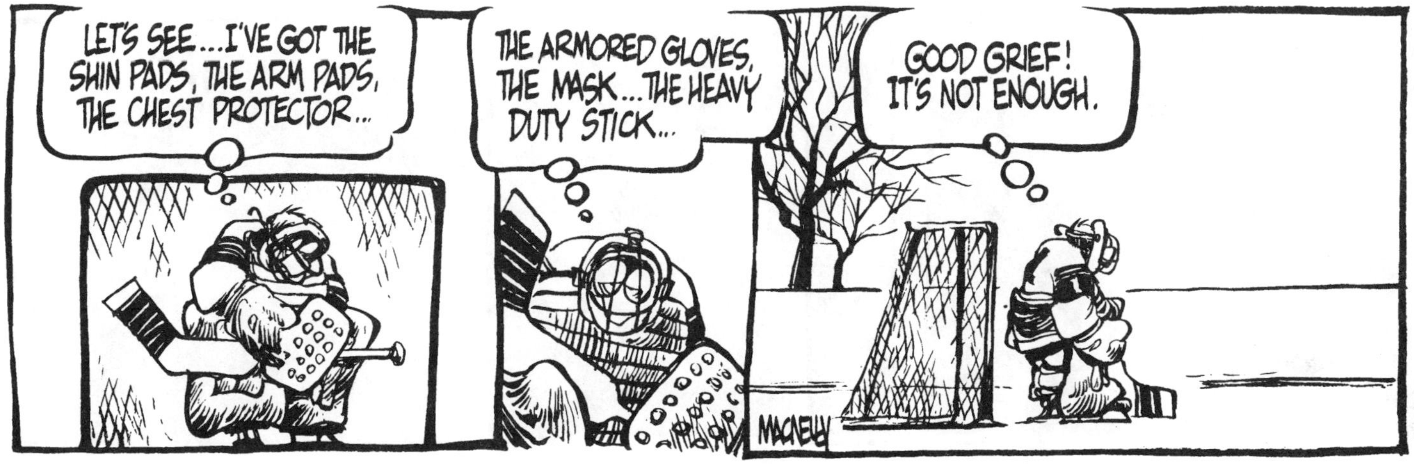
LET'S SEE....I'VE GOT THE SHIN PADS, THE ARM PADS, THE CHEST PROTECTOR...
THE ARMORED GLOVES, THE MASK...THE HEAVY DUTY STICK...
GOOD GRIEF! IT'S NOT ENOUGH.
MACNELLY

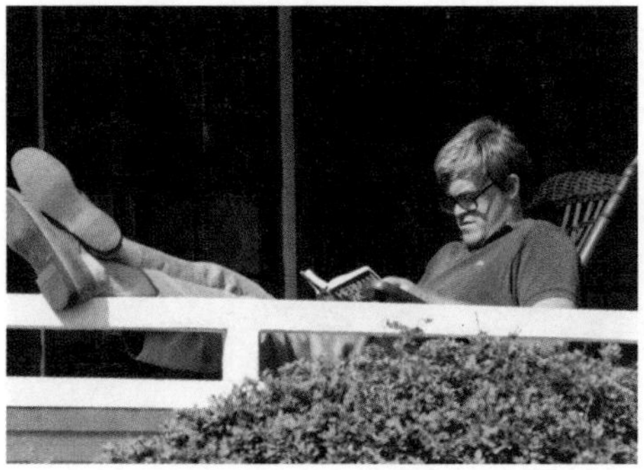

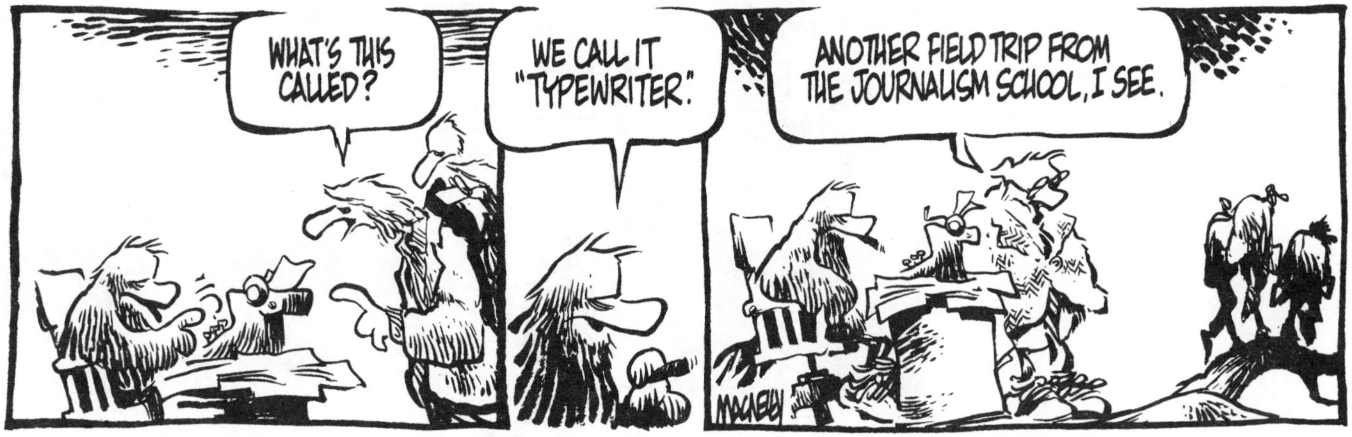
WHAT'S THIS CALLED?
WE CALL IT "TYPEWRITER."
ANOTHER FIELD TRIP FROM THE JOURNALISM SCHOOL, I SEE.
MACNELLY

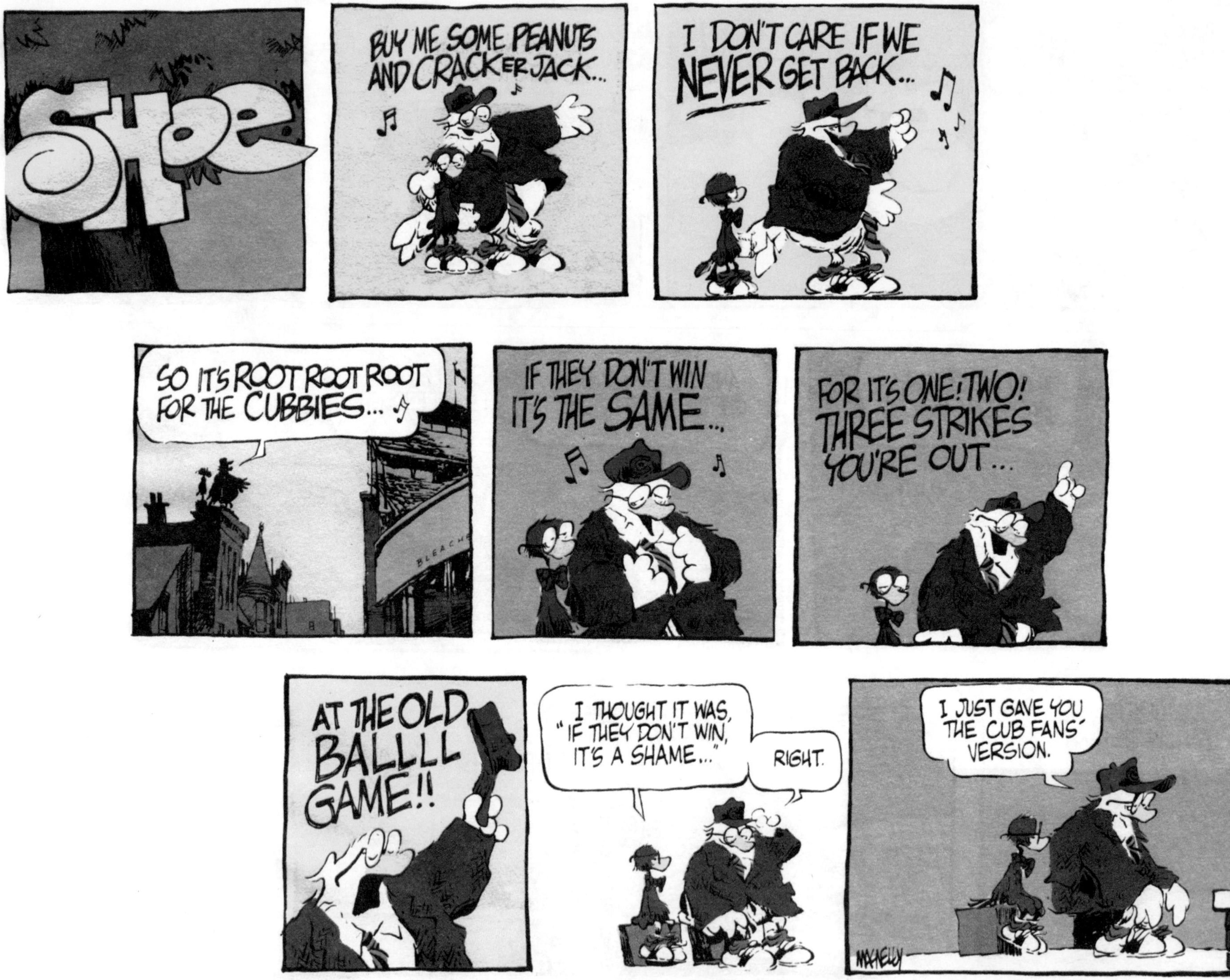
SHOE
BUY ME SOME PEANUTS AND CRACKER JACK...
I DON'T CARE IF WE NEVER GET BACK...
SO IT'S ROOT ROOT ROOT FOR THE CUBBIES...
BLEACH
IF THEY DON'T WIN IT'S THE SAME...
FOR IT'S ONE! TWO! THREE STRIKES YOU'RE OUT...
AT THE OLD BALLLL GAME!!
I THOUGHT IT WAS, "IF THEY DON'T WIN, IT'S A SHAME..."
RIGHT.
I JUST GAVE YOU THE CUB FANS' VERSION.
MACNELLY

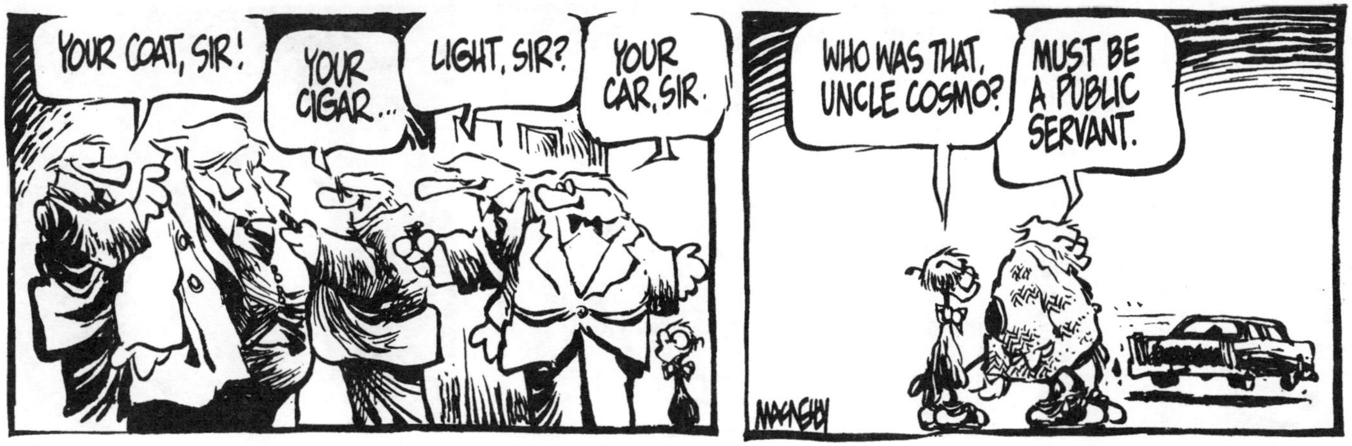
YOUR COAT, SIR!
YOUR CIGAR...
LIGHT, SIR?
YOUR CAR, SIR.
WHO WAS THAT, UNCLE COSMO?
MUST BE A PUBLIC SERVANT.
MACNELLY

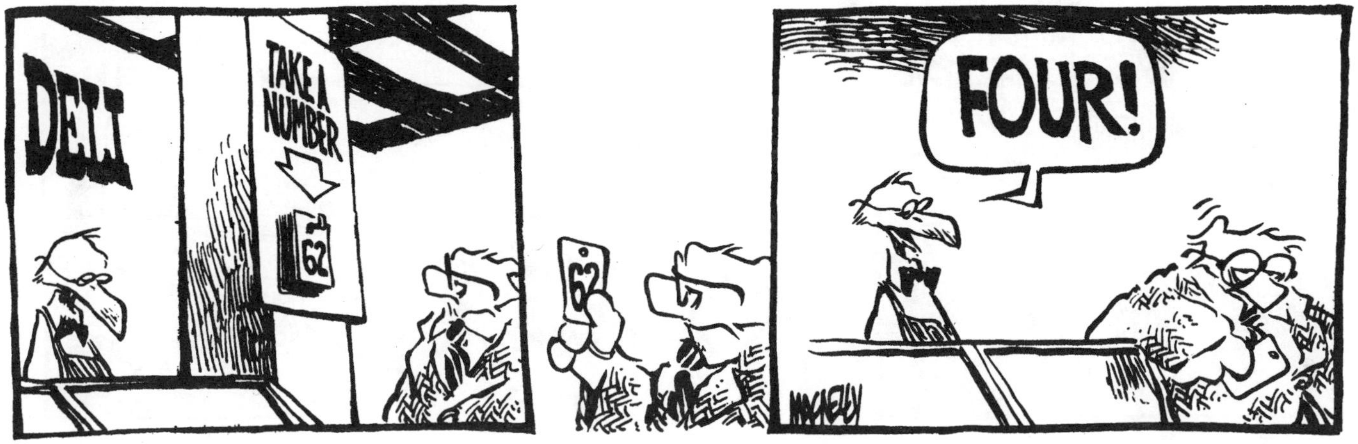
DELI
TAKE A NUMBER
62
62
FOUR!
MACNELLY

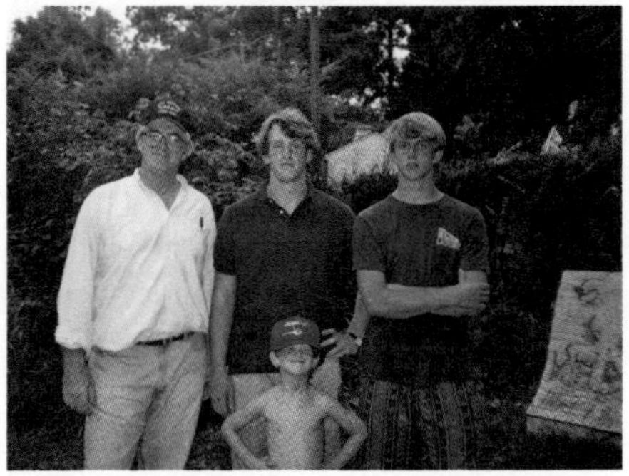

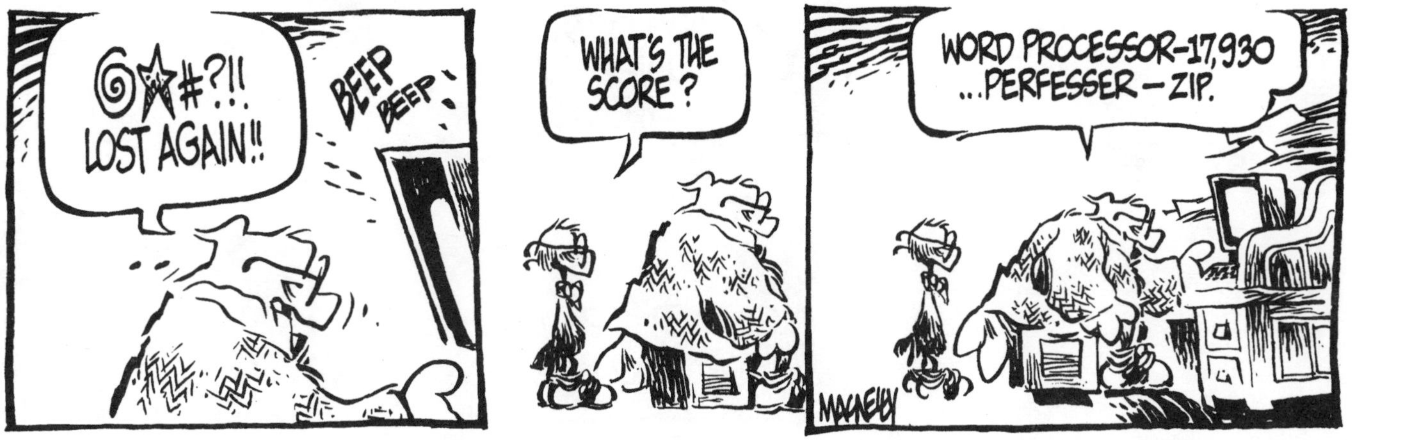
#?!!
LOST AGAIN!!
BEEP
BEEP
WHAT'S THE SCORE?
WORD PROCESSOR–17,930 ...PERFESSER – ZIP.
MACNELLY

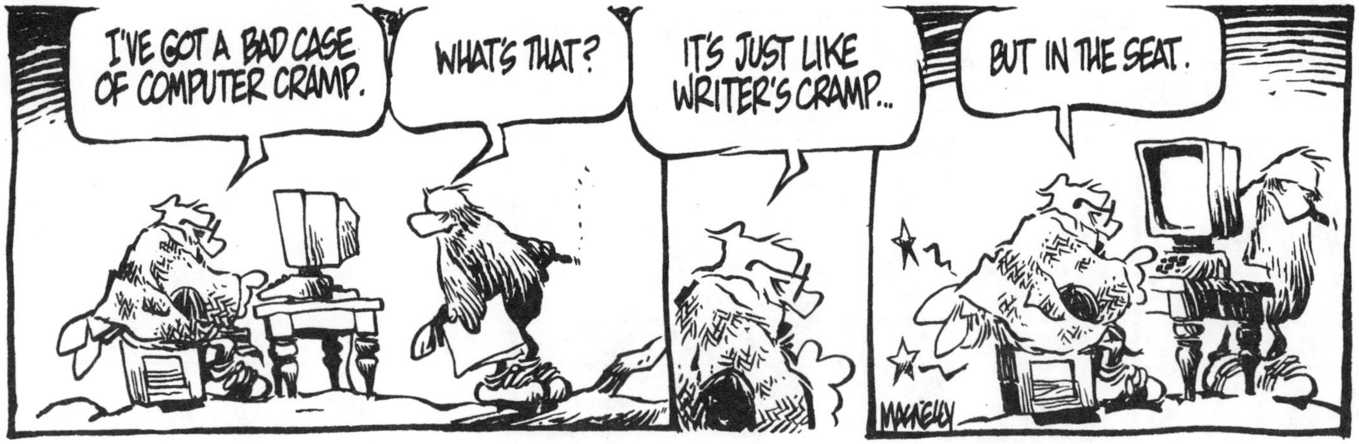
I'VE GOT A BAD CASE OF COMPUTER CRAMP.
WHAT'S THAT?
IT'S JUST LIKE WRITER'S CRAMP...
BUT IN THE SEAT.
MACNELLY

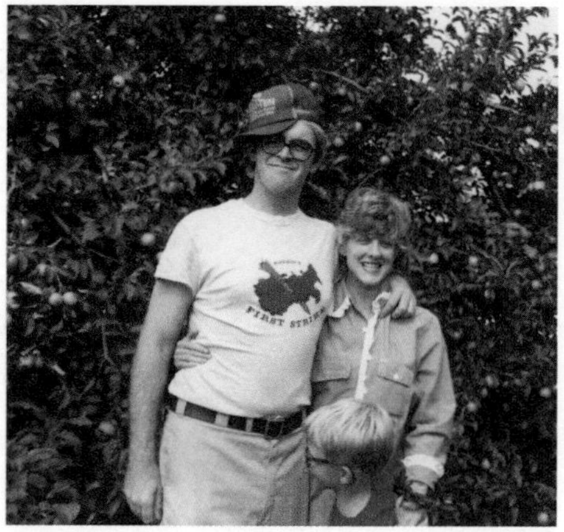

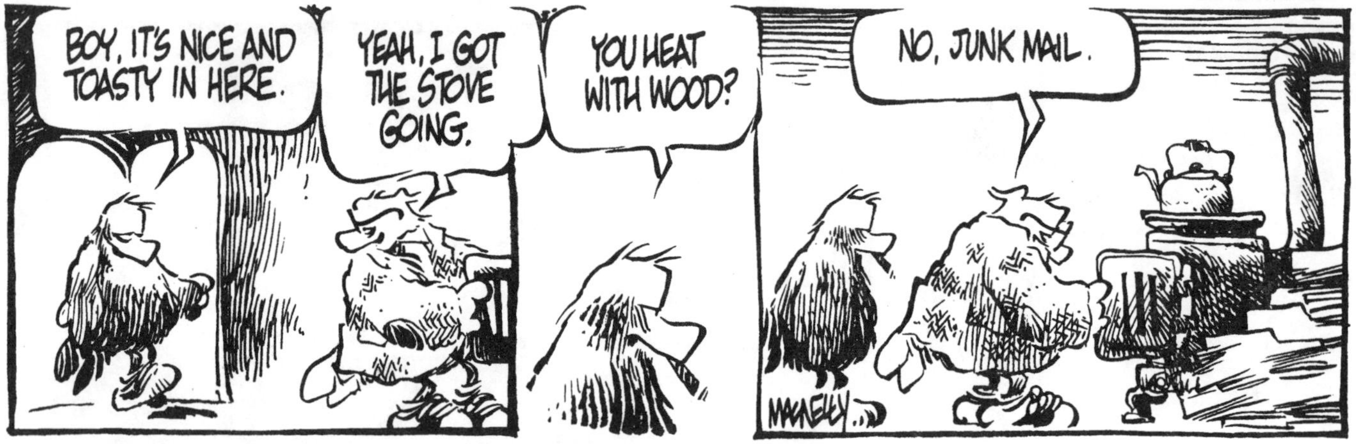
BOY, IT'S NICE AND TOASTY IN HERE.
YEAH, I GOT THE STOVE GOING.
YOU HEAT WITH WOOD?
NO, JUNK MAIL.
MACNELLY

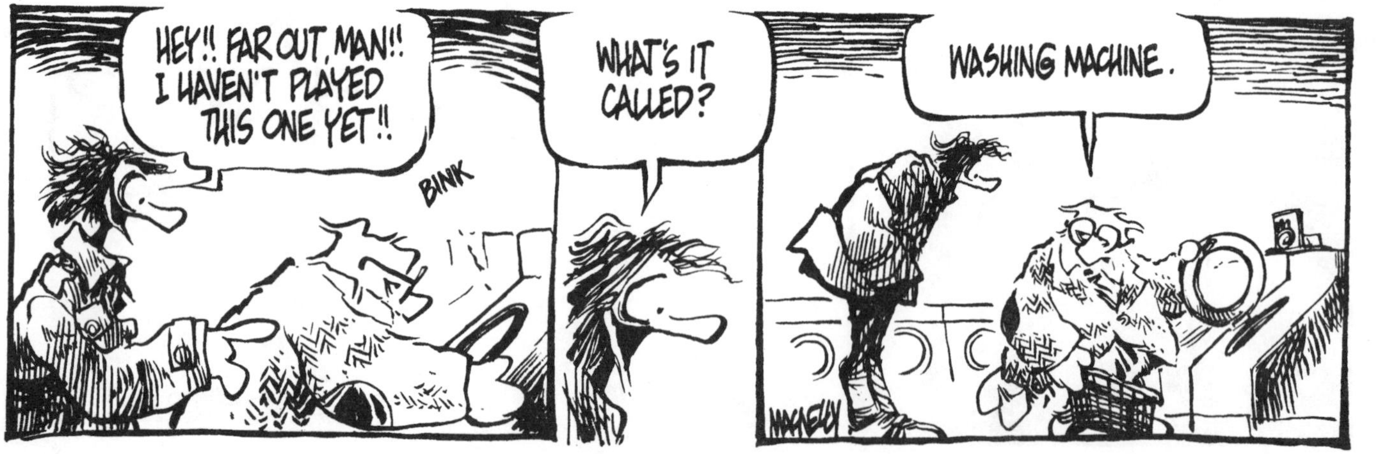
HEY!! FAR OUT, MAN!! I HAVEN'T PLAYED THIS ONE YET!!
BINK
WHAT'S IT CALLED?
WASHING MACHINE.
MACNELLY

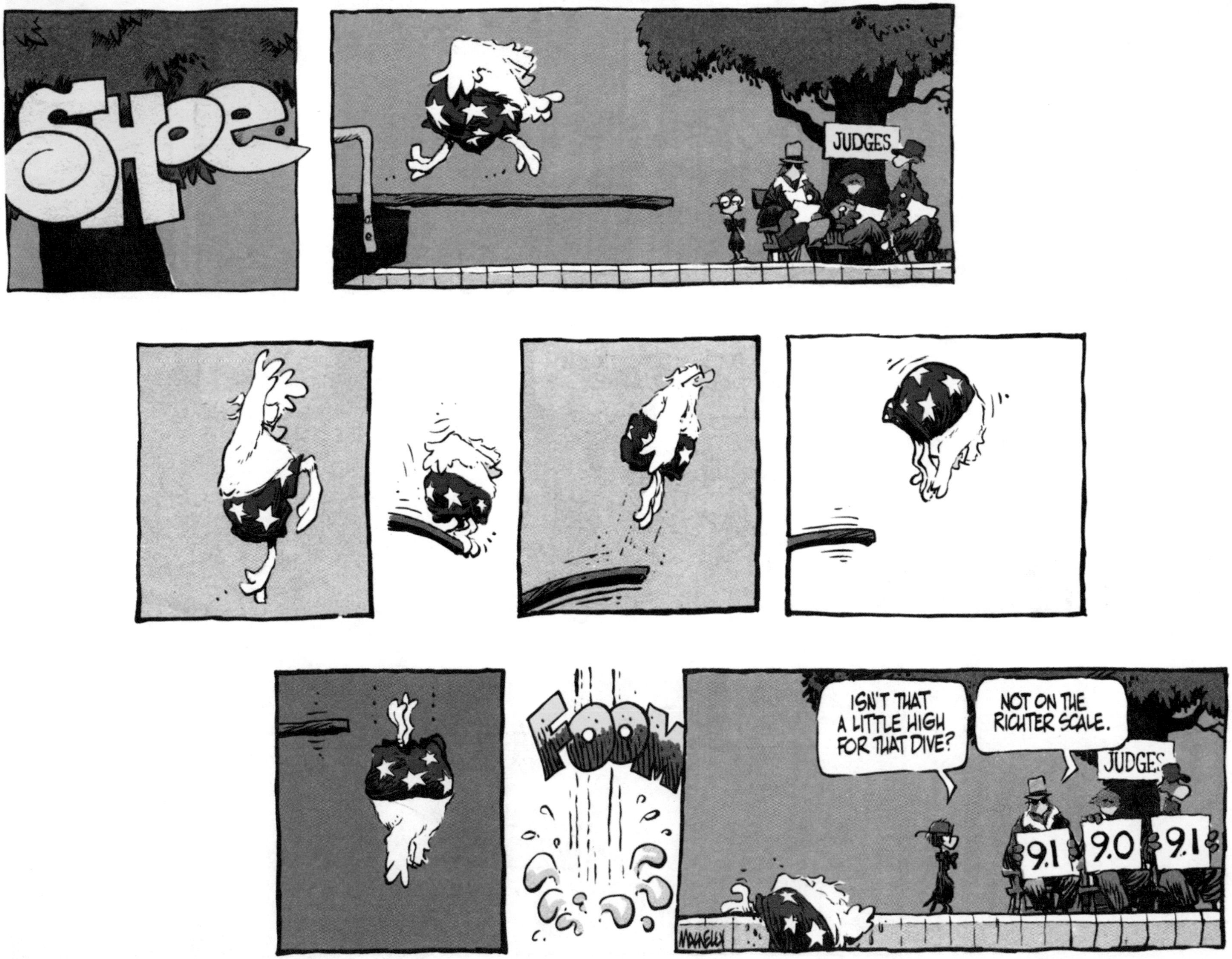
SHOE
JUDGES
FOOM
ISN'T THAT A LITTLE HIGH FOR THAT DIVE?
NOT ON THE RICHTER SCALE.
JUDGES
9.1
9.0
9.1
MACNELLY

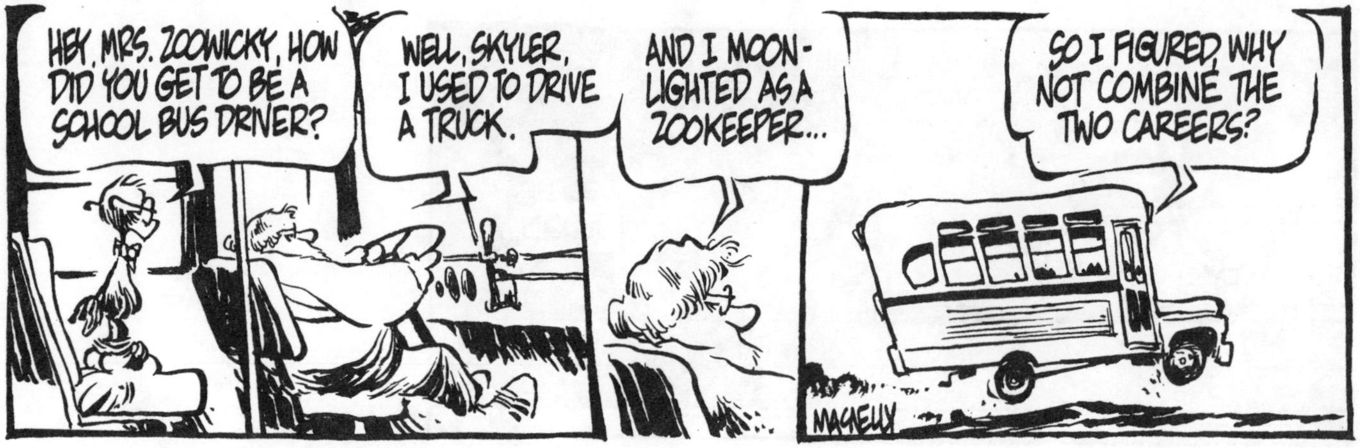
HEY, MRS. ZOOWICKY, HOW DID YOU GET TO BE A SCHOOL BUS DRIVER?
WELL, SKYLER, I USED TO DRIVE A TRUCK.
AND I MOONLIGHTED AS A ZOOKEEPER...
SO I FIGURED, WHY NOT COMBINE THE TWO CAREERS?
MACNELLY

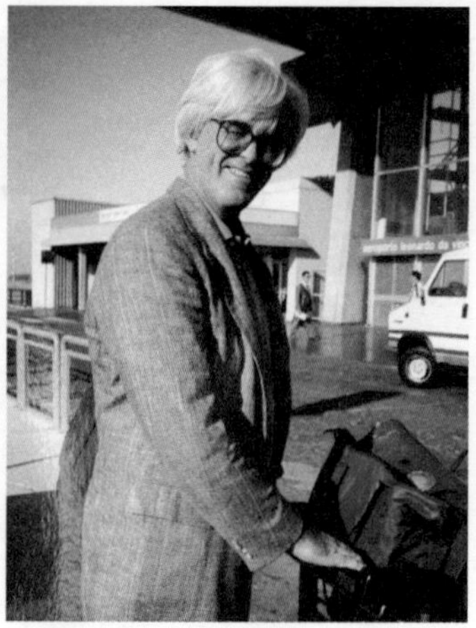

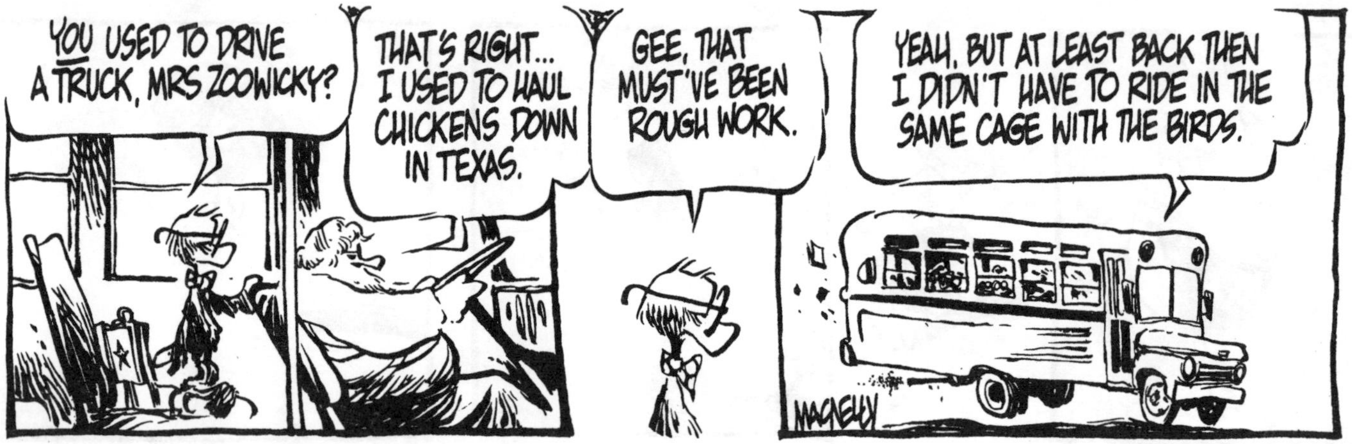
YOU USED TO DRIVE A TRUCK, MRS ZOOWICKY?
THAT'S RIGHT... I USED TO HAUL CHICKENS DOWN IN TEXAS.
GEE, THAT MUST'VE BEEN ROUGH WORK.
YEAH, BUT AT LEAST BACK THEN I DIDN'T HAVE TO RIDE IN THE SAME CAGE WITH THE BIRDS.
MACNELLY

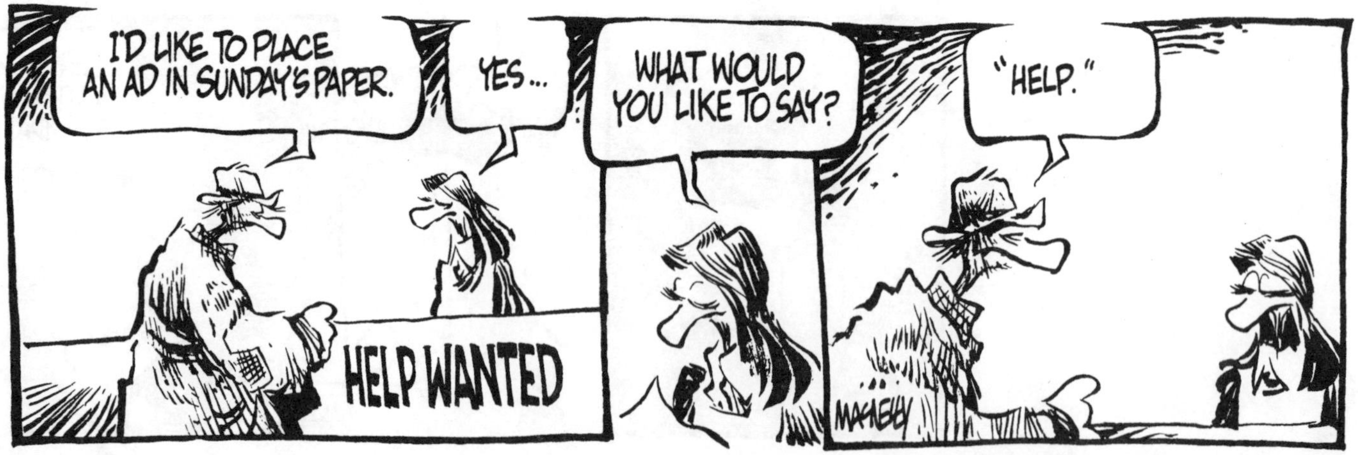
I'D LIKE TO PLACE AN AD IN SUNDAY'S PAPER.
YES...
HELP WANTED
WHAT WOULD YOU LIKE TO SAY?
"HELP."
MACNELLY

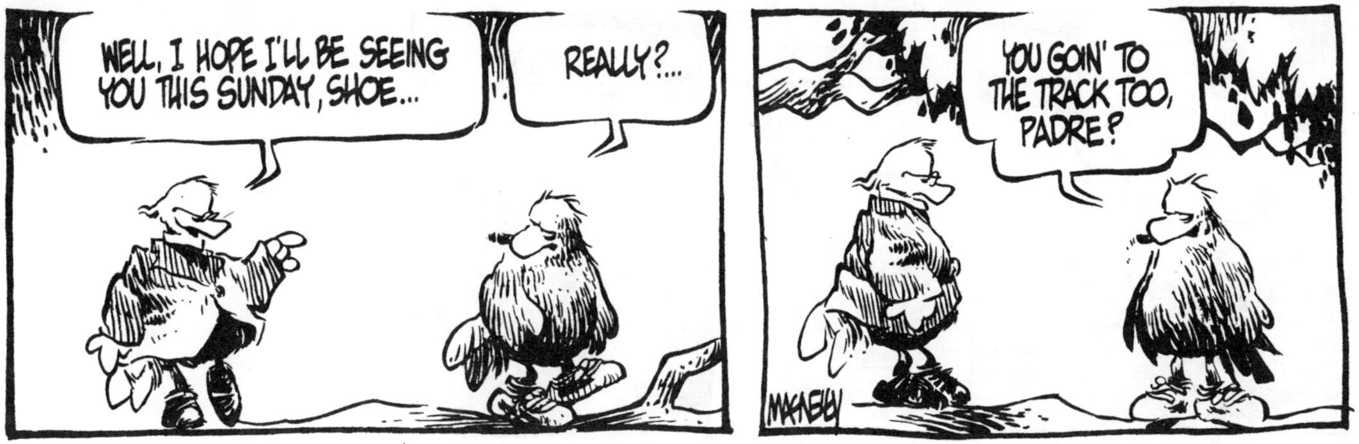
WELL, I HOPE I'LL BE SEEING YOU THIS SUNDAY, SHOE...
REALLY?...
YOU GOIN' TO THE TRACK TOO, PADRE?
MACNELLY

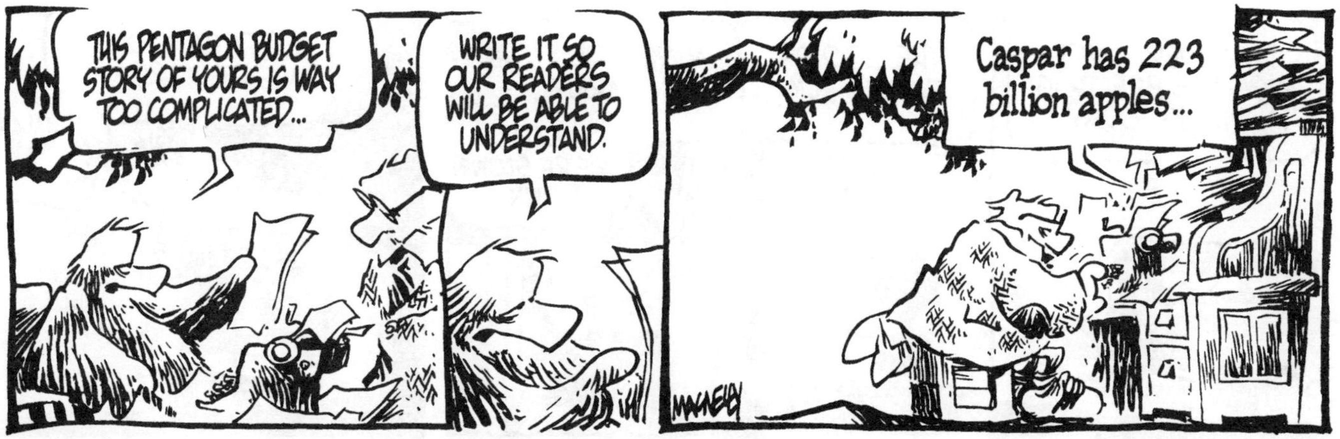
THIS PENTAGON BUDGET STORY OF YOURS IS WAY TOO COMPLICATED...
WRITE IT SO OUR READERS WILL BE ABLE TO UNDERSTAND.
Caspar has 223 billion apples...
MACNELLY

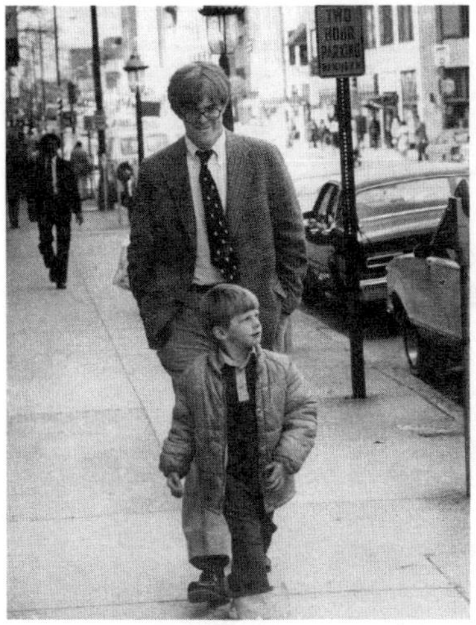

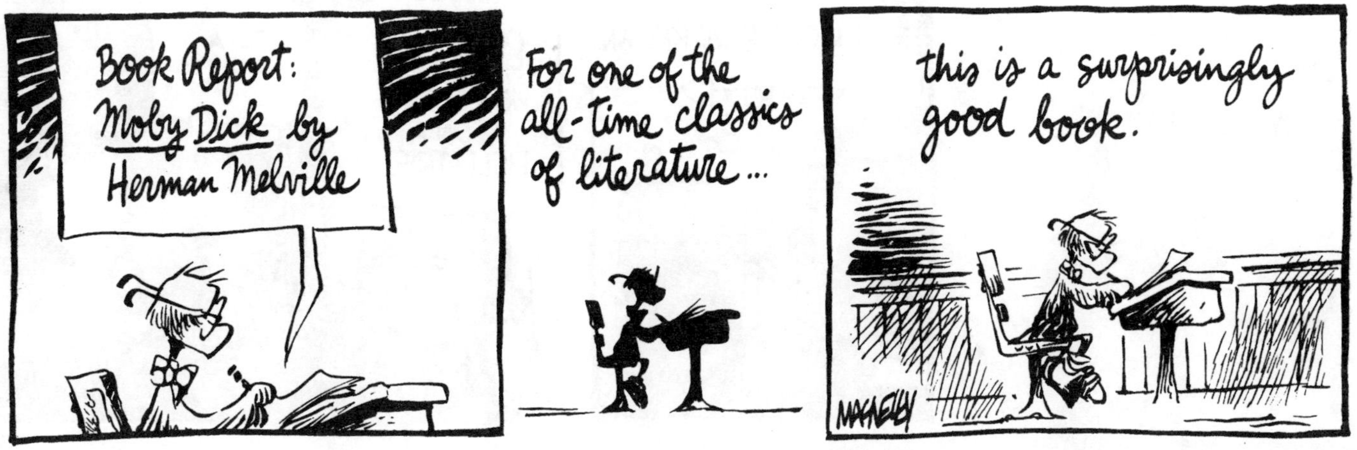
Book Report: Moby Dick by Herman Melville
For one of the all-time classics of literature...
this is a surprisingly good book.
MACNELLY

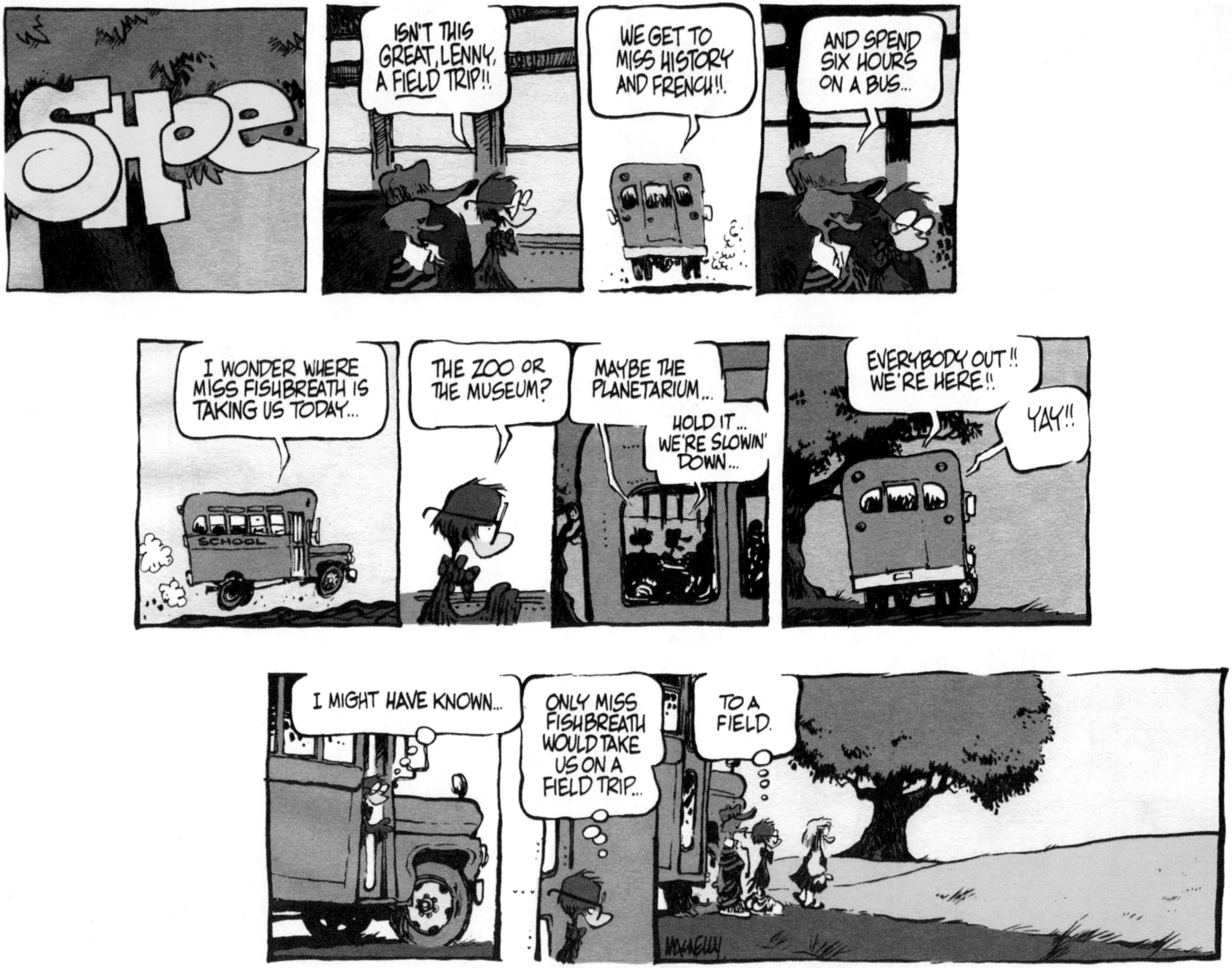
SHOE
ISN'T THIS GREAT, LENNY, A FIELD TRIP!!
WE GET TO MISS HISTORY AND FRENCH!!
AND SPEND SIX HOURS ON A BUS...
I WONDER WHERE MISS FISHBREATH IS TAKING US TODAY...
SCHOOL
THE ZOO OR THE MUSEUM?
MAYBE THE PLANETARIUM...
HOLD IT... WE'RE SLOWIN' DOWN...
EVERYBODY OUT!! WE'RE HERE!!
YAY!!
I MIGHT HAVE KNOWN...
ONLY MISS FISHBREATH WOULD TAKE US ON A FIELD TRIP...
TO A FIELD.

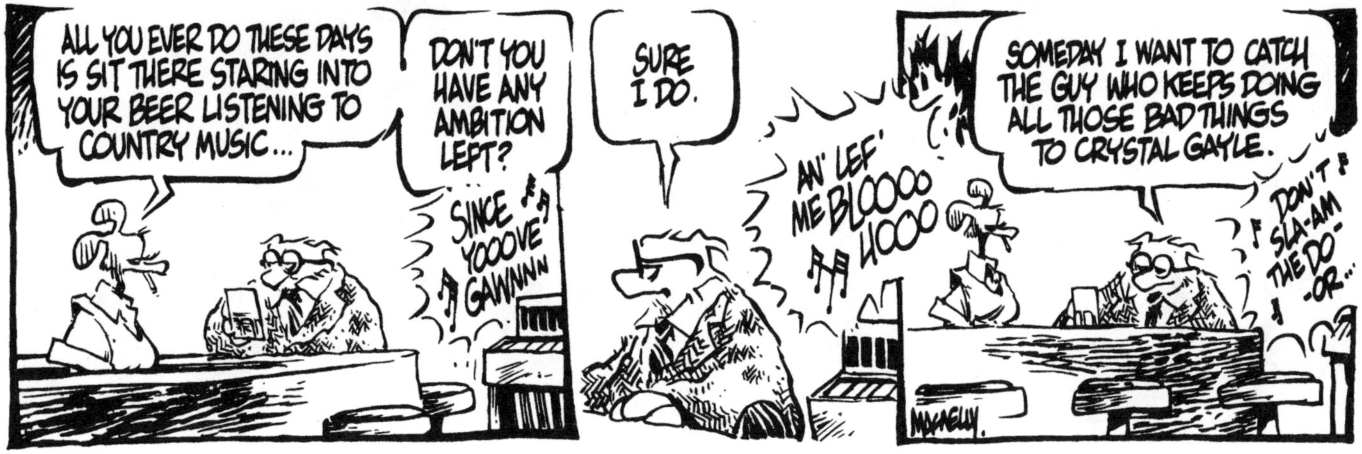
ALL YOU EVER DO THESE DAYS IS SIT THERE STARING INTO YOUR BEER LISTENING TO COUNTRY MUSIC...
DON'T YOU HAVE ANY AMBITION LEFT?
SINCE YOOOVE GAWNNN
SURE I DO.
AN' LEF' ME BLOOOO HOOO
SOMEDAY I WANT TO CATCH THE GUY WHO KEEPS DOING ALL THOSE BAD THINGS TO CRYSTAL GAYLE.
DON'T SLA-AM THE DO-OR...
MACNELLY

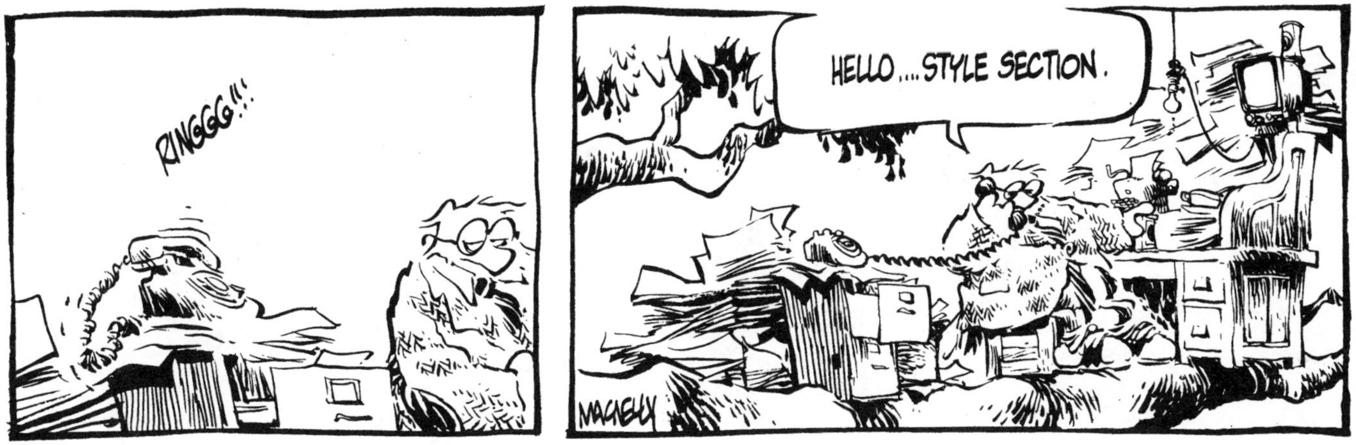
RINGGG!!!
HELLO....STYLE SECTION.
MACNELLY

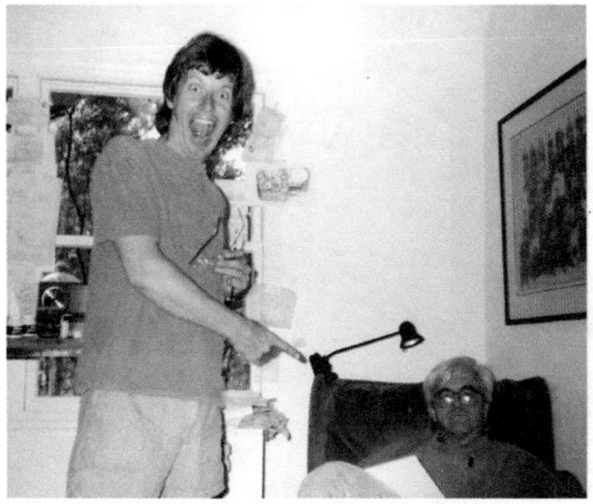

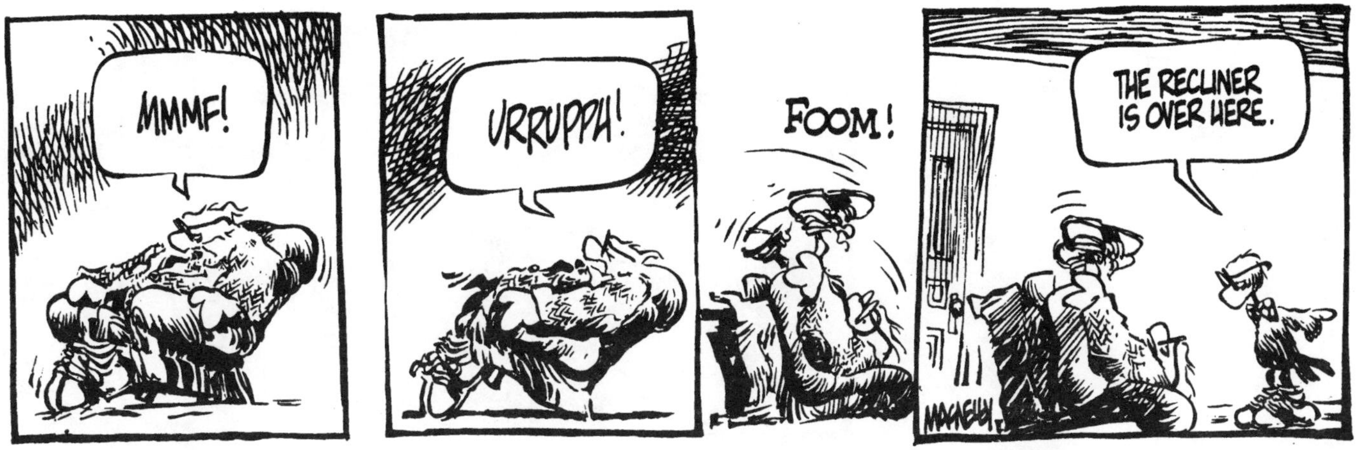
MMMF!
URRUPPH!
FOOM!
THE RECLINER IS OVER HERE.
MACNELLY

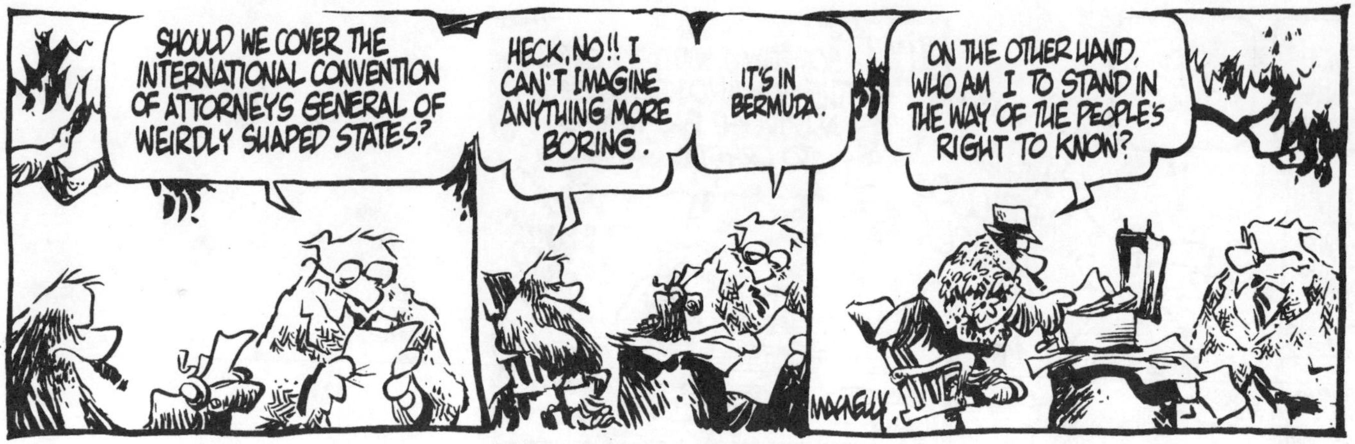
SHOULD WE COVER THE INTERNATIONAL CONVENTION OF ATTORNEYS GENERAL OF WEIRDLY SHAPED STATES?
HECK, NO!! I CAN'T IMAGINE ANYTHING MORE BORING.
IT'S IN BERMUDA.
ON THE OTHER HAND, WHO AM I TO STAND IN THE WAY OF THE PEOPLE'S RIGHT TO KNOW?
MACNELLY

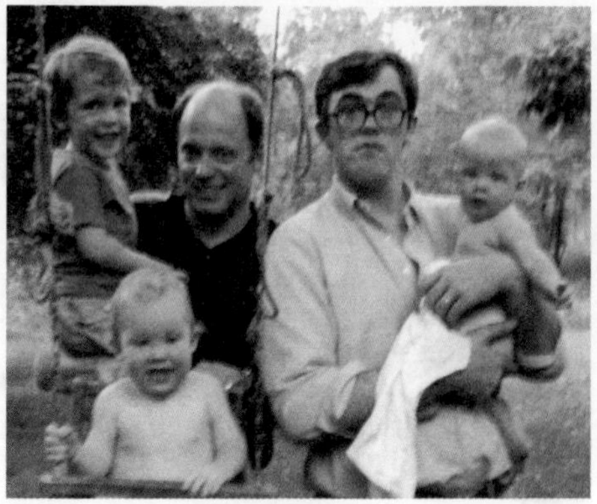

Ross Mackenzie, Jeff, and kids

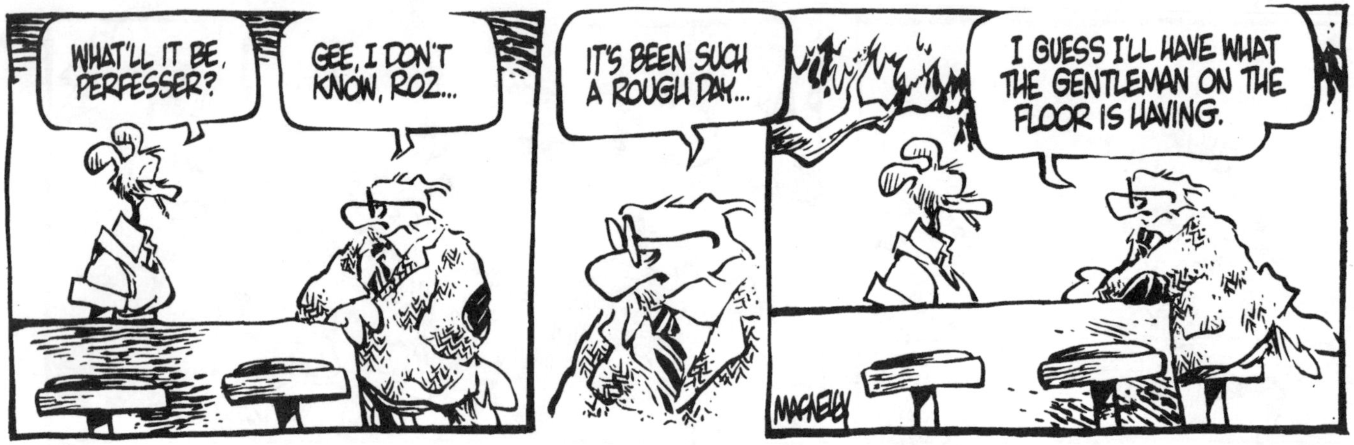
WHAT'LL IT BE, PERFESSER?
GEE, I DON'T KNOW, ROZ...
IT'S BEEN SUCH A ROUGH DAY...
I GUESS I'LL HAVE WHAT THE GENTLEMAN ON THE FLOOR IS HAVING.
MACNELLY

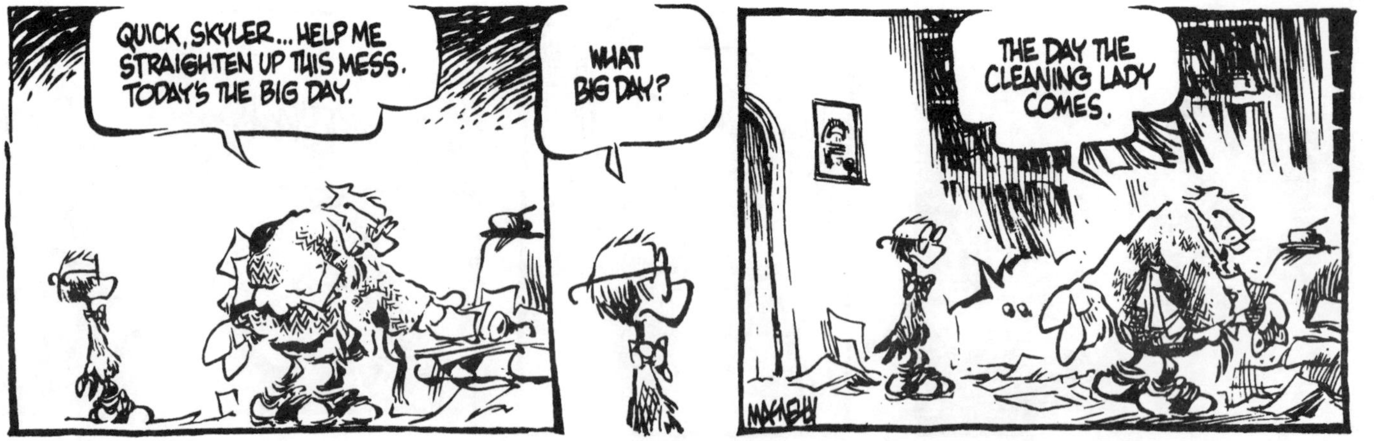
QUICK, SKYLER... HELP ME STRAIGHTEN UP THIS MESS. TODAY'S THE BIG DAY.
WHAT BIG DAY?
THE DAY THE CLEANING LADY COMES.
MACNELLY

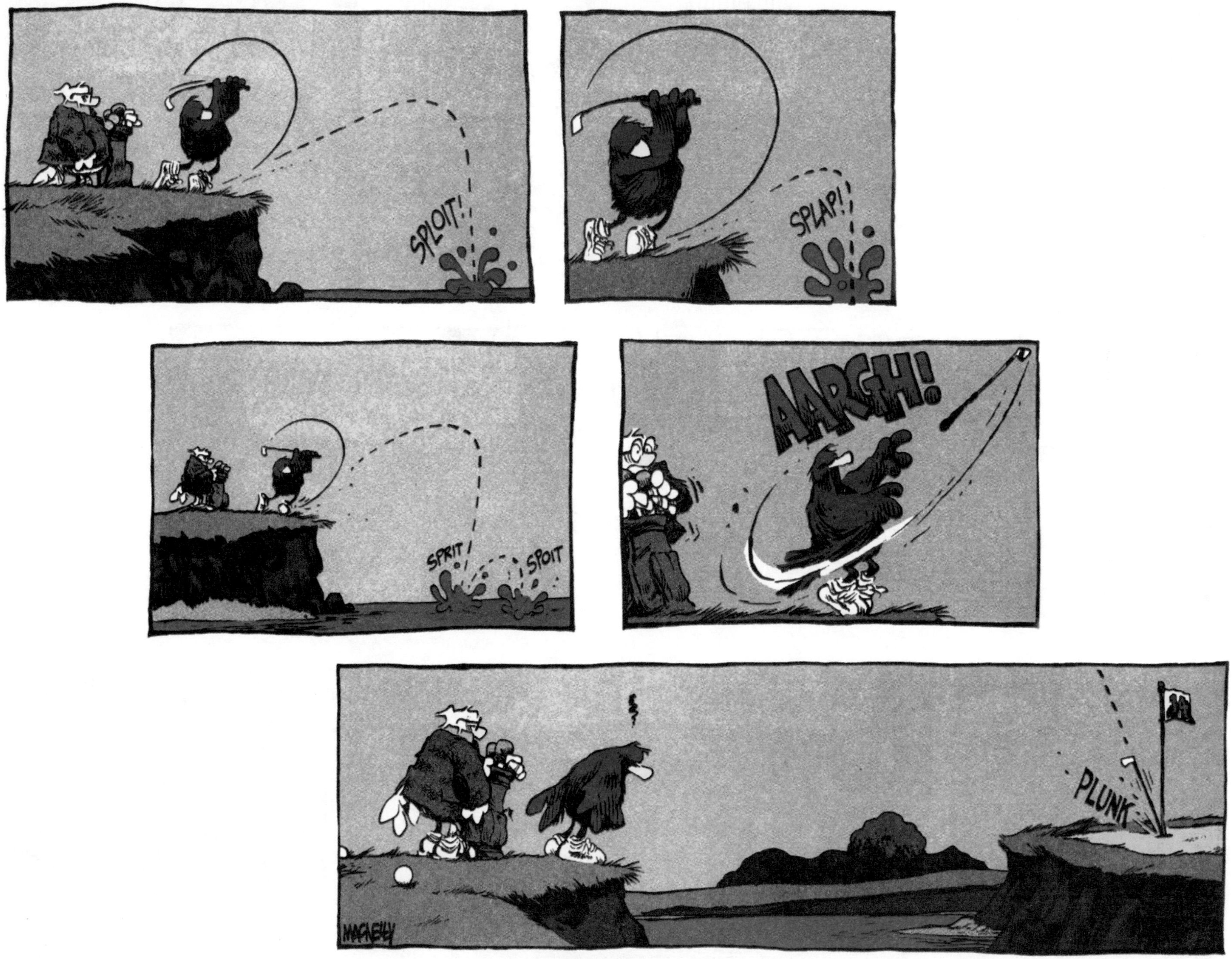
SPLOIT!
SPLAP!
SPRIT
SPOIT
AARGH!
PLUNK
MACNELLY

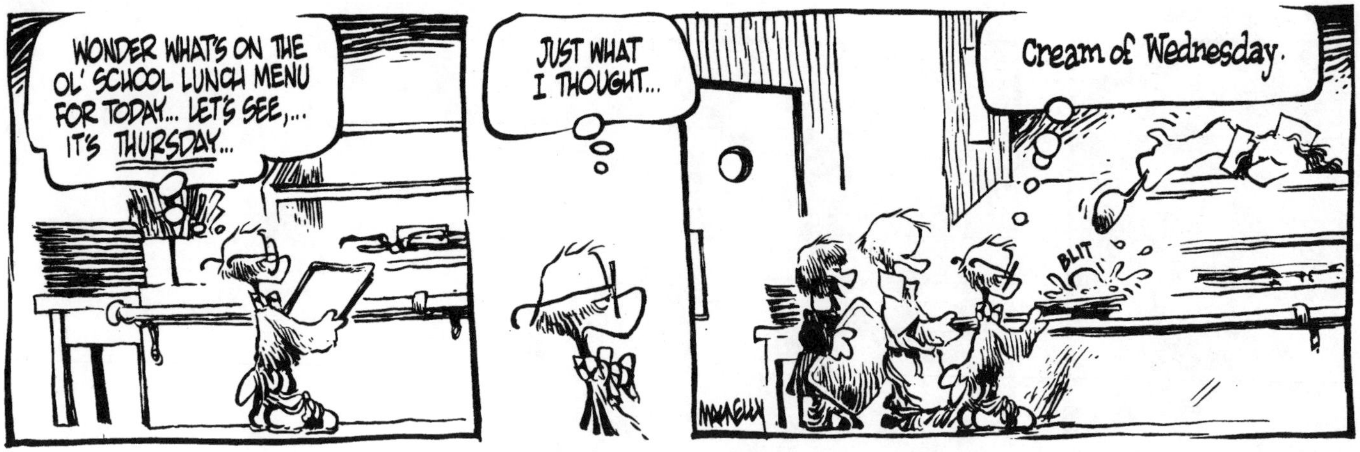
WONDER WHAT'S ON THE OL' SCHOOL LUNCH MENU FOR TODAY... LET'S SEE,... IT'S THURSDAY...
JUST WHAT I THOUGHT...
Cream of Wednesday.
BLIT
MACNELLY

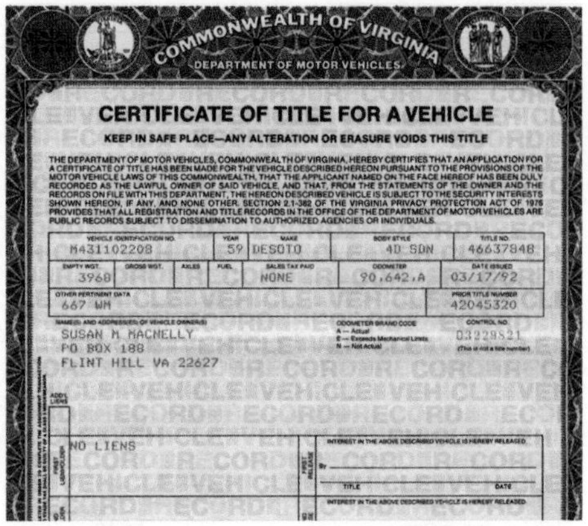
COMMONWEALTH OF VIRGINIA
DEPARTMENT OF MOTOR VEHICLES

CERTIFICATE OF TITLE FOR A VEHICLE

KEEP IN SAFE PLACE—ANY ALTERATION OR ERASURE VOIDS THIS TITLE

THE DEPARTMENT OF MOTOR VEHICLES, COMMONWEALTH OF VIRGINIA, HEREBY CERTIFIES THAT AN APPLICATION FOR A CERTIFICATE OF TITLE HAS BEEN MADE FOR THE VEHICLE DESCRIBED HEREON PURSUANT TO THE PROVISIONS OF THE MOTOR VEHICLE LAWS OF THIS COMMONWEALTH, THAT THE APPLICANT NAMED ON THE FACE HEREOF HAS BEEN DULY RECORDED AS THE LAWFUL OWNER OF SAID VEHICLE, AND THAT, FROM THE STATEMENTS OF THE OWNER AND THE RECORDS ON FILE WITH THIS DEPARTMENT, THE HEREON DESCRIBED VEHICLE IS SUBJECT TO THE SECURITY INTERESTS SHOWN HEREON, IF ANY, AND NONE OTHER. SECTION 2.1-382 OF THE VIRGINIA PRIVACY PROTECTION ACT OF 1976 PROVIDES THAT ALL REGISTRATION AND TITLE RECORDS IN THE OFFICE OF THE DEPARTMENT OF MOTOR VEHICLES ARE PUBLIC RECORDS SUBJECT TO DISSEMINATION TO AUTHORIZED AGENCIES OR INDIVIDUALS.

VEHICLE IDENTIFICATION NO.	YEAR	MAKE	BODY STYLE	TITLE NO.
M431102208	59	DESOTO	4D SDN	46637848

EMPTY WGT.	GROSS WGT.	AXLES	FUEL	SALES TAX PAID	ODOMETER	DATE ISSUED
3968				NONE	90,642,A	03/17/92

OTHER PERTINENT DATA	PRIOR TITLE NUMBER
667 WM	42045320

NAME(S) AND ADDRESS(ES) OF VEHICLE OWNER(S)
SUSAN M MACNELLY
PO BOX 188
FLINT HILL VA 22627

ODOMETER BRAND CODE
A — Actual
E — Exceeds Mechanical Limits
N — Not Actual

CONTROL NO.
03228821
(This is not a title number)

ADD'L LIENS

FIRST LIENHOLDER: NO LIENS

FIRST RELEASE: INTEREST IN THE ABOVE DESCRIBED VEHICLE IS HEREBY RELEASED.
By ____________
TITLE DATE

INTEREST IN THE ABOVE DESCRIBED VEHICLE IS HEREBY RELEASED.

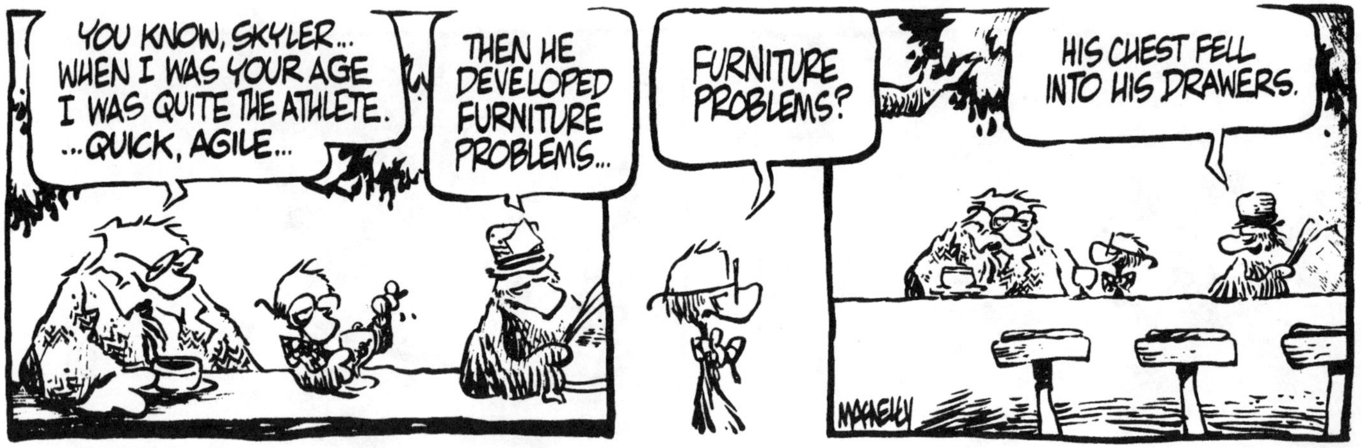
YOU KNOW, SKYLER... WHEN I WAS YOUR AGE I WAS QUITE THE ATHLETE. ...QUICK, AGILE...
THEN HE DEVELOPED FURNITURE PROBLEMS...
FURNITURE PROBLEMS?
HIS CHEST FELL INTO HIS DRAWERS.
MACNELLY

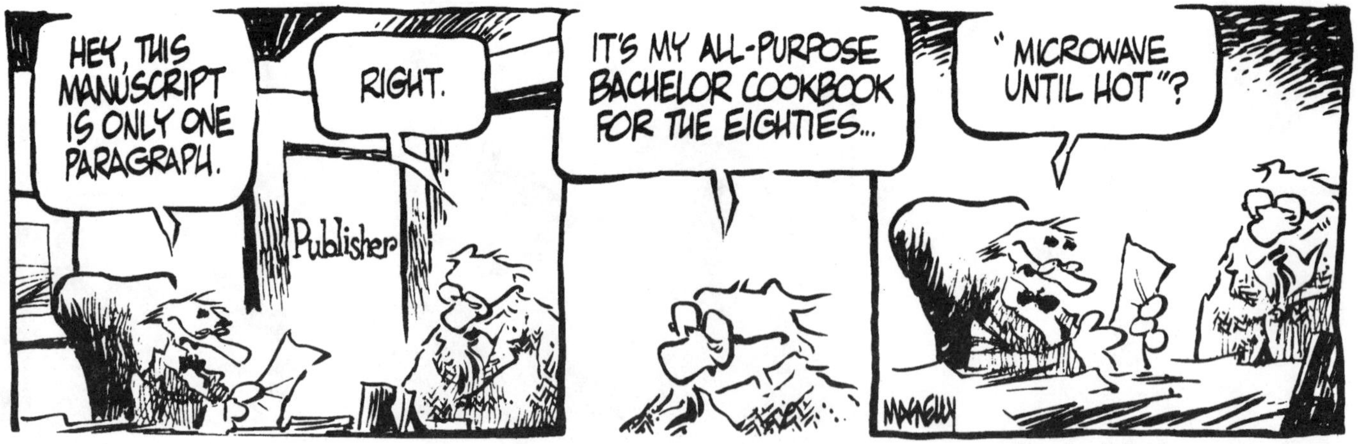
HEY, THIS MANUSCRIPT IS ONLY ONE PARAGRAPH.
RIGHT.
Publisher
IT'S MY ALL-PURPOSE BACHELOR COOKBOOK FOR THE EIGHTIES...
"MICROWAVE UNTIL HOT"?
MACNELLY

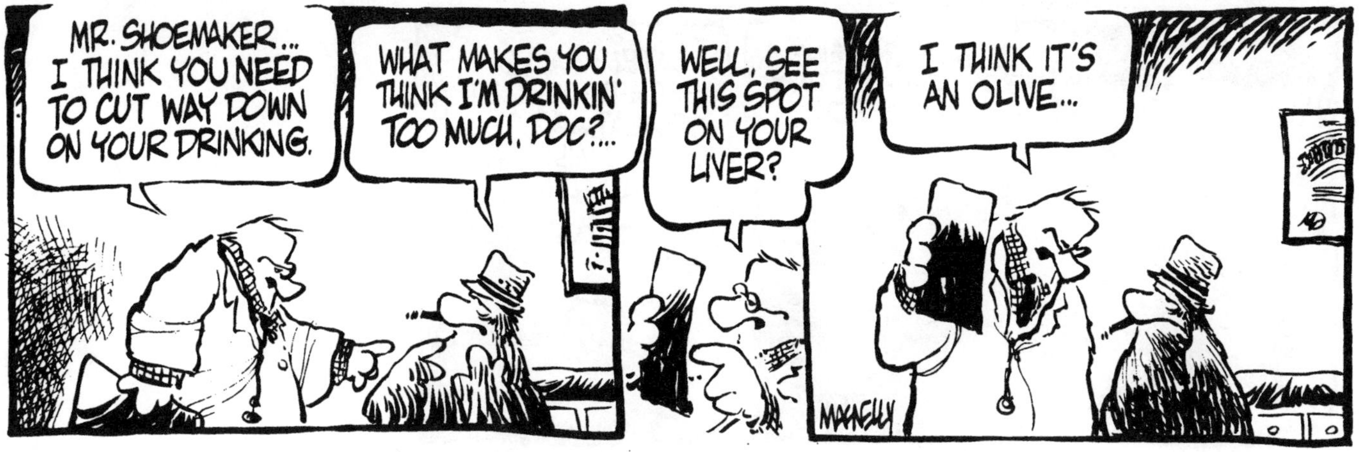
MR. SHOEMAKER... I THINK YOU NEED TO CUT WAY DOWN ON YOUR DRINKING.
WHAT MAKES YOU THINK I'M DRINKIN' TOO MUCH, DOC?...
WELL, SEE THIS SPOT ON YOUR LIVER?
I THINK IT'S AN OLIVE...
MACNELLY

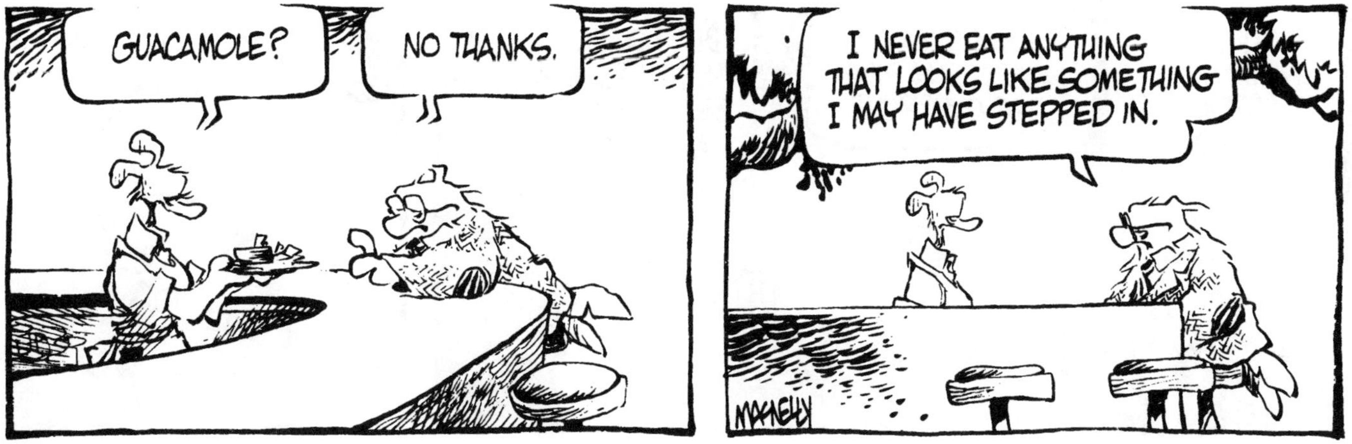
GUACAMOLE?
NO THANKS.
I NEVER EAT ANYTHING THAT LOOKS LIKE SOMETHING I MAY HAVE STEPPED IN.
MACNELLY

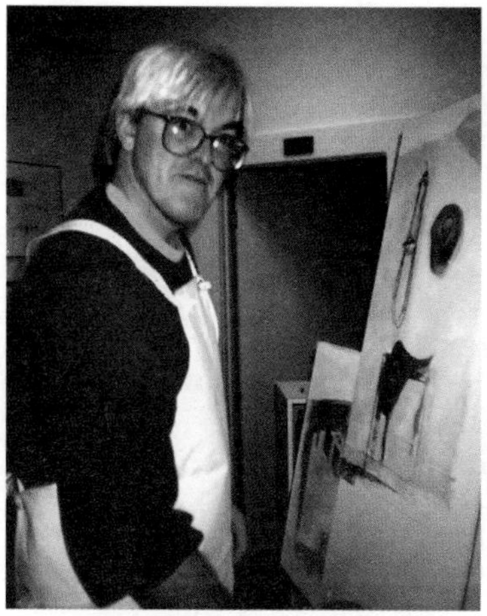

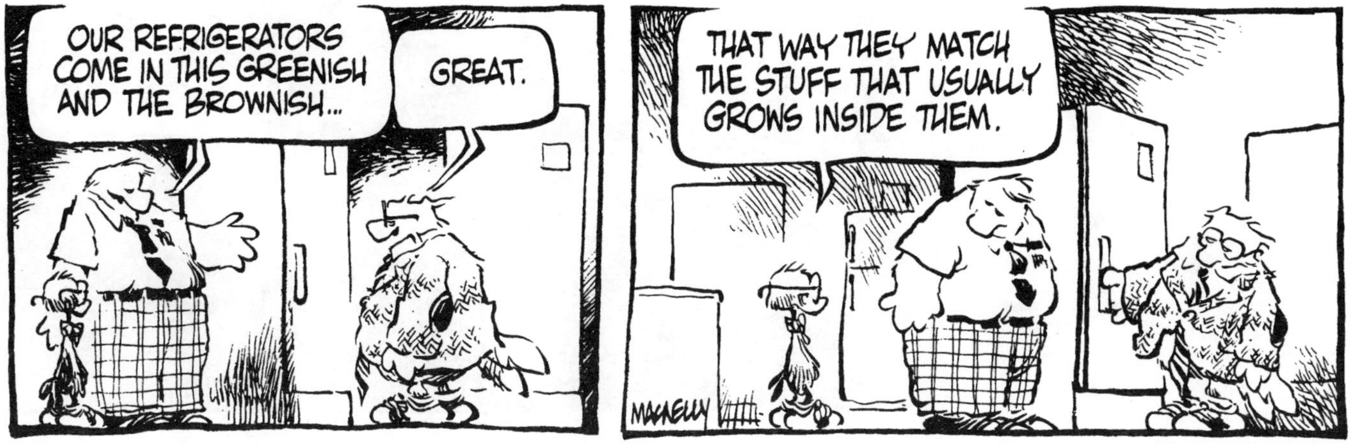
OUR REFRIGERATORS COME IN THIS GREENISH AND THE BROWNISH...
GREAT.
THAT WAY THEY MATCH THE STUFF THAT USUALLY GROWS INSIDE THEM.
MACNELLY

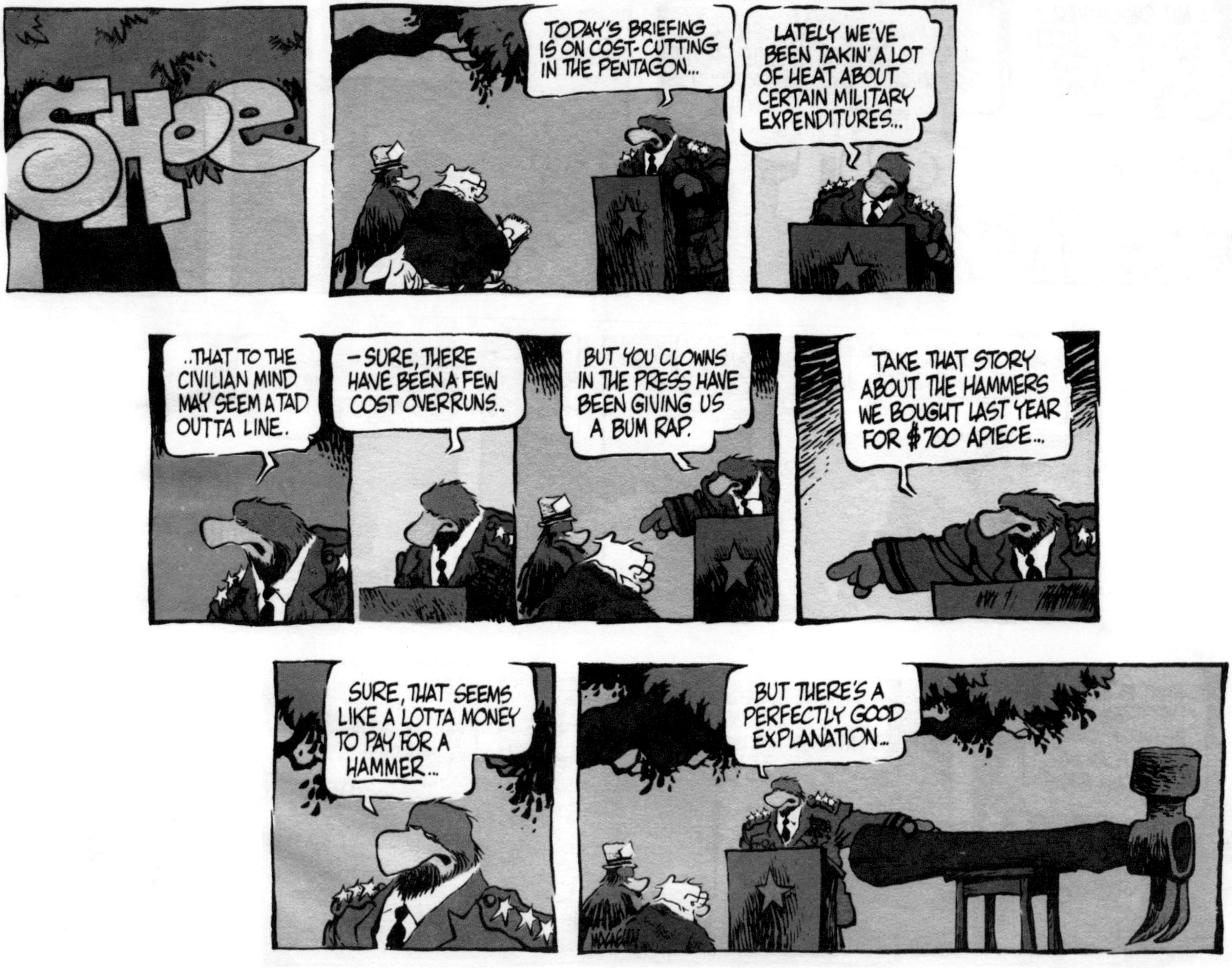
SHOE
TODAY'S BRIEFING IS ON COST-CUTTING IN THE PENTAGON...
LATELY WE'VE BEEN TAKIN' A LOT OF HEAT ABOUT CERTAIN MILITARY EXPENDITURES...
..THAT TO THE CIVILIAN MIND MAY SEEM A TAD OUTTA LINE.
—SURE, THERE HAVE BEEN A FEW COST OVERRUNS..
BUT YOU CLOWNS IN THE PRESS HAVE BEEN GIVING US A BUM RAP.
TAKE THAT STORY ABOUT THE HAMMERS WE BOUGHT LAST YEAR FOR $700 APIECE...
SURE, THAT SEEMS LIKE A LOTTA MONEY TO PAY FOR A HAMMER...
BUT THERE'S A PERFECTLY GOOD EXPLANATION...
MACNELLY

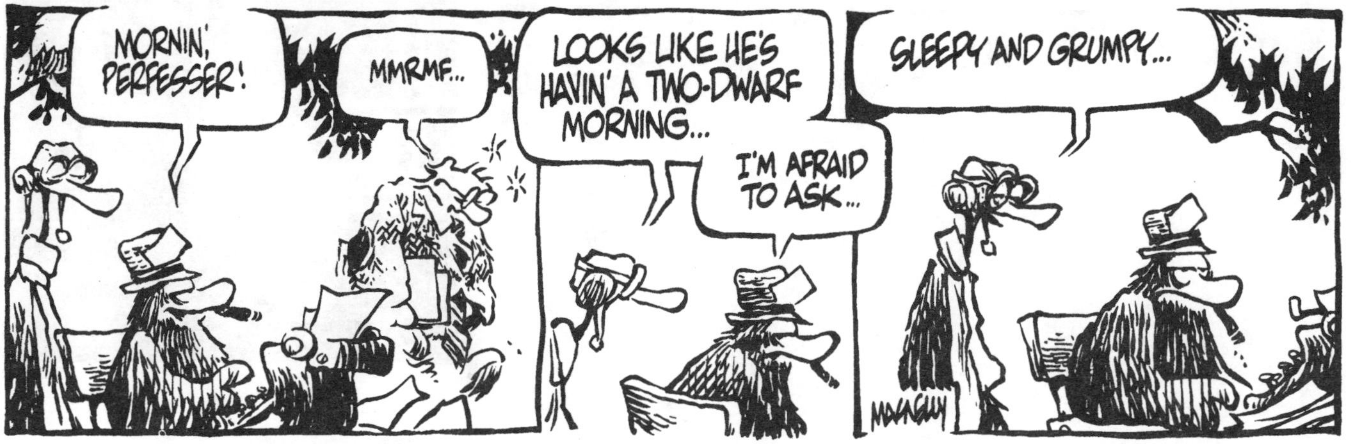
MORNIN', PERFESSER!
MMRMF...
LOOKS LIKE HE'S HAVIN' A TWO-DWARF MORNING...
I'M AFRAID TO ASK...
SLEEPY AND GRUMPY...

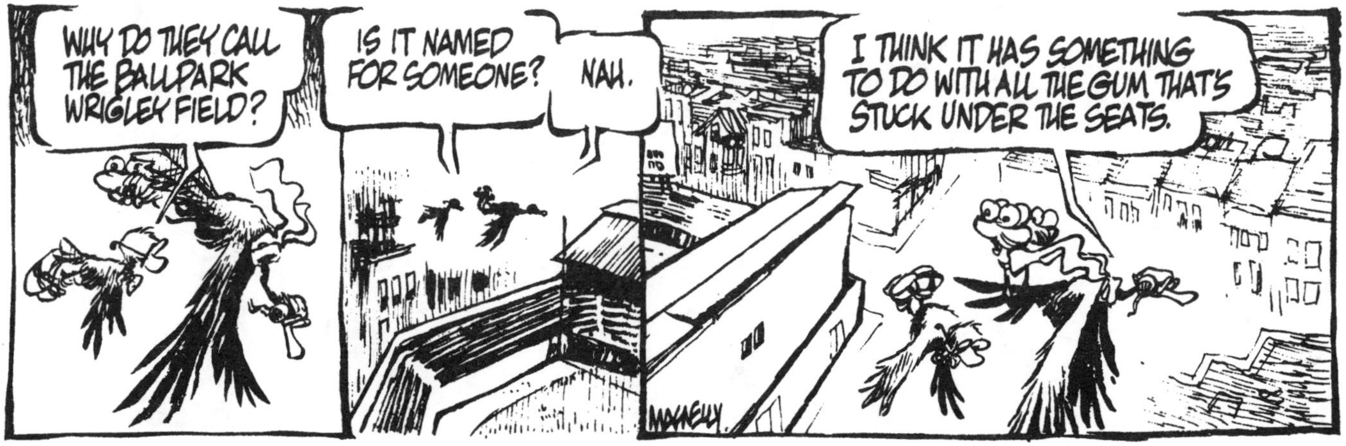
WHY DO THEY CALL THE BALLPARK WRIGLEY FIELD?
IS IT NAMED FOR SOMEONE?
NAH.
I THINK IT HAS SOMETHING TO DO WITH ALL THE GUM THAT'S STUCK UNDER THE SEATS.

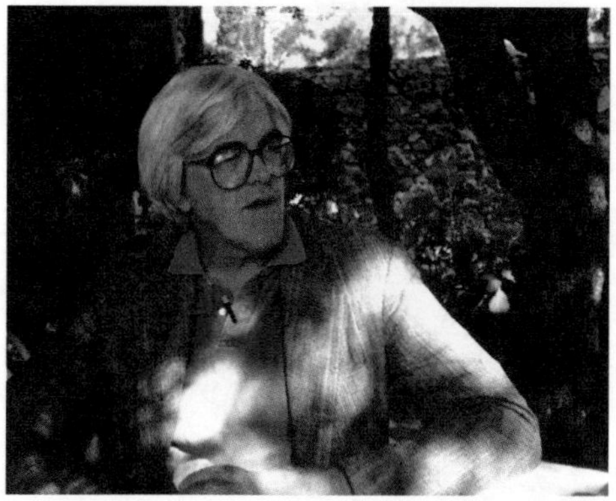

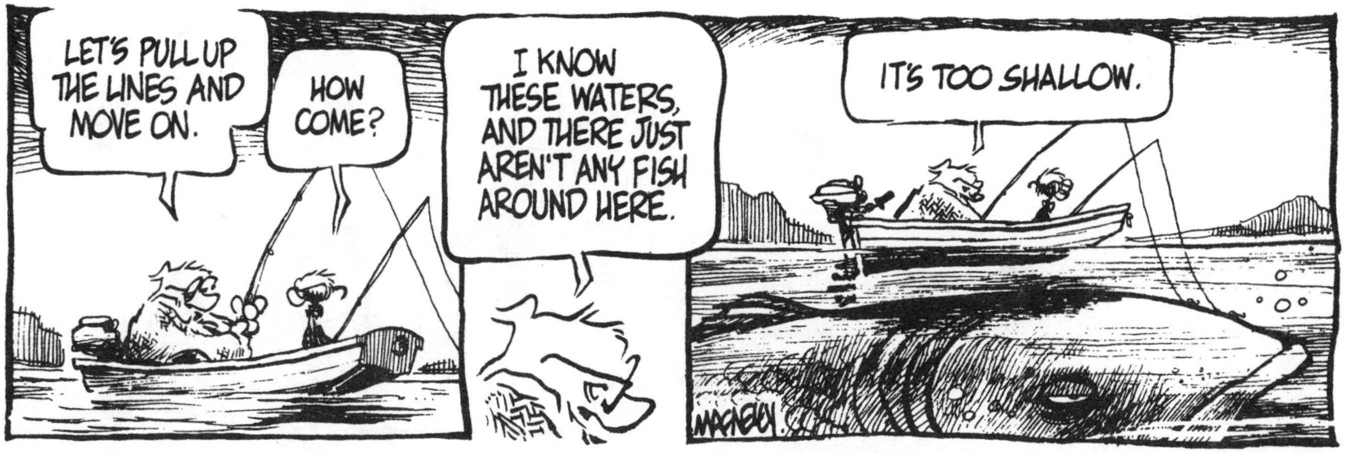
LET'S PULL UP THE LINES AND MOVE ON.
HOW COME?
I KNOW THESE WATERS, AND THERE JUST AREN'T ANY FISH AROUND HERE.
IT'S TOO SHALLOW.

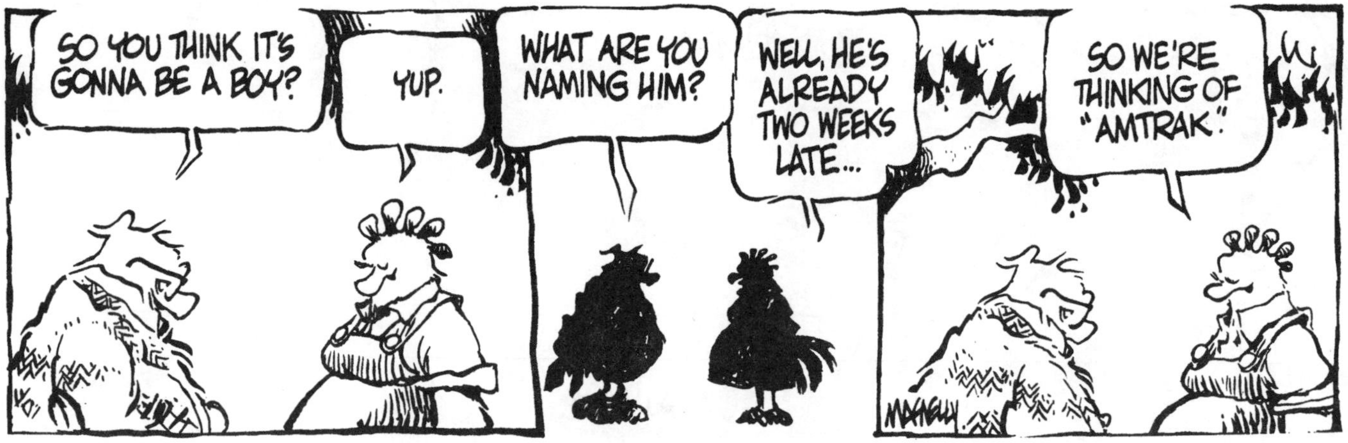
SO YOU THINK IT'S GONNA BE A BOY?
YUP.
WHAT ARE YOU NAMING HIM?
WELL, HE'S ALREADY TWO WEEKS LATE...
SO WE'RE THINKING OF "AMTRAK."
MACNELLY

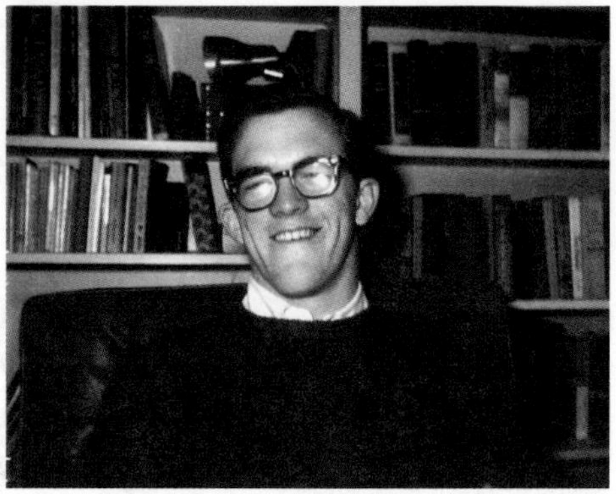

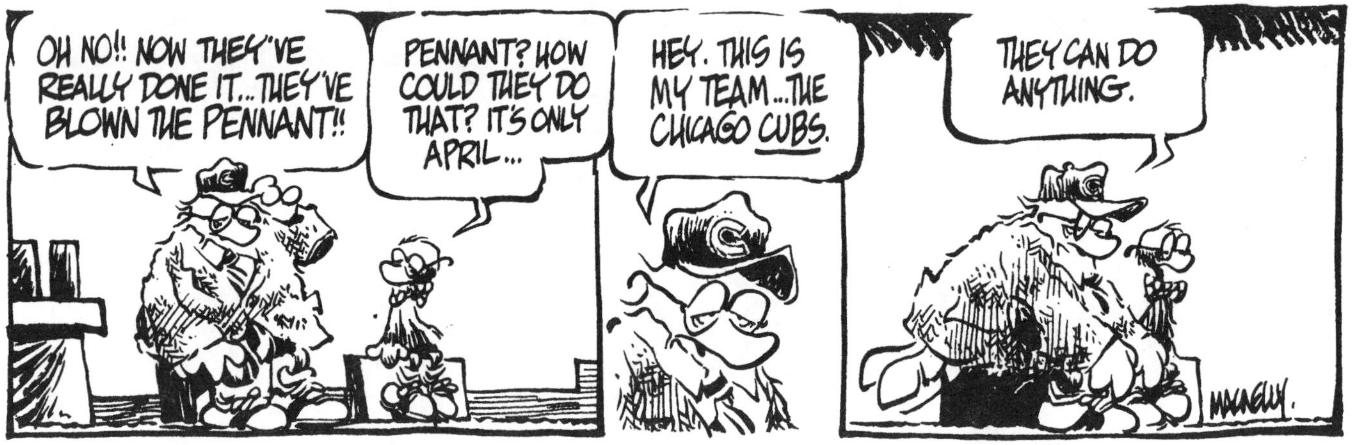
OH NO!! NOW THEY'VE REALLY DONE IT...THEY'VE BLOWN THE PENNANT!!
PENNANT? HOW COULD THEY DO THAT? IT'S ONLY APRIL...
HEY. THIS IS MY TEAM...THE CHICAGO CUBS.
THEY CAN DO ANYTHING.
MACNELLY

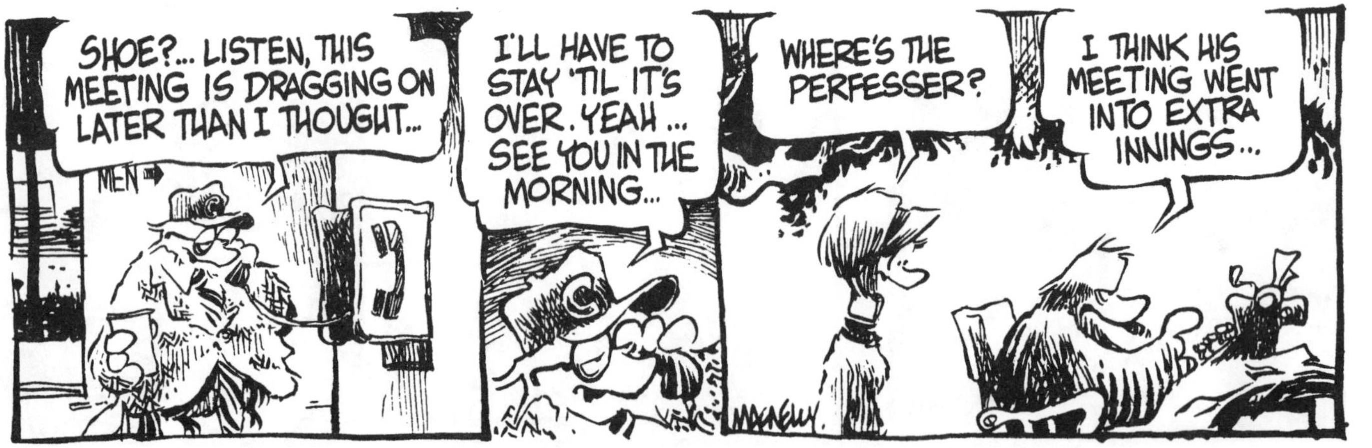
SHOE?... LISTEN, THIS MEETING IS DRAGGING ON LATER THAN I THOUGHT...
MEN
I'LL HAVE TO STAY 'TIL IT'S OVER. YEAH ... SEE YOU IN THE MORNING...
WHERE'S THE PERFESSER?
I THINK HIS MEETING WENT INTO EXTRA INNINGS...
MACNELLY

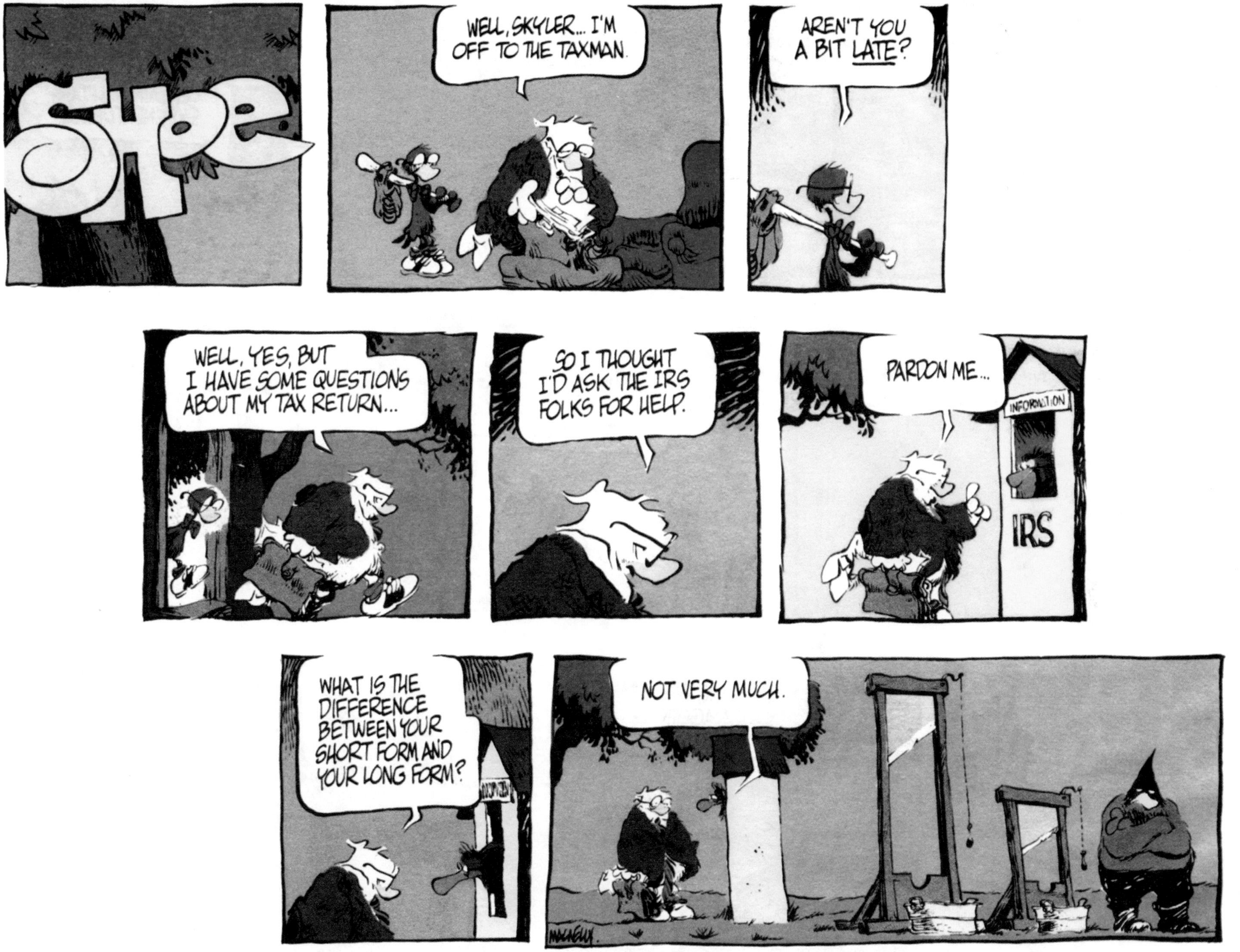
SHOE
WELL, SKYLER... I'M OFF TO THE TAXMAN.
AREN'T YOU A BIT LATE?
WELL, YES, BUT I HAVE SOME QUESTIONS ABOUT MY TAX RETURN...
SO I THOUGHT I'D ASK THE IRS FOLKS FOR HELP.
PARDON ME...
INFORMATION
IRS
WHAT IS THE DIFFERENCE BETWEEN YOUR SHORT FORM AND YOUR LONG FORM?
NOT VERY MUCH.
MACNELLY

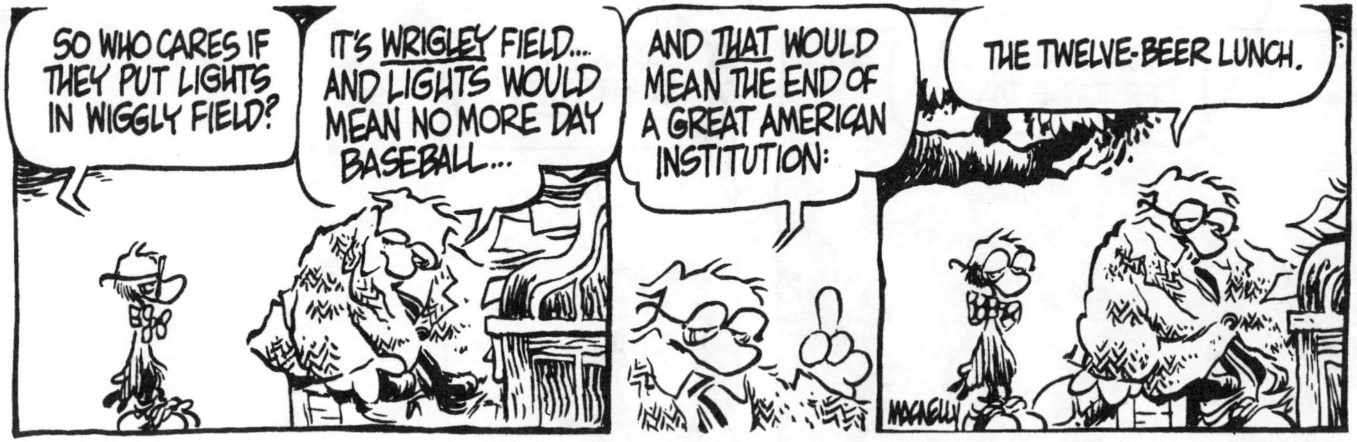
SO WHO CARES IF THEY PUT LIGHTS IN WIGGLY FIELD?
IT'S WRIGLEY FIELD... AND LIGHTS WOULD MEAN NO MORE DAY BASEBALL...
AND THAT WOULD MEAN THE END OF A GREAT AMERICAN INSTITUTION:
THE TWELVE-BEER LUNCH.
MACNELLY

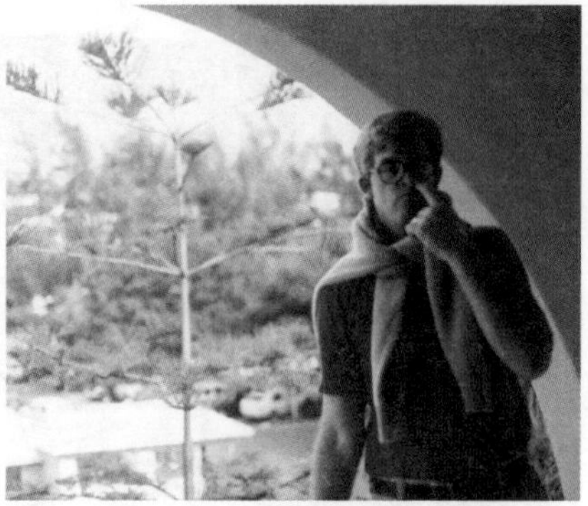

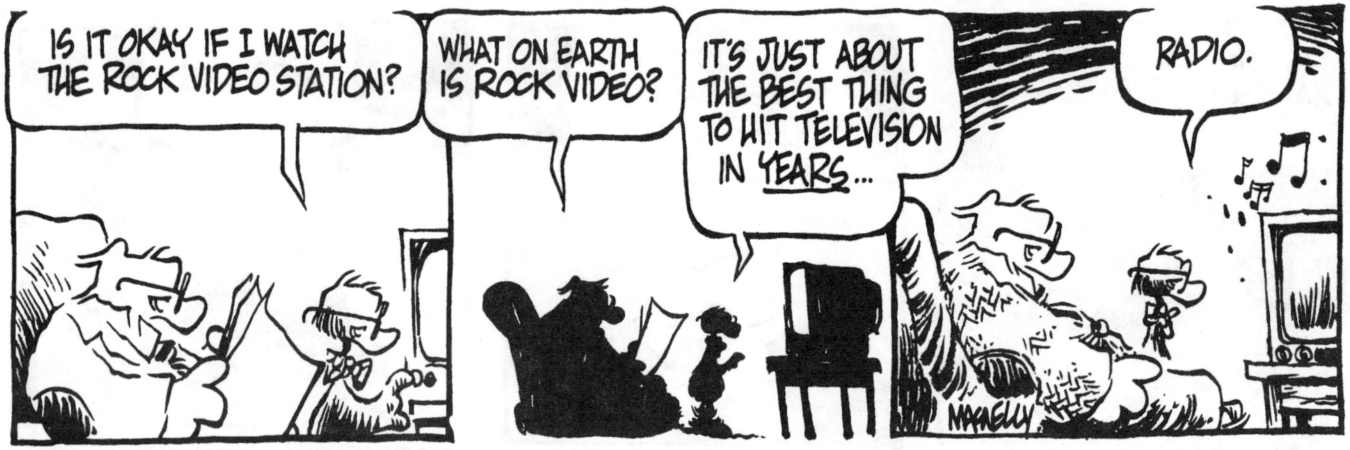
IS IT OKAY IF I WATCH THE ROCK VIDEO STATION?
WHAT ON EARTH IS ROCK VIDEO?
IT'S JUST ABOUT THE BEST THING TO HIT TELEVISION IN YEARS...
RADIO.
MACNELLY

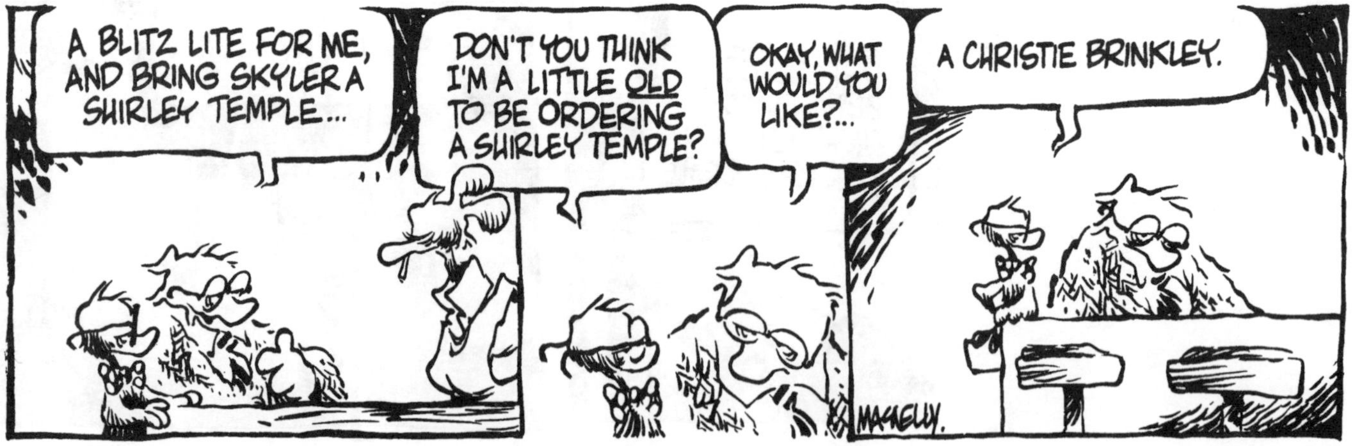
A BLITZ LITE FOR ME, AND BRING SKYLER A SHIRLEY TEMPLE...
DON'T YOU THINK I'M A LITTLE OLD TO BE ORDERING A SHIRLEY TEMPLE?
OKAY, WHAT WOULD YOU LIKE?...
A CHRISTIE BRINKLEY.
MACNELLY.

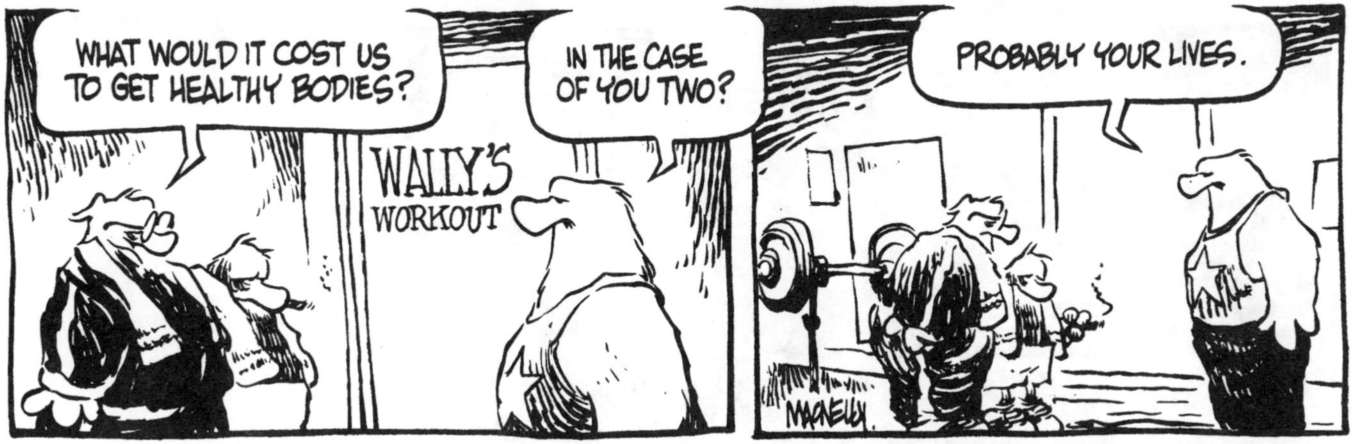
WHAT WOULD IT COST US TO GET HEALTHY BODIES?
WALLY'S WORKOUT
IN THE CASE OF YOU TWO?
PROBABLY YOUR LIVES.
MACNELLY

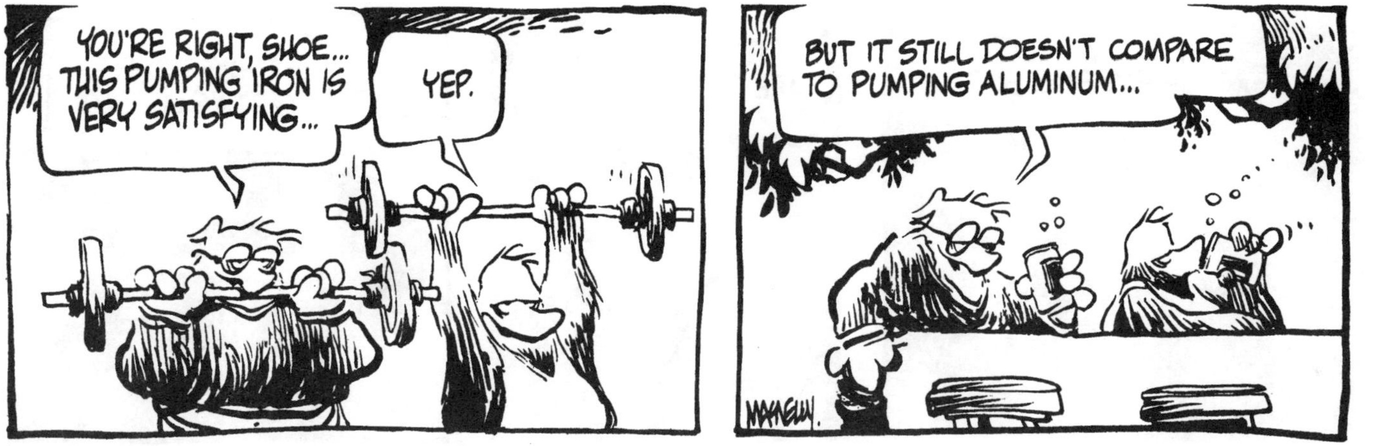
YOU'RE RIGHT, SHOE... THIS PUMPING IRON IS VERY SATISFYING...
YEP.
BUT IT STILL DOESN'T COMPARE TO PUMPING ALUMINUM...
MACNELLY

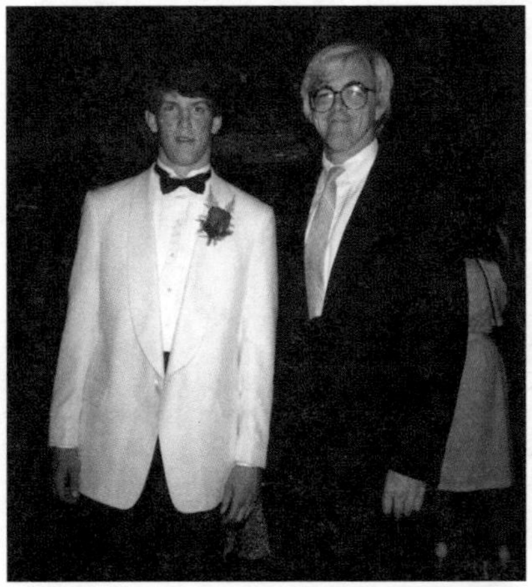

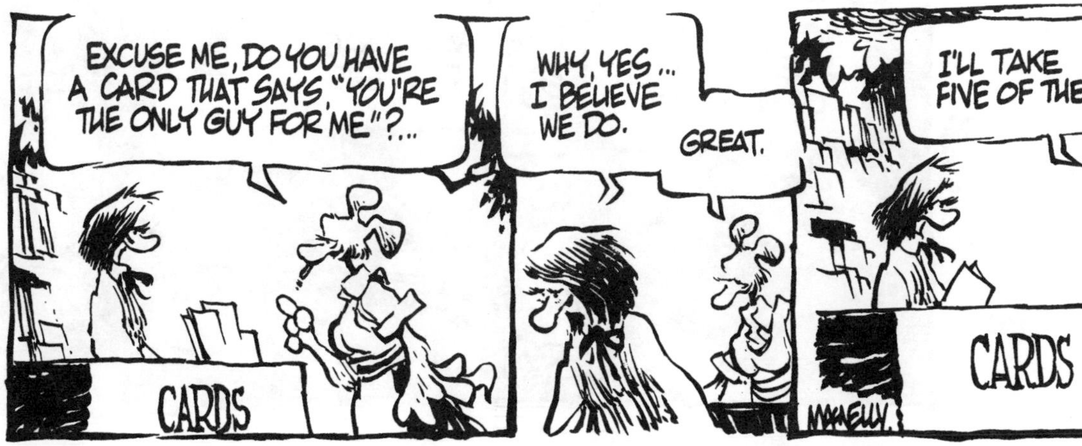
EXCUSE ME, DO YOU HAVE A CARD THAT SAYS, "YOU'RE THE ONLY GUY FOR ME"?...
CARDS
WHY, YES... I BELIEVE WE DO.
GREAT.
I'LL TAKE FIVE OF THEM.
CARDS
MACNELLY

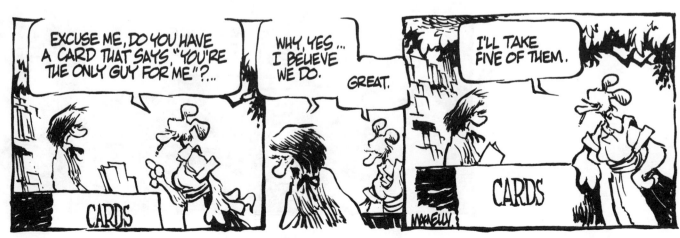

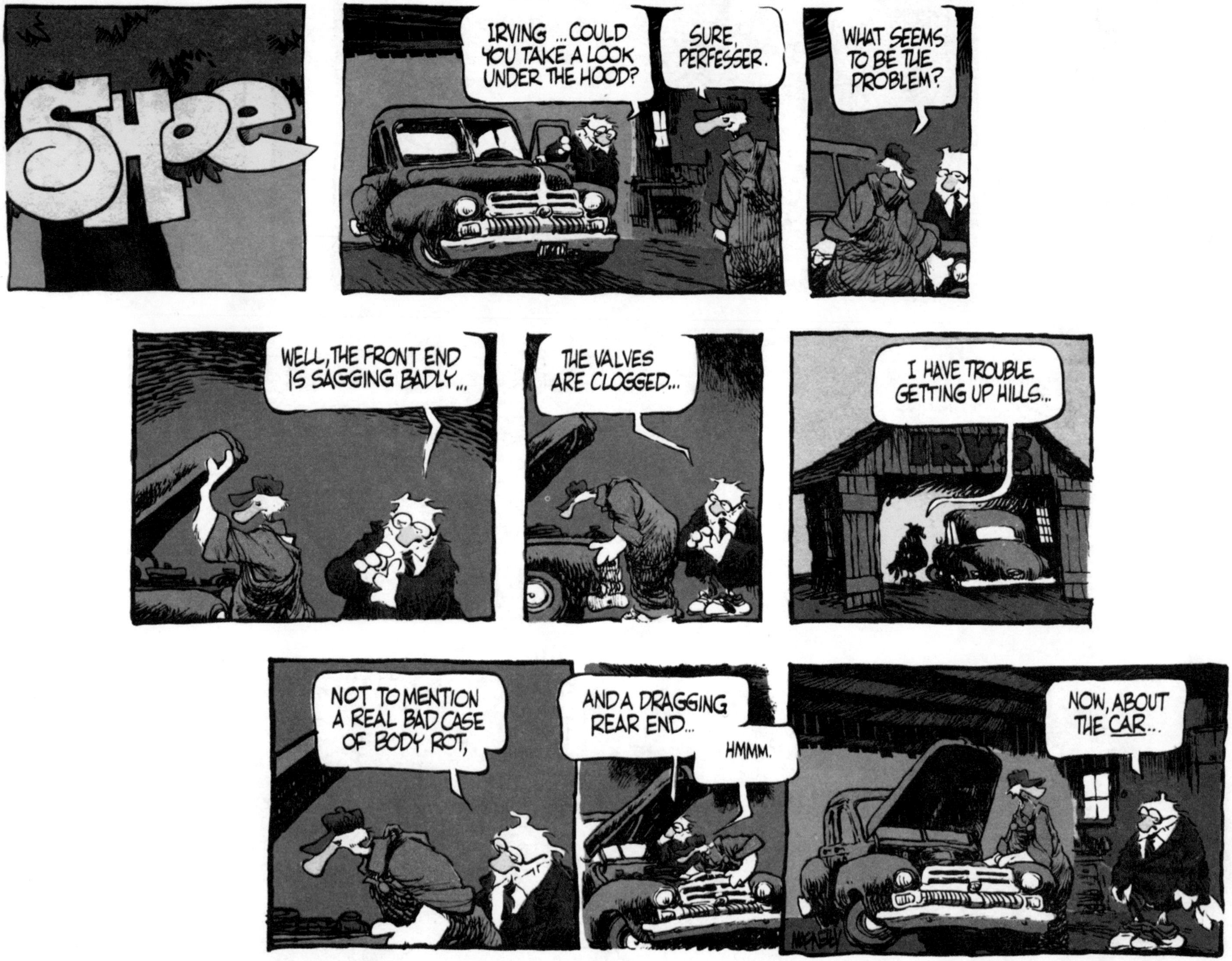
SHOE
IRVING ...COULD YOU TAKE A LOOK UNDER THE HOOD?
SURE, PERFESSER.
WHAT SEEMS TO BE THE PROBLEM?
WELL, THE FRONT END IS SAGGING BADLY...
THE VALVES ARE CLOGGED...
I HAVE TROUBLE GETTING UP HILLS...
IRV'S
NOT TO MENTION A REAL BAD CASE OF BODY ROT,
AND A DRAGGING REAR END...
HMMM.
NOW, ABOUT THE CAR...
MACNELLY

Where are they now?

Muffy Hollandaise
Then: Ultra-preppy summer intern for the *Treetops Tattler Tribune*.

Now: Runs an escort service in Washington, DC. Has a client list the FBI would really like to get its hands on.

Bumpkins the butler
Then: British butler Cosmo Fishhawk inherited from his eccentric uncle.

Now: After leaving Cosmo's employ, Bumpkins made a killing with a dot-com startup. He pulled out just in time and retired to Argentina, which he owns.

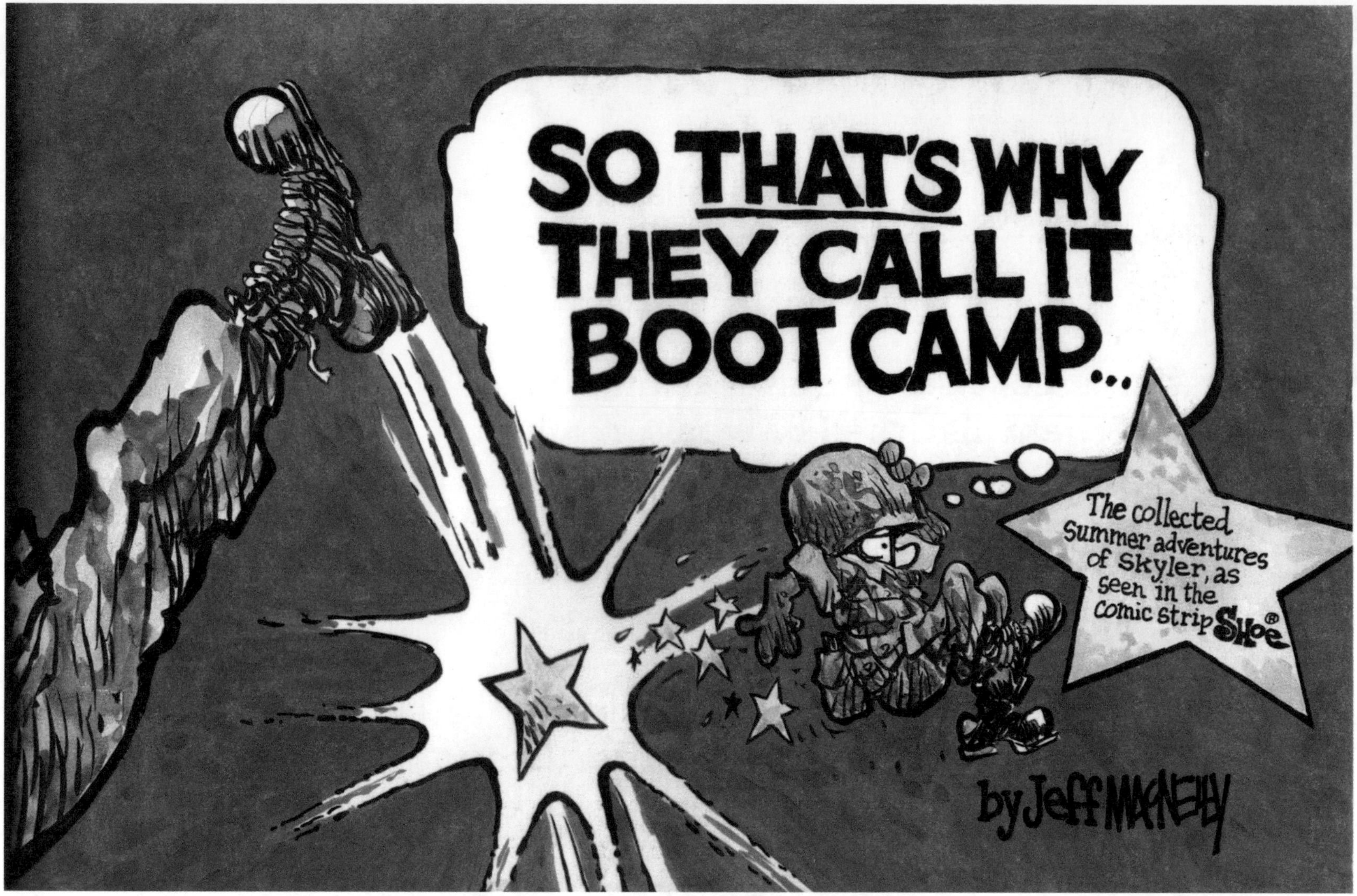
SO THAT'S WHY THEY CALL IT BOOT CAMP...
The collected Summer adventures of Skyler, as seen in the comic strip Shoe®
by Jeff MacNelly

One of the most requested themes of *Shoe* is the "Skyler goes to Camp" series. Jeff put together a collection of camp adventures in 1987 in a book called *So That's Why They Call It Boot Camp*. It was a semiprivate publication with all the proceeds going to the Navy Relief Fund. This section revisits some of Skyler's camp experiences.

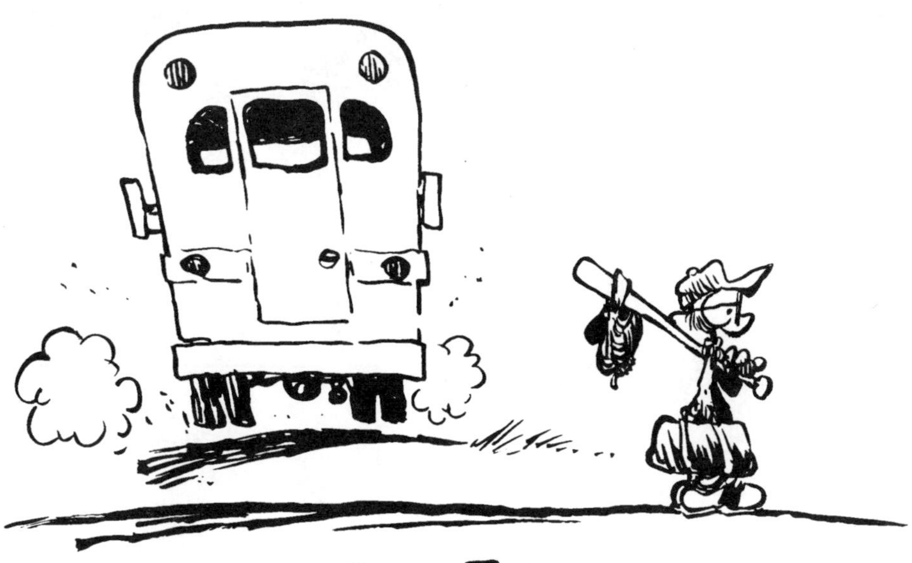

Camp LeJeune

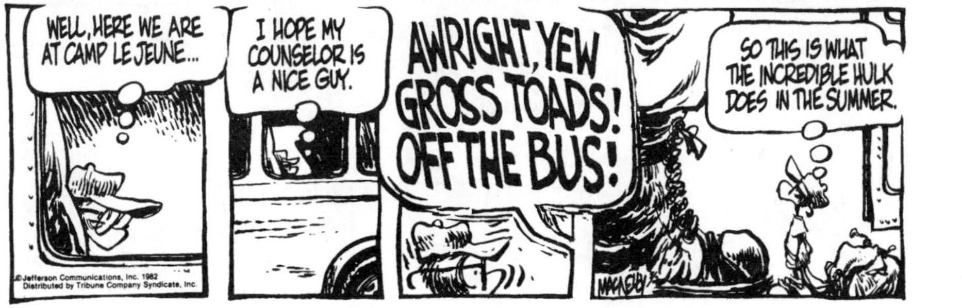

WELL, HERE WE ARE AT CAMP LE JEUNE...
I HOPE MY COUNSELOR IS A NICE GUY.
AWRIGHT, YEW GROSS TOADS! OFF THE BUS!
SO THIS IS WHAT THE INCREDIBLE HULK DOES IN THE SUMMER.
©Jefferson Communications, Inc. 1982 Distributed by Tribune Company Syndicate, Inc.

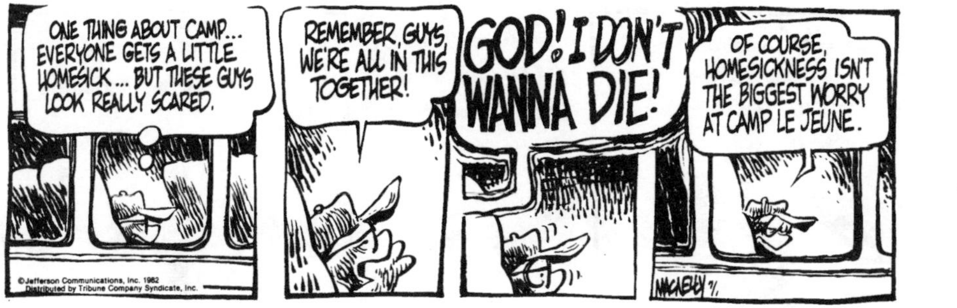

ONE THING ABOUT CAMP... EVERYONE GETS A LITTLE HOMESICK ... BUT THESE GUYS LOOK REALLY SCARED.
REMEMBER, GUYS, WE'RE ALL IN THIS TOGETHER!
GOD! I DON'T WANNA DIE!
OF COURSE, HOMESICKNESS ISN'T THE BIGGEST WORRY AT CAMP LE JEUNE.
©Jefferson Communications, Inc. 1982 Distributed by Tribune Company Syndicate, Inc.

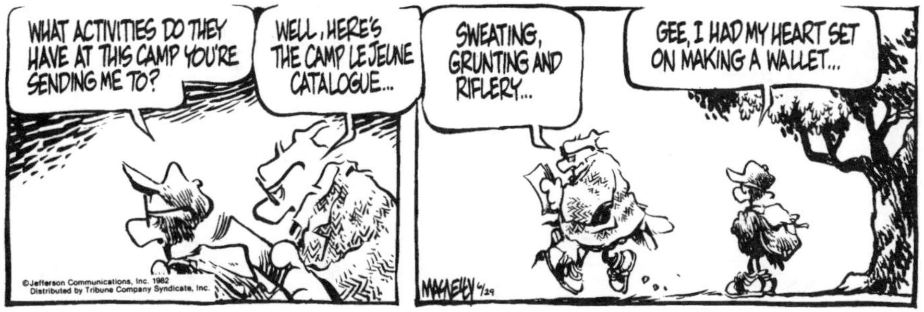

WHAT ACTIVITIES DO THEY HAVE AT THIS CAMP YOU'RE SENDING ME TO?
WELL, HERE'S THE CAMP LE JEUNE CATALOGUE...
SWEATING, GRUNTING AND RIFLERY...
GEE, I HAD MY HEART SET ON MAKING A WALLET...
©Jefferson Communications, Inc. 1982 Distributed by Tribune Company Syndicate, Inc.

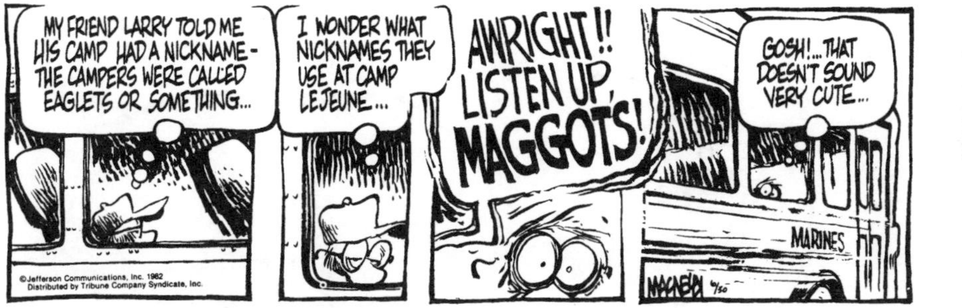

MY FRIEND LARRY TOLD ME HIS CAMP HAD A NICKNAME - THE CAMPERS WERE CALLED EAGLETS OR SOMETHING...
I WONDER WHAT NICKNAMES THEY USE AT CAMP LEJEUNE...
AWRIGHT!! LISTEN UP, MAGGOTS!
GOSH!... THAT DOESN'T SOUND VERY CUTE...
MARINES
©Jefferson Communications, Inc. 1982 Distributed by Tribune Company Syndicate, Inc.

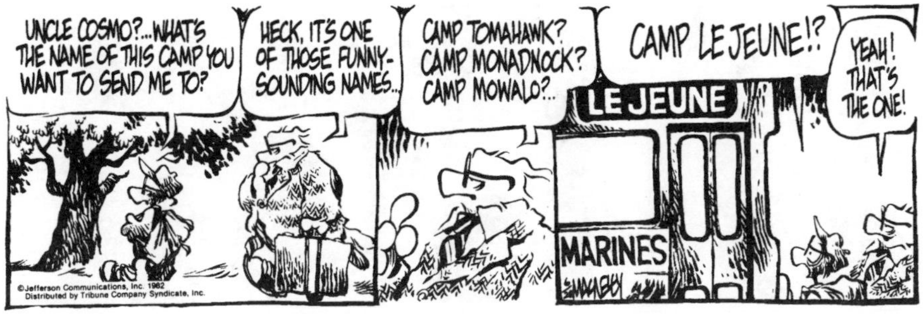

UNCLE COSMO?... WHAT'S THE NAME OF THIS CAMP YOU WANT TO SEND ME TO?
HECK, IT'S ONE OF THOSE FUNNY-SOUNDING NAMES...
CAMP TOMAHAWK? CAMP MONADNOCK? CAMP MOWALO?...
CAMP LE JEUNE!?
YEAH! THAT'S THE ONE!
LE JEUNE
MARINES
©Jefferson Communications, Inc. 1982 Distributed by Tribune Company Syndicate, Inc.

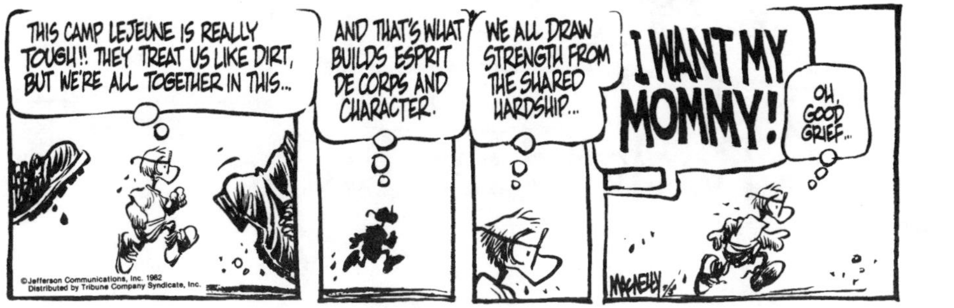

THIS CAMP LEJEUNE IS REALLY TOUGH!! THEY TREAT US LIKE DIRT, BUT WE'RE ALL TOGETHER IN THIS...
AND THAT'S WHAT BUILDS ESPRIT DE CORPS AND CHARACTER.
WE ALL DRAW STRENGTH FROM THE SHARED HARDSHIP...
I WANT MY MOMMY!
OH, GOOD GRIEF...
©Jefferson Communications, Inc. 1982 Distributed by Tribune Company Syndicate, Inc.

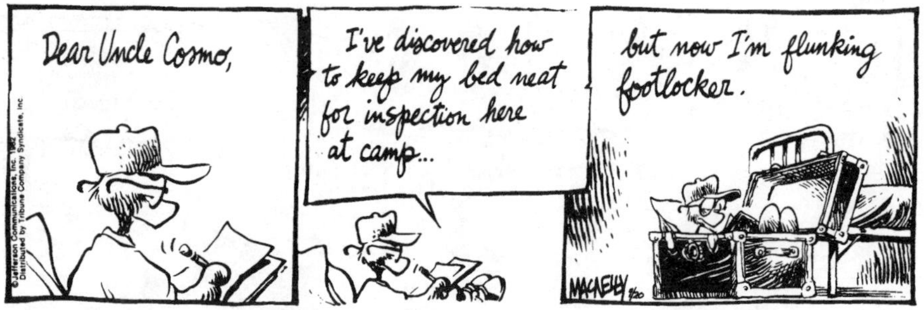
Dear Uncle Cosmo,
I've discovered how to keep my bed neat for inspection here at camp...
but now I'm flunking footlocker.
MACNELLY
©Jefferson Communications, Inc. 1983 Distributed by Tribune Company Syndicate, Inc.

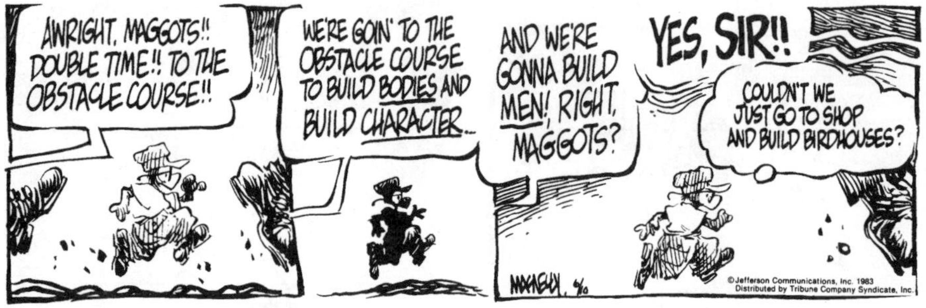
AWRIGHT, MAGGOTS!! DOUBLE TIME!! TO THE OBSTACLE COURSE!!
WE'RE GOIN' TO THE OBSTACLE COURSE TO BUILD BODIES AND BUILD CHARACTER...
AND WE'RE GONNA BUILD MEN! RIGHT, MAGGOTS?
YES, SIR!!
COULDN'T WE JUST GO TO SHOP AND BUILD BIRDHOUSES?
MACNELLY
©Jefferson Communications, Inc. 1983 Distributed by Tribune Company Syndicate, Inc.

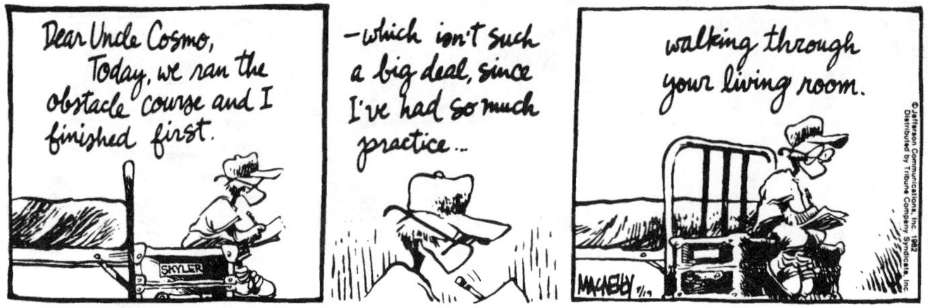
Dear Uncle Cosmo, Today, we ran the obstacle course and I finished first.
—which isn't such a big deal, since I've had so much practice...
walking through your living room.
SKYLER
MACNELLY
©Jefferson Communications, Inc. 1983 Distributed by Tribune Company Syndicate, Inc.

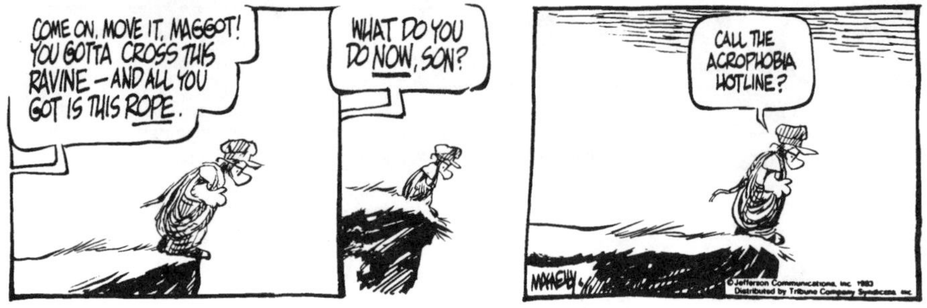
COME ON, MOVE IT, MAGGOT! YOU GOTTA CROSS THIS RAVINE.—AND ALL YOU GOT IS THIS ROPE.
WHAT DO YOU DO NOW, SON?
CALL THE ACROPHOBIA HOTLINE?
MACNELLY
©Jefferson Communications, Inc. 1983 Distributed by Tribune Company Syndicate, Inc.

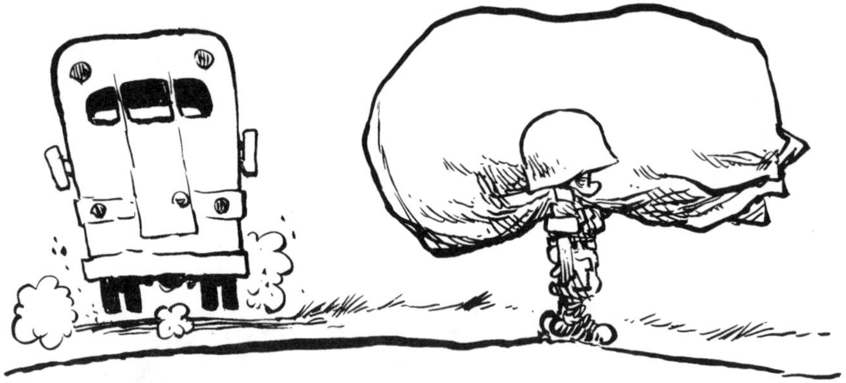

Back to LeJeune

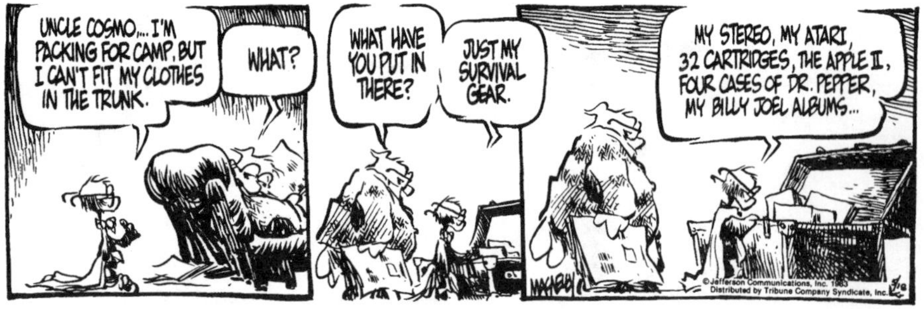
UNCLE COSMO... I'M PACKING FOR CAMP, BUT I CAN'T FIT MY CLOTHES IN THE TRUNK.
WHAT?
WHAT HAVE YOU PUT IN THERE?
JUST MY SURVIVAL GEAR.
MY STEREO, MY ATARI, 32 CARTRIDGES, THE APPLE II, FOUR CASES OF DR. PEPPER, MY BILLY JOEL ALBUMS...
MACNELLY
©Jefferson Communications, Inc. 1983 Distributed by Tribune Company Syndicate, Inc.

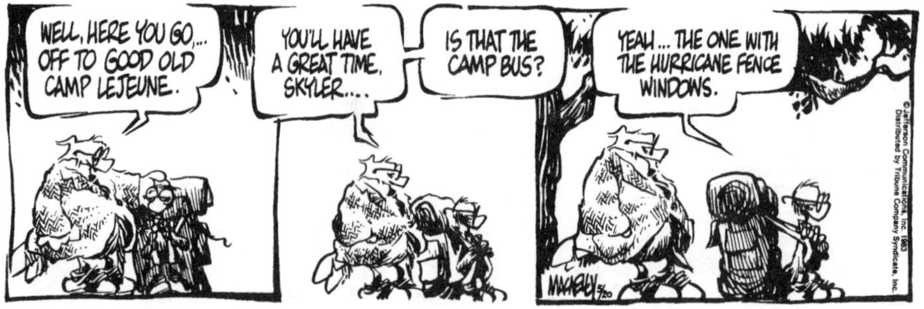
WELL, HERE YOU GO... OFF TO GOOD OLD CAMP LEJEUNE.
YOU'LL HAVE A GREAT TIME, SKYLER....
IS THAT THE CAMP BUS?
YEAH... THE ONE WITH THE HURRICANE FENCE WINDOWS.
MACNELLY
©Jefferson Communications, Inc. 1983 Distributed by Tribune Company Syndicate, Inc.

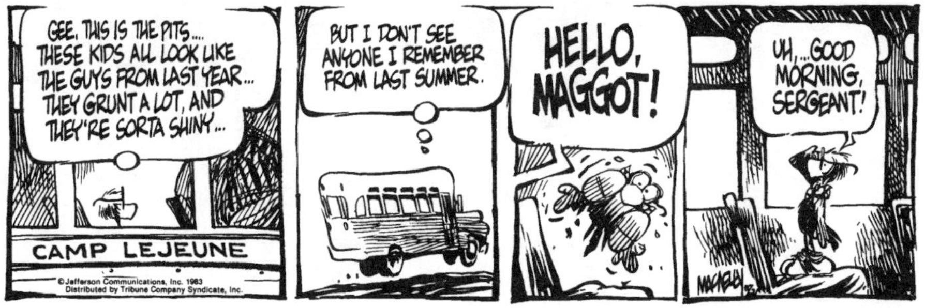
GEE, THIS IS THE PITS.... THESE KIDS ALL LOOK LIKE THE GUYS FROM LAST YEAR... THEY GRUNT A LOT, AND THEY'RE SORTA SHINY...
CAMP LEJEUNE
BUT I DON'T SEE ANYONE I REMEMBER FROM LAST SUMMER.
HELLO, MAGGOT!
UH,...GOOD MORNING, SERGEANT!
©Jefferson Communications, Inc. 1983
Distributed by Tribune Company Syndicate, Inc.

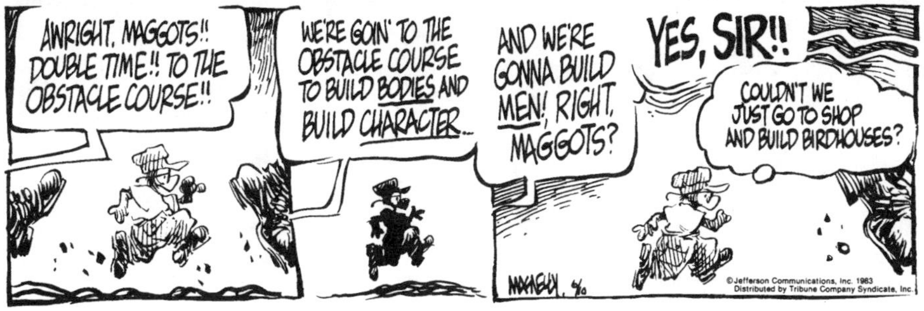
AWRIGHT, MAGGOTS!! DOUBLE TIME!! TO THE OBSTACLE COURSE!!
WE'RE GOIN' TO THE OBSTACLE COURSE TO BUILD BODIES AND BUILD CHARACTER...
AND WE'RE GONNA BUILD MEN! RIGHT, MAGGOTS?
YES, SIR!!
COULDN'T WE JUST GO TO SHOP AND BUILD BIRDHOUSES?
©Jefferson Communications, Inc. 1983
Distributed by Tribune Company Syndicate, Inc.

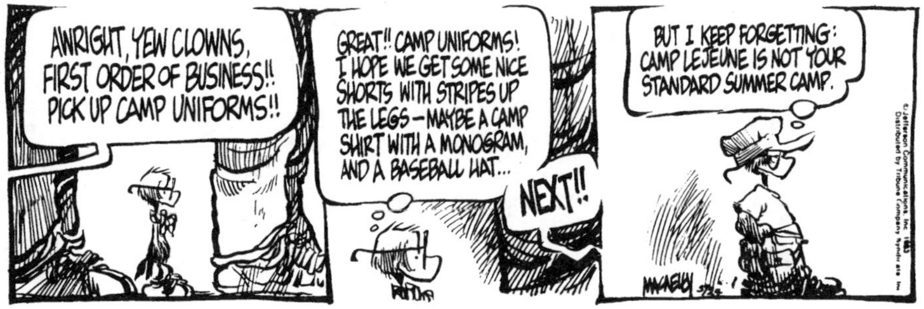
AWRIGHT, YEW CLOWNS, FIRST ORDER OF BUSINESS!! PICK UP CAMP UNIFORMS!!
GREAT!! CAMP UNIFORMS! I HOPE WE GET SOME NICE SHORTS WITH STRIPES UP THE LEGS—MAYBE A CAMP SHIRT WITH A MONOGRAM, AND A BASEBALL HAT...
NEXT!!
BUT I KEEP FORGETTING: CAMP LEJEUNE IS NOT YOUR STANDARD SUMMER CAMP.
©Jefferson Communications, Inc. 1983
Distributed by Tribune Company Syndicate, Inc.

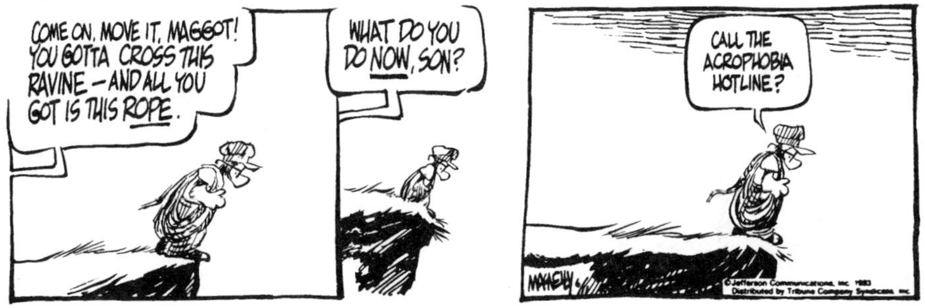
COME ON, MOVE IT, MAGGOT! YOU GOTTA CROSS THIS RAVINE—AND ALL YOU GOT IS THIS ROPE.
WHAT DO YOU DO NOW, SON?
CALL THE ACROPHOBIA HOTLINE?
©Jefferson Communications, Inc. 1983
Distributed by Tribune Company Syndicate, Inc.

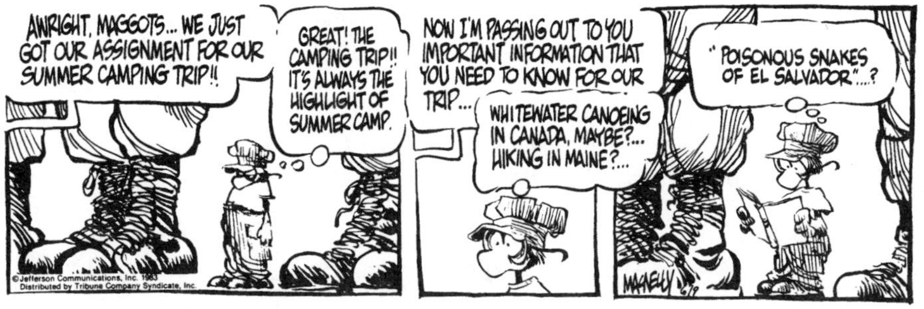
AWRIGHT, MAGGOTS... WE JUST GOT OUR ASSIGNMENT FOR OUR SUMMER CAMPING TRIP!!
GREAT! THE CAMPING TRIP!! IT'S ALWAYS THE HIGHLIGHT OF SUMMER CAMP.
NOW I'M PASSING OUT TO YOU IMPORTANT INFORMATION THAT YOU NEED TO KNOW FOR OUR TRIP...
WHITEWATER CANOEING IN CANADA, MAYBE?... HIKING IN MAINE?...
"POISONOUS SNAKES OF EL SALVADOR"...?
©Jefferson Communications, Inc. 1983
Distributed by Tribune Company Syndicate, Inc.

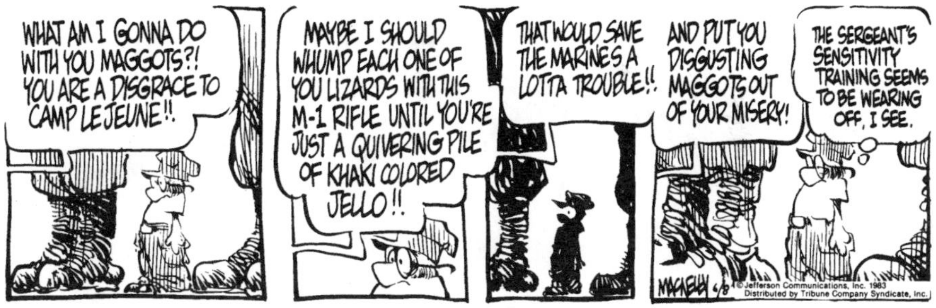
WHAT AM I GONNA DO WITH YOU MAGGOTS?! YOU ARE A DISGRACE TO CAMP LEJEUNE!!
MAYBE I SHOULD WHUMP EACH ONE OF YOU LIZARDS WITH THIS M-1 RIFLE UNTIL YOU'RE JUST A QUIVERING PILE OF KHAKI COLORED JELLO!!
THAT WOULD SAVE THE MARINES A LOTTA TROUBLE!!
AND PUT YOU DISGUSTING MAGGOTS OUT OF YOUR MISERY!
THE SERGEANT'S SENSITIVITY TRAINING SEEMS TO BE WEARING OFF, I SEE.
©Jefferson Communications, Inc. 1983
Distributed by Tribune Company Syndicate, Inc.

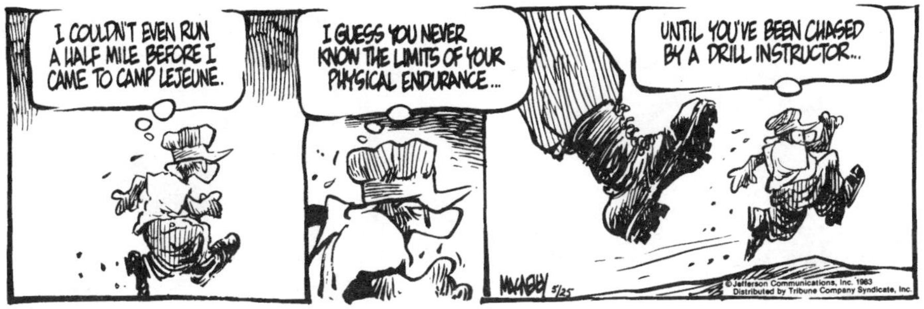
I COULDN'T EVEN RUN A HALF MILE BEFORE I CAME TO CAMP LEJEUNE.
I GUESS YOU NEVER KNOW THE LIMITS OF YOUR PHYSICAL ENDURANCE...
UNTIL YOU'VE BEEN CHASED BY A DRILL INSTRUCTOR...
©Jefferson Communications, Inc. 1983
Distributed by Tribune Company Syndicate, Inc.

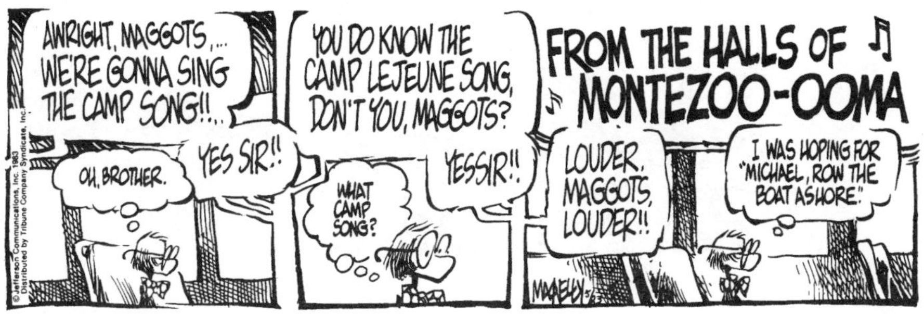
AWRIGHT, MAGGOTS,... WE'RE GONNA SING THE CAMP SONG!!...
OH, BROTHER.
YES SIR!!
YOU DO KNOW THE CAMP LEJEUNE SONG, DON'T YOU, MAGGOTS?
WHAT CAMP SONG?
YESSIR!!
FROM THE HALLS OF MONTEZOO-OOMA
LOUDER, MAGGOTS, LOUDER!!
I WAS HOPING FOR "MICHAEL, ROW THE BOAT ASHORE."
©Jefferson Communications, Inc. 1983
Distributed by Tribune Company Syndicate, Inc.

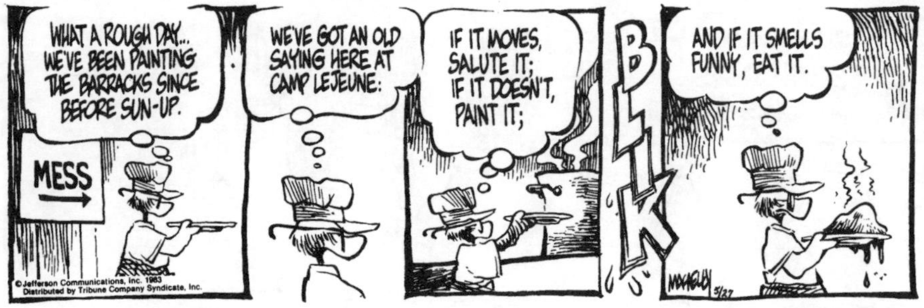
WHAT A ROUGH DAY... WE'VE BEEN PAINTING THE BARRACKS SINCE BEFORE SUN-UP.
MESS
WE'VE GOT AN OLD SAYING HERE AT CAMP LEJEUNE:
IF IT MOVES, SALUTE IT; IF IT DOESN'T, PAINT IT;
BLIK
AND IF IT SMELLS FUNNY, EAT IT.
© Jefferson Communications, Inc. 1983
Distributed by Tribune Company Syndicate, Inc.
MACNELLY 5/27

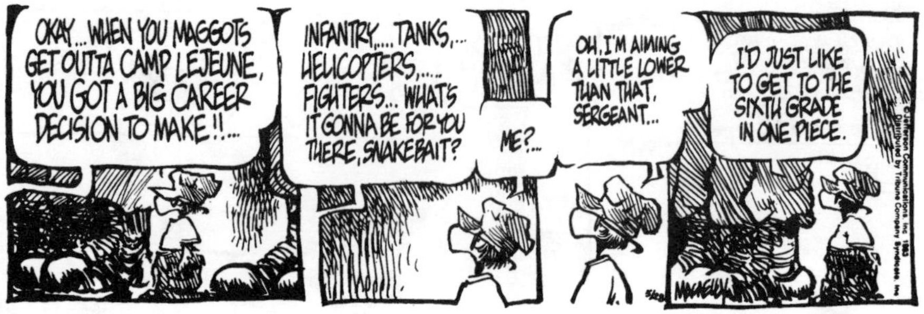
OKAY... WHEN YOU MAGGOTS GET OUTTA CAMP LEJEUNE, YOU GOT A BIG CAREER DECISION TO MAKE!!...
INFANTRY... TANKS,... HELICOPTERS,..... FIGHTERS... WHAT'S IT GONNA BE FOR YOU THERE, SNAKEBAIT?
ME?...
OH, I'M AIMING A LITTLE LOWER THAN THAT, SERGEANT...
I'D JUST LIKE TO GET TO THE SIXTH GRADE IN ONE PIECE.
MACNELLY

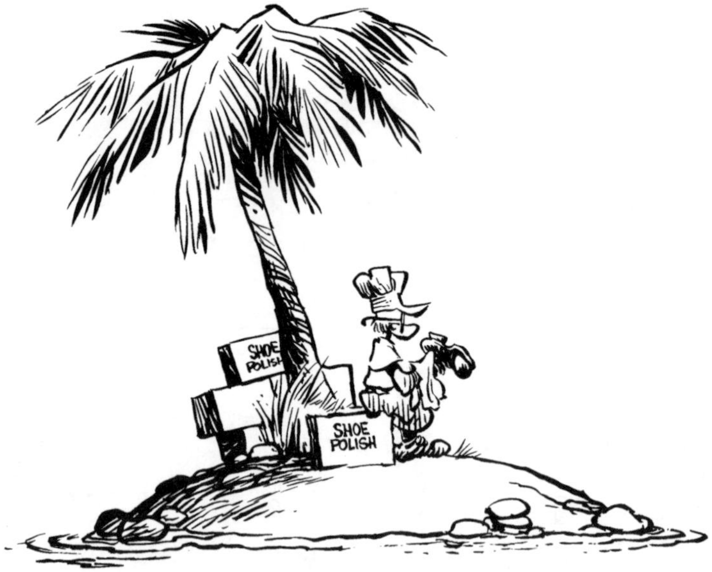

Parris Island

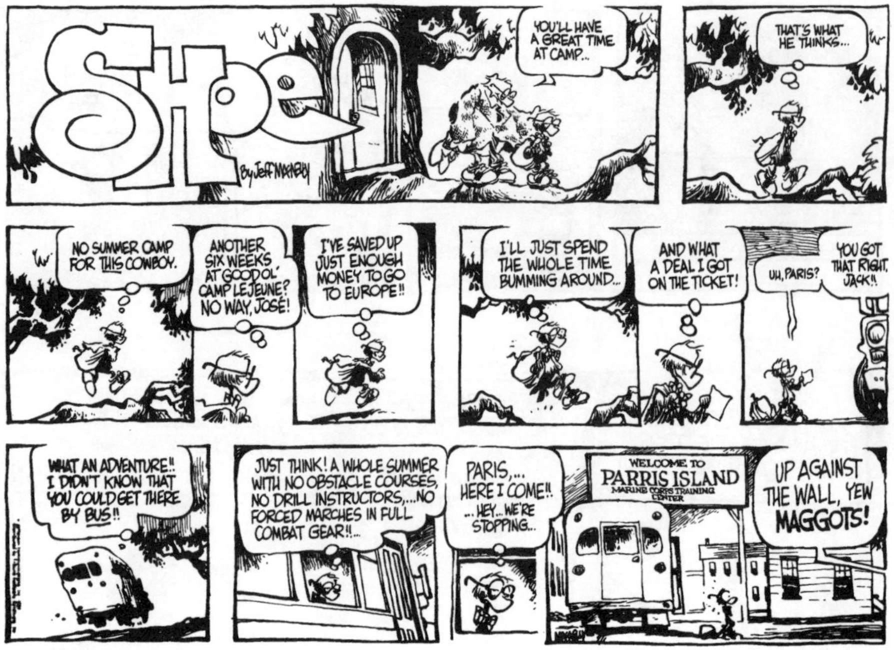
SHOE
By JEFF MACNELLY
YOU'LL HAVE A GREAT TIME AT CAMP...
THAT'S WHAT HE THINKS...
NO SUMMER CAMP FOR THIS COWBOY.
ANOTHER SIX WEEKS AT GOOD OL' CAMP LEJEUNE? NO WAY, JOSÉ!
I'VE SAVED UP JUST ENOUGH MONEY TO GO TO EUROPE!!
I'LL JUST SPEND THE WHOLE TIME BUMMING AROUND...
AND WHAT A DEAL I GOT ON THE TICKET!
UH, PARIS?
YOU GOT THAT RIGHT, JACK!!
WHAT AN ADVENTURE!! I DIDN'T KNOW THAT YOU COULD GET THERE BY BUS!!
JUST THINK! A WHOLE SUMMER WITH NO OBSTACLE COURSES, NO DRILL INSTRUCTORS,...NO FORCED MARCHES IN FULL COMBAT GEAR!!...
PARIS,... HERE I COME!! ...HEY... WE'RE STOPPING...
WELCOME TO PARRIS ISLAND MARINE CORPS TRAINING CENTER
UP AGAINST THE WALL, YEW MAGGOTS!

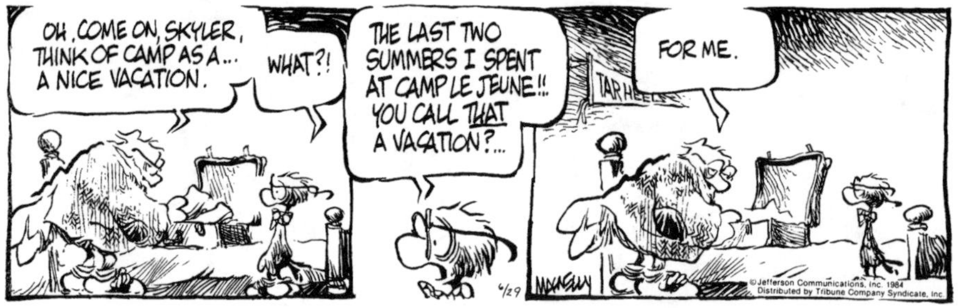
OH, COME ON, SKYLER, THINK OF CAMP AS A... A NICE VACATION.
WHAT?!
THE LAST TWO SUMMERS I SPENT AT CAMP LEJEUNE!! YOU CALL THAT A VACATION?...
TAR HEELS
FOR ME.
MACNELLY 6/29
© Jefferson Communications, Inc. 1984
Distributed by Tribune Company Syndicate, Inc.

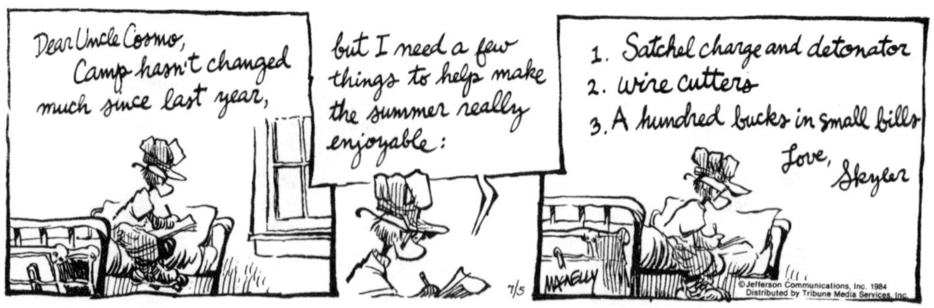
Dear Uncle Cosmo, Camp hasn't changed much since last year,
but I need a few things to help make the summer really enjoyable:
1. Satchel charge and detonator
2. Wire cutters
3. A hundred bucks in small bills
Love, Skyler
MACNELLY 7/5
© Jefferson Communications, Inc. 1984
Distributed by Tribune Media Services, Inc.

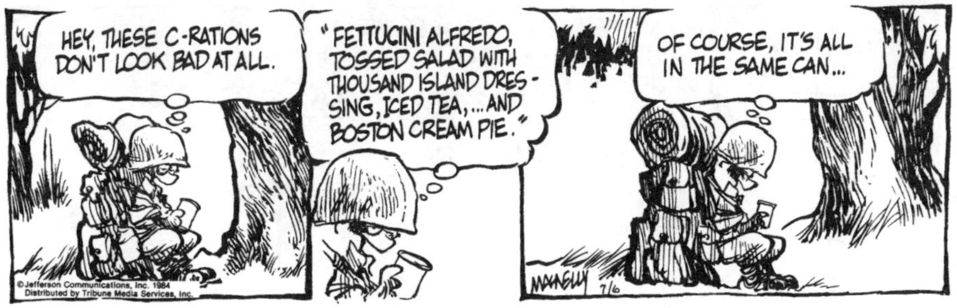
HEY, THESE C-RATIONS DON'T LOOK BAD AT ALL.
"FETTUCINI ALFREDO, TOSSED SALAD WITH THOUSAND ISLAND DRESSING, ICED TEA, ... AND BOSTON CREAM PIE."
OF COURSE, IT'S ALL IN THE SAME CAN...
MACNELLY 7/6
© Jefferson Communications, Inc. 1984
Distributed by Tribune Media Services, Inc.

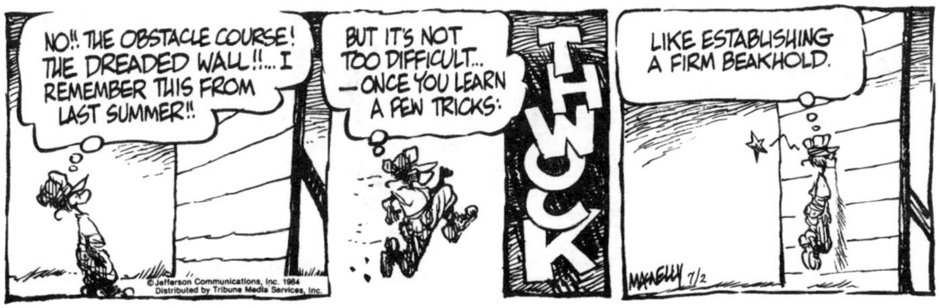
NO!! THE OBSTACLE COURSE! THE DREADED WALL!!... I REMEMBER THIS FROM LAST SUMMER!!
BUT IT'S NOT TOO DIFFICULT... —ONCE YOU LEARN A FEW TRICKS:
THWOCK
LIKE ESTABLISHING A FIRM BEAKHOLD.
MACNELLY 7/2
© Jefferson Communications, Inc. 1984
Distributed by Tribune Media Services, Inc.

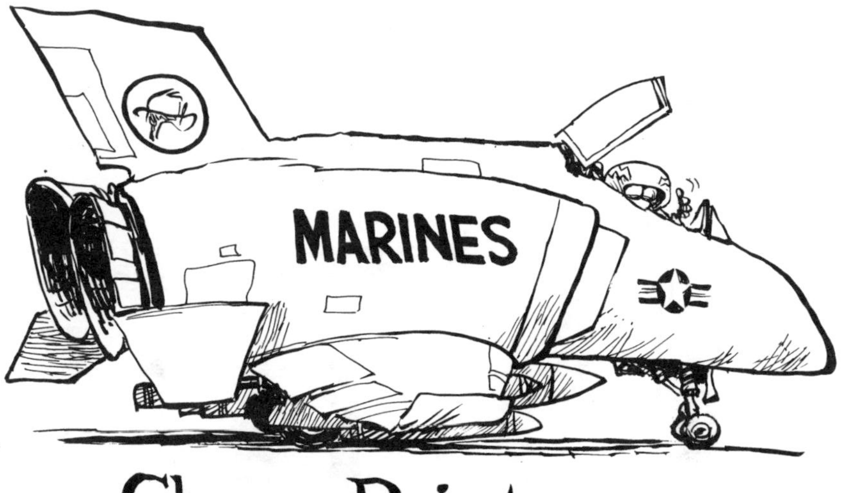
MARINES

Cherry Point

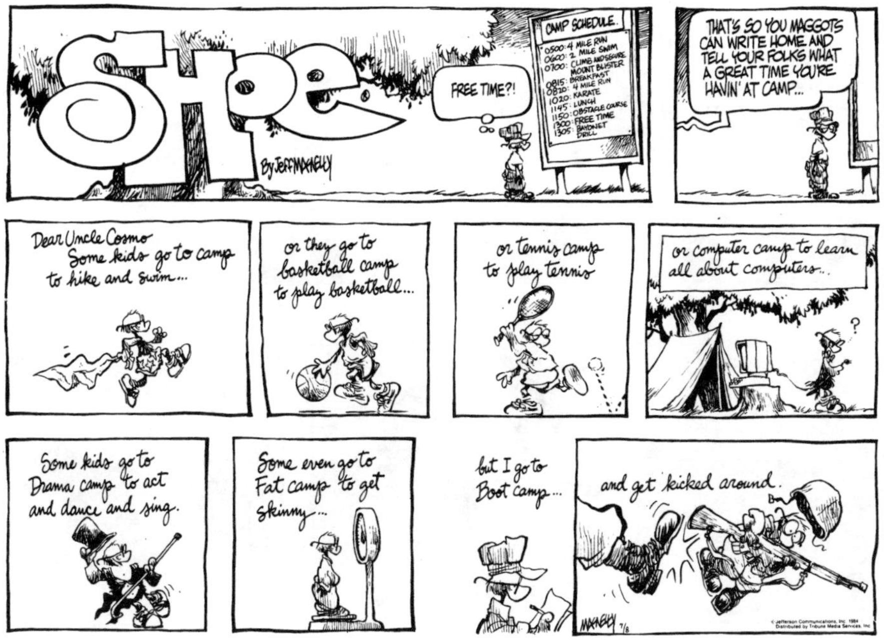
SHOE
By JEFF MACNELLY
FREE TIME?!
CAMP SCHEDULE.
0500: 4 MILE RUN
0600: 2 MILE SWIM
0700: CLIMB AND SECURE MOUNT BLISTER
0815: BREAKFAST
0820: 4 MILE RUN
1020: KARATE
1145: LUNCH
1150: OBSTACLE COURSE
1300: FREE TIME
1305: BAYONET DRILL
THAT'S SO YOU MAGGOTS CAN WRITE HOME AND TELL YOUR FOLKS WHAT A GREAT TIME YOU'RE HAVIN' AT CAMP...
Dear Uncle Cosmo
Some kids go to camp to hike and swim...
or they go to basketball camp to play basketball...
or tennis camp to play tennis
or computer camp to learn all about computers...
Some kids go to Drama camp to act and dance and sing.
Some even go to Fat camp to get skinny...
but I go to Boot camp...
and get kicked around.
MACNELLY 7/8

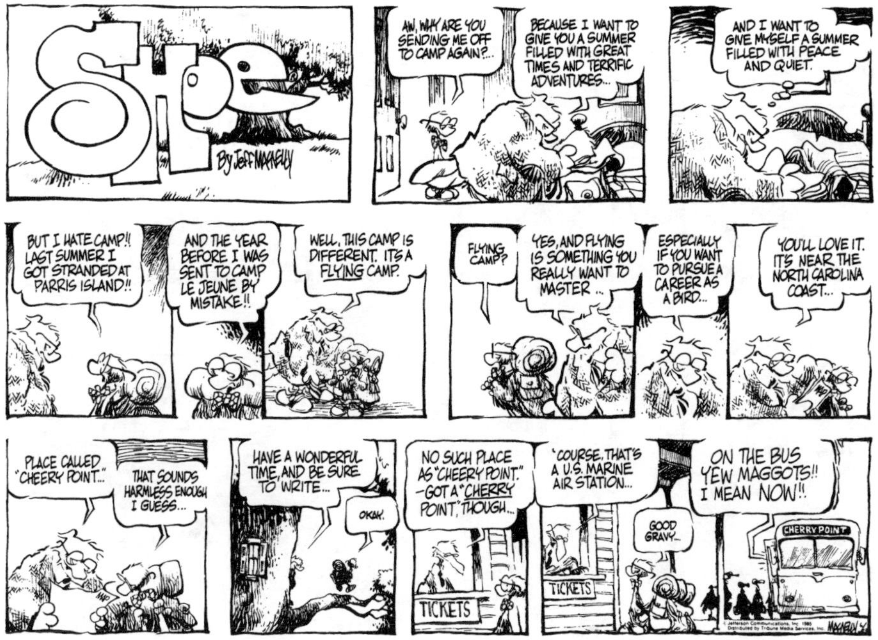
SHOE
By JEFF MACNELLY
AW, WHY ARE YOU SENDING ME OFF TO CAMP AGAIN?...
BECAUSE I WANT TO GIVE YOU A SUMMER FILLED WITH GREAT TIMES AND TERRIFIC ADVENTURES...
AND I WANT TO GIVE MYSELF A SUMMER FILLED WITH PEACE AND QUIET.
BUT I HATE CAMP!! LAST SUMMER I GOT STRANDED AT PARRIS ISLAND!!
AND THE YEAR BEFORE I WAS SENT TO CAMP LE JEUNE BY MISTAKE!!
WELL, THIS CAMP IS DIFFERENT. IT'S A FLYING CAMP.
FLYING CAMP?
YES, AND FLYING IS SOMETHING YOU REALLY WANT TO MASTER...
ESPECIALLY IF YOU WANT TO PURSUE A CAREER AS A BIRD...
YOU'LL LOVE IT. IT'S NEAR THE NORTH CAROLINA COAST...
PLACE CALLED "CHERRY POINT."
THAT SOUNDS HARMLESS ENOUGH I GUESS...
HAVE A WONDERFUL TIME, AND BE SURE TO WRITE...
OKAY.
NO SUCH PLACE AS "CHERRY POINT." —GOT A "CHERRY POINT," THOUGH...
'COURSE, THAT'S A U.S. MARINE AIR STATION...
GOOD GRAVY...
ON THE BUS YEW MAGGOTS!! I MEAN NOW!!
TICKETS
CHERRY POINT
MACNELLY

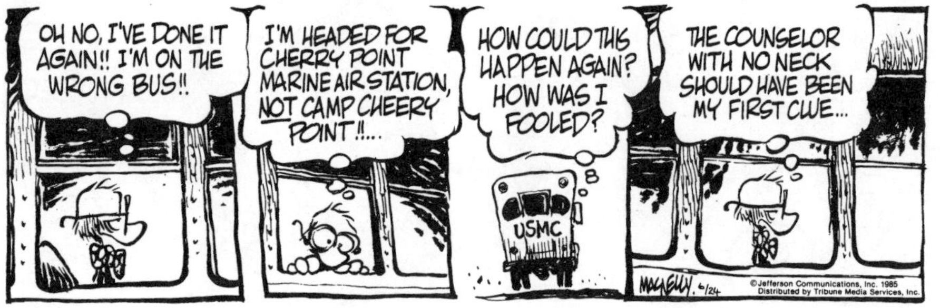
OH NO, I'VE DONE IT AGAIN!! I'M ON THE WRONG BUS!!
I'M HEADED FOR CHERRY POINT MARINE AIR STATION, NOT CAMP CHEERY POINT!!...
HOW COULD THIS HAPPEN AGAIN? HOW WAS I FOOLED?
USMC
THE COUNSELOR WITH NO NECK SHOULD HAVE BEEN MY FIRST CLUE...
MACNELLY 6/24
© Jefferson Communications, Inc. 1985 Distributed by Tribune Media Services, Inc.

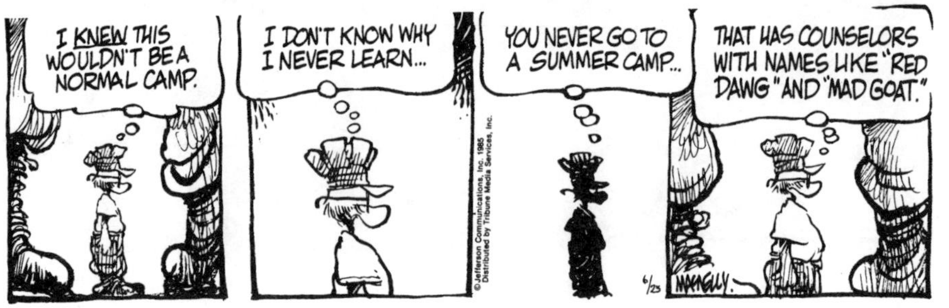
I KNEW THIS WOULDN'T BE A NORMAL CAMP.
I DON'T KNOW WHY I NEVER LEARN...
YOU NEVER GO TO A SUMMER CAMP...
THAT HAS COUNSELORS WITH NAMES LIKE "RED DAWG" AND "MAD GOAT."
© Jefferson Communications, Inc. 1985 Distributed by Tribune Media Services, Inc.
6/25
MACNELLY

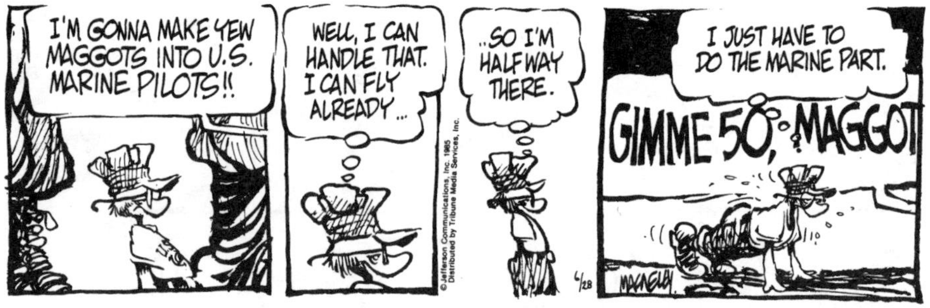
I'M GONNA MAKE YEW MAGGOTS INTO U.S. MARINE PILOTS!!
WELL, I CAN HANDLE THAT. I CAN FLY ALREADY...
..SO I'M HALFWAY THERE.
I JUST HAVE TO DO THE MARINE PART.
GIMME 50, MAGGOT
© Jefferson Communications, Inc. 1985 Distributed by Tribune Media Services, Inc.
6/28
MACNELLY

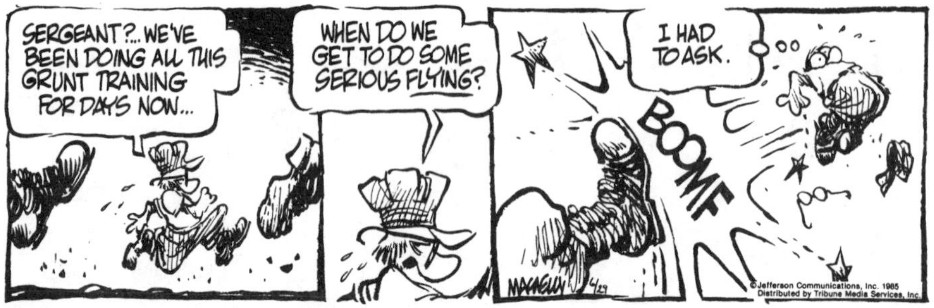
SERGEANT?... WE'VE BEEN DOING ALL THIS GRUNT TRAINING FOR DAYS NOW...
WHEN DO WE GET TO DO SOME SERIOUS FLYING?
I HAD TO ASK.
BOOMF
MACNELLY 6/29
© Jefferson Communications, Inc. 1985 Distributed by Tribune Media Services, Inc.

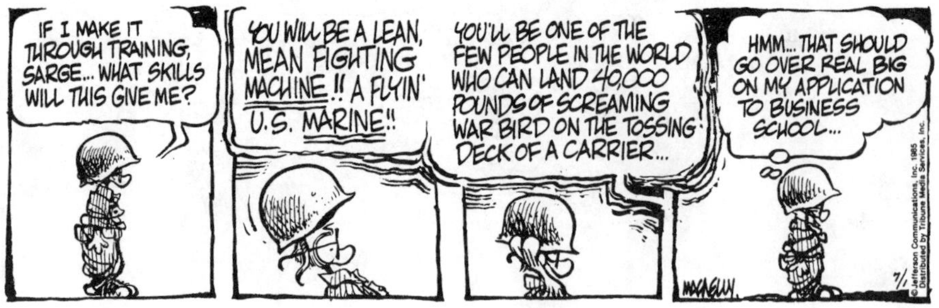
IF I MAKE IT THROUGH TRAINING, SARGE... WHAT SKILLS WILL THIS GIVE ME?
YOU WILL BE A LEAN, MEAN FIGHTING MACHINE!! A FLYIN' U.S. MARINE!!
YOU'LL BE ONE OF THE FEW PEOPLE IN THE WORLD WHO CAN LAND 40,000 POUNDS OF SCREAMING WAR BIRD ON THE TOSSING DECK OF A CARRIER...
HMM... THAT SHOULD GO OVER REAL BIG ON MY APPLICATION TO BUSINESS SCHOOL...
MACNELLY 7/1
© Jefferson Communications, Inc. 1985 Distributed by Tribune Media Services, Inc.

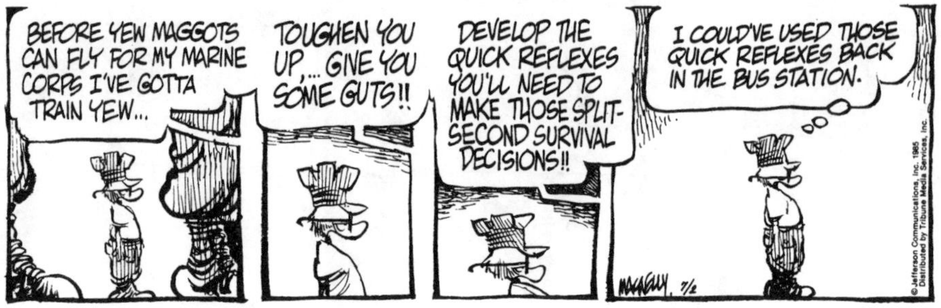
BEFORE YEW MAGGOTS CAN FLY FOR MY MARINE CORPS I'VE GOTTA TRAIN YEW...
TOUGHEN YOU UP,... GIVE YOU SOME GUTS!!
DEVELOP THE QUICK REFLEXES YOU'LL NEED TO MAKE THOSE SPLIT-SECOND SURVIVAL DECISIONS!!
I COULD'VE USED THOSE QUICK REFLEXES BACK IN THE BUS STATION.
MACNELLY 7/2
© Jefferson Communications, Inc. 1985 Distributed by Tribune Media Services, Inc.

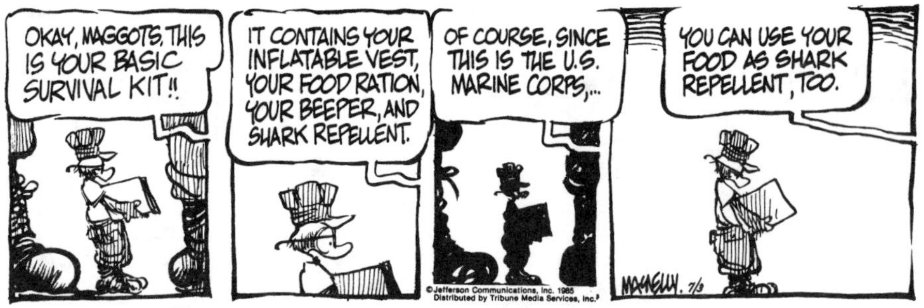
OKAY, MAGGOTS, THIS IS YOUR BASIC SURVIVAL KIT!!
IT CONTAINS YOUR INFLATABLE VEST, YOUR FOOD RATION, YOUR BEEPER, AND SHARK REPELLENT.
OF COURSE, SINCE THIS IS THE U.S. MARINE CORPS,...
YOU CAN USE YOUR FOOD AS SHARK REPELLENT, TOO.
© Jefferson Communications, Inc. 1985 Distributed by Tribune Media Services, Inc.
MACNELLY 7/3

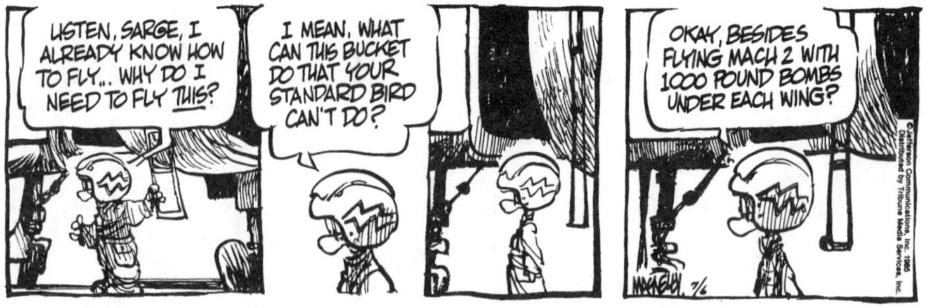
LISTEN, SARGE, I ALREADY KNOW HOW TO FLY... WHY DO I NEED TO FLY THIS?
I MEAN, WHAT CAN THIS BUCKET DO THAT YOUR STANDARD BIRD CAN'T DO?
OKAY, BESIDES FLYING MACH 2 WITH 1000 POUND BOMBS UNDER EACH WING?
MACNELLY 7/6
© Jefferson Communications, Inc. 1985 Distributed by Tribune Media Services, Inc.

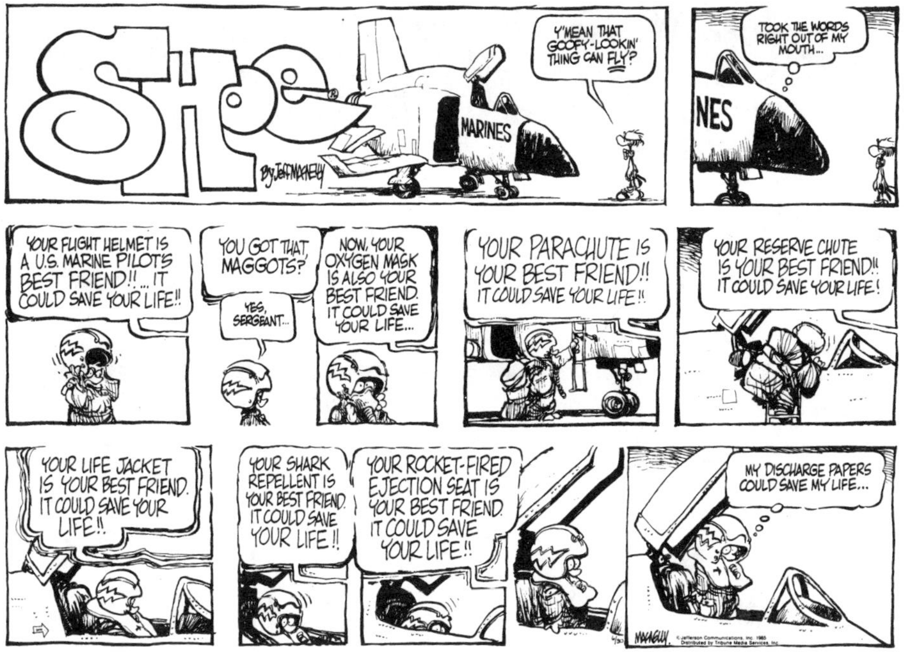
Shoe
By Jeff MacNelly
MARINES
Y'MEAN THAT GOOFY-LOOKIN' THING CAN FLY?
NES
TOOK THE WORDS RIGHT OUT OF MY MOUTH...
YOUR FLIGHT HELMET IS A U.S. MARINE PILOT'S BEST FRIEND!! ... IT COULD SAVE YOUR LIFE!!
YOU GOT THAT, MAGGOTS?
YES, SERGEANT...
NOW, YOUR OXYGEN MASK IS ALSO YOUR BEST FRIEND. IT COULD SAVE YOUR LIFE...
YOUR PARACHUTE IS YOUR BEST FRIEND!! IT COULD SAVE YOUR LIFE!!
YOUR RESERVE CHUTE IS YOUR BEST FRIEND!! IT COULD SAVE YOUR LIFE!
YOUR LIFE JACKET IS YOUR BEST FRIEND. IT COULD SAVE YOUR LIFE!!
YOUR SHARK REPELLENT IS YOUR BEST FRIEND. IT COULD SAVE YOUR LIFE!!
YOUR ROCKET-FIRED EJECTION SEAT IS YOUR BEST FRIEND. IT COULD SAVE YOUR LIFE!!
MY DISCHARGE PAPERS COULD SAVE MY LIFE...
MACNELLY

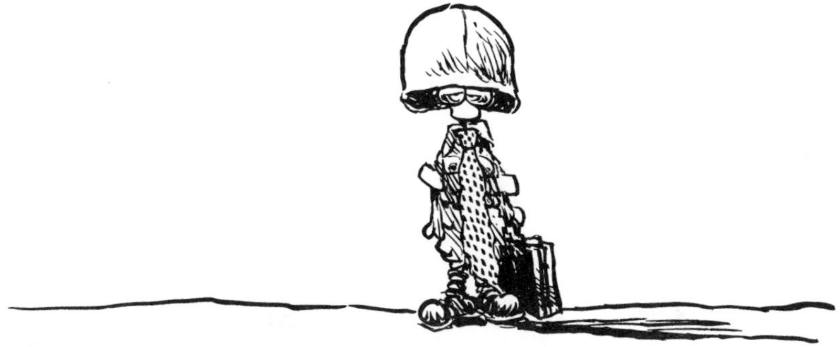

U.S. Marine Corporation

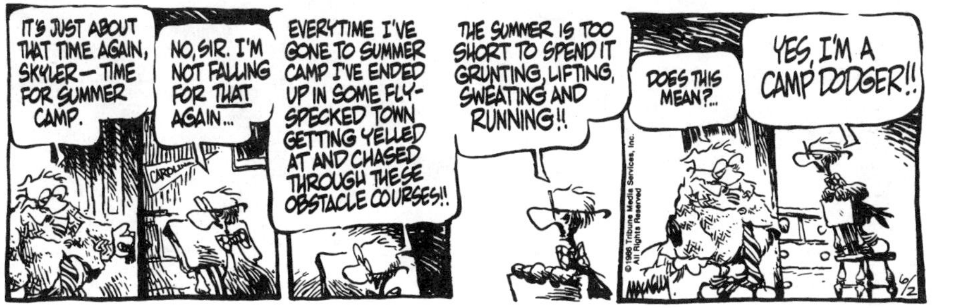
IT'S JUST ABOUT THAT TIME AGAIN, SKYLER— TIME FOR SUMMER CAMP.
NO, SIR. I'M NOT FALLING FOR THAT AGAIN...
EVERYTIME I'VE GONE TO SUMMER CAMP I'VE ENDED UP IN SOME FLY-SPECKED TOWN GETTING YELLED AT AND CHASED THROUGH THESE OBSTACLE COURSES!!
THE SUMMER IS TOO SHORT TO SPEND IT GRUNTING, LIFTING, SWEATING AND RUNNING!!
DOES THIS MEAN?...
YES, I'M A CAMP DODGER!!
MACNELLY
6/2

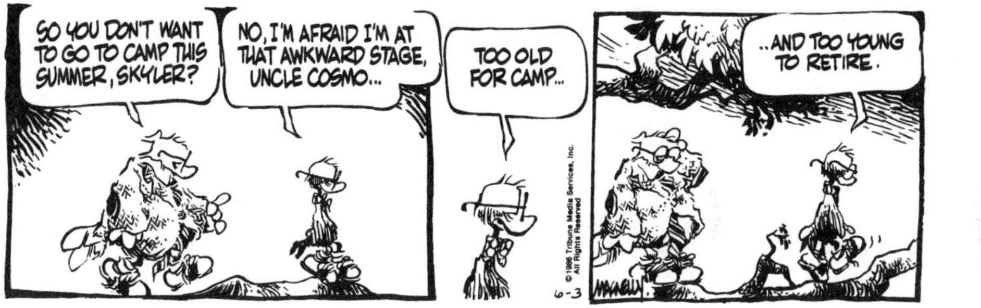
SO YOU DON'T WANT TO GO TO CAMP THIS SUMMER, SKYLER?
NO, I'M AFRAID I'M AT THAT AWKWARD STAGE, UNCLE COSMO...
TOO OLD FOR CAMP...
...AND TOO YOUNG TO RETIRE.
MACNELLY
6-3

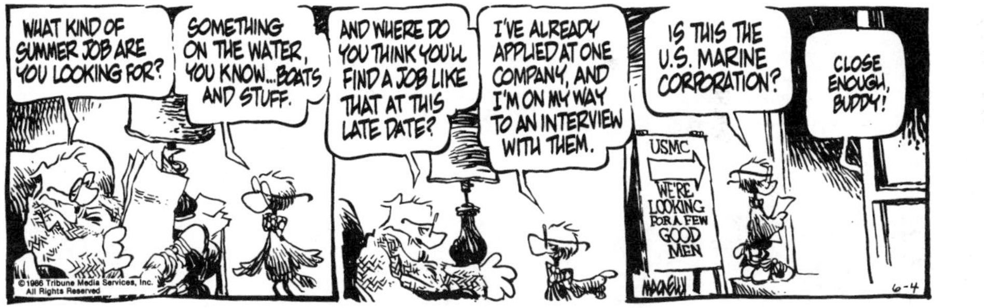
WHAT KIND OF SUMMER JOB ARE YOU LOOKING FOR?
SOMETHING ON THE WATER, YOU KNOW...BOATS AND STUFF.
AND WHERE DO YOU THINK YOU'LL FIND A JOB LIKE THAT AT THIS LATE DATE?
I'VE ALREADY APPLIED AT ONE COMPANY, AND I'M ON MY WAY TO AN INTERVIEW WITH THEM.
USMC
WE'RE LOOKING FOR A FEW GOOD MEN
IS THIS THE U.S. MARINE CORPORATION?
CLOSE ENOUGH, BUDDY!
MACNELLY
6-4

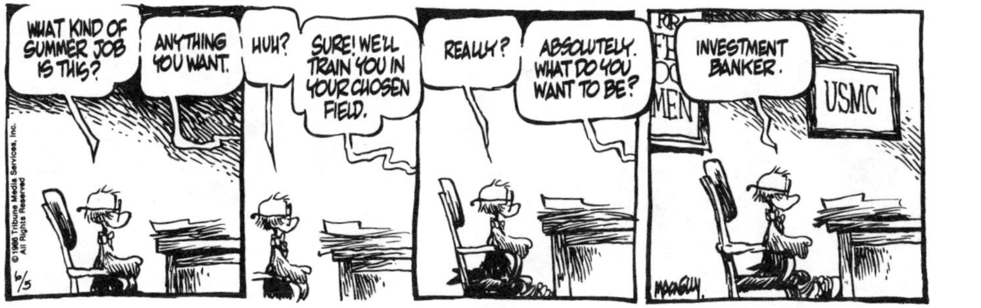
WHAT KIND OF SUMMER JOB IS THIS?
ANYTHING YOU WANT.
HUH?
SURE! WE'LL TRAIN YOU IN YOUR CHOSEN FIELD.
REALLY?
ABSOLUTELY. WHAT DO YOU WANT TO BE?
INVESTMENT BANKER.
USMC
MACNELLY
6/5

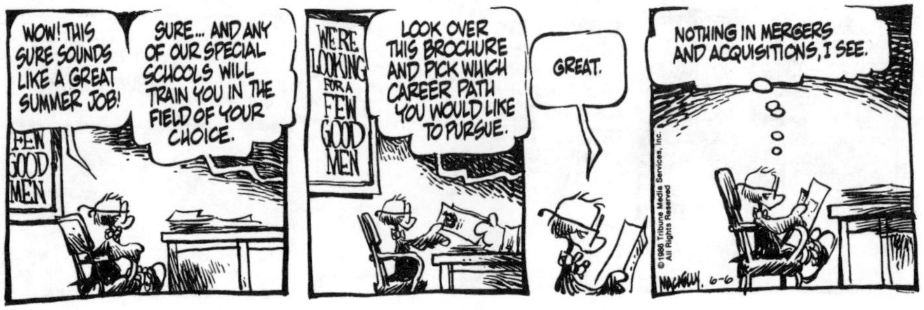
WOW! THIS SURE SOUNDS LIKE A GREAT SUMMER JOB!
SURE... AND ANY OF OUR SPECIAL SCHOOLS WILL TRAIN YOU IN THE FIELD OF YOUR CHOICE.
WE'RE LOOKING FOR A FEW GOOD MEN
LOOK OVER THIS BROCHURE AND PICK WHICH CAREER PATH YOU WOULD LIKE TO PURSUE.
GREAT.
NOTHING IN MERGERS AND ACQUISITIONS, I SEE.

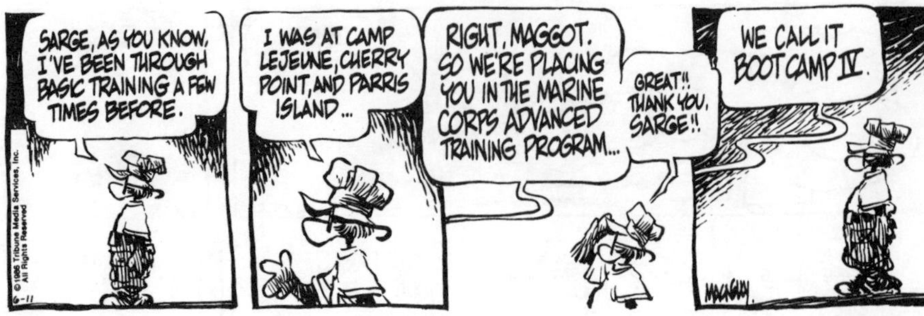
SARGE, AS YOU KNOW, I'VE BEEN THROUGH BASIC TRAINING A FEW TIMES BEFORE.
I WAS AT CAMP LEJEUNE, CHERRY POINT, AND PARRIS ISLAND...
RIGHT, MAGGOT. SO WE'RE PLACING YOU IN THE MARINE CORPS ADVANCED TRAINING PROGRAM...
GREAT!! THANK YOU, SARGE!!
WE CALL IT BOOT CAMP IV.

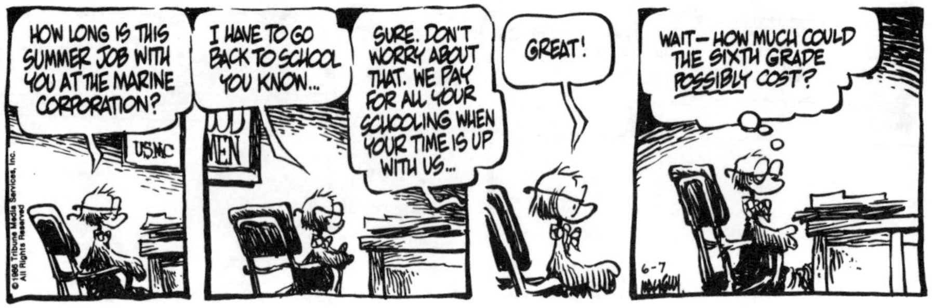
HOW LONG IS THIS SUMMER JOB WITH YOU AT THE MARINE CORPORATION?
USMC
I HAVE TO GO BACK TO SCHOOL YOU KNOW...
SURE. DON'T WORRY ABOUT THAT. WE PAY FOR ALL YOUR SCHOOLING WHEN YOUR TIME IS UP WITH US...
GREAT!
WAIT– HOW MUCH COULD THE SIXTH GRADE POSSIBLY COST?

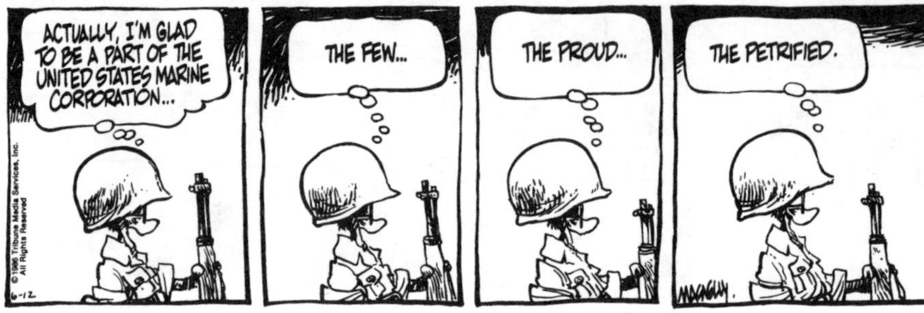
ACTUALLY, I'M GLAD TO BE A PART OF THE UNITED STATES MARINE CORPORATION...
THE FEW...
THE PROUD...
THE PETRIFIED.

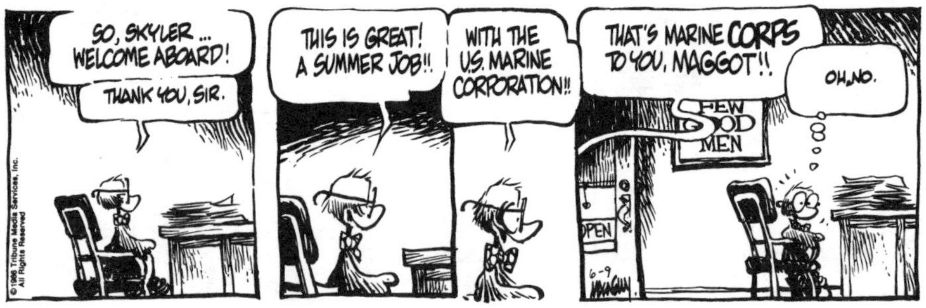
SO, SKYLER ... WELCOME ABOARD!
THANK YOU, SIR.
THIS IS GREAT! A SUMMER JOB!!
WITH THE U.S. MARINE CORPORATION!!
THAT'S MARINE CORPS TO YOU, MAGGOT!!
OH, NO.
FEW GOOD MEN
OPEN

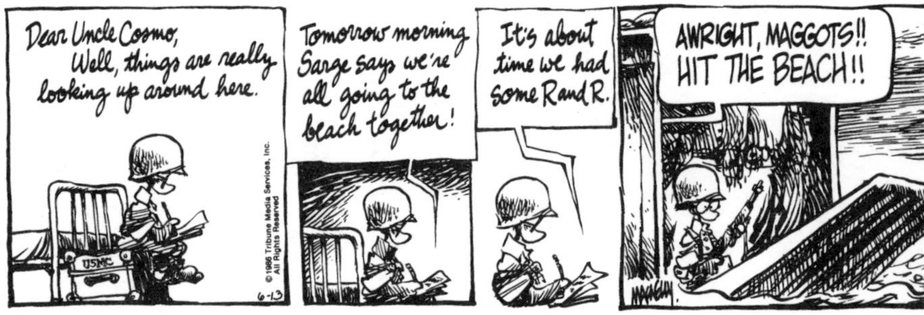
Dear Uncle Cosmo, Well, things are really looking up around here.
Tomorrow morning Sarge says we're all going to the beach together!
It's about time we had some R and R.
AWRIGHT, MAGGOTS!! HIT THE BEACH!!
USMC

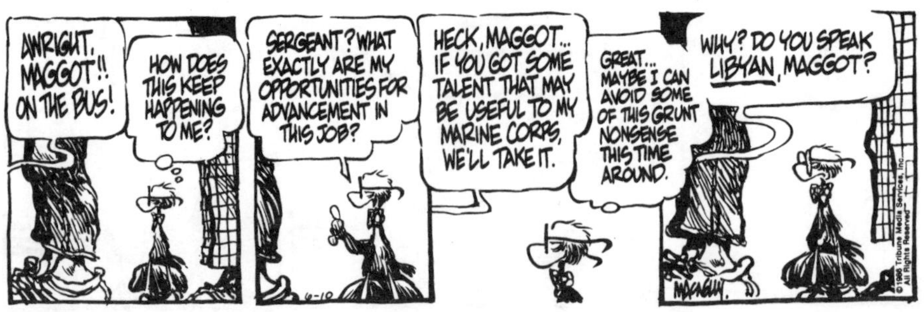
AWRIGHT, MAGGOT!! ON THE BUS!
HOW DOES THIS KEEP HAPPENING TO ME?
SERGEANT? WHAT EXACTLY ARE MY OPPORTUNITIES FOR ADVANCEMENT IN THIS JOB?
HECK, MAGGOT... IF YOU GOT SOME TALENT THAT MAY BE USEFUL TO MY MARINE CORPS, WE'LL TAKE IT.
GREAT... MAYBE I CAN AVOID SOME OF THIS GRUNT NONSENSE THIS TIME AROUND.
WHY? DO YOU SPEAK LIBYAN, MAGGOT?

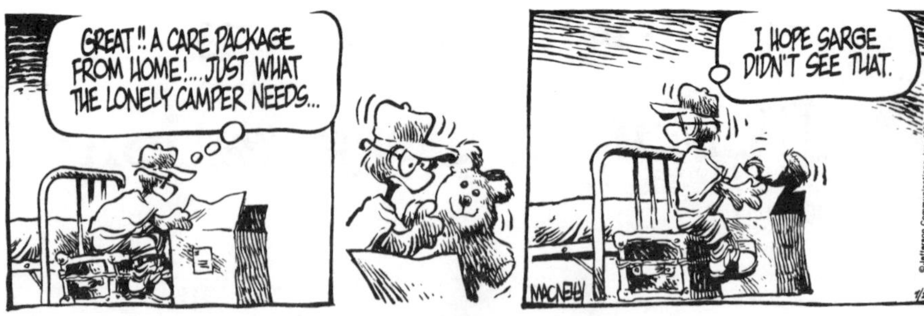
GREAT!! A CARE PACKAGE FROM HOME!... JUST WHAT THE LONELY CAMPER NEEDS...
I HOPE SARGE DIDN'T SEE THAT.

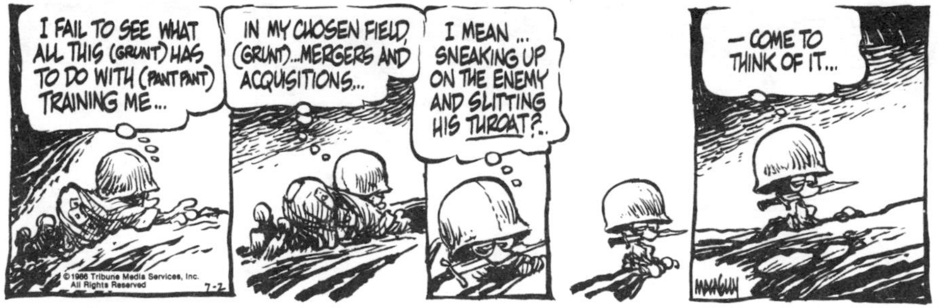
I FAIL TO SEE WHAT ALL THIS (GRUNT) HAS TO DO WITH (PANT PANT) TRAINING ME...
IN MY CHOSEN FIELD, (GRUNT)...MERGERS AND ACQUISITIONS...
I MEAN ... SNEAKING UP ON THE ENEMY AND SLITTING HIS THROAT?...
— COME TO THINK OF IT...
© 1986 Tribune Media Services, Inc. All Rights Reserved
7-2

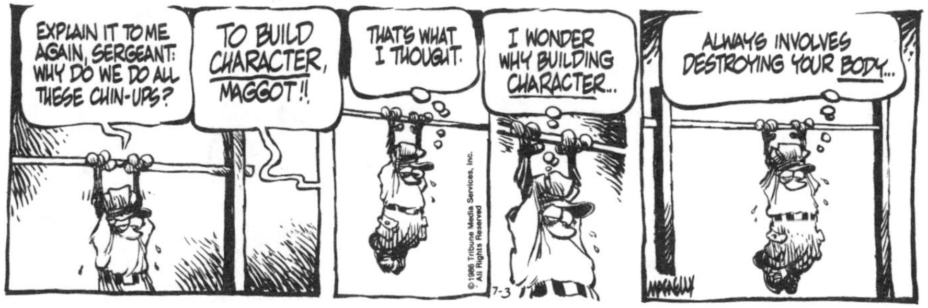
EXPLAIN IT TO ME AGAIN, SERGEANT: WHY DO WE DO ALL THESE CHIN-UPS?
TO BUILD CHARACTER, MAGGOT!!
THAT'S WHAT I THOUGHT.
I WONDER WHY BUILDING CHARACTER...
ALWAYS INVOLVES DESTROYING YOUR BODY...
© 1986 Tribune Media Services, Inc. All Rights Reserved
7-3

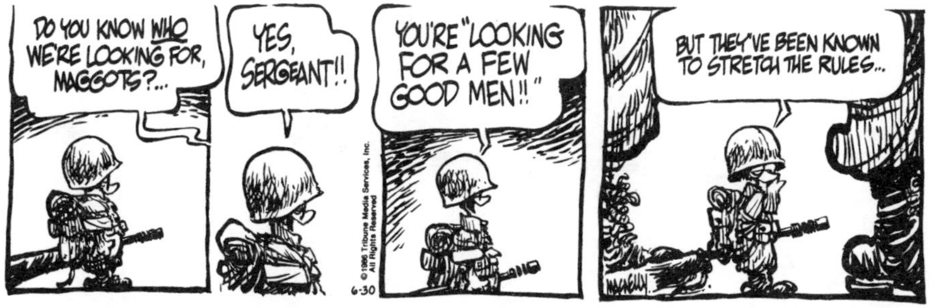
DO YOU KNOW WHO WE'RE LOOKING FOR, MAGGOTS?...
YES, SERGEANT!!
YOU'RE "LOOKING FOR A FEW GOOD MEN!!"
BUT THEY'VE BEEN KNOWN TO STRETCH THE RULES...
© 1986 Tribune Media Services, Inc. All Rights Reserved
6-30

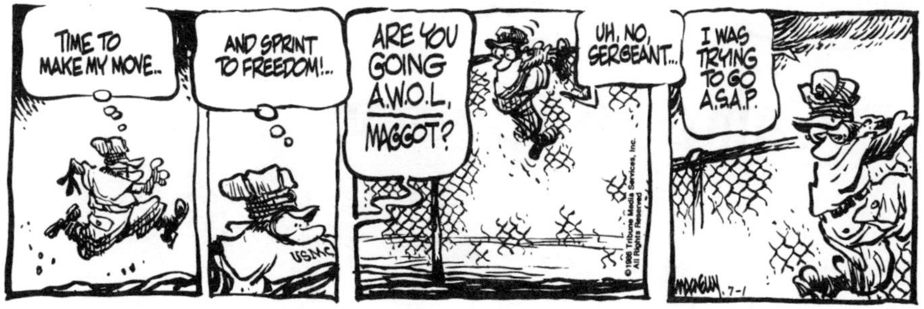
TIME TO MAKE MY MOVE..
AND SPRINT TO FREEDOM!...
USMC
ARE YOU GOING A.W.O.L., MAGGOT?
UH, NO, SERGEANT...
I WAS TRYING TO GO A.S.A.P.
© 1986 Tribune Media Services, Inc. All Rights Reserved
7-1

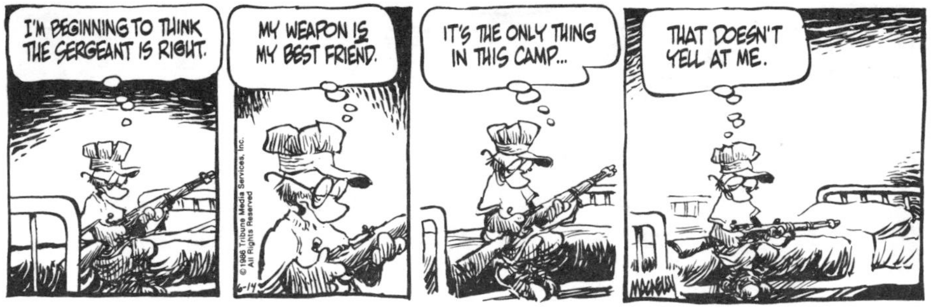
I'M BEGINNING TO THINK THE SERGEANT IS RIGHT.
MY WEAPON IS MY BEST FRIEND.
IT'S THE ONLY THING IN THIS CAMP...
THAT DOESN'T YELL AT ME.
© 1986 Tribune Media Services, Inc. All Rights Reserved
6-14

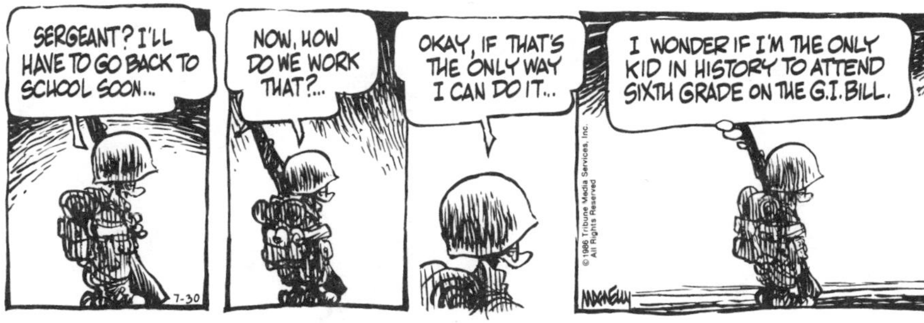
SERGEANT? I'LL HAVE TO GO BACK TO SCHOOL SOON...
NOW, HOW DO WE WORK THAT?...
OKAY, IF THAT'S THE ONLY WAY I CAN DO IT...
I WONDER IF I'M THE ONLY KID IN HISTORY TO ATTEND SIXTH GRADE ON THE G.I. BILL.
© 1986 Tribune Media Services, Inc. All Rights Reserved
7-30

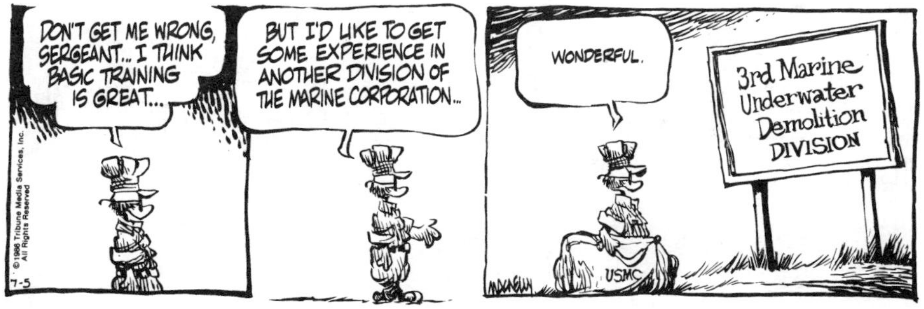
DON'T GET ME WRONG, SERGEANT... I THINK BASIC TRAINING IS GREAT...
BUT I'D LIKE TO GET SOME EXPERIENCE IN ANOTHER DIVISION OF THE MARINE CORPORATION...
WONDERFUL.
3rd Marine Underwater Demolition DIVISION
USMC
© 1986 Tribune Media Services, Inc. All Rights Reserved
7-5

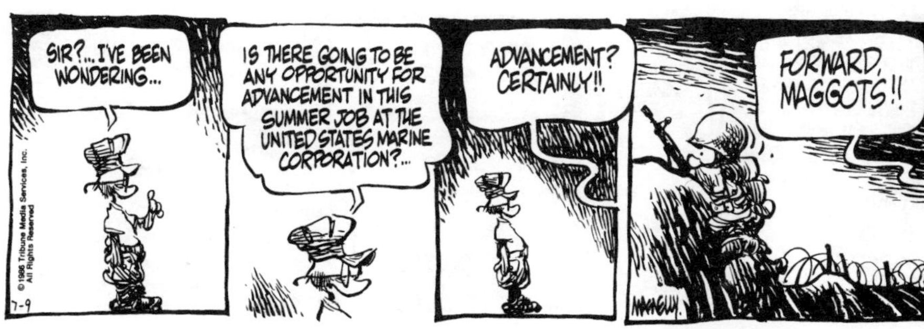
SIR?... I'VE BEEN WONDERING...
IS THERE GOING TO BE ANY OPPORTUNITY FOR ADVANCEMENT IN THIS SUMMER JOB AT THE UNITED STATES MARINE CORPORATION?...
ADVANCEMENT? CERTAINLY!!
FORWARD, MAGGOTS!!
© 1986 Tribune Media Services, Inc. All Rights Reserved
7-9

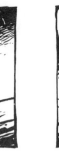

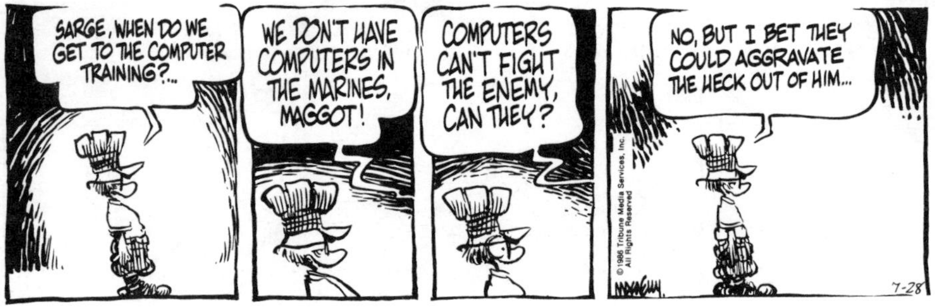
SARGE, WHEN DO WE GET TO THE COMPUTER TRAINING?...
WE DON'T HAVE COMPUTERS IN THE MARINES, MAGGOT!
COMPUTERS CAN'T FIGHT THE ENEMY, CAN THEY?
NO, BUT I BET THEY COULD AGGRAVATE THE HECK OUT OF HIM...
© 1986 Tribune Media Services, Inc. All Rights Reserved
7-28

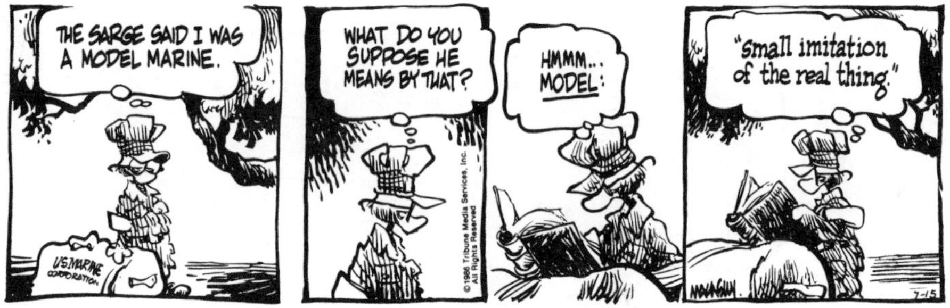
THE SARGE SAID I WAS A MODEL MARINE.
U.S. MARINE CORPORATION
WHAT DO YOU SUPPOSE HE MEANS BY THAT?
© 1986 Tribune Media Services, Inc. All Rights Reserved
HMMM... MODEL:
"small imitation of the real thing."
7-15

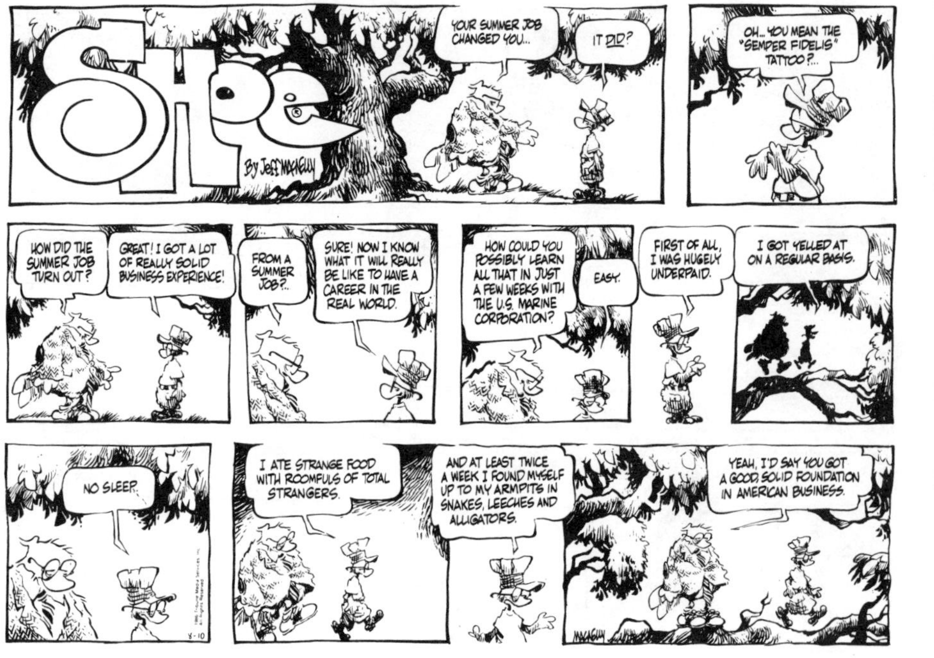
SHOE
By Jeff MacNelly
YOUR SUMMER JOB CHANGED YOU...
IT DID?
OH... YOU MEAN THE "SEMPER FIDELIS" TATTOO?...
HOW DID THE SUMMER JOB TURN OUT?
GREAT! I GOT A LOT OF REALLY SOLID BUSINESS EXPERIENCE!
FROM A SUMMER JOB?..
SURE! NOW I KNOW WHAT IT WILL REALLY BE LIKE TO HAVE A CAREER IN THE REAL WORLD.
HOW COULD YOU POSSIBLY LEARN ALL THAT IN JUST A FEW WEEKS WITH THE U.S. MARINE CORPORATION?
EASY.
FIRST OF ALL, I WAS HUGELY UNDERPAID.
I GOT YELLED AT ON A REGULAR BASIS.
NO SLEEP.
I ATE STRANGE FOOD WITH ROOMFULS OF TOTAL STRANGERS.
AND AT LEAST TWICE A WEEK I FOUND MYSELF UP TO MY ARMPITS IN SNAKES, LEECHES AND ALLIGATORS.
YEAH, I'D SAY YOU GOT A GOOD, SOLID FOUNDATION IN AMERICAN BUSINESS.
8-10

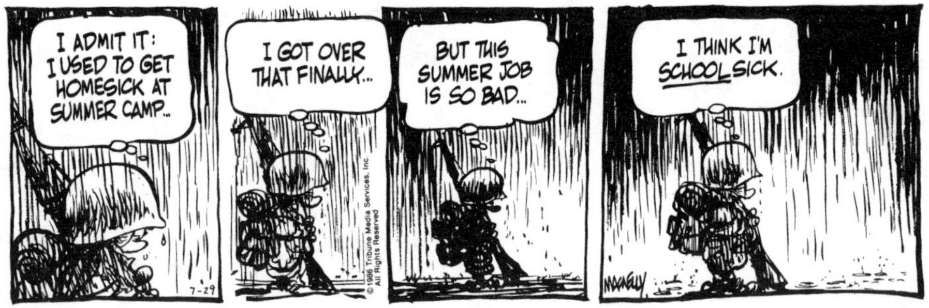
I ADMIT IT: I USED TO GET HOMESICK AT SUMMER CAMP...
7-29
I GOT OVER THAT FINALLY...
© 1986 Tribune Media Services, Inc. All Rights Reserved
BUT THIS SUMMER JOB IS SO BAD...
I THINK I'M SCHOOL SICK.

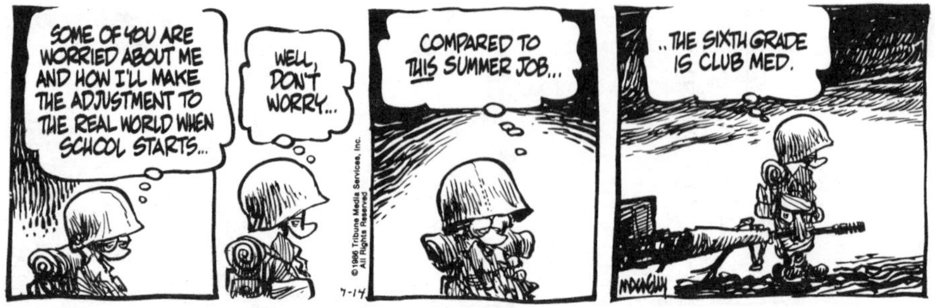
SOME OF YOU ARE WORRIED ABOUT ME AND HOW I'LL MAKE THE ADJUSTMENT TO THE REAL WORLD WHEN SCHOOL STARTS...
WELL, DON'T WORRY...
© 1986 Tribune Media Services, Inc. All Rights Reserved
7-14
COMPARED TO THIS SUMMER JOB...
...THE SIXTH GRADE IS CLUB MED.

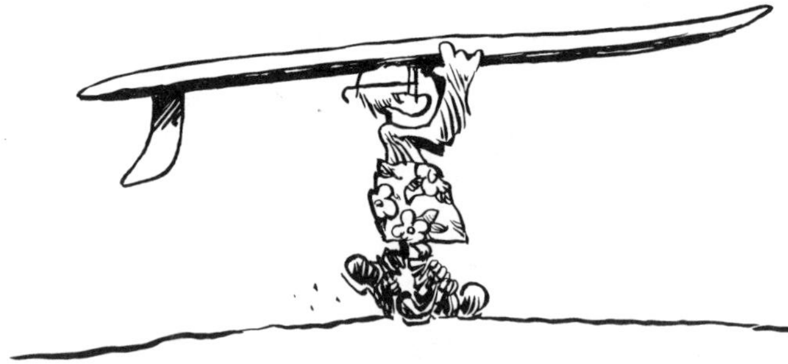

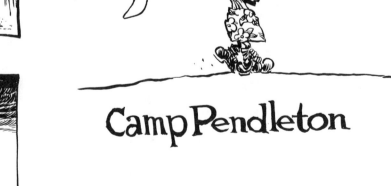

Camp Pendleton

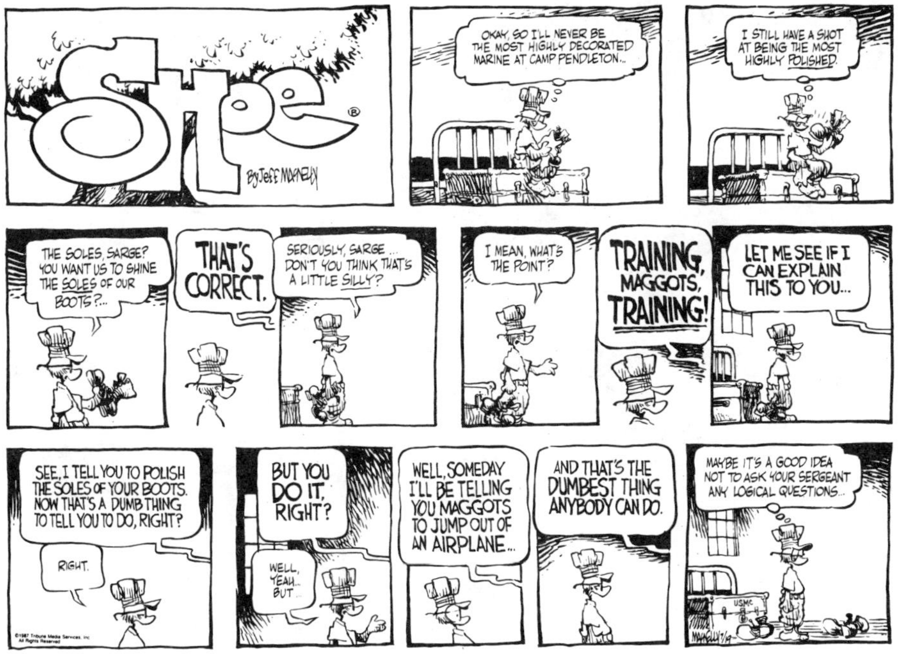

Shoe
By Jeff MacNelly
OKAY, SO I'LL NEVER BE THE MOST HIGHLY DECORATED MARINE AT CAMP PENDLETON...
I STILL HAVE A SHOT AT BEING THE MOST HIGHLY POLISHED.
THE SOLES, SARGE? YOU WANT US TO SHINE THE SOLES OF OUR BOOTS?...
THAT'S CORRECT.
SERIOUSLY, SARGE... DON'T YOU THINK THAT'S A LITTLE SILLY?
I MEAN, WHAT'S THE POINT?
TRAINING, MAGGOTS, TRAINING!
LET ME SEE IF I CAN EXPLAIN THIS TO YOU...
SEE, I TELL YOU TO POLISH THE SOLES OF YOUR BOOTS. NOW THAT'S A DUMB THING TO TELL YOU TO DO, RIGHT?
RIGHT.
BUT YOU DO IT, RIGHT?
WELL, YEAH... BUT...
WELL, SOMEDAY I'LL BE TELLING YOU MAGGOTS TO JUMP OUT OF AN AIRPLANE...
AND THAT'S THE DUMBEST THING ANYBODY CAN DO.
MAYBE IT'S A GOOD IDEA NOT TO ASK YOUR SERGEANT ANY LOGICAL QUESTIONS...
USMC
©1987 Tribune Media Services, Inc. All Rights Reserved

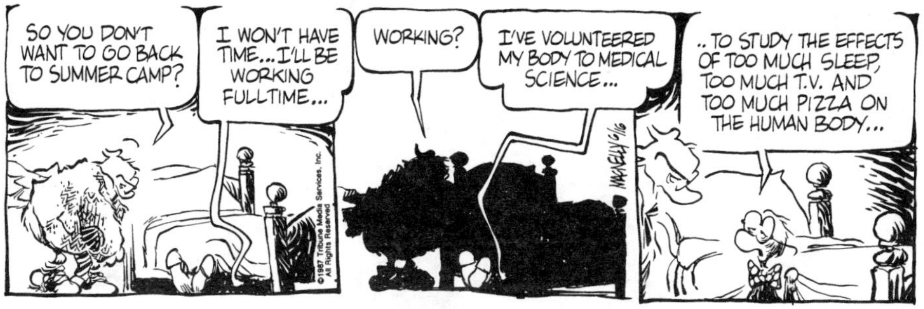

SO YOU DON'T WANT TO GO BACK TO SUMMER CAMP?
I WON'T HAVE TIME... I'LL BE WORKING FULLTIME...
WORKING?
I'VE VOLUNTEERED MY BODY TO MEDICAL SCIENCE...
.. TO STUDY THE EFFECTS OF TOO MUCH SLEEP, TOO MUCH T.V. AND TOO MUCH PIZZA ON THE HUMAN BODY...
©1987 Tribune Media Services, Inc. All Rights Reserved
MACNELLY 6/16

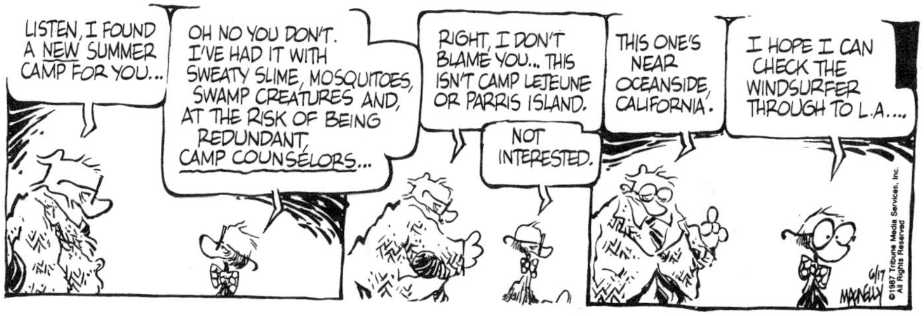

LISTEN, I FOUND A NEW SUMMER CAMP FOR YOU...
OH NO YOU DON'T. I'VE HAD IT WITH SWEATY SLIME, MOSQUITOES, SWAMP CREATURES AND, AT THE RISK OF BEING REDUNDANT, CAMP COUNSELORS...
RIGHT, I DON'T BLAME YOU... THIS ISN'T CAMP LEJEUNE OR PARRIS ISLAND.
NOT INTERESTED.
THIS ONE'S NEAR OCEANSIDE, CALIFORNIA.
I HOPE I CAN CHECK THE WINDSURFER THROUGH TO L.A....
©1987 Tribune Media Services, Inc. All Rights Reserved
MACNELLY 6/17

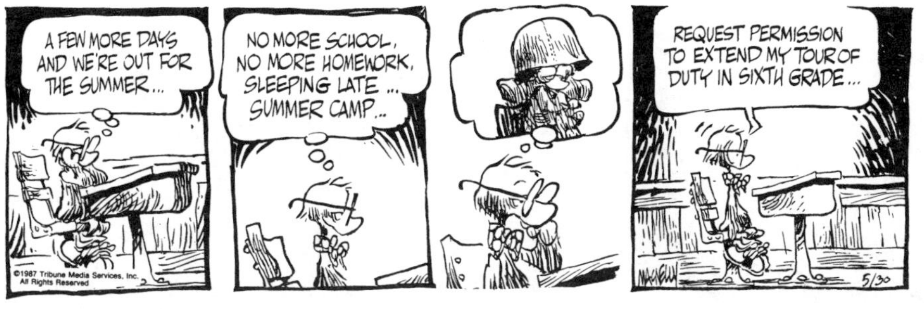

A FEW MORE DAYS AND WE'RE OUT FOR THE SUMMER...
NO MORE SCHOOL, NO MORE HOMEWORK, SLEEPING LATE ... SUMMER CAMP...
REQUEST PERMISSION TO EXTEND MY TOUR OF DUTY IN SIXTH GRADE...
©1987 Tribune Media Services, Inc. All Rights Reserved
MACNELLY 5/30

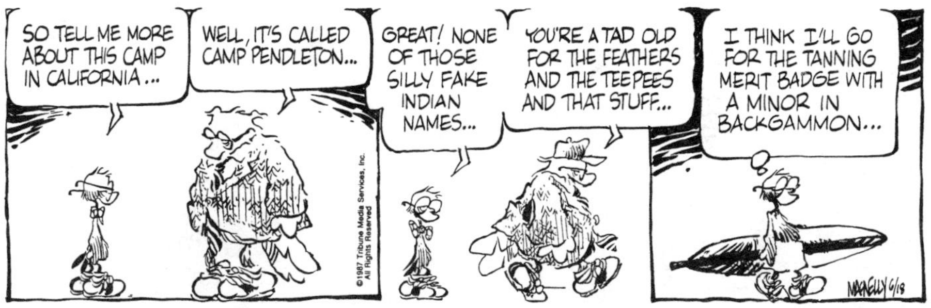

SO TELL ME MORE ABOUT THIS CAMP IN CALIFORNIA...
WELL, IT'S CALLED CAMP PENDLETON...
GREAT! NONE OF THOSE SILLY FAKE INDIAN NAMES...
YOU'RE A TAD OLD FOR THE FEATHERS AND THE TEEPEES AND THAT STUFF...
I THINK I'LL GO FOR THE TANNING MERIT BADGE WITH A MINOR IN BACKGAMMON...
©1987 Tribune Media Services, Inc. All Rights Reserved
MACNELLY 6/18

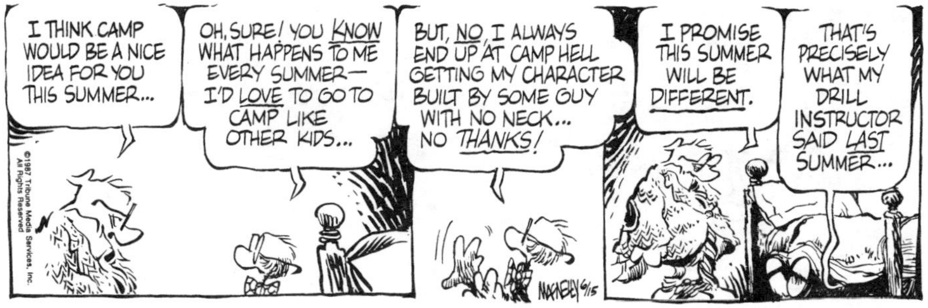

I THINK CAMP WOULD BE A NICE IDEA FOR YOU THIS SUMMER...
OH, SURE! YOU KNOW WHAT HAPPENS TO ME EVERY SUMMER— I'D LOVE TO GO TO CAMP LIKE OTHER KIDS...
BUT, NO, I ALWAYS END UP AT CAMP HELL GETTING MY CHARACTER BUILT BY SOME GUY WITH NO NECK... NO THANKS!
I PROMISE THIS SUMMER WILL BE DIFFERENT.
THAT'S PRECISELY WHAT MY DRILL INSTRUCTOR SAID LAST SUMMER...
©1987 Tribune Media Services, Inc. All Rights Reserved
MACNELLY 6/15

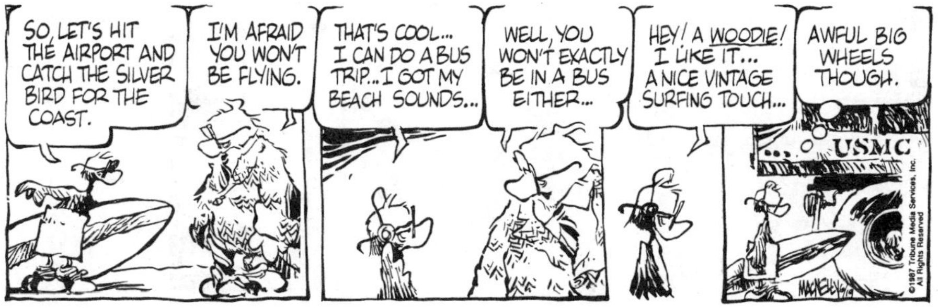

SO, LET'S HIT THE AIRPORT AND CATCH THE SILVER BIRD FOR THE COAST.
I'M AFRAID YOU WON'T BE FLYING.
THAT'S COOL... I CAN DO A BUS TRIP... I GOT MY BEACH SOUNDS...
WELL, YOU WON'T EXACTLY BE IN A BUS EITHER...
HEY! A WOODIE! I LIKE IT... A NICE VINTAGE SURFING TOUCH...
AWFUL BIG WHEELS THOUGH.
USMC
©1987 Tribune Media Services, Inc. All Rights Reserved

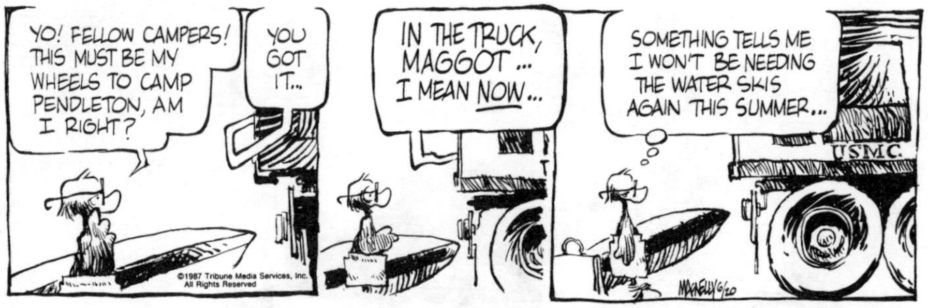
YO! FELLOW CAMPERS! THIS MUST BE MY WHEELS TO CAMP PENDLETON, AM I RIGHT?
YOU GOT IT..
IN THE TRUCK, MAGGOT ... I MEAN NOW...
SOMETHING TELLS ME I WON'T BE NEEDING THE WATER SKIS AGAIN THIS SUMMER...
USMC
©1987 Tribune Media Services, Inc. All Rights Reserved
MACNELLY 6/20

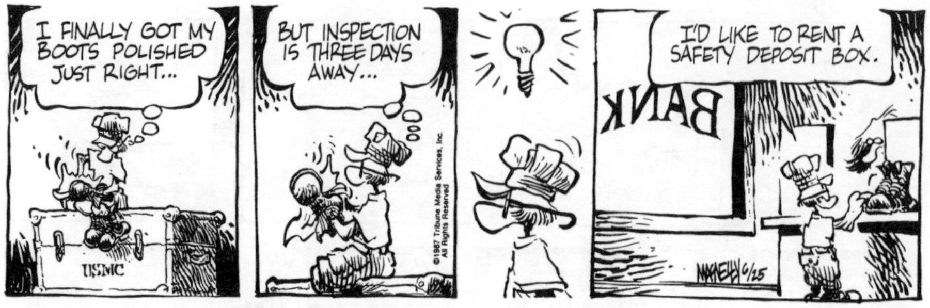
I FINALLY GOT MY BOOTS POLISHED JUST RIGHT...
USMC
BUT INSPECTION IS THREE DAYS AWAY...
©1987 Tribune Media Services, Inc. All Rights Reserved
I'D LIKE TO RENT A SAFETY DEPOSIT BOX.
BANK
MACNELLY 6/25

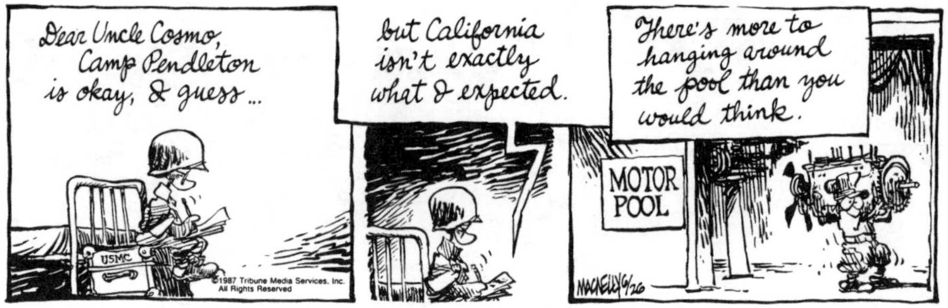
Dear Uncle Cosmo, Camp Pendleton is okay, I guess...
USMC
©1987 Tribune Media Services, Inc. All Rights Reserved
but California isn't exactly what I expected.
There's more to hanging around the pool than you would think.
MOTOR POOL
MACNELLY 6/26

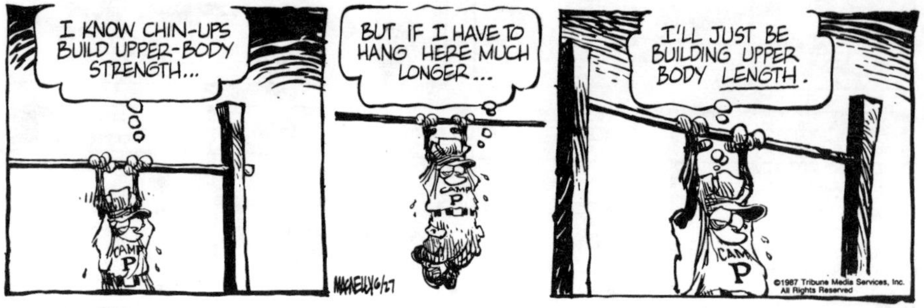
I KNOW CHIN-UPS BUILD UPPER-BODY STRENGTH...
BUT IF I HAVE TO HANG HERE MUCH LONGER...
MACNELLY 6/27
I'LL JUST BE BUILDING UPPER BODY LENGTH.
©1987 Tribune Media Services, Inc. All Rights Reserved

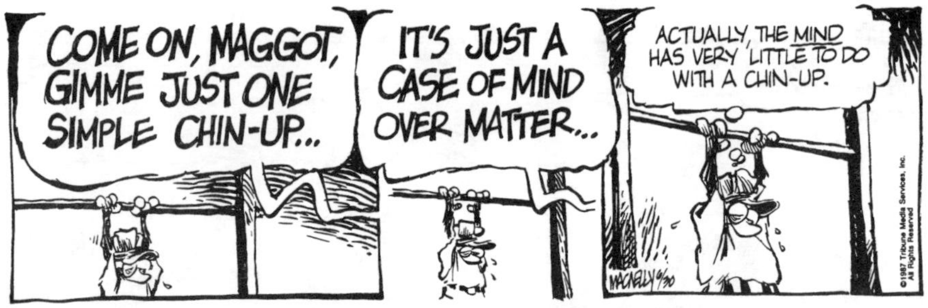
COME ON, MAGGOT, GIMME JUST ONE SIMPLE CHIN-UP...
IT'S JUST A CASE OF MIND OVER MATTER...
ACTUALLY, THE MIND HAS VERY LITTLE TO DO WITH A CHIN-UP.
MACNELLY 6/30
©1987 Tribune Media Services, Inc. All Rights Reserved

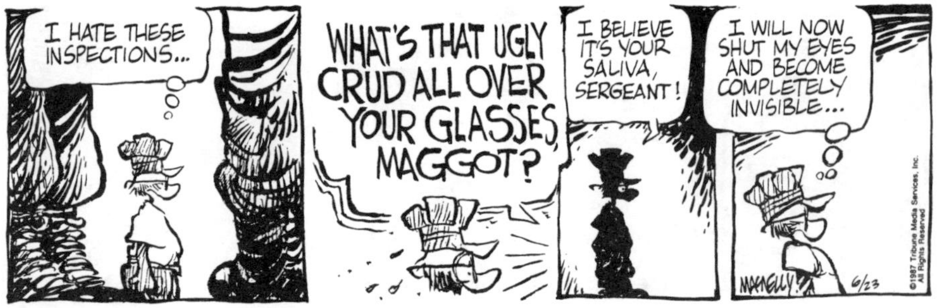
I HATE THESE INSPECTIONS...
WHAT'S THAT UGLY CRUD ALL OVER YOUR GLASSES, MAGGOT?
I BELIEVE IT'S YOUR SALIVA, SERGEANT!
I WILL NOW SHUT MY EYES AND BECOME COMPLETELY INVISIBLE...
MACNELLY 6/23
©1987 Tribune Media Services, Inc. All Rights Reserved

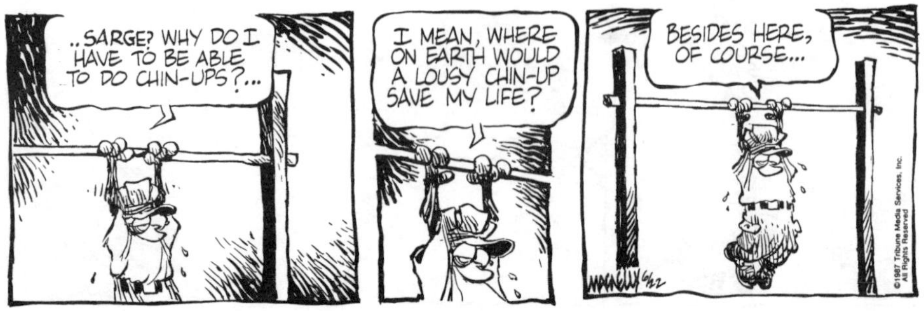
..SARGE? WHY DO I HAVE TO BE ABLE TO DO CHIN-UPS?...
I MEAN, WHERE ON EARTH WOULD A LOUSY CHIN-UP SAVE MY LIFE?
BESIDES HERE, OF COURSE...
MACNELLY 6/22
©1987 Tribune Media Services, Inc. All Rights Reserved

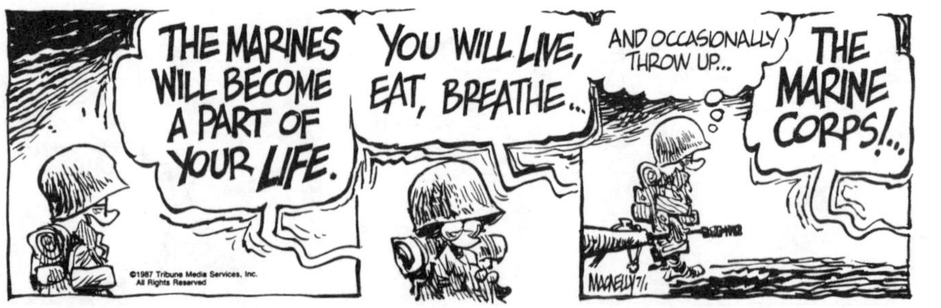
THE MARINES WILL BECOME A PART OF YOUR LIFE.
©1987 Tribune Media Services, Inc. All Rights Reserved
YOU WILL LIVE, EAT, BREATHE...
AND OCCASIONALLY THROW UP...
THE MARINE CORPS!..
MACNELLY 7/1

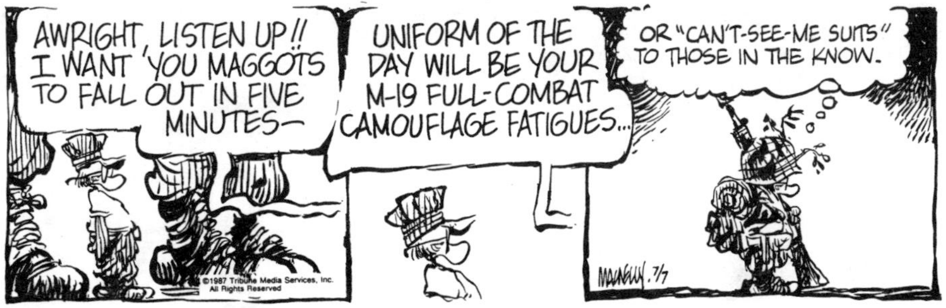
AWRIGHT, LISTEN UP!! I WANT YOU MAGGOTS TO FALL OUT IN FIVE MINUTES—
UNIFORM OF THE DAY WILL BE YOUR M-19 FULL-COMBAT CAMOUFLAGE FATIGUES...
OR "CAN'T-SEE-ME SUITS" TO THOSE IN THE KNOW.
©1987 Tribune Media Services, Inc. All Rights Reserved

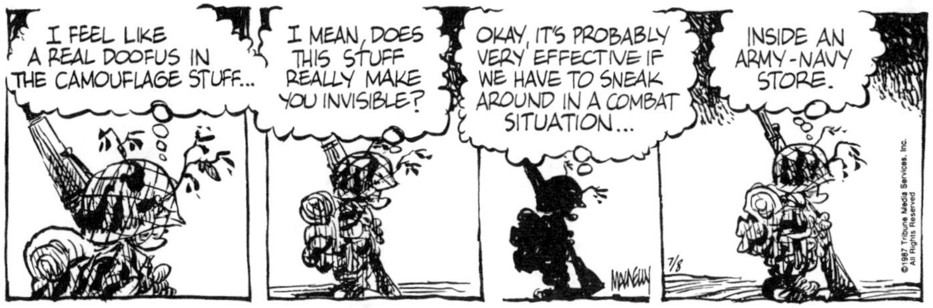
I FEEL LIKE A REAL DOOFUS IN THE CAMOUFLAGE STUFF...
I MEAN, DOES THIS STUFF REALLY MAKE YOU INVISIBLE?
OKAY, IT'S PROBABLY VERY EFFECTIVE IF WE HAVE TO SNEAK AROUND IN A COMBAT SITUATION...
INSIDE AN ARMY-NAVY STORE.
©1987 Tribune Media Services, Inc. All Rights Reserved

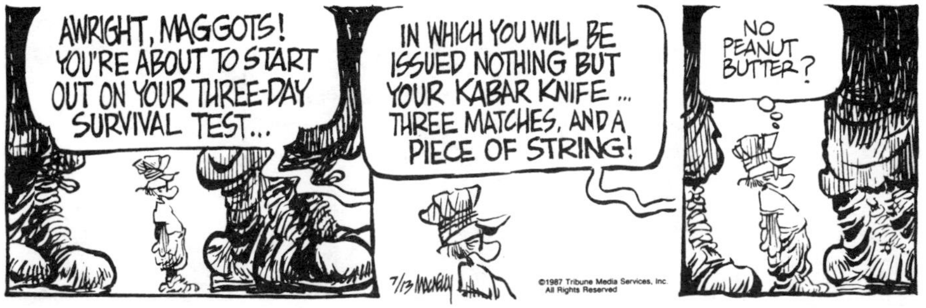
AWRIGHT, MAGGOTS! YOU'RE ABOUT TO START OUT ON YOUR THREE-DAY SURVIVAL TEST...
IN WHICH YOU WILL BE ISSUED NOTHING BUT YOUR KABAR KNIFE... THREE MATCHES, AND A PIECE OF STRING!
NO PEANUT BUTTER?
©1987 Tribune Media Services, Inc. All Rights Reserved

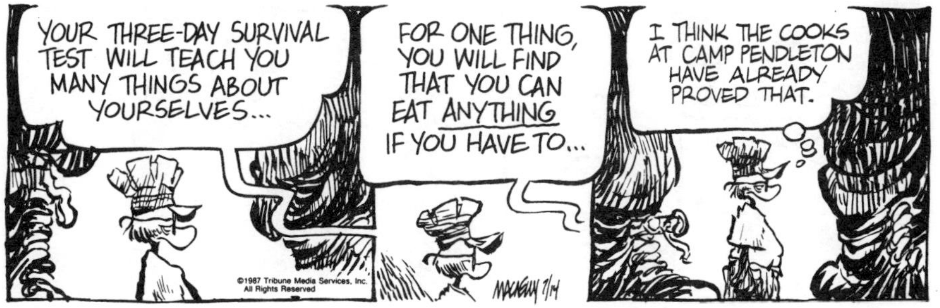
YOUR THREE-DAY SURVIVAL TEST WILL TEACH YOU MANY THINGS ABOUT YOURSELVES...
FOR ONE THING, YOU WILL FIND THAT YOU CAN EAT ANYTHING IF YOU HAVE TO...
I THINK THE COOKS AT CAMP PENDLETON HAVE ALREADY PROVED THAT.
©1987 Tribune Media Services, Inc. All Rights Reserved

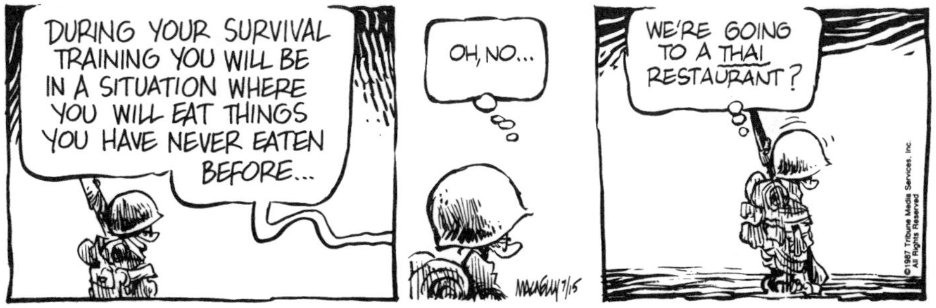
DURING YOUR SURVIVAL TRAINING YOU WILL BE IN A SITUATION WHERE YOU WILL EAT THINGS YOU HAVE NEVER EATEN BEFORE...
OH, NO...
WE'RE GOING TO A THAI RESTAURANT?
©1987 Tribune Media Services, Inc. All Rights Reserved

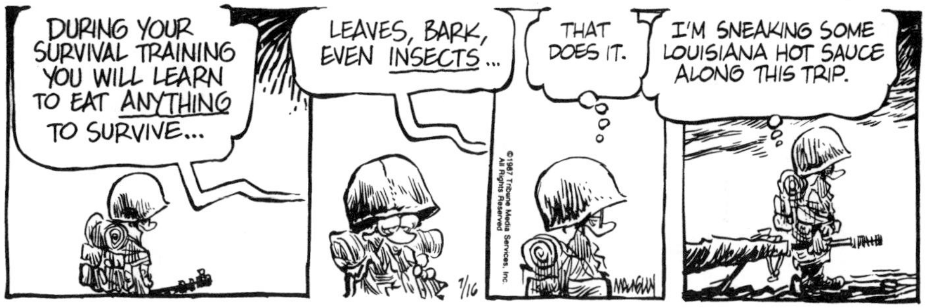
DURING YOUR SURVIVAL TRAINING YOU WILL LEARN TO EAT ANYTHING TO SURVIVE...
LEAVES, BARK, EVEN INSECTS...
THAT DOES IT.
I'M SNEAKING SOME LOUISIANA HOT SAUCE ALONG THIS TRIP.
©1987 Tribune Media Services, Inc. All Rights Reserved

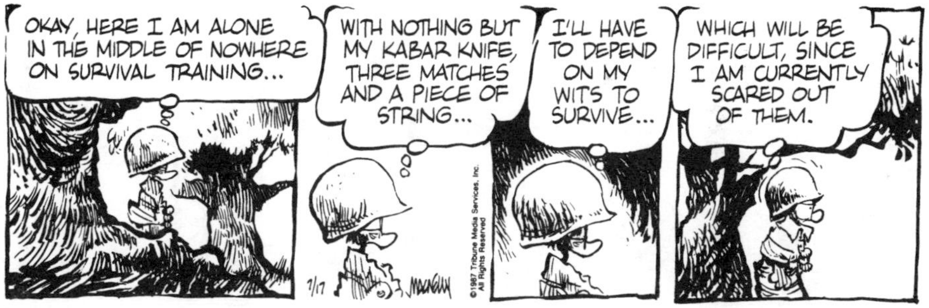
OKAY, HERE I AM ALONE IN THE MIDDLE OF NOWHERE ON SURVIVAL TRAINING...
WITH NOTHING BUT MY KABAR KNIFE, THREE MATCHES AND A PIECE OF STRING...
I'LL HAVE TO DEPEND ON MY WITS TO SURVIVE...
WHICH WILL BE DIFFICULT, SINCE I AM CURRENTLY SCARED OUT OF THEM.
©1987 Tribune Media Services, Inc. All Rights Reserved

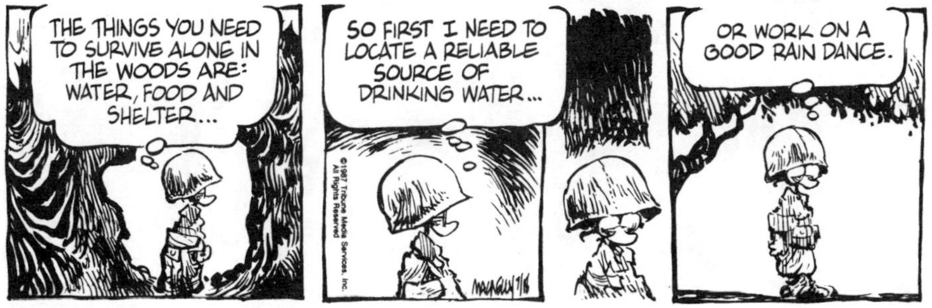
THE THINGS YOU NEED TO SURVIVE ALONE IN THE WOODS ARE: WATER, FOOD AND SHELTER...
SO FIRST I NEED TO LOCATE A RELIABLE SOURCE OF DRINKING WATER...
OR WORK ON A GOOD RAIN DANCE.
©1987 Tribune Media Services, Inc. All Rights Reserved

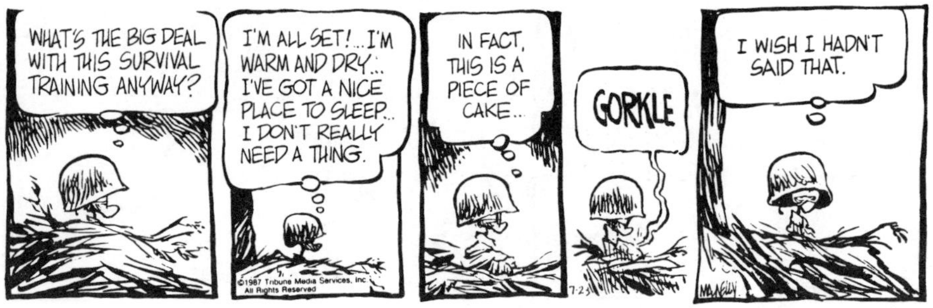
WHAT'S THE BIG DEAL WITH THIS SURVIVAL TRAINING ANYWAY?
I'M ALL SET!...I'M WARM AND DRY... I'VE GOT A NICE PLACE TO SLEEP... I DON'T REALLY NEED A THING.
IN FACT, THIS IS A PIECE OF CAKE...
GORKLE
I WISH I HADN'T SAID THAT.
©1987 Tribune Media Services, Inc. All Rights Reserved

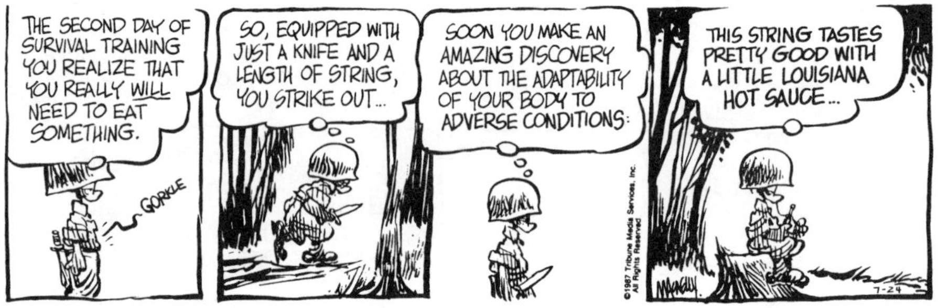
THE SECOND DAY OF SURVIVAL TRAINING YOU REALIZE THAT YOU REALLY WILL NEED TO EAT SOMETHING.
GORKLE
SO, EQUIPPED WITH JUST A KNIFE AND A LENGTH OF STRING, YOU STRIKE OUT...
SOON YOU MAKE AN AMAZING DISCOVERY ABOUT THE ADAPTABILITY OF YOUR BODY TO ADVERSE CONDITIONS:
THIS STRING TASTES PRETTY GOOD WITH A LITTLE LOUISIANA HOT SAUCE...
©1987 Tribune Media Services, Inc. All Rights Reserved

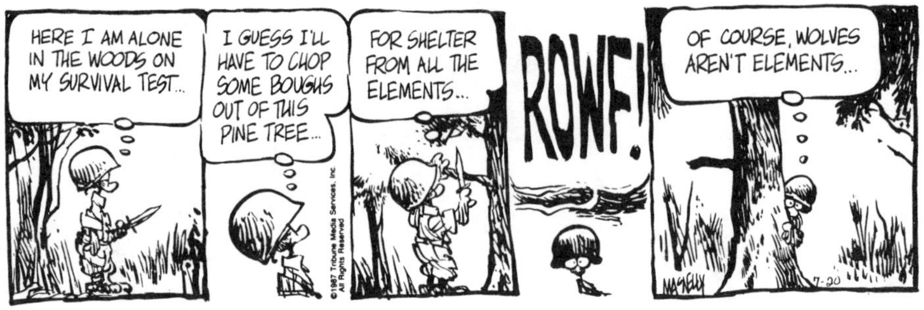
HERE I AM ALONE IN THE WOODS ON MY SURVIVAL TEST...
I GUESS I'LL HAVE TO CHOP SOME BOUGHS OUT OF THIS PINE TREE...
FOR SHELTER FROM ALL THE ELEMENTS...
ROWF!
OF COURSE, WOLVES AREN'T ELEMENTS...
©1987 Tribune Media Services, Inc. All Rights Reserved

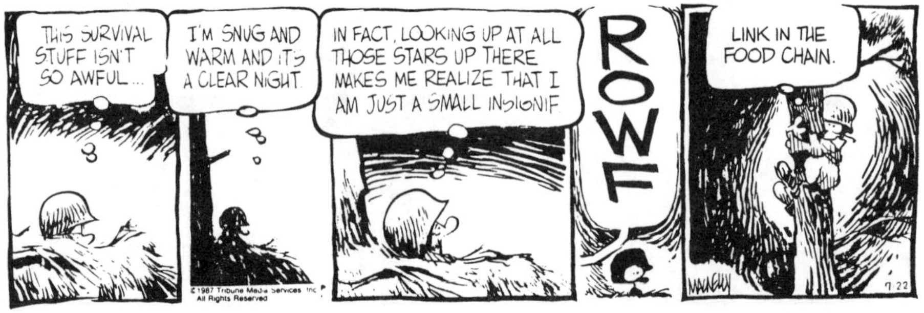
THIS SURVIVAL STUFF ISN'T SO AWFUL...
I'M SNUG AND WARM AND IT'S A CLEAR NIGHT.
IN FACT, LOOKING UP AT ALL THOSE STARS UP THERE MAKES ME REALIZE THAT I AM JUST A SMALL INSIGNIF
ROWF
LINK IN THE FOOD CHAIN.
©1987 Tribune Media Services, Inc. All Rights Reserved

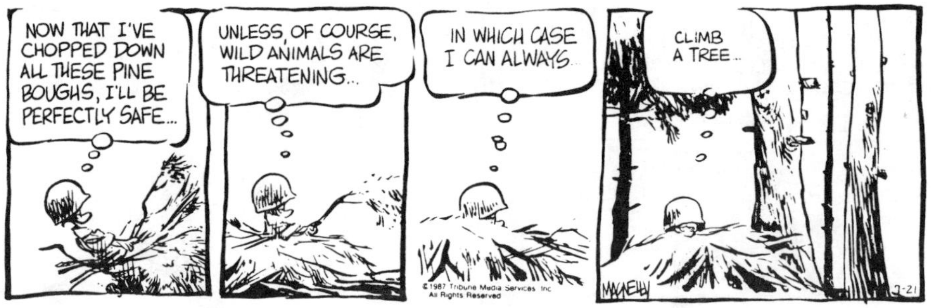
NOW THAT I'VE CHOPPED DOWN ALL THESE PINE BOUGHS, I'LL BE PERFECTLY SAFE...
UNLESS, OF COURSE, WILD ANIMALS ARE THREATENING...
IN WHICH CASE I CAN ALWAYS...
CLIMB A TREE...
©1987 Tribune Media Services, Inc. All Rights Reserved

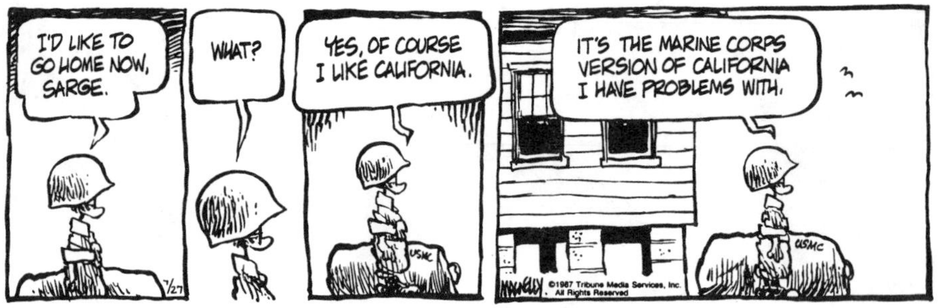
I'D LIKE TO GO HOME NOW, SARGE.
WHAT?
YES, OF COURSE I LIKE CALIFORNIA.
IT'S THE MARINE CORPS VERSION OF CALIFORNIA I HAVE PROBLEMS WITH.
USMC
©1987 Tribune Media Services, Inc. All Rights Reserved

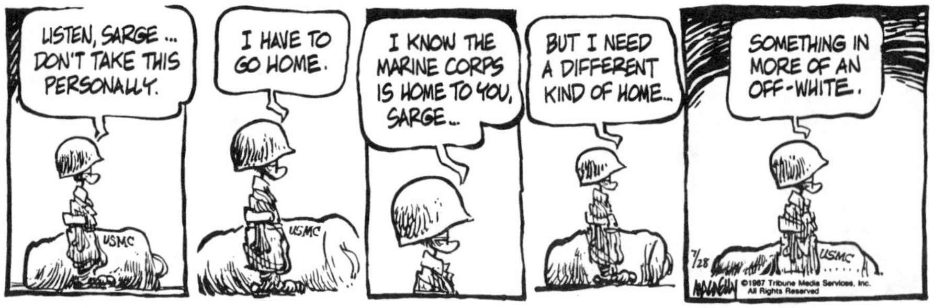
LISTEN, SARGE ... DON'T TAKE THIS PERSONALLY.
I HAVE TO GO HOME.
I KNOW THE MARINE CORPS IS HOME TO YOU, SARGE...
BUT I NEED A DIFFERENT KIND OF HOME...
SOMETHING IN MORE OF AN OFF-WHITE.
USMC
©1987 Tribune Media Services, Inc. All Rights Reserved

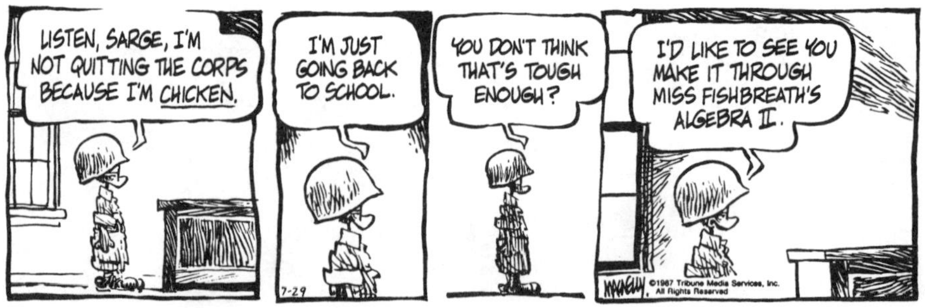
LISTEN, SARGE, I'M NOT QUITTING THE CORPS BECAUSE I'M CHICKEN.
I'M JUST GOING BACK TO SCHOOL.
YOU DON'T THINK THAT'S TOUGH ENOUGH?
I'D LIKE TO SEE YOU MAKE IT THROUGH MISS FISHBREATH'S ALGEBRA II.
©1987 Tribune Media Services, Inc. All Rights Reserved

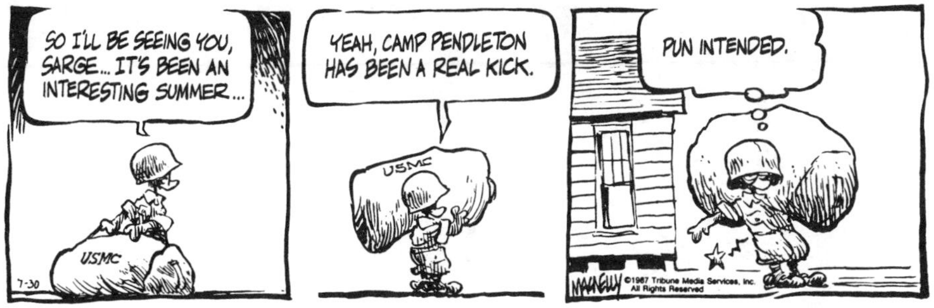
SO I'LL BE SEEING YOU, SARGE... IT'S BEEN AN INTERESTING SUMMER...
YEAH, CAMP PENDLETON HAS BEEN A REAL KICK.
PUN INTENDED.
USMC
7-30
MACNELLY
©1987 Tribune Media Services, Inc. All Rights Reserved

From the original book:

Dedicated to all who sacrifice in service to their country — especially to those who served in Vietnam, those who are still missing, my friends in the 4th Allied P.O.W. Wing, and the devoted families of all of the above.

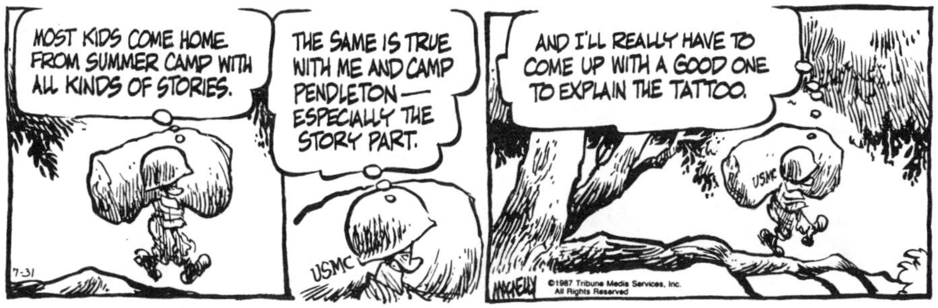
MOST KIDS COME HOME FROM SUMMER CAMP WITH ALL KINDS OF STORIES.
THE SAME IS TRUE WITH ME AND CAMP PENDLETON — ESPECIALLY THE STORY PART.
AND I'LL REALLY HAVE TO COME UP WITH A GOOD ONE TO EXPLAIN THE TATTOO.
USMC
7-31
MACNELLY
©1987 Tribune Media Services, Inc. All Rights Reserved

All royalties from this book go to the Navy Relief Fund.

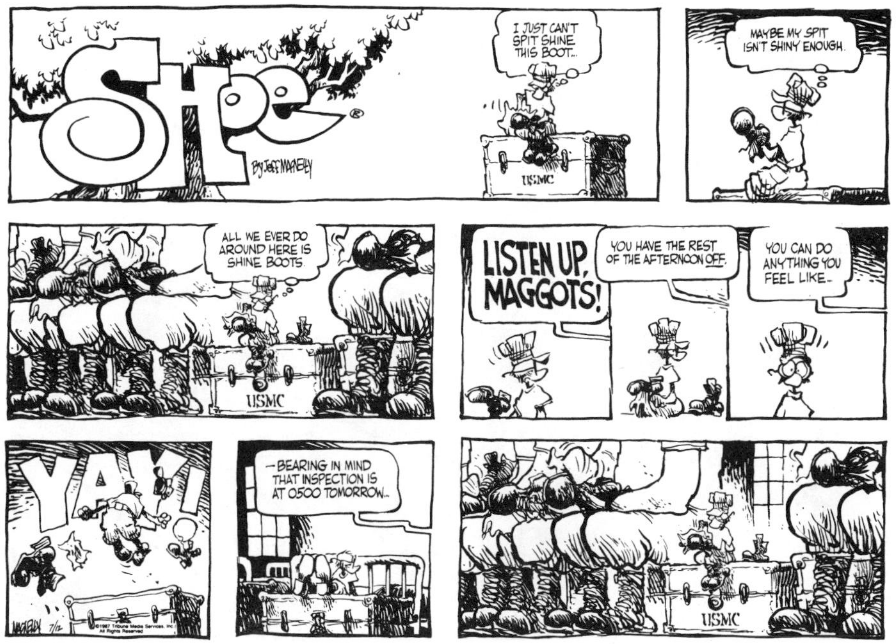
Shoe®
By JEFF MACNELLY
I JUST CAN'T SPIT SHINE THIS BOOT...
USMC
MAYBE MY SPIT ISN'T SHINY ENOUGH.
ALL WE EVER DO AROUND HERE IS SHINE BOOTS.
USMC
LISTEN UP, MAGGOTS!
YOU HAVE THE REST OF THE AFTERNOON OFF.
YOU CAN DO ANYTHING YOU FEEL LIKE...
YAY!
MACNELLY 7/12
©1987 Tribune Media Services, Inc. All Rights Reserved
—BEARING IN MIND THAT INSPECTION IS AT 0500 TOMORROW...
USMC

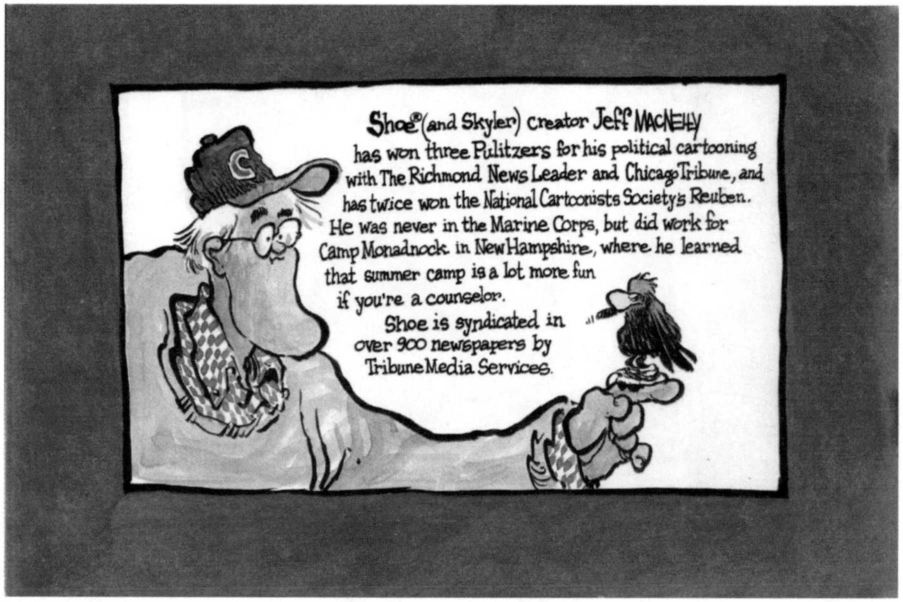
Shoe® (and Skyler) creator Jeff MACNELLY has won three Pulitzers for his political cartooning with The Richmond News Leader and Chicago Tribune, and has twice won the National Cartoonists Society's Reuben. He was never in the Marine Corps, but did work for Camp Monadnock in New Hampshire, where he learned that summer camp is a lot more fun if you're a counselor.
Shoe is syndicated in over 900 newspapers by Tribune Media Services.

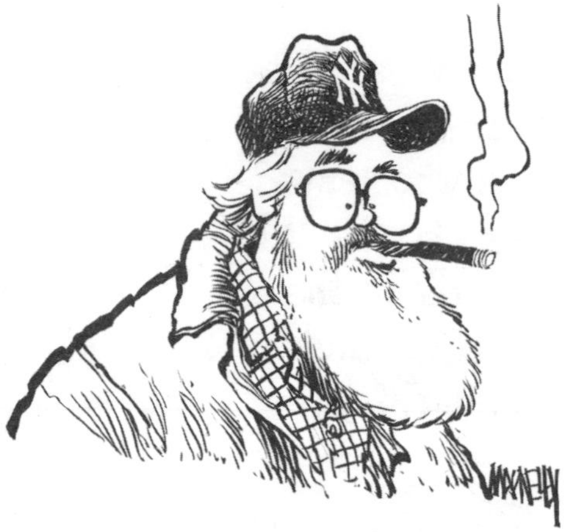

The '90s

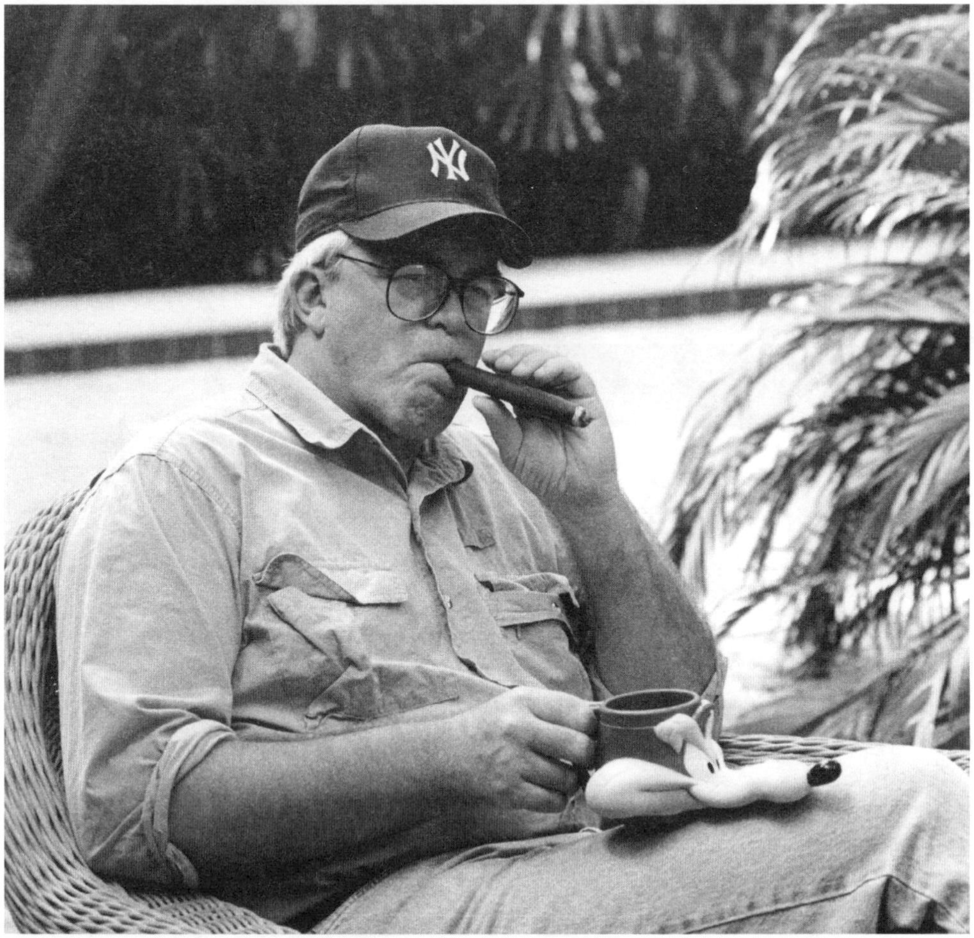

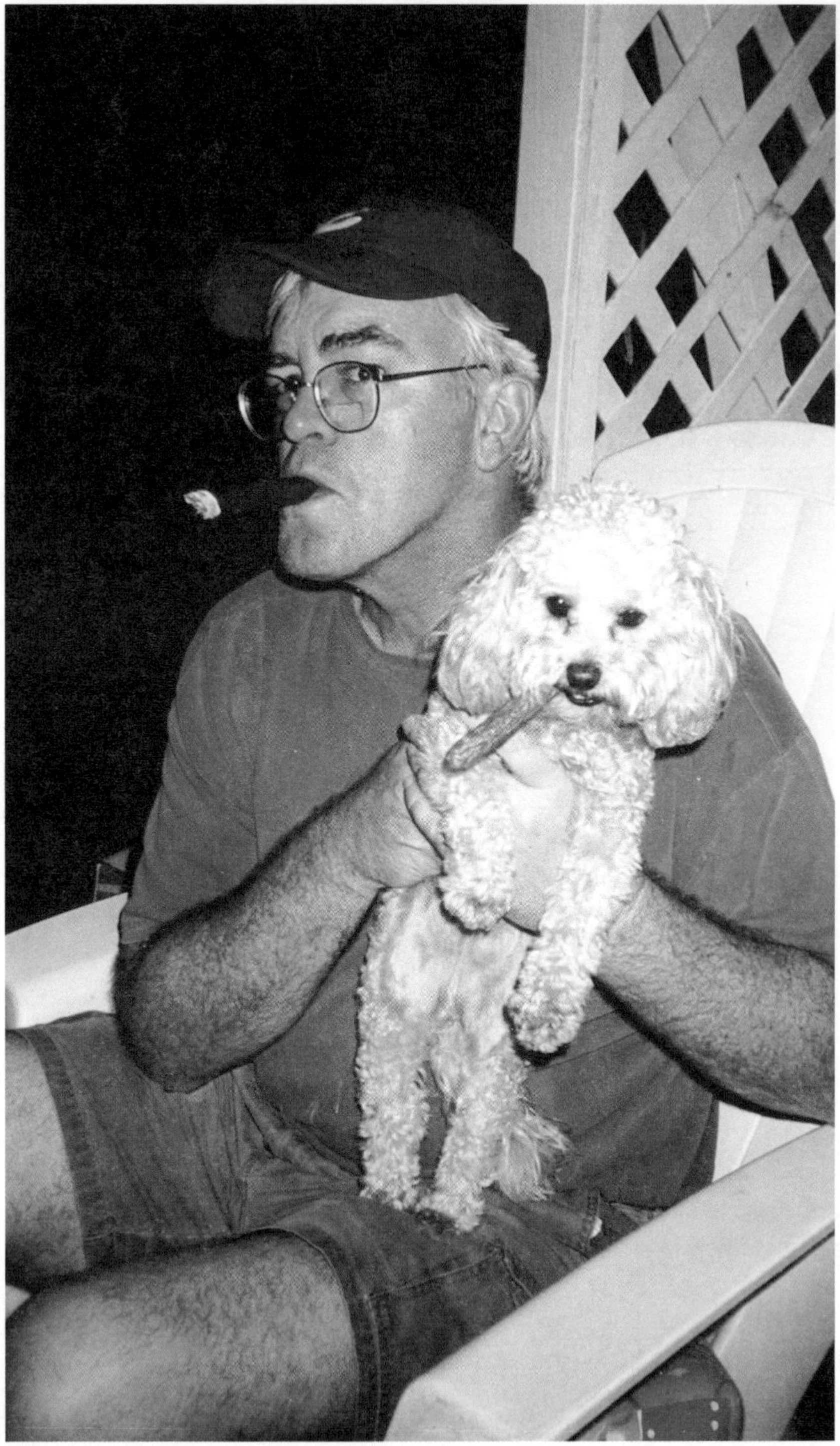

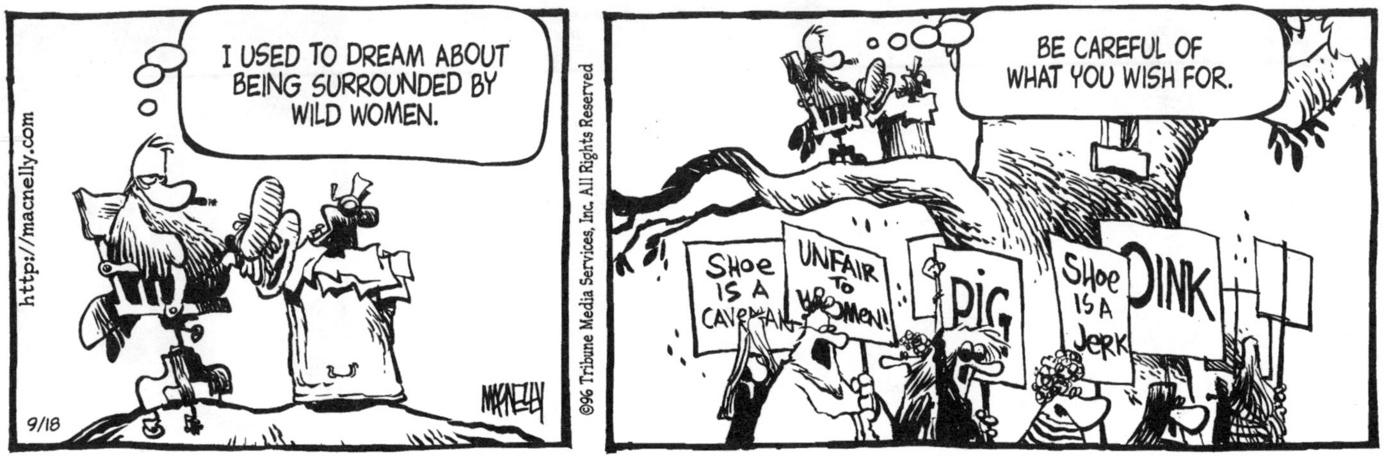

I USED TO DREAM ABOUT BEING SURROUNDED BY WILD WOMEN.
BE CAREFUL OF WHAT YOU WISH FOR.
SHoe IS A
UNFAIR TO
PIG
SHoe IS A JERK
OINK
http://macnelly.com
9/18
MACNELLY
©96 Tribune Media Services, Inc. All Rights Reserved

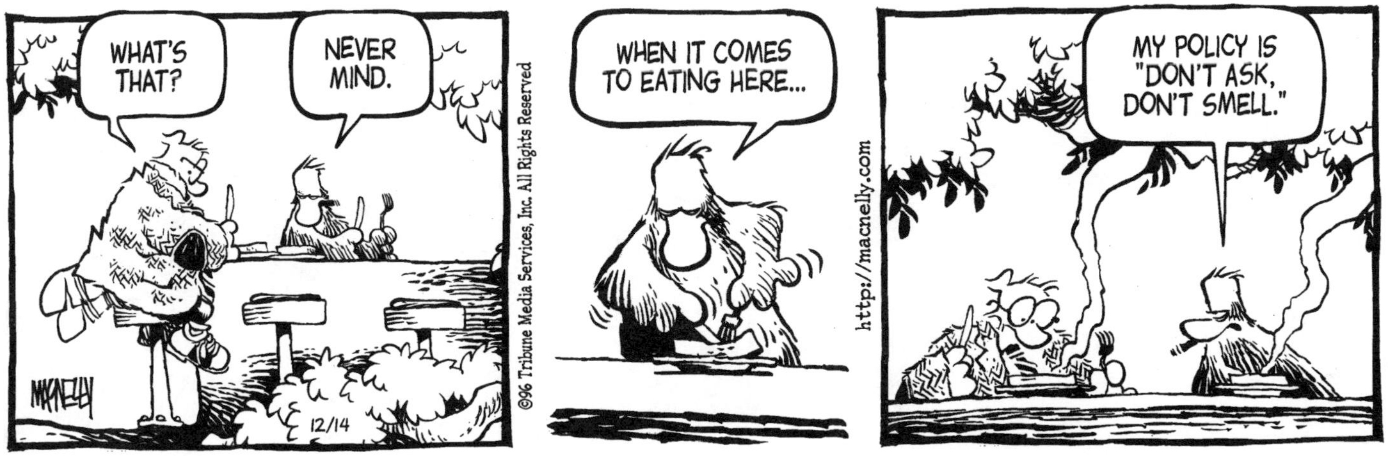

WHAT'S THAT?
NEVER MIND.
WHEN IT COMES TO EATING HERE...
MY POLICY IS "DON'T ASK, DON'T SMELL."
MACNELLY
12/14
©96 Tribune Media Services, Inc. All Rights Reserved
http://macnelly.com

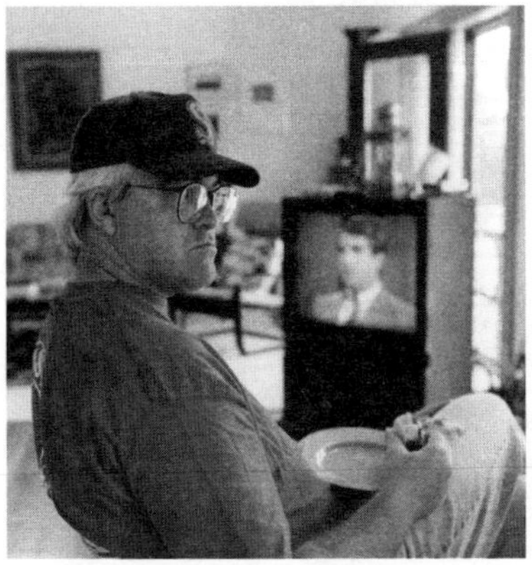

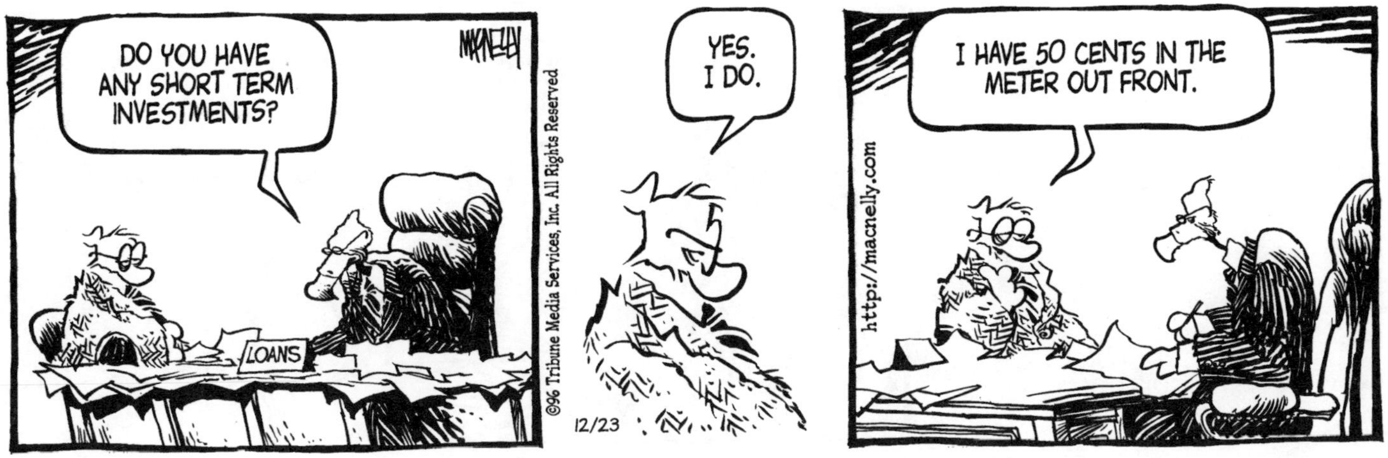

DO YOU HAVE ANY SHORT TERM INVESTMENTS?
LOANS
MACNELLY
YES. I DO.
I HAVE 50 CENTS IN THE METER OUT FRONT.
©96 Tribune Media Services, Inc. All Rights Reserved
12/23
http://macnelly.com

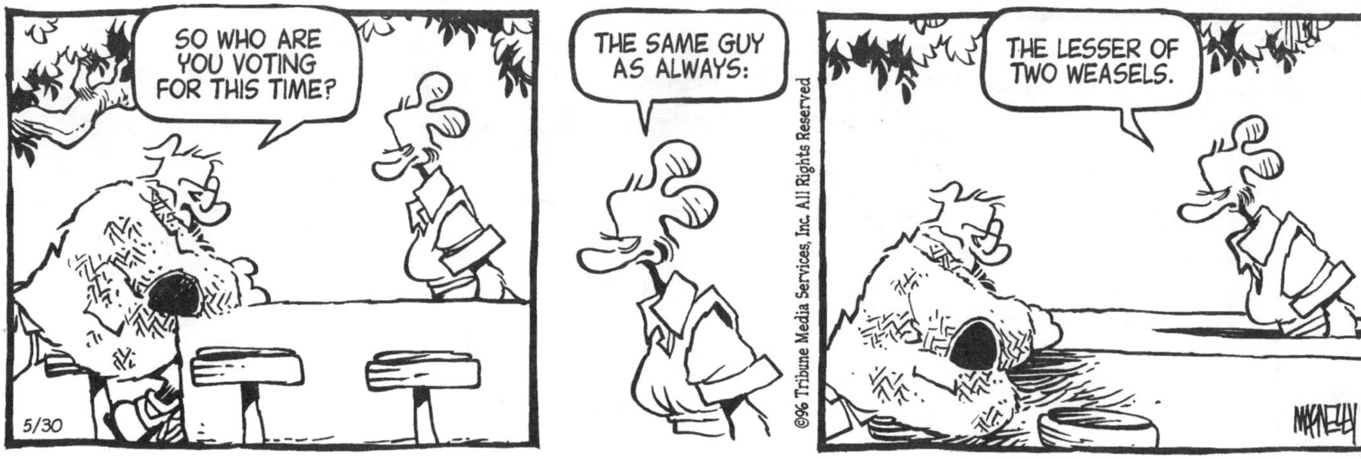
SO WHO ARE YOU VOTING FOR THIS TIME?
THE SAME GUY AS ALWAYS:
THE LESSER OF TWO WEASELS.
5/30
©96 Tribune Media Services, Inc. All Rights Reserved
MACNELLY

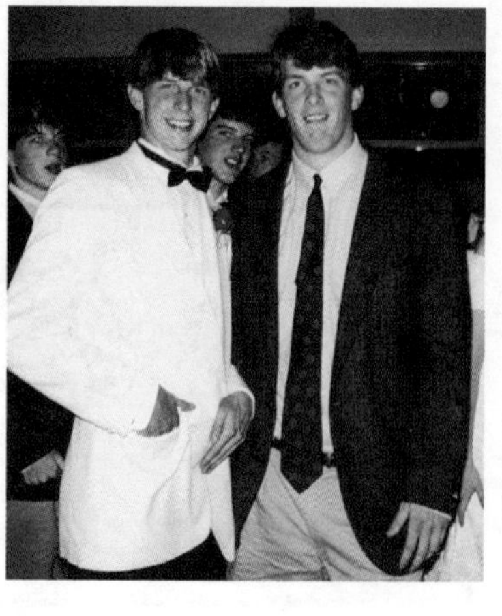

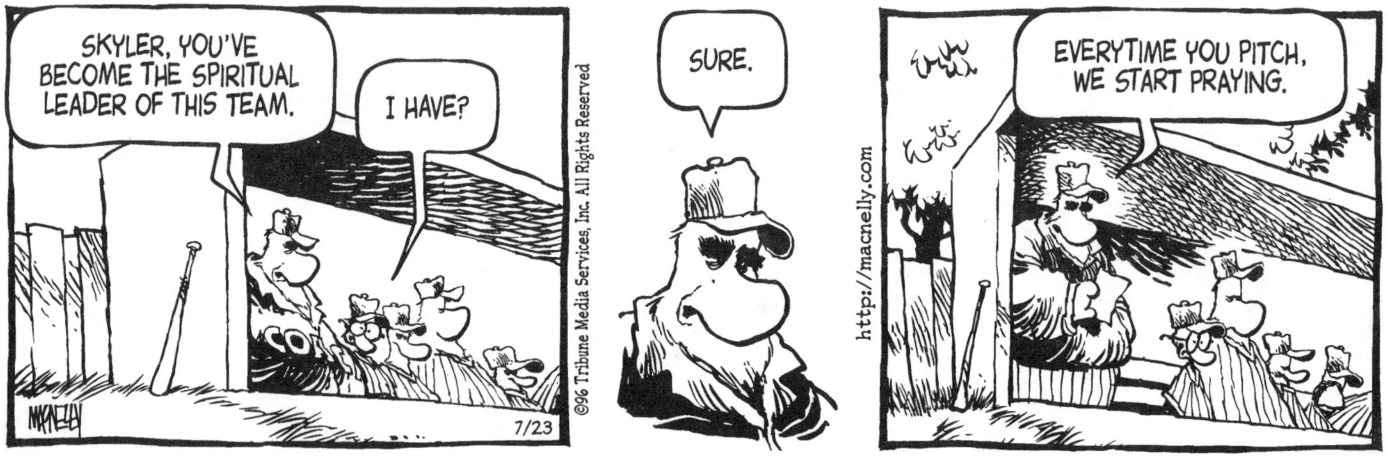
SKYLER, YOU'VE BECOME THE SPIRITUAL LEADER OF THIS TEAM.
I HAVE?
SURE.
EVERYTIME YOU PITCH, WE START PRAYING.
MACNELLY
7/23
©96 Tribune Media Services, Inc. All Rights Reserved
http://macnelly.com

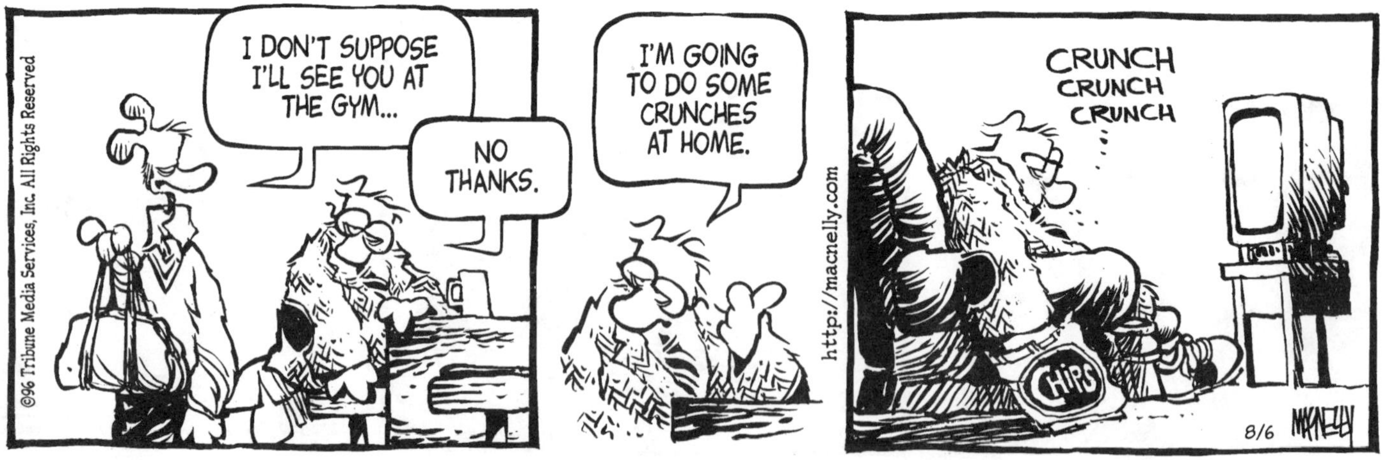
I DON'T SUPPOSE I'LL SEE YOU AT THE GYM...
NO THANKS.
I'M GOING TO DO SOME CRUNCHES AT HOME.
CRUNCH
CRUNCH
CRUNCH
CHIPS
8/6
MACNELLY
©96 Tribune Media Services, Inc. All Rights Reserved
http://macnelly.com

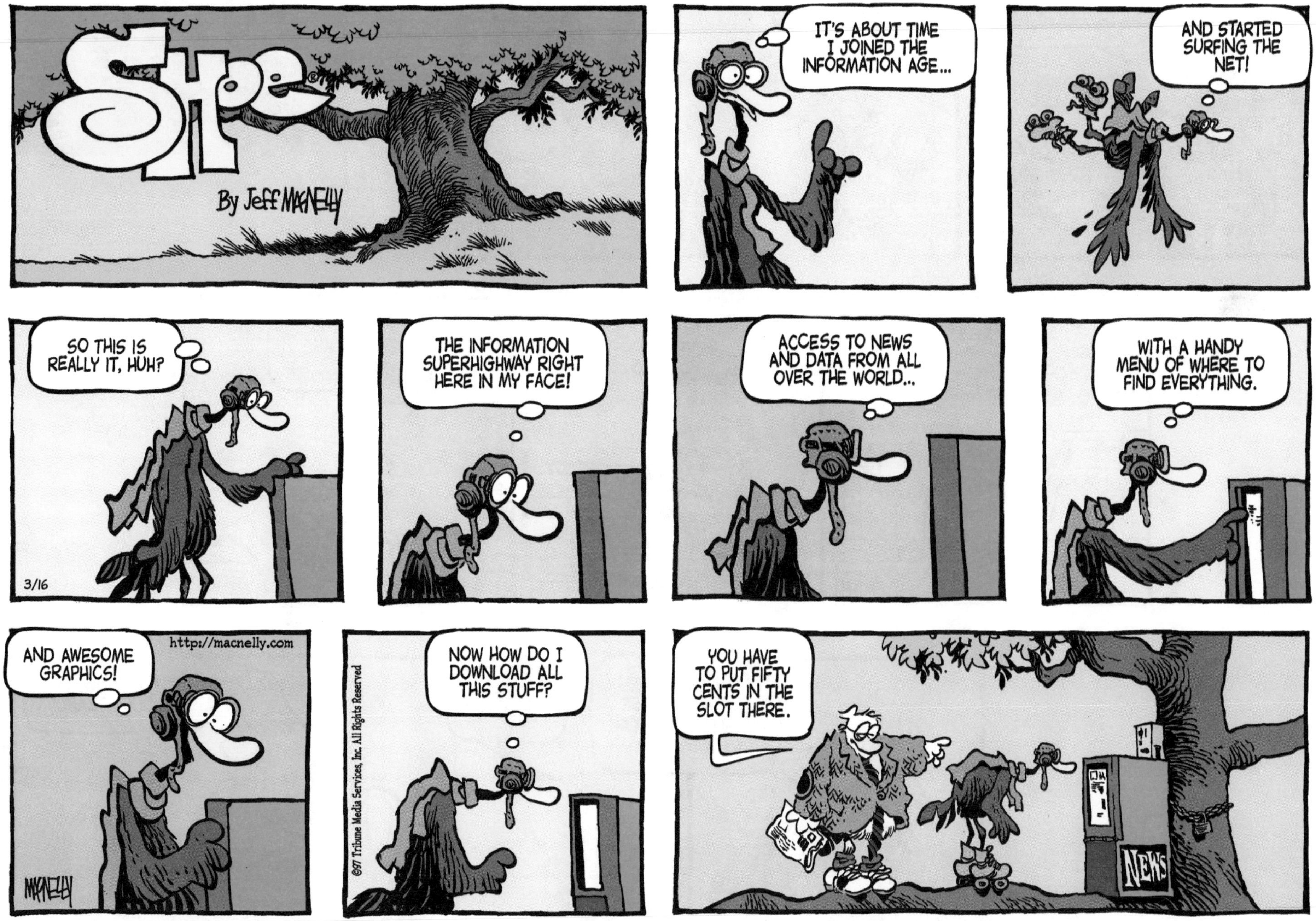
SHOE®
By Jeff MacNelly
IT'S ABOUT TIME I JOINED THE INFORMATION AGE...
AND STARTED SURFING THE NET!
SO THIS IS REALLY IT, HUH?
3/16
THE INFORMATION SUPERHIGHWAY RIGHT HERE IN MY FACE!
ACCESS TO NEWS AND DATA FROM ALL OVER THE WORLD...
WITH A HANDY MENU OF WHERE TO FIND EVERYTHING.
http://macnelly.com
AND AWESOME GRAPHICS!
MacNelly
©97 Tribune Media Services, Inc. All Rights Reserved
NOW HOW DO I DOWNLOAD ALL THIS STUFF?
YOU HAVE TO PUT FIFTY CENTS IN THE SLOT THERE.
NEWS

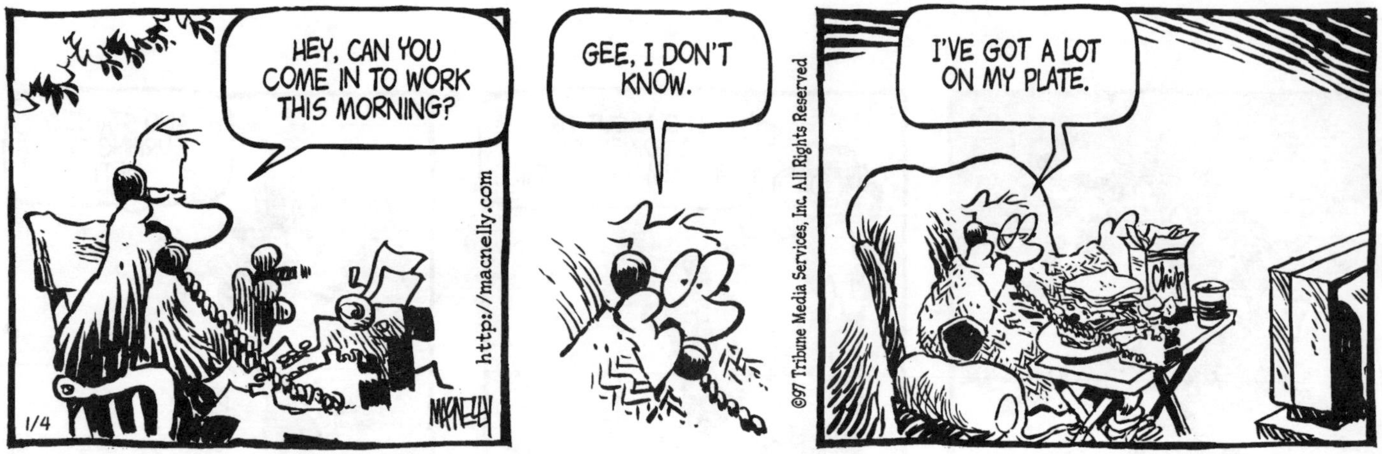
1/4
HEY, CAN YOU COME IN TO WORK THIS MORNING?
http://macnelly.com
MACNELLY
GEE, I DON'T KNOW.
©97 Tribune Media Services, Inc. All Rights Reserved
I'VE GOT A LOT ON MY PLATE.
Chips

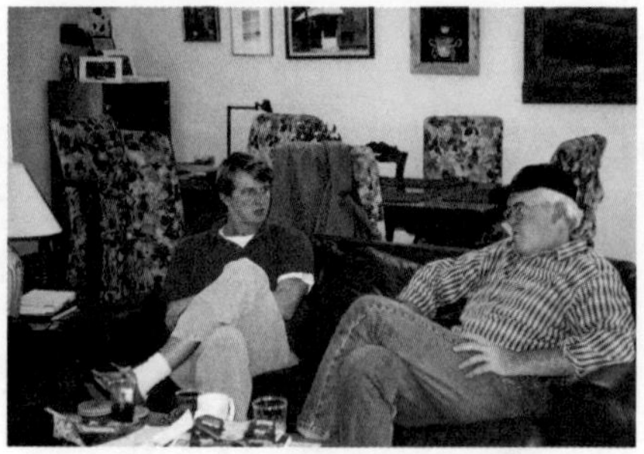

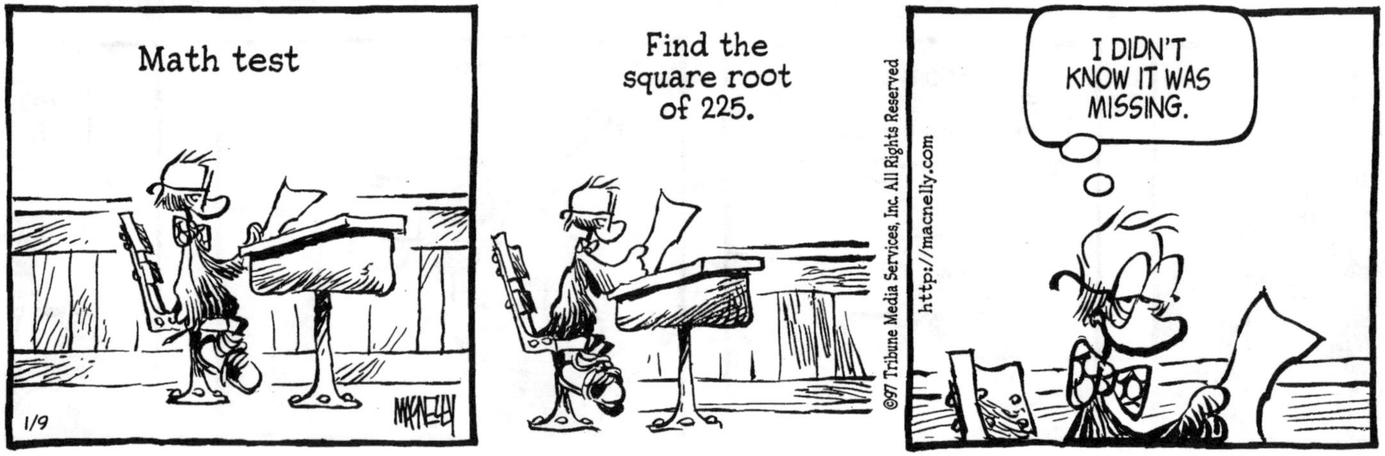
Math test
1/9
MACNELLY
Find the square root of 225.
©97 Tribune Media Services, Inc. All Rights Reserved
http://macnelly.com
I DIDN'T KNOW IT WAS MISSING.

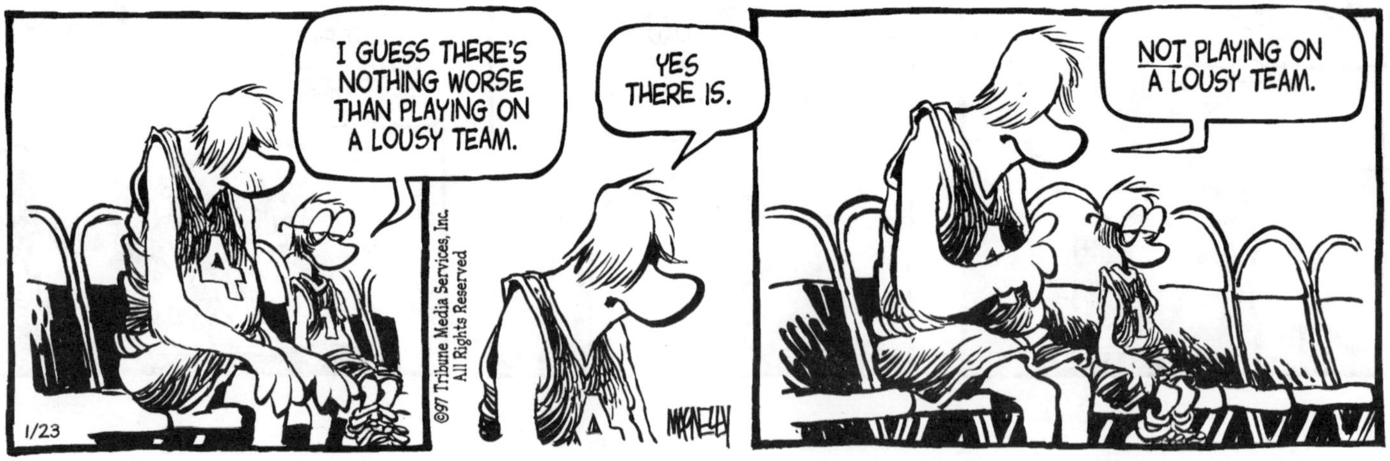
I GUESS THERE'S NOTHING WORSE THAN PLAYING ON A LOUSY TEAM.
1/23
©97 Tribune Media Services, Inc. All Rights Reserved
YES THERE IS.
MACNELLY
NOT PLAYING ON A LOUSY TEAM.

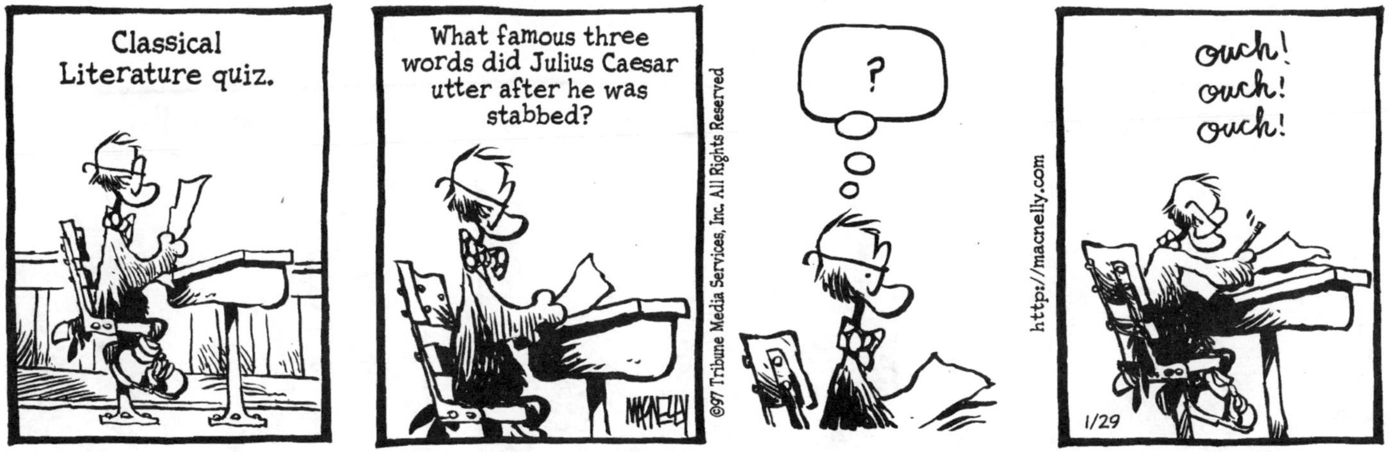
Classical Literature quiz.
What famous three words did Julius Caesar utter after he was stabbed?
MACNELLY
©97 Tribune Media Services, Inc. All Rights Reserved
?
http://macnelly.com
ouch! ouch! ouch!
1/29

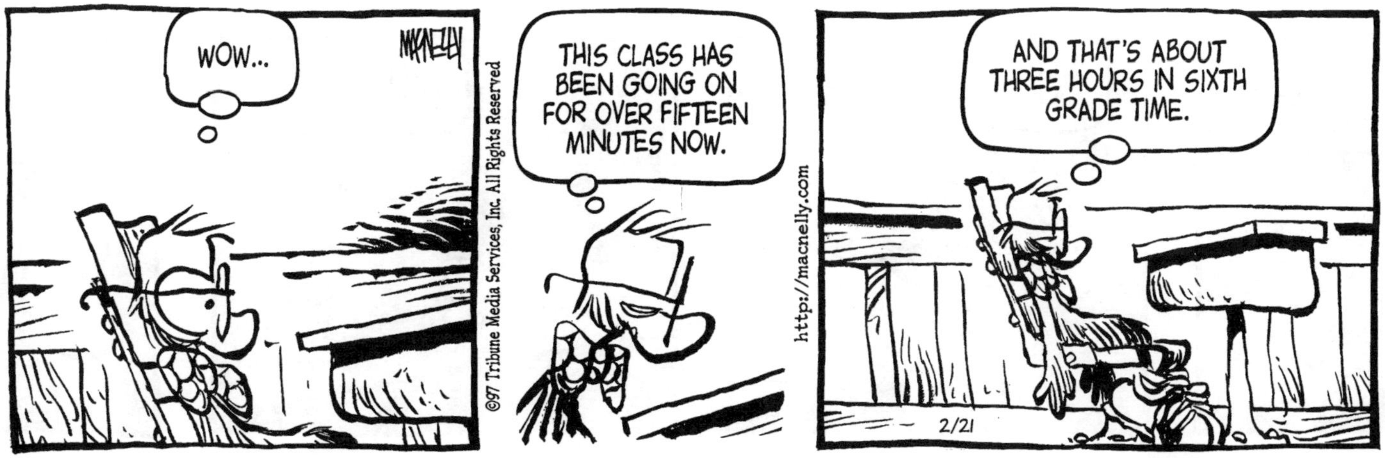
WOW...
MACNELLY
©97 Tribune Media Services, Inc. All Rights Reserved
THIS CLASS HAS BEEN GOING ON FOR OVER FIFTEEN MINUTES NOW.
http://macnelly.com
AND THAT'S ABOUT THREE HOURS IN SIXTH GRADE TIME.
2/21

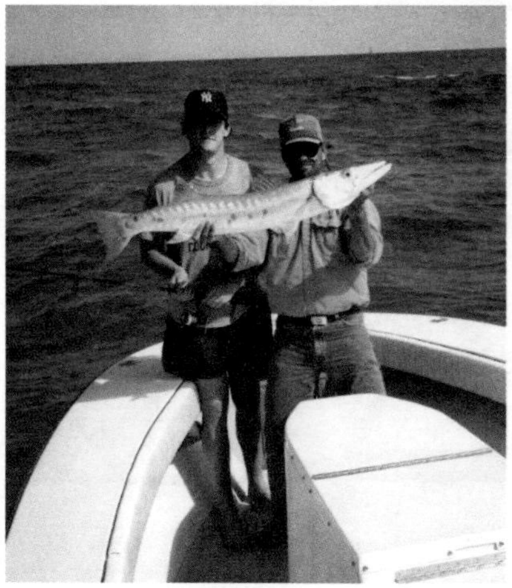

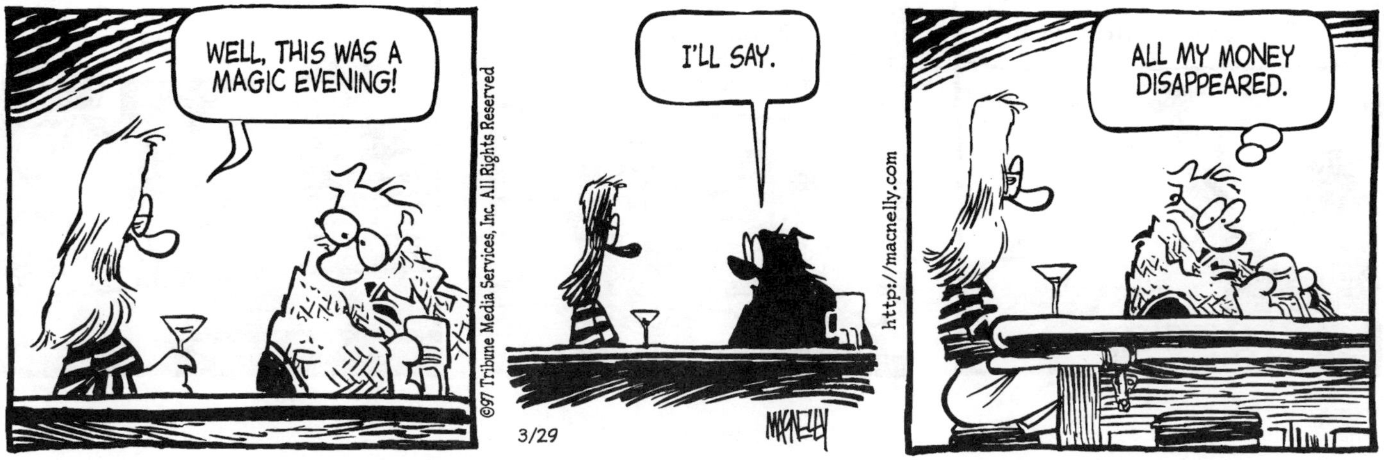
WELL, THIS WAS A MAGIC EVENING!
©97 Tribune Media Services, Inc. All Rights Reserved
I'LL SAY.
3/29
MACNELLY
http://macnelly.com
ALL MY MONEY DISAPPEARED.

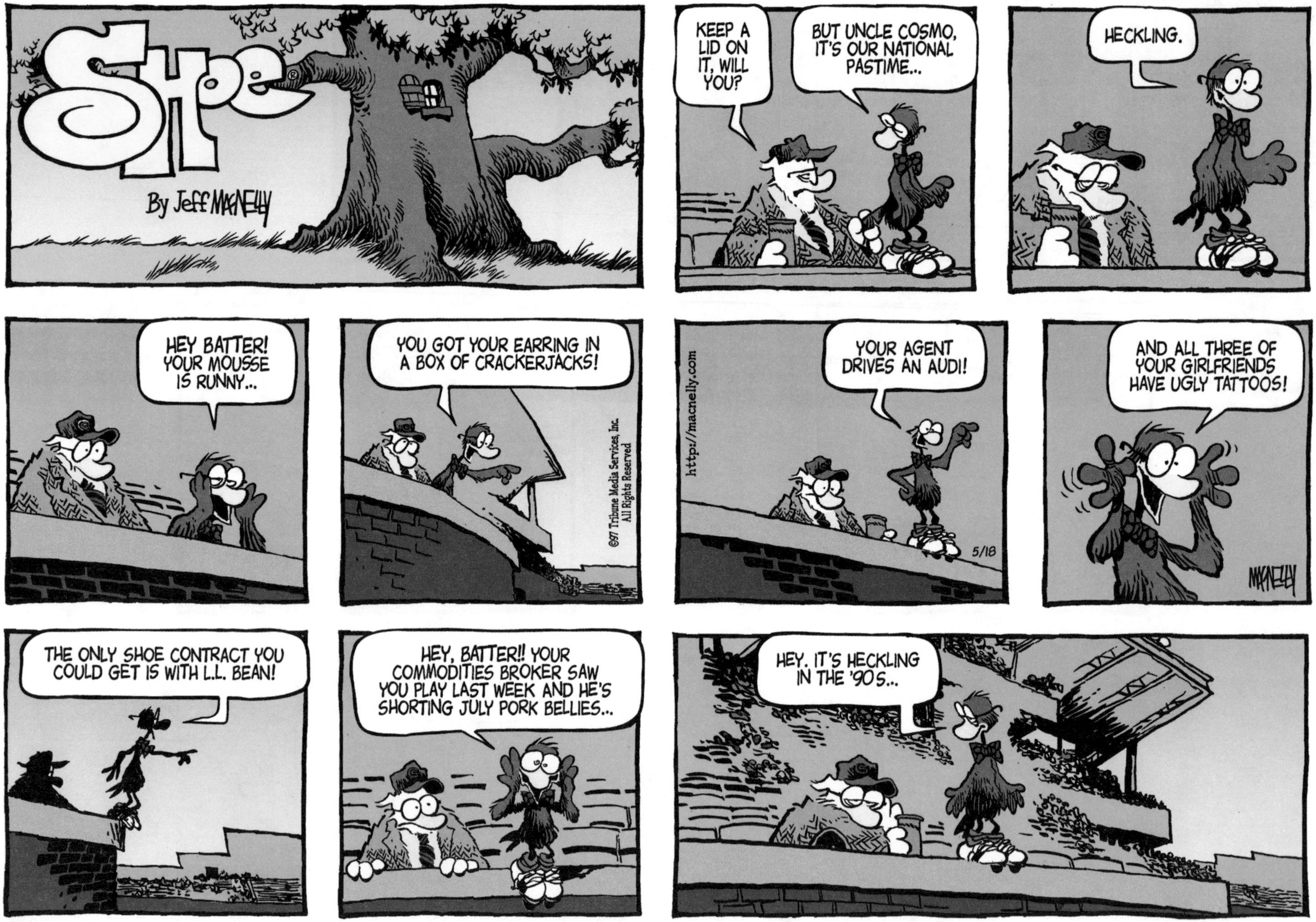
SHOE
By Jeff MACNELLY
KEEP A LID ON IT, WILL YOU?
BUT UNCLE COSMO, IT'S OUR NATIONAL PASTIME...
HECKLING.
HEY BATTER! YOUR MOUSSE IS RUNNY...
YOU GOT YOUR EARRING IN A BOX OF CRACKERJACKS!
©97 Tribune Media Services, Inc. All Rights Reserved
http://macnelly.com
YOUR AGENT DRIVES AN AUDI!
5/18
AND ALL THREE OF YOUR GIRLFRIENDS HAVE UGLY TATTOOS!
MACNELLY
THE ONLY SHOE CONTRACT YOU COULD GET IS WITH L.L. BEAN!
HEY, BATTER!! YOUR COMMODITIES BROKER SAW YOU PLAY LAST WEEK AND HE'S SHORTING JULY PORK BELLIES...
HEY. IT'S HECKLING IN THE '90S...

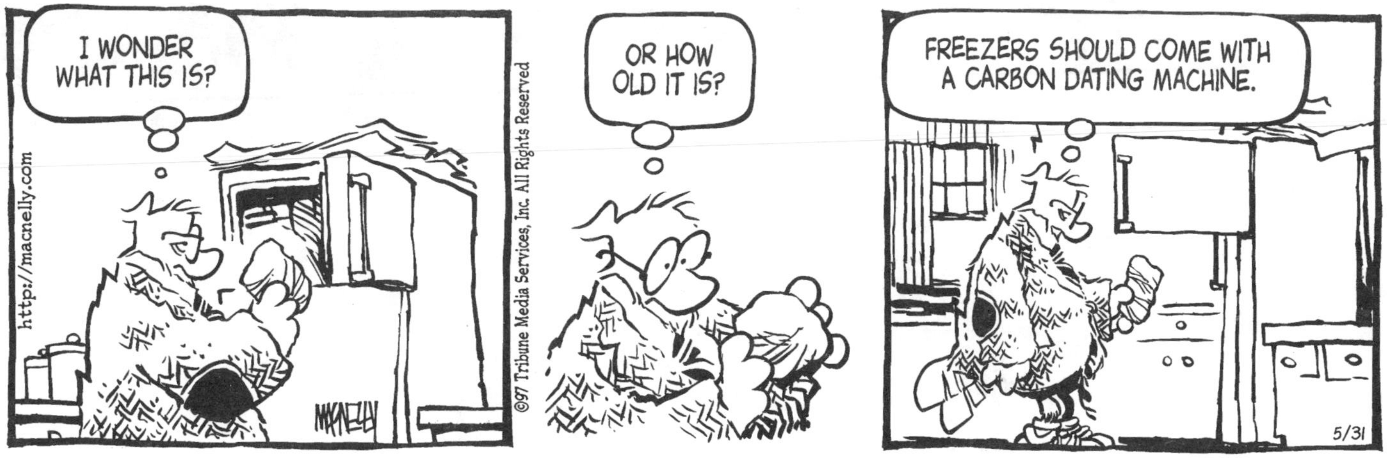
I WONDER WHAT THIS IS?
OR HOW OLD IT IS?
FREEZERS SHOULD COME WITH A CARBON DATING MACHINE.
http://macnelly.com
©97 Tribune Media Services, Inc. All Rights Reserved
MACNELLY
5/31

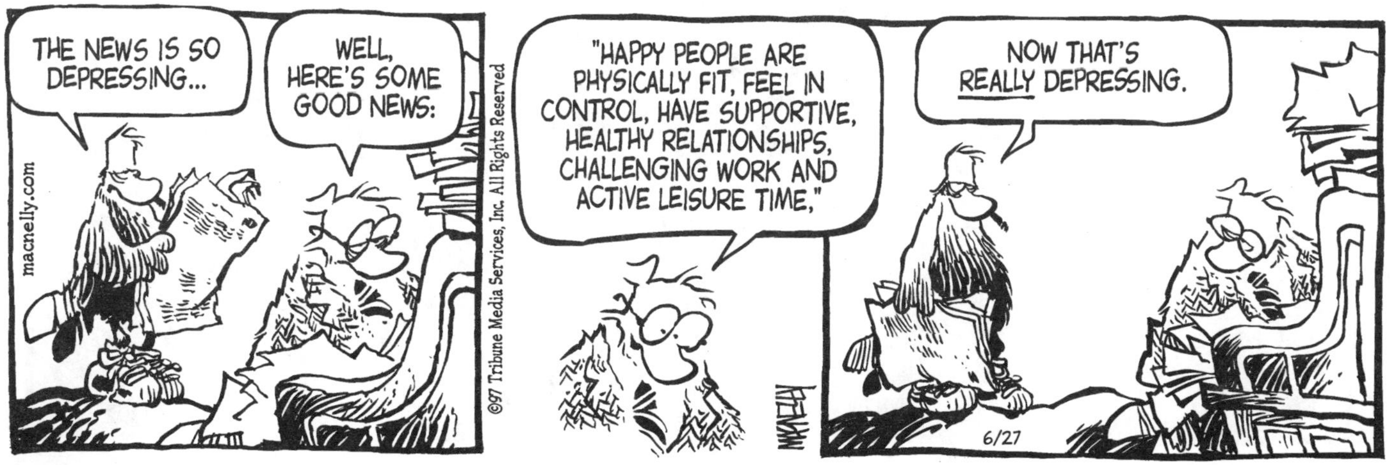
THE NEWS IS SO DEPRESSING...
WELL, HERE'S SOME GOOD NEWS:
"HAPPY PEOPLE ARE PHYSICALLY FIT, FEEL IN CONTROL, HAVE SUPPORTIVE, HEALTHY RELATIONSHIPS, CHALLENGING WORK AND ACTIVE LEISURE TIME,"
NOW THAT'S REALLY DEPRESSING.
macnelly.com
©97 Tribune Media Services, Inc. All Rights Reserved
MACNELLY
6/27

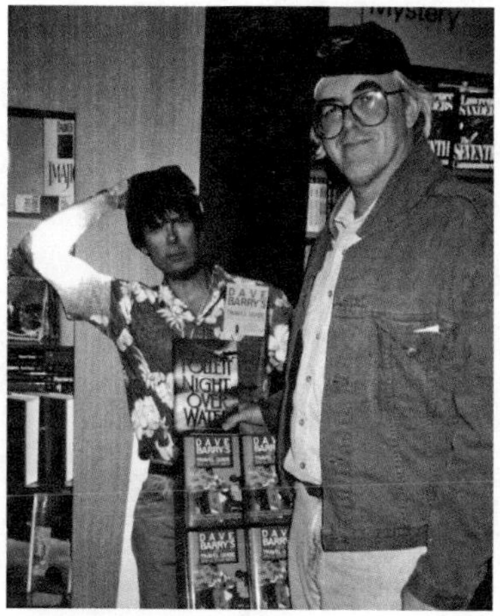
Mystery

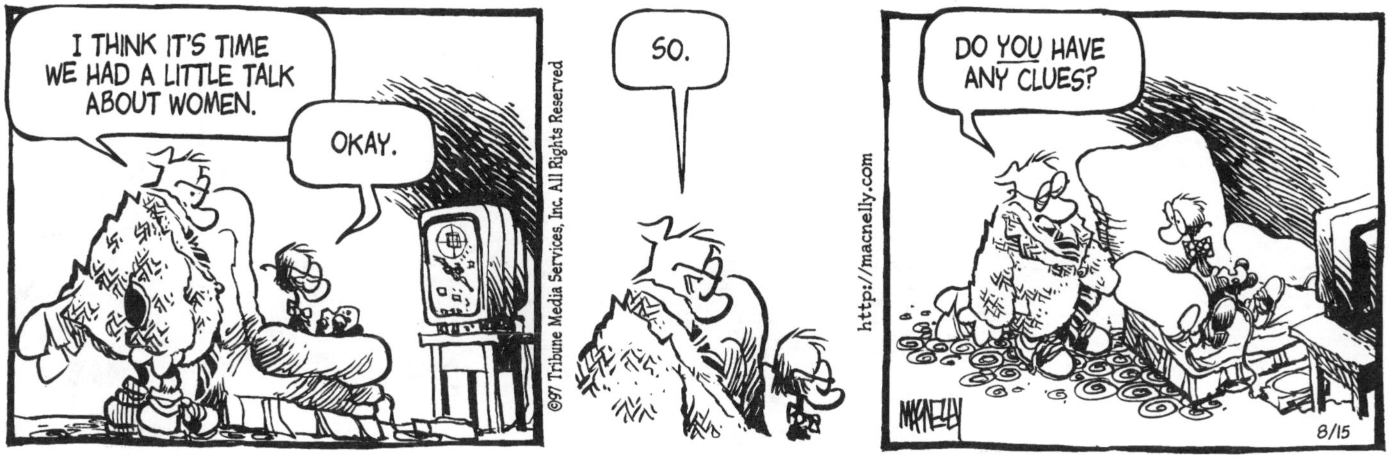
I THINK IT'S TIME WE HAD A LITTLE TALK ABOUT WOMEN.
OKAY.
SO.
DO YOU HAVE ANY CLUES?
©97 Tribune Media Services, Inc. All Rights Reserved
http://macnelly.com
MACNELLY
8/15

AS FOR THESE FUND-RAISING QUESTIONS...
WHAT I DID WAS PERFECTLY LEGAL.
AND I'LL NEVER DO IT AGAIN.
http://macnelly.com
4/21
MACNELLY
©97 Tribune Media Services, Inc. All Rights Reserved

COUGARS
COUGARS
57

I SEE THERE'S A NEW PROGRAM TO GIVE FOOD TO THE HOMELESS...
YEAH.
I WISH THEY'D STOP BEATING AROUND THE BUSH...
AND GIVE HOMES TO THE HOMELESS.
The SNEWS
MACNELLY
©97 Tribune Media Services, Inc. All Rights Reserved
http://macnelly.com
4/29

YES, A LOT OF PEOPLE ASK ME THAT.
BOOKS
MEET THE AUTHOR
THE RESTROOM IS DOWN THE HALL ON THE RIGHT.
MEET THE AUTHOR
MACNELLY
©97 Tribune Media Services, Inc. All Rights Reserved
http://macnelly.com
5/30

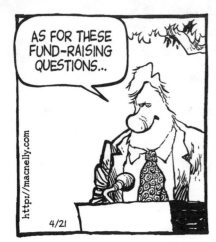

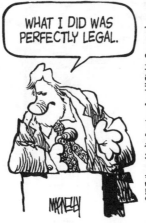

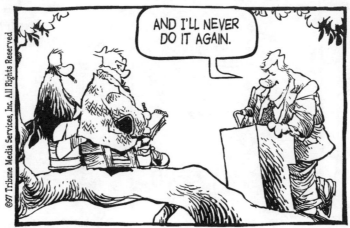

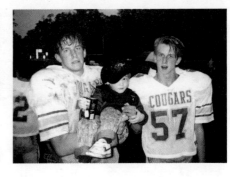

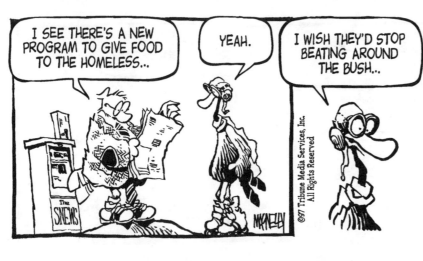

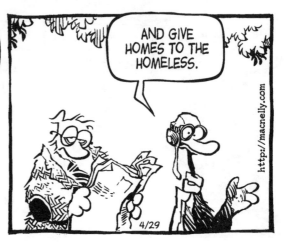

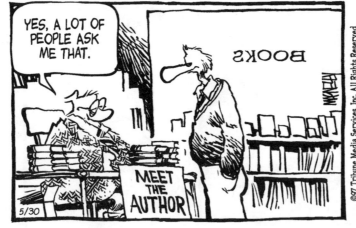

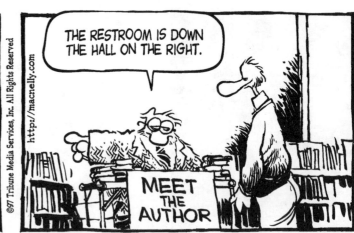

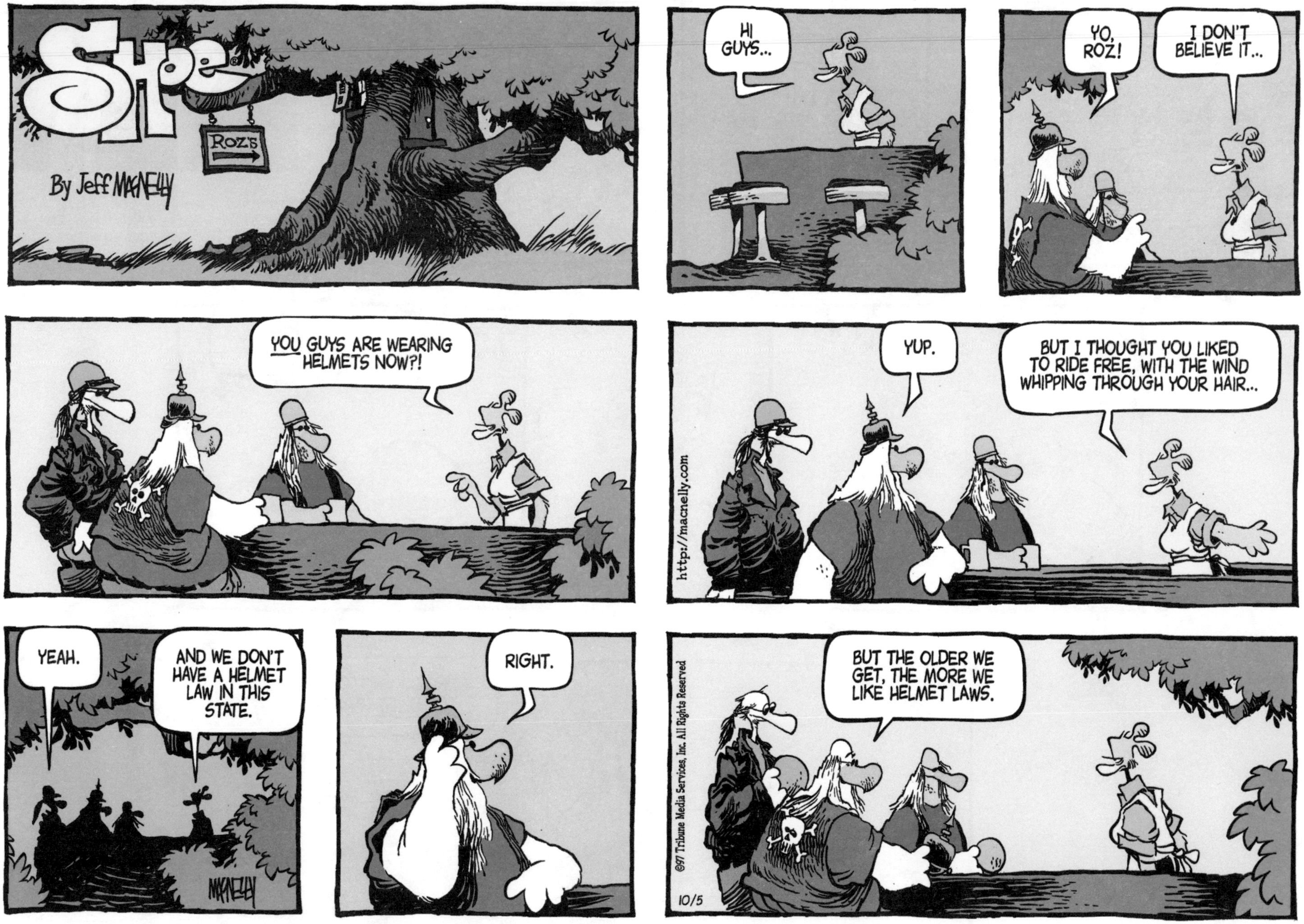
SHOE®
By Jeff MacNelly
ROZ'S
HI GUYS...
YO, ROZ!
I DON'T BELIEVE IT...
YOU GUYS ARE WEARING HELMETS NOW?!
YUP.
BUT I THOUGHT YOU LIKED TO RIDE FREE, WITH THE WIND WHIPPING THROUGH YOUR HAIR...
http://macnelly.com
YEAH.
AND WE DON'T HAVE A HELMET LAW IN THIS STATE.
MACNELLY
RIGHT.
©97 Tribune Media Services, Inc. All Rights Reserved
BUT THE OLDER WE GET, THE MORE WE LIKE HELMET LAWS.
10/5

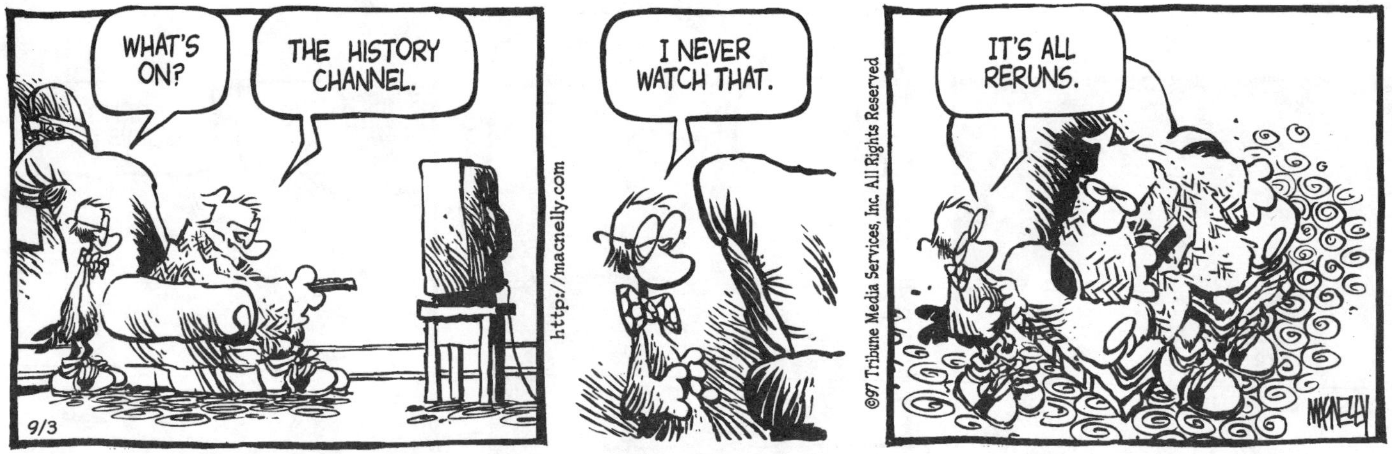
WHAT'S ON?
THE HISTORY CHANNEL.
http://macnelly.com
I NEVER WATCH THAT.
©97 Tribune Media Services, Inc. All Rights Reserved
IT'S ALL RERUNS.
MACNELLY
9/3

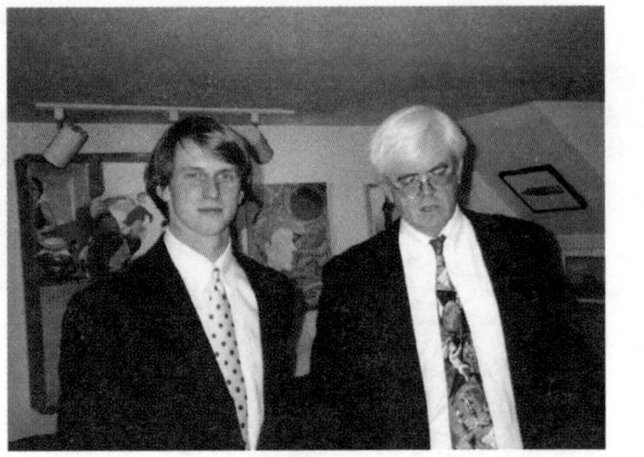

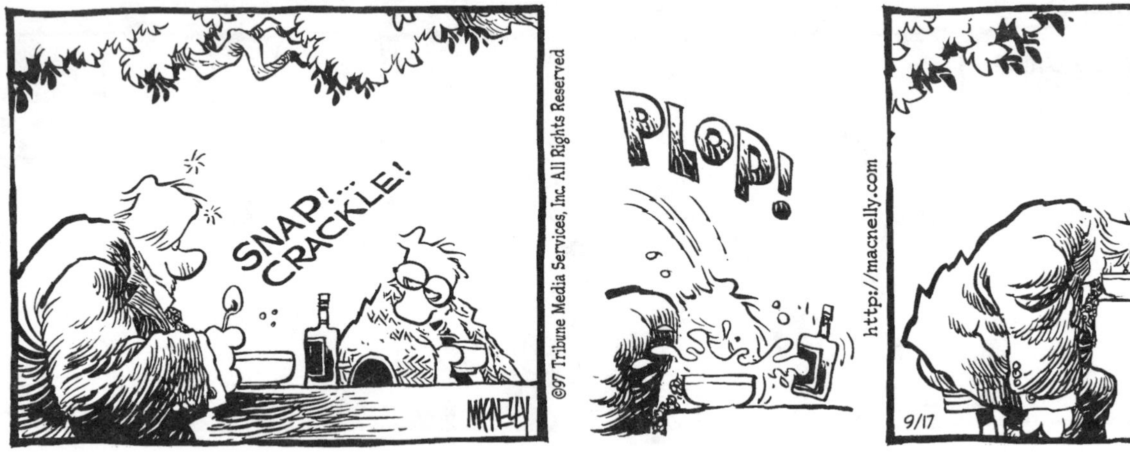
SNAP!... CRACKLE!
MACNELLY
©97 Tribune Media Services, Inc. All Rights Reserved
PLOP!
http://macnelly.com
RICE WHISKEYS.
9/17

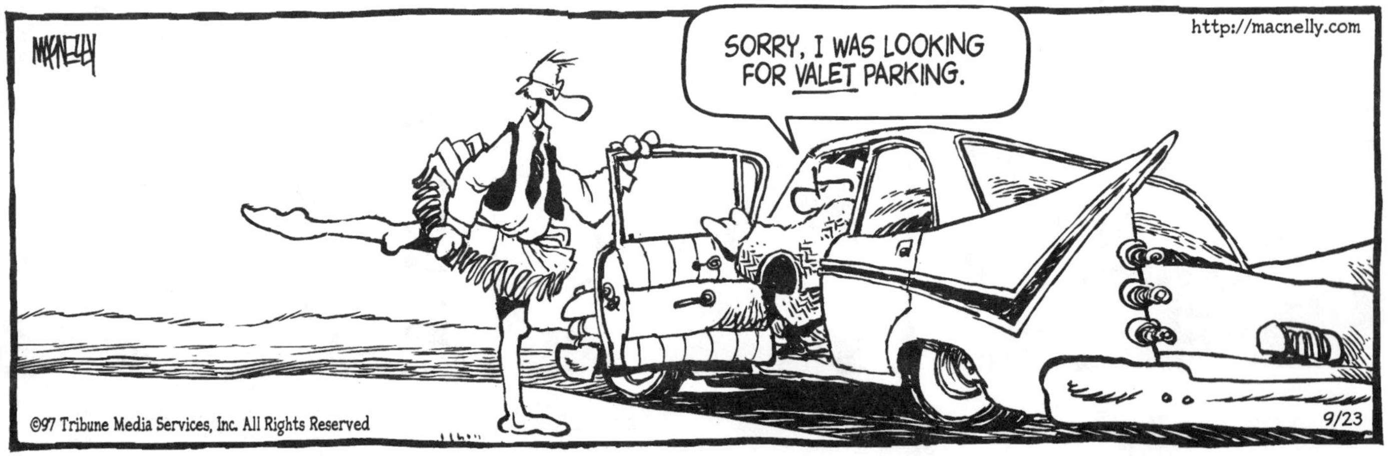
MACNELLY
SORRY, I WAS LOOKING FOR VALET PARKING.
http://macnelly.com
©97 Tribune Media Services, Inc. All Rights Reserved
9/23

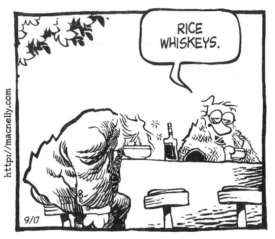

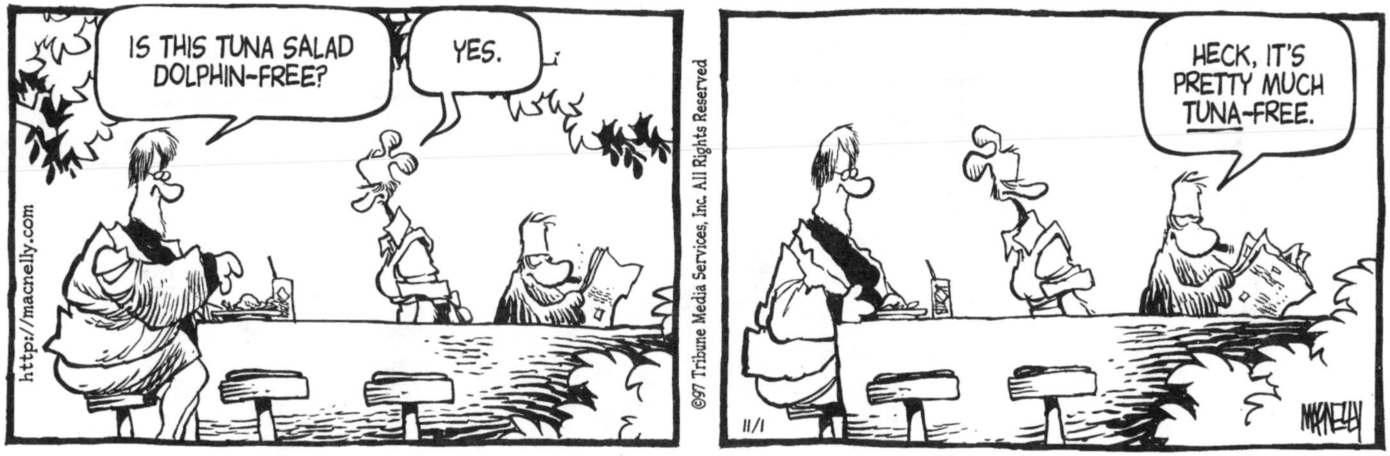
IS THIS TUNA SALAD DOLPHIN-FREE?
YES.
HECK, IT'S PRETTY MUCH TUNA-FREE.
http://macnelly.com
©97 Tribune Media Services, Inc. All Rights Reserved
11/1
MACNELLY

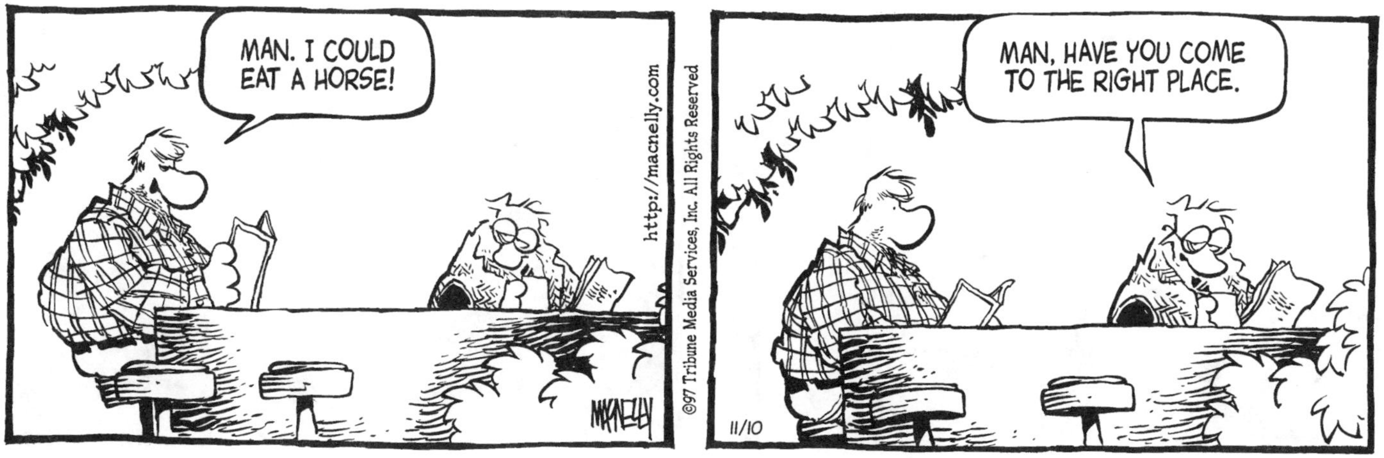
MAN. I COULD EAT A HORSE!
MAN, HAVE YOU COME TO THE RIGHT PLACE.
http://macnelly.com
©97 Tribune Media Services, Inc. All Rights Reserved
11/10
MACNELLY

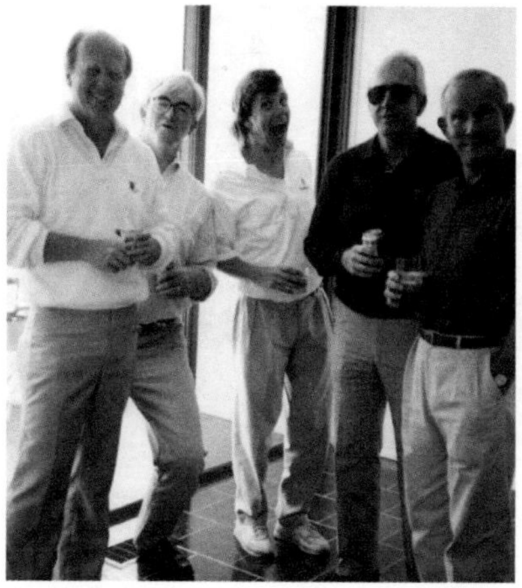

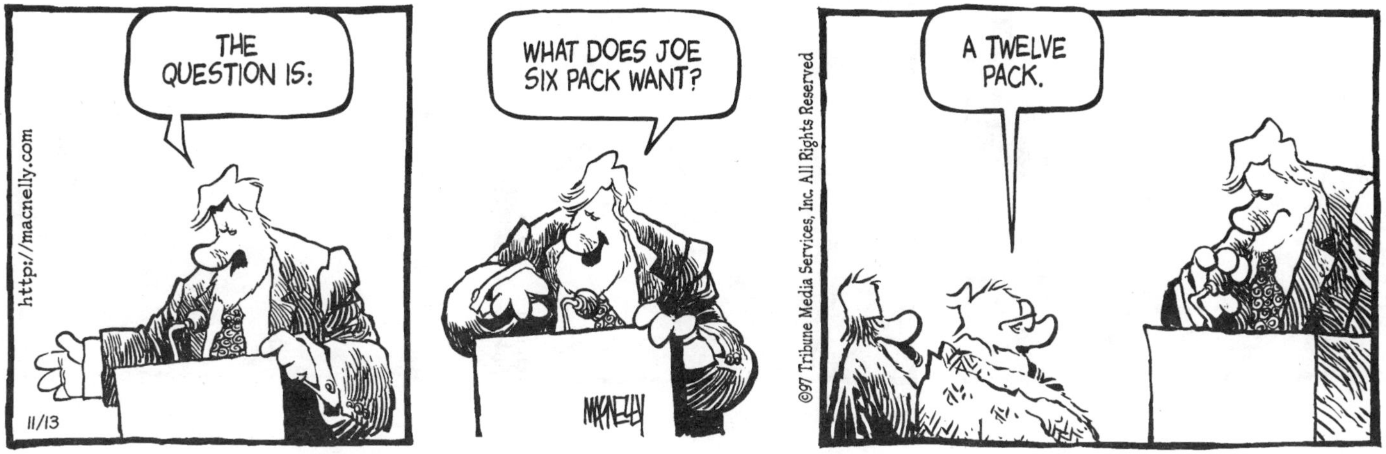
THE QUESTION IS:
WHAT DOES JOE SIX PACK WANT?
A TWELVE PACK.
http://macnelly.com
©97 Tribune Media Services, Inc. All Rights Reserved
11/13
MACNELLY

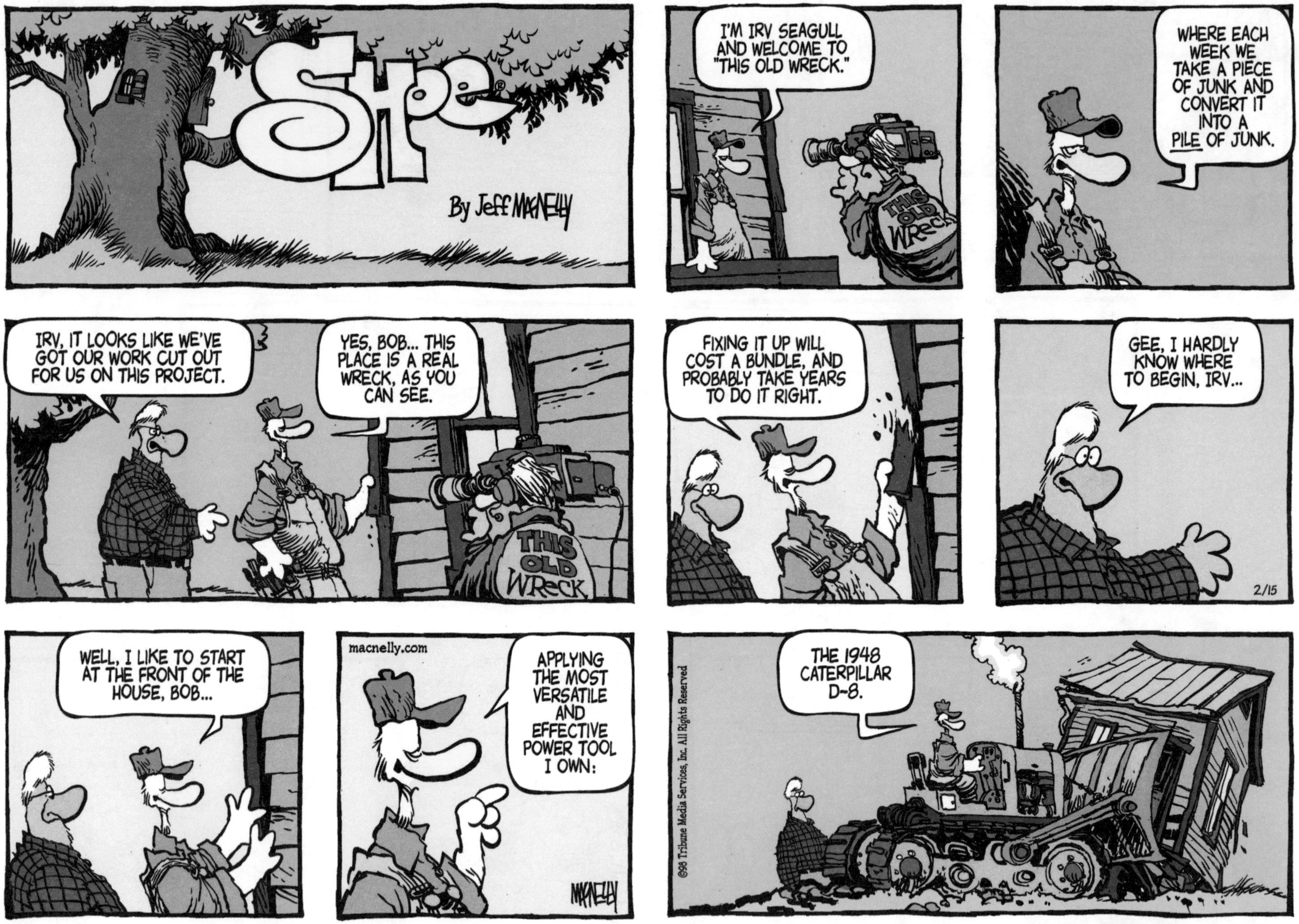
Shoe®
By Jeff MacNelly
I'M IRV SEAGULL AND WELCOME TO "THIS OLD WRECK."
THIS OLD WRECK
WHERE EACH WEEK WE TAKE A PIECE OF JUNK AND CONVERT IT INTO A PILE OF JUNK.
IRV, IT LOOKS LIKE WE'VE GOT OUR WORK CUT OUT FOR US ON THIS PROJECT.
YES, BOB... THIS PLACE IS A REAL WRECK, AS YOU CAN SEE.
THIS OLD WRECK
FIXING IT UP WILL COST A BUNDLE, AND PROBABLY TAKE YEARS TO DO IT RIGHT.
GEE, I HARDLY KNOW WHERE TO BEGIN, IRV...
2/15
WELL, I LIKE TO START AT THE FRONT OF THE HOUSE, BOB...
macnelly.com
APPLYING THE MOST VERSATILE AND EFFECTIVE POWER TOOL I OWN:
MACNELLY
©98 Tribune Media Services, Inc. All Rights Reserved
THE 1948 CATERPILLAR D-8.

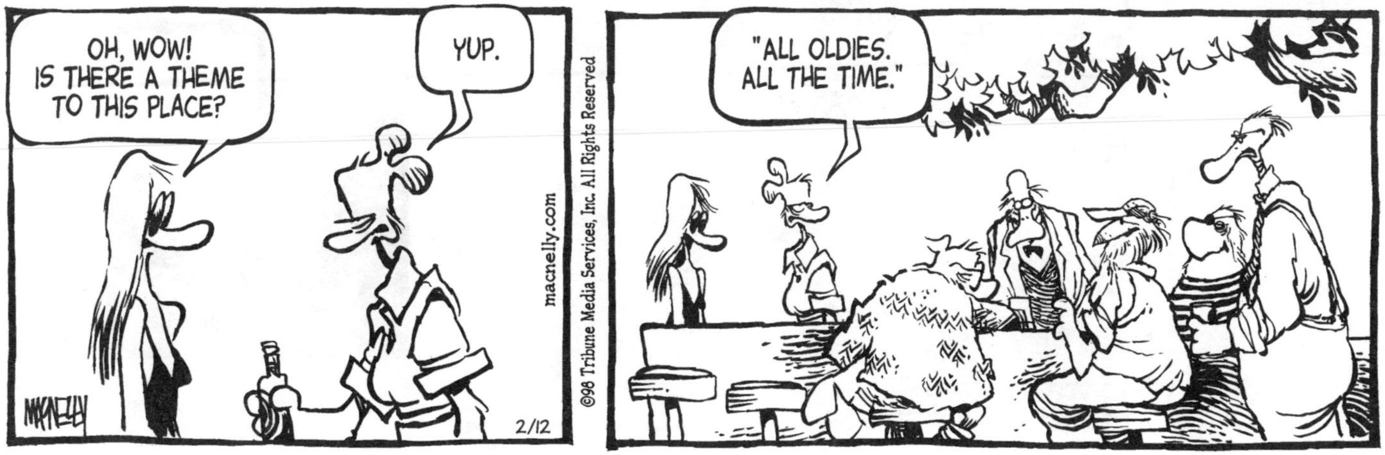
OH, WOW! IS THERE A THEME TO THIS PLACE?
YUP.
MACNELLY
2/12
macnelly.com
©98 Tribune Media Services, Inc. All Rights Reserved
"ALL OLDIES. ALL THE TIME."

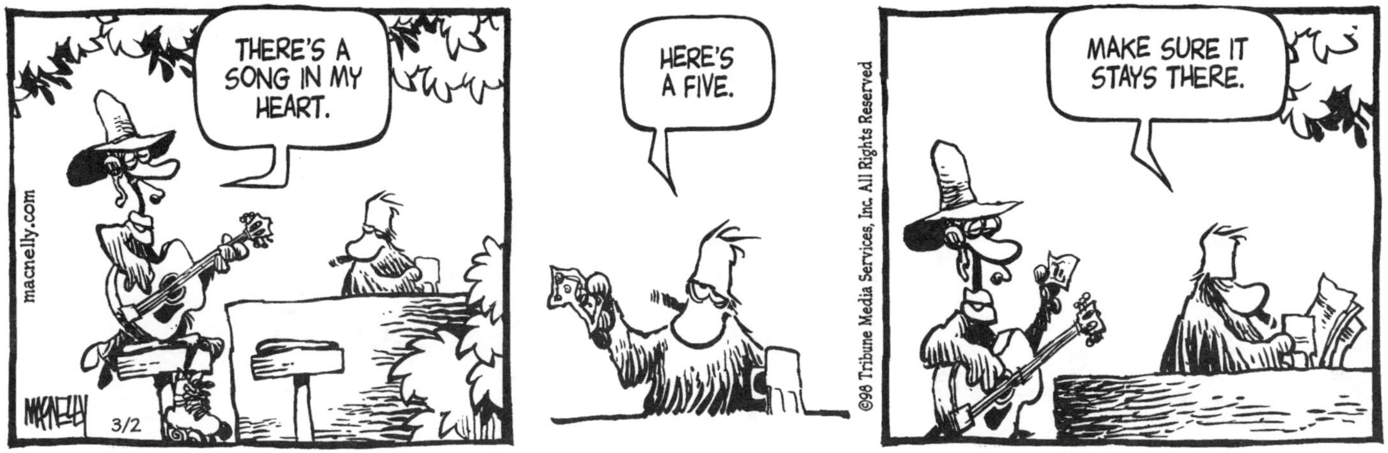
THERE'S A SONG IN MY HEART.
macnelly.com
MACNELLY
3/2
HERE'S A FIVE.
©98 Tribune Media Services, Inc. All Rights Reserved
MAKE SURE IT STAYS THERE.

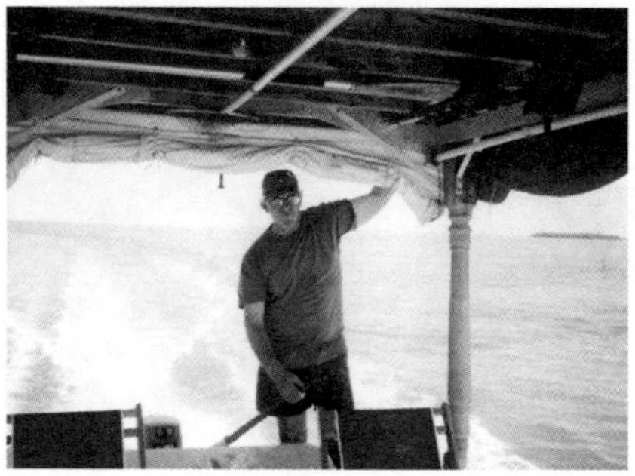

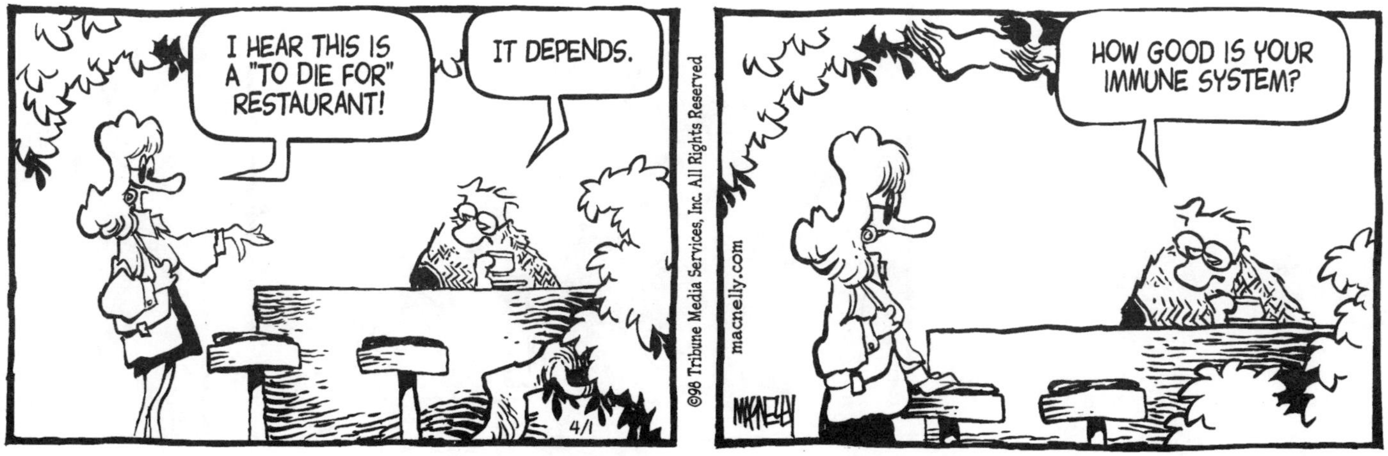
I HEAR THIS IS A "TO DIE FOR" RESTAURANT!
IT DEPENDS.
4/1
©98 Tribune Media Services, Inc. All Rights Reserved
macnelly.com
MACNELLY
HOW GOOD IS YOUR IMMUNE SYSTEM?

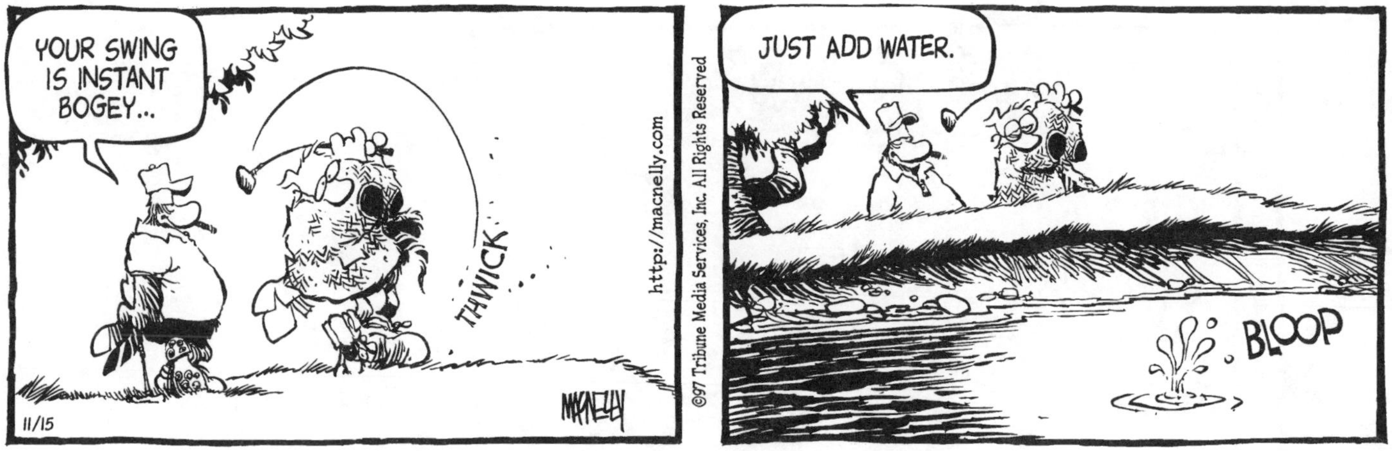
YOUR SWING IS INSTANT BOGEY...
THWICK
11/15
MACNELLY
http://macnelly.com
©97 Tribune Media Services, Inc. All Rights Reserved
JUST ADD WATER.
BLOOP

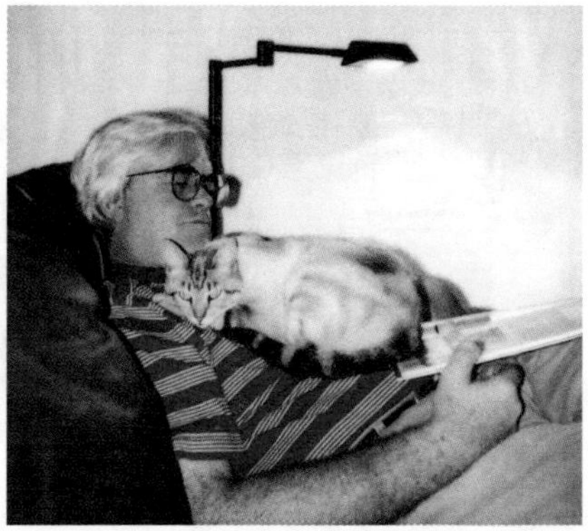

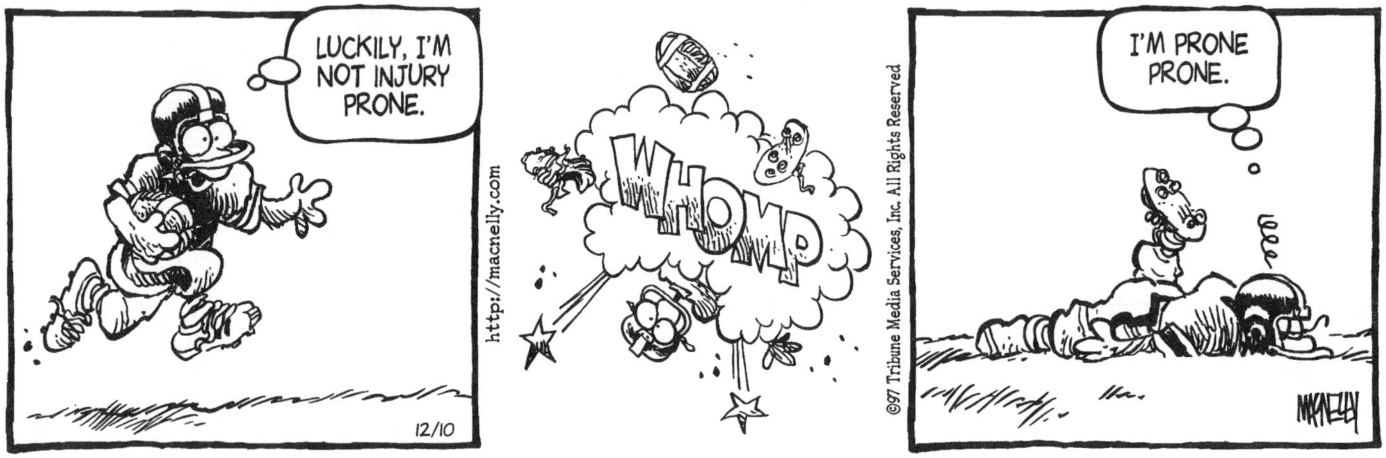
LUCKILY, I'M NOT INJURY PRONE.
12/10
http://macnelly.com
WHOMP
©97 Tribune Media Services, Inc. All Rights Reserved
I'M PRONE PRONE.
MACNELLY

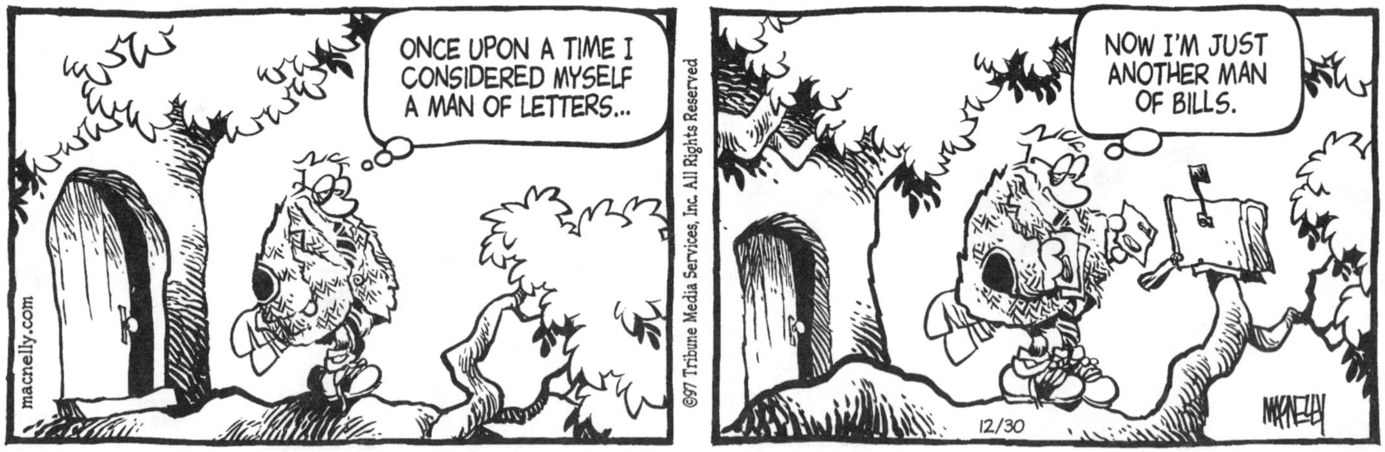
ONCE UPON A TIME I CONSIDERED MYSELF A MAN OF LETTERS...
macnelly.com
©97 Tribune Media Services, Inc. All Rights Reserved
NOW I'M JUST ANOTHER MAN OF BILLS.
12/30
MACNELLY

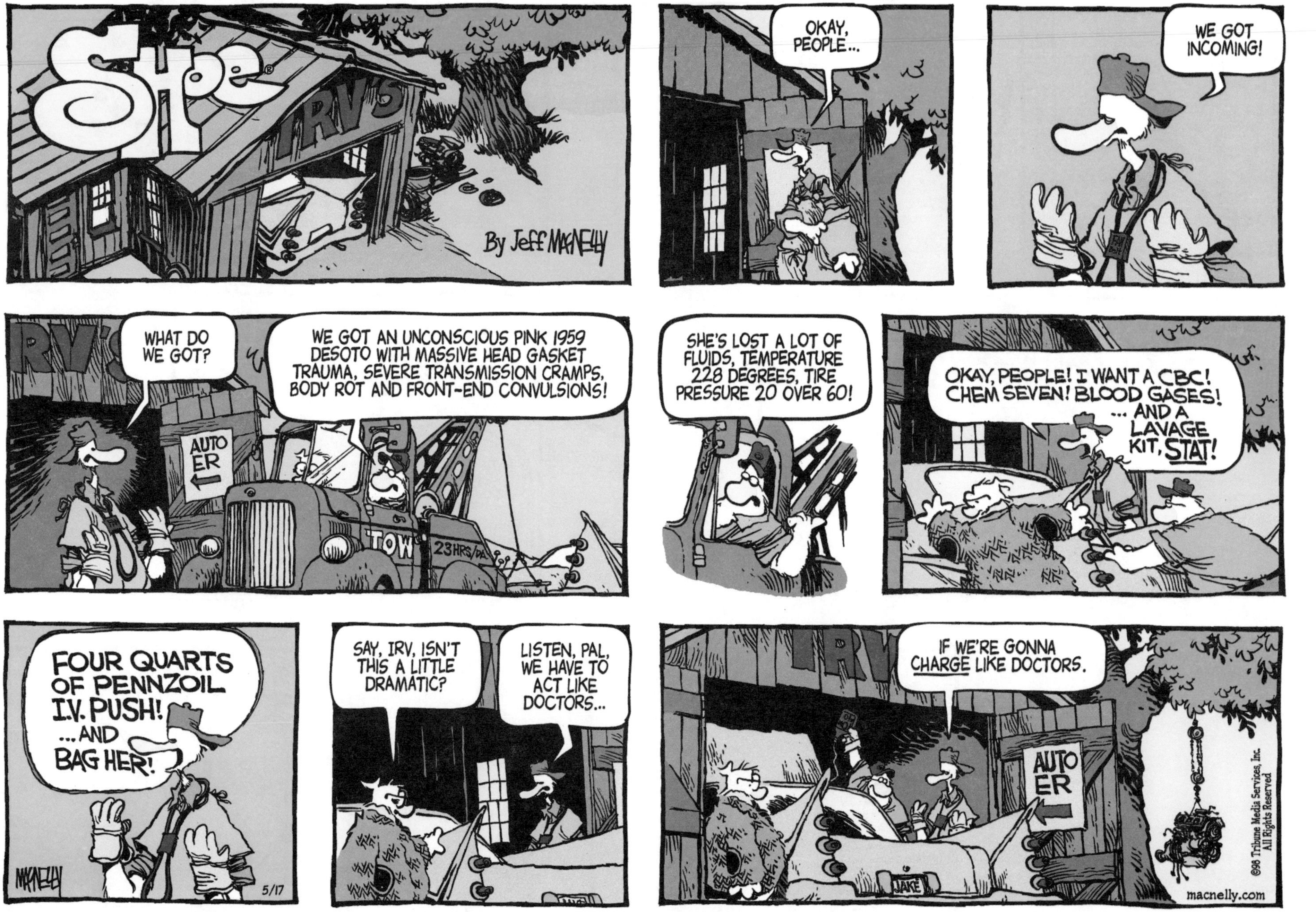
Shoe®
IRV'S
By Jeff MacNelly
OKAY, PEOPLE...
WE GOT INCOMING!
WHAT DO WE GOT?
WE GOT AN UNCONSCIOUS PINK 1959 DESOTO WITH MASSIVE HEAD GASKET TRAUMA, SEVERE TRANSMISSION CRAMPS, BODY ROT AND FRONT-END CONVULSIONS!
AUTO ER
TOW
23 HRS/DA
SHE'S LOST A LOT OF FLUIDS, TEMPERATURE 228 DEGREES, TIRE PRESSURE 20 OVER 60!
OKAY, PEOPLE! I WANT A CBC! CHEM SEVEN! BLOOD GASES! ... AND A LAVAGE KIT, STAT!
FOUR QUARTS OF PENNZOIL I.V. PUSH! ... AND BAG HER!
MACNELLY
5/17
SAY, IRV, ISN'T THIS A LITTLE DRAMATIC?
LISTEN, PAL, WE HAVE TO ACT LIKE DOCTORS...
IF WE'RE GONNA CHARGE LIKE DOCTORS.
AUTO ER
JAKE
©98 Tribune Media Services, Inc. All Rights Reserved
macnelly.com

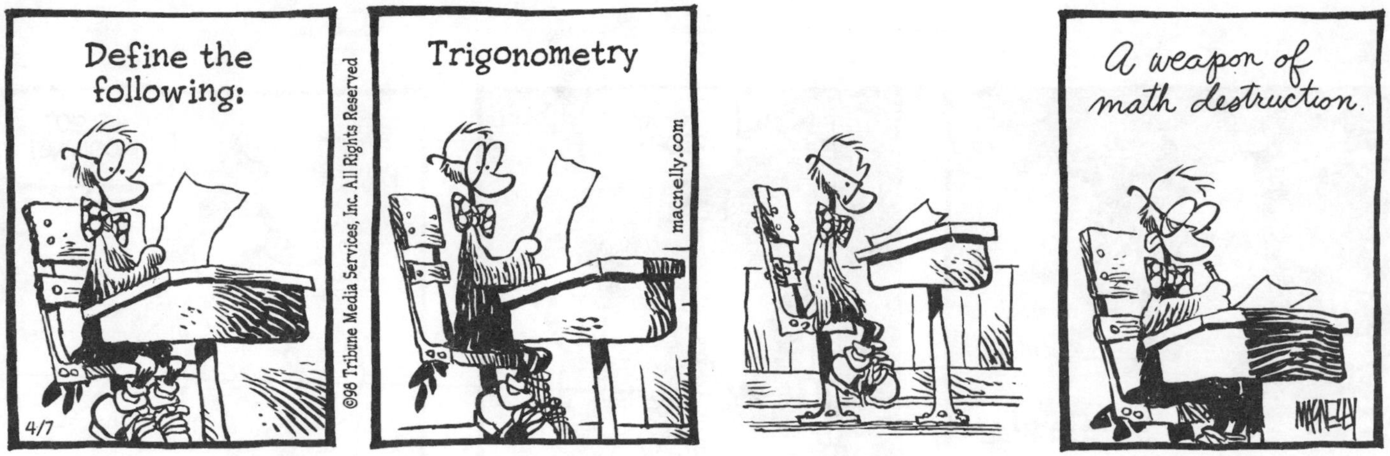
Define the following:
4/7
©98 Tribune Media Services, Inc. All Rights Reserved
Trigonometry
macnelly.com
A weapon of math destruction.
MACNELLY

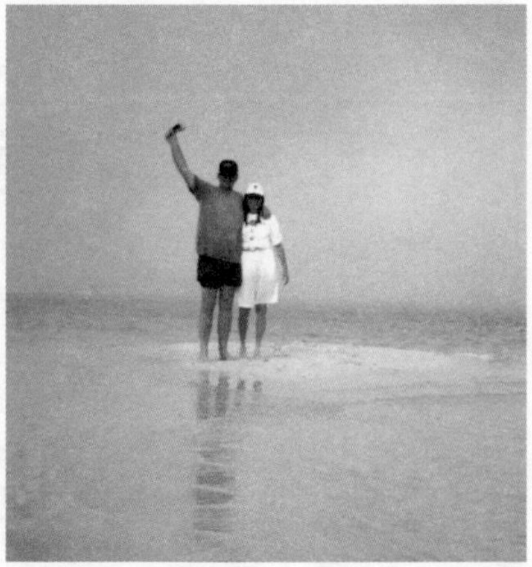

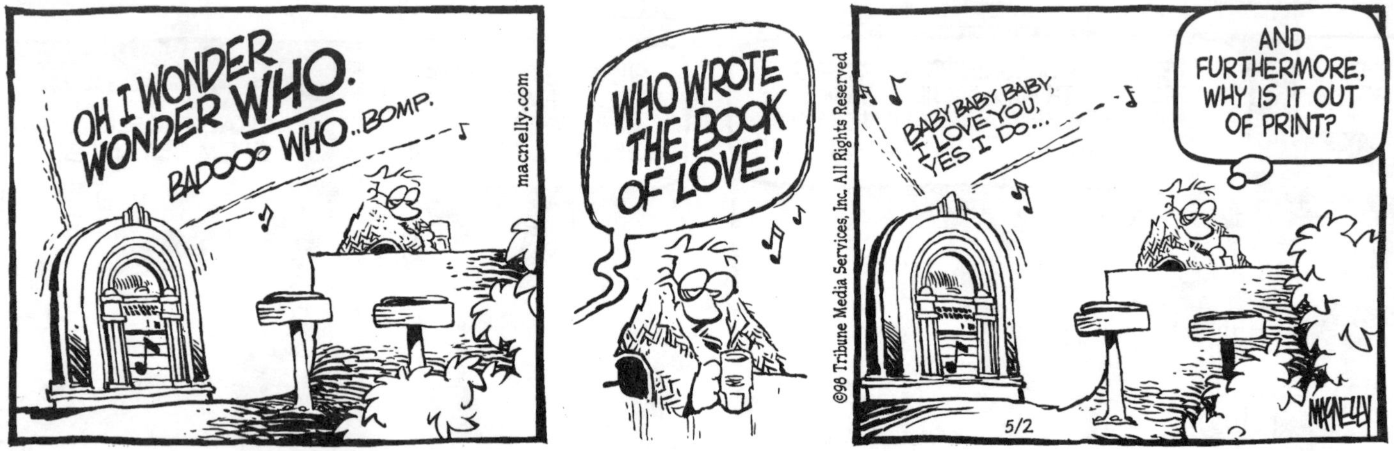
OH I WONDER WONDER WHO.
BADOOO WHO..BOMP.
macnelly.com
WHO WROTE THE BOOK OF LOVE!
©98 Tribune Media Services, Inc. All Rights Reserved
BABY BABY BABY, I LOVE YOU, YES I DO...
AND FURTHERMORE, WHY IS IT OUT OF PRINT?
5/2
MACNELLY

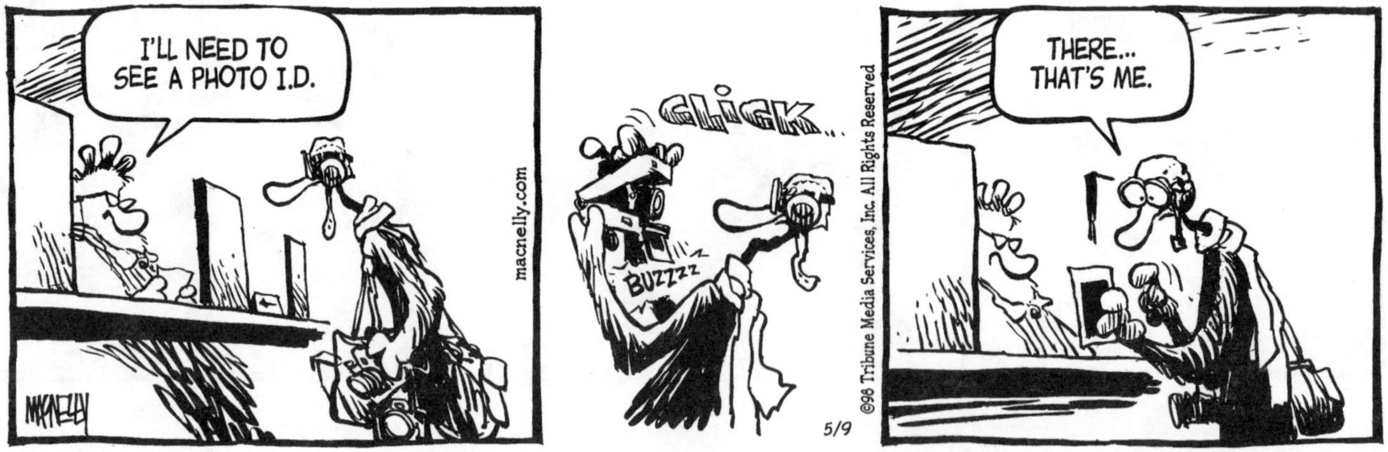
I'LL NEED TO SEE A PHOTO I.D.
MACNELLY
macnelly.com
CLICK..
BUZZZZ
5/9
©98 Tribune Media Services, Inc. All Rights Reserved
THERE... THAT'S ME.

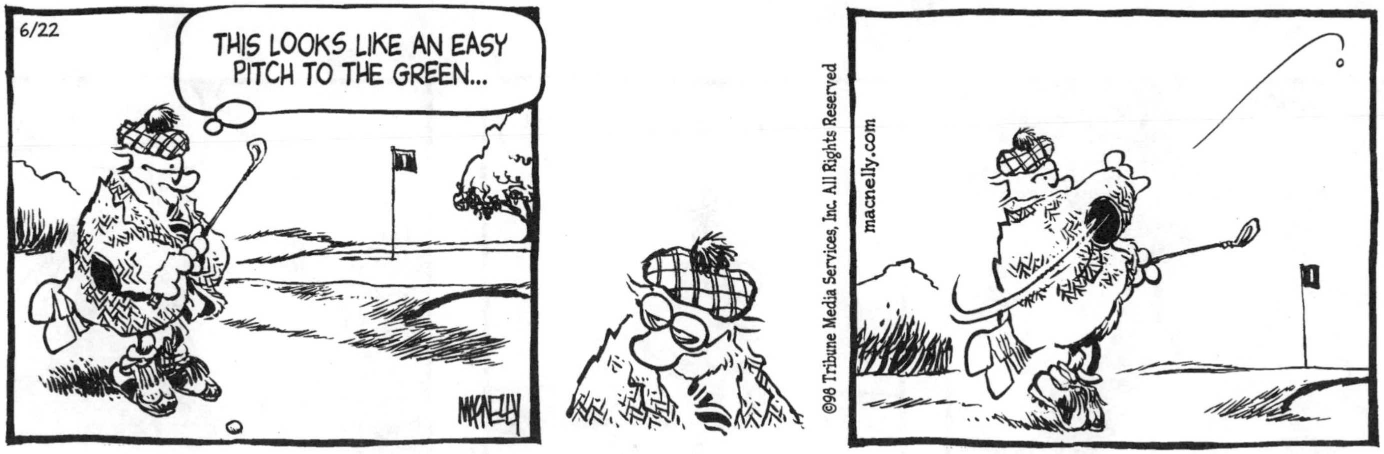
6/22
THIS LOOKS LIKE AN EASY PITCH TO THE GREEN...
©98 Tribune Media Services, Inc. All Rights Reserved
macnelly.com

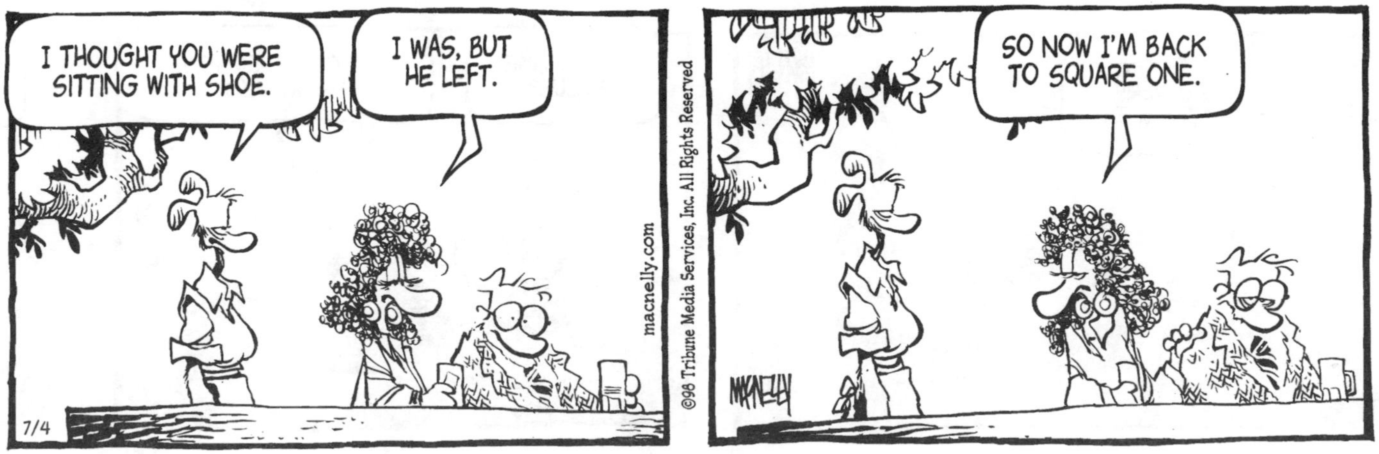
I THOUGHT YOU WERE SITTING WITH SHOE.
I WAS, BUT HE LEFT.
SO NOW I'M BACK TO SQUARE ONE.
7/4
macnelly.com
©98 Tribune Media Services, Inc. All Rights Reserved

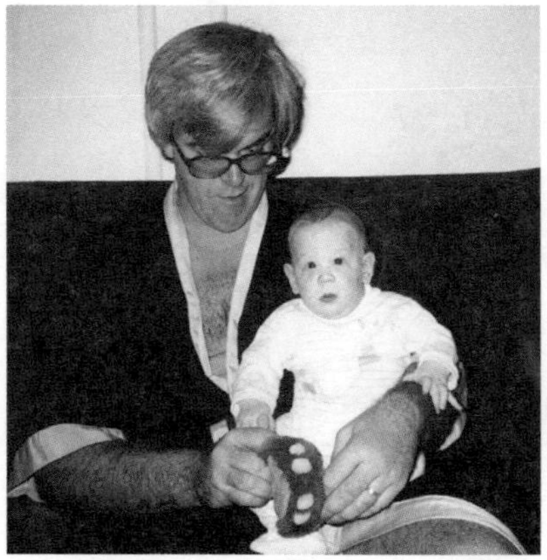

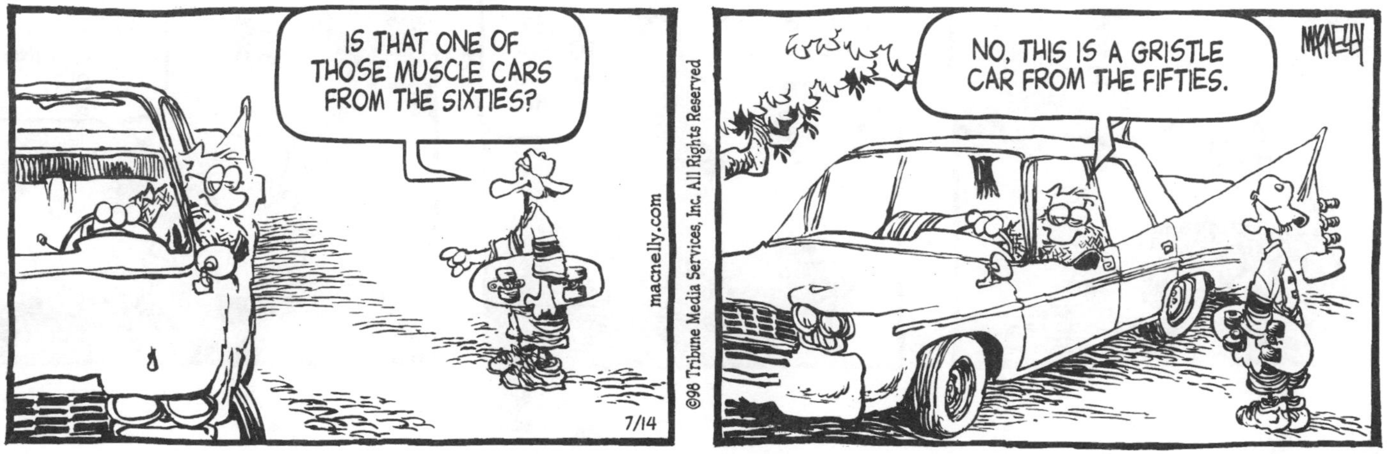
IS THAT ONE OF THOSE MUSCLE CARS FROM THE SIXTIES?
NO, THIS IS A GRISTLE CAR FROM THE FIFTIES.
7/14
macnelly.com
©98 Tribune Media Services, Inc. All Rights Reserved

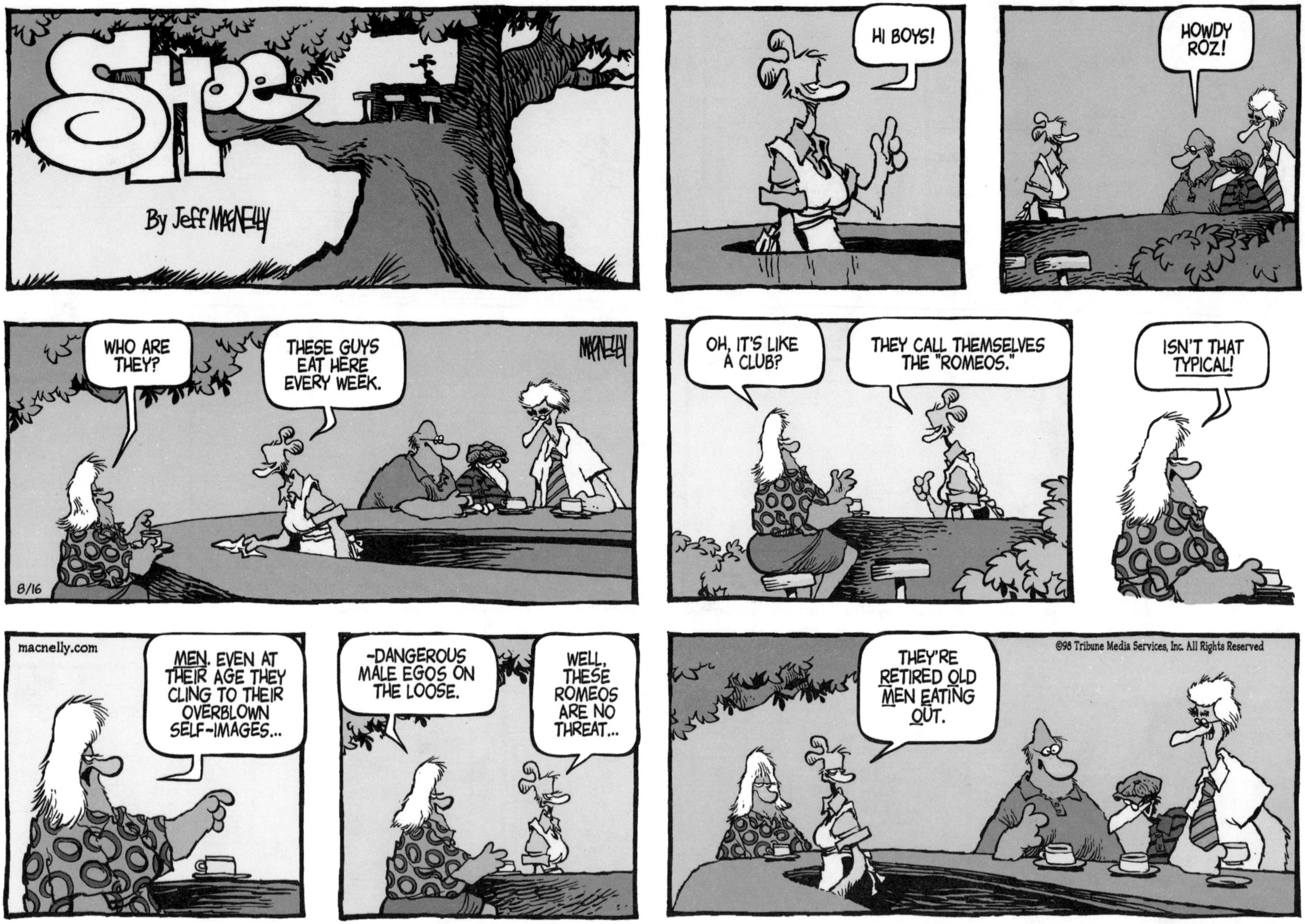
SHOE
By Jeff MacNelly
HI BOYS!
HOWDY ROZ!
WHO ARE THEY?
THESE GUYS EAT HERE EVERY WEEK.
MacNelly
8/16
OH, IT'S LIKE A CLUB?
THEY CALL THEMSELVES THE "ROMEOS."
ISN'T THAT TYPICAL!
macnelly.com
MEN. EVEN AT THEIR AGE THEY CLING TO THEIR OVERBLOWN SELF-IMAGES...
-DANGEROUS MALE EGOS ON THE LOOSE.
WELL, THESE ROMEOS ARE NO THREAT...
©98 Tribune Media Services, Inc. All Rights Reserved
THEY'RE RETIRED OLD MEN EATING OUT.

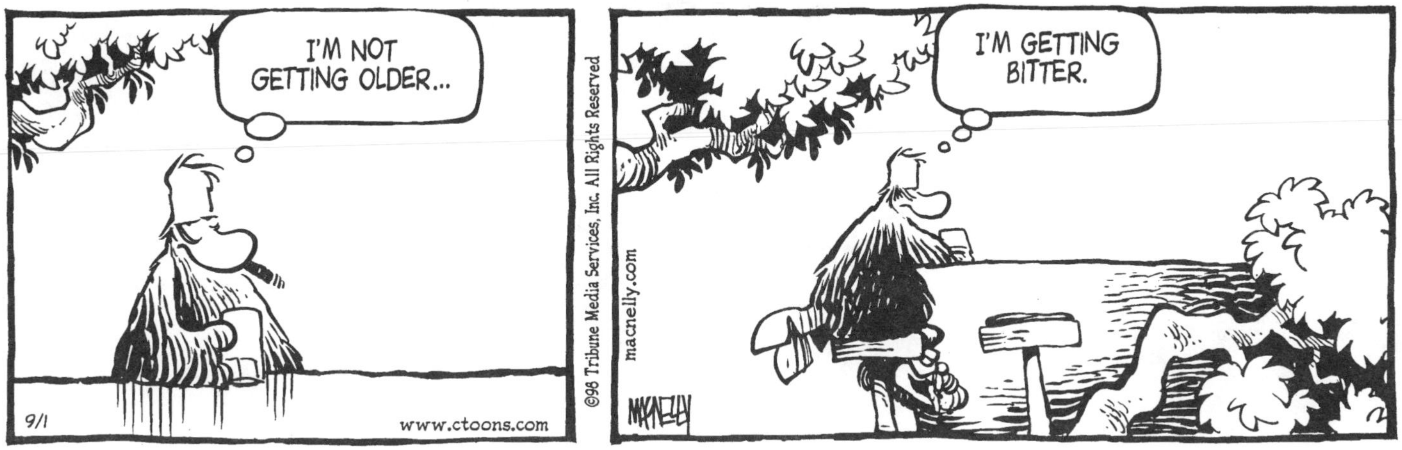
I'M NOT GETTING OLDER...
9/1
www.ctoons.com
©98 Tribune Media Services, Inc. All Rights Reserved
macnelly.com
MACNELLY
I'M GETTING BITTER.

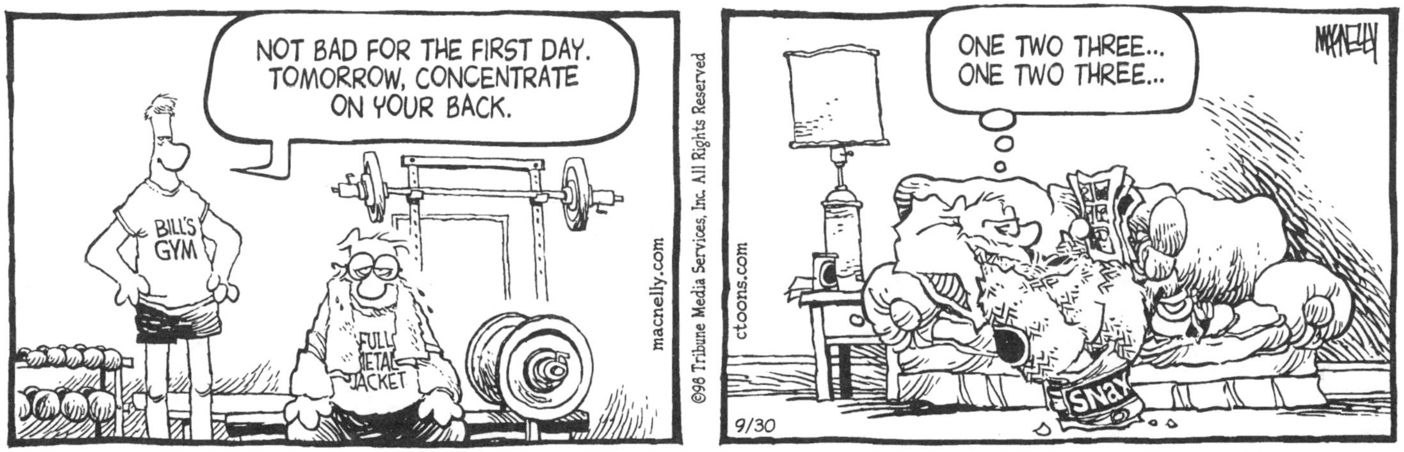
NOT BAD FOR THE FIRST DAY. TOMORROW, CONCENTRATE ON YOUR BACK.
BILL'S GYM
FULL METAL JACKET
macnelly.com
©98 Tribune Media Services, Inc. All Rights Reserved
ctoons.com
MACNELLY
ONE TWO THREE... ONE TWO THREE...
SNAX
9/30

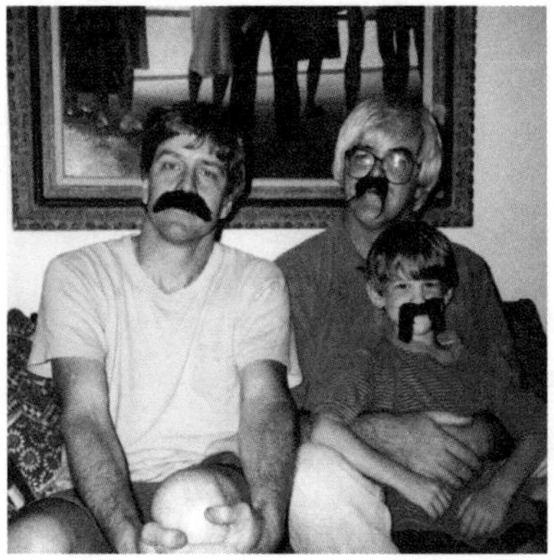

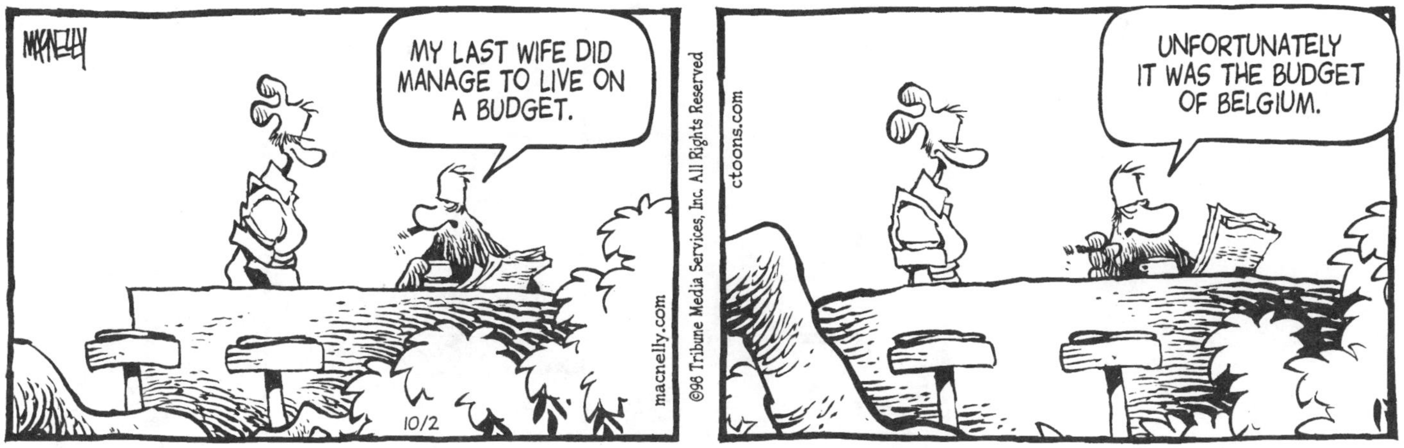
MACNELLY
MY LAST WIFE DID MANAGE TO LIVE ON A BUDGET.
10/2
macnelly.com
©98 Tribune Media Services, Inc. All Rights Reserved
ctoons.com
UNFORTUNATELY IT WAS THE BUDGET OF BELGIUM.

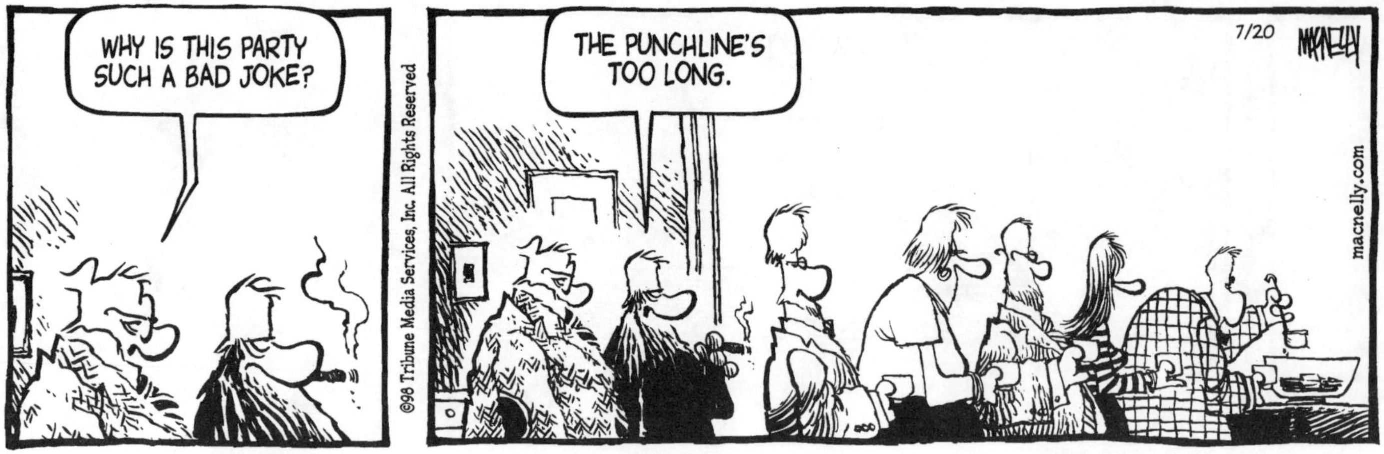
WHY IS THIS PARTY SUCH A BAD JOKE?
©98 Tribune Media Services, Inc. All Rights Reserved
THE PUNCHLINE'S TOO LONG.
7/20
MACNELLY
macnelly.com

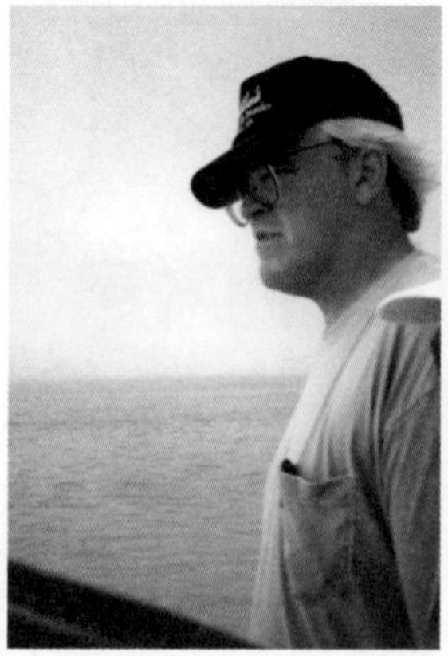

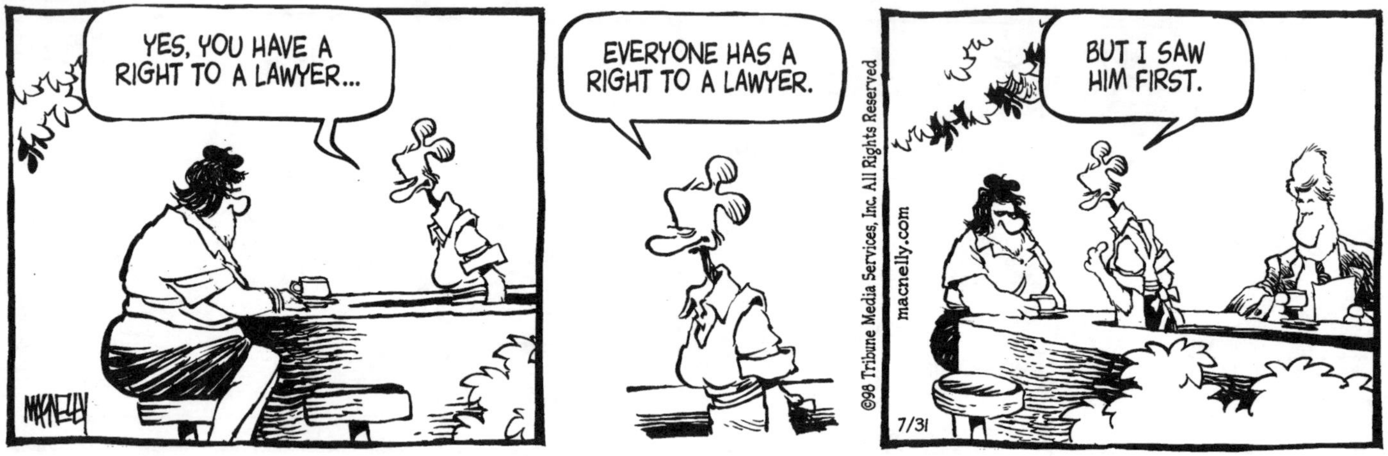
YES, YOU HAVE A RIGHT TO A LAWYER...
MACNELLY
EVERYONE HAS A RIGHT TO A LAWYER.
©98 Tribune Media Services, Inc. All Rights Reserved
macnelly.com
BUT I SAW HIM FIRST.
7/31

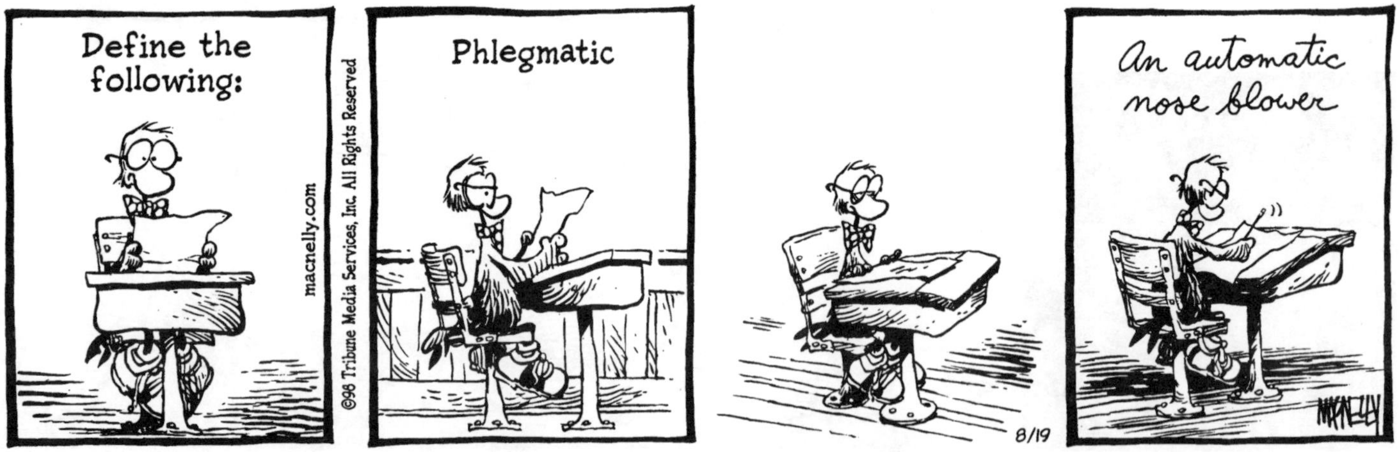
Define the following:
macnelly.com
©98 Tribune Media Services, Inc. All Rights Reserved
Phlegmatic
8/19
An automatic nose blower
MACNELLY

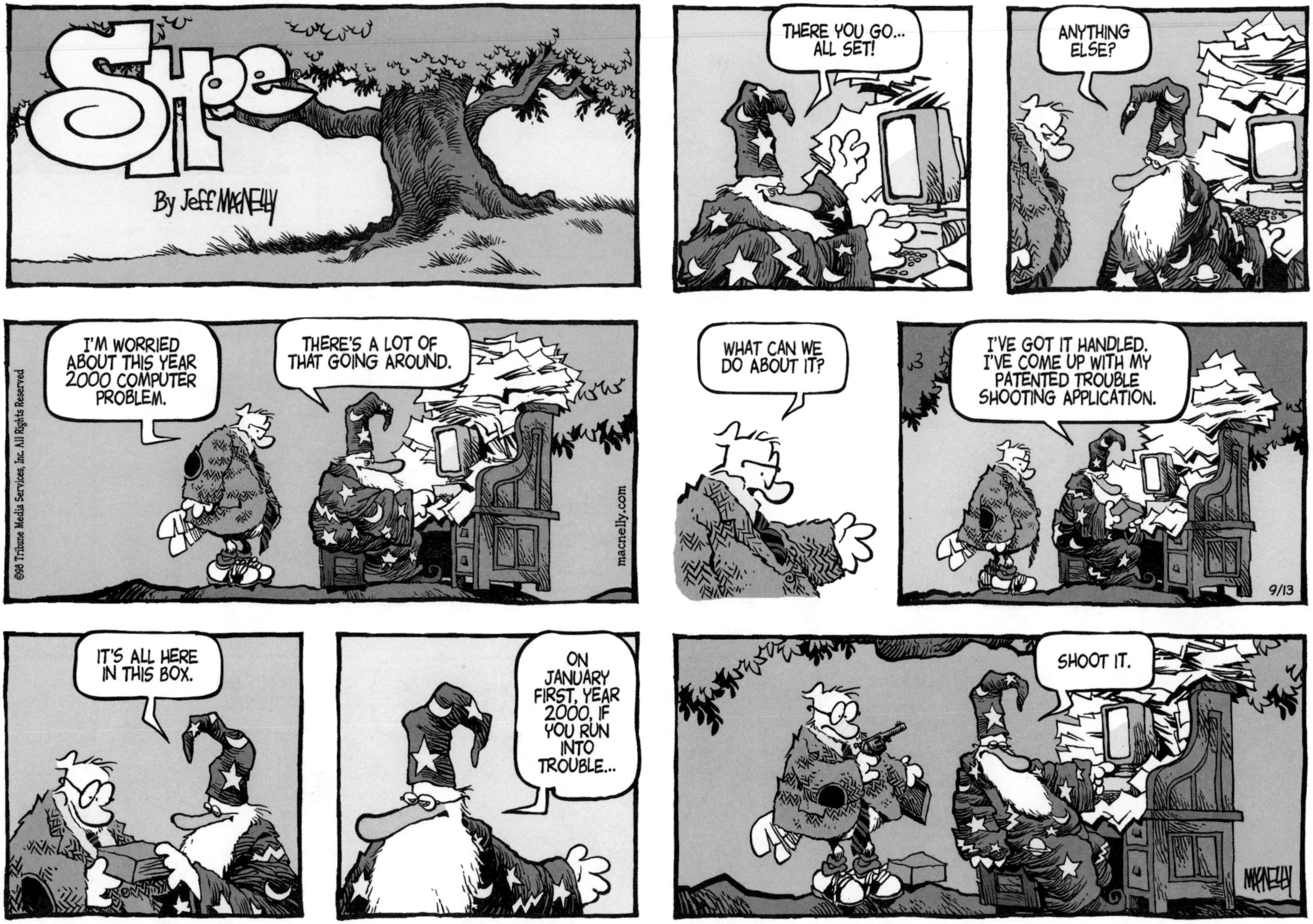
SHOE
By Jeff MacNelly
THERE YOU GO... ALL SET!
ANYTHING ELSE?
I'M WORRIED ABOUT THIS YEAR 2000 COMPUTER PROBLEM.
THERE'S A LOT OF THAT GOING AROUND.
©98 Tribune Media Services, Inc. All Rights Reserved
macnelly.com
WHAT CAN WE DO ABOUT IT?
I'VE GOT IT HANDLED. I'VE COME UP WITH MY PATENTED TROUBLE SHOOTING APPLICATION.
9/13
IT'S ALL HERE IN THIS BOX.
ON JANUARY FIRST, YEAR 2000, IF YOU RUN INTO TROUBLE...
SHOOT IT.
MACNELLY

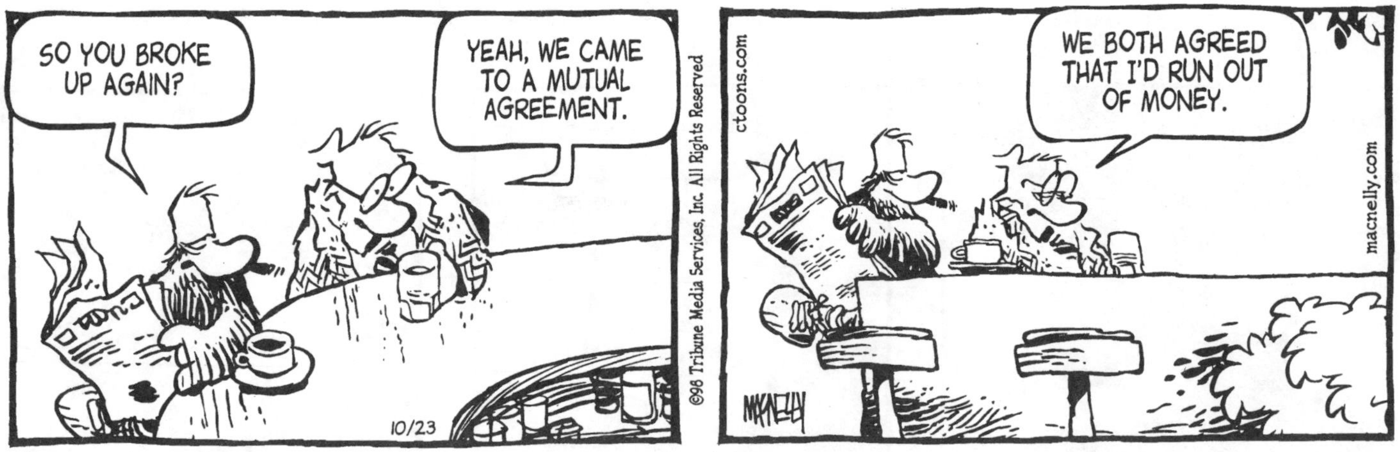
SO YOU BROKE UP AGAIN?
YEAH, WE CAME TO A MUTUAL AGREEMENT.
10/23
©98 Tribune Media Services, Inc. All Rights Reserved
ctoons.com
WE BOTH AGREED THAT I'D RUN OUT OF MONEY.
macnelly.com
MACNELLY

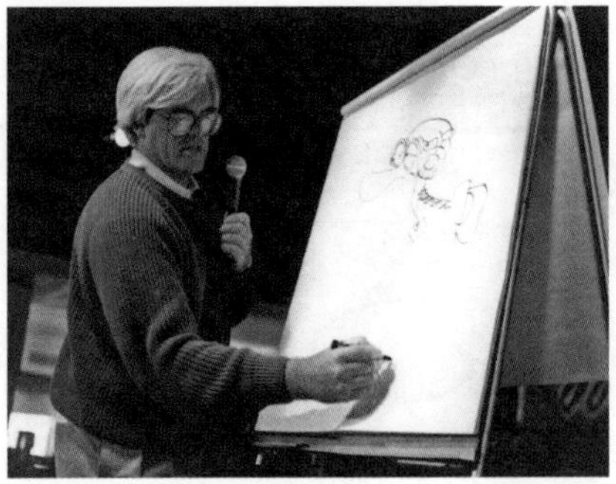

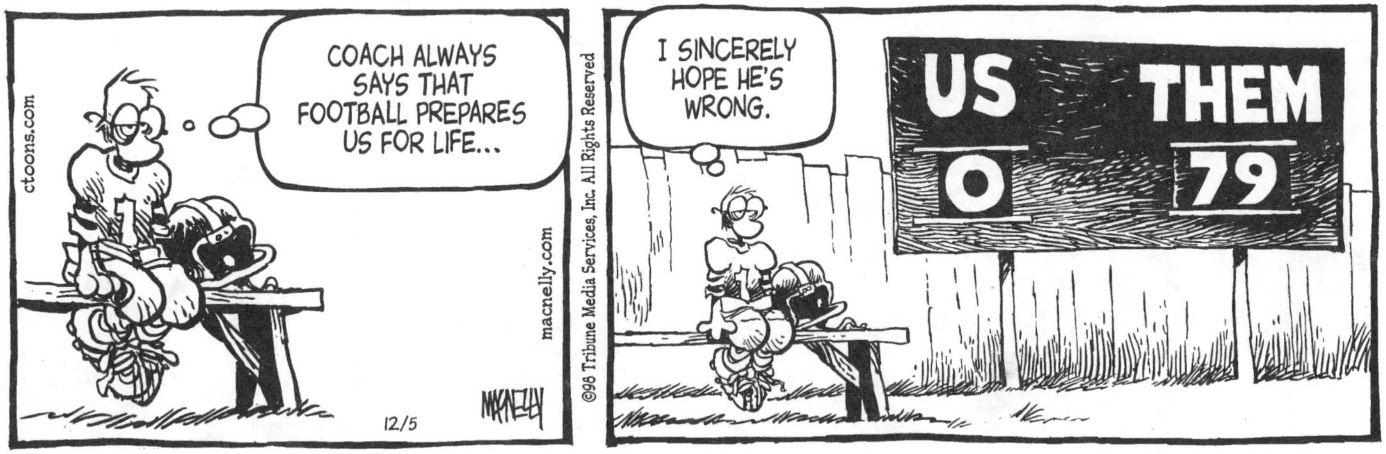
ctoons.com
COACH ALWAYS SAYS THAT FOOTBALL PREPARES US FOR LIFE...
macnelly.com
12/5
MACNELLY
©98 Tribune Media Services, Inc. All Rights Reserved
I SINCERELY HOPE HE'S WRONG.
US
THEM
0
79

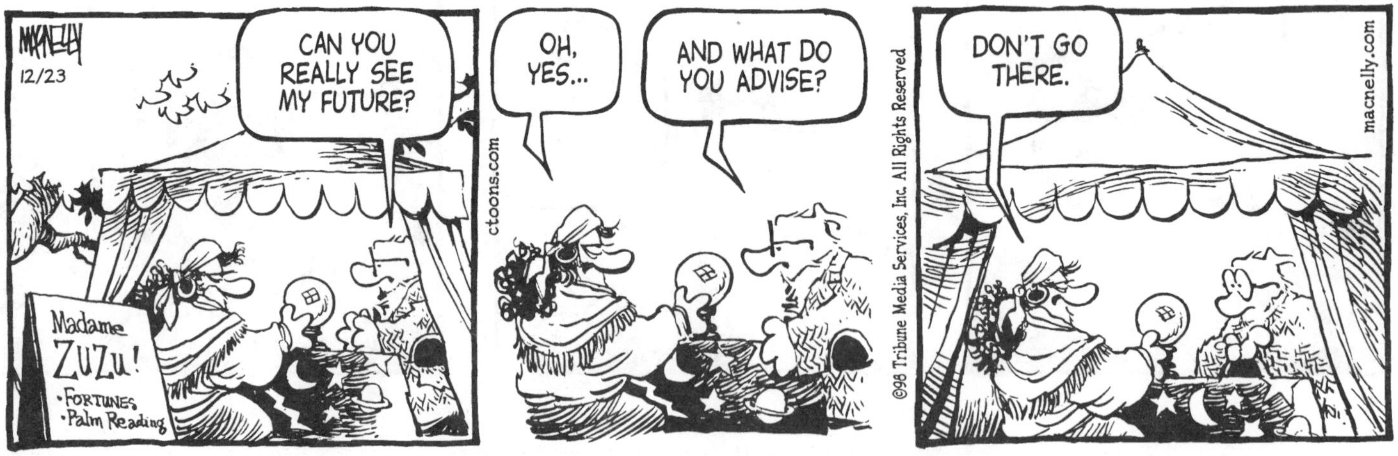
MACNELLY
12/23
CAN YOU REALLY SEE MY FUTURE?
Madame ZuZu!
• FORTUNES
• Palm Reading
ctoons.com
OH, YES...
AND WHAT DO YOU ADVISE?
©98 Tribune Media Services, Inc. All Rights Reserved
DON'T GO THERE.
macnelly.com

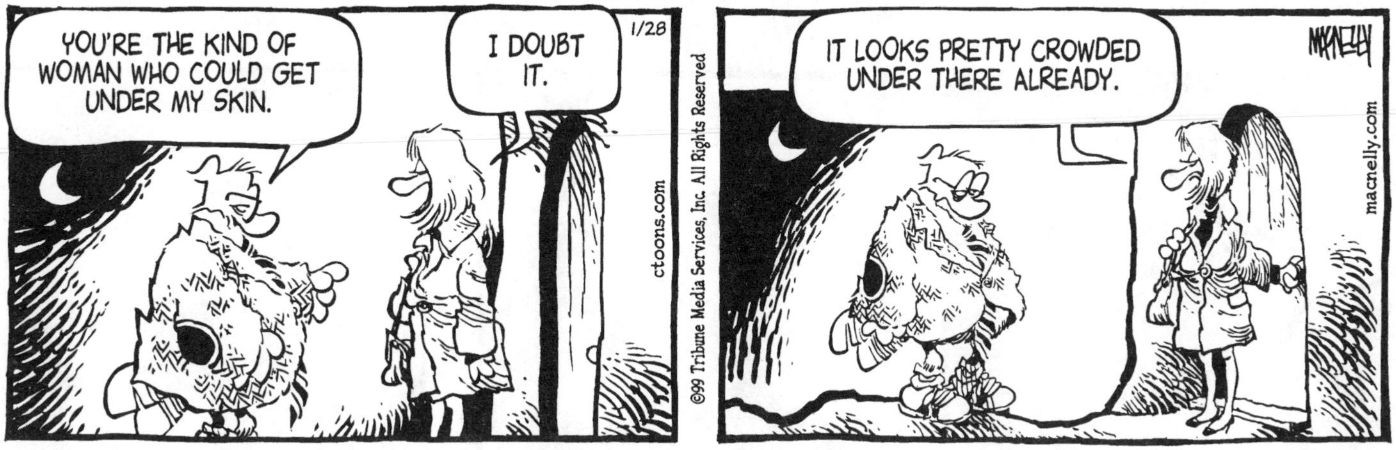
YOU'RE THE KIND OF WOMAN WHO COULD GET UNDER MY SKIN.
I DOUBT IT.
1/28
ctoons.com
©99 Tribune Media Services, Inc. All Rights Reserved
IT LOOKS PRETTY CROWDED UNDER THERE ALREADY.
MACNELLY
macnelly.com

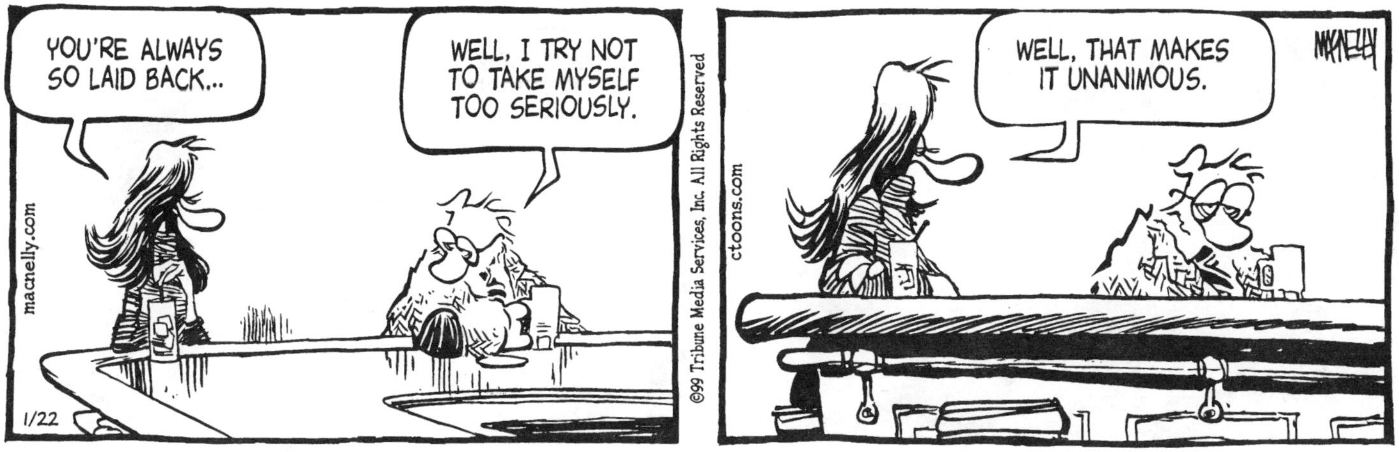
YOU'RE ALWAYS SO LAID BACK...
WELL, I TRY NOT TO TAKE MYSELF TOO SERIOUSLY.
macnelly.com
1/22
©99 Tribune Media Services, Inc. All Rights Reserved
ctoons.com
WELL, THAT MAKES IT UNANIMOUS.
MACNELLY

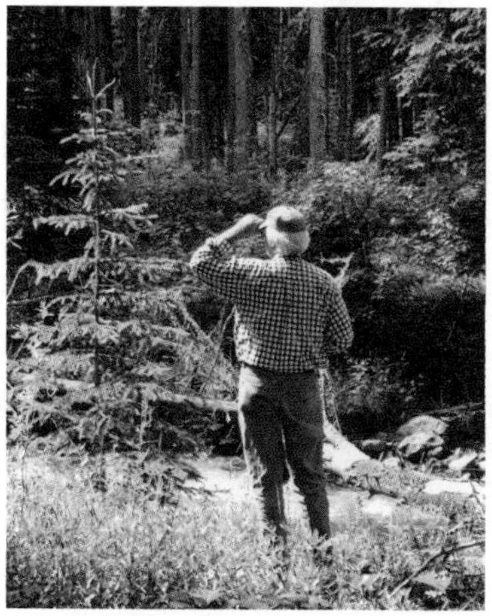

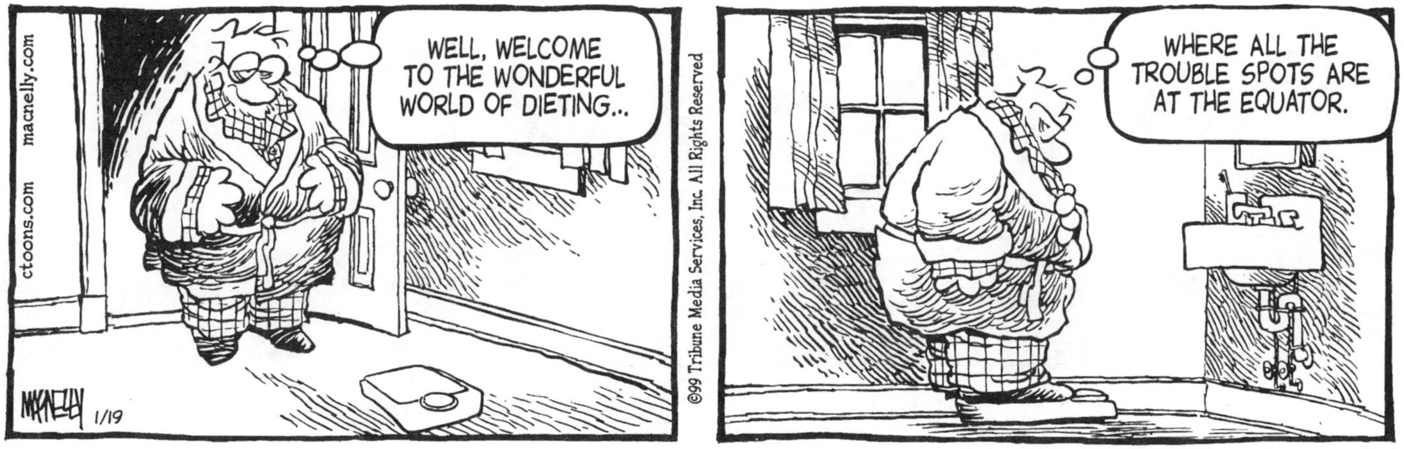
ctoons.com macnelly.com
WELL, WELCOME TO THE WONDERFUL WORLD OF DIETING...
MACNELLY 1/19
©99 Tribune Media Services, Inc. All Rights Reserved
WHERE ALL THE TROUBLE SPOTS ARE AT THE EQUATOR.

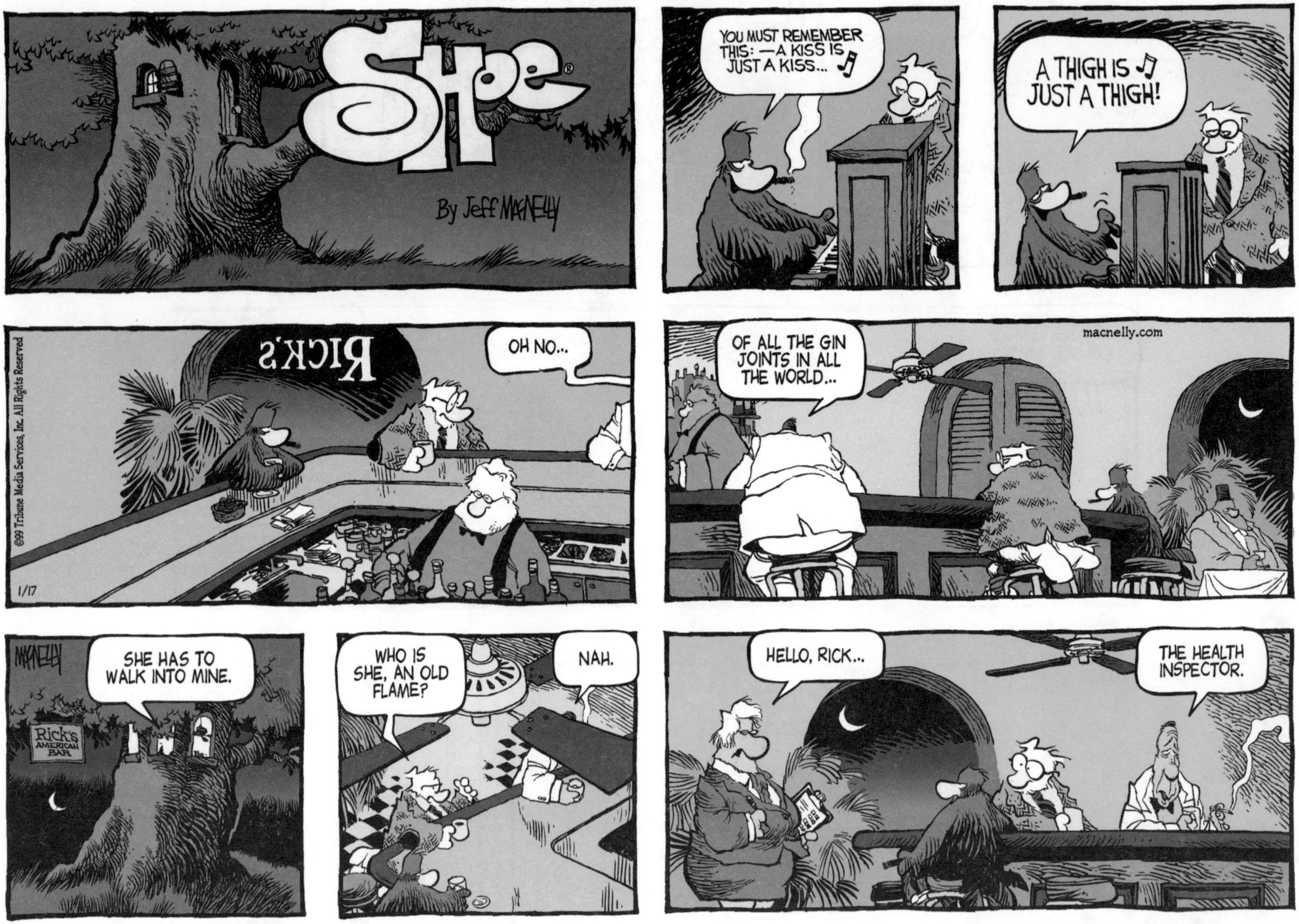
Shoe®
By Jeff MacNelly
YOU MUST REMEMBER THIS: —A KISS IS JUST A KISS...
A THIGH IS JUST A THIGH!
RICK'S
OH NO...
©99 Tribune Media Services, Inc. All Rights Reserved
1/17
macnelly.com
OF ALL THE GIN JOINTS IN ALL THE WORLD...
MACNELLY
SHE HAS TO WALK INTO MINE.
Rick's AMERICAN BAR
WHO IS SHE, AN OLD FLAME?
NAH.
HELLO, RICK...
THE HEALTH INSPECTOR.

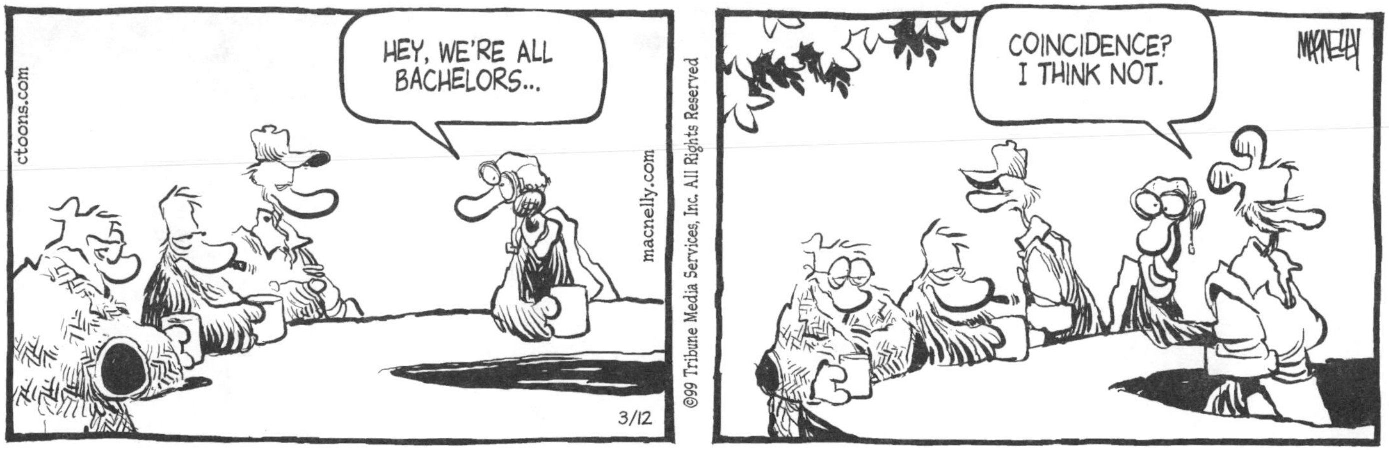
ctoons.com
HEY, WE'RE ALL BACHELORS...
macnelly.com
3/12
©99 Tribune Media Services, Inc. All Rights Reserved
COINCIDENCE? I THINK NOT.
MACNELLY

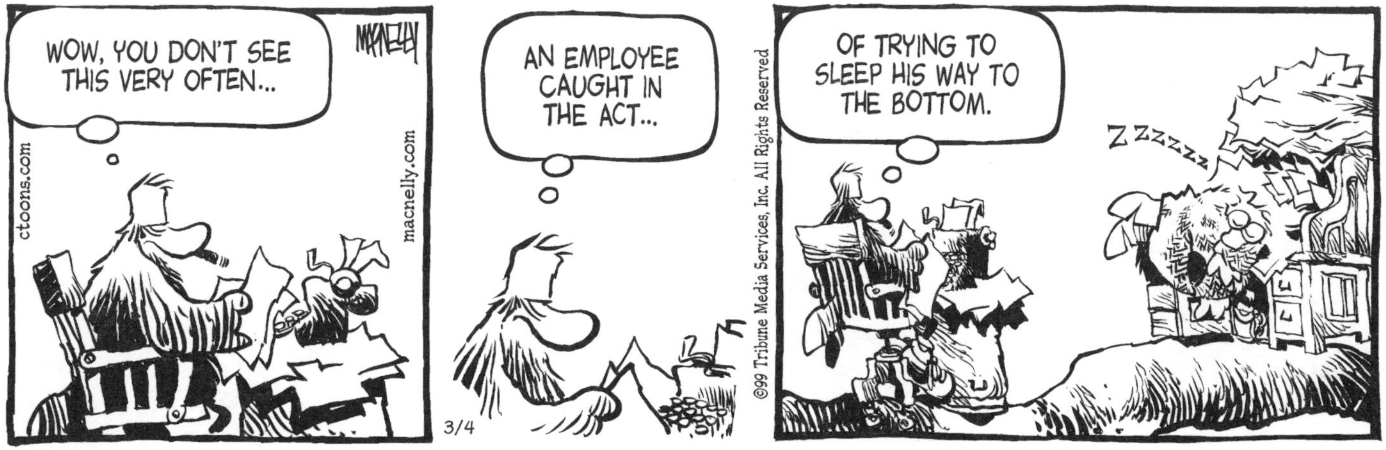
WOW, YOU DON'T SEE THIS VERY OFTEN...
MACNELLY
ctoons.com
macnelly.com
AN EMPLOYEE CAUGHT IN THE ACT...
3/4
©99 Tribune Media Services, Inc. All Rights Reserved
OF TRYING TO SLEEP HIS WAY TO THE BOTTOM.
ZZZZZZ

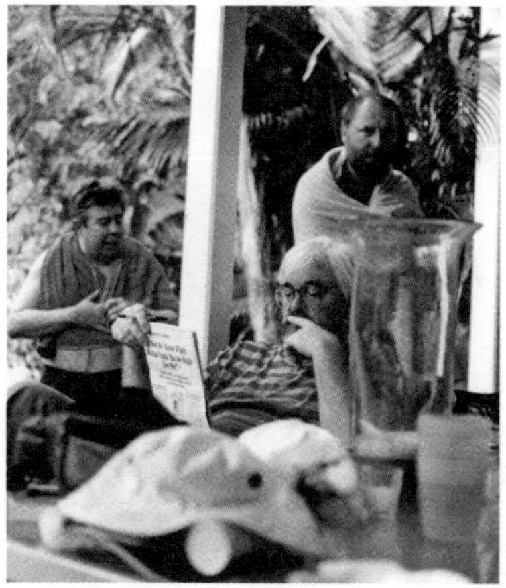

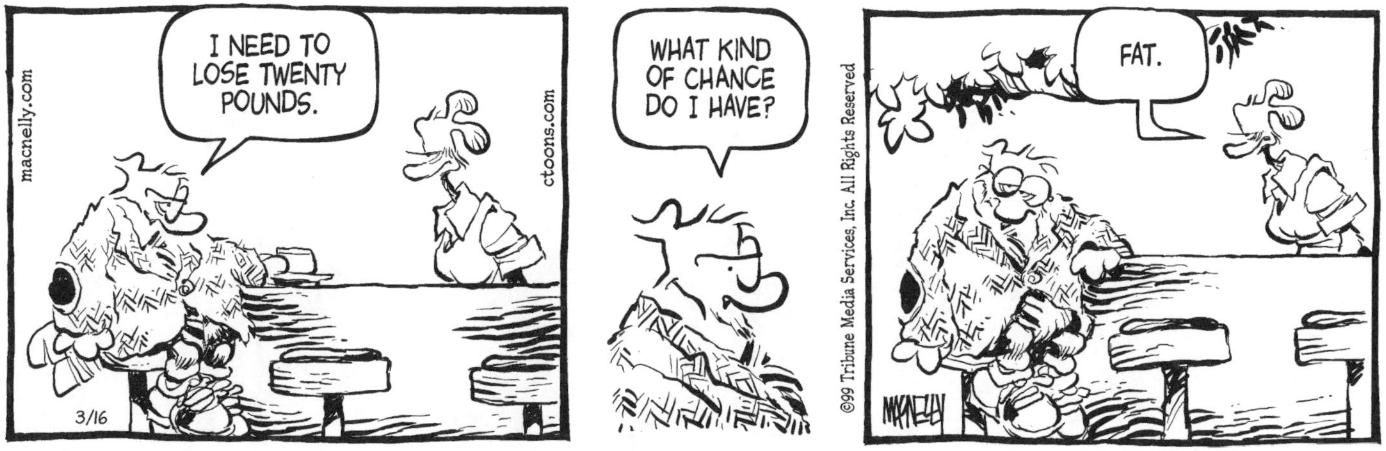
macnelly.com
I NEED TO LOSE TWENTY POUNDS.
ctoons.com
3/16
WHAT KIND OF CHANCE DO I HAVE?
©99 Tribune Media Services, Inc. All Rights Reserved
FAT.
MACNELLY

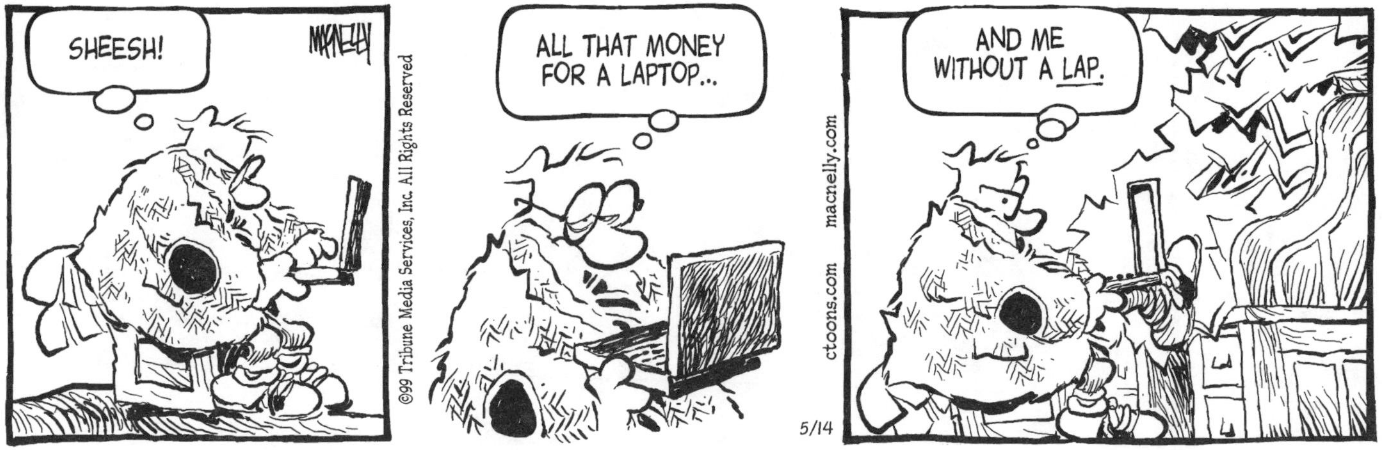
SHEESH!
MACNELLY
©99 Tribune Media Services, Inc. All Rights Reserved
ALL THAT MONEY FOR A LAPTOP...
macnelly.com
ctoons.com
5/14
AND ME WITHOUT A LAP.

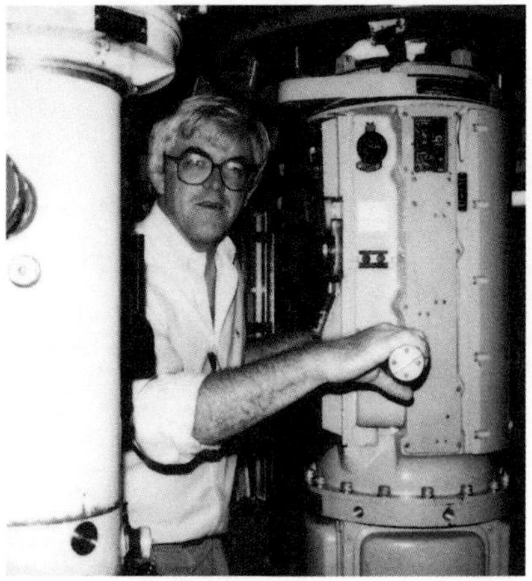

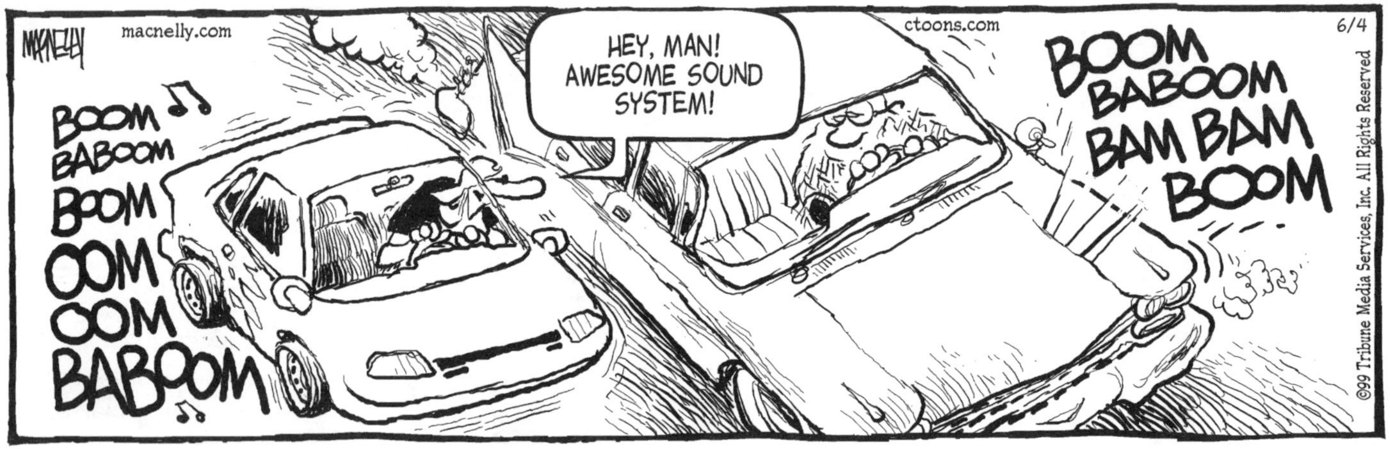
MACNELLY
macnelly.com
ctoons.com
6/4
BOOM BABOOM BOOM OOM OOM BABOOM
HEY, MAN! AWESOME SOUND SYSTEM!
BOOM BABOOM BAM BAM BOOM
©99 Tribune Media Services, Inc. All Rights Reserved

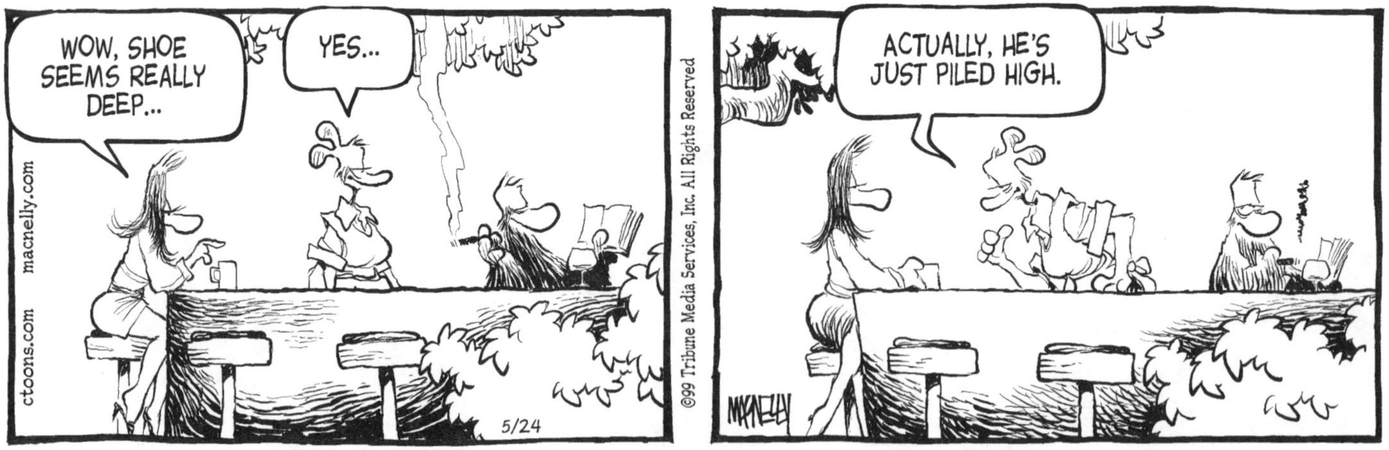
macnelly.com
ctoons.com
WOW, SHOE SEEMS REALLY DEEP...
YES...
5/24
©99 Tribune Media Services, Inc. All Rights Reserved
ACTUALLY, HE'S JUST PILED HIGH.
MACNELLY

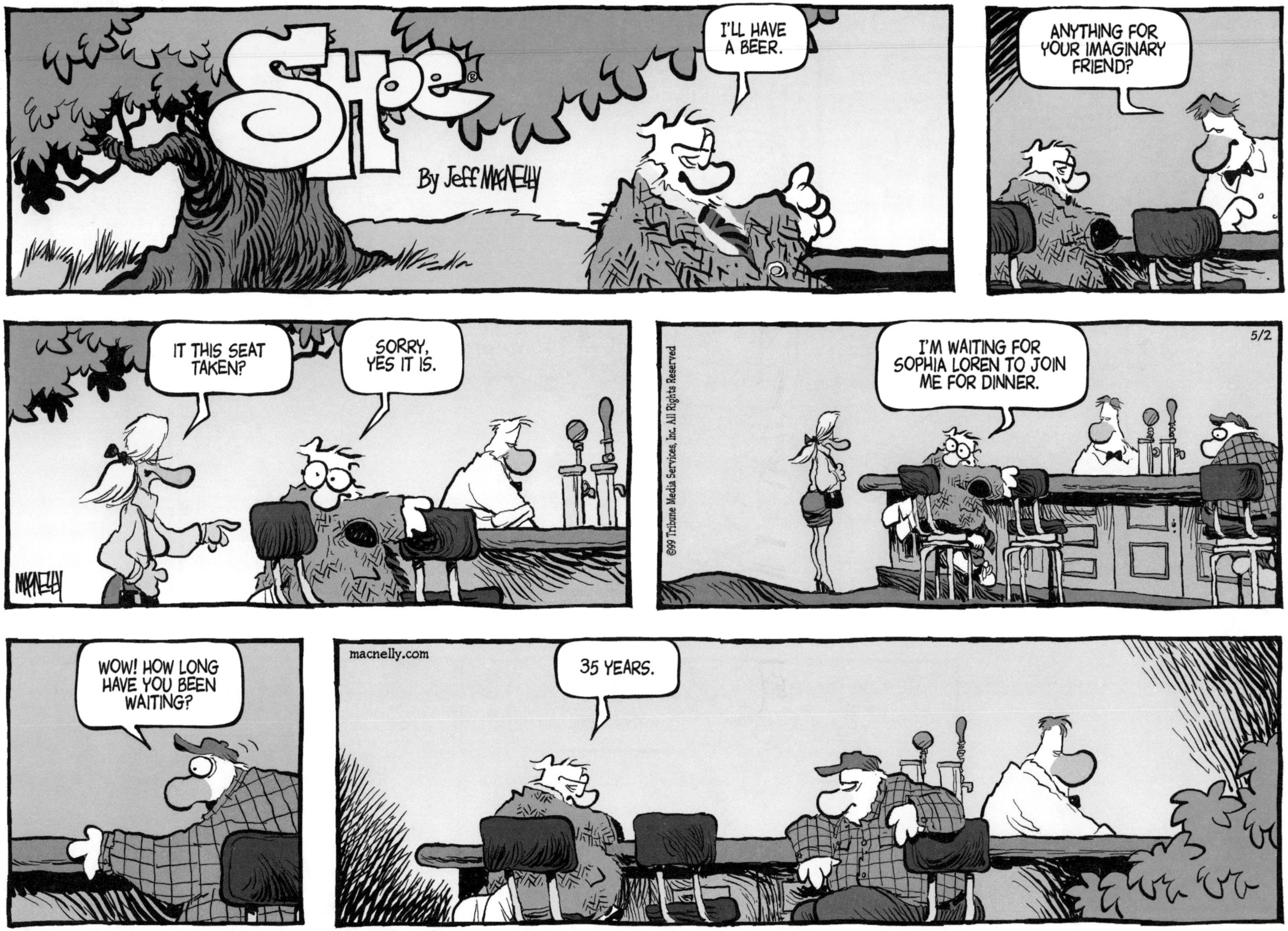
Shoe®
By Jeff MacNelly
I'LL HAVE A BEER.
ANYTHING FOR YOUR IMAGINARY FRIEND?
IT THIS SEAT TAKEN?
SORRY, YES IT IS.
MacNelly
©99 Tribune Media Services, Inc. All Rights Reserved
5/2
I'M WAITING FOR SOPHIA LOREN TO JOIN ME FOR DINNER.
WOW! HOW LONG HAVE YOU BEEN WAITING?
macnelly.com
35 YEARS.

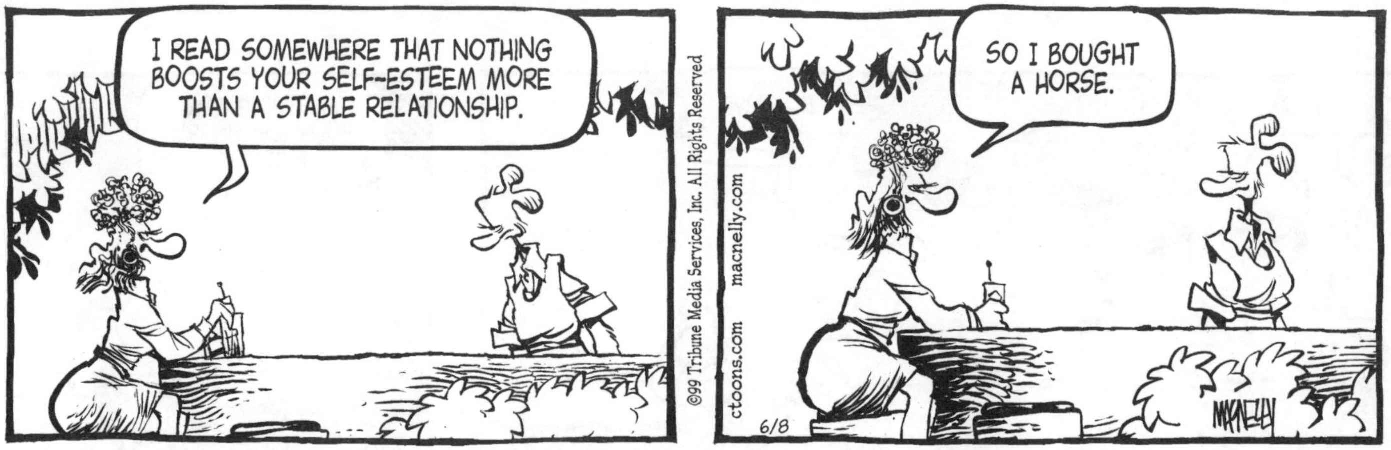
I READ SOMEWHERE THAT NOTHING BOOSTS YOUR SELF-ESTEEM MORE THAN A STABLE RELATIONSHIP.
©99 Tribune Media Services, Inc. All Rights Reserved
ctoons.com macnelly.com
6/8
SO I BOUGHT A HORSE.
MACNELLY

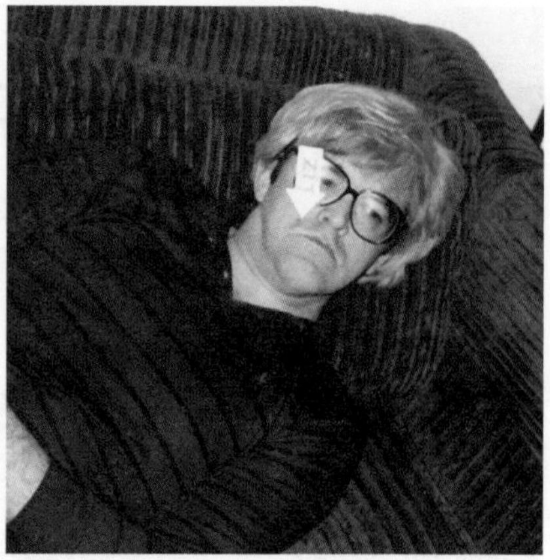

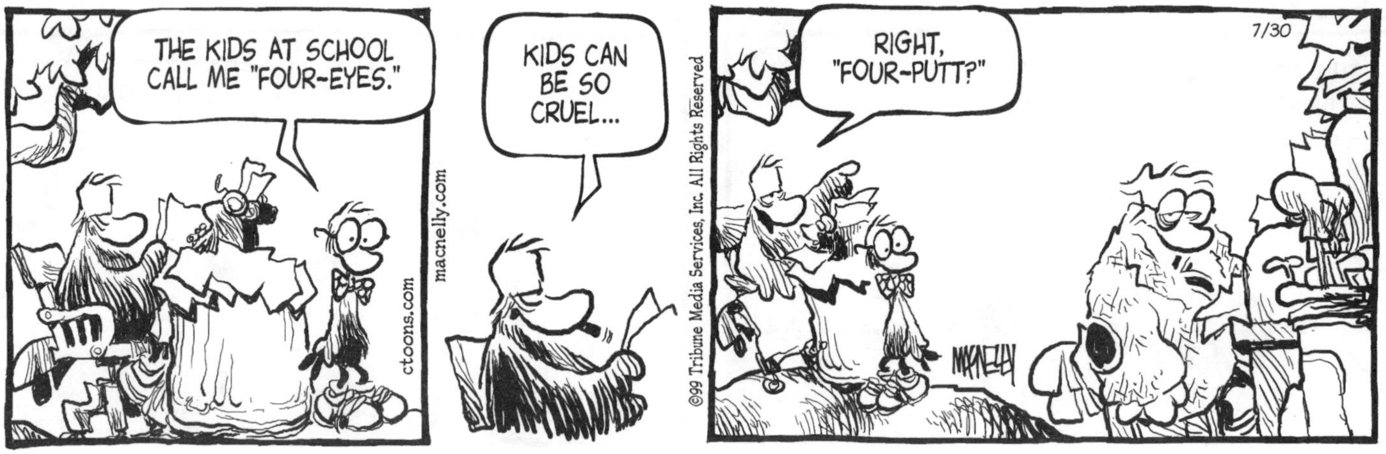
THE KIDS AT SCHOOL CALL ME "FOUR-EYES."
macnelly.com
ctoons.com
KIDS CAN BE SO CRUEL...
©99 Tribune Media Services, Inc. All Rights Reserved
7/30
RIGHT, "FOUR-PUTT?"
MACNELLY

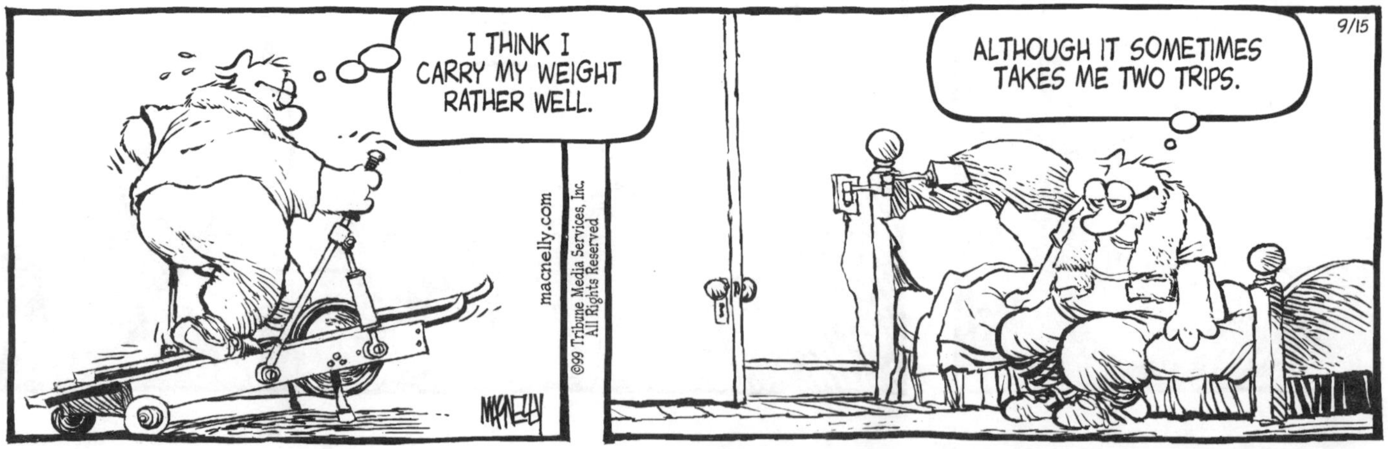
I THINK I CARRY MY WEIGHT RATHER WELL.
MACNELLY
macnelly.com
©99 Tribune Media Services, Inc. All Rights Reserved
9/15
ALTHOUGH IT SOMETIMES TAKES ME TWO TRIPS.

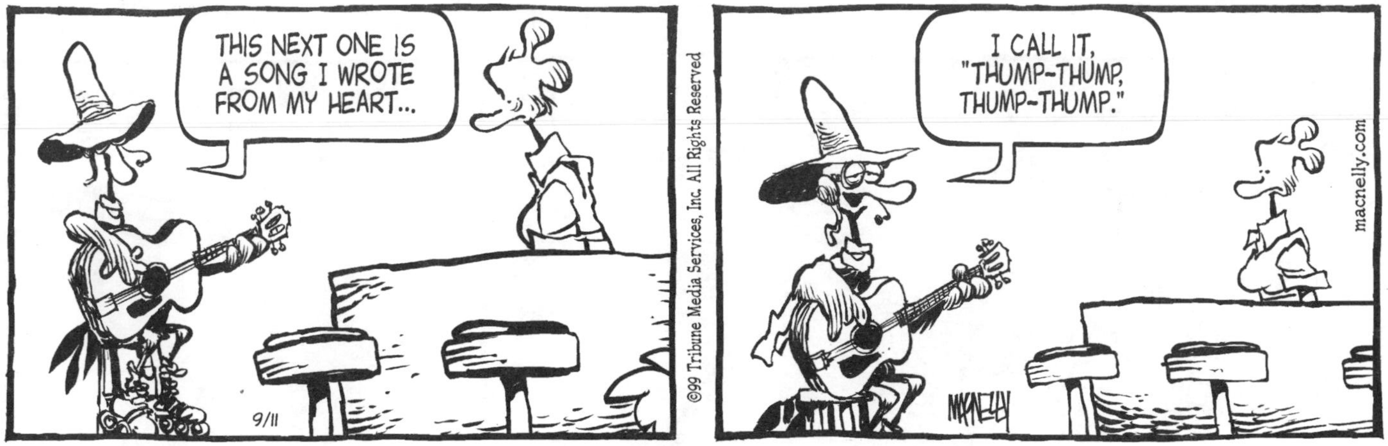
THIS NEXT ONE IS A SONG I WROTE FROM MY HEART...
9/11
©99 Tribune Media Services, Inc. All Rights Reserved
I CALL IT, "THUMP-THUMP, THUMP-THUMP."
macnelly.com

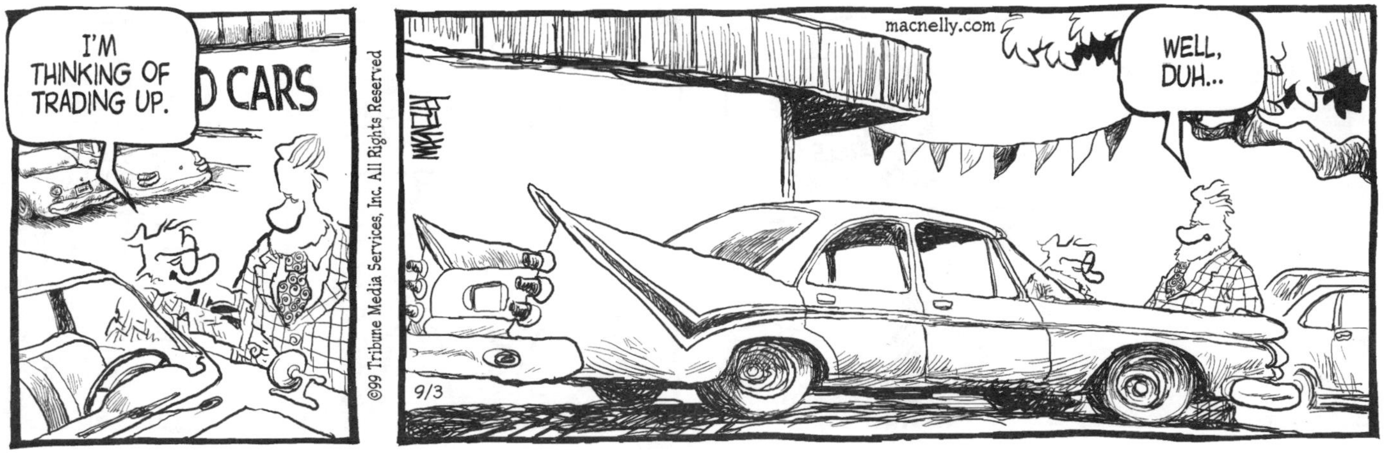
I'M THINKING OF TRADING UP.
D CARS
©99 Tribune Media Services, Inc. All Rights Reserved
macnelly.com
WELL, DUH...
9/3

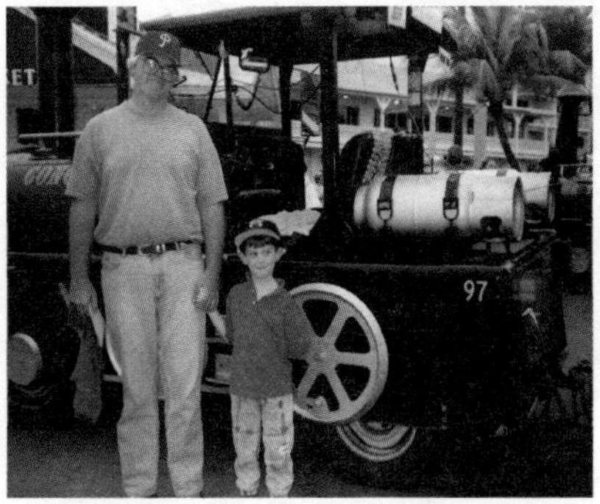
97

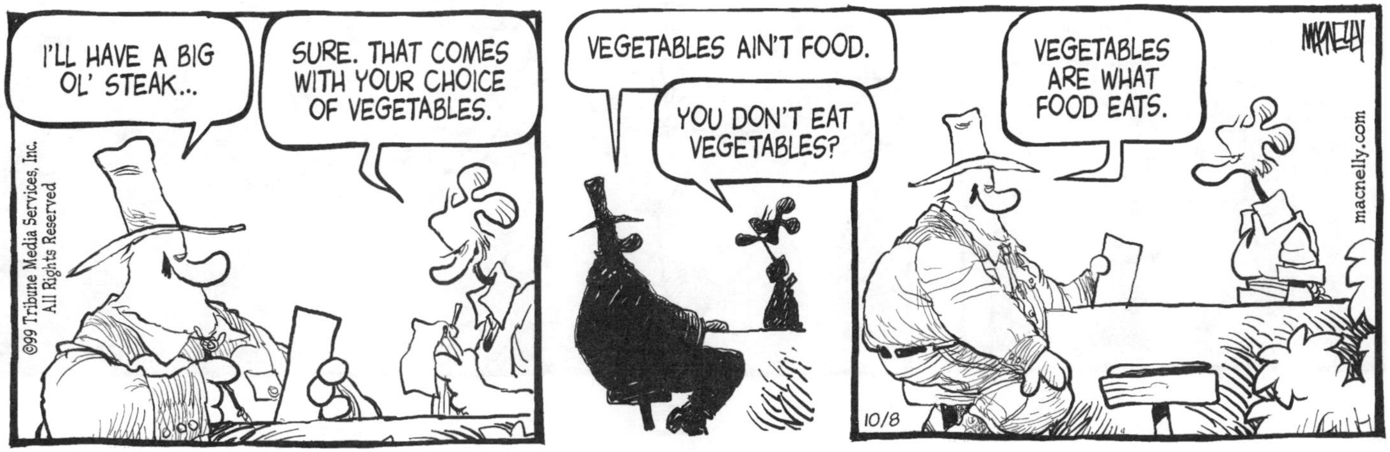
I'LL HAVE A BIG OL' STEAK...
SURE. THAT COMES WITH YOUR CHOICE OF VEGETABLES.
©99 Tribune Media Services, Inc. All Rights Reserved
VEGETABLES AIN'T FOOD.
YOU DON'T EAT VEGETABLES?
VEGETABLES ARE WHAT FOOD EATS.
macnelly.com
10/8

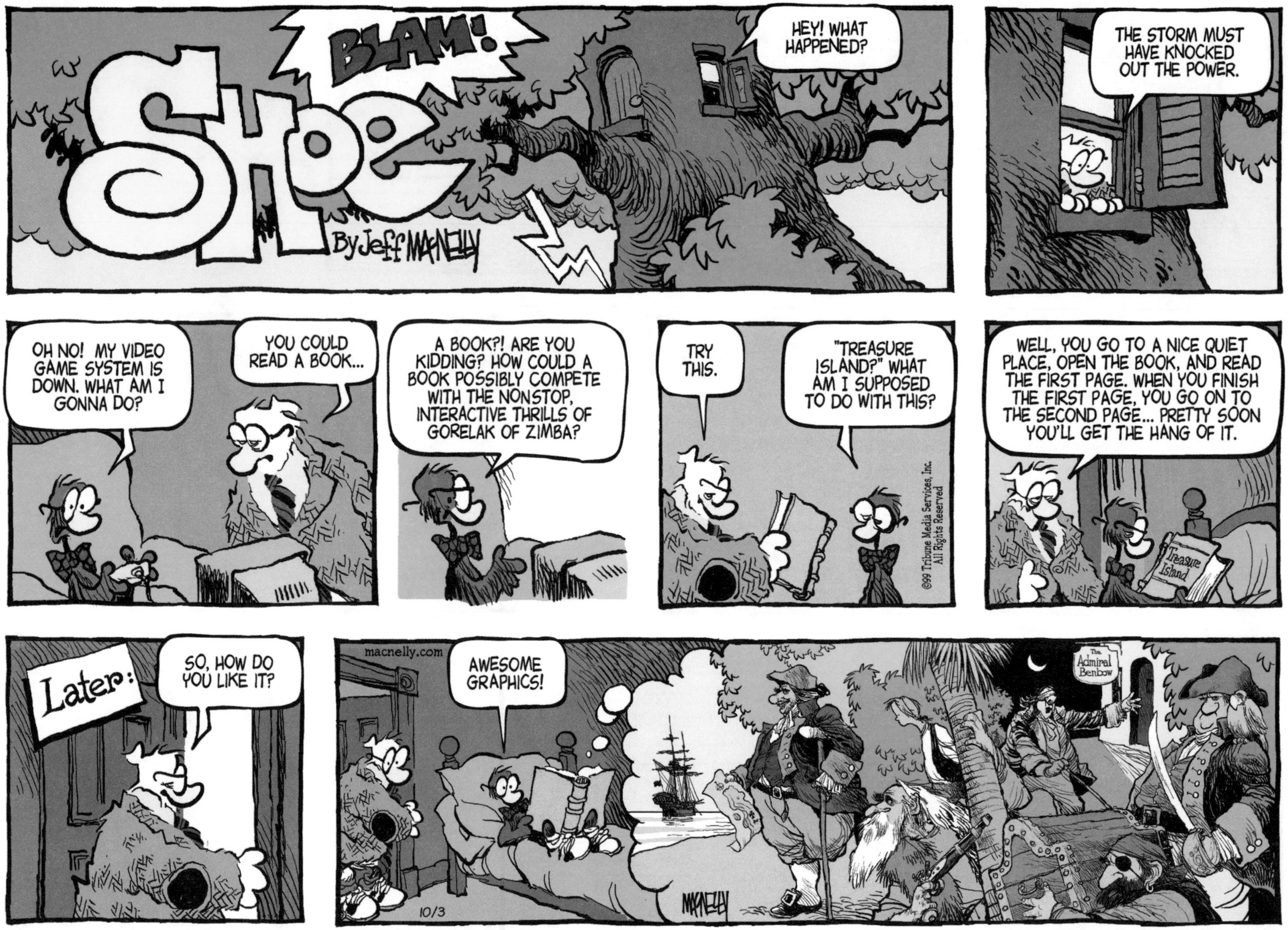

BLAM!
SHOE
By Jeff MacNELLY
HEY! WHAT HAPPENED?
THE STORM MUST HAVE KNOCKED OUT THE POWER.
OH NO! MY VIDEO GAME SYSTEM IS DOWN. WHAT AM I GONNA DO?
YOU COULD READ A BOOK...
A BOOK?! ARE YOU KIDDING? HOW COULD A BOOK POSSIBLY COMPETE WITH THE NONSTOP, INTERACTIVE THRILLS OF GORELAK OF ZIMBA?
TRY THIS.
"TREASURE ISLAND?" WHAT AM I SUPPOSED TO DO WITH THIS?
©99 Tribune Media Services, Inc. All Rights Reserved
WELL, YOU GO TO A NICE QUIET PLACE, OPEN THE BOOK, AND READ THE FIRST PAGE. WHEN YOU FINISH THE FIRST PAGE, YOU GO ON TO THE SECOND PAGE... PRETTY SOON YOU'LL GET THE HANG OF IT.
Treasure Island
Later:
SO, HOW DO YOU LIKE IT?
macnelly.com
AWESOME GRAPHICS!
The Admiral Benbow
MacNELLY
10/3

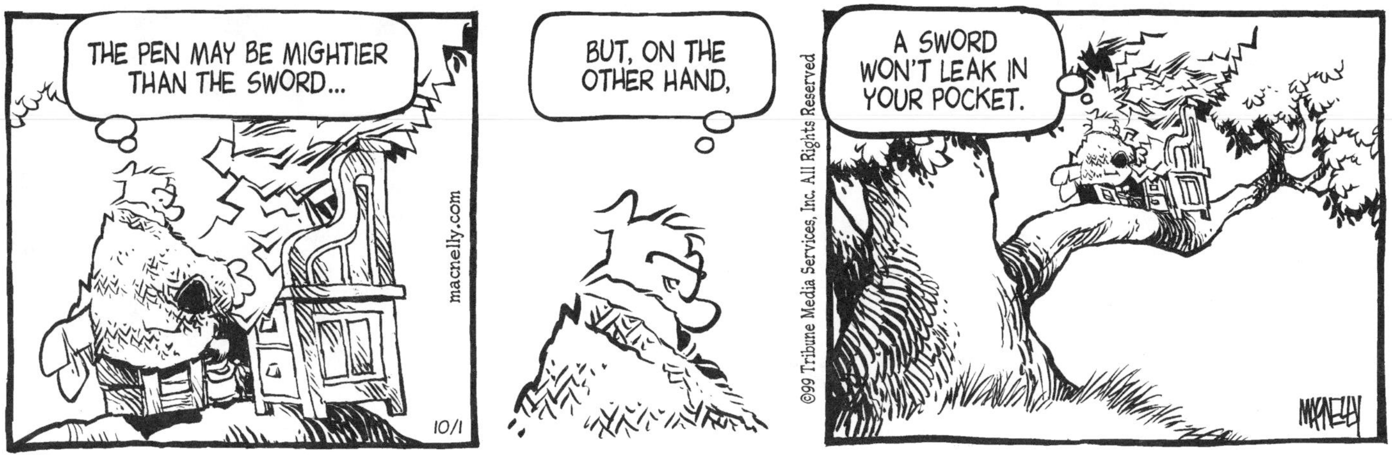
THE PEN MAY BE MIGHTIER THAN THE SWORD...
macnelly.com
10/1
BUT, ON THE OTHER HAND,
©99 Tribune Media Services, Inc. All Rights Reserved
A SWORD WON'T LEAK IN YOUR POCKET.
MACNELLY

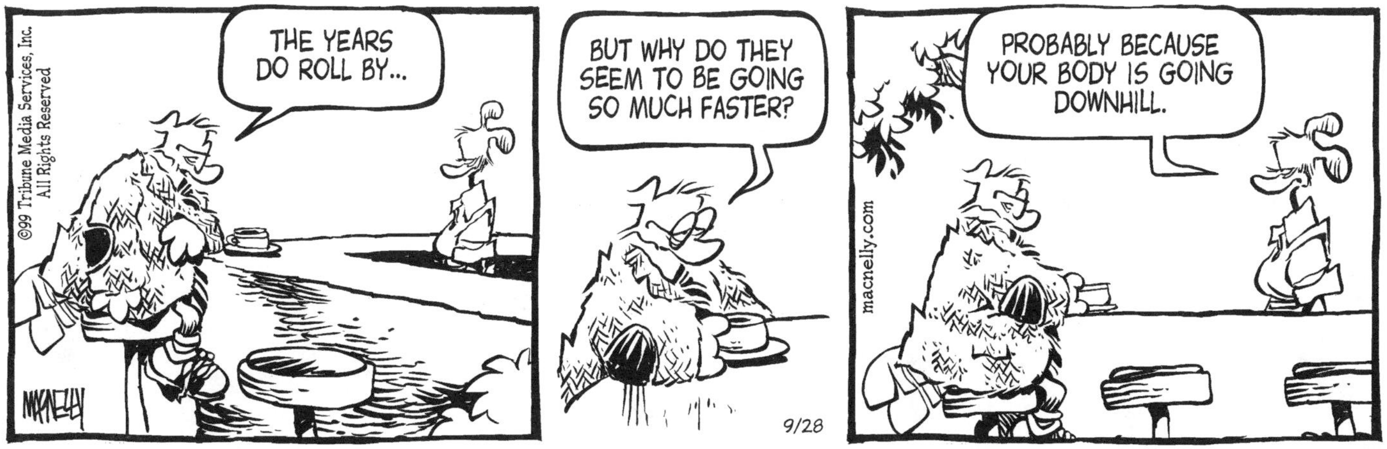
©99 Tribune Media Services, Inc. All Rights Reserved
THE YEARS DO ROLL BY...
MACNELLY
BUT WHY DO THEY SEEM TO BE GOING SO MUCH FASTER?
9/28
macnelly.com
PROBABLY BECAUSE YOUR BODY IS GOING DOWNHILL.

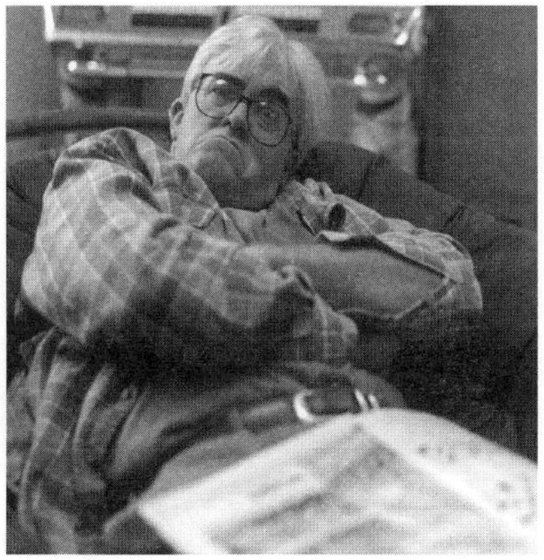

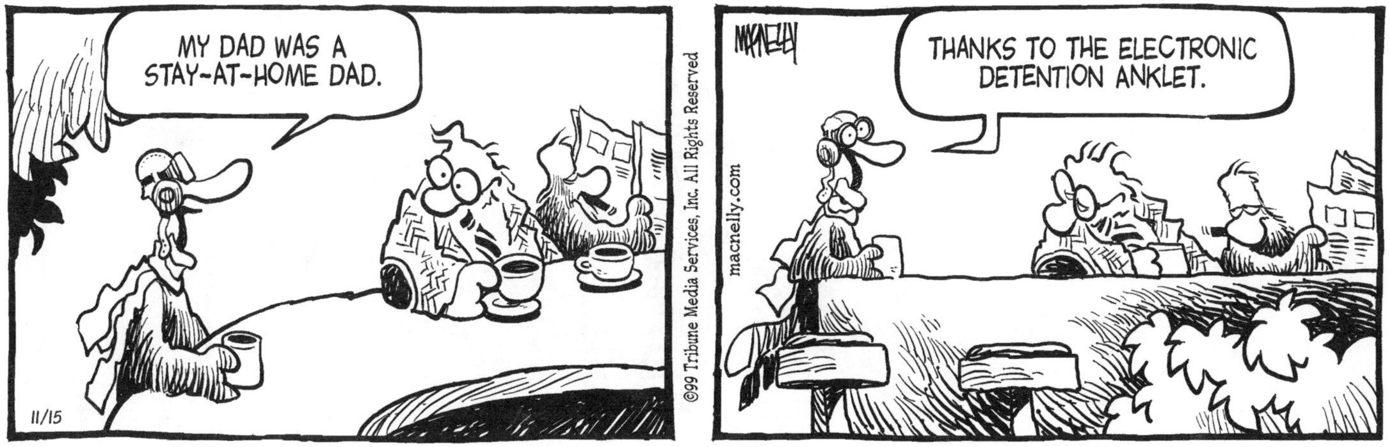
MY DAD WAS A STAY-AT-HOME DAD.
11/15
©99 Tribune Media Services, Inc. All Rights Reserved
macnelly.com
MACNELLY
THANKS TO THE ELECTRONIC DETENTION ANKLET.

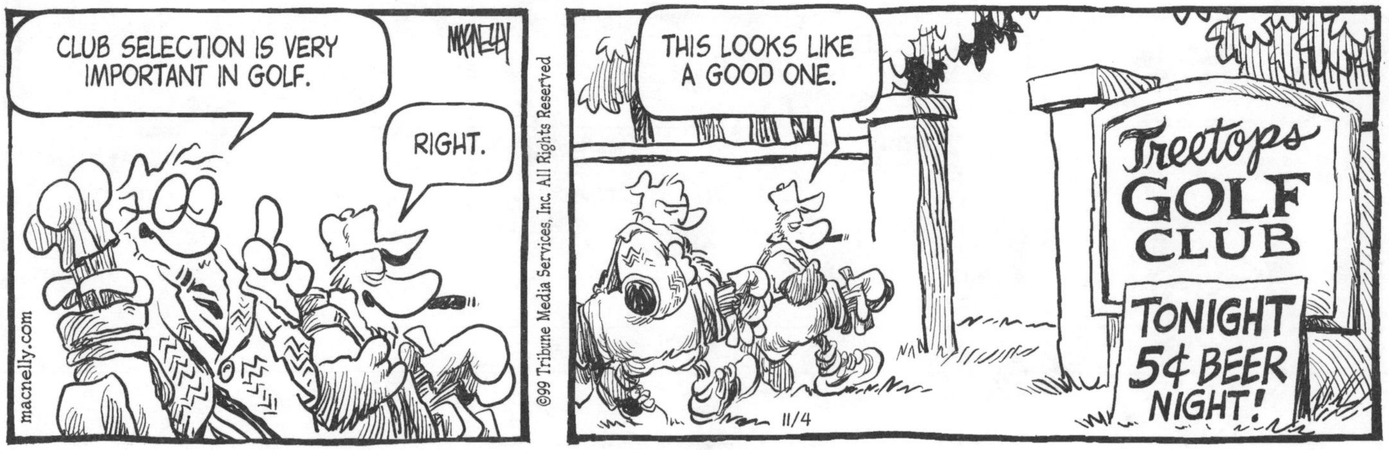
CLUB SELECTION IS VERY IMPORTANT IN GOLF.
RIGHT.
THIS LOOKS LIKE A GOOD ONE.
Treetops GOLF CLUB
TONIGHT 5¢ BEER NIGHT!
MACNELLY
macnelly.com
©99 Tribune Media Services, Inc. All Rights Reserved
11/4

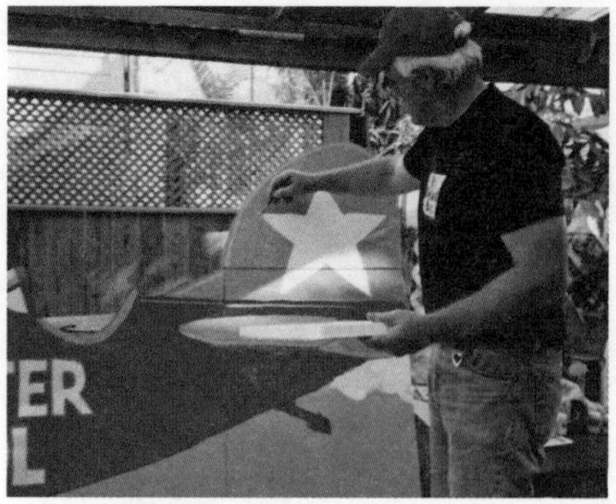

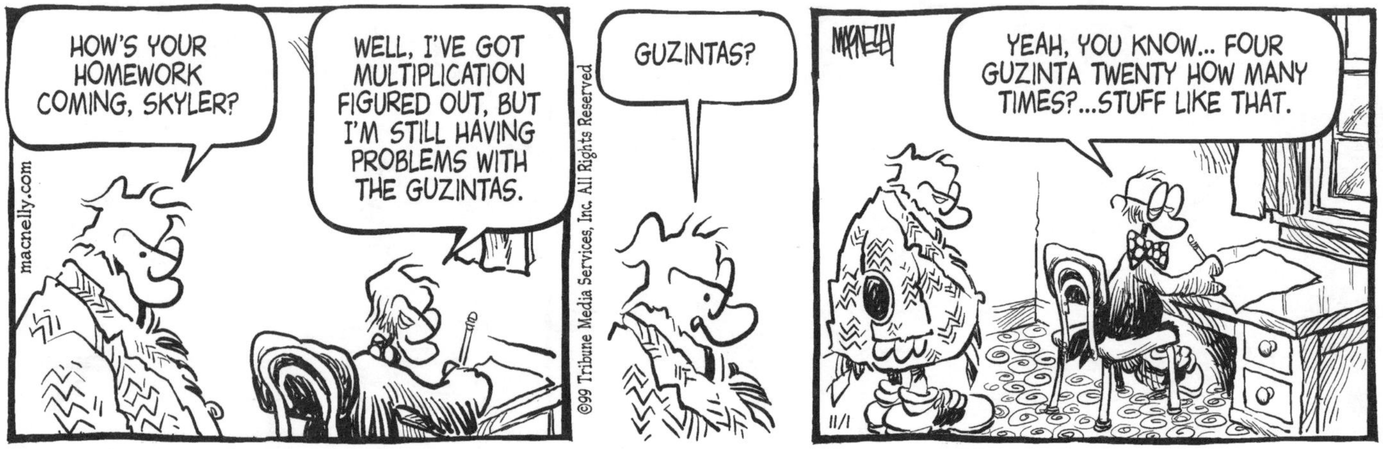
HOW'S YOUR HOMEWORK COMING, SKYLER?
WELL, I'VE GOT MULTIPLICATION FIGURED OUT, BUT I'M STILL HAVING PROBLEMS WITH THE GUZINTAS.
GUZINTAS?
YEAH, YOU KNOW... FOUR GUZINTA TWENTY HOW MANY TIMES?...STUFF LIKE THAT.
MACNELLY
macnelly.com
©99 Tribune Media Services, Inc. All Rights Reserved
11/1

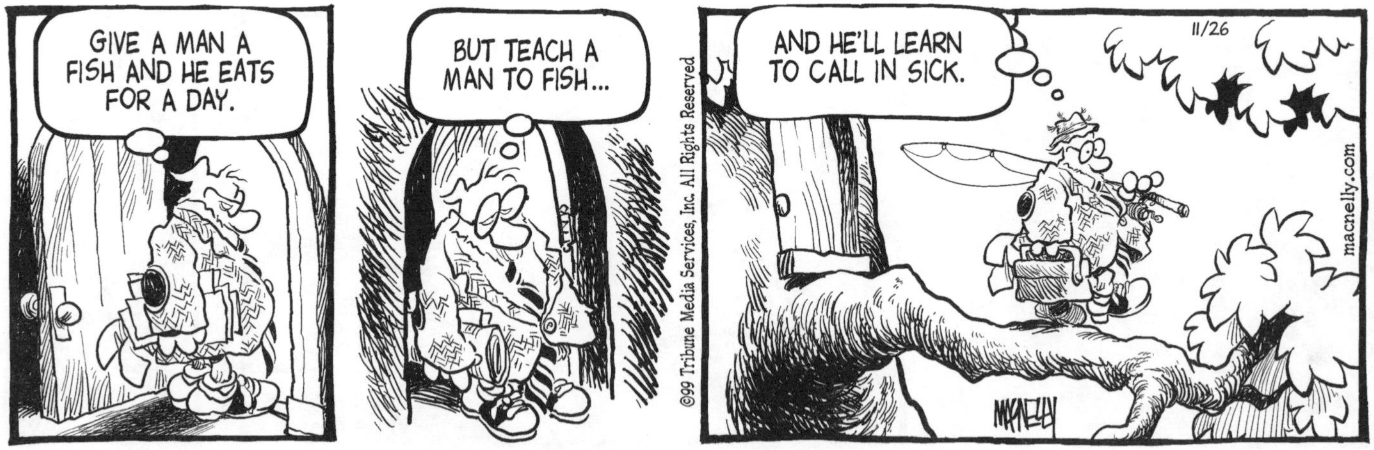
GIVE A MAN A FISH AND HE EATS FOR A DAY.
BUT TEACH A MAN TO FISH...
AND HE'LL LEARN TO CALL IN SICK.
11/26
MACNELLY
macnelly.com
©99 Tribune Media Services, Inc. All Rights Reserved

About Jake

Without a doubt, the hardest thing Jeff MacNelly had to deal with in his life was the death of his oldest son, Jake.

Jake was living in Aspen and working at my studio. I had gotten him a job as editorial cartoonist for the *Aspen Times* and they really loved his work. He was well on his way to becoming a heavyweight in the editoral cartoon business when he died in a climbing accident.

A rescue team had brought him down from the scene of the accident and I rushed to the hospital for updates on his condition. All his friends were gathered there, too. I talked to Jeff on the phone every fifteen minutes all afternoon. The reports got grimmer and grimmer. Finally I had to tell Jeff that Jake had died. It was the hardest thing I'd ever had to do.

In retrospect, this was the day Jeff started dying.

—Chris Cassatt

Below is the story that appeared in the *Aspen Times Daily*:

Aspen Times editorial cartoonist Jeffrey "Jake" MacNelly, son of Pulitzer Prize-winning cartoonist Jeff MacNelly, died Saturday, October 12, 1996, in a climbing accident on Independence Pass. Jake MacNelly, 24, was climbing at Diehard Rock about nine miles east of Aspen, when he fell about 75 feet, according to witnesses. The accident occurred at about 1 p.m.

Witnesses told the Pitkin County Sheriff's Department that Jake had climbed to the top of the rock and set a rope to rappel down. He took one step and fell, they said. An Aspen ambulance crew and 15 members of Mountain Rescue Aspen evacuated MacNelly, who was treated for massive trauma at Aspen Valley Hospital before he was pronounced dead.

This is the last photo taken of Jake MacNelly. I took it in the alley behind my studio in Aspen a couple of days before he died.

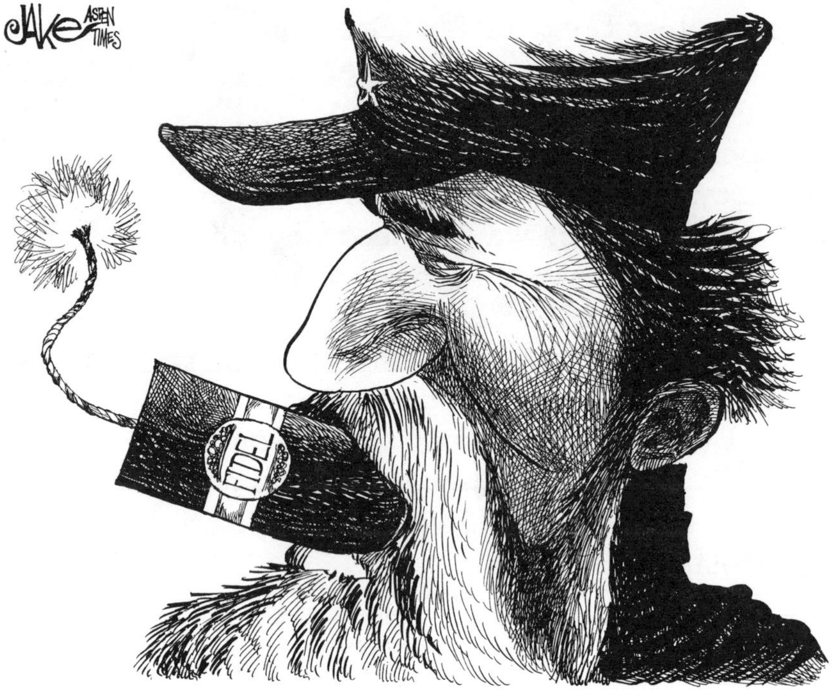
JAKE ASPEN TIMES
FIDEL

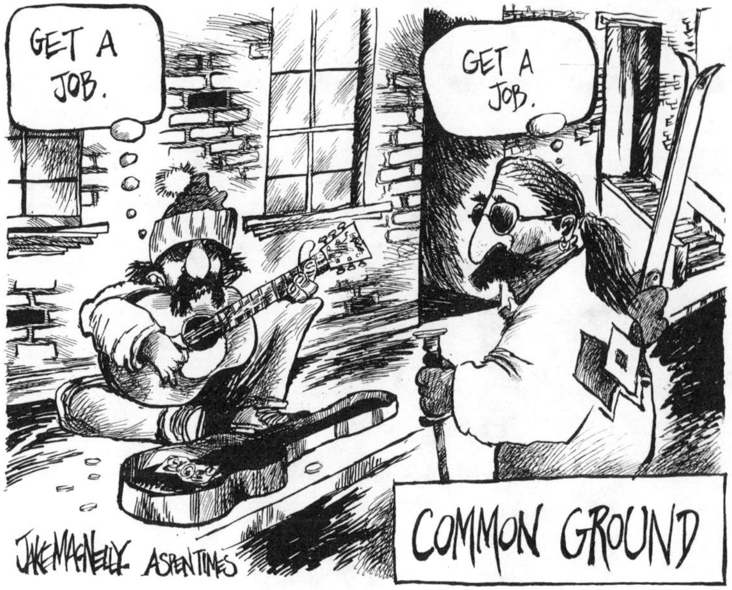
GET A JOB.
GET A JOB.
JAKE MACNELLY ASPEN TIMES
COMMON GROUND

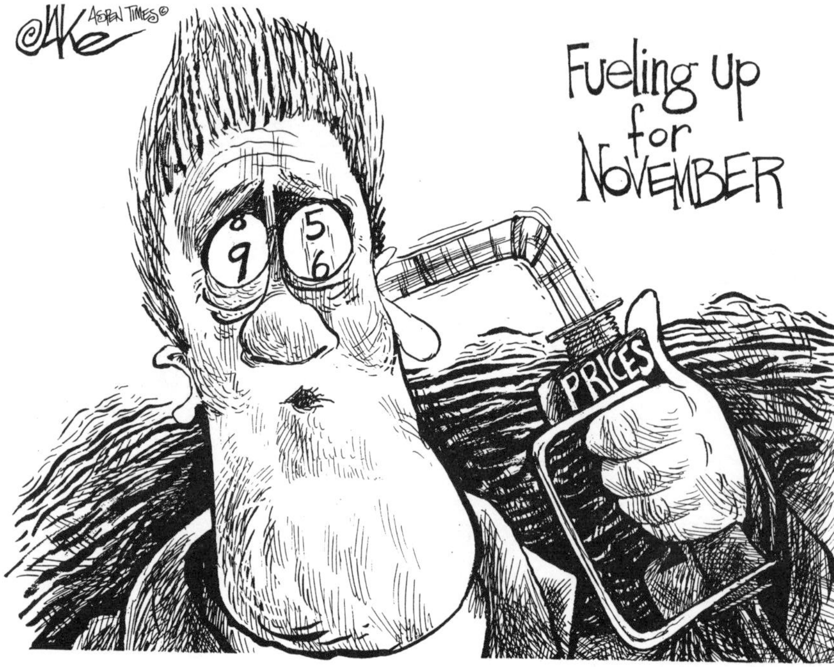
JAKE ASPEN TIMES©
Fueling up for NOVEMBER
PRICES

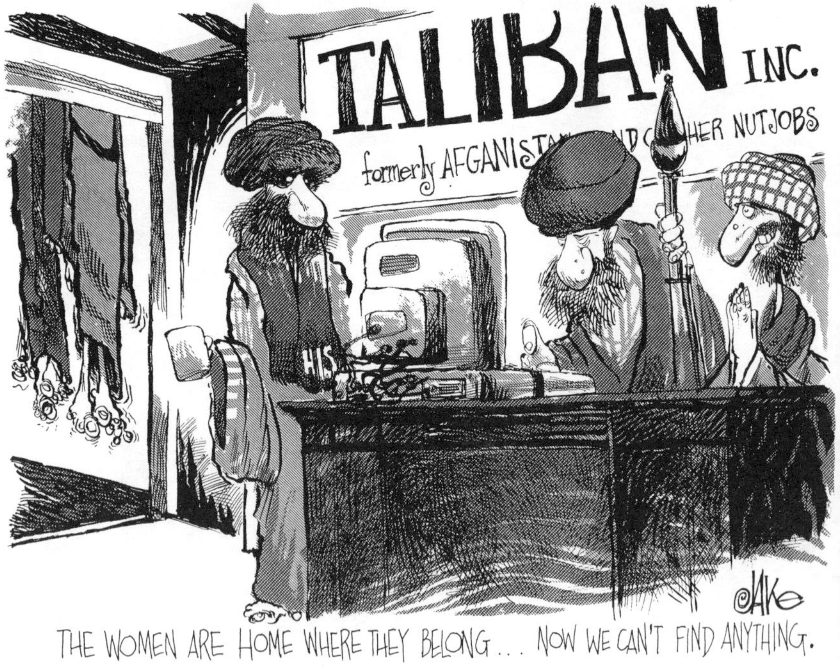
TALIBAN INC.
HIS
JAKE
THE WOMEN ARE HOME WHERE THEY BELONG... NOW WE CAN'T FIND ANYTHING.

This cartoon is the last one Jake did. It was dated 10/10/96. Jake died on the twelfth.

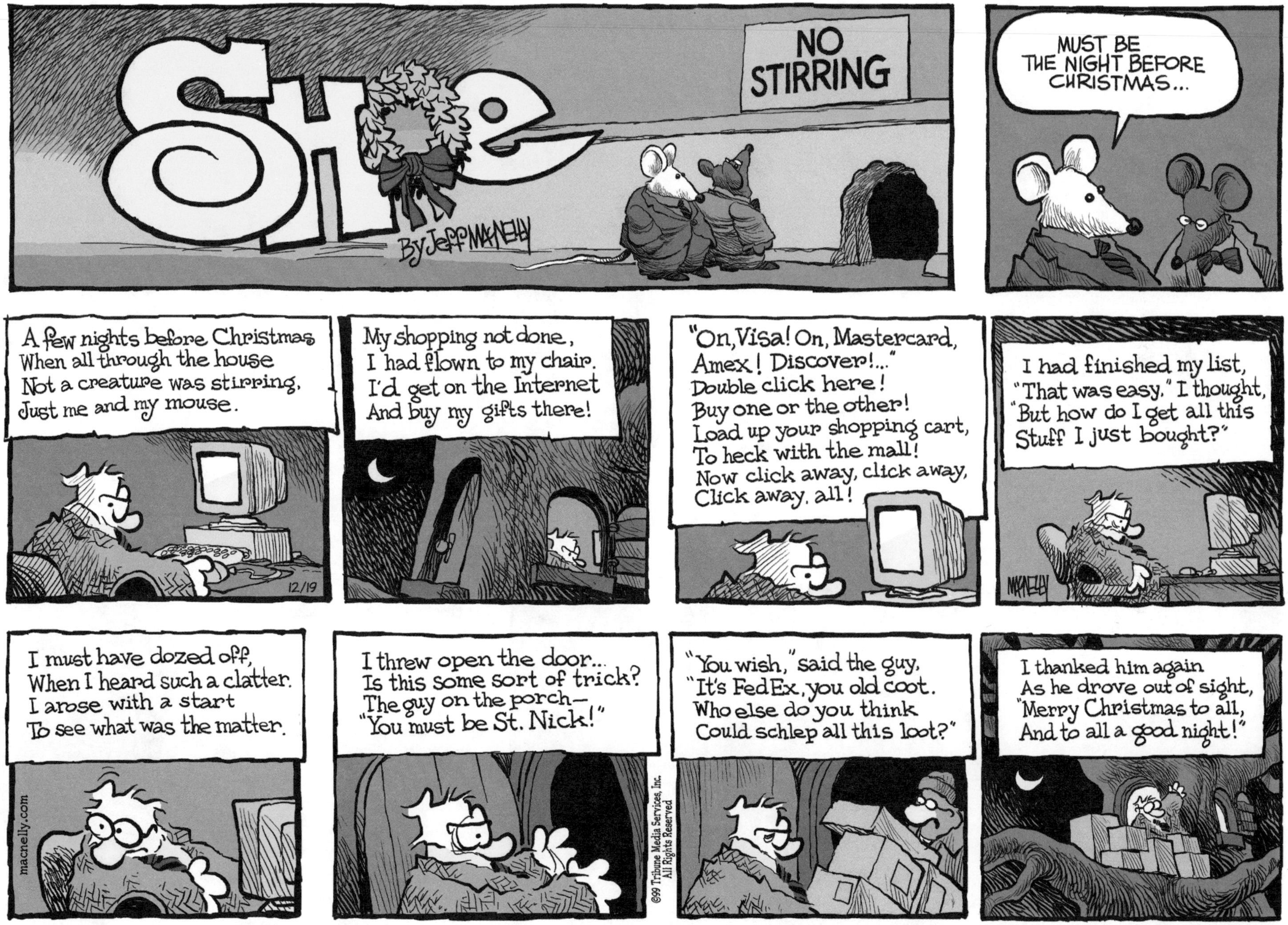
NO STIRRING
Shoe
By Jeff MacNelly
MUST BE THE NIGHT BEFORE CHRISTMAS...
A few nights before Christmas
When all through the house
Not a creature was stirring,
Just me and my mouse.
12/19
My shopping not done,
I had flown to my chair.
I'd get on the Internet
And buy my gifts there!
"On, Visa! On, Mastercard,
Amex! Discover!..."
Double click here!
Buy one or the other!
Load up your shopping cart,
To heck with the mall!
Now click away, click away,
Click away, all!
I had finished my list,
"That was easy," I thought,
"But how do I get all this
Stuff I just bought?"
MacNelly
I must have dozed off,
When I heard such a clatter.
I arose with a start
To see what was the matter.
macnelly.com
I threw open the door...
Is this some sort of trick?
The guy on the porch—
"You must be St. Nick!"
©99 Tribune Media Services, Inc.
All Rights Reserved
"You wish," said the guy,
"It's FedEx, you old coot.
Who else do you think
Could schlep all this loot?"
I thanked him again
As he drove out of sight,
"Merry Christmas to all,
And to all a good night!"

Carrying On in the New Century

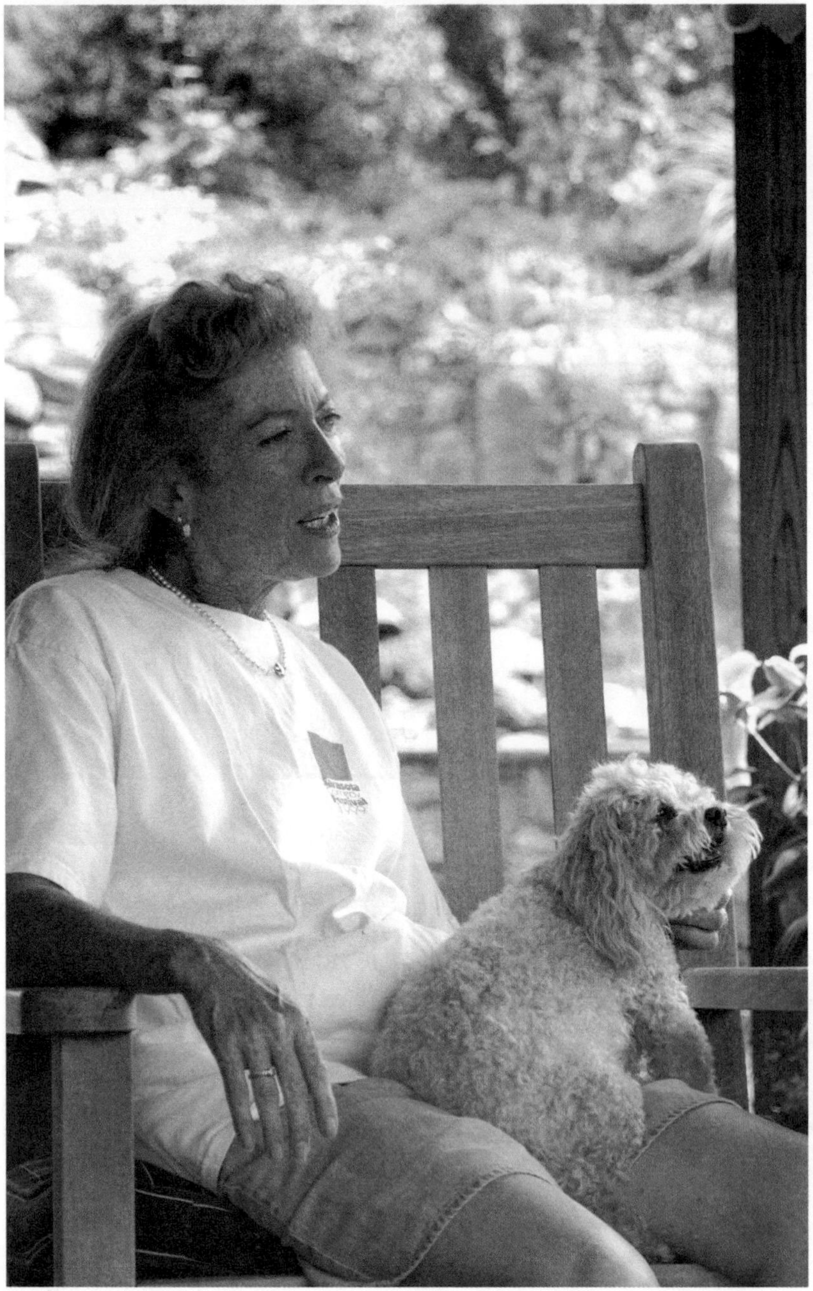

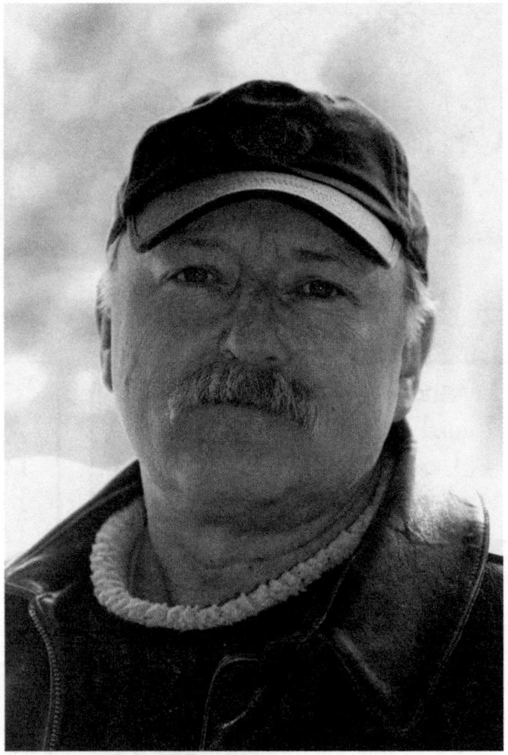

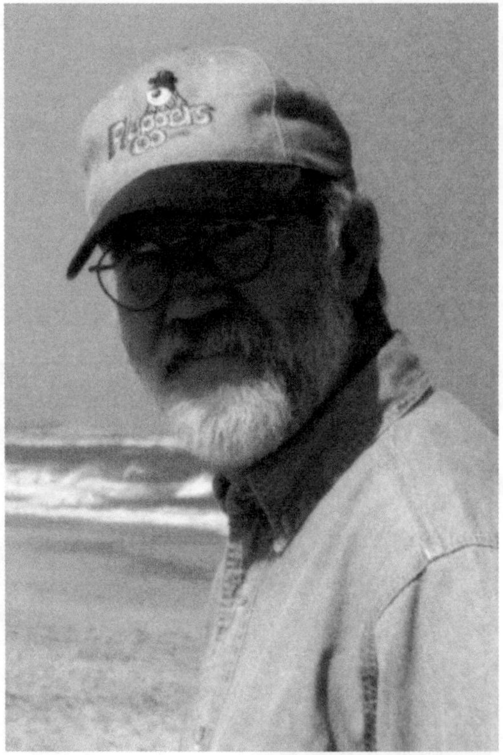

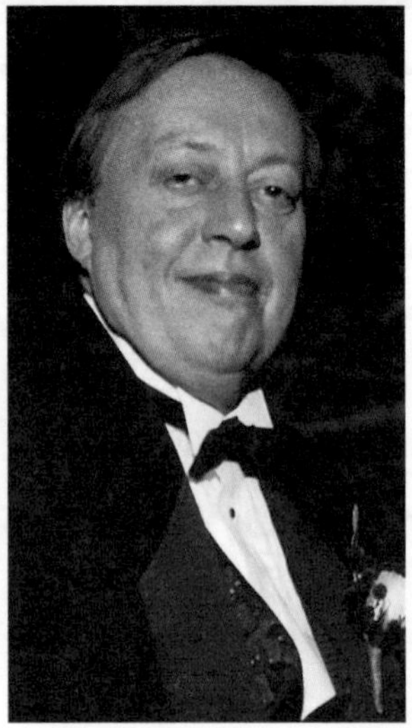

The creative team, handpicked by Jeff himself, carries on the *Shoe* tradition after his untimely death from cancer in June 2000.

Chris Cassatt (top center), Jeff's right-hand man of more than ten years, is lead dog. Gary Brookins (top right), artist extraordinaire, is finish man and co-conspirator. Susie MacNelly (left), is field marshal, bean counter, owner, guiding light, cook, trainer, and final word. Our fabulous gag writers are Bill Linden of Chicago (bottom center), and Doug Gamble of Carmel, California (bottom right).

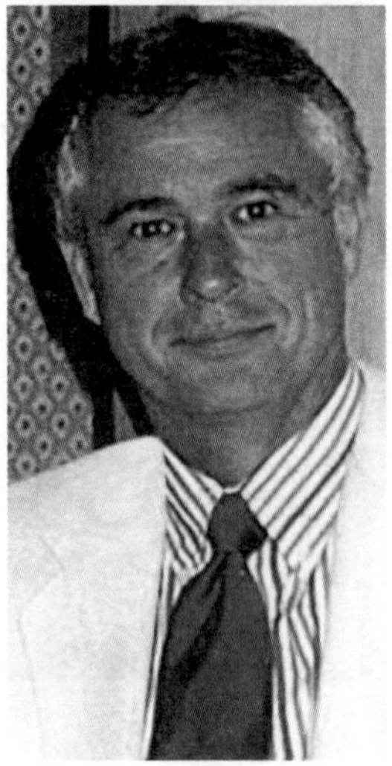

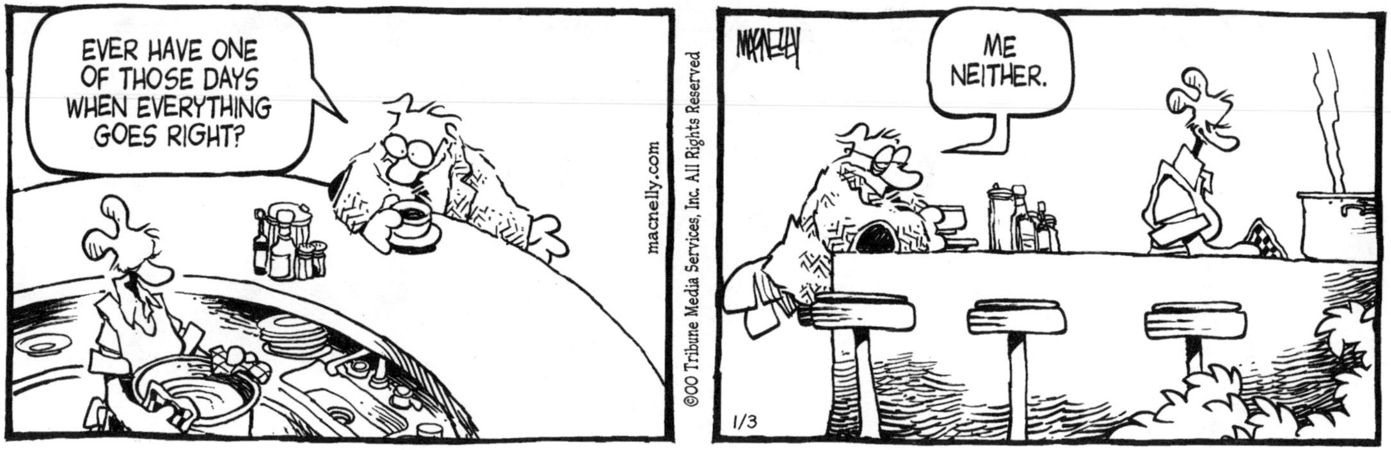
EVER HAVE ONE OF THOSE DAYS WHEN EVERYTHING GOES RIGHT?
macnelly.com
©00 Tribune Media Services, Inc. All Rights Reserved
ME NEITHER.
1/3

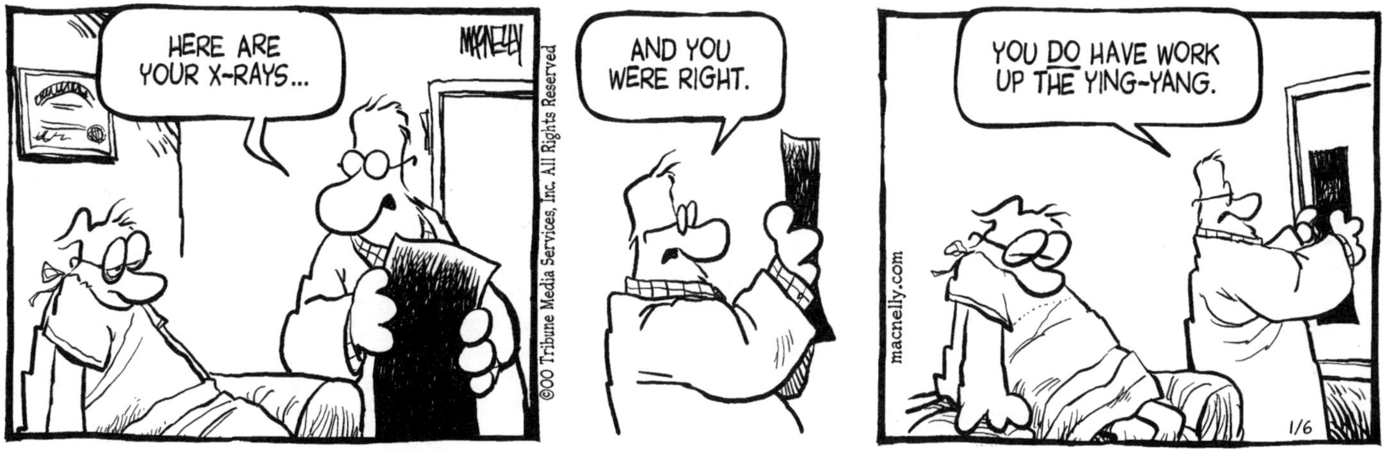
HERE ARE YOUR X-RAYS...
©00 Tribune Media Services, Inc. All Rights Reserved
AND YOU WERE RIGHT.
macnelly.com
YOU DO HAVE WORK UP THE YING-YANG.
1/6

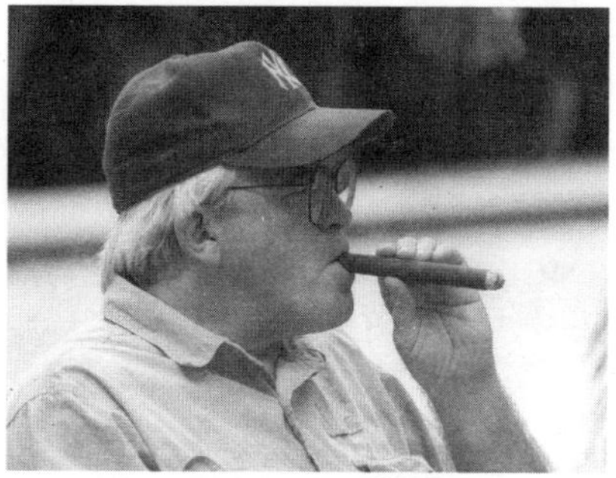

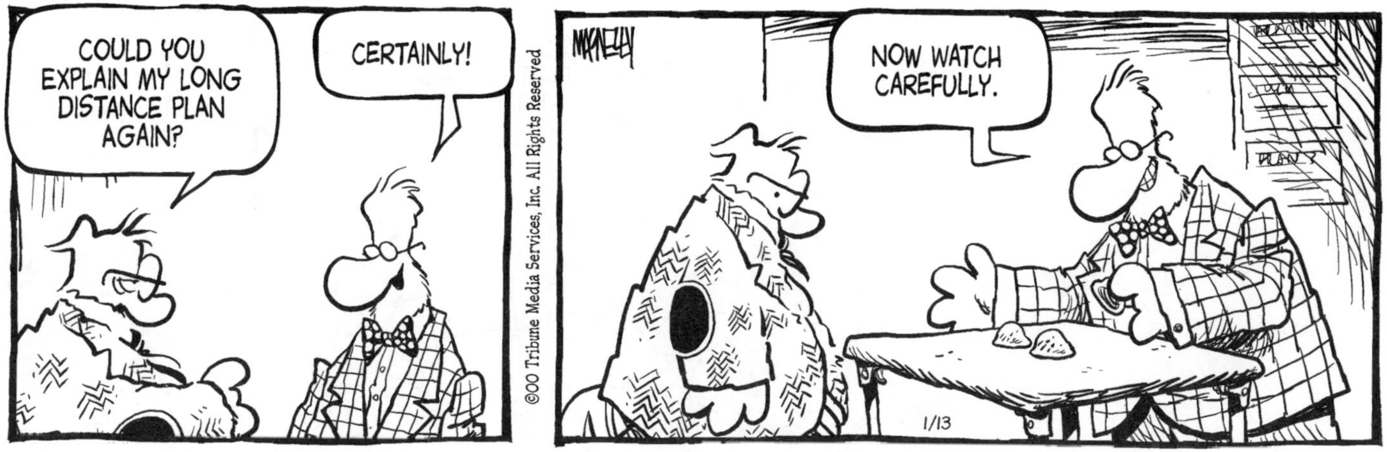
COULD YOU EXPLAIN MY LONG DISTANCE PLAN AGAIN?
CERTAINLY!
©00 Tribune Media Services, Inc. All Rights Reserved
NOW WATCH CAREFULLY.
1/13

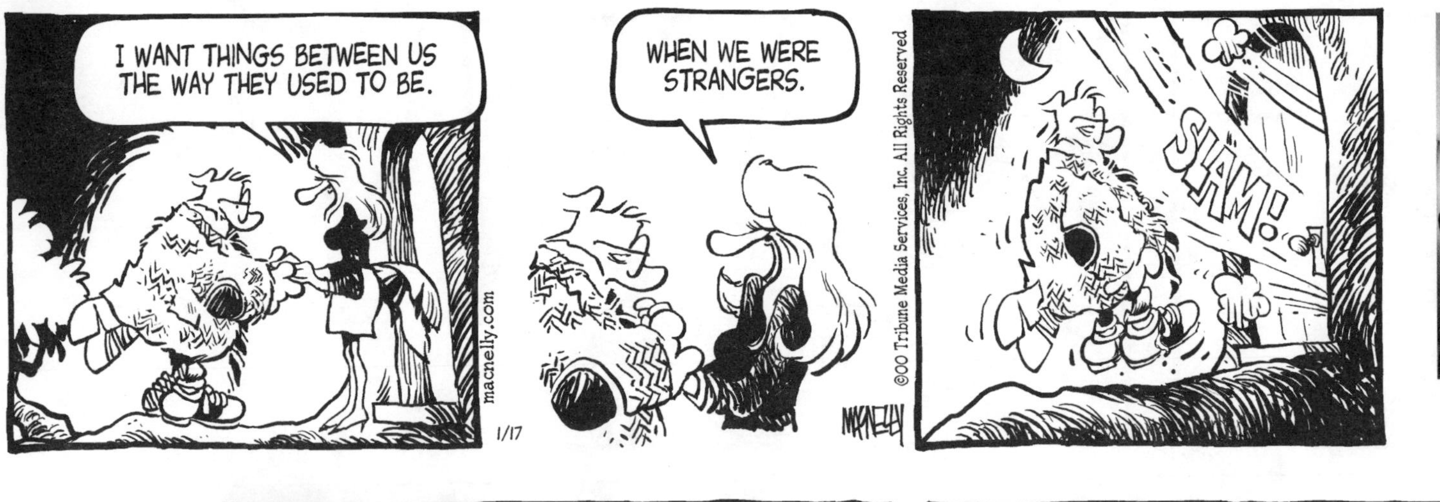
I WANT THINGS BETWEEN US THE WAY THEY USED TO BE.
macnelly.com
1/17
WHEN WE WERE STRANGERS.
MACNELLY
©00 Tribune Media Services, Inc. All Rights Reserved
SLAM!

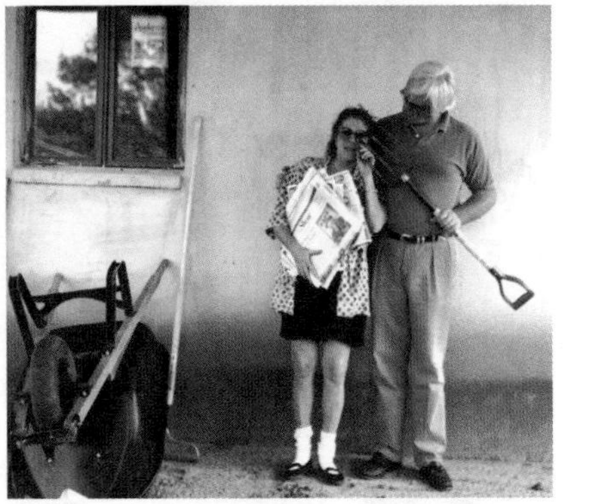

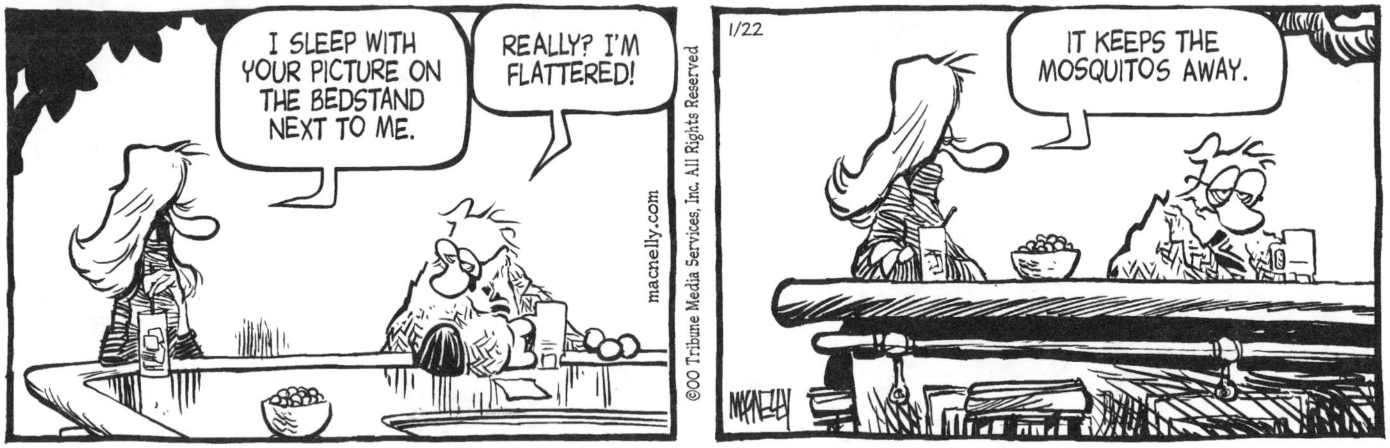
I SLEEP WITH YOUR PICTURE ON THE BEDSTAND NEXT TO ME.
REALLY? I'M FLATTERED!
macnelly.com
©00 Tribune Media Services, Inc. All Rights Reserved
1/22
IT KEEPS THE MOSQUITOS AWAY.
MACNELLY

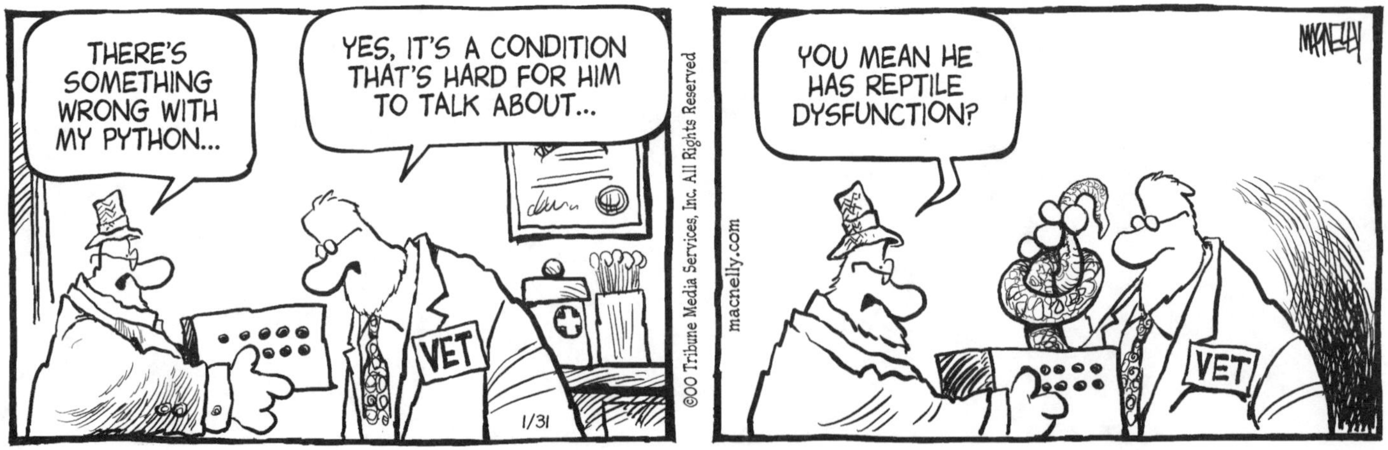
THERE'S SOMETHING WRONG WITH MY PYTHON...
YES, IT'S A CONDITION THAT'S HARD FOR HIM TO TALK ABOUT...
VET
1/31
©00 Tribune Media Services, Inc. All Rights Reserved
macnelly.com
YOU MEAN HE HAS REPTILE DYSFUNCTION?
MACNELLY
VET

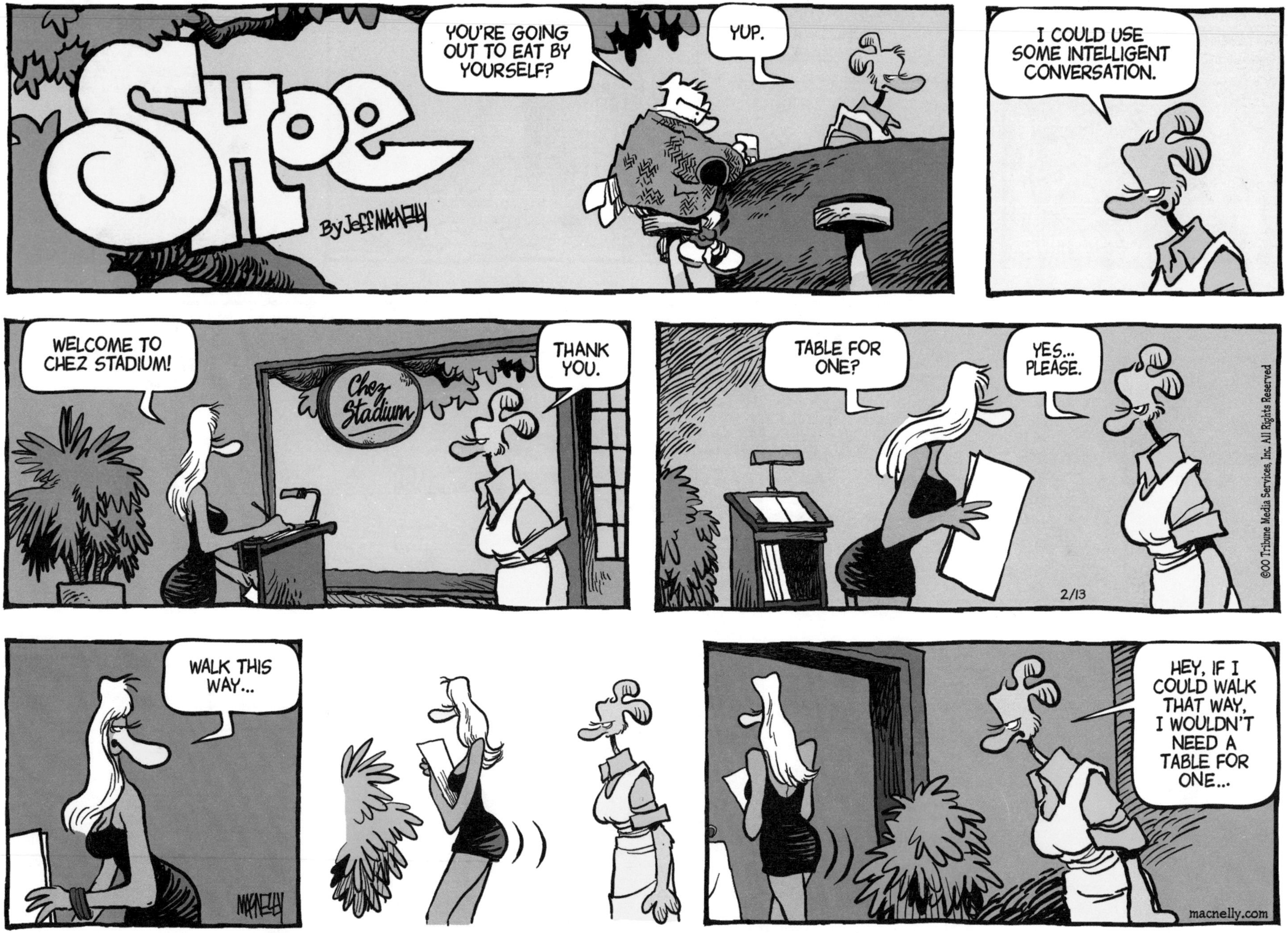
SHOE
By Jeff MacNelly
YOU'RE GOING OUT TO EAT BY YOURSELF?
YUP.
I COULD USE SOME INTELLIGENT CONVERSATION.
WELCOME TO CHEZ STADIUM!
Chez Stadium
THANK YOU.
TABLE FOR ONE?
YES... PLEASE.
©00 Tribune Media Services, Inc. All Rights Reserved
2/13
WALK THIS WAY...
MacNelly
HEY, IF I COULD WALK THAT WAY, I WOULDN'T NEED A TABLE FOR ONE...
macnelly.com

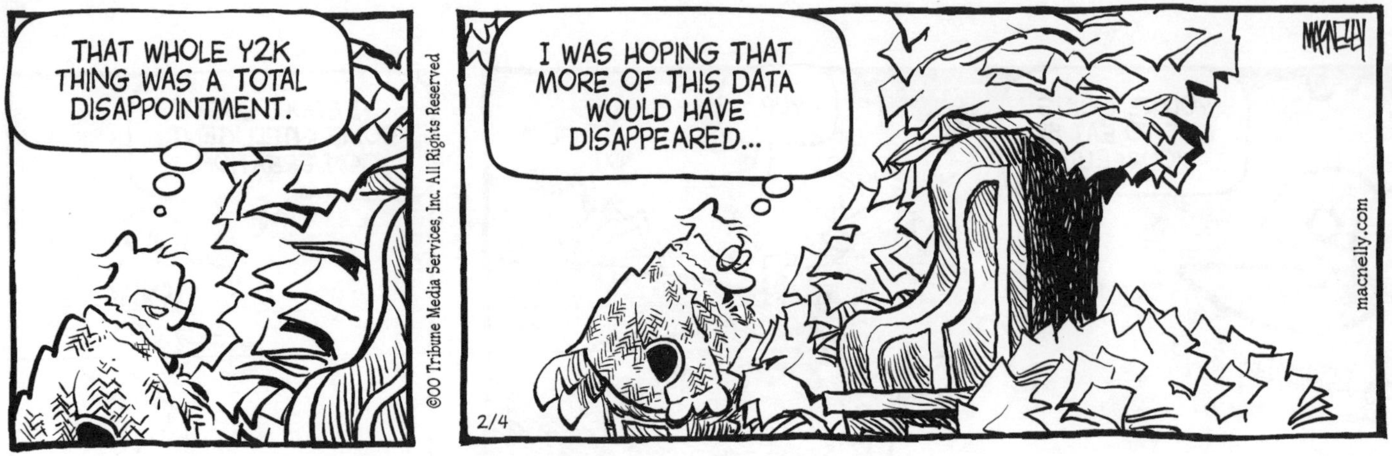
THAT WHOLE Y2K THING WAS A TOTAL DISAPPOINTMENT.
©00 Tribune Media Services, Inc. All Rights Reserved
I WAS HOPING THAT MORE OF THIS DATA WOULD HAVE DISAPPEARED...
2/4
macnelly.com

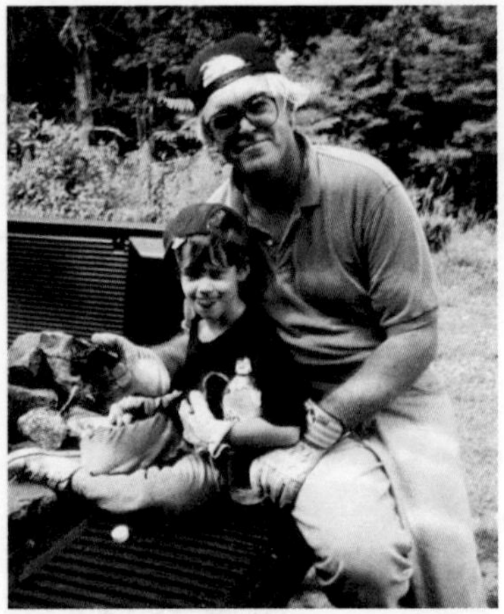

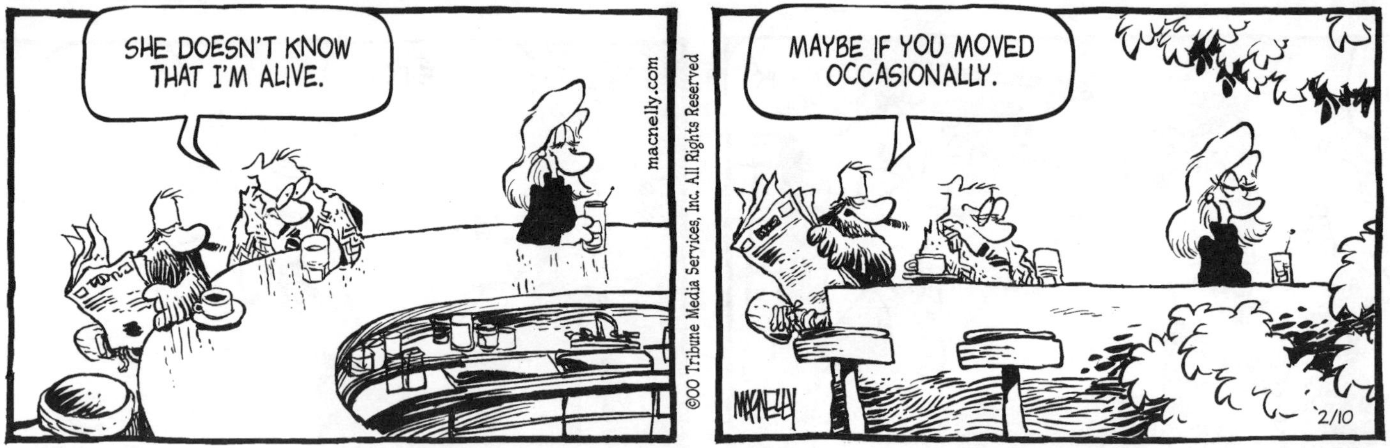
SHE DOESN'T KNOW THAT I'M ALIVE.
macnelly.com
©00 Tribune Media Services, Inc. All Rights Reserved
MAYBE IF YOU MOVED OCCASIONALLY.
2/10

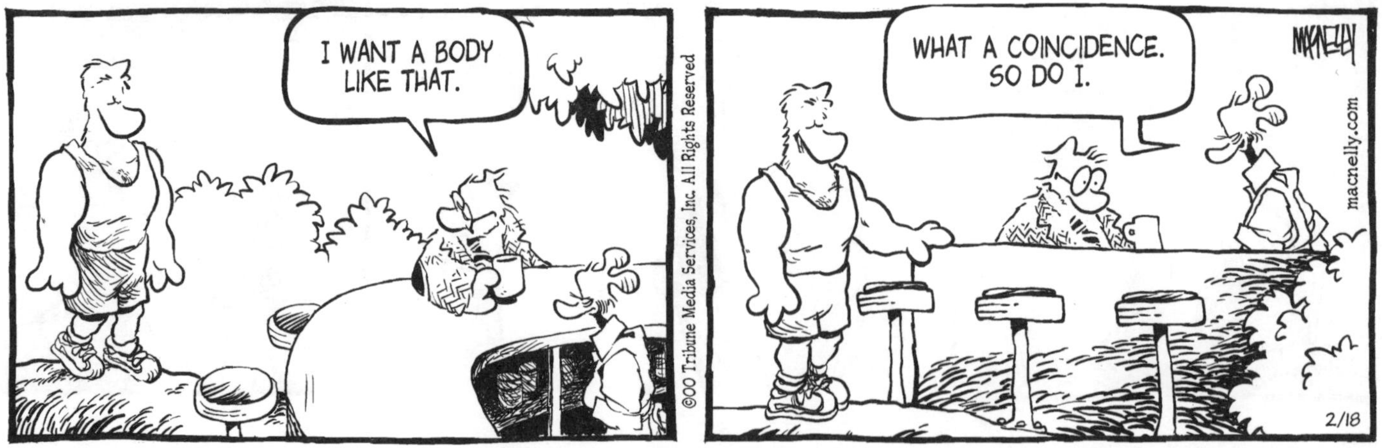
I WANT A BODY LIKE THAT.
©00 Tribune Media Services, Inc. All Rights Reserved
WHAT A COINCIDENCE. SO DO I.
macnelly.com
2/18

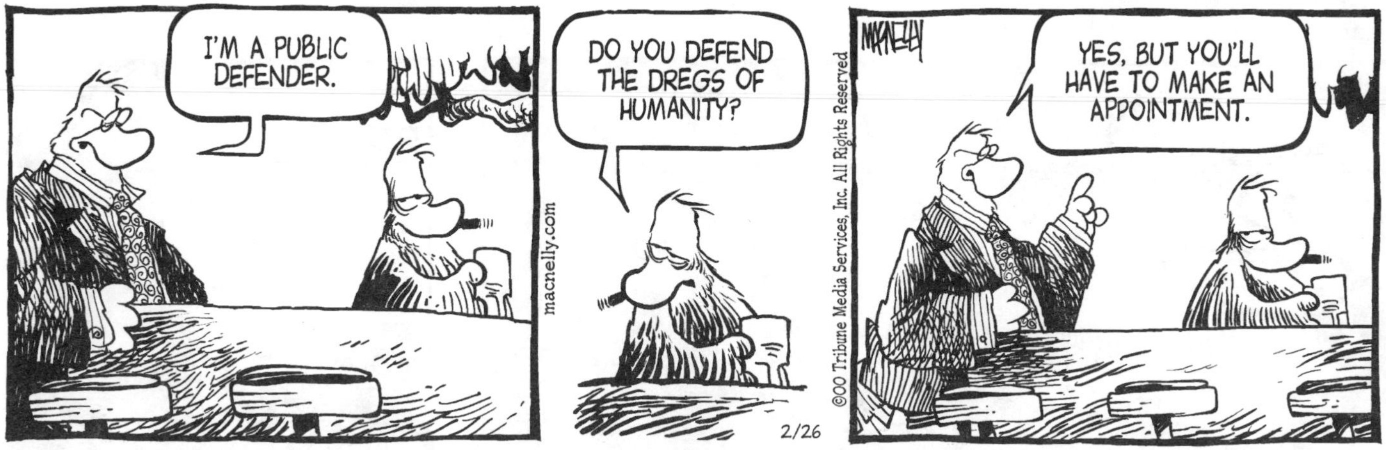
I'M A PUBLIC DEFENDER.
DO YOU DEFEND THE DREGS OF HUMANITY?
YES, BUT YOU'LL HAVE TO MAKE AN APPOINTMENT.
macnelly.com
©00 Tribune Media Services, Inc. All Rights Reserved
2/26

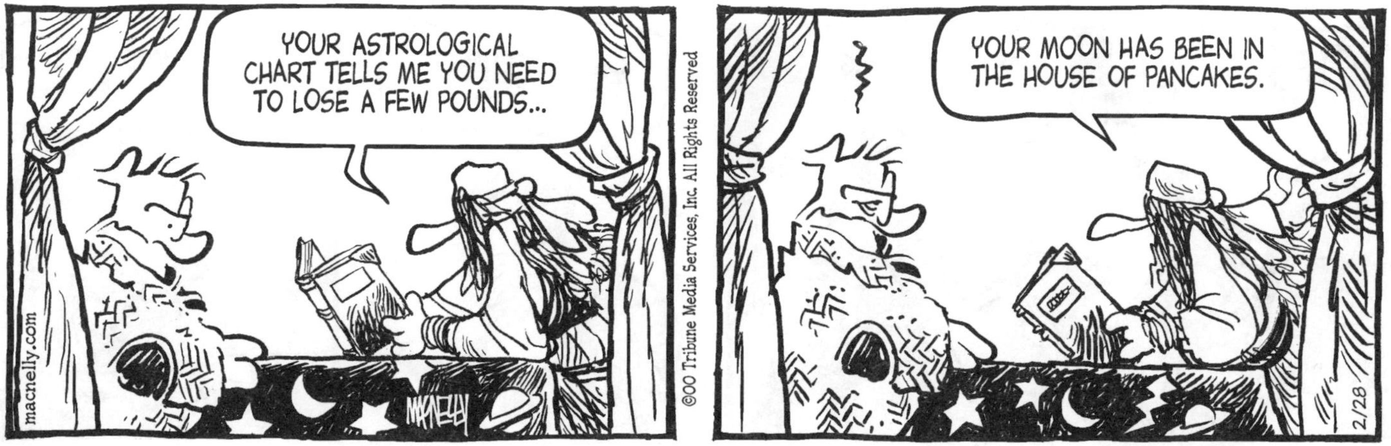
YOUR ASTROLOGICAL CHART TELLS ME YOU NEED TO LOSE A FEW POUNDS...
YOUR MOON HAS BEEN IN THE HOUSE OF PANCAKES.
macnelly.com
©00 Tribune Media Services, Inc. All Rights Reserved
2/28

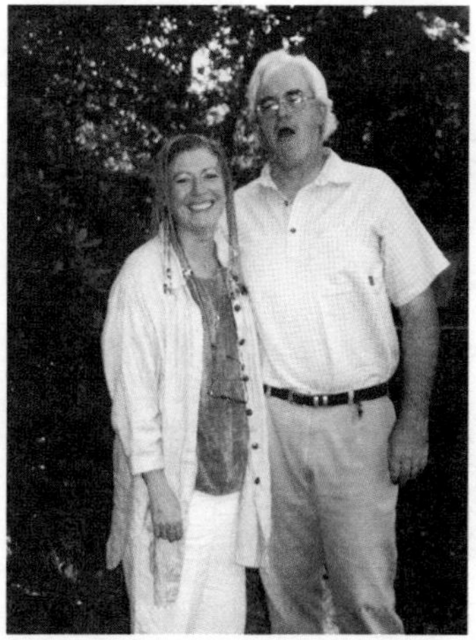

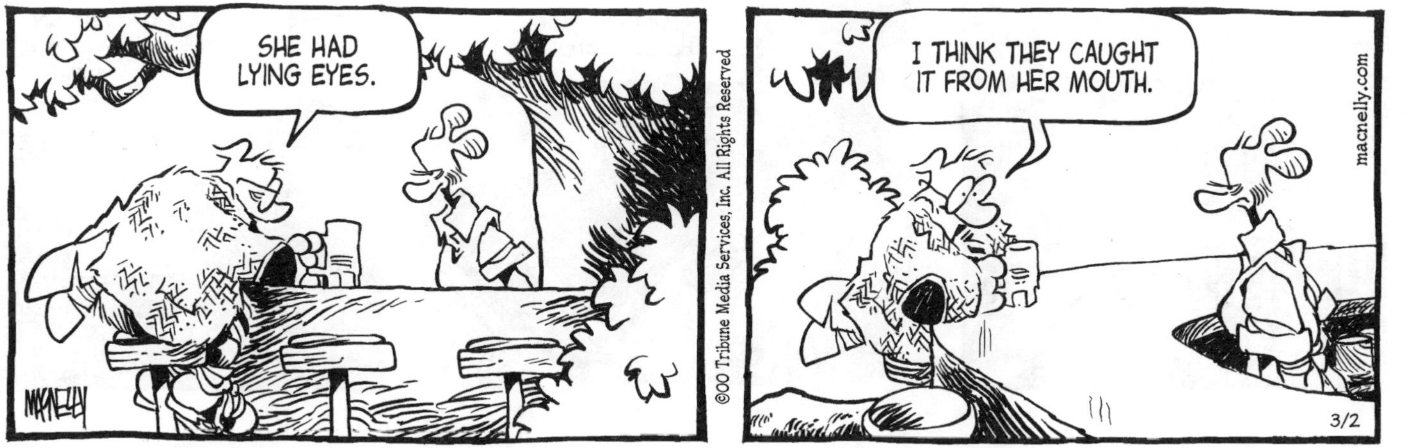
SHE HAD LYING EYES.
I THINK THEY CAUGHT IT FROM HER MOUTH.
©00 Tribune Media Services, Inc. All Rights Reserved
macnelly.com
3/2

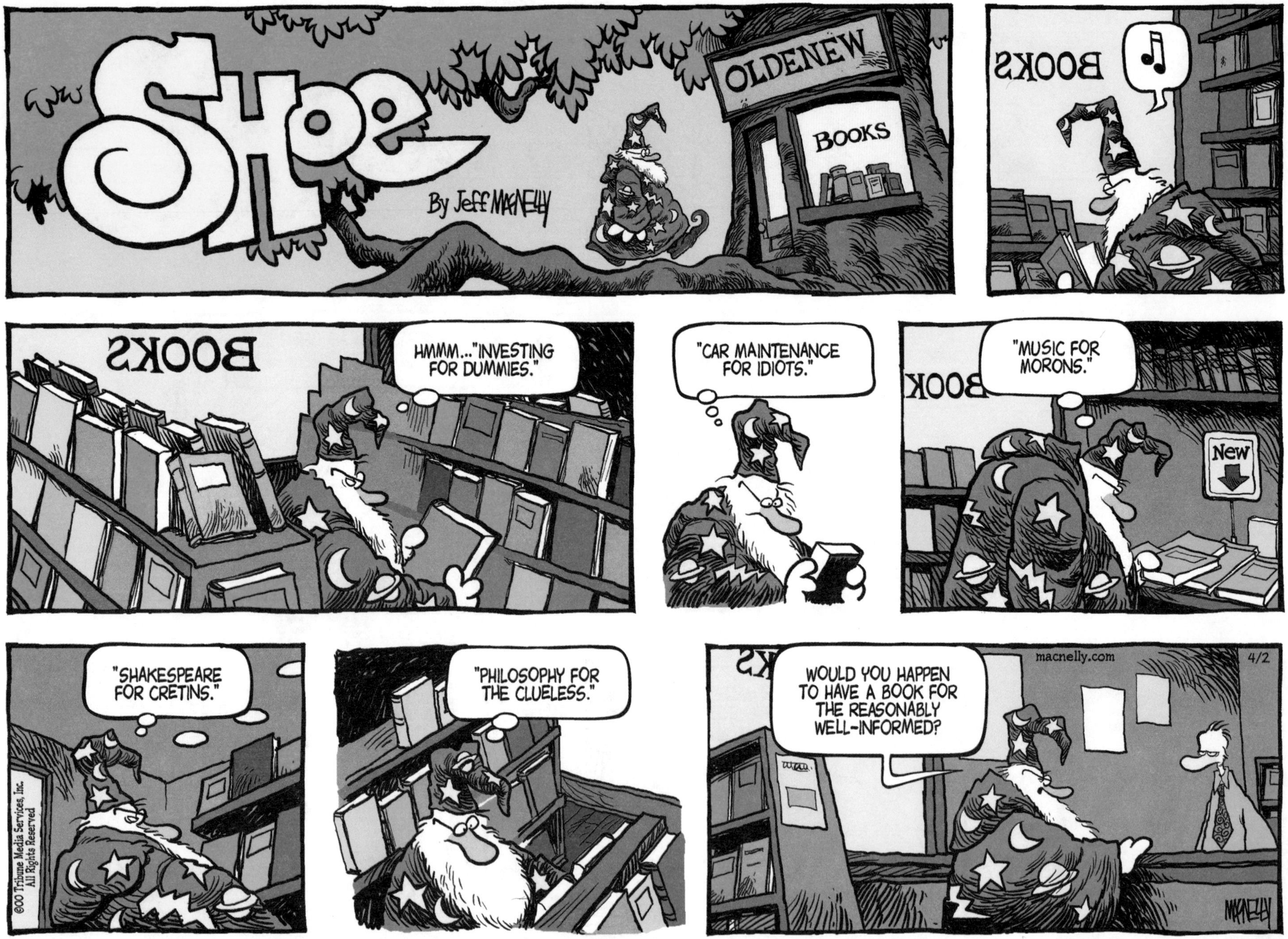
Shoe
By Jeff MacNelly
OLDENEW
BOOKS
HMMM..."INVESTING FOR DUMMIES."
"CAR MAINTENANCE FOR IDIOTS."
"MUSIC FOR MORONS."
"SHAKESPEARE FOR CRETINS."
"PHILOSOPHY FOR THE CLUELESS."
WOULD YOU HAPPEN TO HAVE A BOOK FOR THE REASONABLY WELL-INFORMED?
macnelly.com
4/2
MACNELLY
©00 Tribune Media Services, Inc. All Rights Reserved

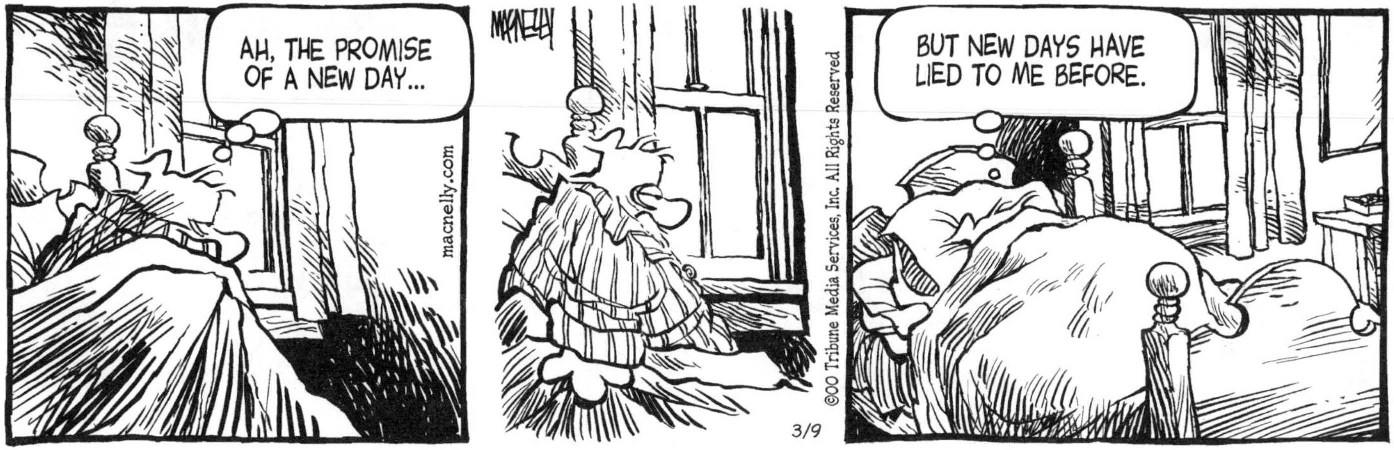
AH, THE PROMISE OF A NEW DAY...
macnelly.com
MACNELLY
©00 Tribune Media Services, Inc. All Rights Reserved
3/9
BUT NEW DAYS HAVE LIED TO ME BEFORE.

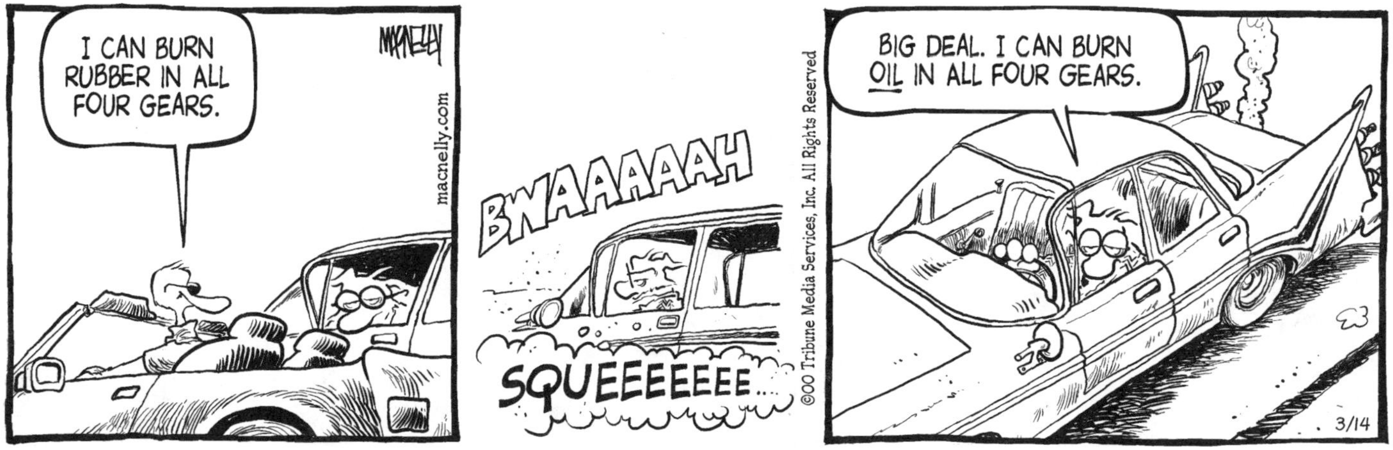
I CAN BURN RUBBER IN ALL FOUR GEARS.
MACNELLY
macnelly.com
BWAAAAAAH
SQUEEEEEEE...
©00 Tribune Media Services, Inc. All Rights Reserved
BIG DEAL. I CAN BURN OIL IN ALL FOUR GEARS.
3/14

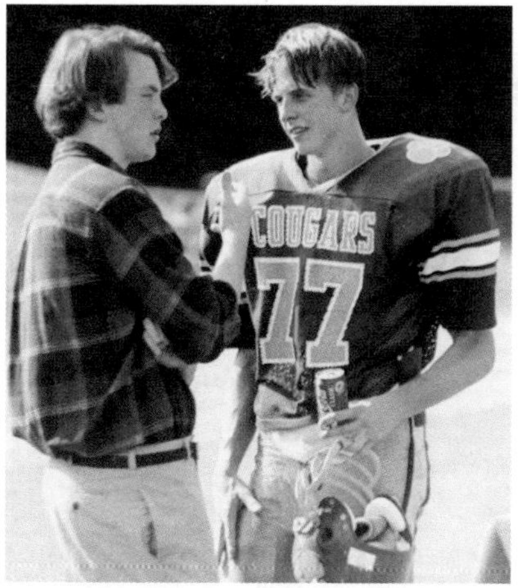
COUGARS
77

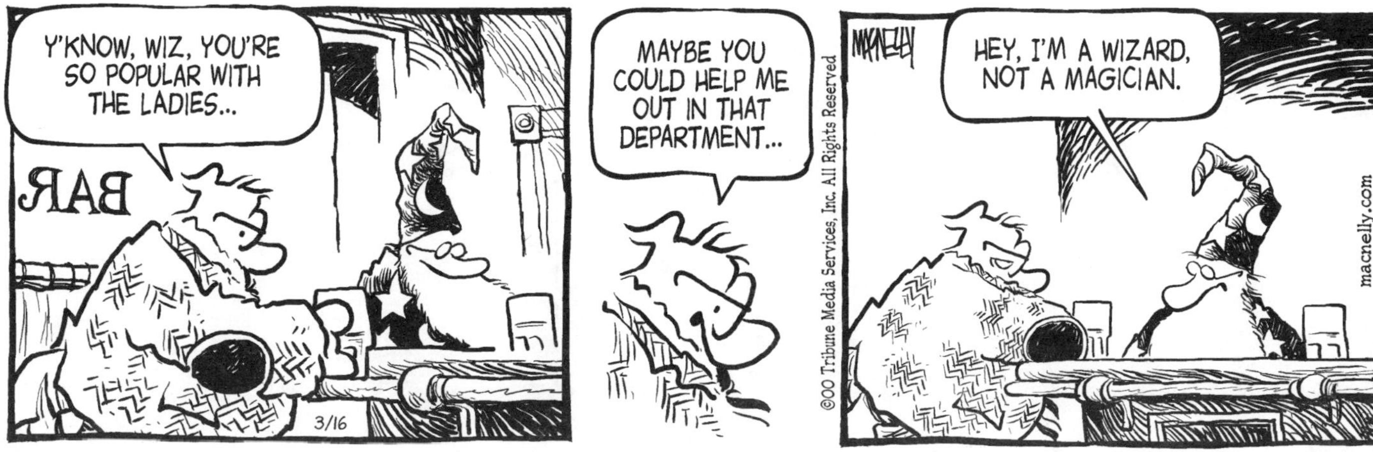
Y'KNOW, WIZ, YOU'RE SO POPULAR WITH THE LADIES...
BAR
3/16
MAYBE YOU COULD HELP ME OUT IN THAT DEPARTMENT...
©00 Tribune Media Services, Inc. All Rights Reserved
MACNELLY
HEY, I'M A WIZARD, NOT A MAGICIAN.
macnelly.com

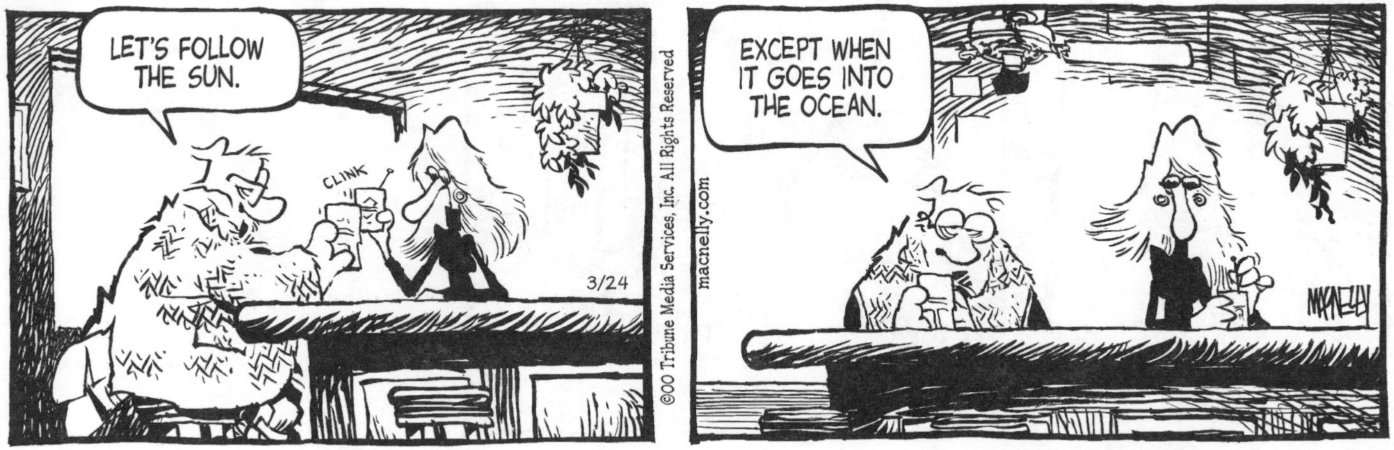
LET'S FOLLOW THE SUN.
CLINK
3/24
©00 Tribune Media Services, Inc. All Rights Reserved
macnelly.com
EXCEPT WHEN IT GOES INTO THE OCEAN.
MACNELLY

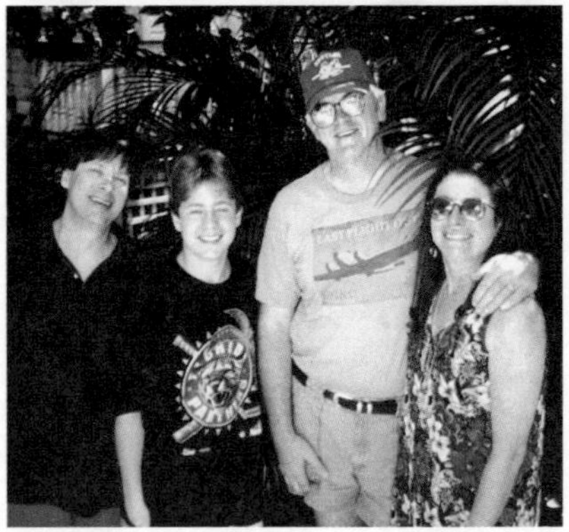

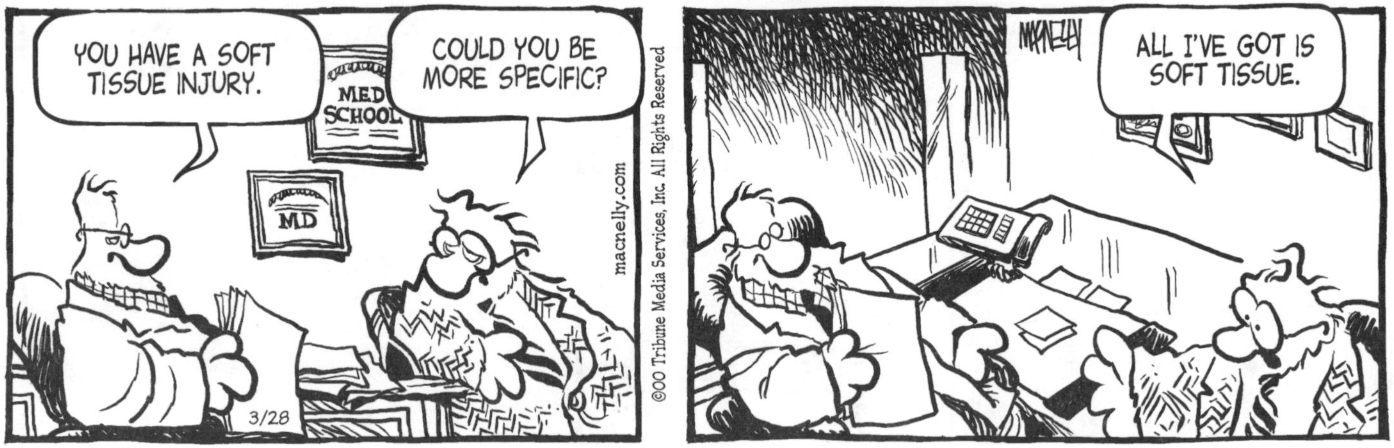
YOU HAVE A SOFT TISSUE INJURY.
MED SCHOOL
MD
COULD YOU BE MORE SPECIFIC?
3/28
©00 Tribune Media Services, Inc. All Rights Reserved
macnelly.com
MACNELLY
ALL I'VE GOT IS SOFT TISSUE.

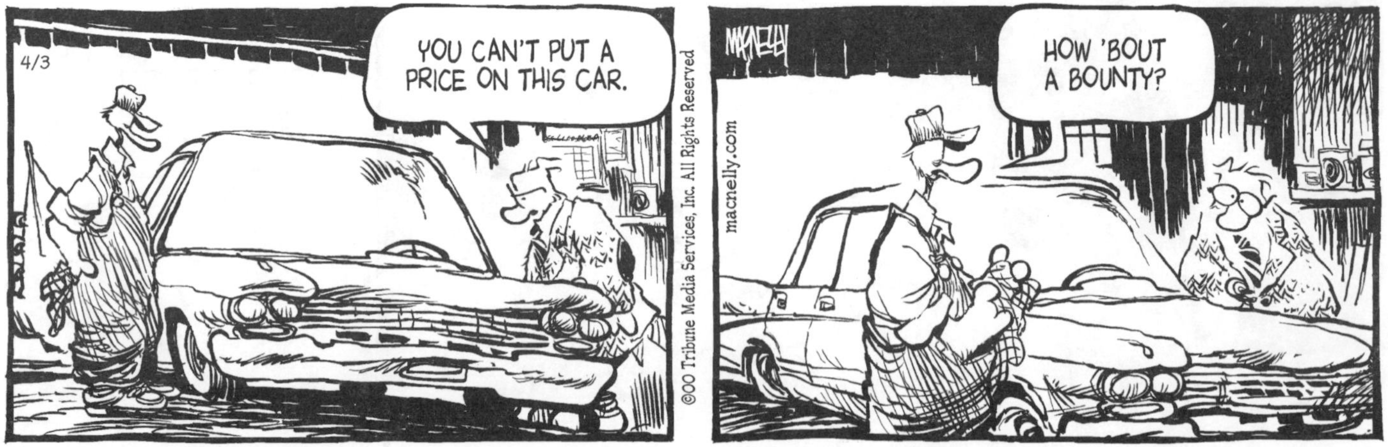
4/3
YOU CAN'T PUT A PRICE ON THIS CAR.
©00 Tribune Media Services, Inc. All Rights Reserved
macnelly.com
MACNELLY
HOW 'BOUT A BOUNTY?

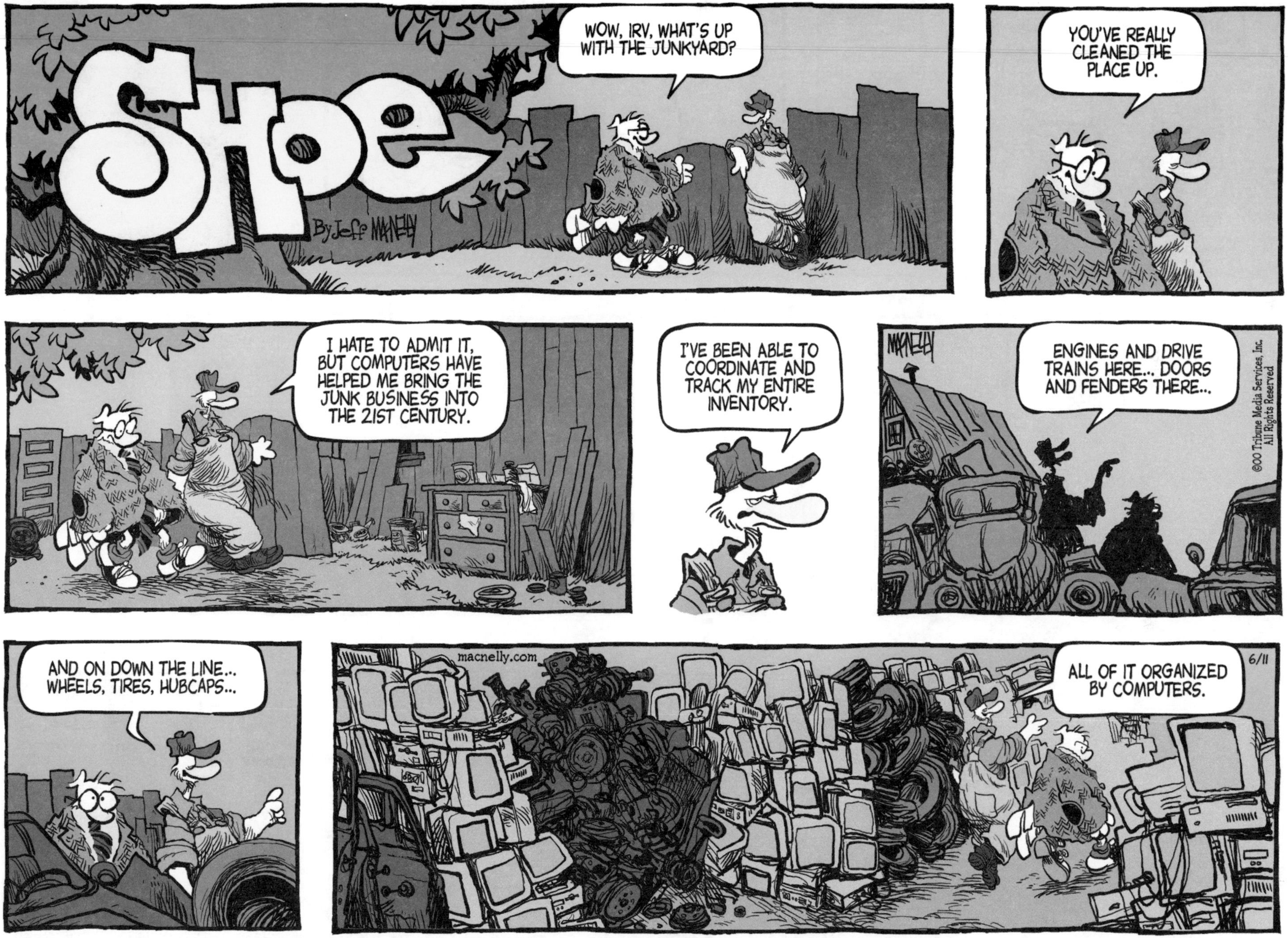
SHOE
By Jeff MacNelly
WOW, IRV, WHAT'S UP WITH THE JUNKYARD?
YOU'VE REALLY CLEANED THE PLACE UP.
I HATE TO ADMIT IT, BUT COMPUTERS HAVE HELPED ME BRING THE JUNK BUSINESS INTO THE 21ST CENTURY.
I'VE BEEN ABLE TO COORDINATE AND TRACK MY ENTIRE INVENTORY.
MACNELLY
ENGINES AND DRIVE TRAINS HERE... DOORS AND FENDERS THERE...
©00 Tribune Media Services, Inc. All Rights Reserved
AND ON DOWN THE LINE... WHEELS, TIRES, HUBCAPS...
macnelly.com
6/11
ALL OF IT ORGANIZED BY COMPUTERS.

This was the last Sunday Jeff drew.

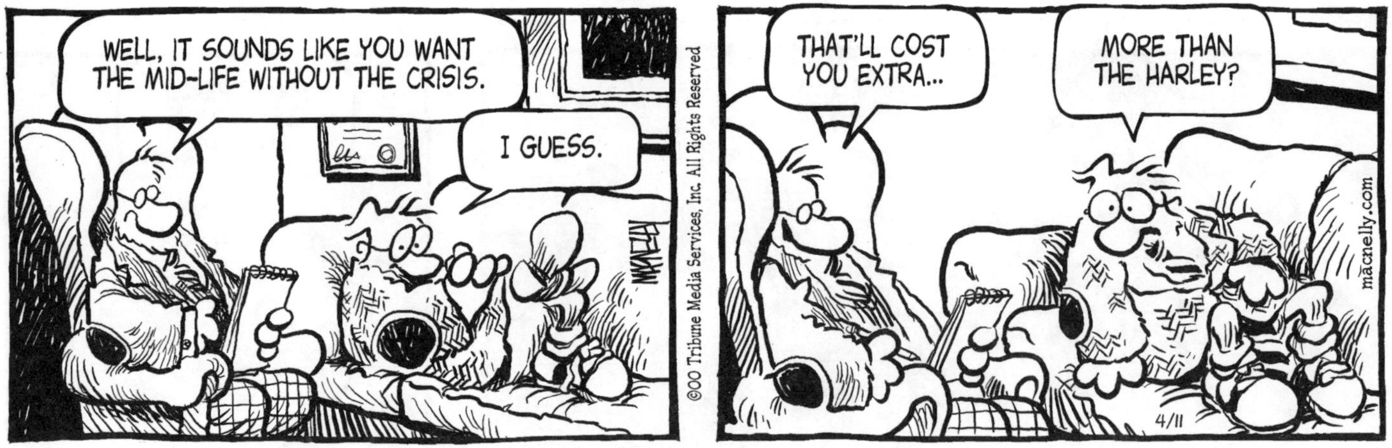
WELL, IT SOUNDS LIKE YOU WANT THE MID-LIFE WITHOUT THE CRISIS.
I GUESS.
©00 Tribune Media Services, Inc. All Rights Reserved
THAT'LL COST YOU EXTRA...
MORE THAN THE HARLEY?
macnelly.com
4/11

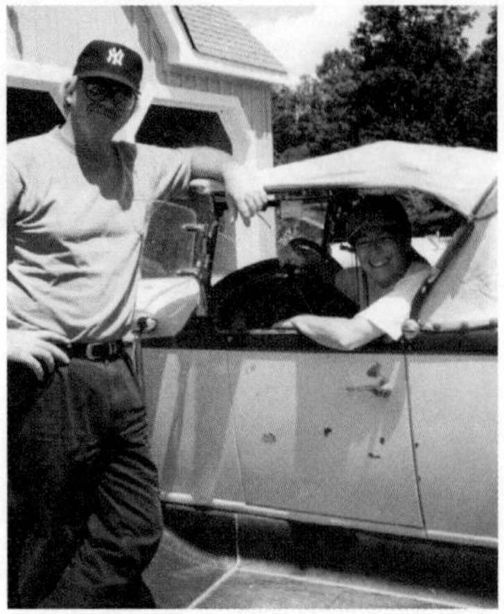

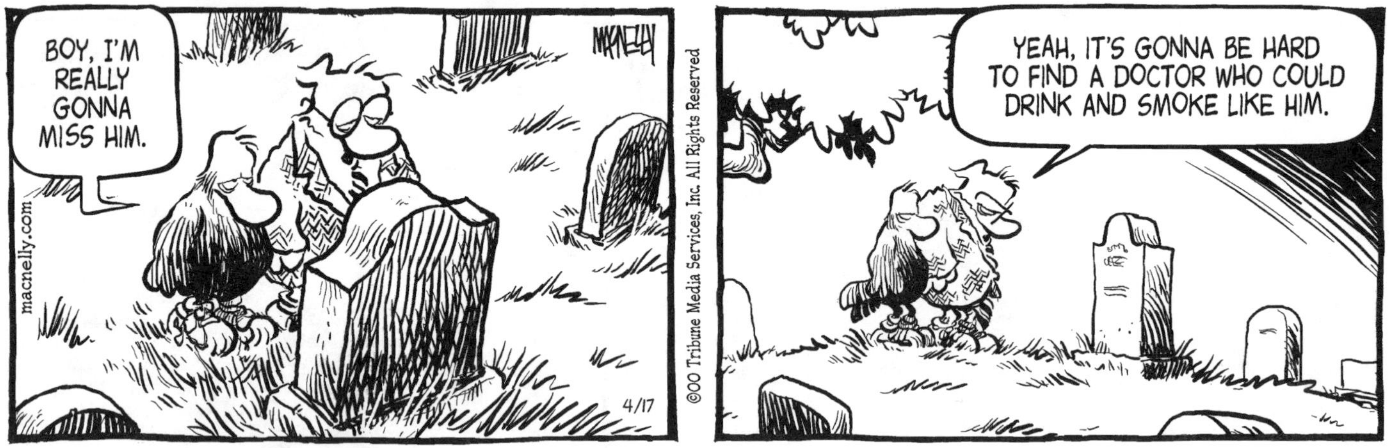
BOY, I'M REALLY GONNA MISS HIM.
macnelly.com
4/17
©00 Tribune Media Services, Inc. All Rights Reserved
YEAH, IT'S GONNA BE HARD TO FIND A DOCTOR WHO COULD DRINK AND SMOKE LIKE HIM.

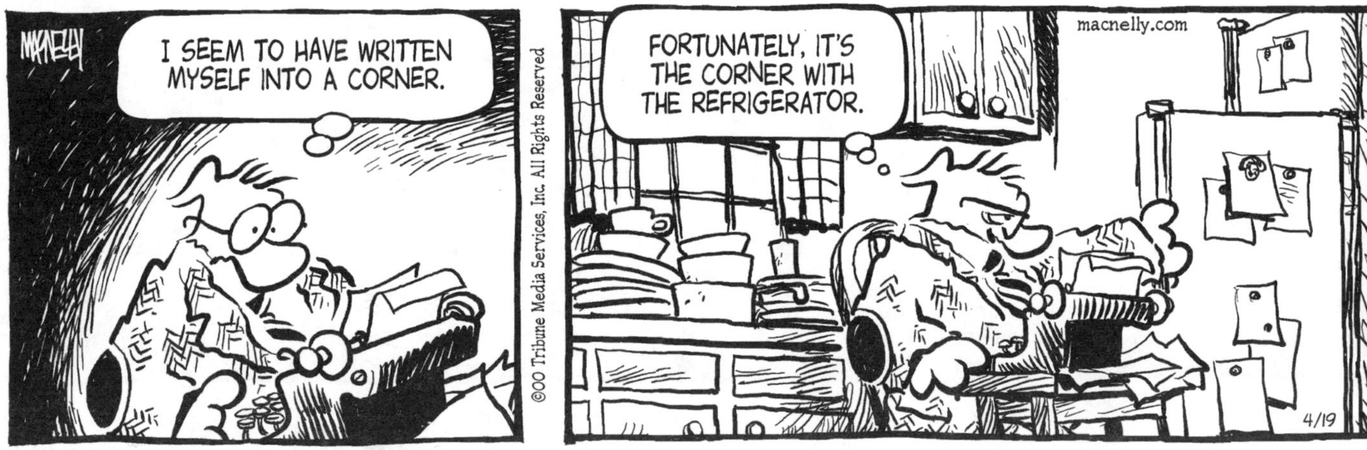
I SEEM TO HAVE WRITTEN MYSELF INTO A CORNER.
©00 Tribune Media Services, Inc. All Rights Reserved
FORTUNATELY, IT'S THE CORNER WITH THE REFRIGERATOR.
macnelly.com
4/19

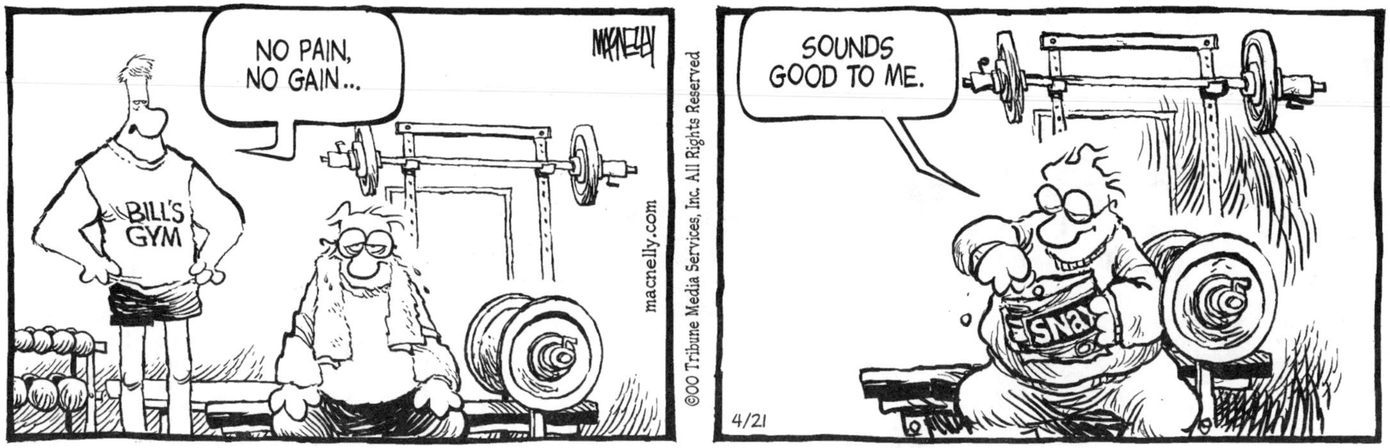
NO PAIN, NO GAIN...
BILL'S GYM
MACNELLY
macnelly.com
©00 Tribune Media Services, Inc. All Rights Reserved
SOUNDS GOOD TO ME.
SNAX
4/21

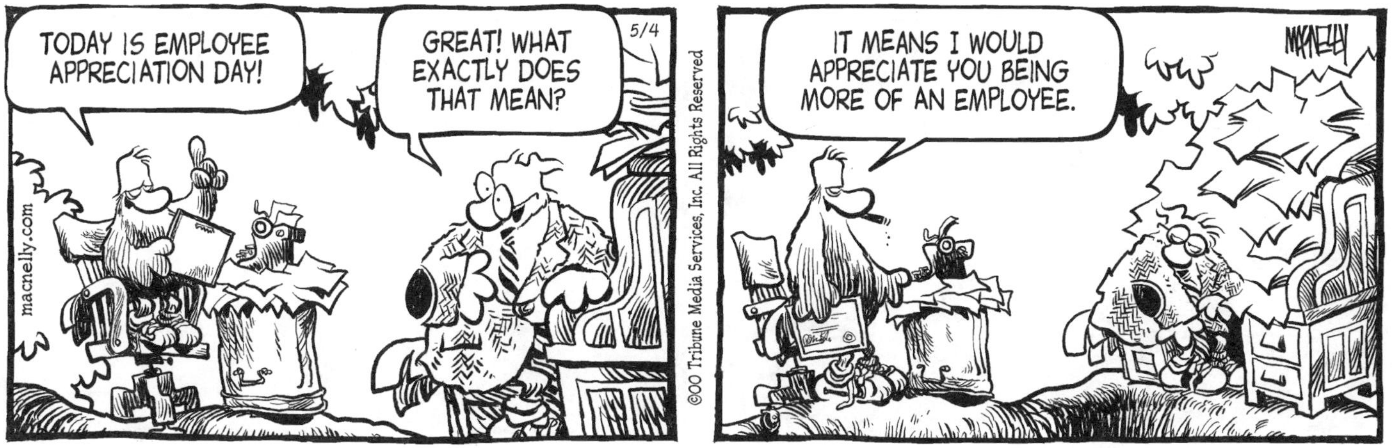
TODAY IS EMPLOYEE APPRECIATION DAY!
GREAT! WHAT EXACTLY DOES THAT MEAN?
5/4
macnelly.com
©00 Tribune Media Services, Inc. All Rights Reserved
IT MEANS I WOULD APPRECIATE YOU BEING MORE OF AN EMPLOYEE.
MACNELLY

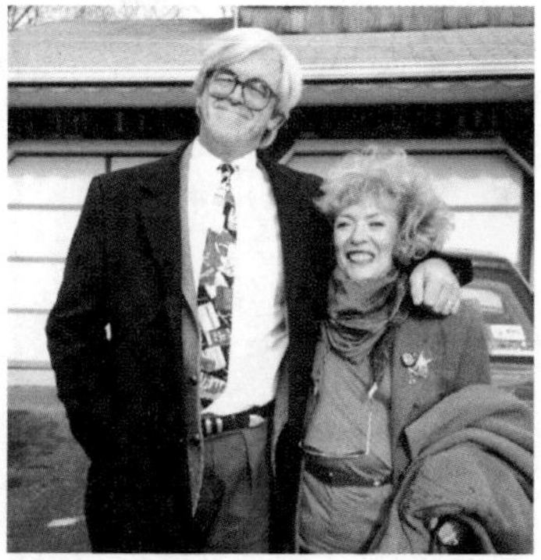

Jeff and sister-in-law Roberta

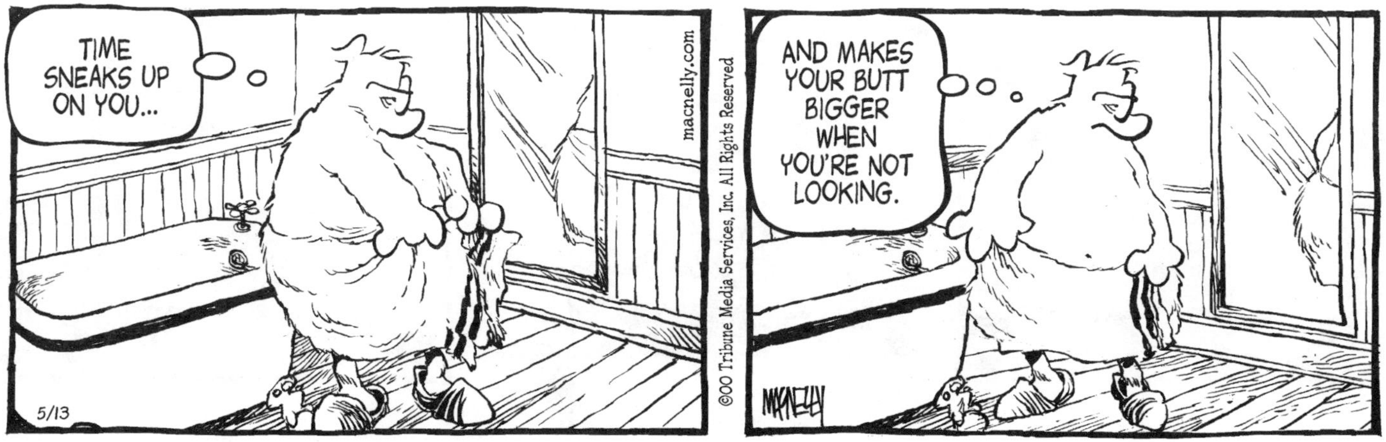
TIME SNEAKS UP ON YOU...
5/13
macnelly.com
©00 Tribune Media Services, Inc. All Rights Reserved
AND MAKES YOUR BUTT BIGGER WHEN YOU'RE NOT LOOKING.
MACNELLY

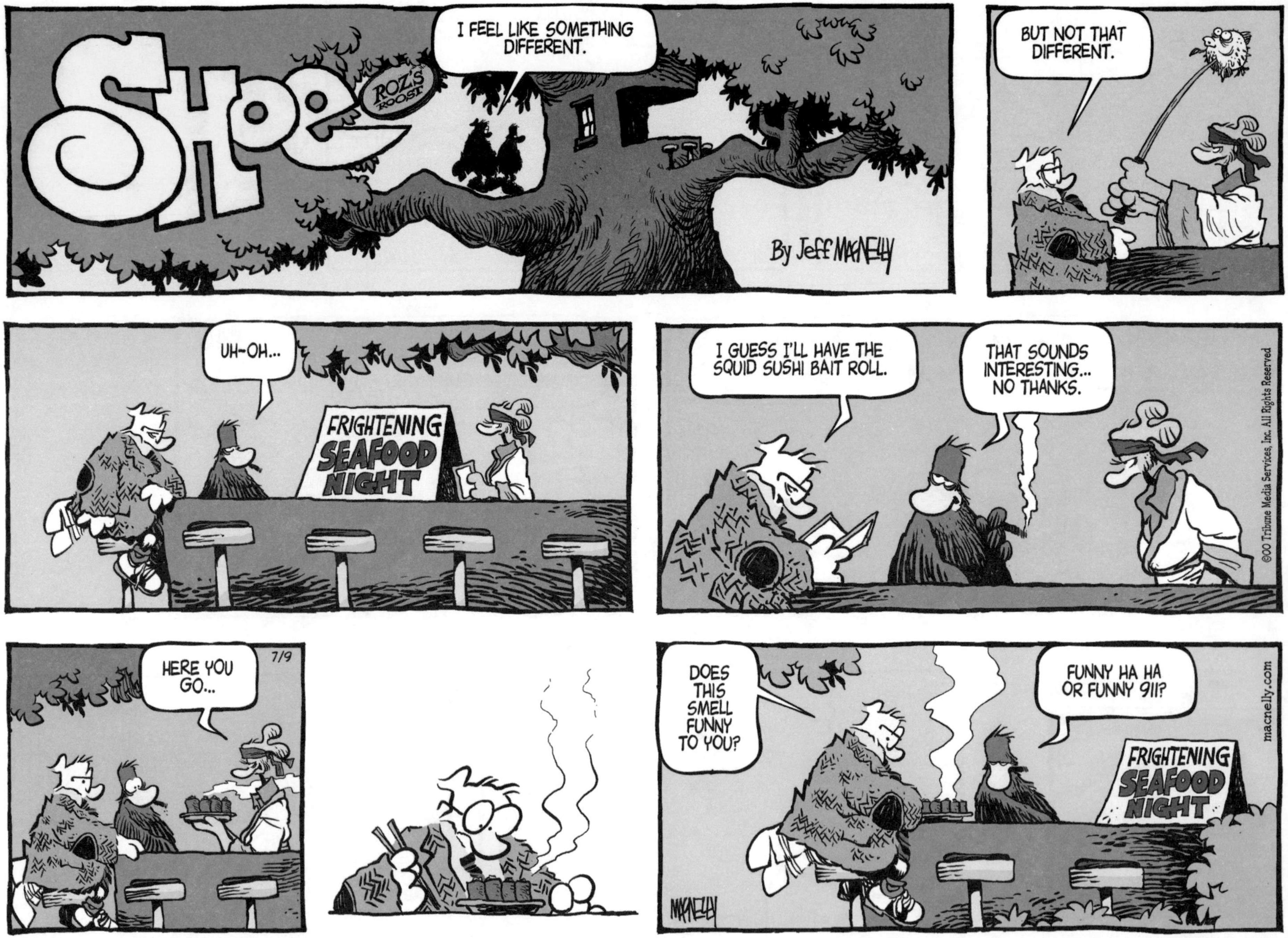
SHOE
ROZ'S ROOST
I FEEL LIKE SOMETHING DIFFERENT.
By Jeff MacNelly
BUT NOT THAT DIFFERENT.
UH-OH...
FRIGHTENING SEAFOOD NIGHT
I GUESS I'LL HAVE THE SQUID SUSHI BAIT ROLL.
THAT SOUNDS INTERESTING... NO THANKS.
©00 Tribune Media Services, Inc. All Rights Reserved
HERE YOU GO...
7/9
DOES THIS SMELL FUNNY TO YOU?
FUNNY HA HA OR FUNNY 911?
FRIGHTENING SEAFOOD NIGHT
MacNelly
macnelly.com

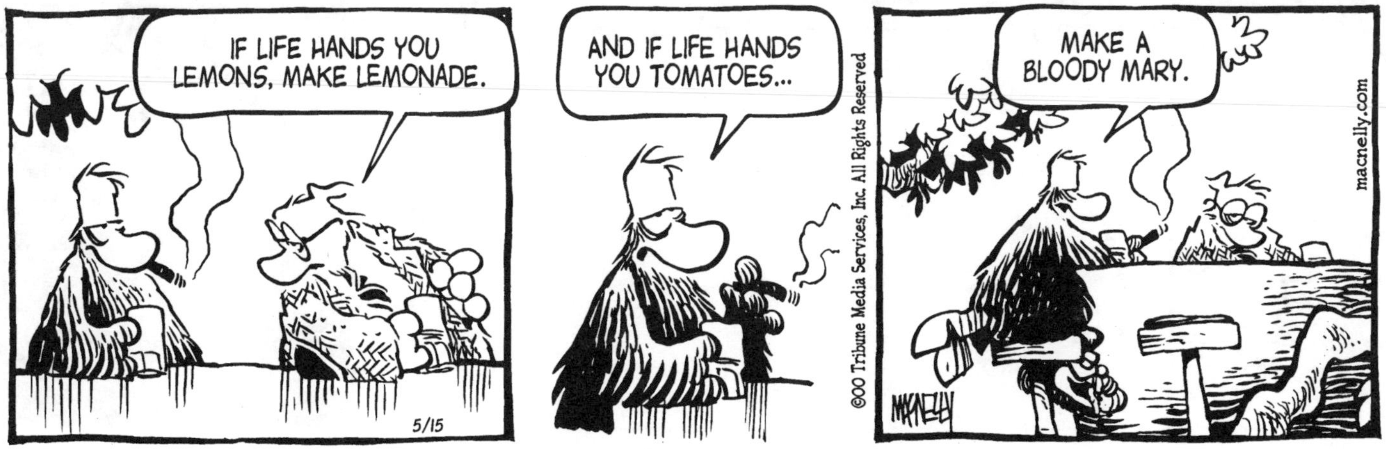
IF LIFE HANDS YOU LEMONS, MAKE LEMONADE.
5/15
AND IF LIFE HANDS YOU TOMATOES...
©00 Tribune Media Services, Inc. All Rights Reserved
MAKE A BLOODY MARY.
MACNELLY
macnelly.com

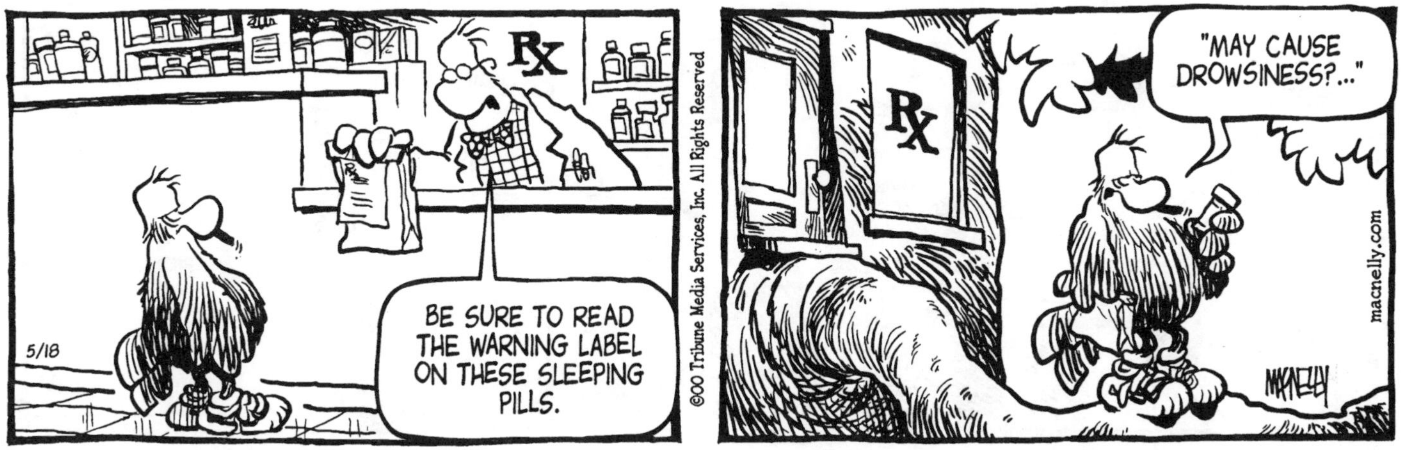
RX
5/18
BE SURE TO READ THE WARNING LABEL ON THESE SLEEPING PILLS.
©00 Tribune Media Services, Inc. All Rights Reserved
RX
"MAY CAUSE DROWSINESS?..."
MACNELLY
macnelly.com

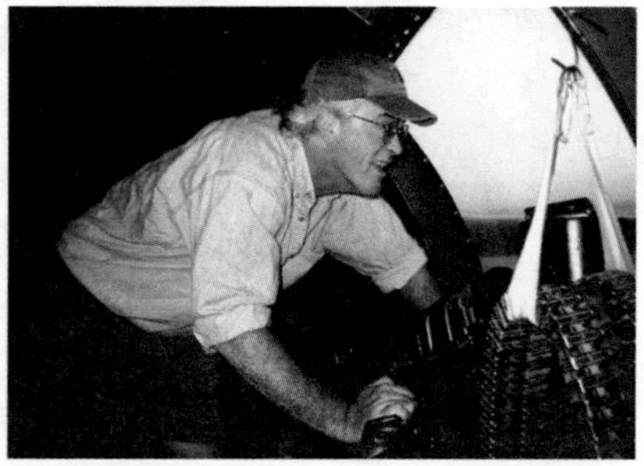

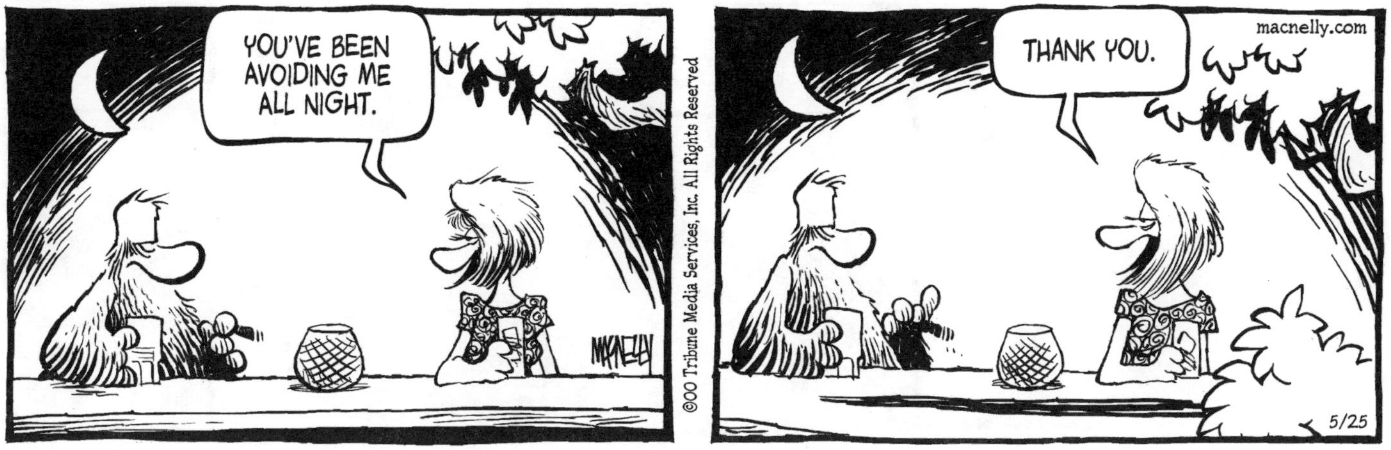
YOU'VE BEEN AVOIDING ME ALL NIGHT.
MACNELLY
©00 Tribune Media Services, Inc. All Rights Reserved
macnelly.com
THANK YOU.
5/25

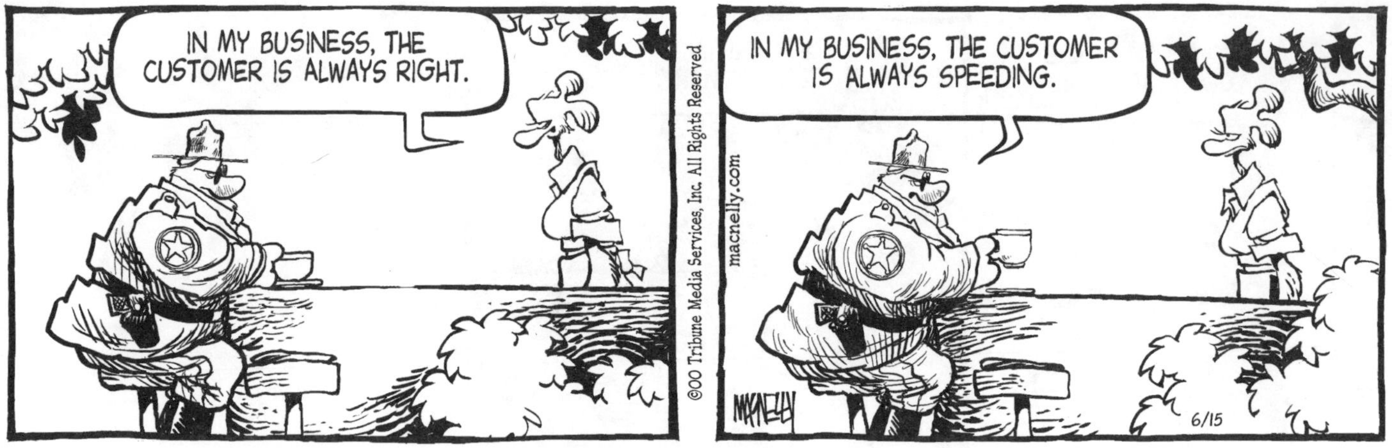
IN MY BUSINESS, THE CUSTOMER IS ALWAYS RIGHT.
IN MY BUSINESS, THE CUSTOMER IS ALWAYS SPEEDING.
©00 Tribune Media Services, Inc. All Rights Reserved
macnelly.com
MACNELLY
6/15

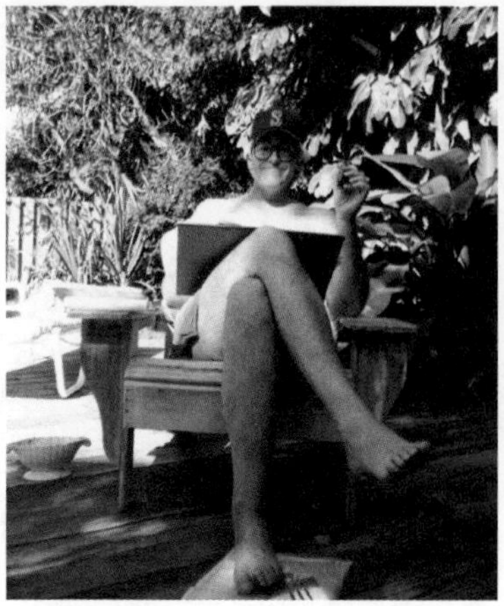

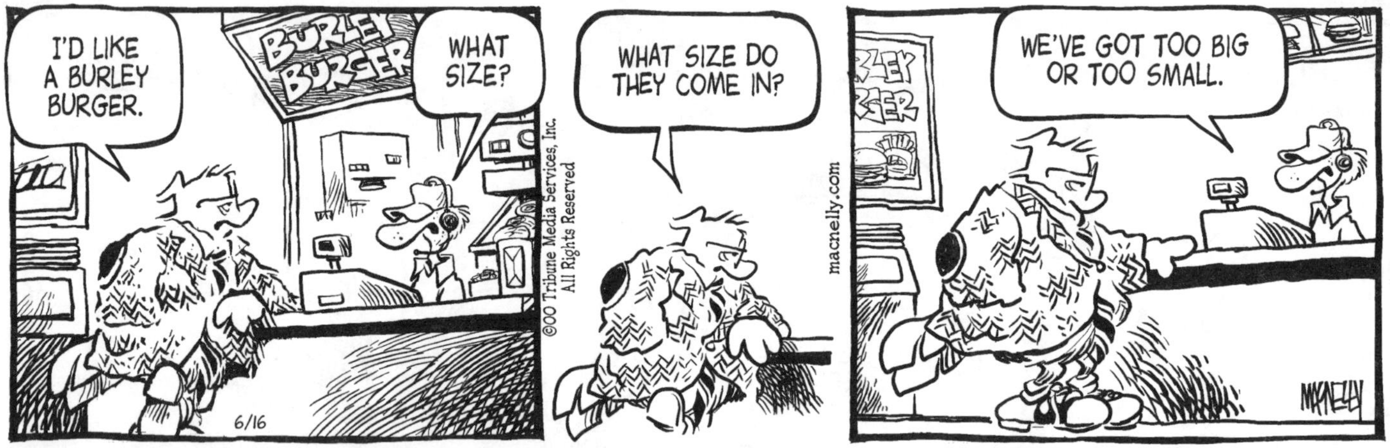
I'D LIKE A BURLEY BURGER.
BURLEY BURGER
WHAT SIZE?
6/16
©00 Tribune Media Services, Inc. All Rights Reserved
WHAT SIZE DO THEY COME IN?
macnelly.com
WE'VE GOT TOO BIG OR TOO SMALL.
MACNELLY

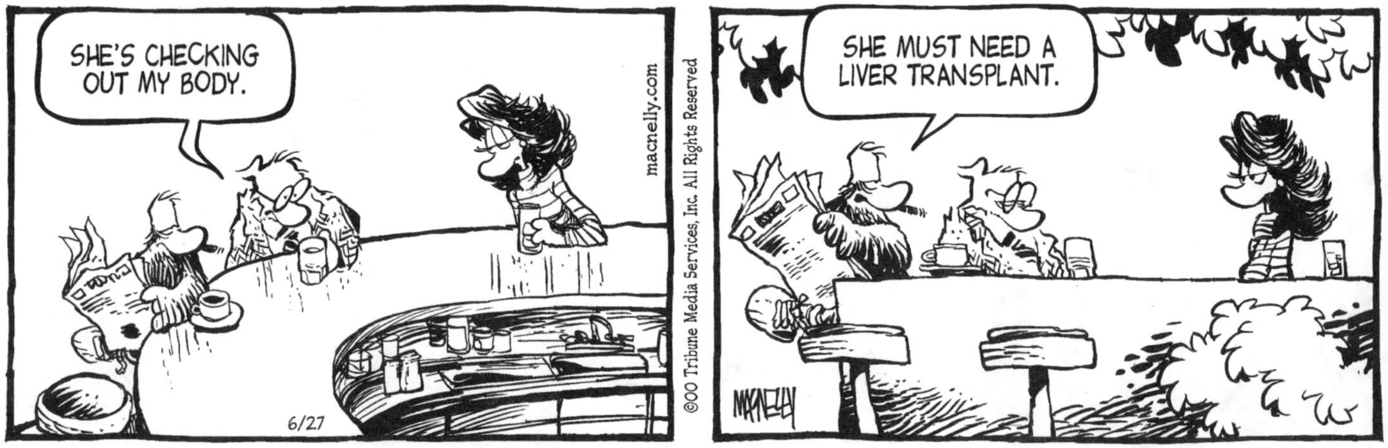
SHE'S CHECKING OUT MY BODY.
macnelly.com
6/27
©00 Tribune Media Services, Inc. All Rights Reserved
SHE MUST NEED A LIVER TRANSPLANT.
MACNELLY

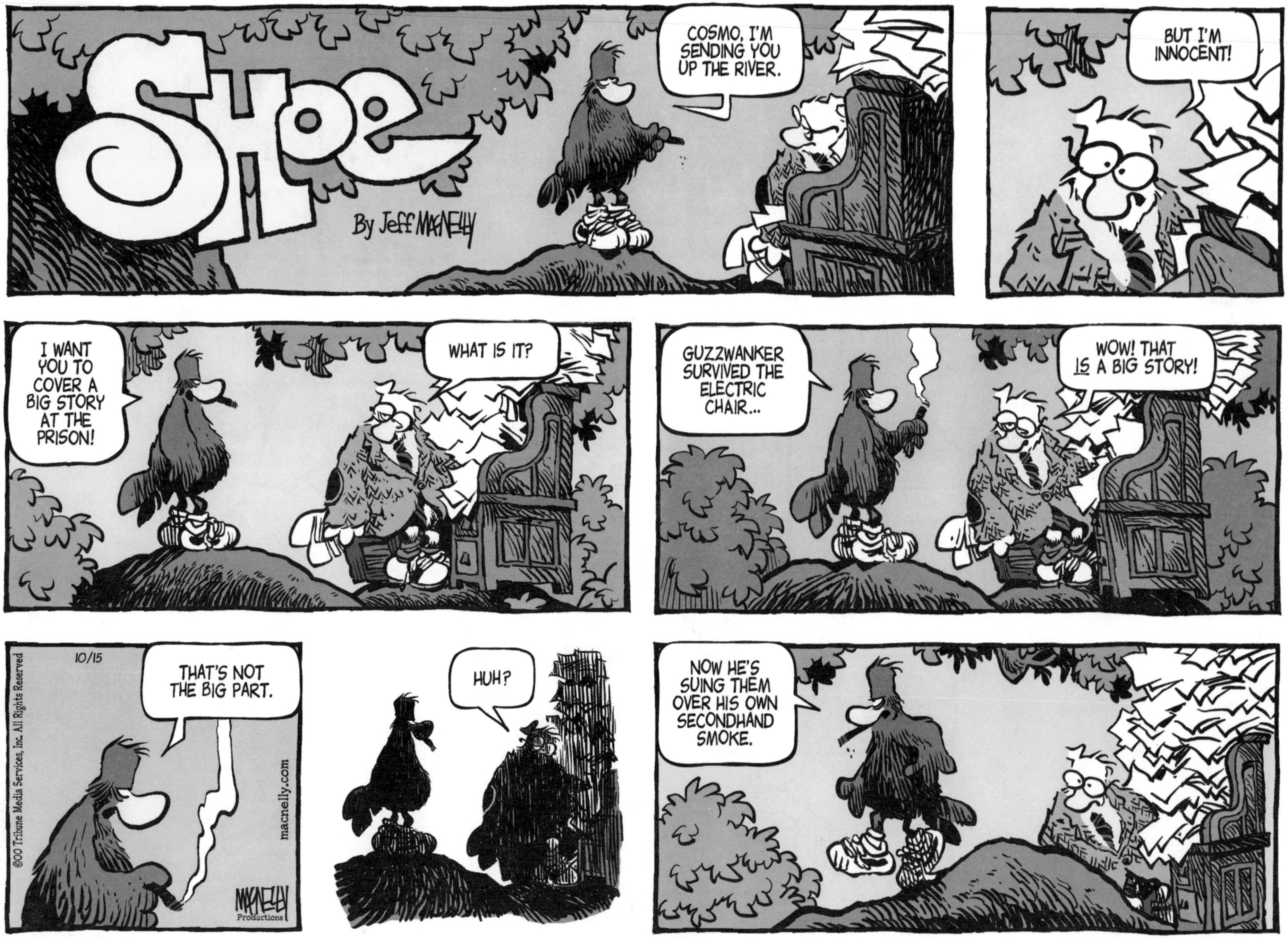
SHOE
By Jeff MacNelly
COSMO, I'M SENDING YOU UP THE RIVER.
BUT I'M INNOCENT!
I WANT YOU TO COVER A BIG STORY AT THE PRISON!
WHAT IS IT?
GUZZWANKER SURVIVED THE ELECTRIC CHAIR...
WOW! THAT IS A BIG STORY!
10/15
©00 Tribune Media Services, Inc. All Rights Reserved
THAT'S NOT THE BIG PART.
macnelly.com
MACNELLY Productions
HUH?
NOW HE'S SUING THEM OVER HIS OWN SECONDHAND SMOKE.

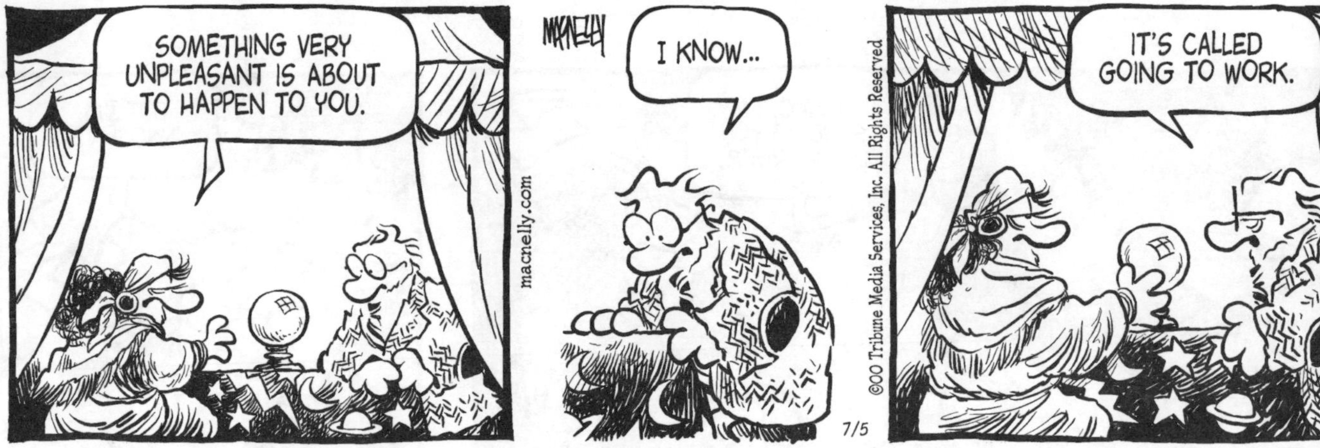
SOMETHING VERY UNPLEASANT IS ABOUT TO HAPPEN TO YOU.
macnelly.com
I KNOW...
7/5
©00 Tribune Media Services, Inc. All Rights Reserved
IT'S CALLED GOING TO WORK.

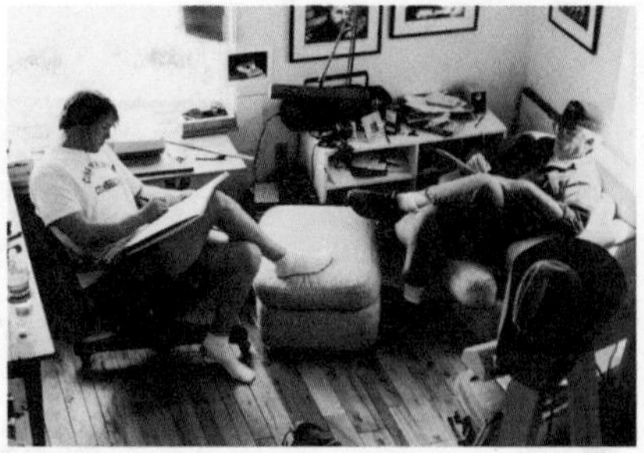

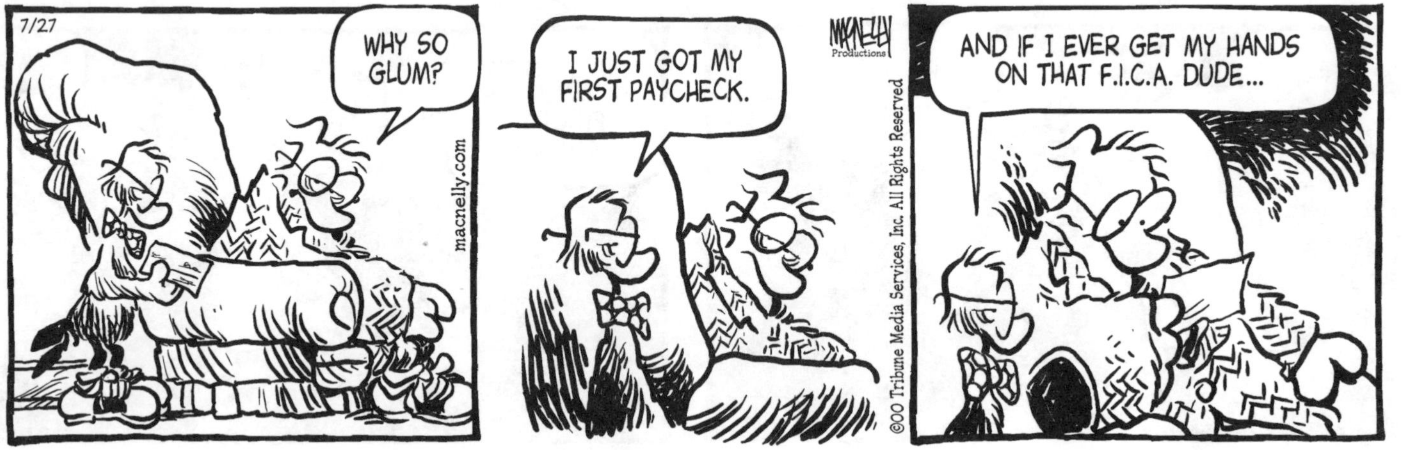
7/27
WHY SO GLUM?
macnelly.com
I JUST GOT MY FIRST PAYCHECK.
Productions
©00 Tribune Media Services, Inc. All Rights Reserved
AND IF I EVER GET MY HANDS ON THAT F.I.C.A. DUDE...

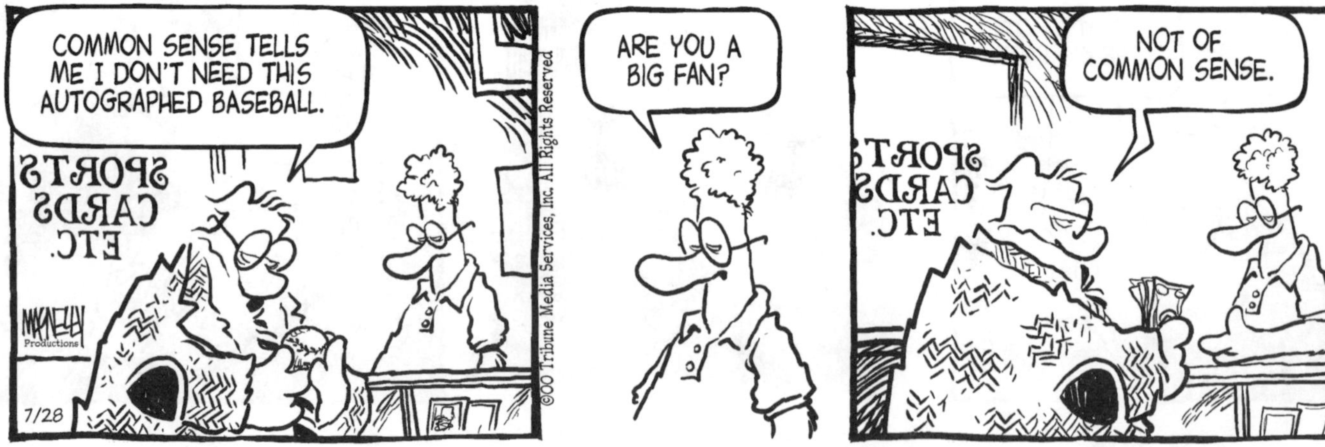
COMMON SENSE TELLS ME I DON'T NEED THIS AUTOGRAPHED BASEBALL.
Productions
7/28
©00 Tribune Media Services, Inc. All Rights Reserved
ARE YOU A BIG FAN?
NOT OF COMMON SENSE.
macnelly.com

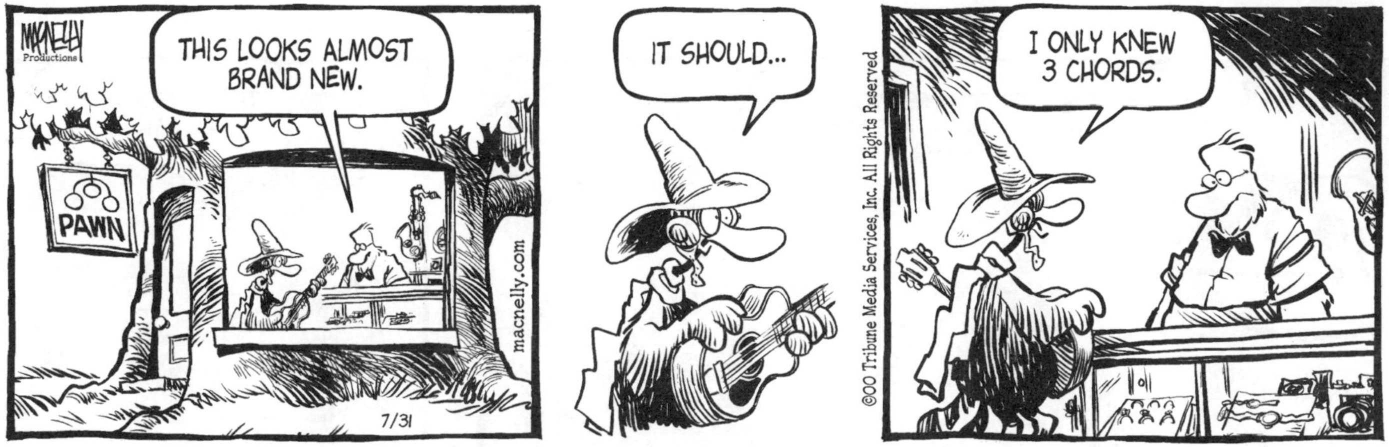
MACNELLY Productions
THIS LOOKS ALMOST BRAND NEW.
PAWN
macnelly.com
7/31
IT SHOULD...
©00 Tribune Media Services, Inc. All Rights Reserved
I ONLY KNEW 3 CHORDS.

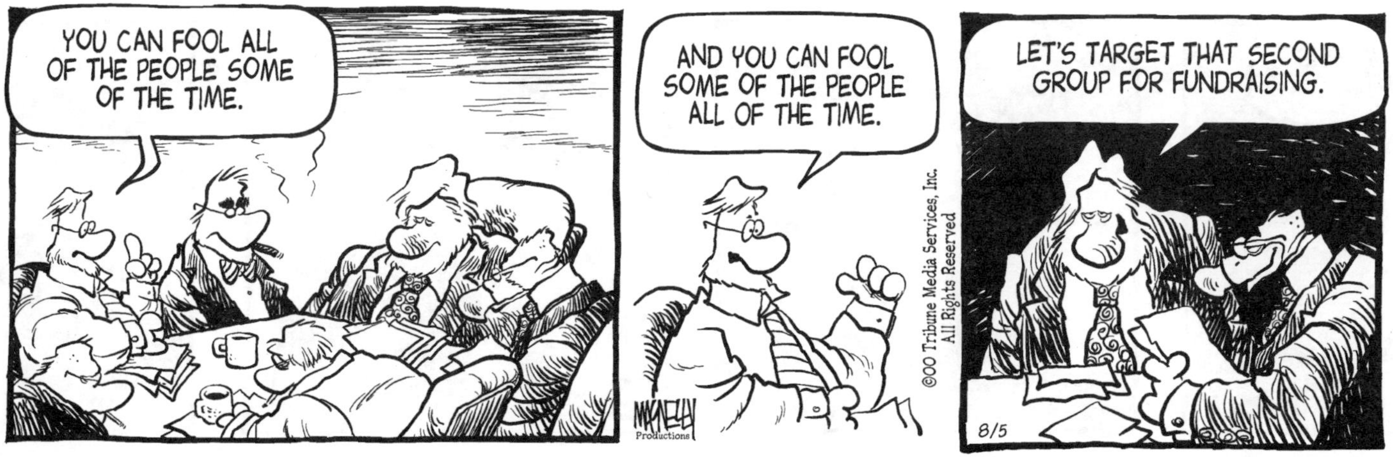
YOU CAN FOOL ALL OF THE PEOPLE SOME OF THE TIME.
AND YOU CAN FOOL SOME OF THE PEOPLE ALL OF THE TIME.
MACNELLY Productions
©00 Tribune Media Services, Inc. All Rights Reserved
LET'S TARGET THAT SECOND GROUP FOR FUNDRAISING.
8/5

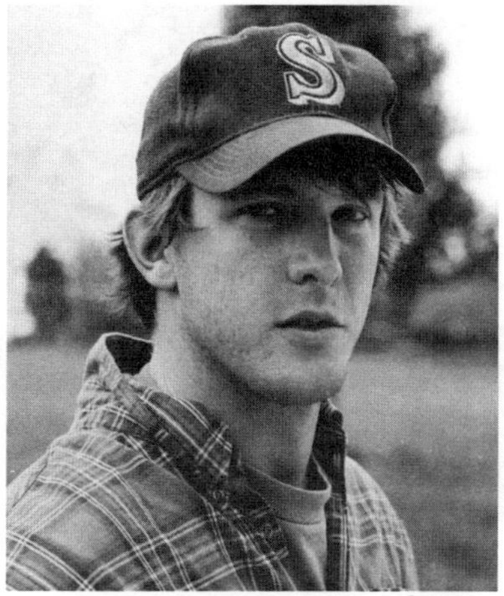

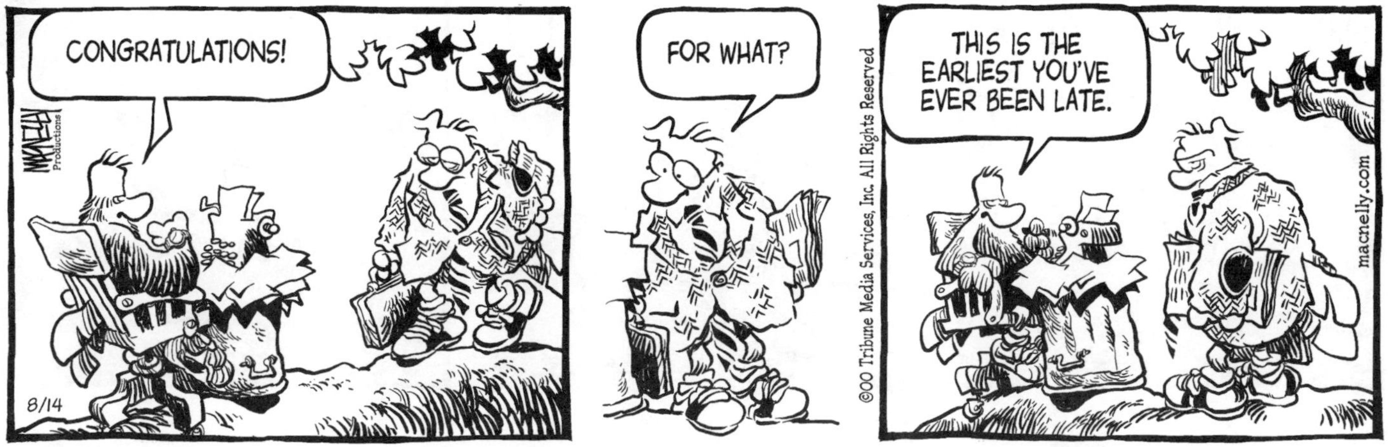
CONGRATULATIONS!
MACNELLY Productions
8/14
FOR WHAT?
©00 Tribune Media Services, Inc. All Rights Reserved
THIS IS THE EARLIEST YOU'VE EVER BEEN LATE.
macnelly.com

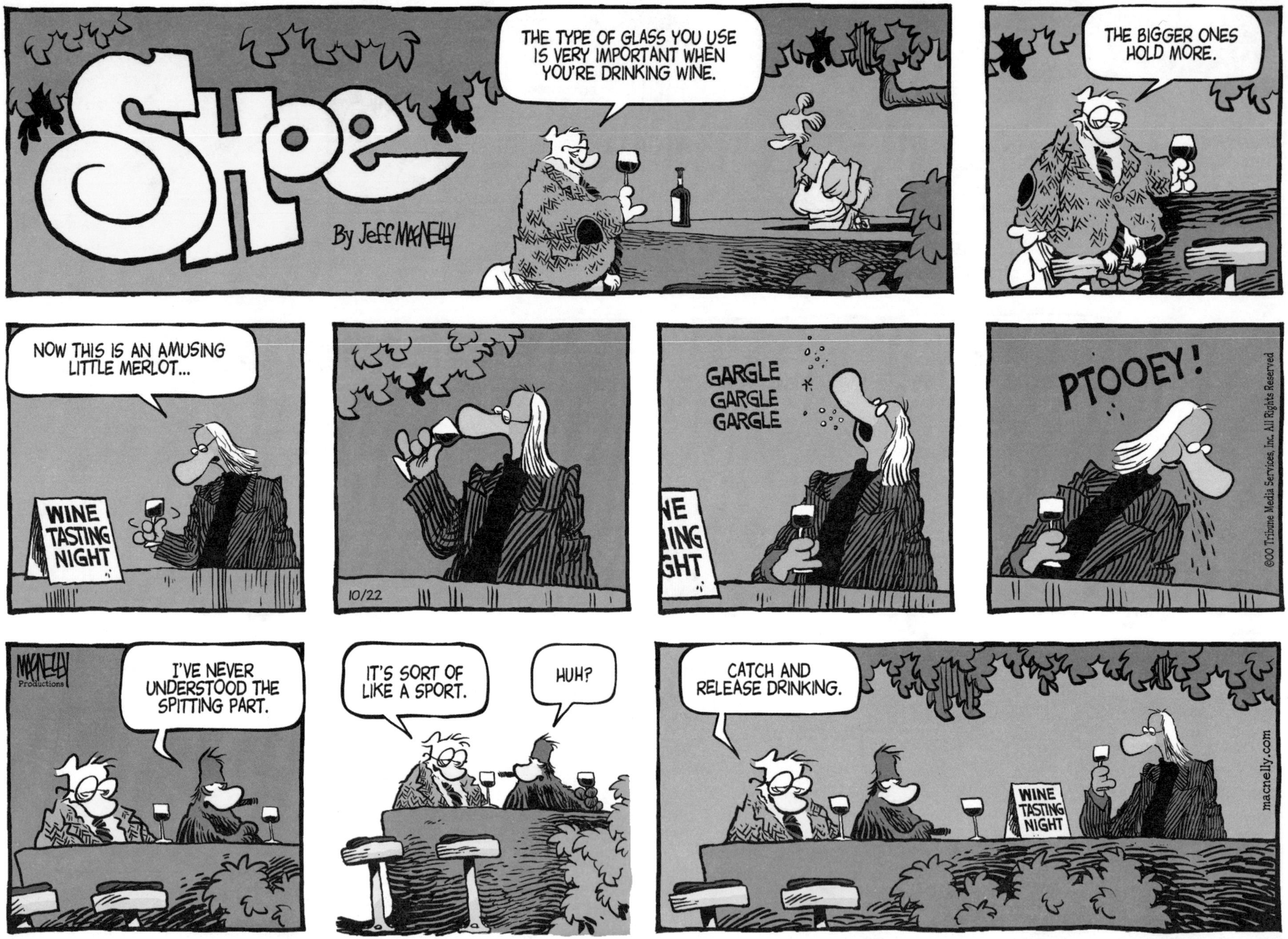
SHOE
By Jeff MacNelly
THE TYPE OF GLASS YOU USE IS VERY IMPORTANT WHEN YOU'RE DRINKING WINE.
THE BIGGER ONES HOLD MORE.
NOW THIS IS AN AMUSING LITTLE MERLOT...
WINE TASTING NIGHT
10/22
GARGLE GARGLE GARGLE
PTOOEY!
©00 Tribune Media Services, Inc. All Rights Reserved
MacNelly Productions
I'VE NEVER UNDERSTOOD THE SPITTING PART.
IT'S SORT OF LIKE A SPORT.
HUH?
CATCH AND RELEASE DRINKING.
WINE TASTING NIGHT
macnelly.com

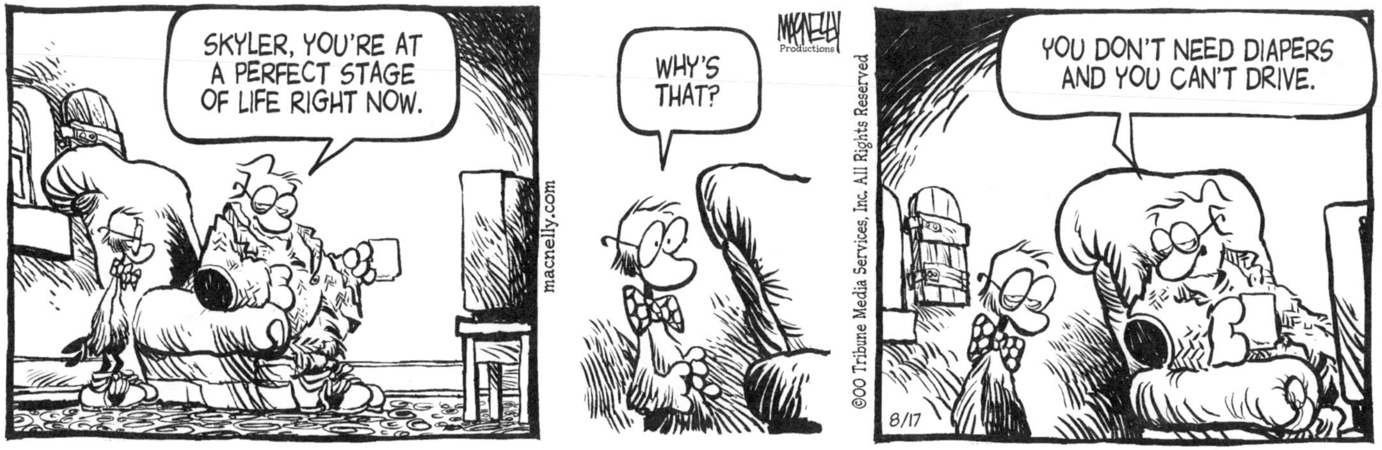
SKYLER, YOU'RE AT A PERFECT STAGE OF LIFE RIGHT NOW.
WHY'S THAT?
YOU DON'T NEED DIAPERS AND YOU CAN'T DRIVE.
MACNELLY Productions
macnelly.com
©00 Tribune Media Services, Inc. All Rights Reserved
8/17

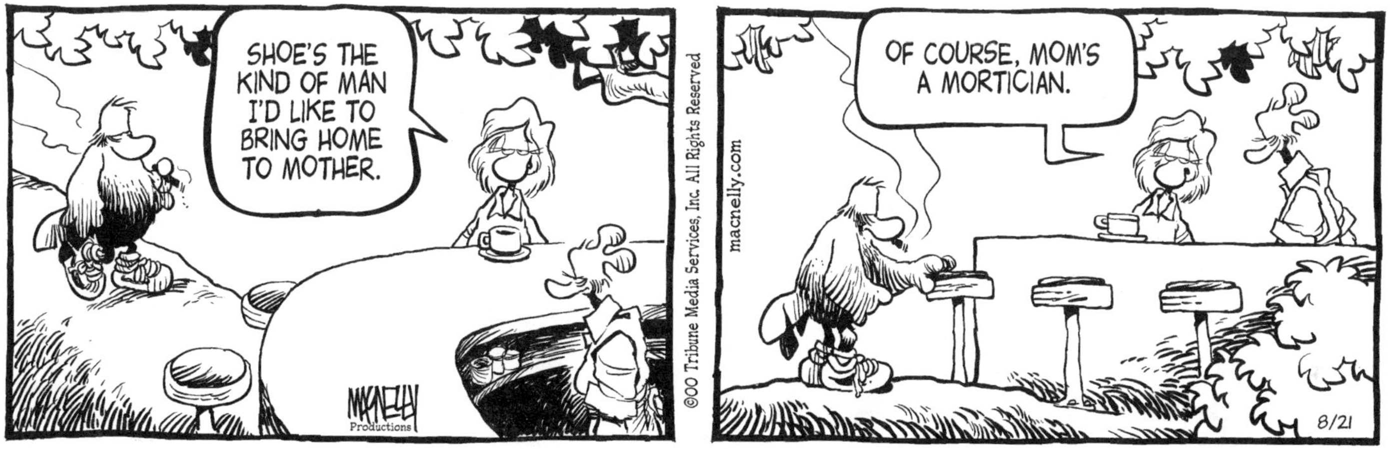
SHOE'S THE KIND OF MAN I'D LIKE TO BRING HOME TO MOTHER.
OF COURSE, MOM'S A MORTICIAN.
MACNELLY Productions
©00 Tribune Media Services, Inc. All Rights Reserved
macnelly.com
8/21

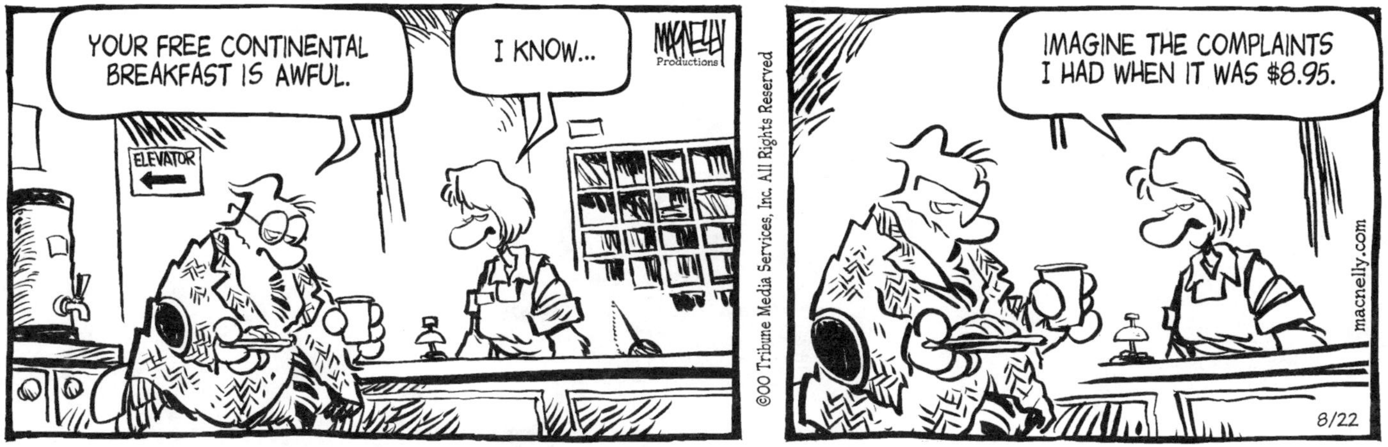
YOUR FREE CONTINENTAL BREAKFAST IS AWFUL.
I KNOW...
ELEVATOR
IMAGINE THE COMPLAINTS I HAD WHEN IT WAS $8.95.
MACNELLY Productions
©00 Tribune Media Services, Inc. All Rights Reserved
macnelly.com
8/22

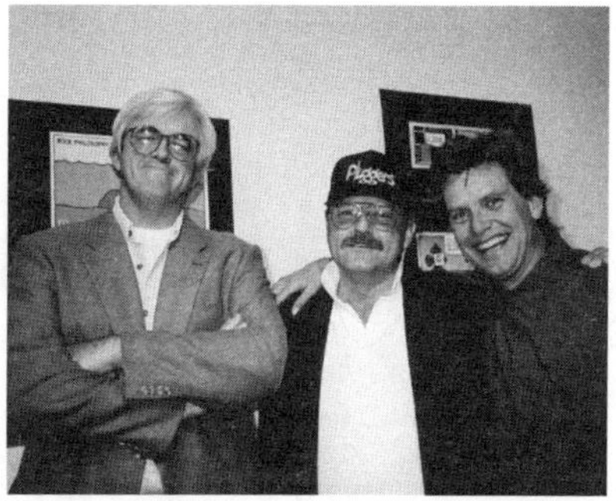

The Three Amigos: Jeff, Chris Cassatt, and Mike Peters at their gallery opening in Aspen in 1994

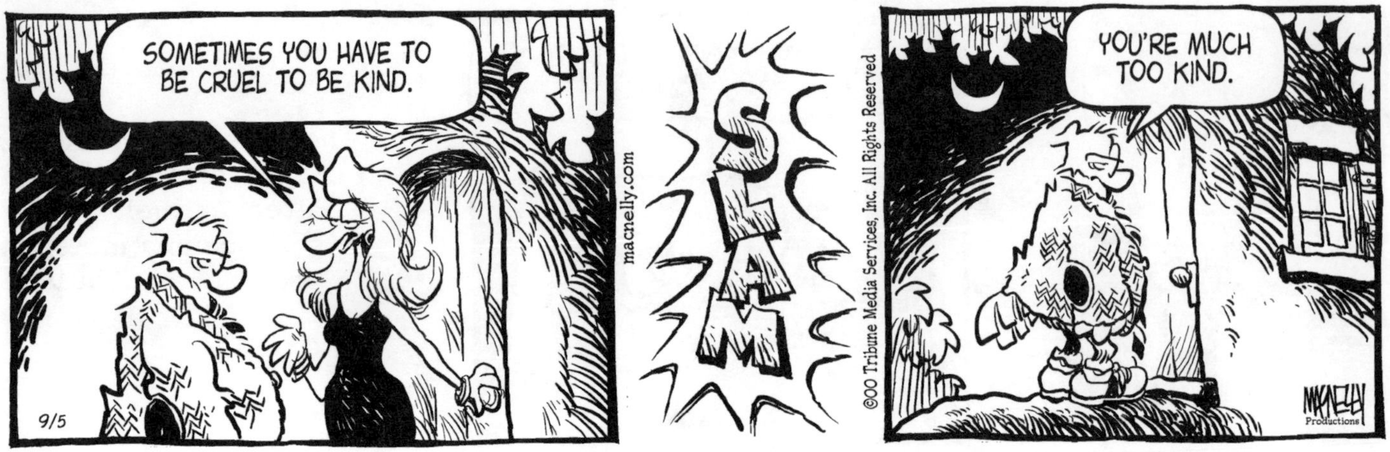
SOMETIMES YOU HAVE TO BE CRUEL TO BE KIND.
9/5
macnelly.com
SLAM
©00 Tribune Media Services, Inc. All Rights Reserved
YOU'RE MUCH TOO KIND.
MACNELLY Productions

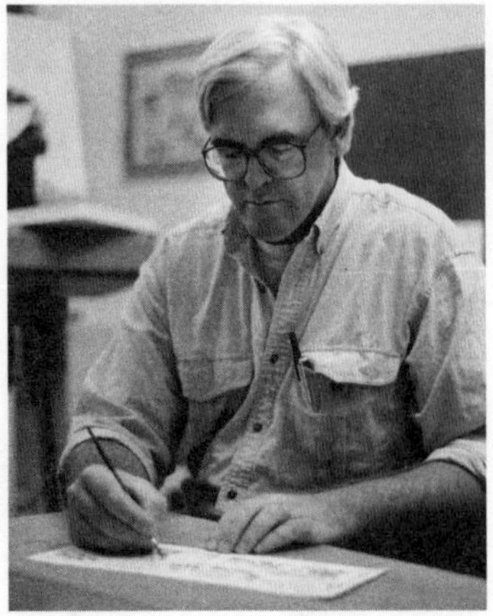

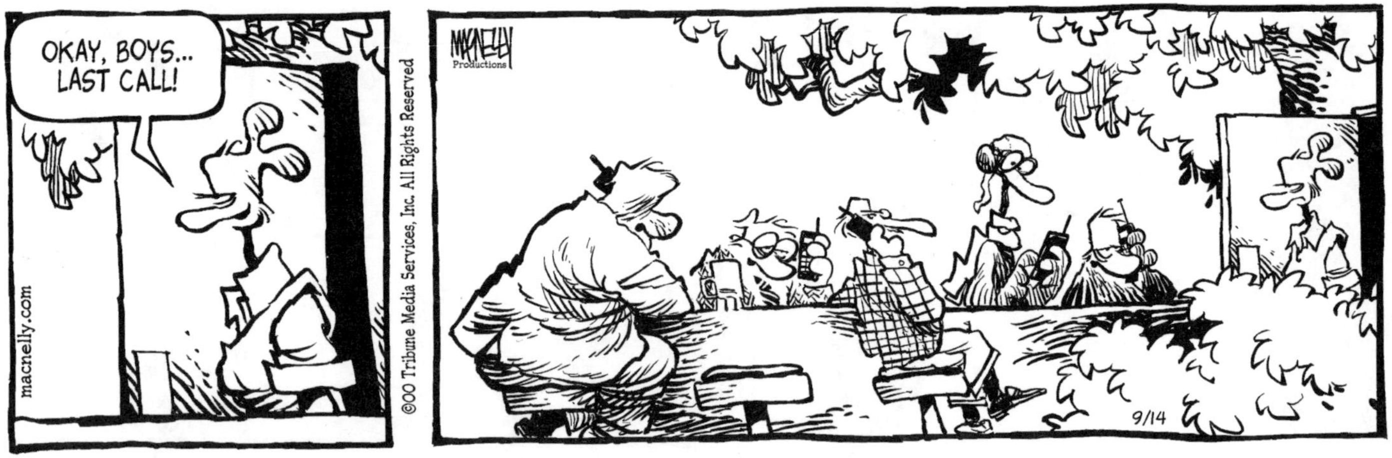
OKAY, BOYS... LAST CALL!
macnelly.com
©00 Tribune Media Services, Inc. All Rights Reserved
MACNELLY Productions
9/14

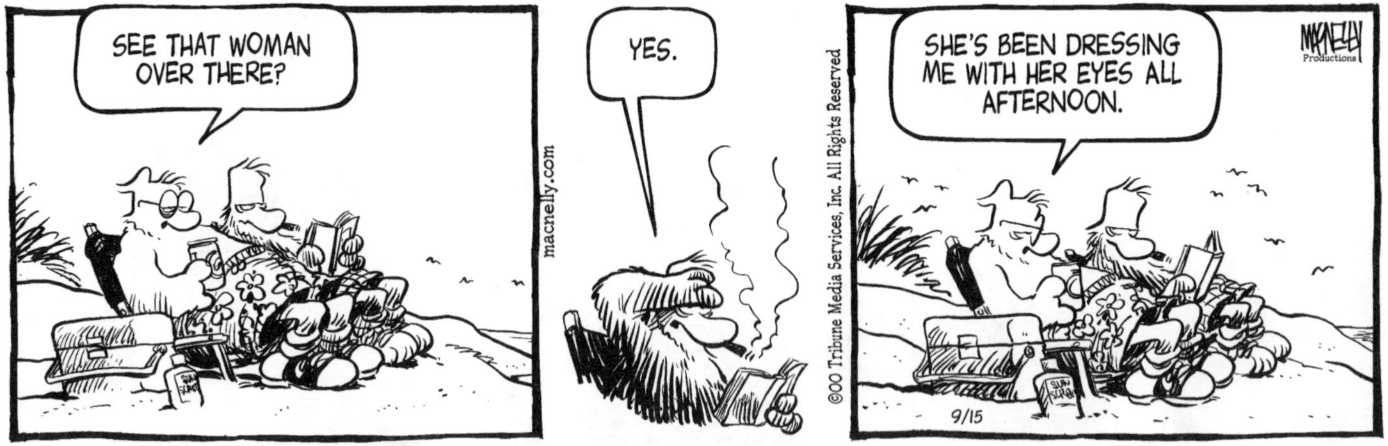
SEE THAT WOMAN OVER THERE?
macnelly.com
YES.
©00 Tribune Media Services, Inc. All Rights Reserved
SHE'S BEEN DRESSING ME WITH HER EYES ALL AFTERNOON.
MACNELLY Productions
9/15

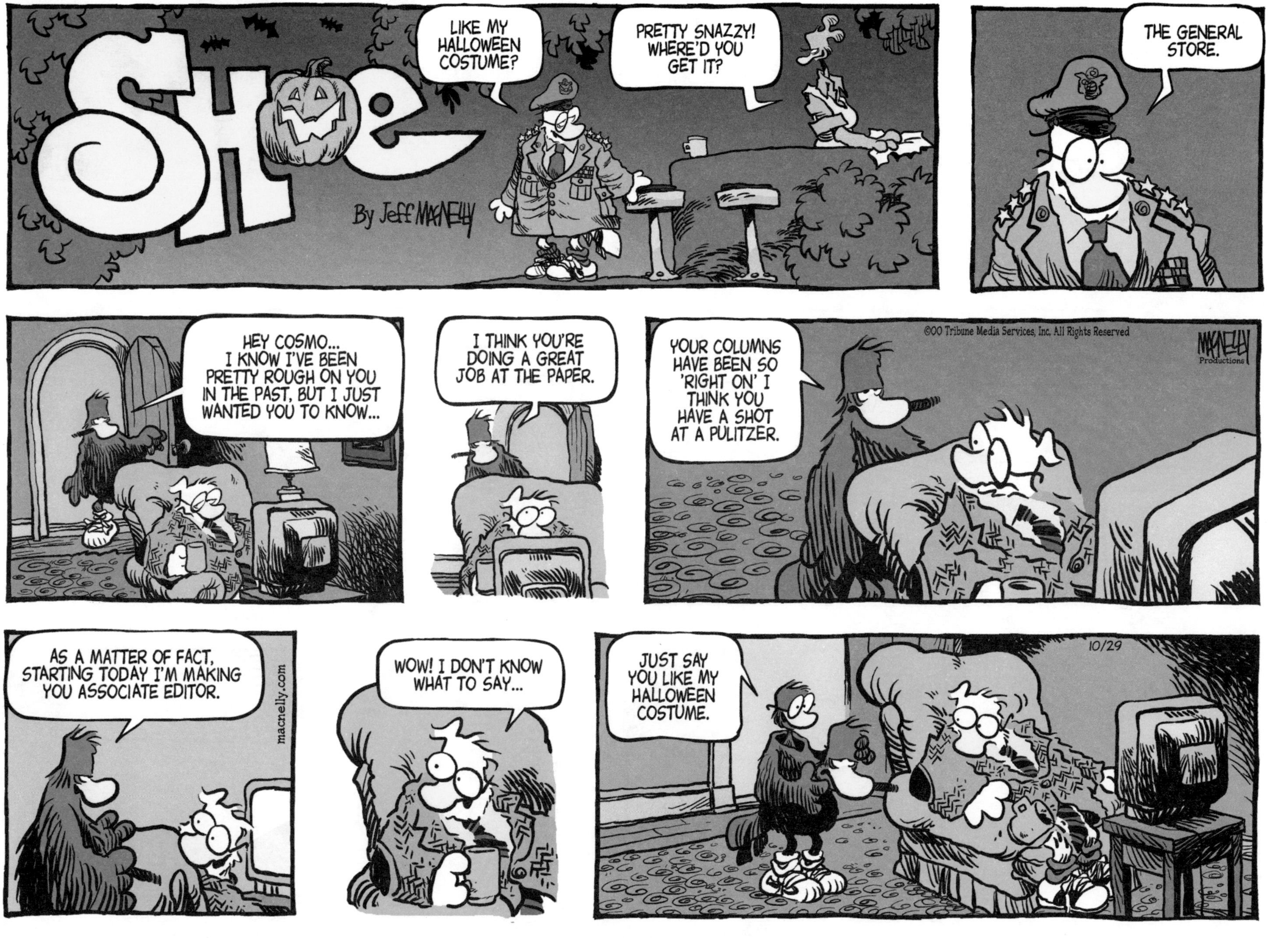

SHOE
By Jeff MacNELLY
LIKE MY HALLOWEEN COSTUME?
PRETTY SNAZZY! WHERE'D YOU GET IT?
THE GENERAL STORE.
HEY COSMO... I KNOW I'VE BEEN PRETTY ROUGH ON YOU IN THE PAST, BUT I JUST WANTED YOU TO KNOW...
I THINK YOU'RE DOING A GREAT JOB AT THE PAPER.
©00 Tribune Media Services, Inc. All Rights Reserved
MacNELLY Productions
YOUR COLUMNS HAVE BEEN SO 'RIGHT ON' I THINK YOU HAVE A SHOT AT A PULITZER.
AS A MATTER OF FACT, STARTING TODAY I'M MAKING YOU ASSOCIATE EDITOR.
macnelly.com
WOW! I DON'T KNOW WHAT TO SAY...
10/29
JUST SAY YOU LIKE MY HALLOWEEN COSTUME.

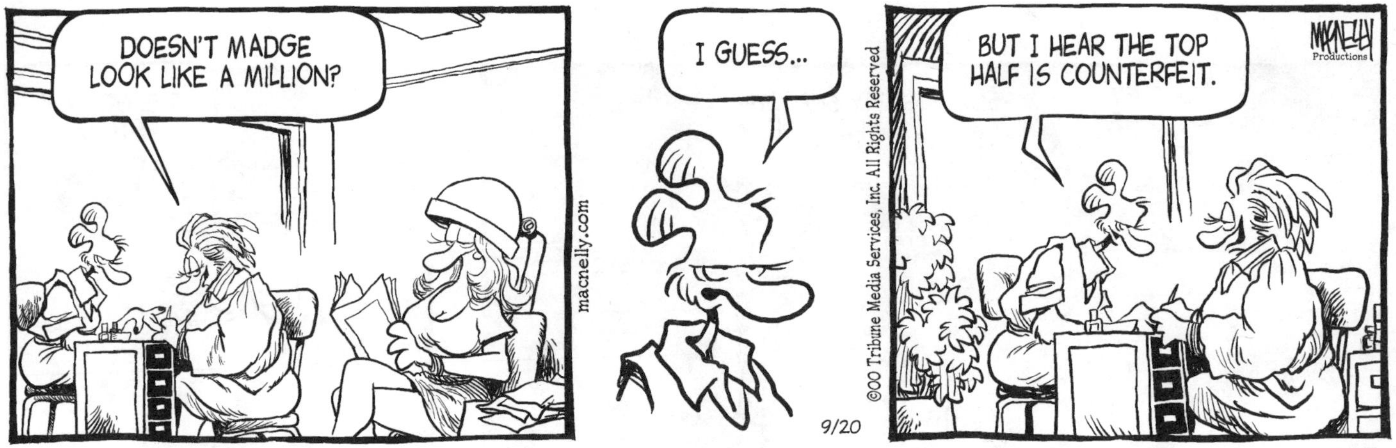
DOESN'T MADGE LOOK LIKE A MILLION?
I GUESS...
BUT I HEAR THE TOP HALF IS COUNTERFEIT.
macnelly.com
9/20
©00 Tribune Media Services, Inc. All Rights Reserved

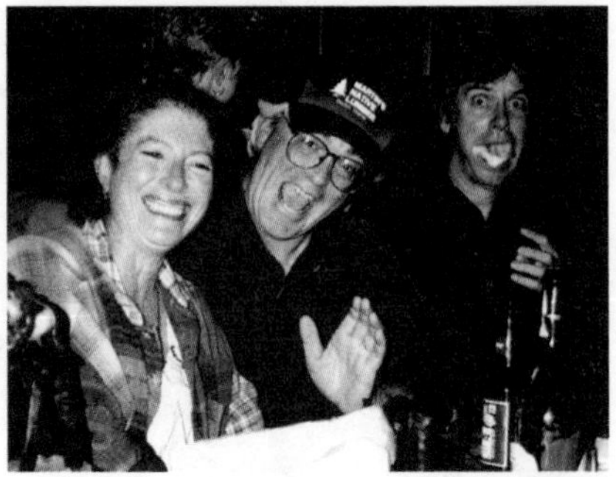

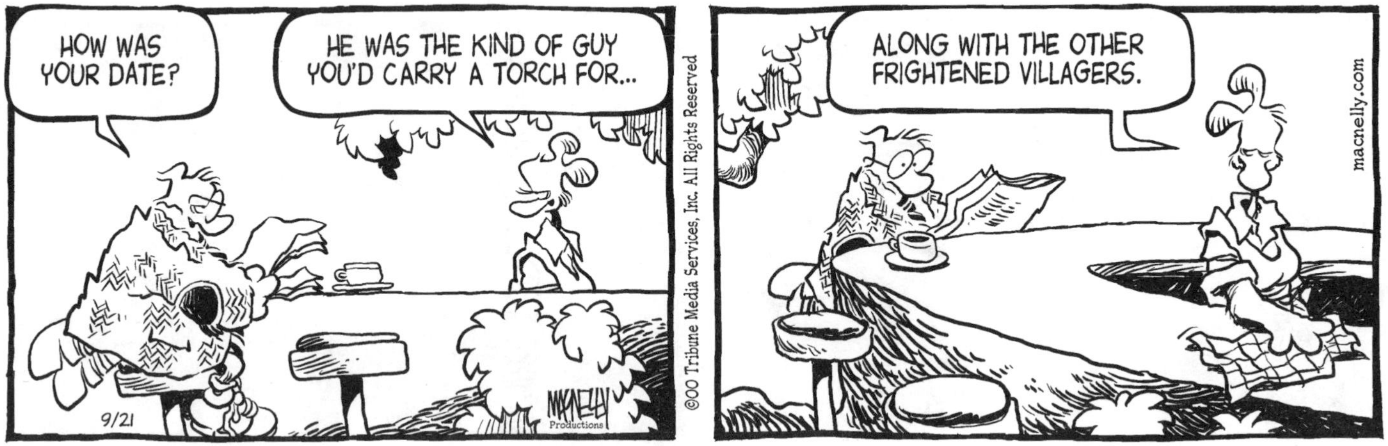
HOW WAS YOUR DATE?
HE WAS THE KIND OF GUY YOU'D CARRY A TORCH FOR...
ALONG WITH THE OTHER FRIGHTENED VILLAGERS.
9/21
©00 Tribune Media Services, Inc. All Rights Reserved
macnelly.com

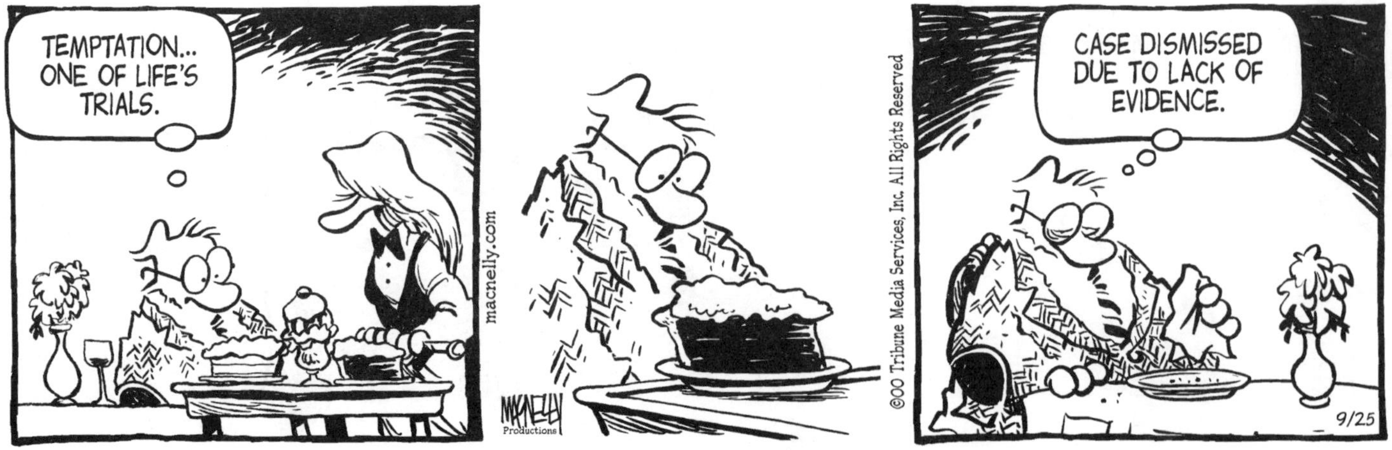
TEMPTATION... ONE OF LIFE'S TRIALS.
macnelly.com
CASE DISMISSED DUE TO LACK OF EVIDENCE.
©00 Tribune Media Services, Inc. All Rights Reserved
9/25

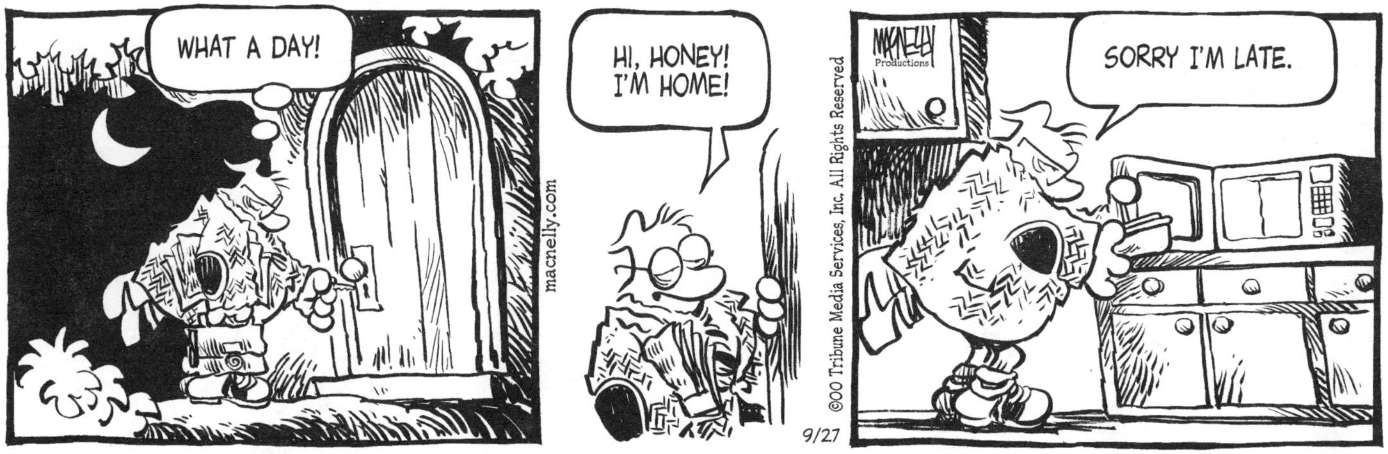
WHAT A DAY!
HI, HONEY! I'M HOME!
SORRY I'M LATE.
macnelly.com
©00 Tribune Media Services, Inc. All Rights Reserved
9/27

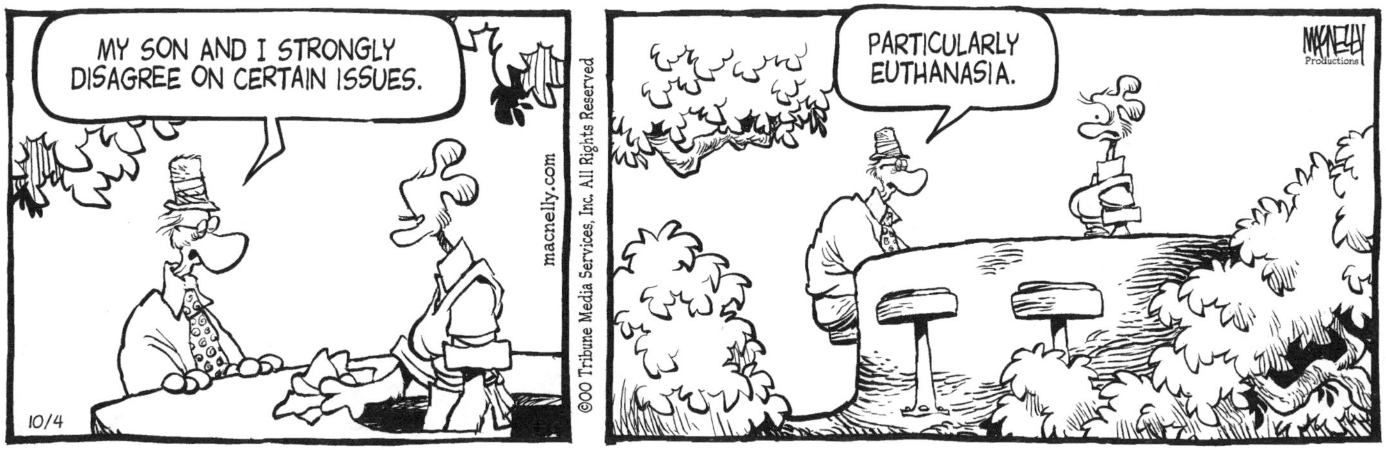
MY SON AND I STRONGLY DISAGREE ON CERTAIN ISSUES.
PARTICULARLY EUTHANASIA.
macnelly.com
©00 Tribune Media Services, Inc. All Rights Reserved
10/4

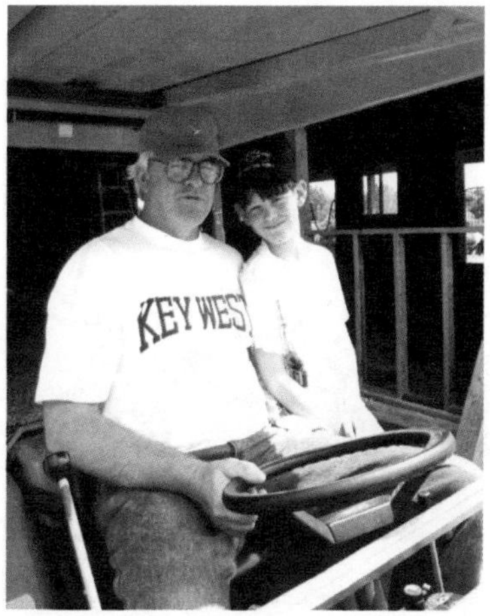
KEY WEST

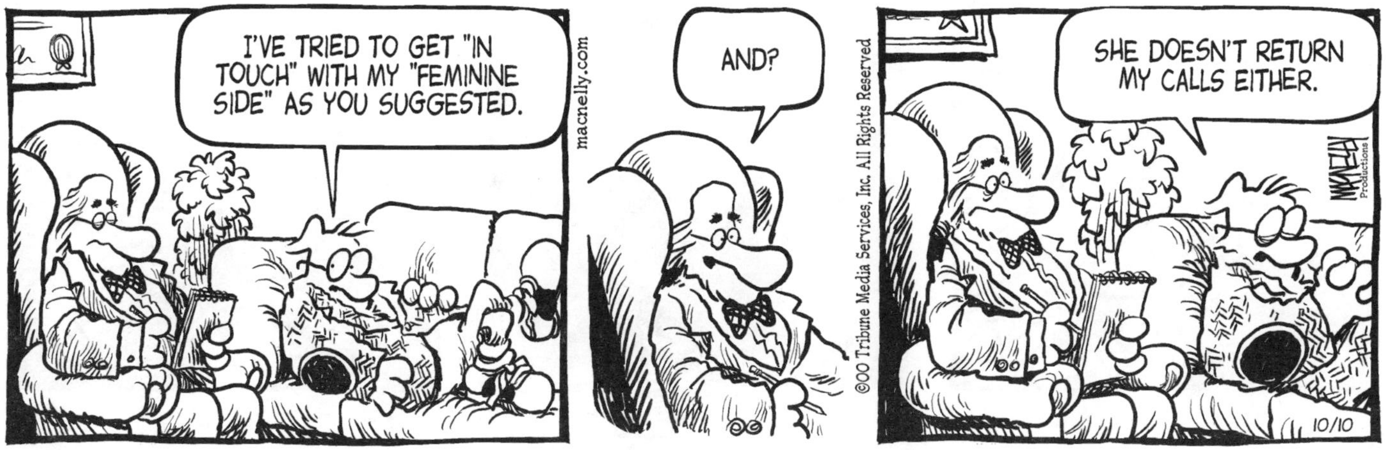
I'VE TRIED TO GET "IN TOUCH" WITH MY "FEMININE SIDE" AS YOU SUGGESTED.
AND?
SHE DOESN'T RETURN MY CALLS EITHER.
macnelly.com
©00 Tribune Media Services, Inc. All Rights Reserved
10/10

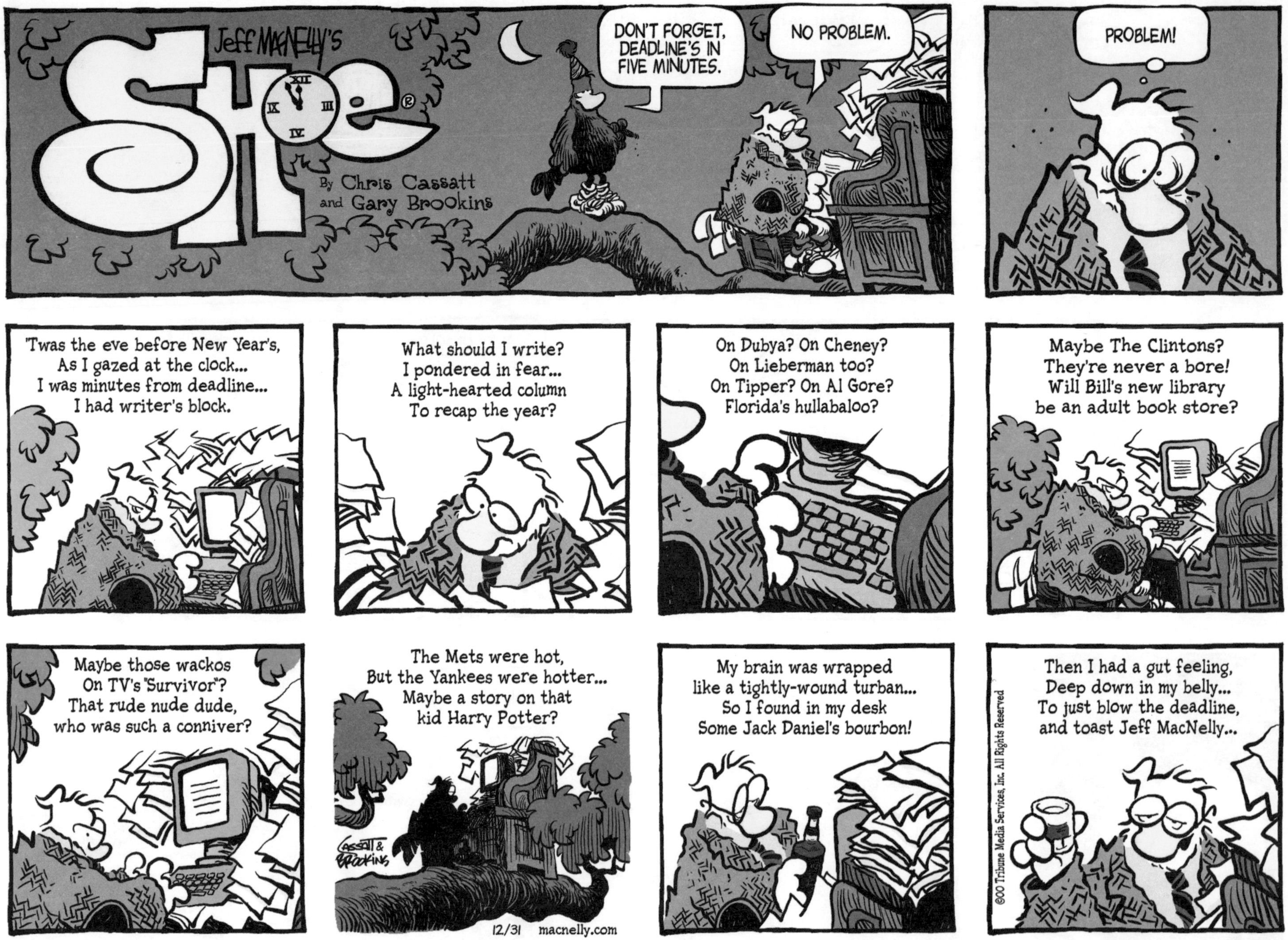
Jeff MacNelly's
Shoe®
By Chris Cassatt and Gary Brookins
DON'T FORGET, DEADLINE'S IN FIVE MINUTES.
NO PROBLEM.
PROBLEM!
'Twas the eve before New Year's, As I gazed at the clock... I was minutes from deadline... I had writer's block.
What should I write? I pondered in fear... A light-hearted column To recap the year?
On Dubya? On Cheney? On Lieberman too? On Tipper? On Al Gore? Florida's hullabaloo?
Maybe The Clintons? They're never a bore! Will Bill's new library be an adult book store?
Maybe those wackos On TV's "Survivor"? That rude nude dude, who was such a conniver?
The Mets were hot, But the Yankees were hotter... Maybe a story on that kid Harry Potter?
Cassatt & Brookins
12/31 macnelly.com
My brain was wrapped like a tightly-wound turban... So I found in my desk Some Jack Daniel's bourbon!
©00 Tribune Media Services, Inc. All Rights Reserved
Then I had a gut feeling, Deep down in my belly... To just blow the deadline, and toast Jeff MacNelly...

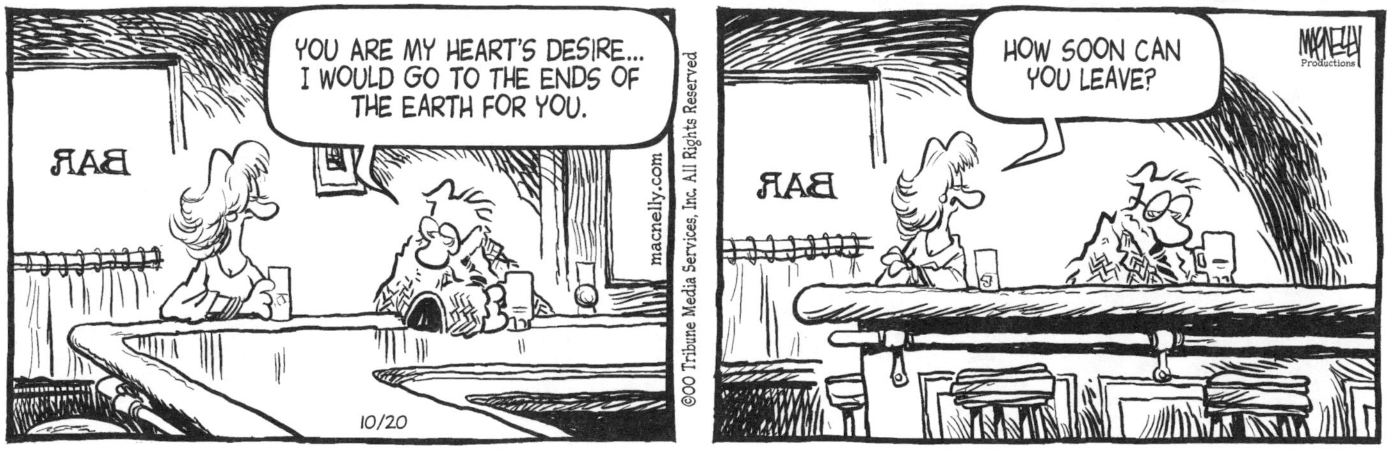
YOU ARE MY HEART'S DESIRE... I WOULD GO TO THE ENDS OF THE EARTH FOR YOU.
BAR
10/20
macnelly.com
©00 Tribune Media Services, Inc. All Rights Reserved
HOW SOON CAN YOU LEAVE?
MACNELLY Productions
BAR

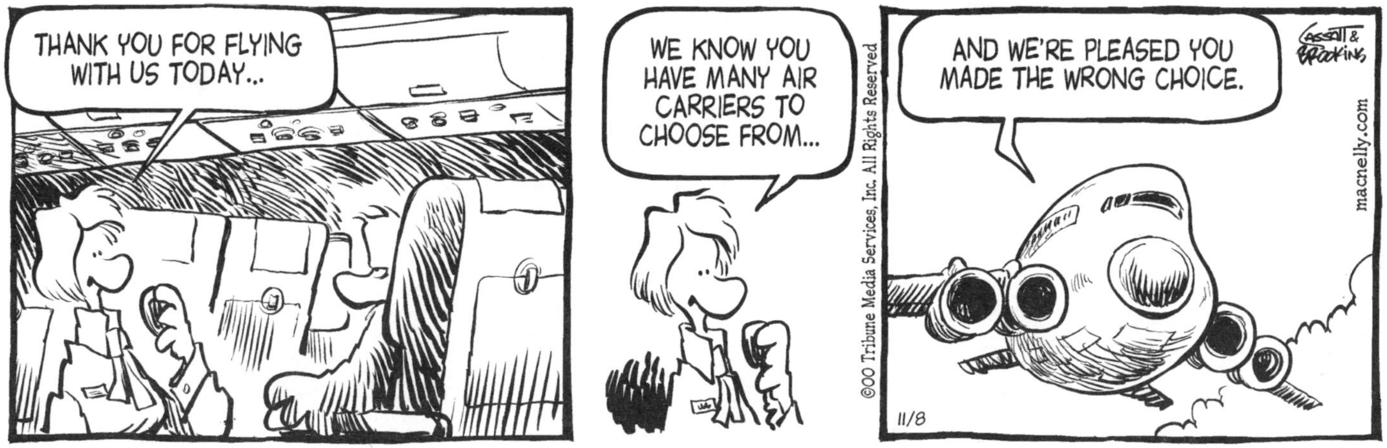
THANK YOU FOR FLYING WITH US TODAY...
WE KNOW YOU HAVE MANY AIR CARRIERS TO CHOOSE FROM...
©00 Tribune Media Services, Inc. All Rights Reserved
AND WE'RE PLEASED YOU MADE THE WRONG CHOICE.
CASSATT & BROOKINS
macnelly.com
11/8

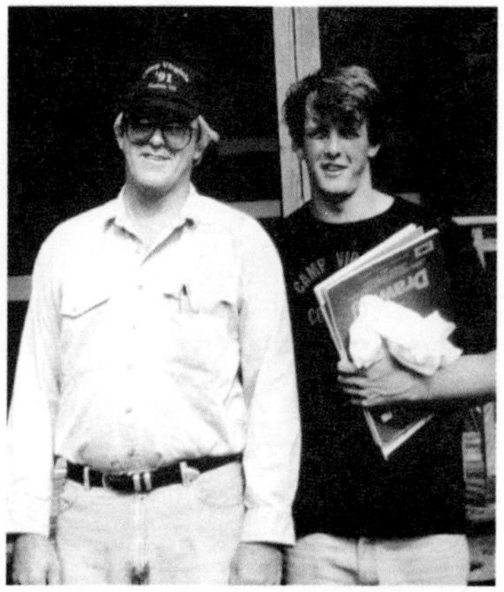

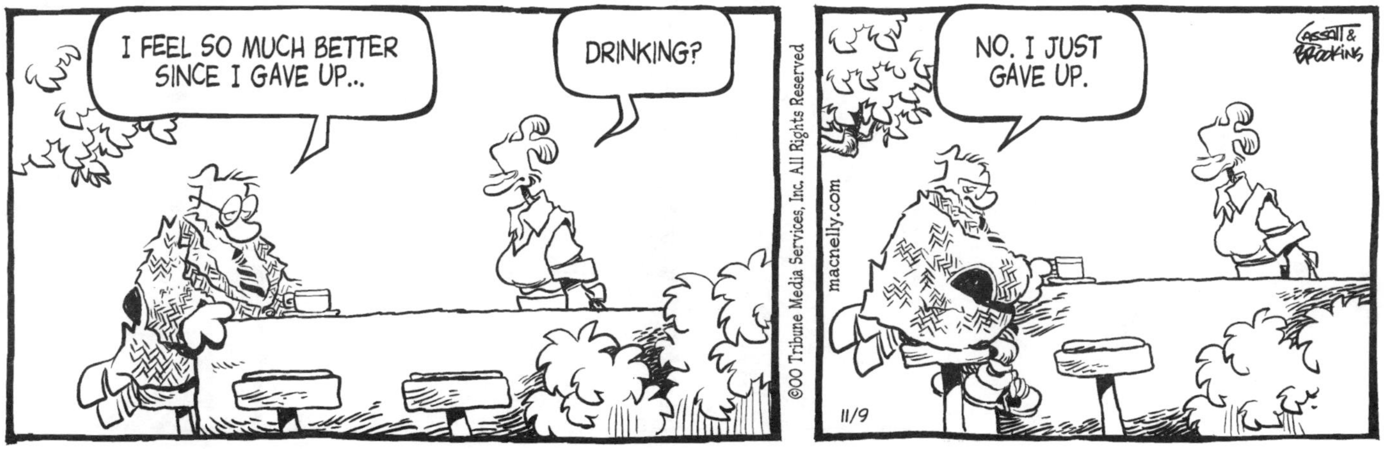
I FEEL SO MUCH BETTER SINCE I GAVE UP...
DRINKING?
©00 Tribune Media Services, Inc. All Rights Reserved
macnelly.com
NO. I JUST GAVE UP.
CASSATT & BROOKINS
11/9

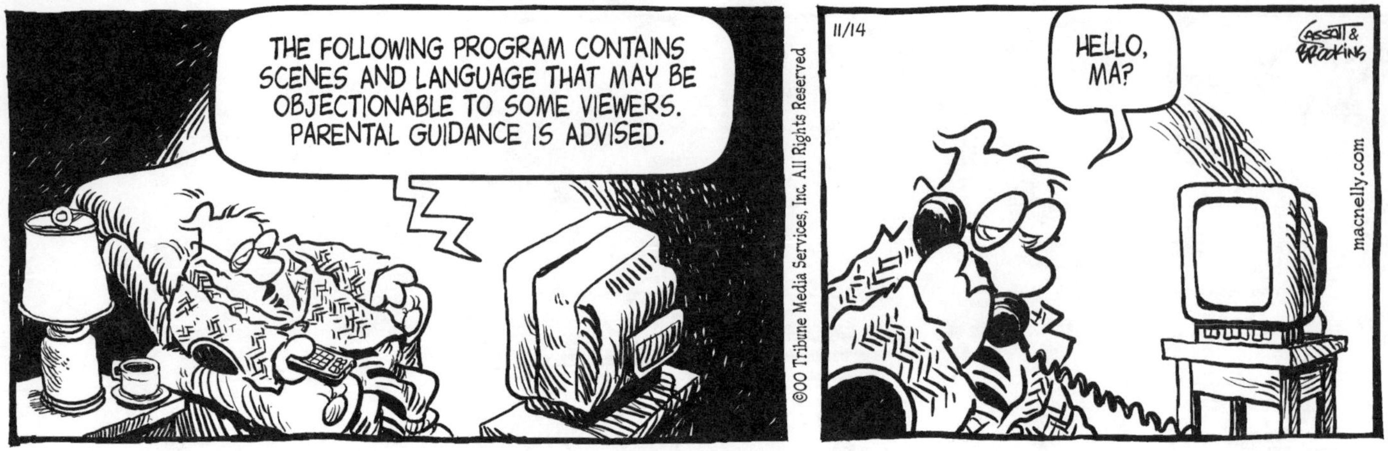
THE FOLLOWING PROGRAM CONTAINS SCENES AND LANGUAGE THAT MAY BE OBJECTIONABLE TO SOME VIEWERS. PARENTAL GUIDANCE IS ADVISED.
©00 Tribune Media Services, Inc. All Rights Reserved
11/14
HELLO, MA?
CASSATT & BROOKINS
macnelly.com

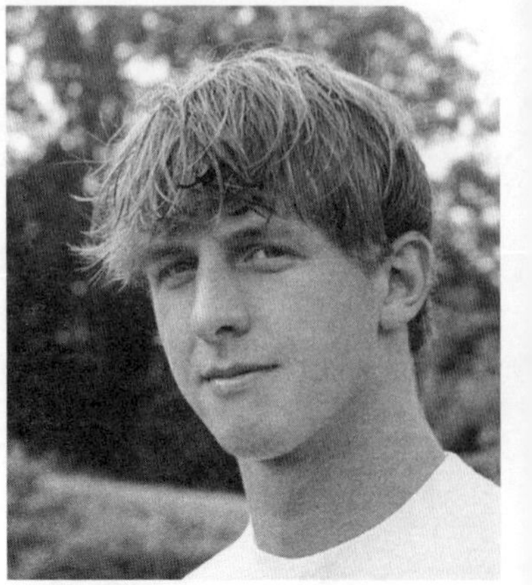

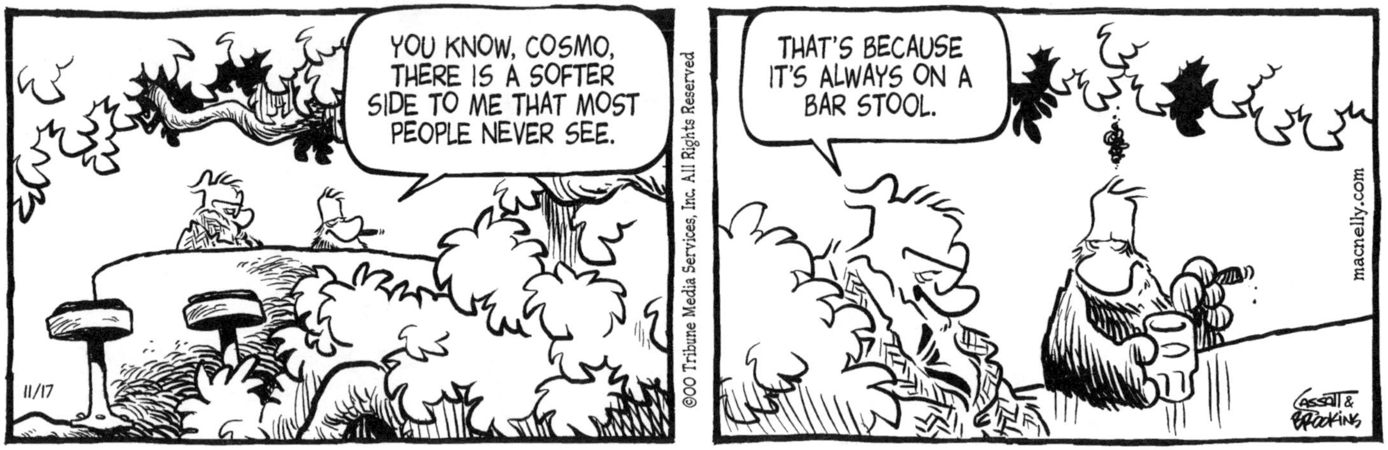
YOU KNOW, COSMO, THERE IS A SOFTER SIDE TO ME THAT MOST PEOPLE NEVER SEE.
11/17
©00 Tribune Media Services, Inc. All Rights Reserved
THAT'S BECAUSE IT'S ALWAYS ON A BAR STOOL.
macnelly.com
CASSATT & BROOKINS

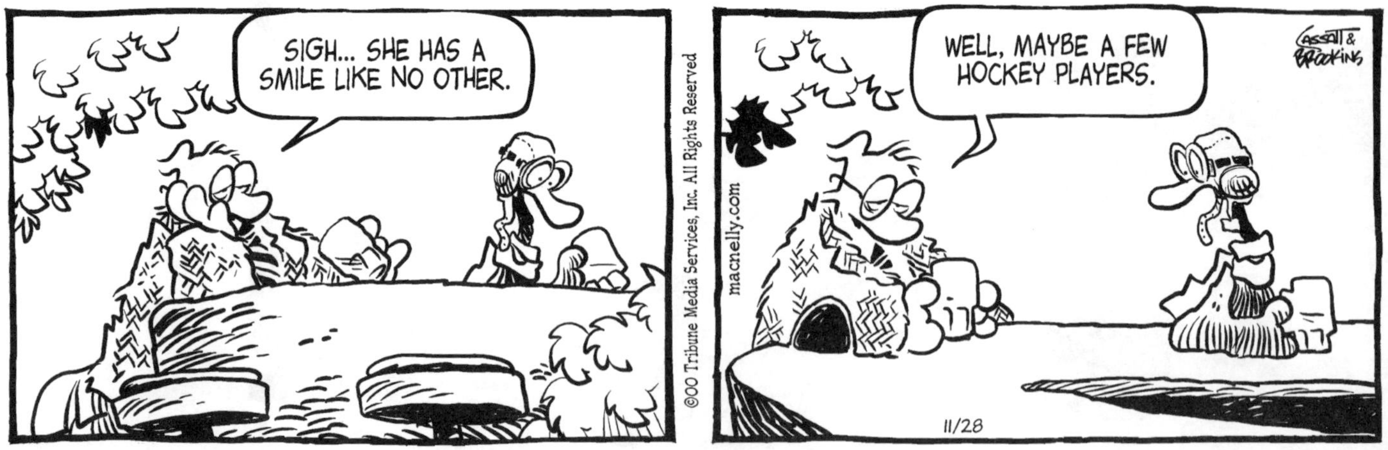
SIGH... SHE HAS A SMILE LIKE NO OTHER.
©00 Tribune Media Services, Inc. All Rights Reserved
macnelly.com
WELL, MAYBE A FEW HOCKEY PLAYERS.
CASSATT & BROOKINS
11/28

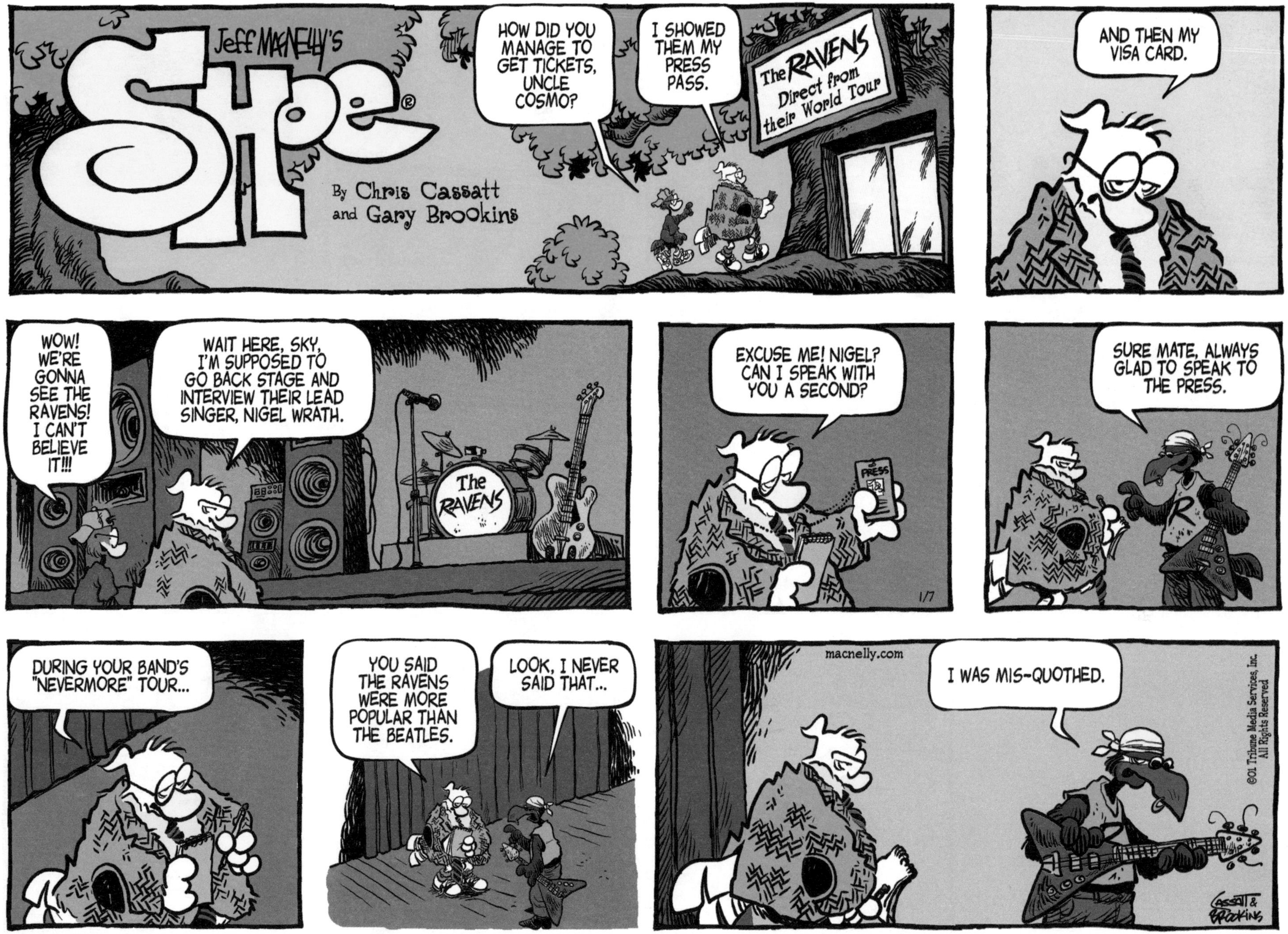
JEFF MACNELLY'S
SHOE®
By Chris Cassatt
and Gary Brookins
HOW DID YOU MANAGE TO GET TICKETS, UNCLE COSMO?
I SHOWED THEM MY PRESS PASS.
The RAVENS Direct from their World Tour
AND THEN MY VISA CARD.
WOW! WE'RE GONNA SEE THE RAVENS! I CAN'T BELIEVE IT!!!
WAIT HERE, SKY, I'M SUPPOSED TO GO BACK STAGE AND INTERVIEW THEIR LEAD SINGER, NIGEL WRATH.
The RAVENS
EXCUSE ME! NIGEL? CAN I SPEAK WITH YOU A SECOND?
PRESS
1/7
SURE MATE, ALWAYS GLAD TO SPEAK TO THE PRESS.
DURING YOUR BAND'S "NEVERMORE" TOUR...
YOU SAID THE RAVENS WERE MORE POPULAR THAN THE BEATLES.
LOOK, I NEVER SAID THAT...
macnelly.com
I WAS MIS-QUOTHED.
©01 Tribune Media Services, Inc. All Rights Reserved
CASSATT & BROOKINS

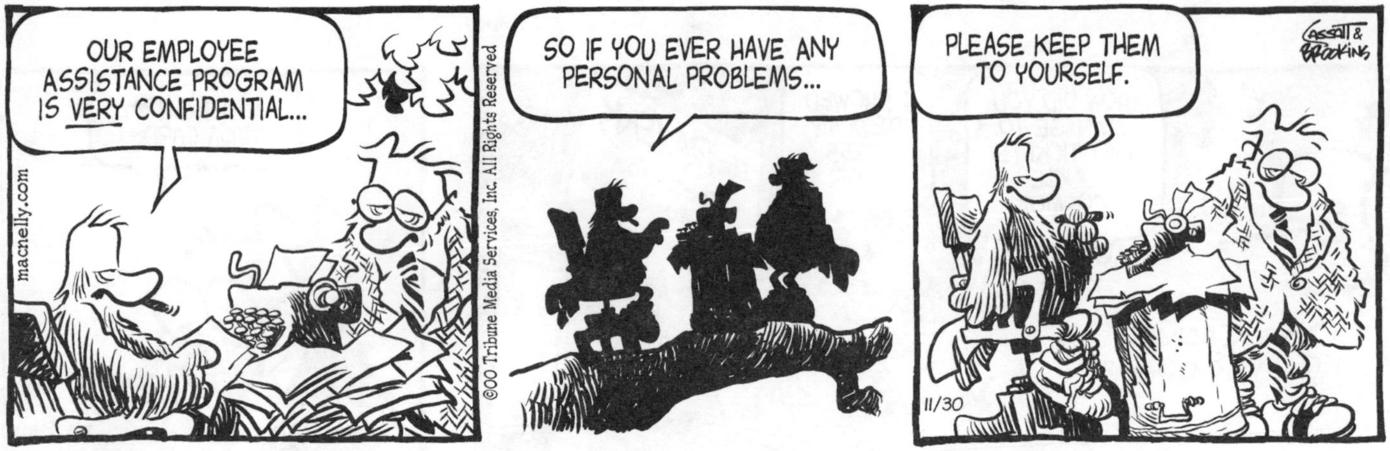
OUR EMPLOYEE ASSISTANCE PROGRAM IS VERY CONFIDENTIAL...
SO IF YOU EVER HAVE ANY PERSONAL PROBLEMS...
PLEASE KEEP THEM TO YOURSELF.
CASSATT & BROOKINS
11/30
macnelly.com
©00 Tribune Media Services, Inc. All Rights Reserved

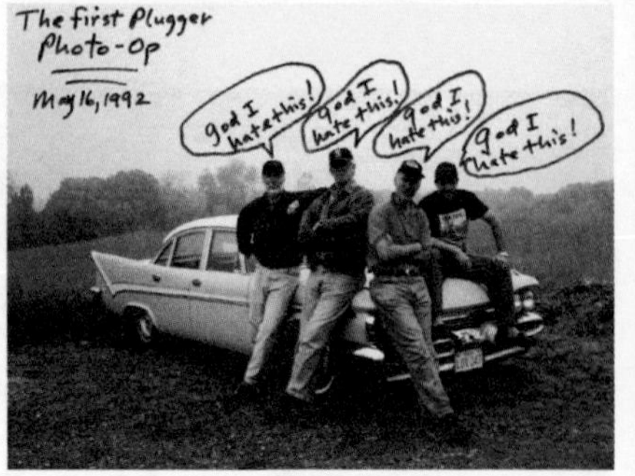
The first Plugger Photo-Op
May 16, 1992
god I hate this!
god I hate this!
god I hate this!
god I hate this!

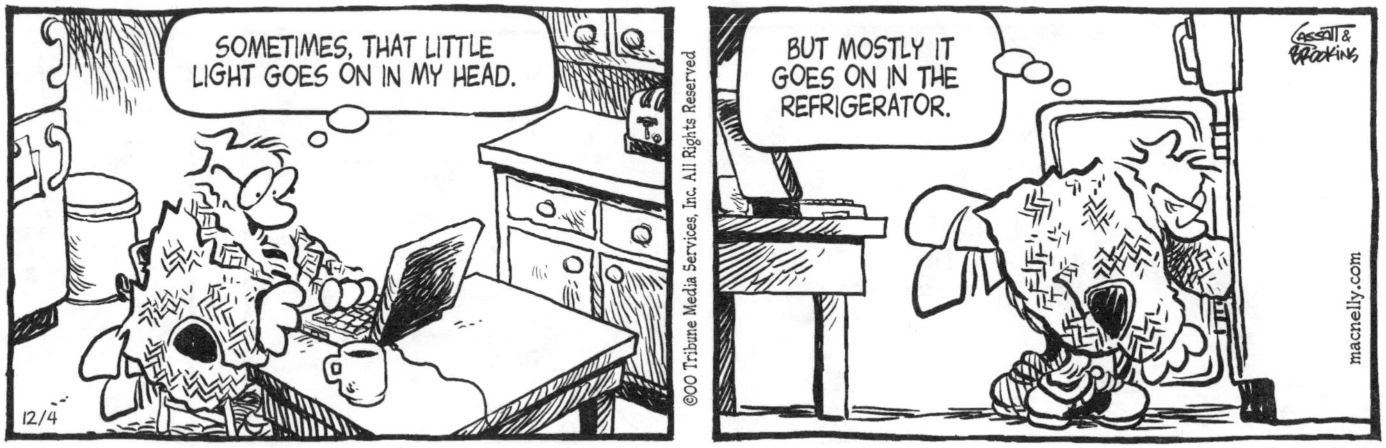
SOMETIMES, THAT LITTLE LIGHT GOES ON IN MY HEAD.
BUT MOSTLY IT GOES ON IN THE REFRIGERATOR.
CASSATT & BROOKINS
12/4
macnelly.com
©00 Tribune Media Services, Inc. All Rights Reserved

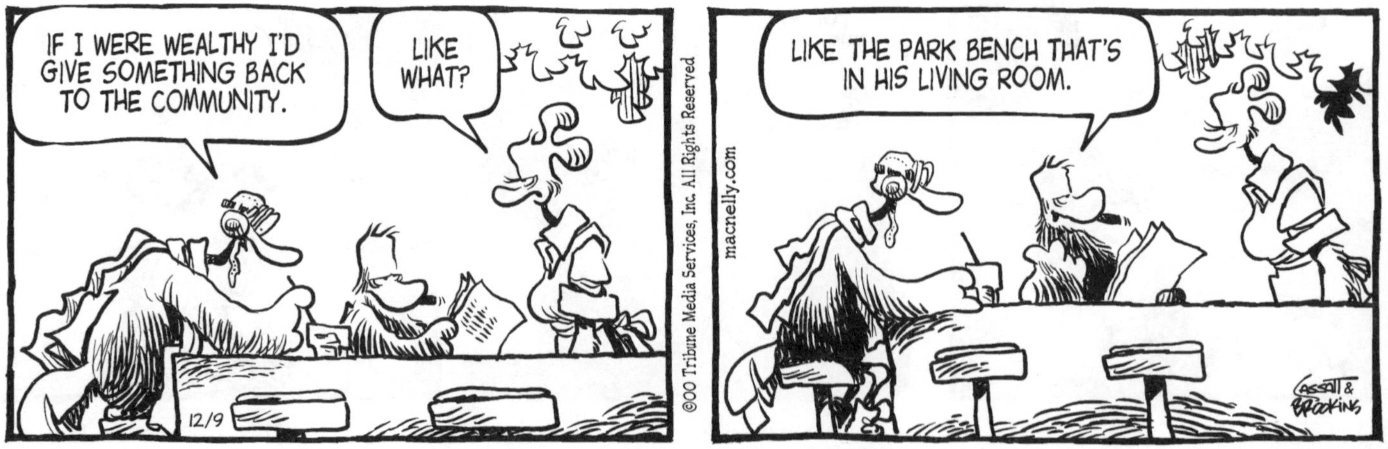
IF I WERE WEALTHY I'D GIVE SOMETHING BACK TO THE COMMUNITY.
LIKE WHAT?
LIKE THE PARK BENCH THAT'S IN HIS LIVING ROOM.
CASSATT & BROOKINS
12/9
macnelly.com
©00 Tribune Media Services, Inc. All Rights Reserved

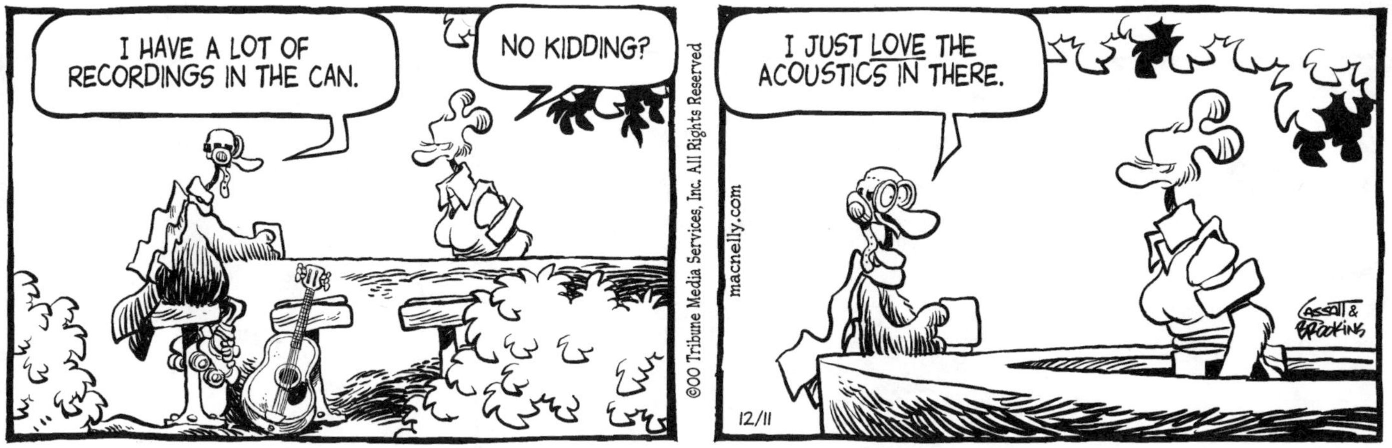
I HAVE A LOT OF RECORDINGS IN THE CAN.
NO KIDDING?
©00 Tribune Media Services, Inc. All Rights Reserved
macnelly.com
I JUST LOVE THE ACOUSTICS IN THERE.
CASSATT & BROOKINS
12/11

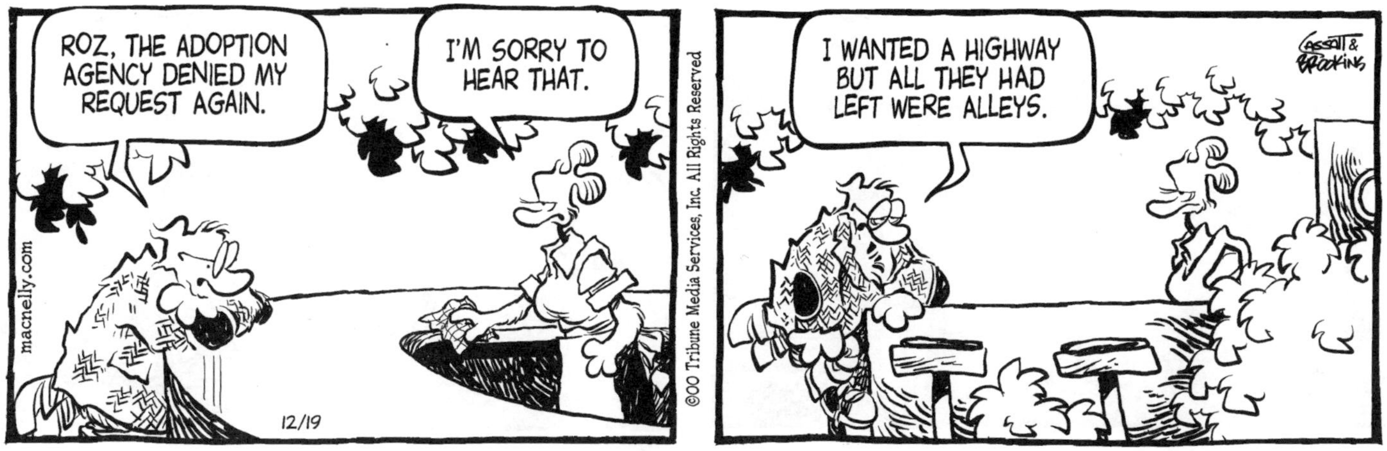
ROZ, THE ADOPTION AGENCY DENIED MY REQUEST AGAIN.
I'M SORRY TO HEAR THAT.
macnelly.com
12/19
©00 Tribune Media Services, Inc. All Rights Reserved
I WANTED A HIGHWAY BUT ALL THEY HAD LEFT WERE ALLEYS.
CASSATT & BROOKINS

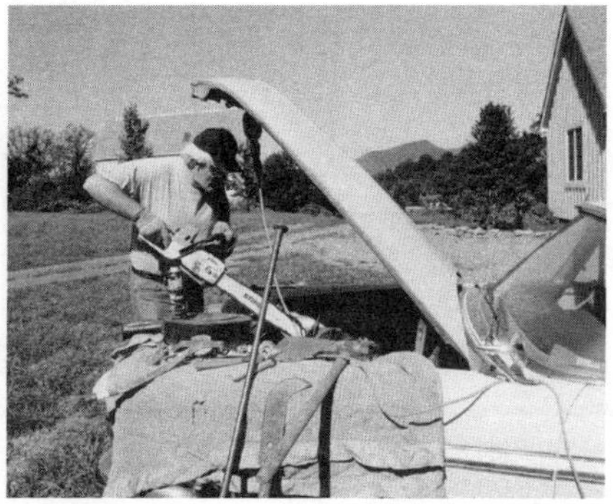

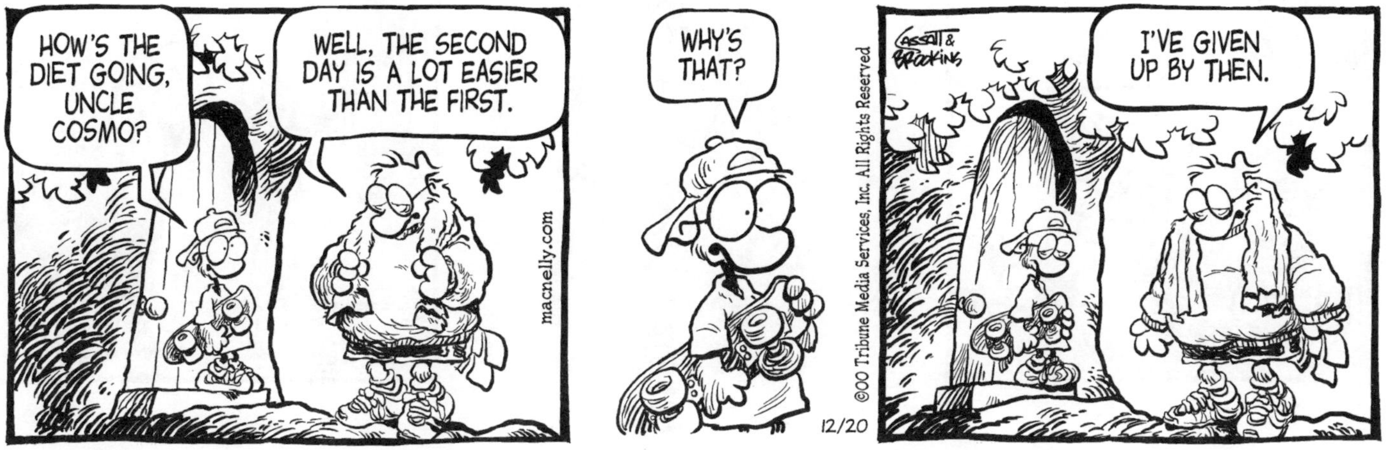
HOW'S THE DIET GOING, UNCLE COSMO?
WELL, THE SECOND DAY IS A LOT EASIER THAN THE FIRST.
macnelly.com
WHY'S THAT?
12/20
©00 Tribune Media Services, Inc. All Rights Reserved
CASSATT & BROOKINS
I'VE GIVEN UP BY THEN.

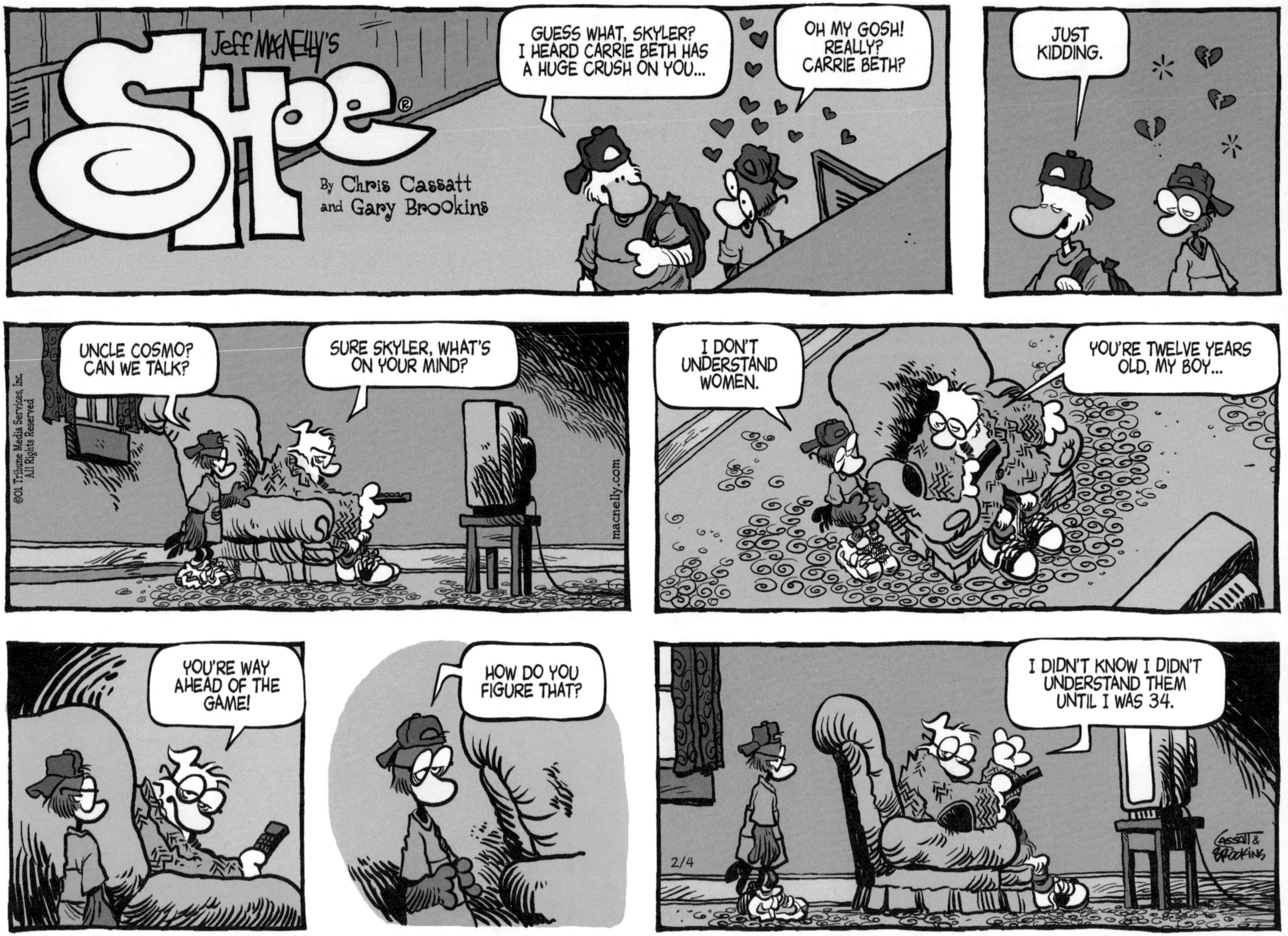
Jeff MacNelly's
Shoe®
By Chris Cassatt and Gary Brookins
GUESS WHAT, SKYLER? I HEARD CARRIE BETH HAS A HUGE CRUSH ON YOU...
OH MY GOSH! REALLY? CARRIE BETH?
JUST KIDDING.
©01 Tribune Media Services, Inc. All Rights Reserved
UNCLE COSMO? CAN WE TALK?
SURE SKYLER, WHAT'S ON YOUR MIND?
macnelly.com
I DON'T UNDERSTAND WOMEN.
YOU'RE TWELVE YEARS OLD, MY BOY...
YOU'RE WAY AHEAD OF THE GAME!
HOW DO YOU FIGURE THAT?
I DIDN'T KNOW I DIDN'T UNDERSTAND THEM UNTIL I WAS 34.
2/4
CASSATT & BROOKINS

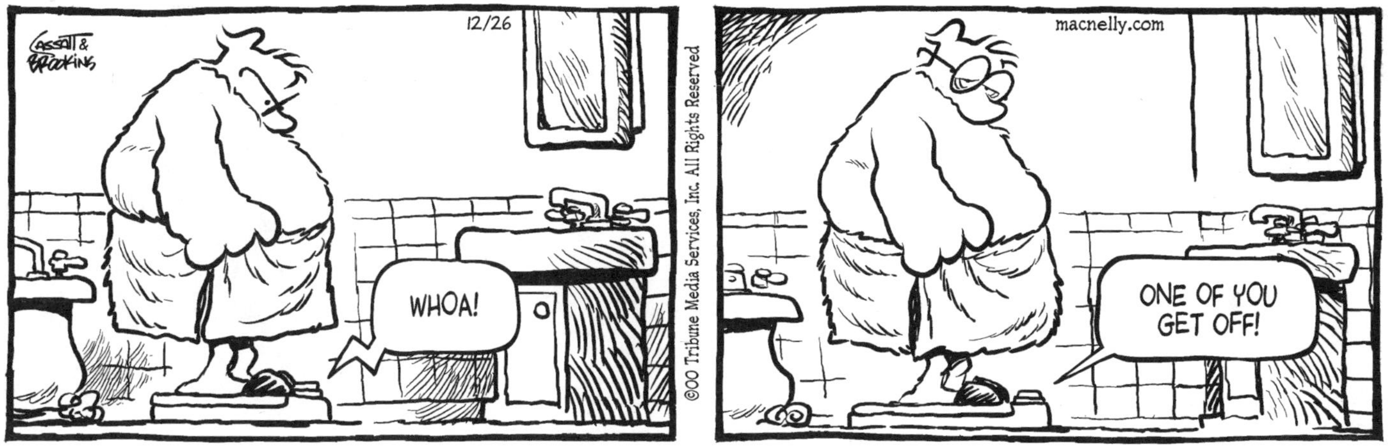
12/26
macnelly.com
©00 Tribune Media Services, Inc. All Rights Reserved
WHOA!
ONE OF YOU GET OFF!

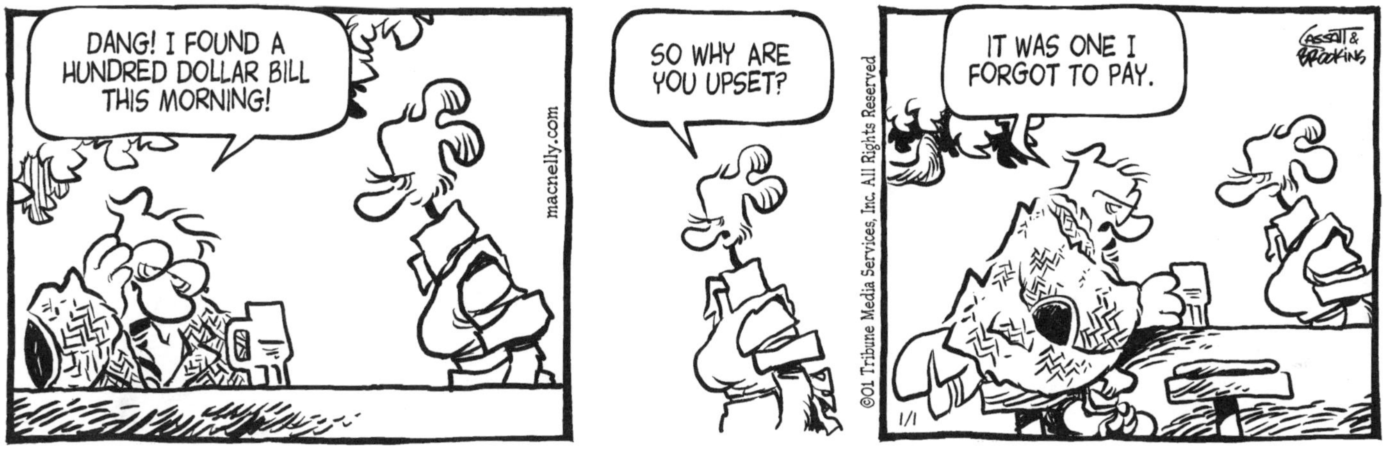
DANG! I FOUND A HUNDRED DOLLAR BILL THIS MORNING!
macnelly.com
SO WHY ARE YOU UPSET?
©01 Tribune Media Services, Inc. All Rights Reserved
IT WAS ONE I FORGOT TO PAY.
1/1

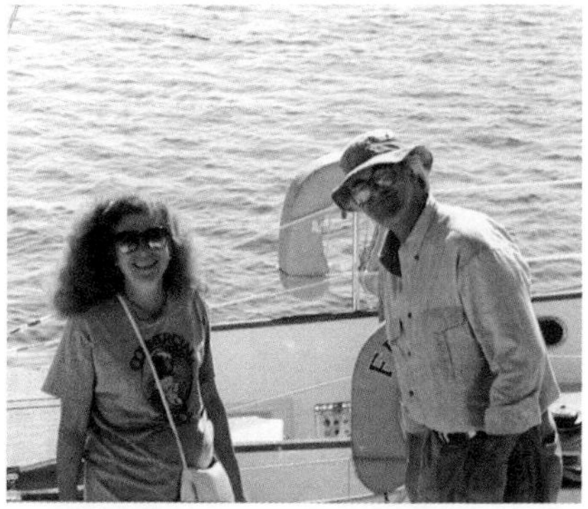

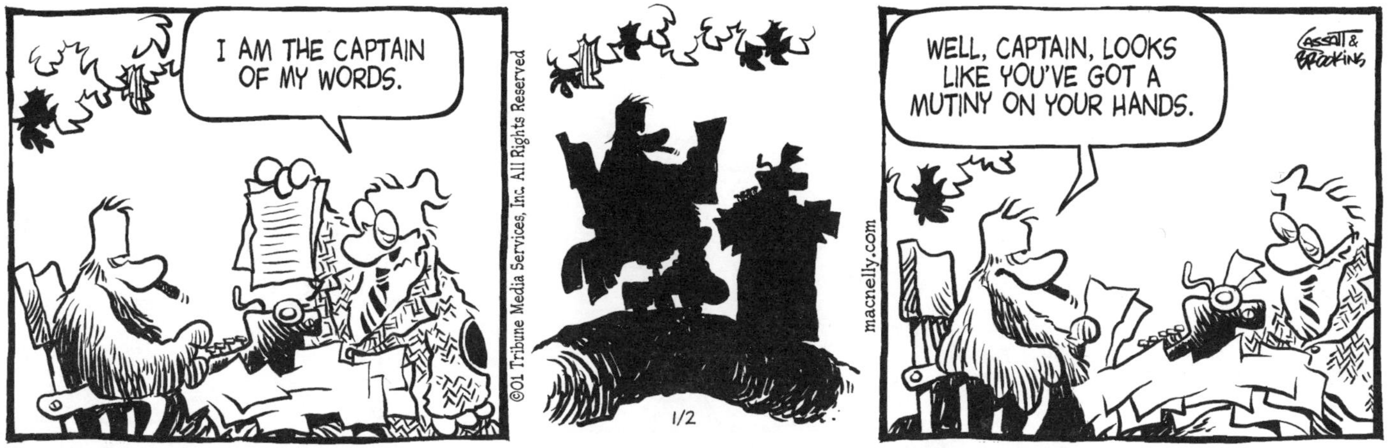
I AM THE CAPTAIN OF MY WORDS.
©01 Tribune Media Services, Inc. All Rights Reserved
1/2
macnelly.com
WELL, CAPTAIN, LOOKS LIKE YOU'VE GOT A MUTINY ON YOUR HANDS.

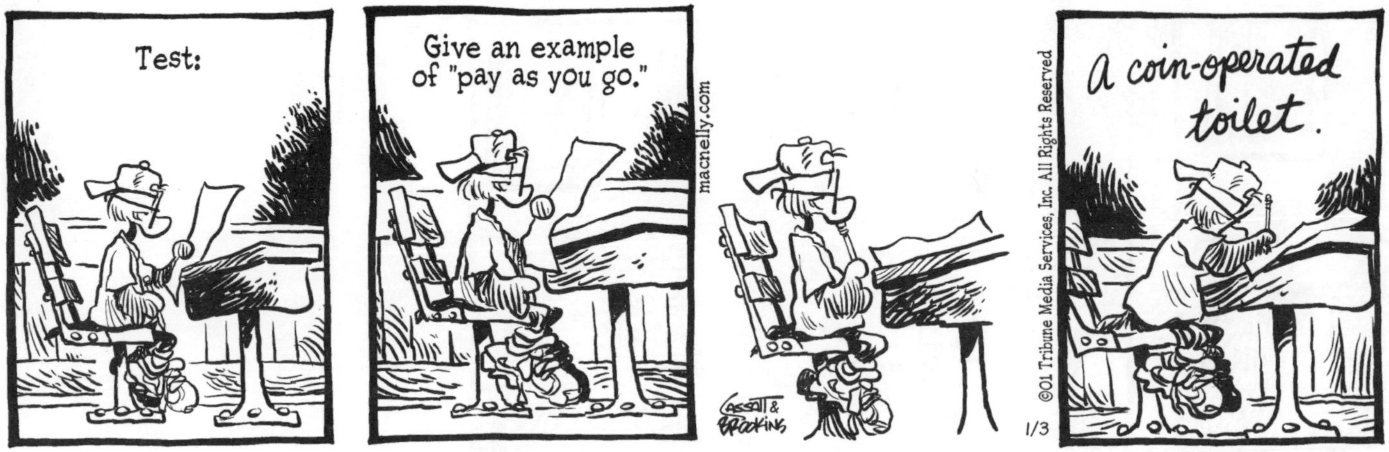

Test:
Give an example of "pay as you go."
macnelly.com
CASSATT & BROOKINS
©01 Tribune Media Services, Inc. All Rights Reserved
1/3
A coin-operated toilet.

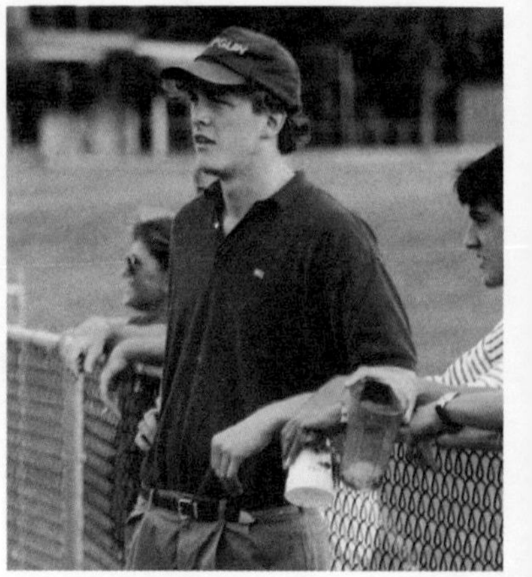

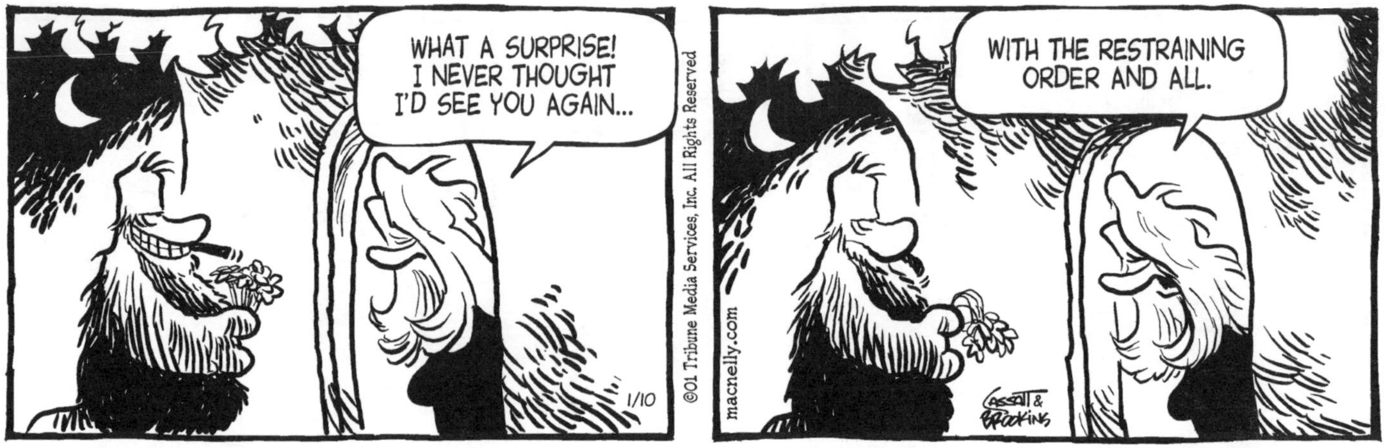

WHAT A SURPRISE! I NEVER THOUGHT I'D SEE YOU AGAIN...
1/10
©01 Tribune Media Services, Inc. All Rights Reserved
macnelly.com
WITH THE RESTRAINING ORDER AND ALL.
CASSATT & BROOKINS

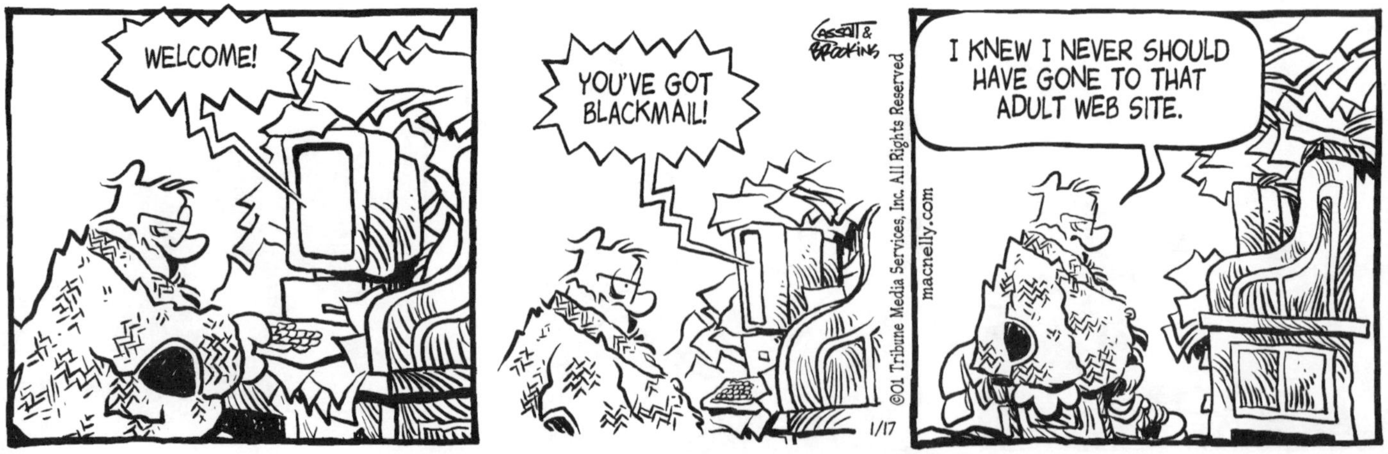

WELCOME!
CASSATT & BROOKINS
YOU'VE GOT BLACKMAIL!
©01 Tribune Media Services, Inc. All Rights Reserved
1/17
macnelly.com
I KNEW I NEVER SHOULD HAVE GONE TO THAT ADULT WEB SITE.

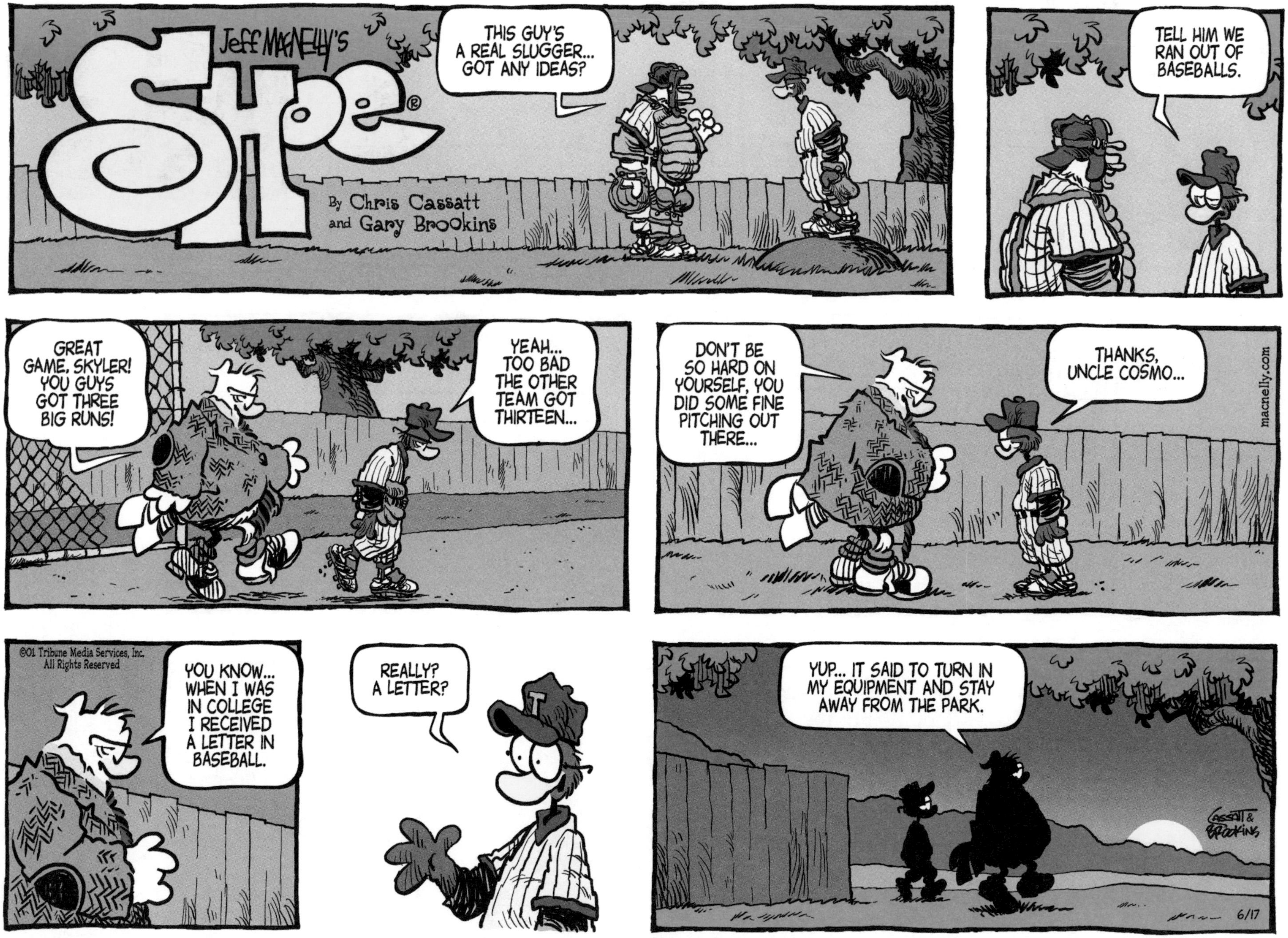
JEFF MACNELLY'S
SHOE®
By Chris Cassatt and Gary Brookins
THIS GUY'S A REAL SLUGGER... GOT ANY IDEAS?
TELL HIM WE RAN OUT OF BASEBALLS.
GREAT GAME, SKYLER! YOU GUYS GOT THREE BIG RUNS!
YEAH... TOO BAD THE OTHER TEAM GOT THIRTEEN...
DON'T BE SO HARD ON YOURSELF, YOU DID SOME FINE PITCHING OUT THERE...
THANKS, UNCLE COSMO...
macnelly.com
©01 Tribune Media Services, Inc. All Rights Reserved
YOU KNOW... WHEN I WAS IN COLLEGE I RECEIVED A LETTER IN BASEBALL.
REALLY? A LETTER?
YUP... IT SAID TO TURN IN MY EQUIPMENT AND STAY AWAY FROM THE PARK.
CASSATT & BROOKINS
6/17

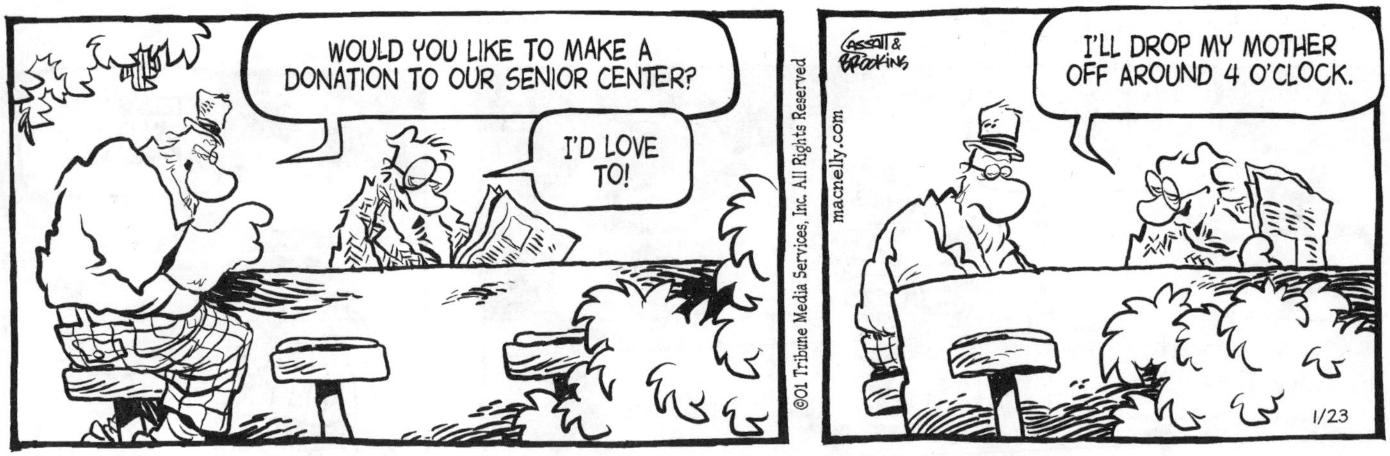
WOULD YOU LIKE TO MAKE A DONATION TO OUR SENIOR CENTER?
I'D LOVE TO!
©01 Tribune Media Services, Inc. All Rights Reserved
macnelly.com
CASSATT & BROOKINS
I'LL DROP MY MOTHER OFF AROUND 4 O'CLOCK.
1/23

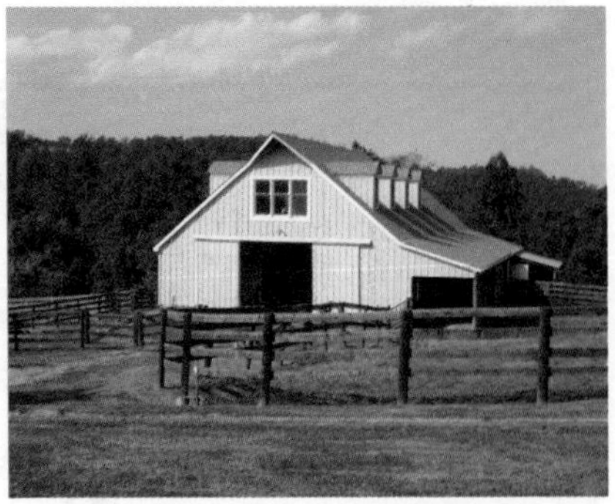

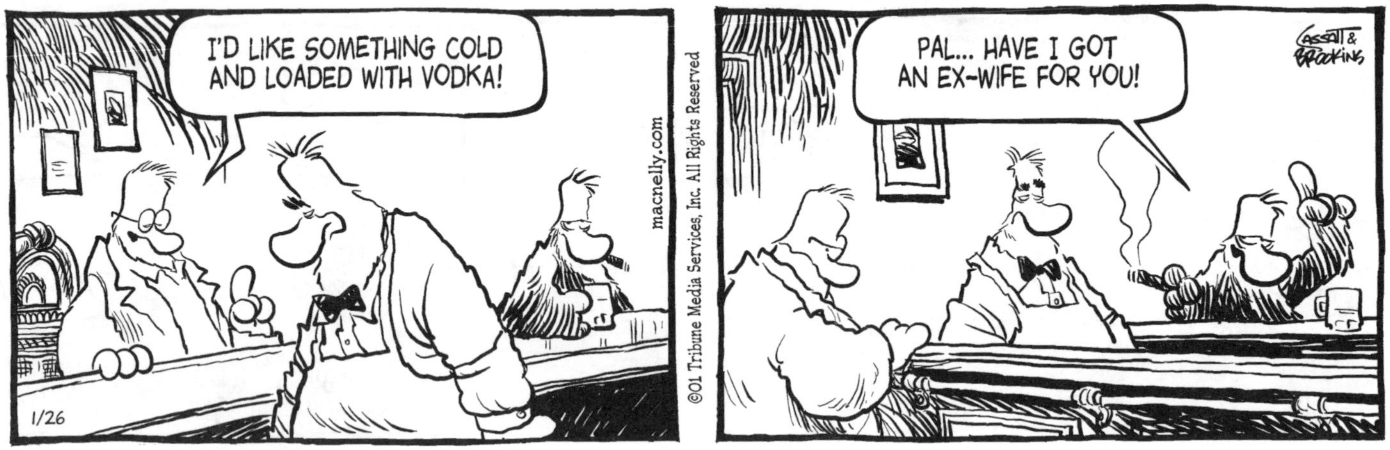
I'D LIKE SOMETHING COLD AND LOADED WITH VODKA!
1/26
macnelly.com
©01 Tribune Media Services, Inc. All Rights Reserved
CASSATT & BROOKINS
PAL... HAVE I GOT AN EX-WIFE FOR YOU!

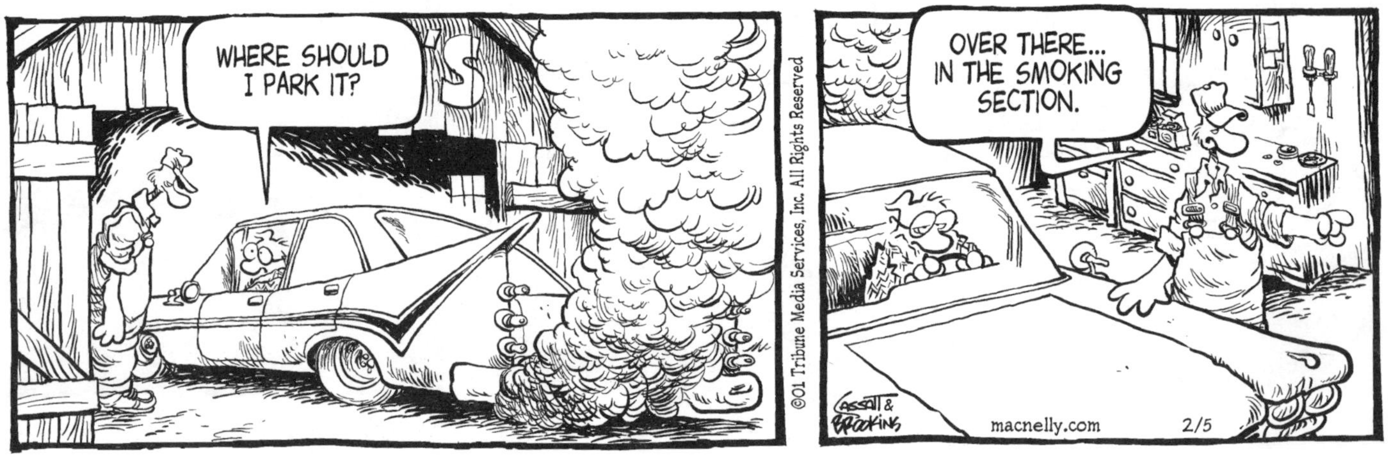
WHERE SHOULD I PARK IT?
©01 Tribune Media Services, Inc. All Rights Reserved
OVER THERE... IN THE SMOKING SECTION.
CASSATT & BROOKINS
macnelly.com
2/5

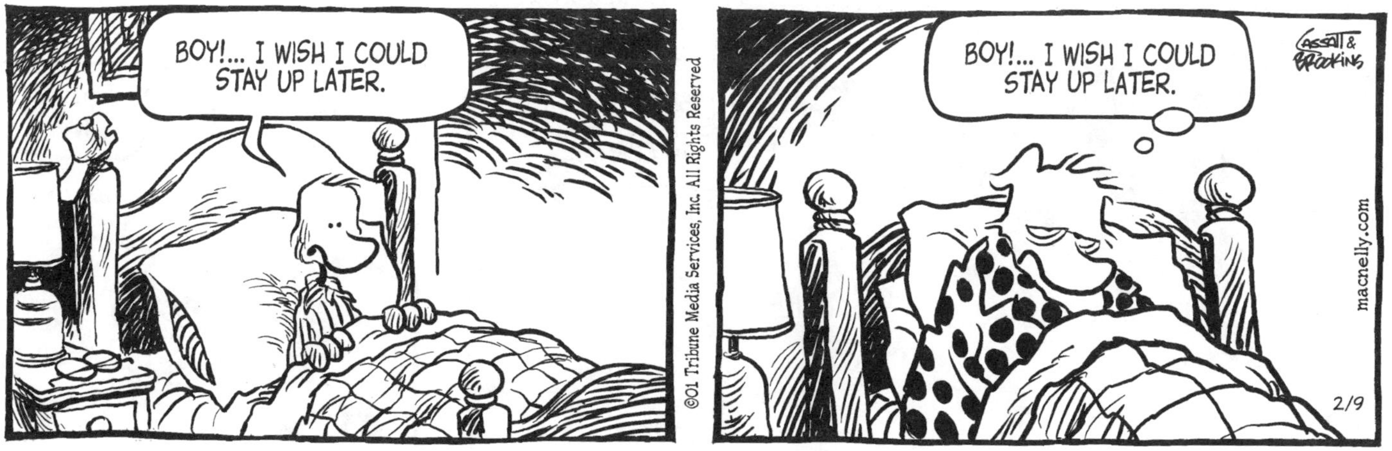
BOY!... I WISH I COULD STAY UP LATER.
©01 Tribune Media Services, Inc. All Rights Reserved
BOY!... I WISH I COULD STAY UP LATER.
CASSATT & BROOKINS
macnelly.com
2/9

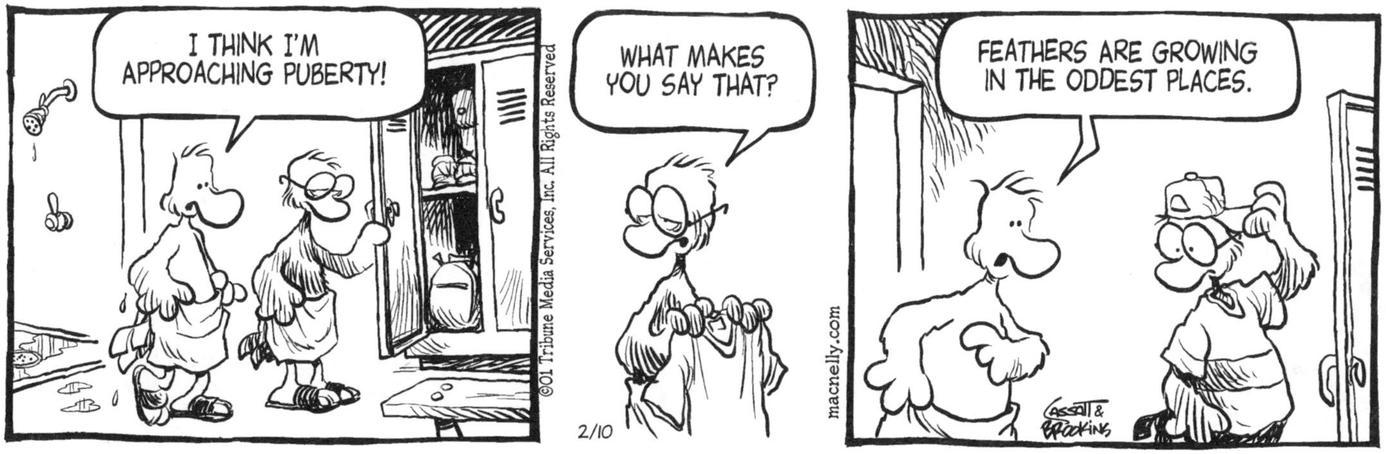
I THINK I'M APPROACHING PUBERTY!
©01 Tribune Media Services, Inc. All Rights Reserved
WHAT MAKES YOU SAY THAT?
2/10
macnelly.com
FEATHERS ARE GROWING IN THE ODDEST PLACES.
CASSATT & BROOKINS

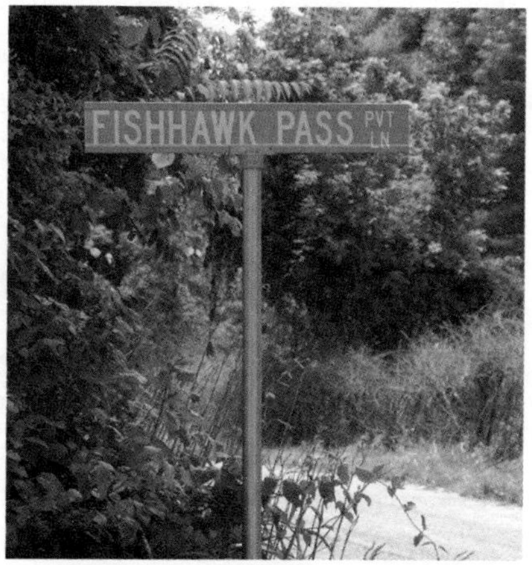
FISHHAWK PASS PVT LN

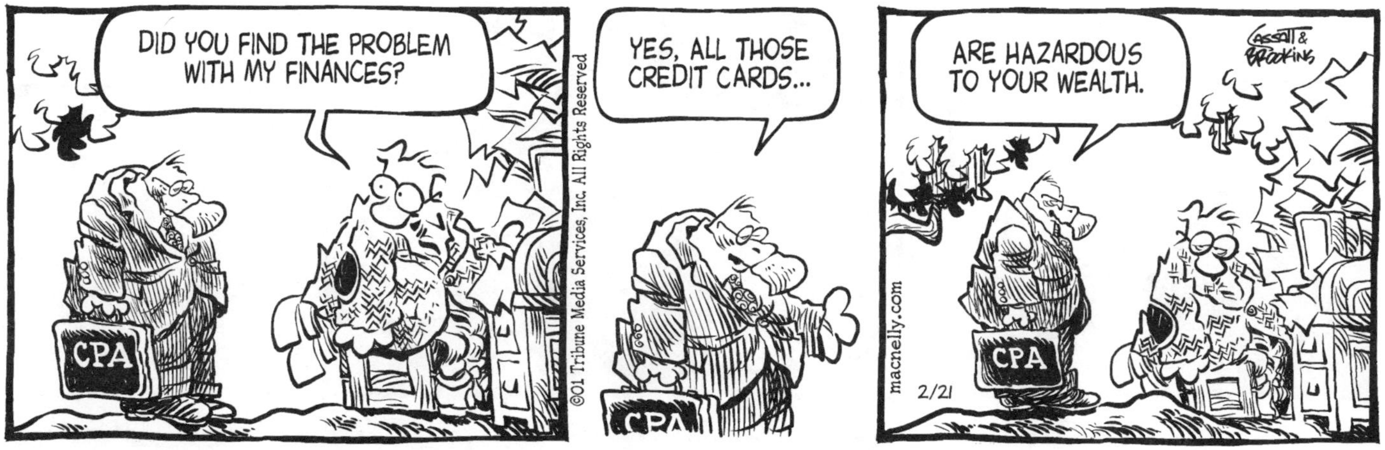
DID YOU FIND THE PROBLEM WITH MY FINANCES?
CPA
©01 Tribune Media Services, Inc. All Rights Reserved
YES, ALL THOSE CREDIT CARDS...
ARE HAZARDOUS TO YOUR WEALTH.
CASSATT & BROOKINS
macnelly.com
2/21
CPA

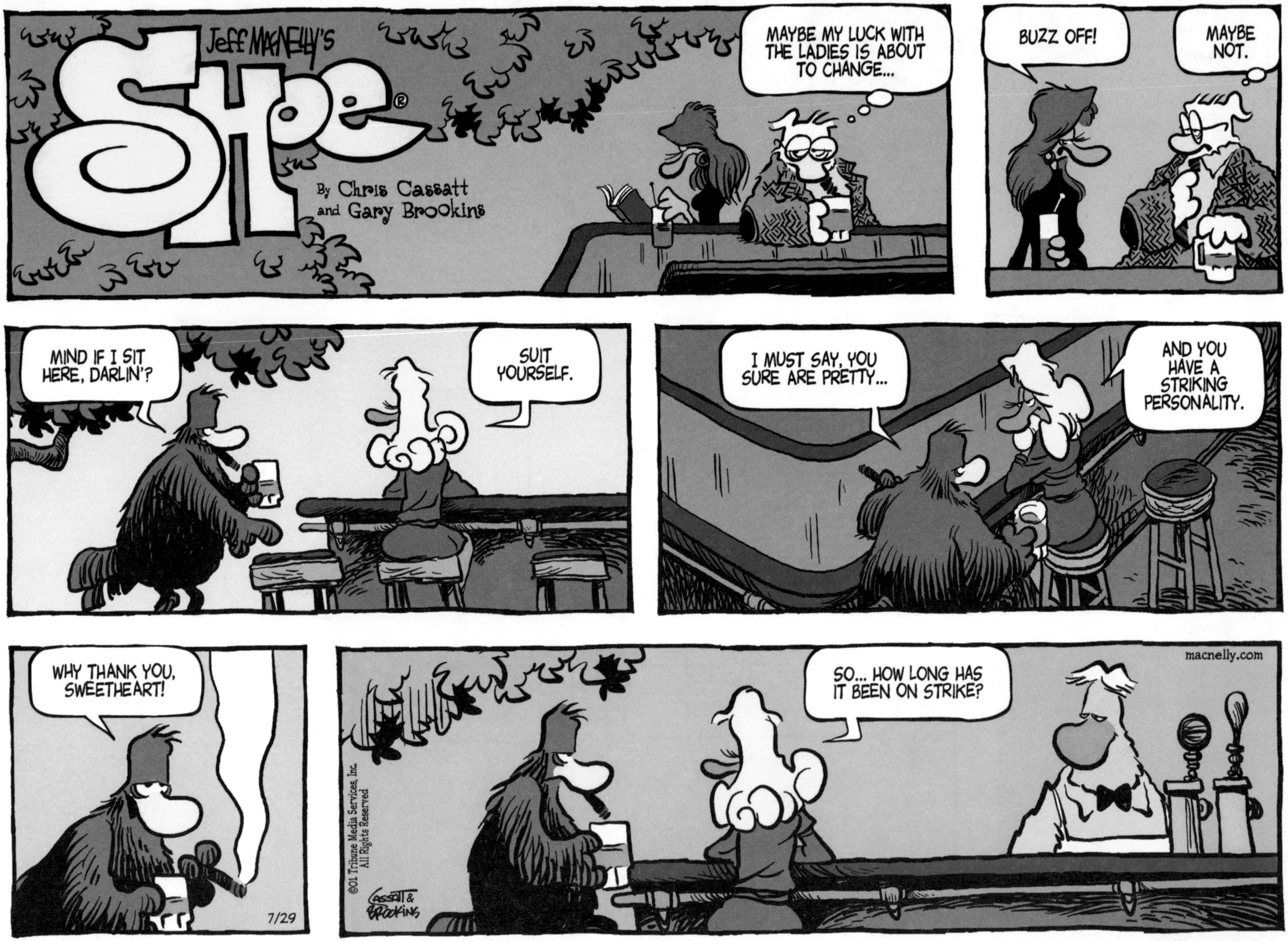
JEFF MACNELLY'S
SHOE
By Chris Cassatt
and Gary Brookins
MAYBE MY LUCK WITH THE LADIES IS ABOUT TO CHANGE...
BUZZ OFF!
MAYBE NOT.
MIND IF I SIT HERE, DARLIN'?
SUIT YOURSELF.
I MUST SAY, YOU SURE ARE PRETTY...
AND YOU HAVE A STRIKING PERSONALITY.
WHY THANK YOU, SWEETHEART!
7/29
macnelly.com
SO... HOW LONG HAS IT BEEN ON STRIKE?
©01 Tribune Media Services, Inc.
All Rights Reserved
CASSATT & BROOKINS

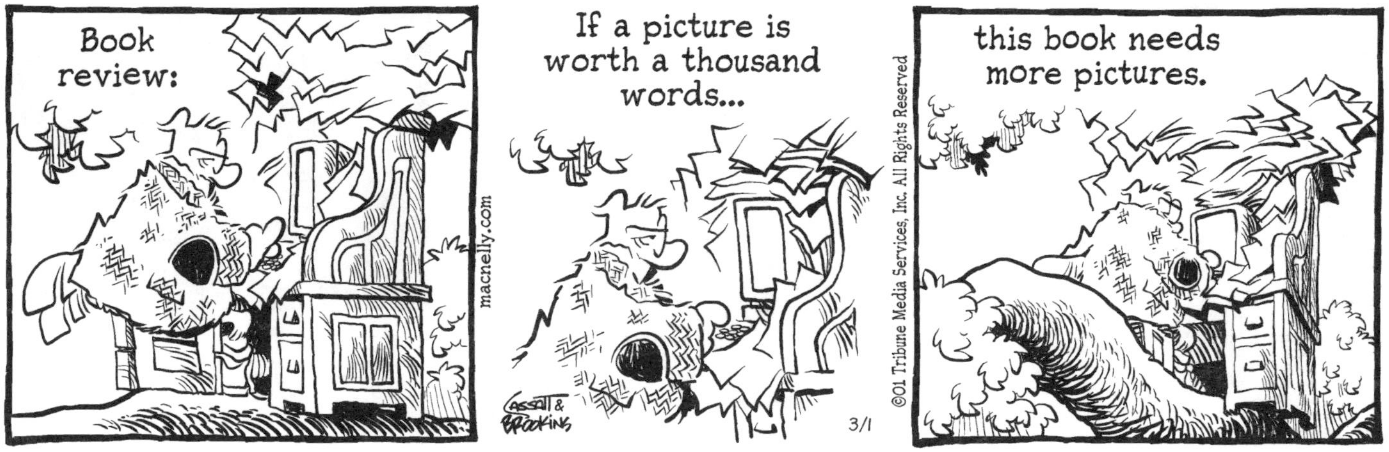
Book review:
If a picture is worth a thousand words...
this book needs more pictures.
macnelly.com
CASSATT & BROOKINS
3/1
©01 Tribune Media Services, Inc. All Rights Reserved

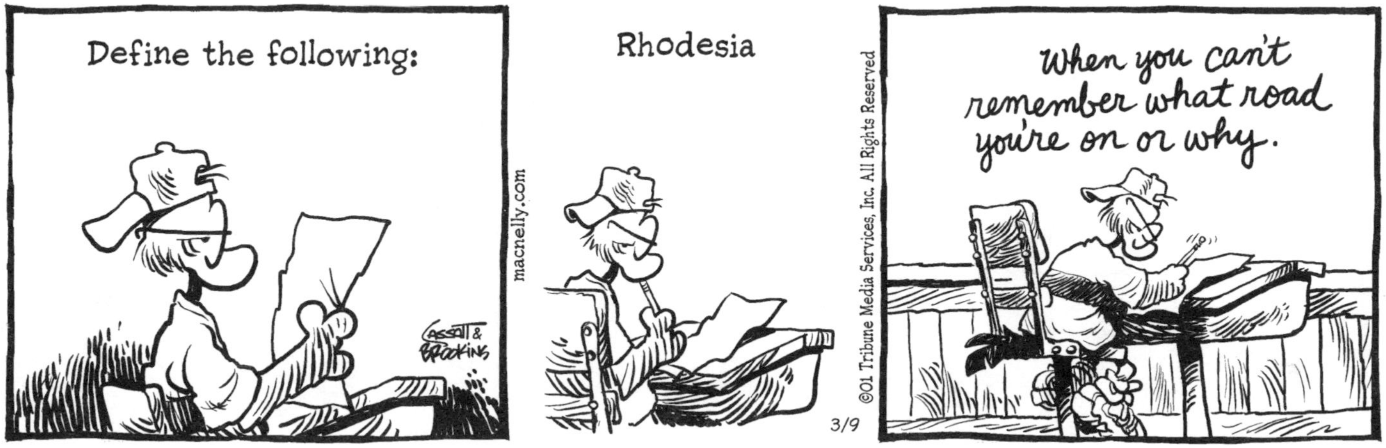
Define the following:
CASSATT & BROOKINS
macnelly.com
Rhodesia
3/9
©01 Tribune Media Services, Inc. All Rights Reserved
When you can't remember what road you're on or why.

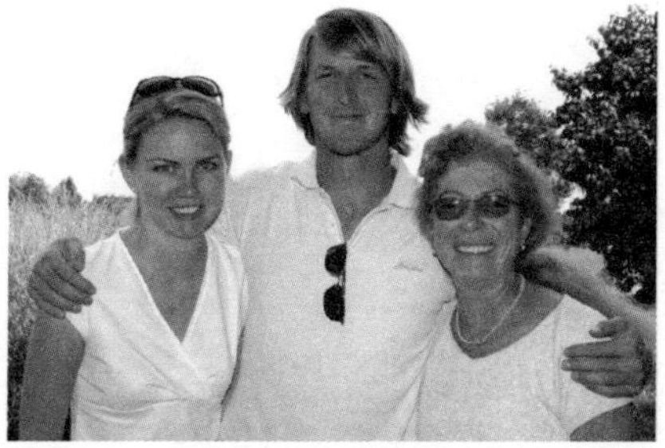

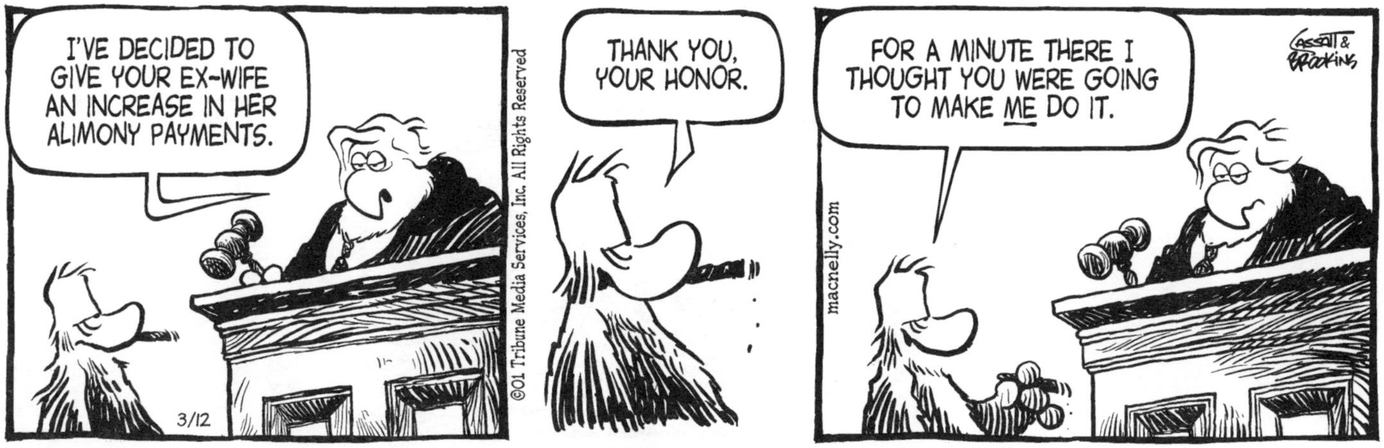
I'VE DECIDED TO GIVE YOUR EX-WIFE AN INCREASE IN HER ALIMONY PAYMENTS.
3/12
©01 Tribune Media Services, Inc. All Rights Reserved
THANK YOU, YOUR HONOR.
macnelly.com
FOR A MINUTE THERE I THOUGHT YOU WERE GOING TO MAKE ME DO IT.
CASSATT & BROOKINS

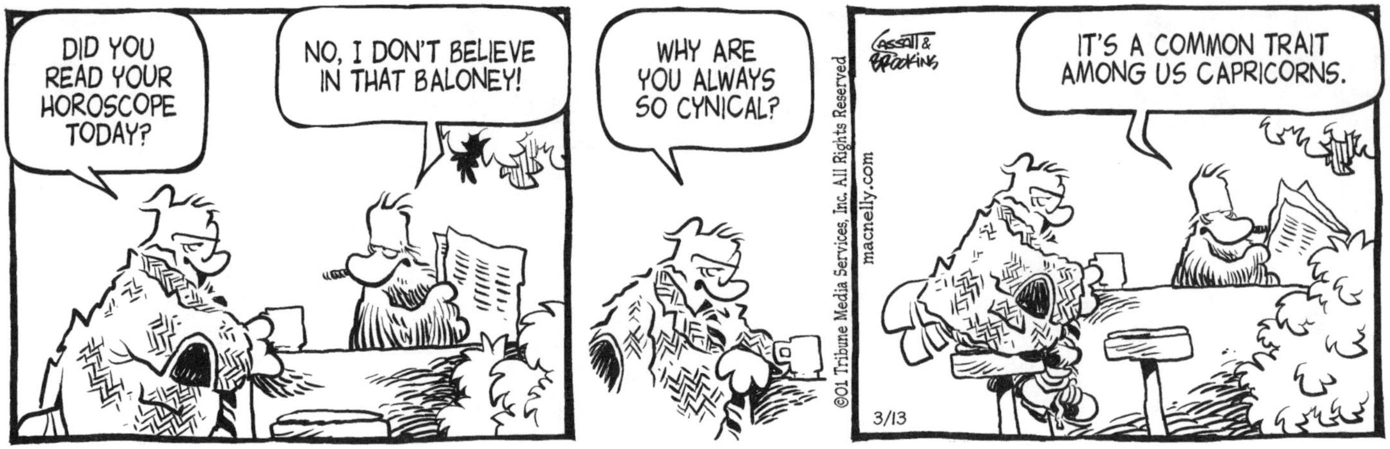
DID YOU READ YOUR HOROSCOPE TODAY?
NO, I DON'T BELIEVE IN THAT BALONEY!
WHY ARE YOU ALWAYS SO CYNICAL?
©01 Tribune Media Services, Inc. All Rights Reserved
macnelly.com
CASSATT & BROOKINS
IT'S A COMMON TRAIT AMONG US CAPRICORNS.
3/13

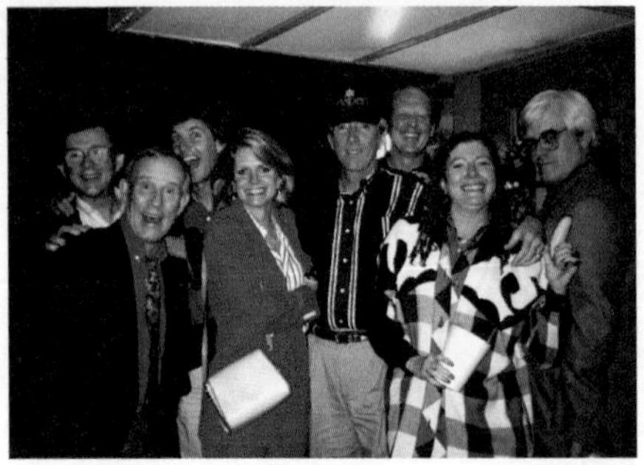

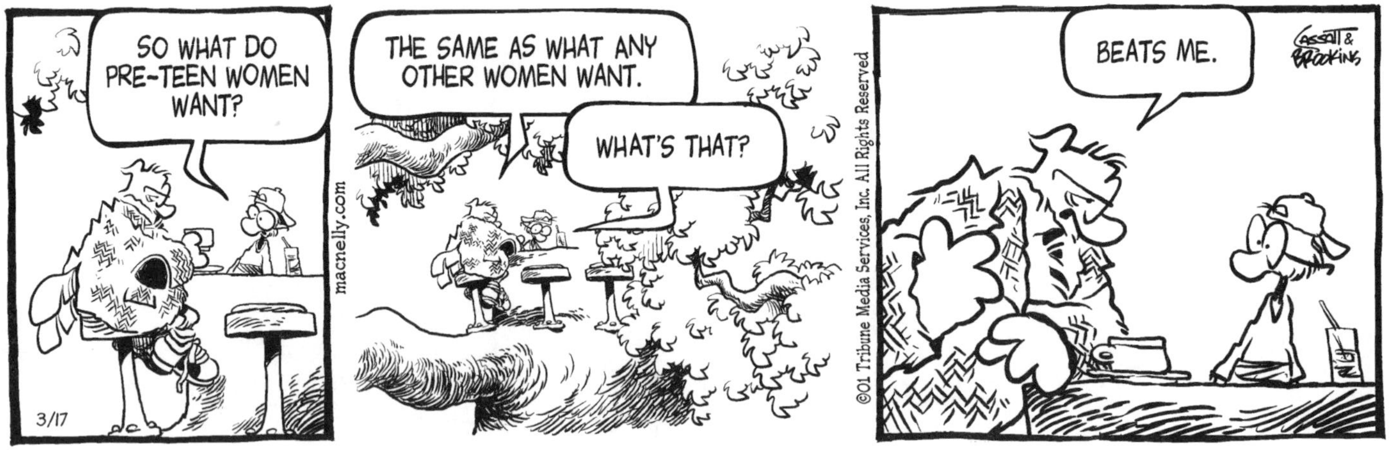
SO WHAT DO PRE-TEEN WOMEN WANT?
3/17
macnelly.com
THE SAME AS WHAT ANY OTHER WOMEN WANT.
WHAT'S THAT?
©01 Tribune Media Services, Inc. All Rights Reserved
BEATS ME.
CASSATT & BROOKINS

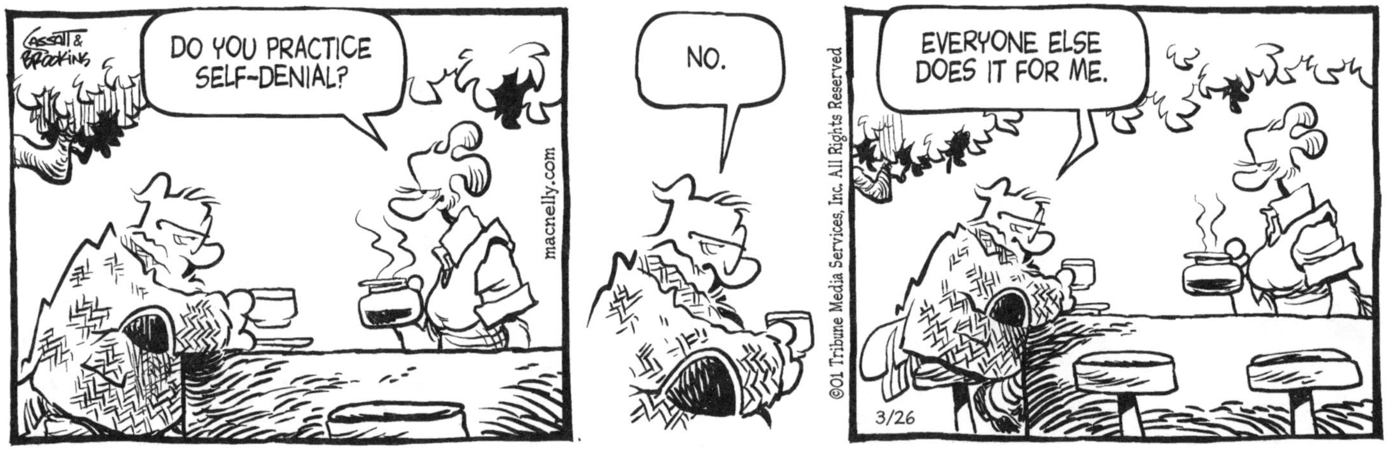
CASSATT & BROOKINS
DO YOU PRACTICE SELF-DENIAL?
macnelly.com
NO.
©01 Tribune Media Services, Inc. All Rights Reserved
EVERYONE ELSE DOES IT FOR ME.
3/26

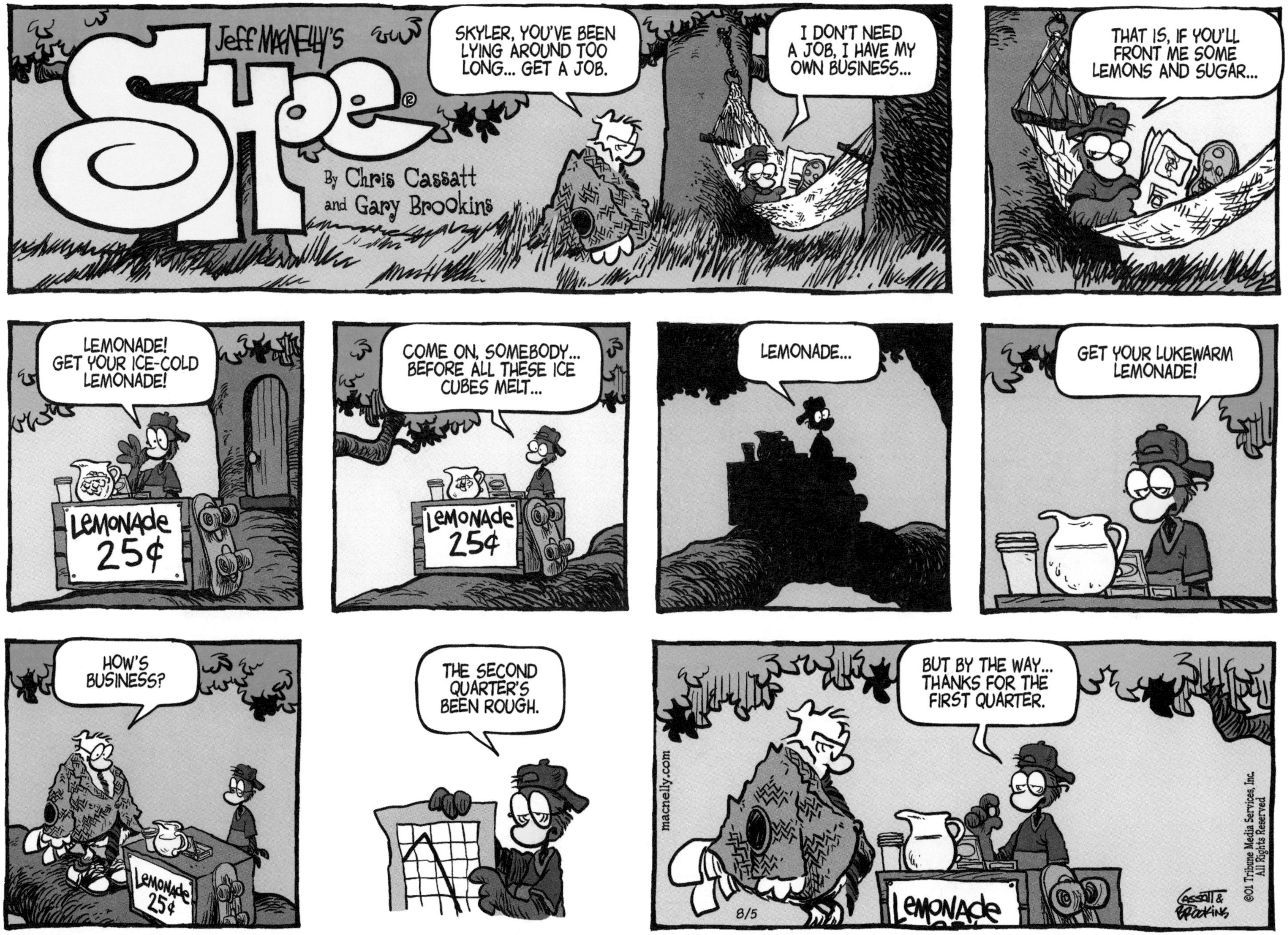
Jeff MacNelly's
Shoe®
By Chris Cassatt
and Gary Brookins
SKYLER, YOU'VE BEEN LYING AROUND TOO LONG... GET A JOB.
I DON'T NEED A JOB, I HAVE MY OWN BUSINESS...
THAT IS, IF YOU'LL FRONT ME SOME LEMONS AND SUGAR...
LEMONADE! GET YOUR ICE-COLD LEMONADE!
LEMONADE 25¢
COME ON, SOMEBODY... BEFORE ALL THESE ICE CUBES MELT...
LEMONADE 25¢
LEMONADE...
GET YOUR LUKEWARM LEMONADE!
HOW'S BUSINESS?
LEMONADE 25¢
THE SECOND QUARTER'S BEEN ROUGH.
macnelly.com
BUT BY THE WAY... THANKS FOR THE FIRST QUARTER.
LEMONADE
8/5
CASSATT & BROOKINS
©01 Tribune Media Services, Inc. All Rights Reserved

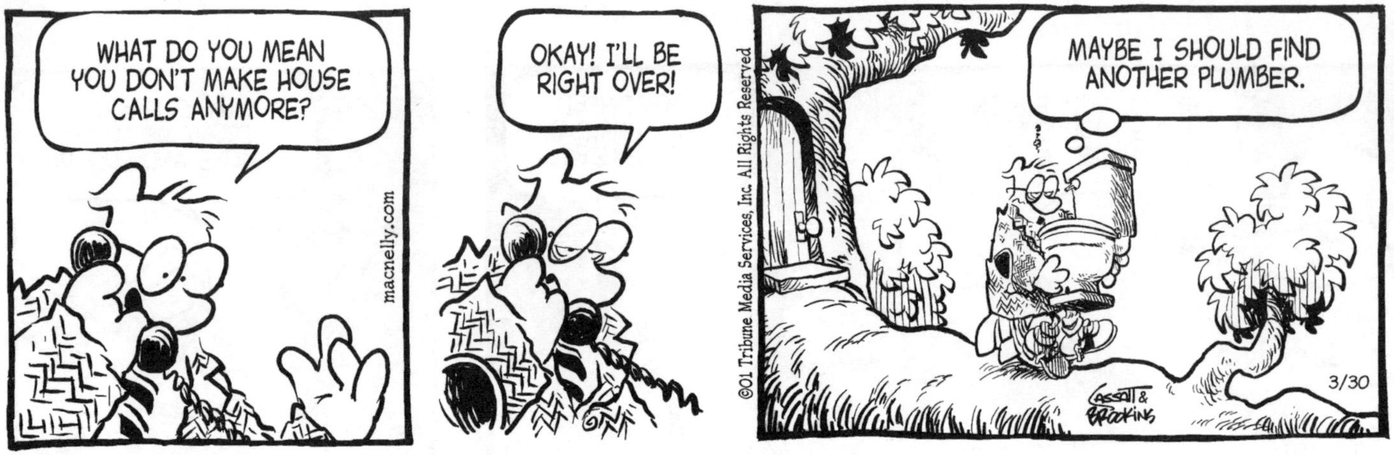

WHAT DO YOU MEAN YOU DON'T MAKE HOUSE CALLS ANYMORE?
macnelly.com
OKAY! I'LL BE RIGHT OVER!
©01 Tribune Media Services, Inc. All Rights Reserved
MAYBE I SHOULD FIND ANOTHER PLUMBER.
CASSATT & BROOKINS
3/30

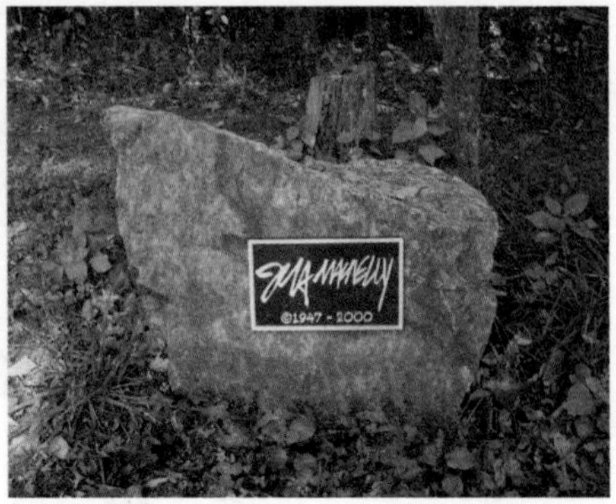

©1947 - 2000

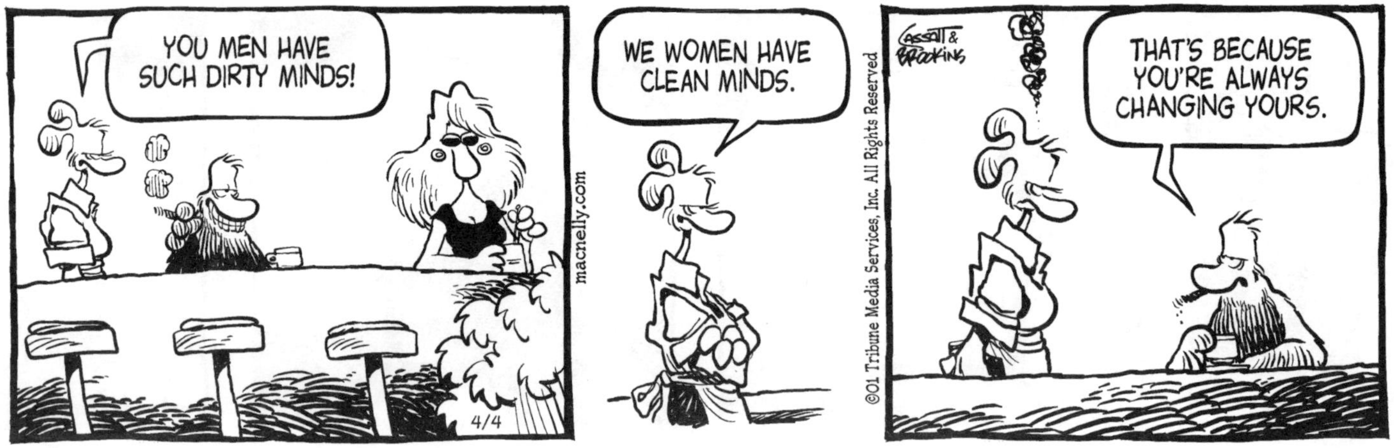

YOU MEN HAVE SUCH DIRTY MINDS!
macnelly.com
4/4
WE WOMEN HAVE CLEAN MINDS.
©01 Tribune Media Services, Inc. All Rights Reserved
CASSATT & BROOKINS
THAT'S BECAUSE YOU'RE ALWAYS CHANGING YOURS.

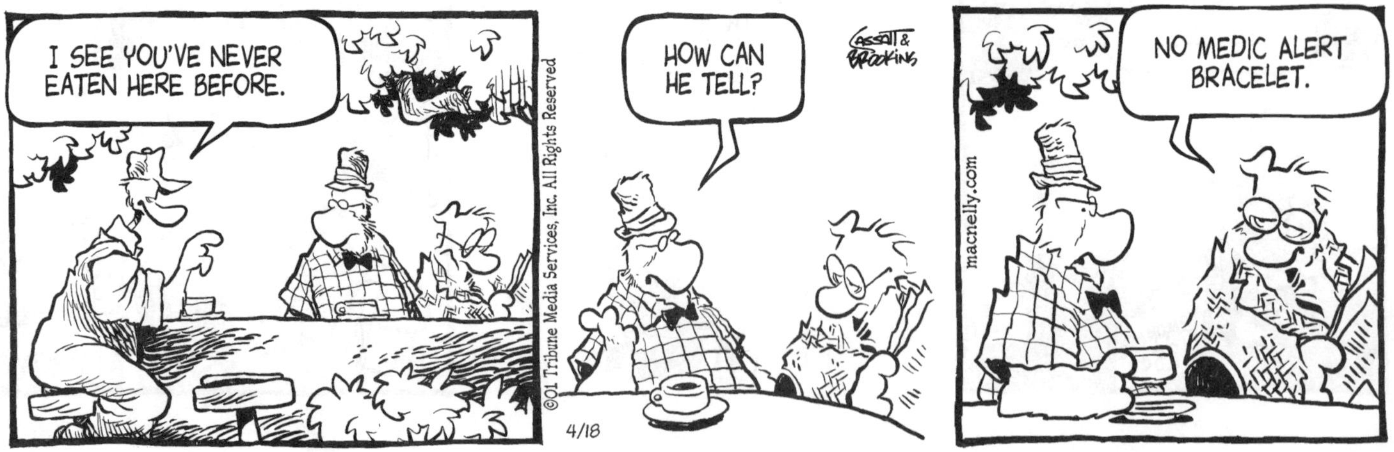

I SEE YOU'VE NEVER EATEN HERE BEFORE.
©01 Tribune Media Services, Inc. All Rights Reserved
HOW CAN HE TELL?
4/18
CASSATT & BROOKINS
macnelly.com
NO MEDIC ALERT BRACELET.

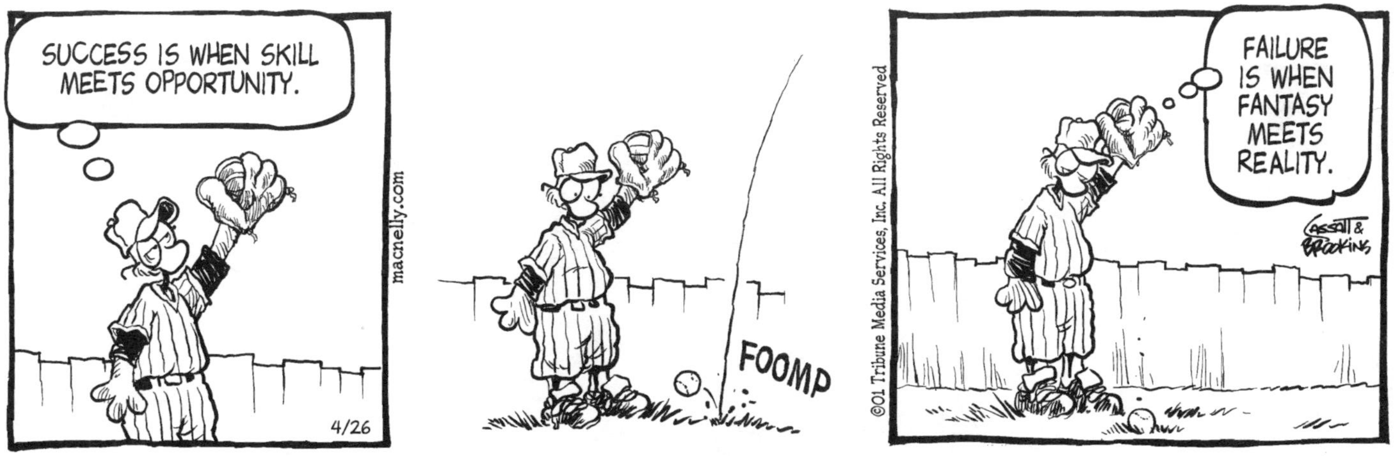
SUCCESS IS WHEN SKILL MEETS OPPORTUNITY.
macnelly.com
4/26
FOOMP
©01 Tribune Media Services, Inc. All Rights Reserved
FAILURE IS WHEN FANTASY MEETS REALITY.
CASSATT & BROOKINS

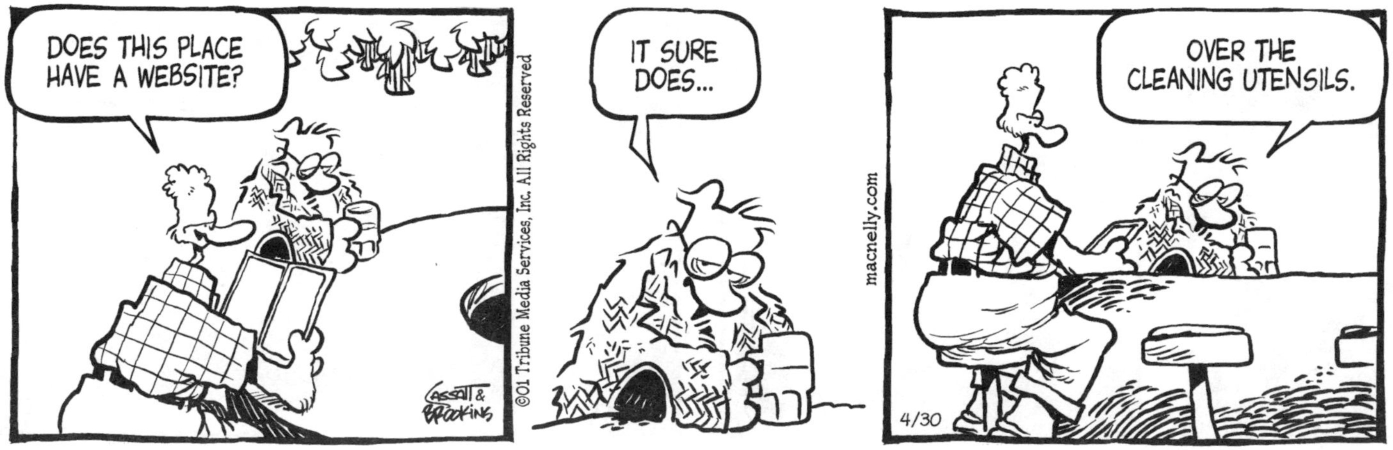
DOES THIS PLACE HAVE A WEBSITE?
CASSATT & BROOKINS
©01 Tribune Media Services, Inc. All Rights Reserved
IT SURE DOES...
macnelly.com
OVER THE CLEANING UTENSILS.
4/30

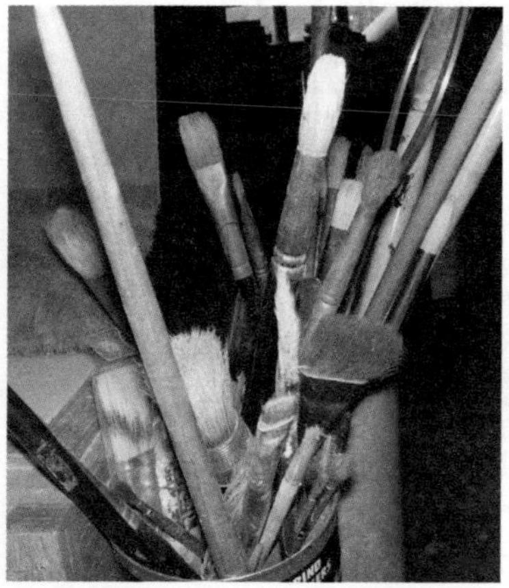

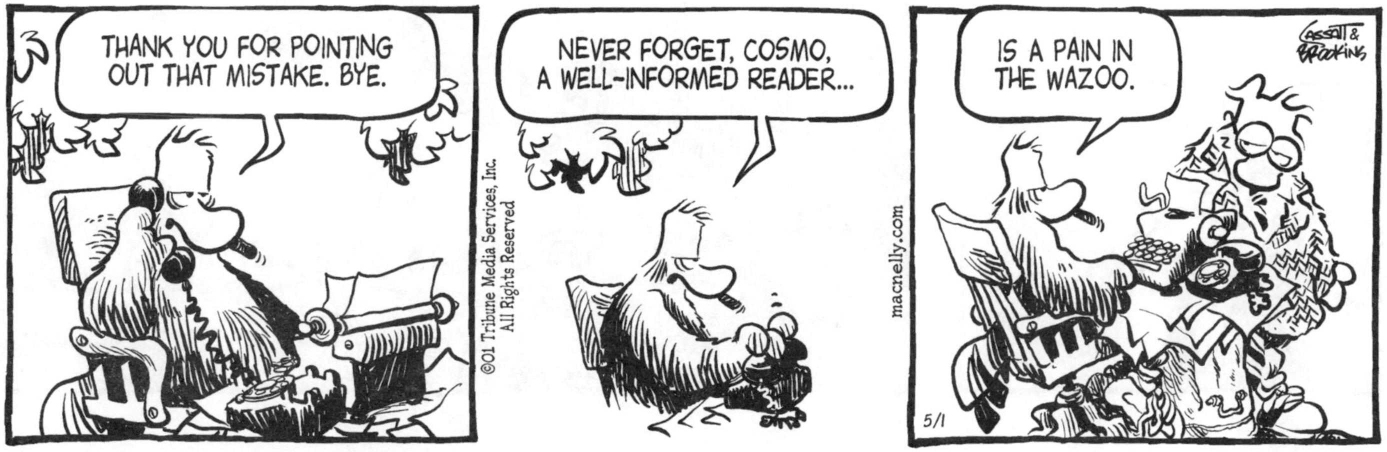
THANK YOU FOR POINTING OUT THAT MISTAKE. BYE.
©01 Tribune Media Services, Inc. All Rights Reserved
NEVER FORGET, COSMO, A WELL-INFORMED READER...
macnelly.com
IS A PAIN IN THE WAZOO.
CASSATT & BROOKINS
5/1

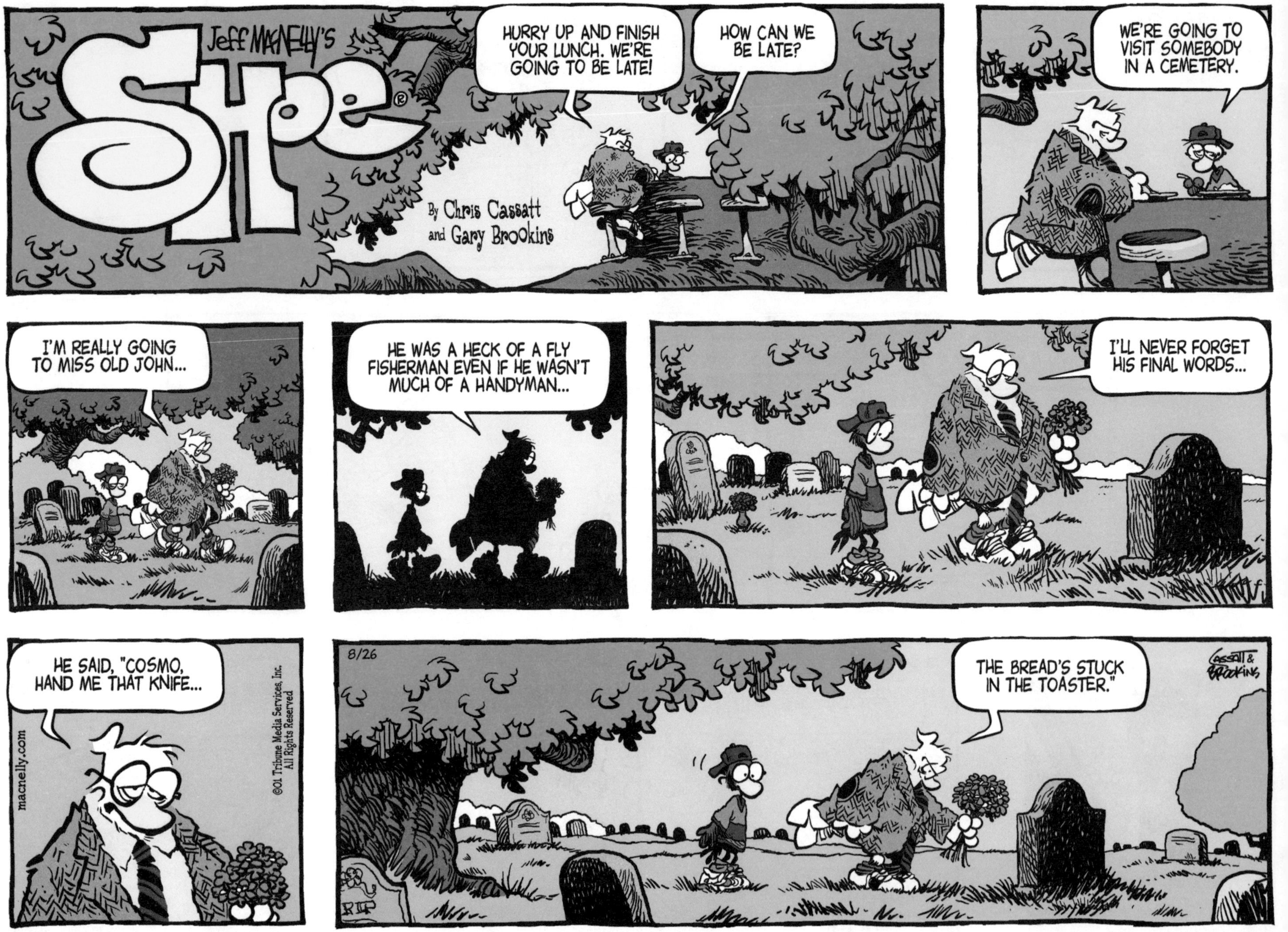
Jeff MacNelly's
Shoe
By Chris Cassatt and Gary Brookins
HURRY UP AND FINISH YOUR LUNCH. WE'RE GOING TO BE LATE!
HOW CAN WE BE LATE?
WE'RE GOING TO VISIT SOMEBODY IN A CEMETERY.
I'M REALLY GOING TO MISS OLD JOHN...
HE WAS A HECK OF A FLY FISHERMAN EVEN IF HE WASN'T MUCH OF A HANDYMAN...
I'LL NEVER FORGET HIS FINAL WORDS...
HE SAID, "COSMO, HAND ME THAT KNIFE...
macnelly.com
©01 Tribune Media Services, Inc. All Rights Reserved
8/26
THE BREAD'S STUCK IN THE TOASTER."
CASSATT & BROOKINS
RIP

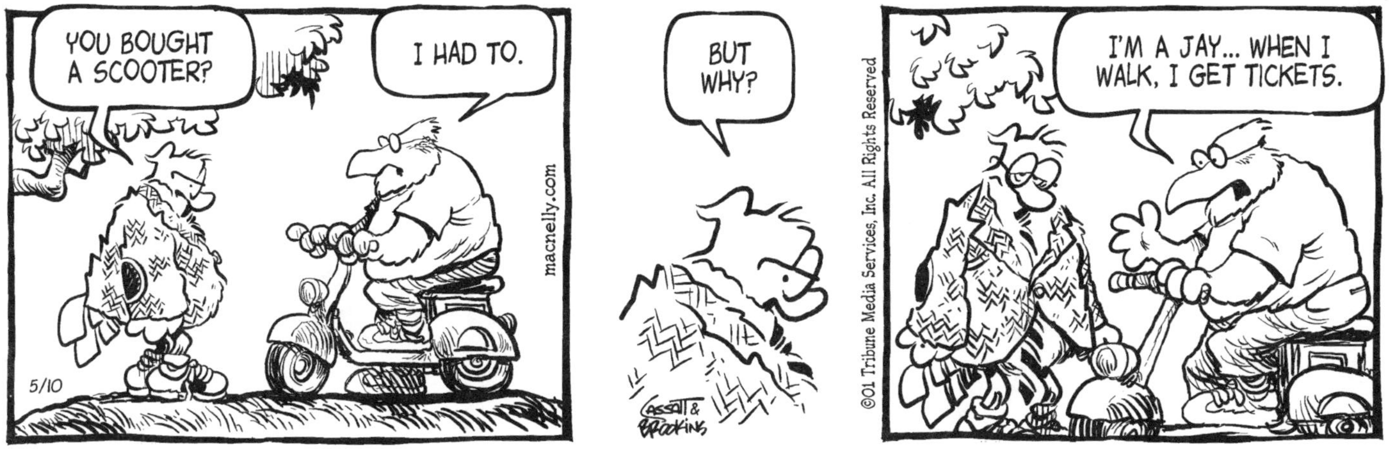
YOU BOUGHT A SCOOTER?
I HAD TO.
BUT WHY?
I'M A JAY... WHEN I WALK, I GET TICKETS.
5/10
macnelly.com
©01 Tribune Media Services, Inc. All Rights Reserved

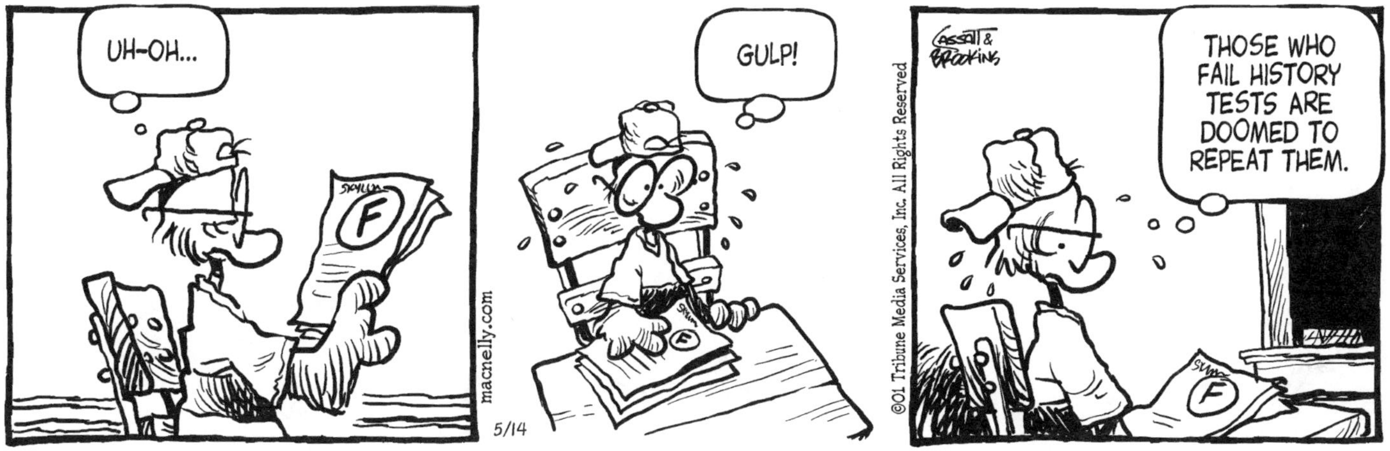
UH-OH...
GULP!
THOSE WHO FAIL HISTORY TESTS ARE DOOMED TO REPEAT THEM.
F
5/14
macnelly.com
©01 Tribune Media Services, Inc. All Rights Reserved

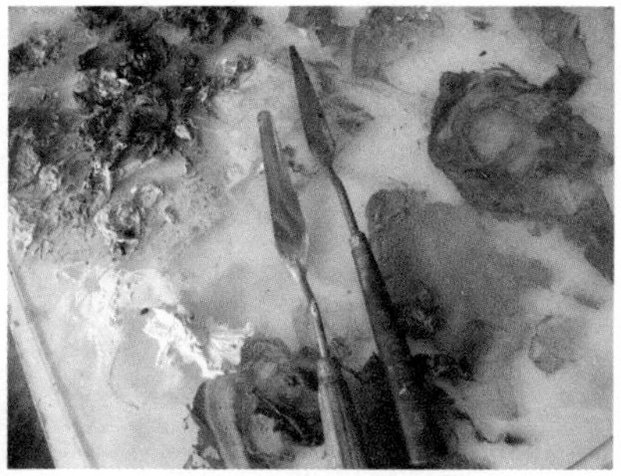

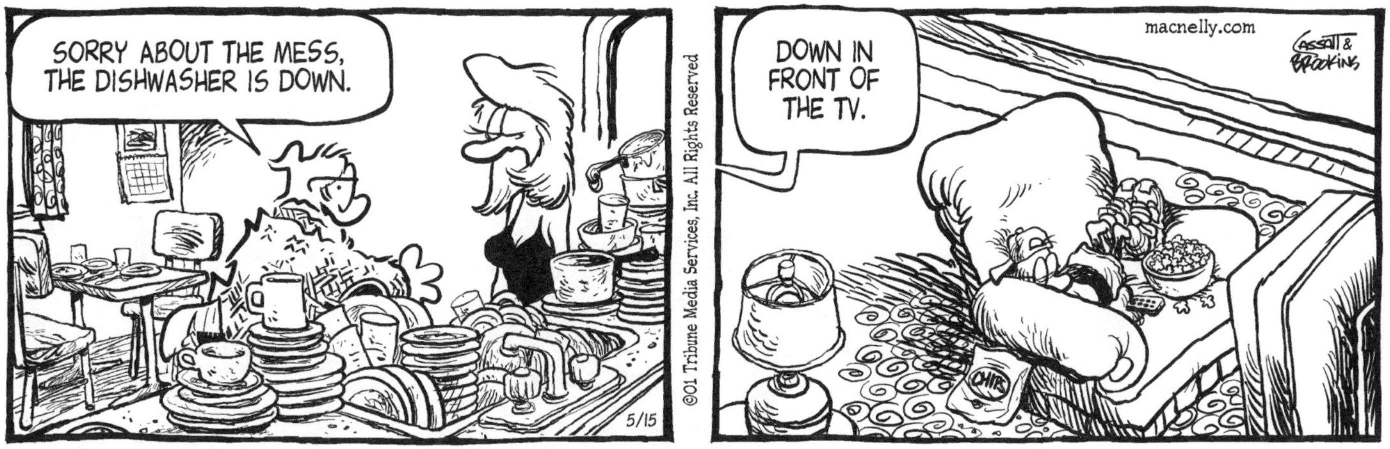
SORRY ABOUT THE MESS, THE DISHWASHER IS DOWN.
DOWN IN FRONT OF THE TV.
CHIPS
5/15
macnelly.com
©01 Tribune Media Services, Inc. All Rights Reserved

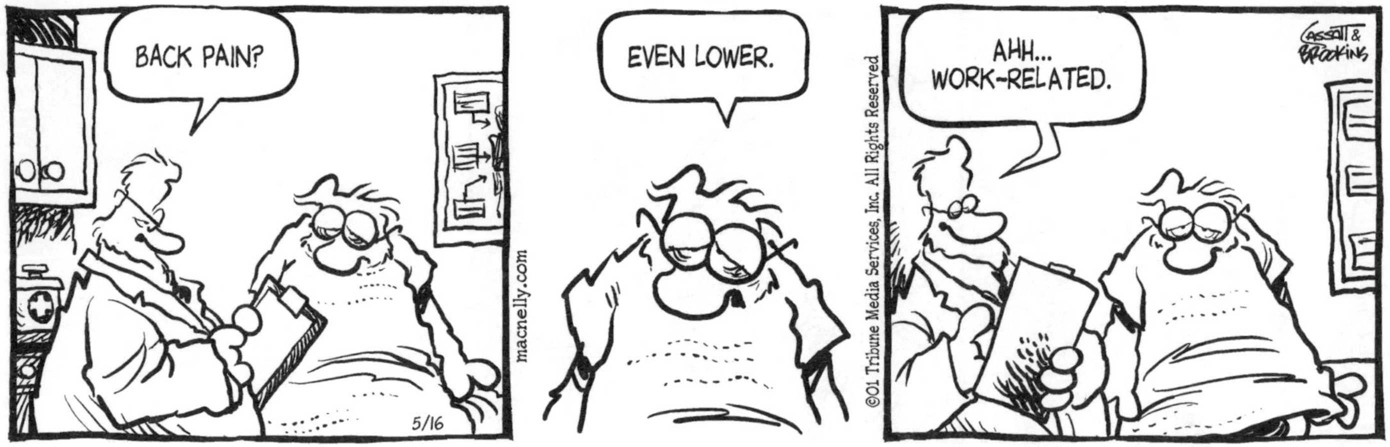
BACK PAIN?
5/16
macnelly.com
EVEN LOWER.
©01 Tribune Media Services, Inc. All Rights Reserved
AHH... WORK-RELATED.
CASSATT & BROOKINS

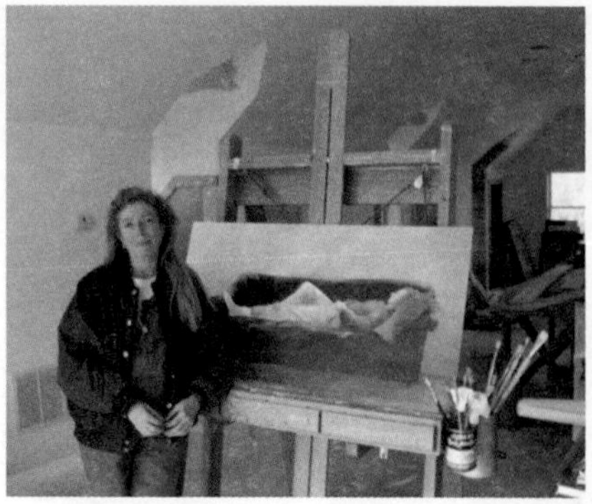

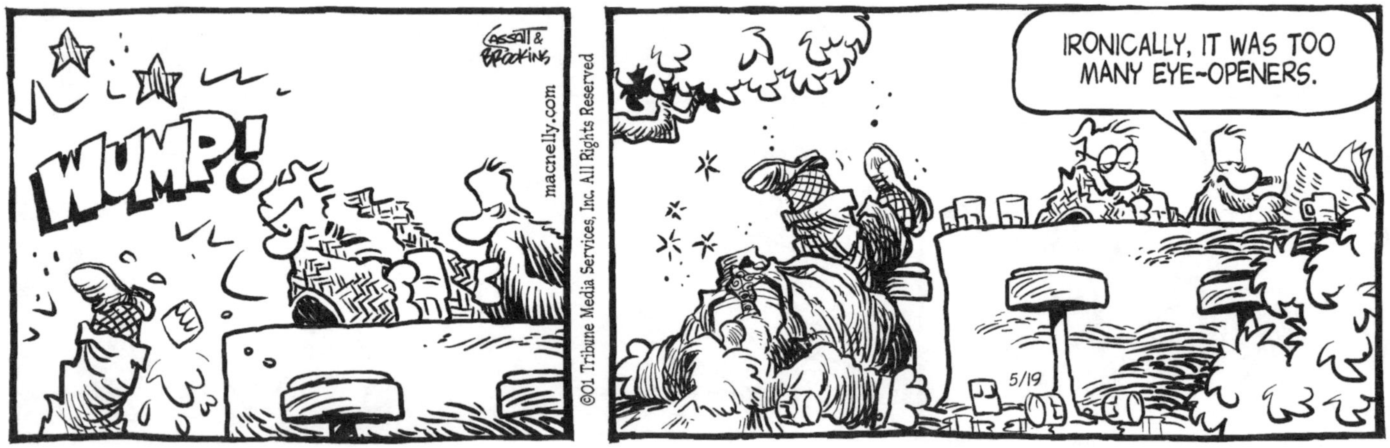
CASSATT & BROOKINS
WUMP!
macnelly.com
©01 Tribune Media Services, Inc. All Rights Reserved
IRONICALLY, IT WAS TOO MANY EYE-OPENERS.
5/19

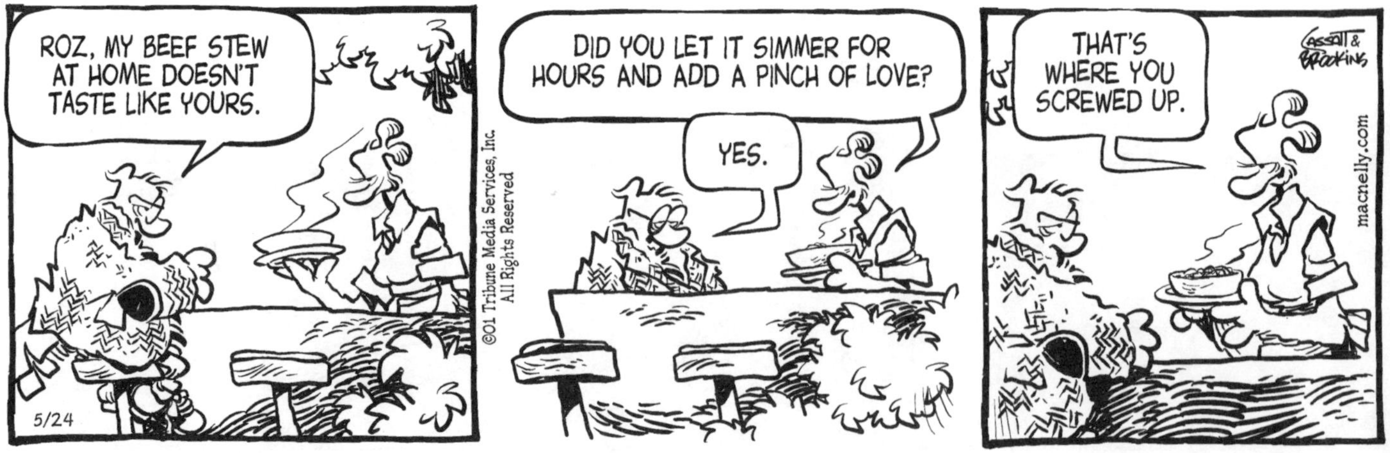
ROZ, MY BEEF STEW AT HOME DOESN'T TASTE LIKE YOURS.
5/24
©01 Tribune Media Services, Inc. All Rights Reserved
DID YOU LET IT SIMMER FOR HOURS AND ADD A PINCH OF LOVE?
YES.
THAT'S WHERE YOU SCREWED UP.
CASSATT & BROOKINS
macnelly.com

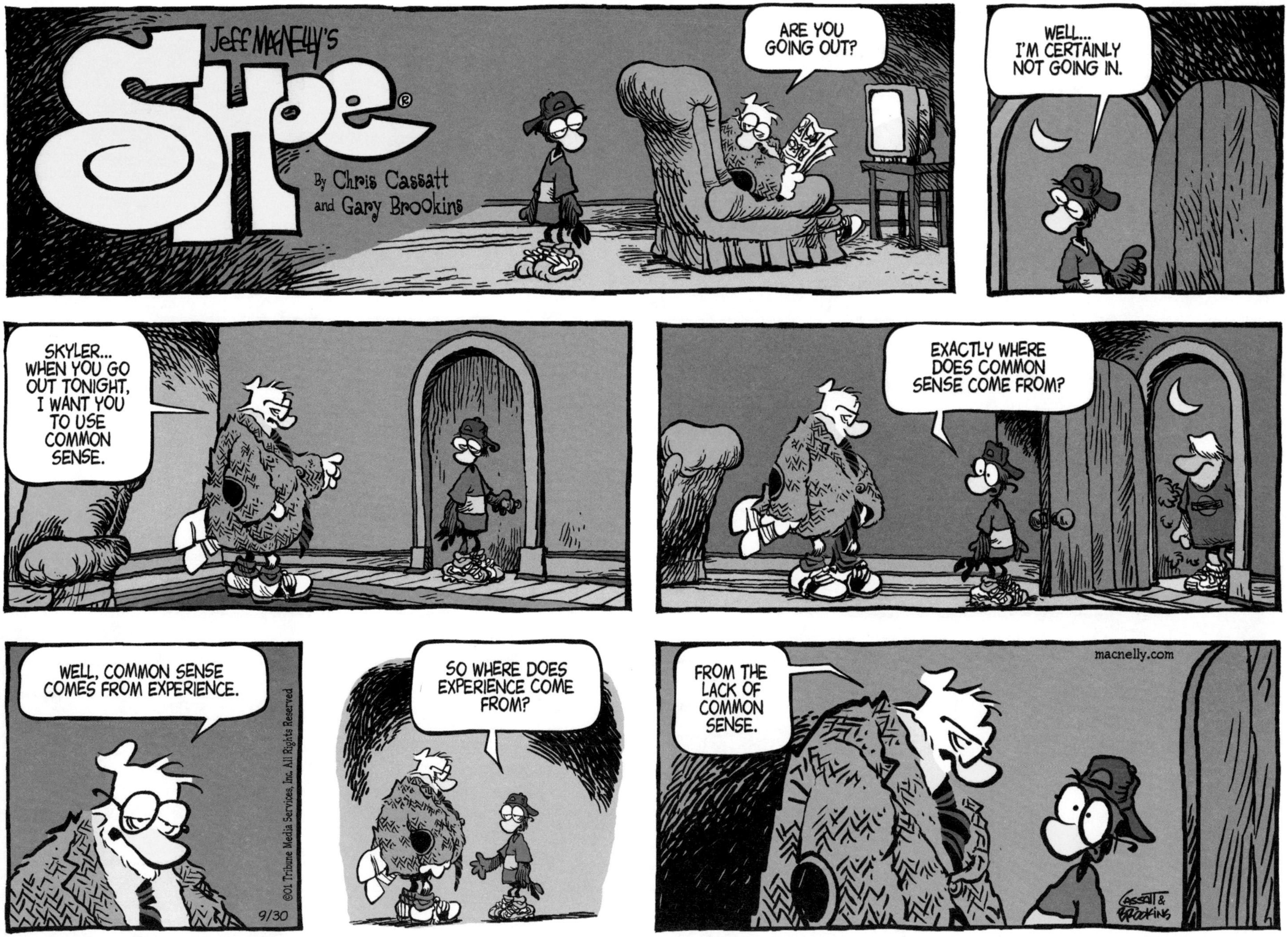
JEFF MACNELLY'S
SHOE®
By Chris Cassatt and Gary Brookins
ARE YOU GOING OUT?
WELL... I'M CERTAINLY NOT GOING IN.
SKYLER... WHEN YOU GO OUT TONIGHT, I WANT YOU TO USE COMMON SENSE.
EXACTLY WHERE DOES COMMON SENSE COME FROM?
WELL, COMMON SENSE COMES FROM EXPERIENCE.
©01 Tribune Media Services, Inc. All Rights Reserved
9/30
SO WHERE DOES EXPERIENCE COME FROM?
macnelly.com
FROM THE LACK OF COMMON SENSE.
CASSATT & BROOKINS

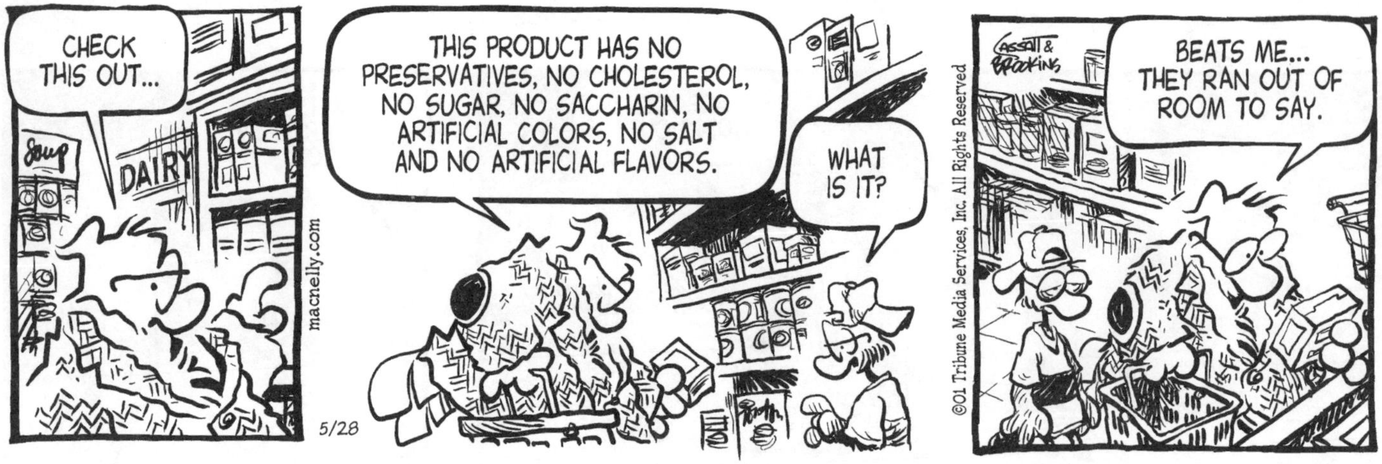
CHECK THIS OUT...
Soup
DAIRY
macnelly.com
5/28
THIS PRODUCT HAS NO PRESERVATIVES, NO CHOLESTEROL, NO SUGAR, NO SACCHARIN, NO ARTIFICIAL COLORS, NO SALT AND NO ARTIFICIAL FLAVORS.
WHAT IS IT?
©01 Tribune Media Services, Inc. All Rights Reserved
CASSATT & BROOKINS
BEATS ME... THEY RAN OUT OF ROOM TO SAY.

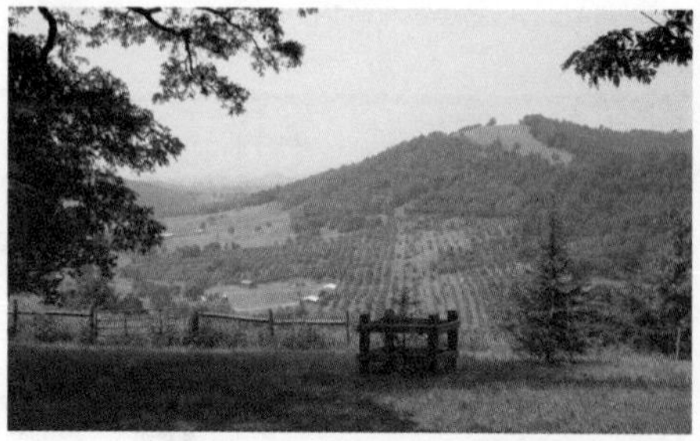

The view from "Jake's Place" where the ashes of both Jake and Jeff are scattered

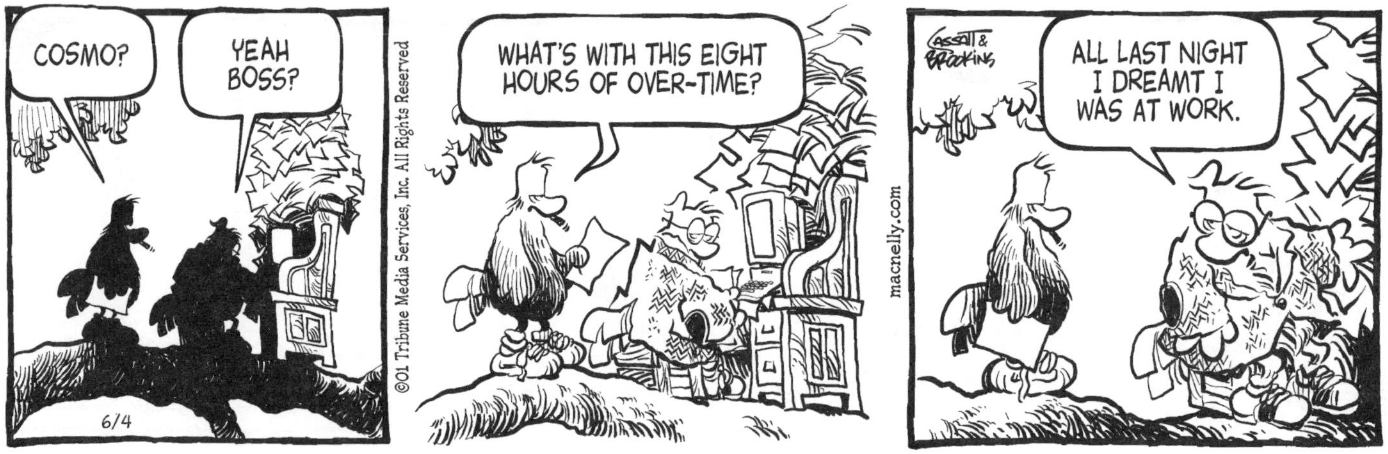
COSMO?
YEAH BOSS?
6/4
©01 Tribune Media Services, Inc. All Rights Reserved
WHAT'S WITH THIS EIGHT HOURS OF OVER-TIME?
macnelly.com
CASSATT & BROOKINS
ALL LAST NIGHT I DREAMT I WAS AT WORK.

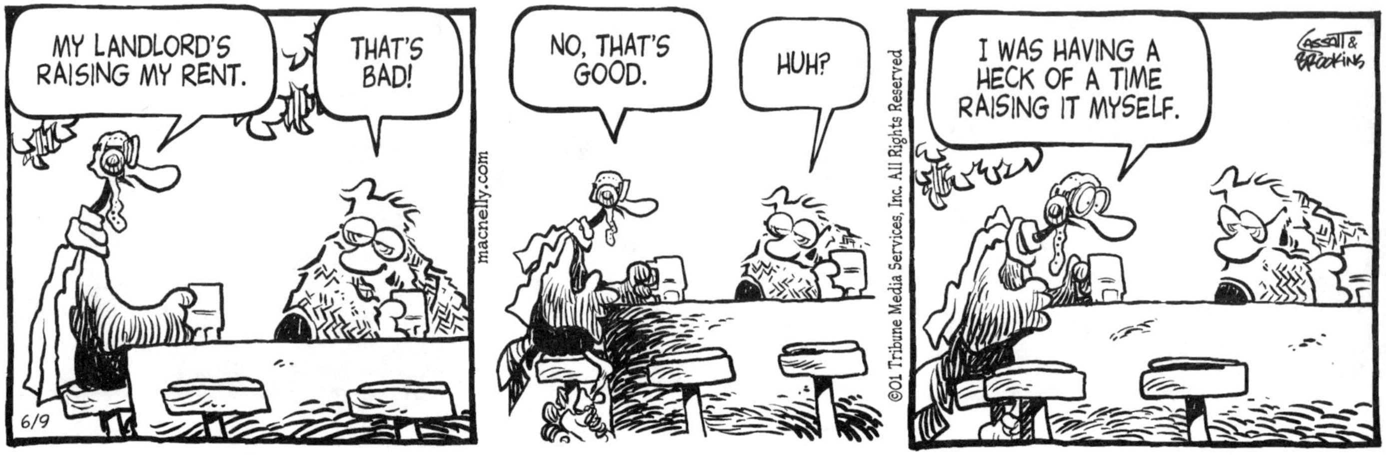
MY LANDLORD'S RAISING MY RENT.
THAT'S BAD!
6/9
macnelly.com
NO, THAT'S GOOD.
HUH?
©01 Tribune Media Services, Inc. All Rights Reserved
CASSATT & BROOKINS
I WAS HAVING A HECK OF A TIME RAISING IT MYSELF.

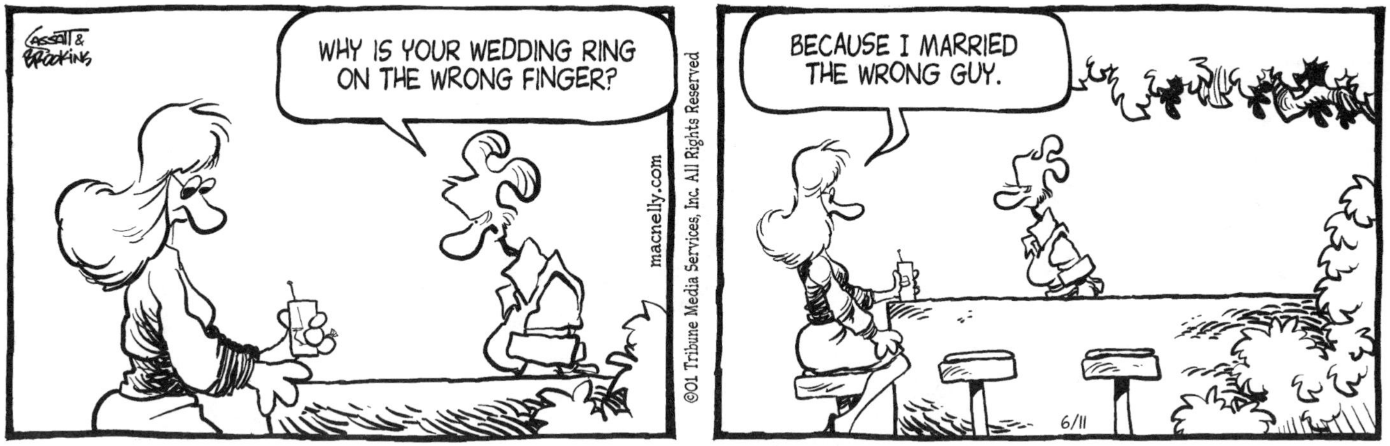
CASSATT & BROOKINS
WHY IS YOUR WEDDING RING ON THE WRONG FINGER?
macnelly.com
©01 Tribune Media Services, Inc. All Rights Reserved
BECAUSE I MARRIED THE WRONG GUY.
6/11

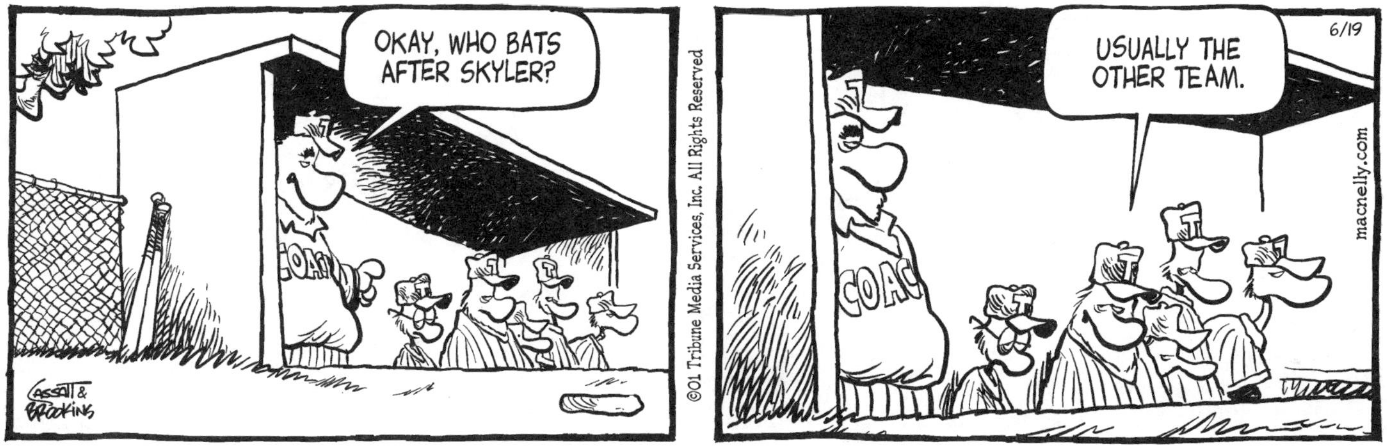
OKAY, WHO BATS AFTER SKYLER?
CASSATT & BROOKINS
©01 Tribune Media Services, Inc. All Rights Reserved
USUALLY THE OTHER TEAM.
6/19
macnelly.com

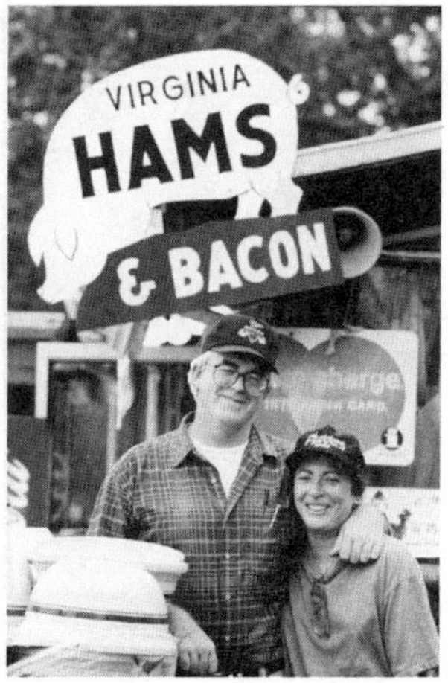
VIRGINIA
HAMS
& BACON

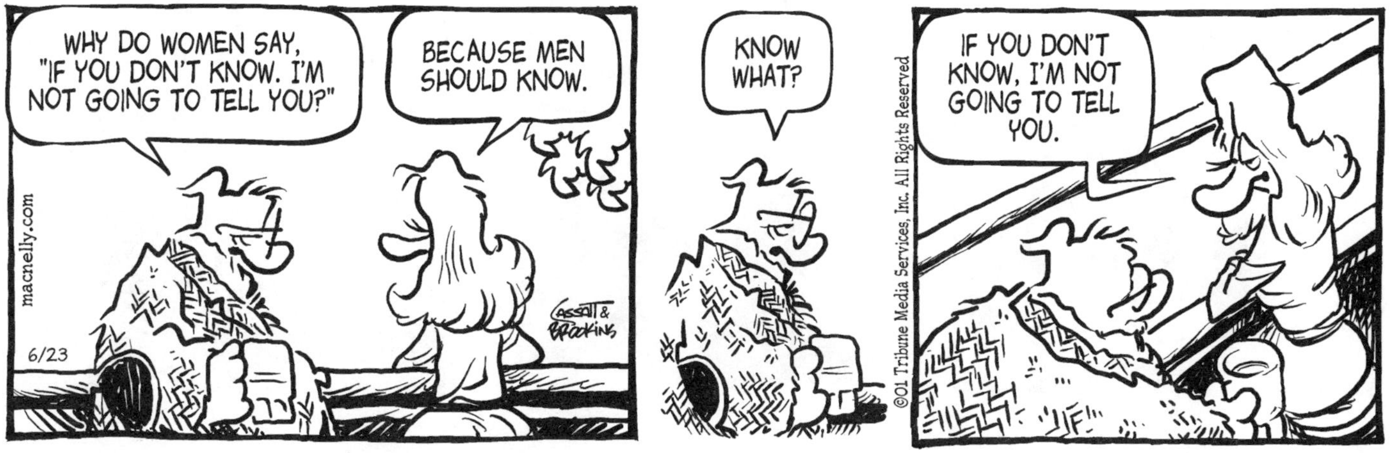
WHY DO WOMEN SAY, "IF YOU DON'T KNOW. I'M NOT GOING TO TELL YOU?"
BECAUSE MEN SHOULD KNOW.
macnelly.com
6/23
CASSATT & BROOKINS
KNOW WHAT?
©01 Tribune Media Services, Inc. All Rights Reserved
IF YOU DON'T KNOW, I'M NOT GOING TO TELL YOU.

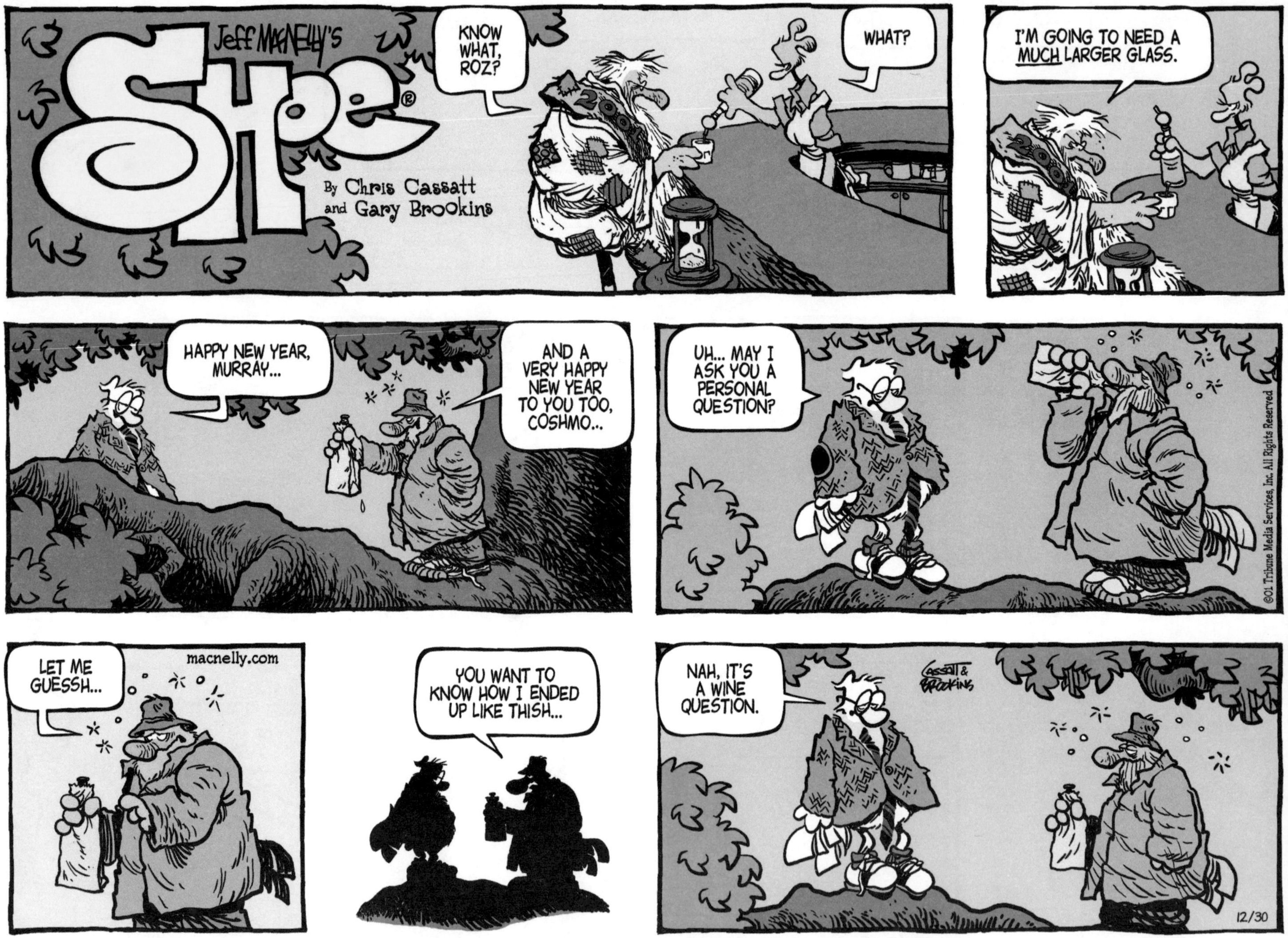
JEFF MACNELLY'S
SHOE®
By Chris Cassatt
and Gary Brookins
KNOW WHAT, ROZ?
WHAT?
I'M GOING TO NEED A MUCH LARGER GLASS.
HAPPY NEW YEAR, MURRAY...
AND A VERY HAPPY NEW YEAR TO YOU TOO, COSHMO...
UH... MAY I ASK YOU A PERSONAL QUESTION?
©01 Tribune Media Services, Inc. All Rights Reserved
LET ME GUESSH...
macnelly.com
YOU WANT TO KNOW HOW I ENDED UP LIKE THISH...
NAH, IT'S A WINE QUESTION.
CASSATT & BROOKINS
12/30

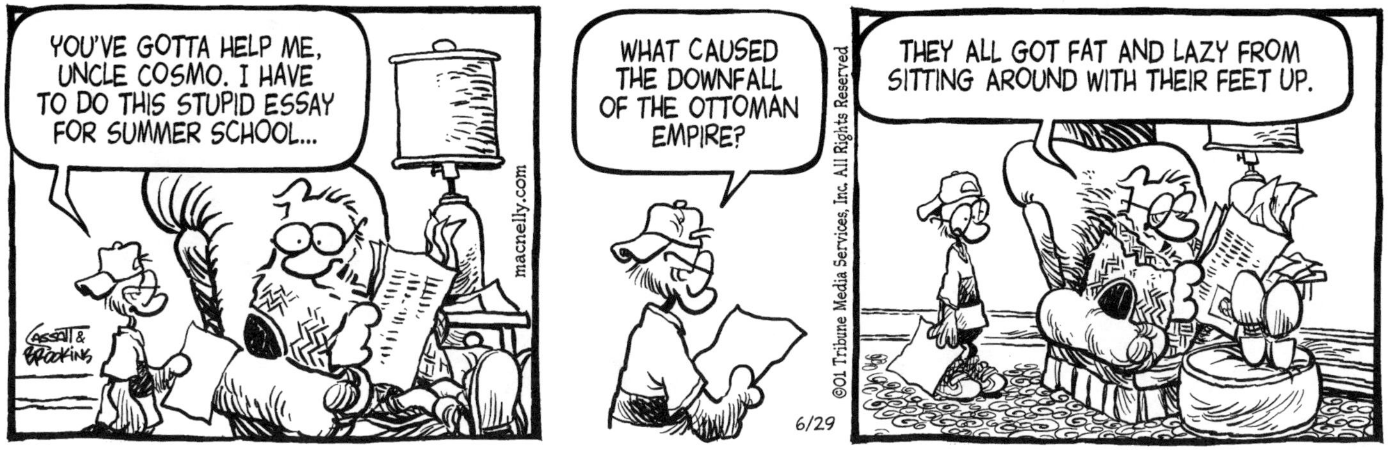
YOU'VE GOTTA HELP ME, UNCLE COSMO. I HAVE TO DO THIS STUPID ESSAY FOR SUMMER SCHOOL...
CASSATT & BROOKINS
macnelly.com
WHAT CAUSED THE DOWNFALL OF THE OTTOMAN EMPIRE?
6/29
©01 Tribune Media Services, Inc. All Rights Reserved
THEY ALL GOT FAT AND LAZY FROM SITTING AROUND WITH THEIR FEET UP.

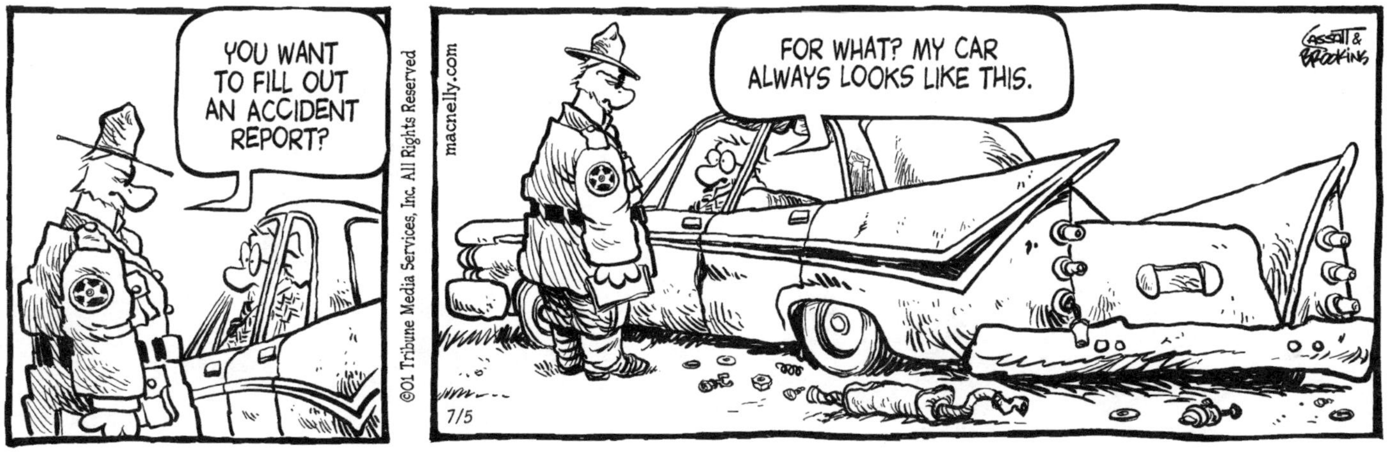
YOU WANT TO FILL OUT AN ACCIDENT REPORT?
©01 Tribune Media Services, Inc. All Rights Reserved
macnelly.com
FOR WHAT? MY CAR ALWAYS LOOKS LIKE THIS.
CASSATT & BROOKINS
7/5

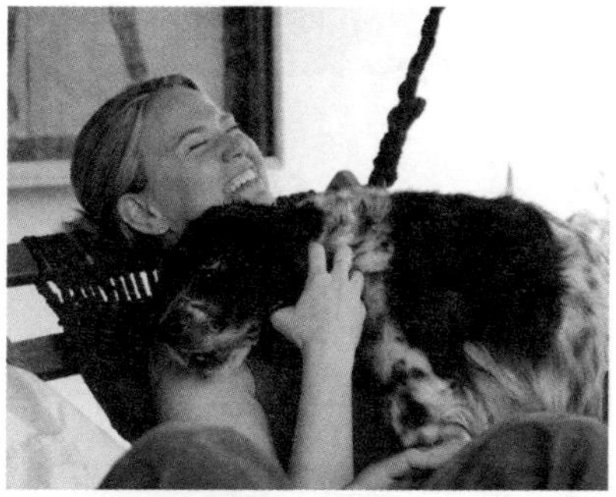

Katie and Doofus.

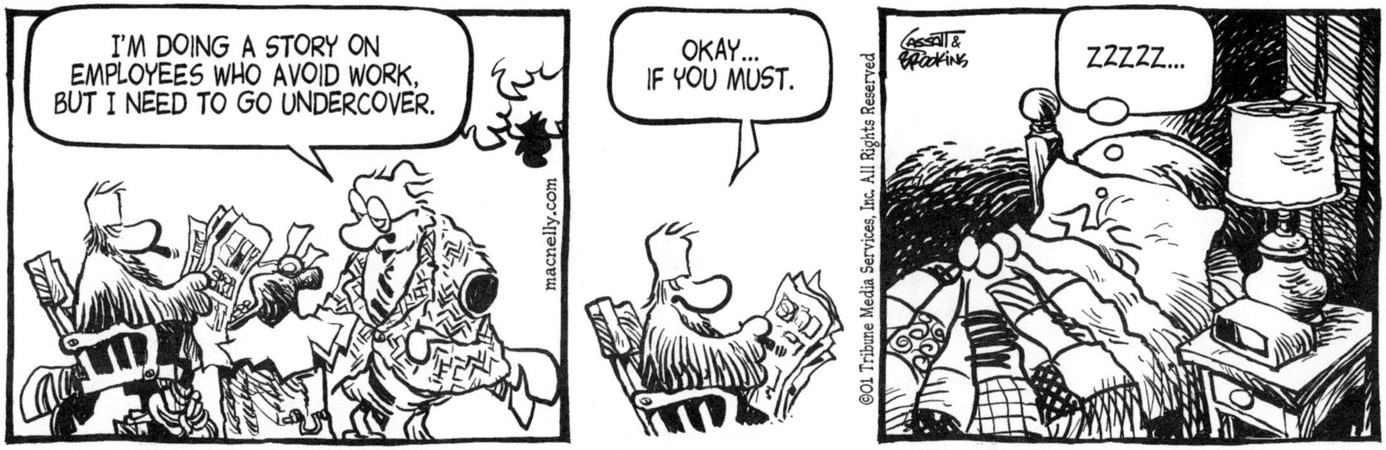
I'M DOING A STORY ON EMPLOYEES WHO AVOID WORK, BUT I NEED TO GO UNDERCOVER.
macnelly.com
OKAY... IF YOU MUST.
©01 Tribune Media Services, Inc. All Rights Reserved
CASSATT & BROOKINS
ZZZZZ...

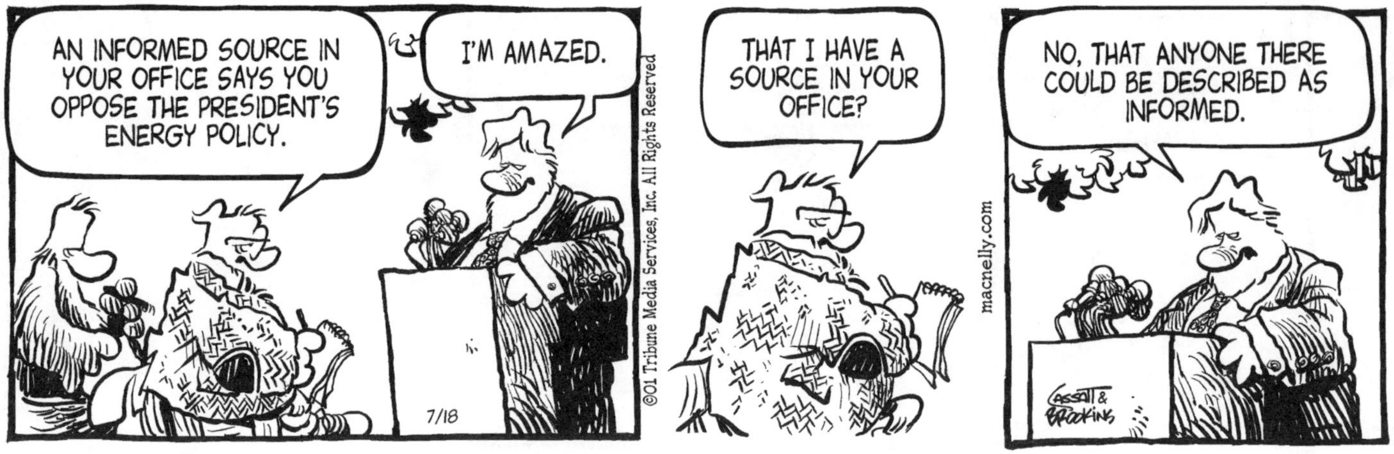
AN INFORMED SOURCE IN YOUR OFFICE SAYS YOU OPPOSE THE PRESIDENT'S ENERGY POLICY.
I'M AMAZED.
7/18
©01 Tribune Media Services, Inc. All Rights Reserved
THAT I HAVE A SOURCE IN YOUR OFFICE?
macnelly.com
NO, THAT ANYONE THERE COULD BE DESCRIBED AS INFORMED.
CASSATT & BROOKINS

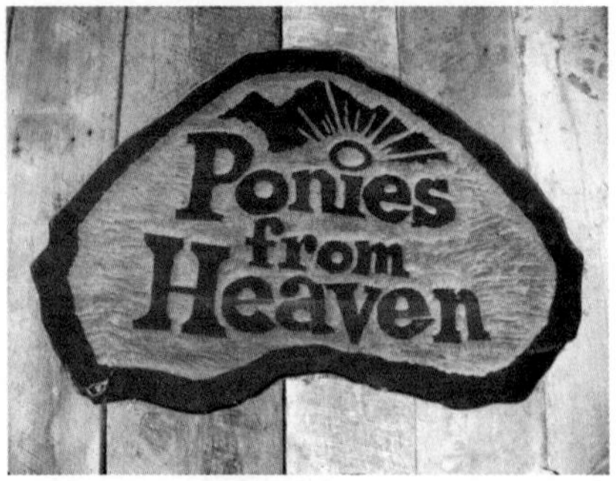
Ponies from Heaven

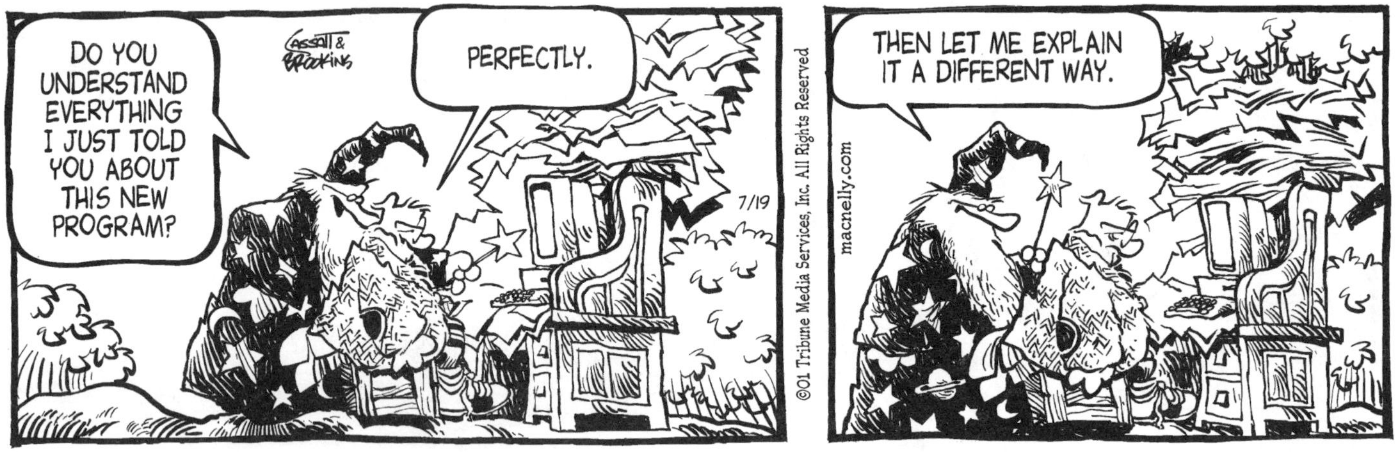
DO YOU UNDERSTAND EVERYTHING I JUST TOLD YOU ABOUT THIS NEW PROGRAM?
CASSATT & BROOKINS
PERFECTLY.
7/19
©01 Tribune Media Services, Inc. All Rights Reserved
macnelly.com
THEN LET ME EXPLAIN IT A DIFFERENT WAY.

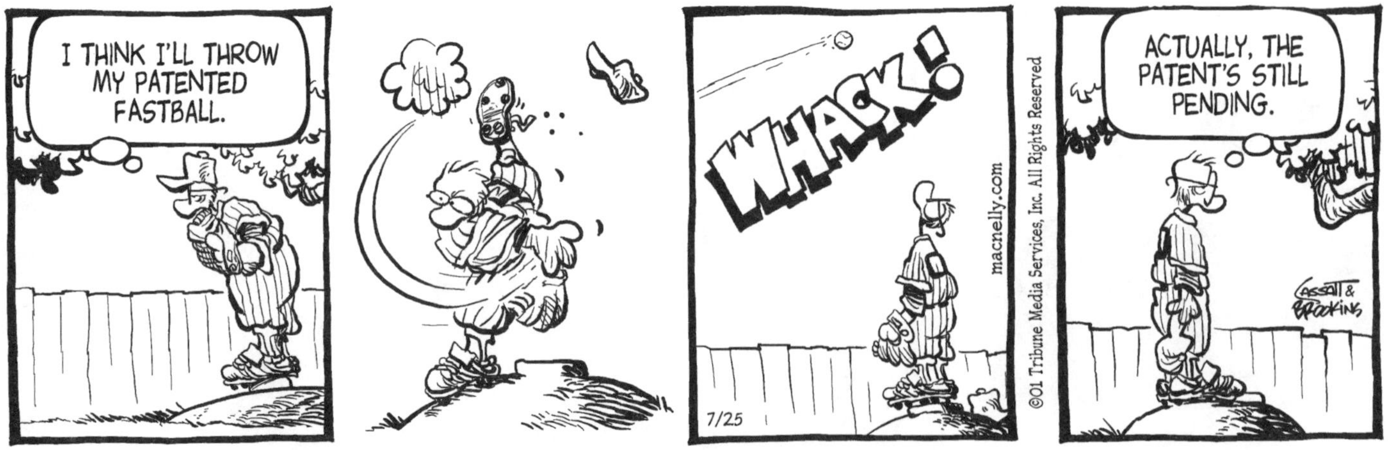
I THINK I'LL THROW MY PATENTED FASTBALL.
WHACK!
7/25
macnelly.com
©01 Tribune Media Services, Inc. All Rights Reserved
ACTUALLY, THE PATENT'S STILL PENDING.
CASSATT & BROOKINS

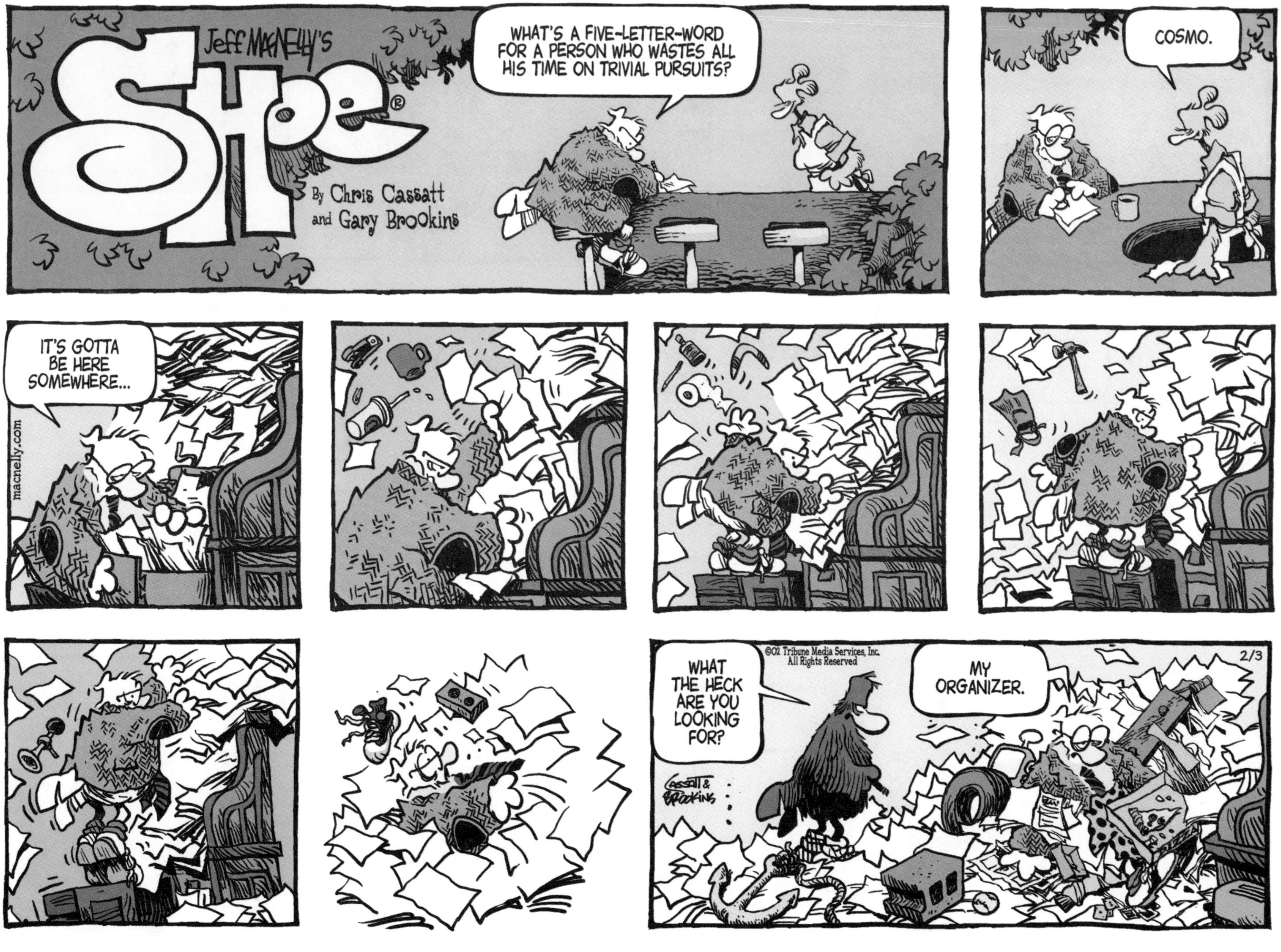

Jeff MacNelly's
Shoe
By Chris Cassatt and Gary Brookins
WHAT'S A FIVE-LETTER-WORD FOR A PERSON WHO WASTES ALL HIS TIME ON TRIVIAL PURSUITS?
COSMO.
IT'S GOTTA BE HERE SOMEWHERE...
macnelly.com
©02 Tribune Media Services, Inc. All Rights Reserved
2/3
WHAT THE HECK ARE YOU LOOKING FOR?
MY ORGANIZER.
CASSATT & BROOKINS

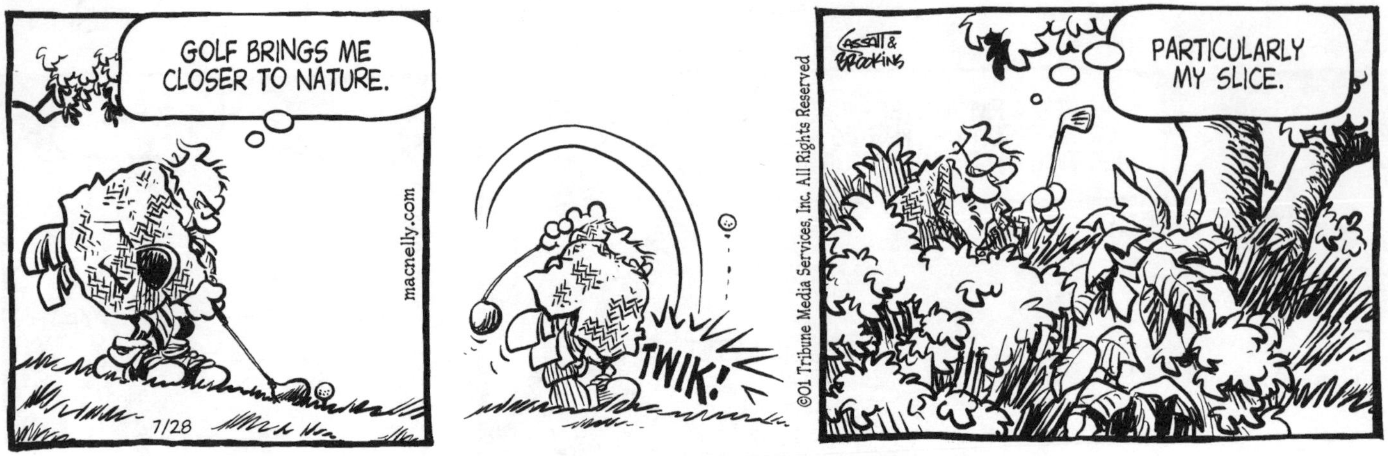
GOLF BRINGS ME CLOSER TO NATURE.
7/28
macnelly.com
TWIK!
©01 Tribune Media Services, Inc. All Rights Reserved
CASSATT & BROOKINS
PARTICULARLY MY SLICE.

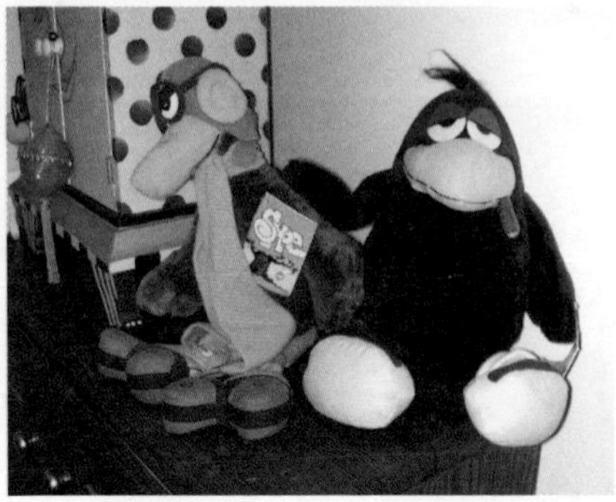

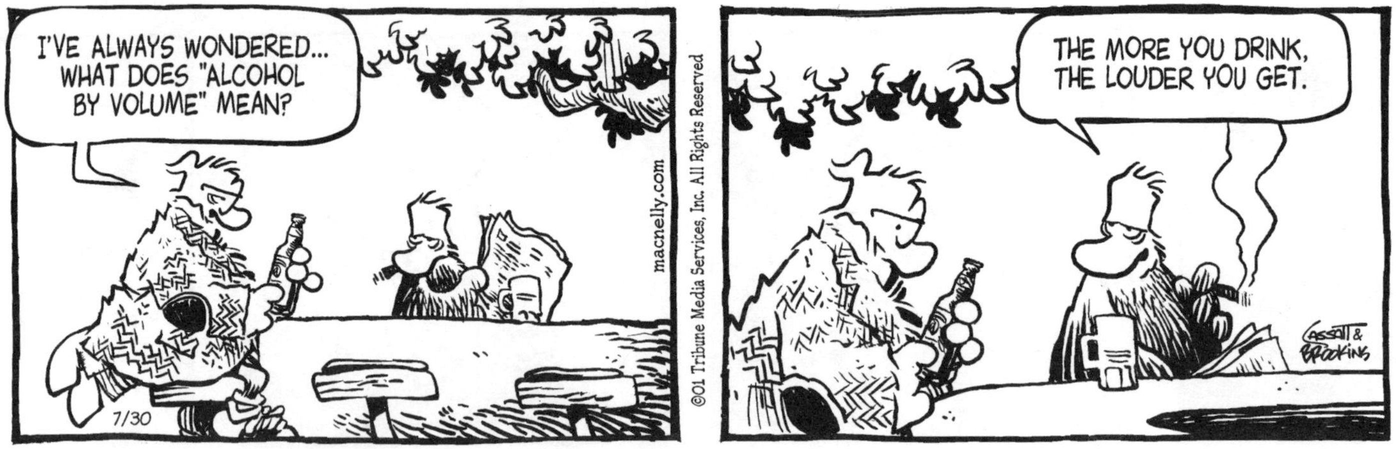
I'VE ALWAYS WONDERED... WHAT DOES "ALCOHOL BY VOLUME" MEAN?
7/30
macnelly.com
©01 Tribune Media Services, Inc. All Rights Reserved
THE MORE YOU DRINK, THE LOUDER YOU GET.
CASSATT & BROOKINS

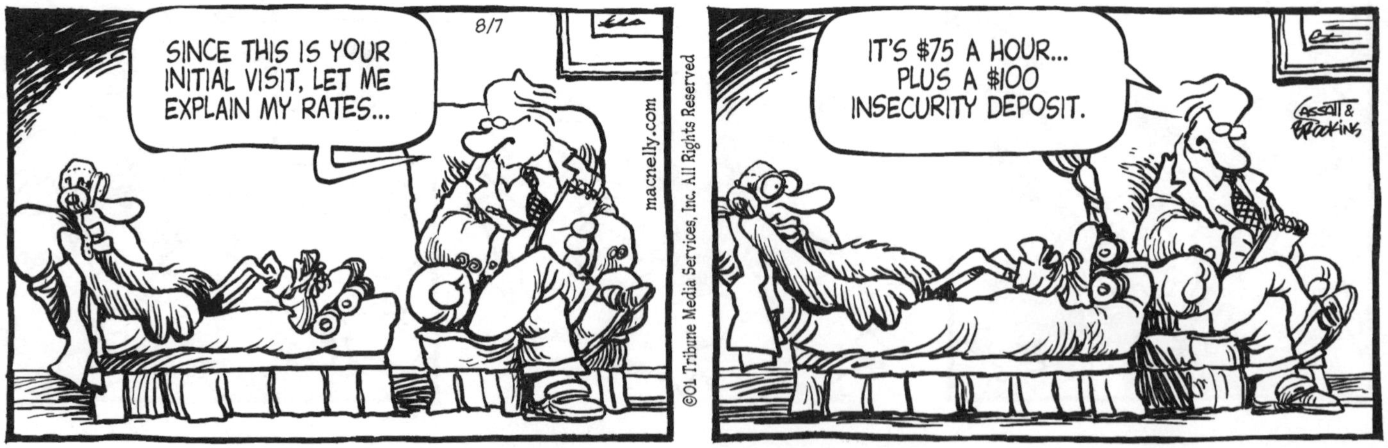
SINCE THIS IS YOUR INITIAL VISIT, LET ME EXPLAIN MY RATES...
8/7
macnelly.com
©01 Tribune Media Services, Inc. All Rights Reserved
IT'S $75 A HOUR... PLUS A $100 INSECURITY DEPOSIT.
CASSATT & BROOKINS

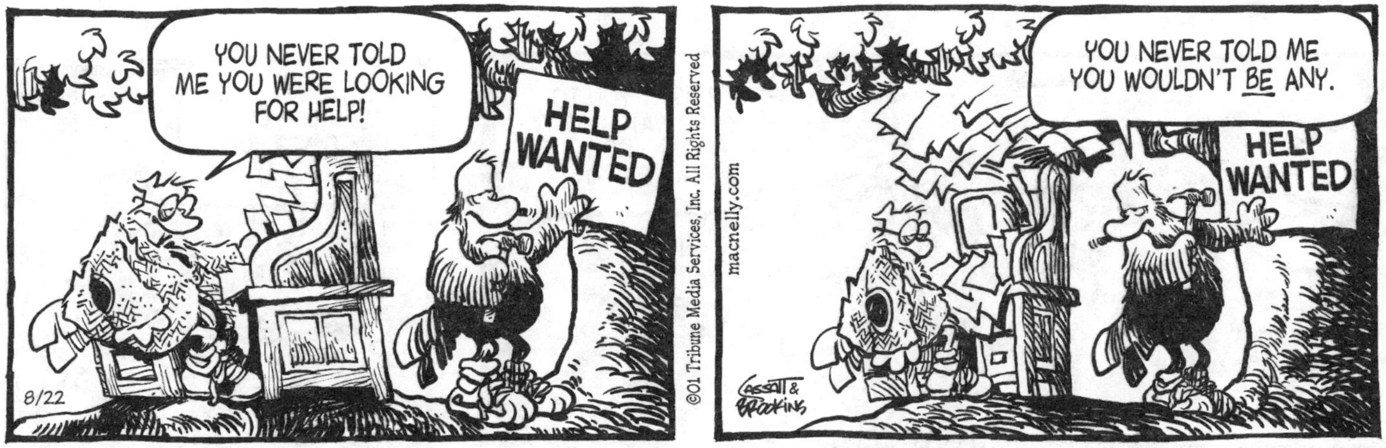
YOU NEVER TOLD ME YOU WERE LOOKING FOR HELP!
HELP WANTED
8/22
©01 Tribune Media Services, Inc. All Rights Reserved
macnelly.com
YOU NEVER TOLD ME YOU WOULDN'T BE ANY.
HELP WANTED
CASSATT & BROOKINS

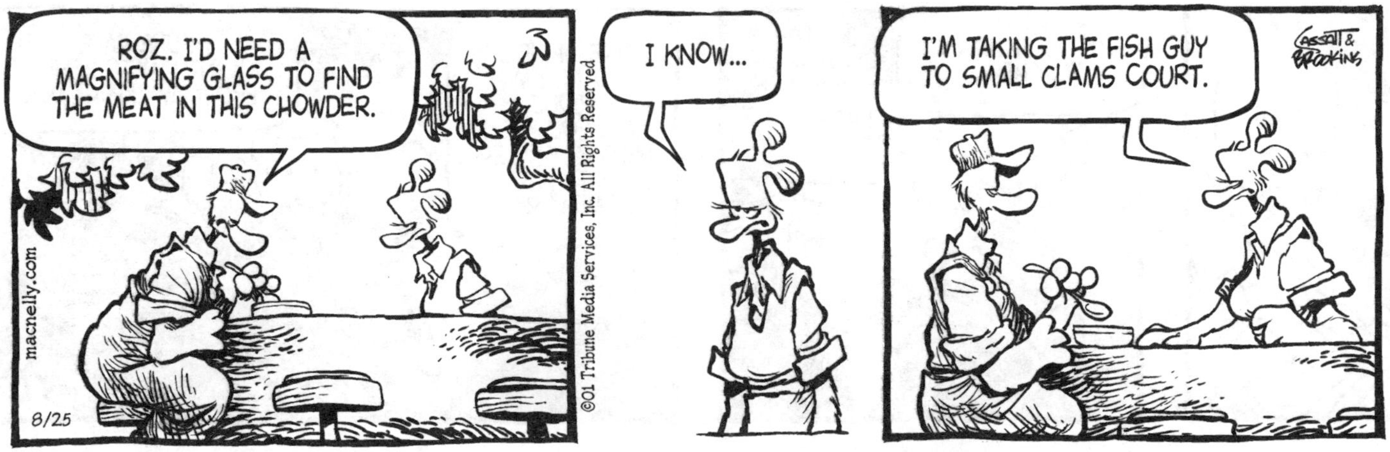
ROZ. I'D NEED A MAGNIFYING GLASS TO FIND THE MEAT IN THIS CHOWDER.
macnelly.com
8/25
©01 Tribune Media Services, Inc. All Rights Reserved
I KNOW...
I'M TAKING THE FISH GUY TO SMALL CLAMS COURT.
CASSATT & BROOKINS

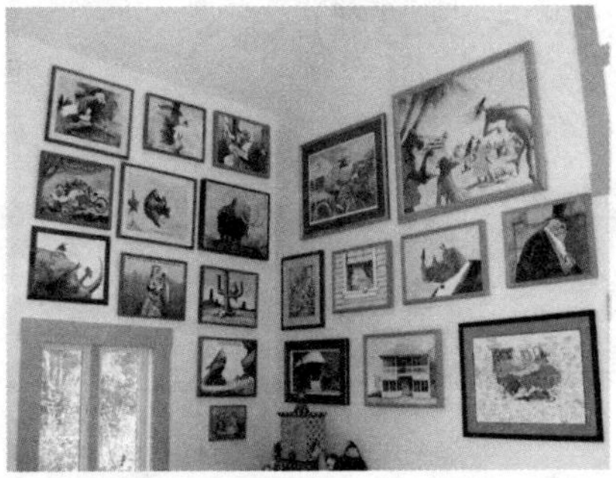

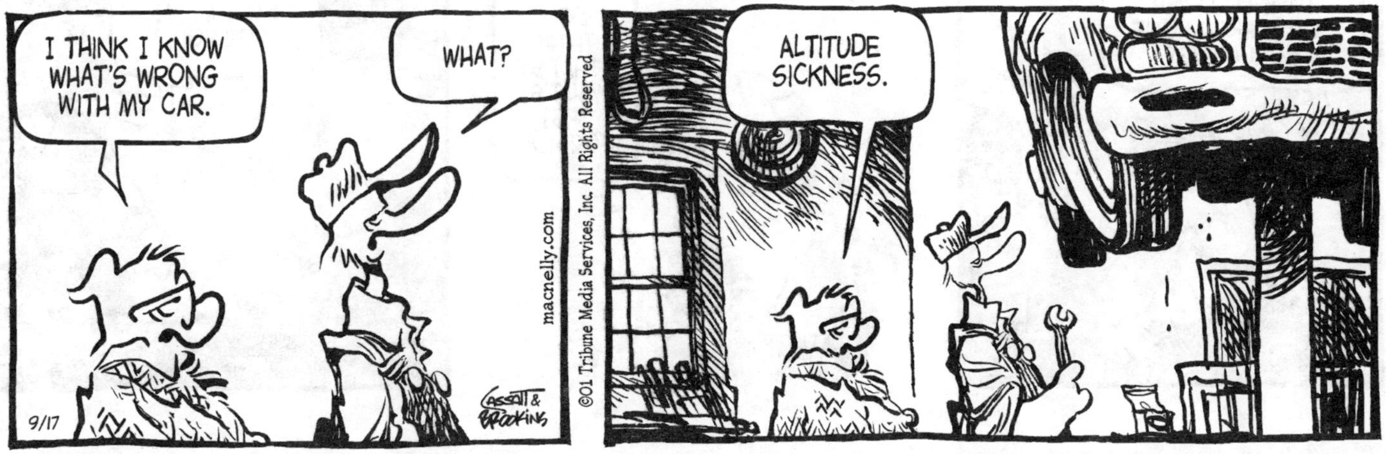
I THINK I KNOW WHAT'S WRONG WITH MY CAR.
WHAT?
9/17
macnelly.com
CASSATT & BROOKINS
©01 Tribune Media Services, Inc. All Rights Reserved
ALTITUDE SICKNESS.

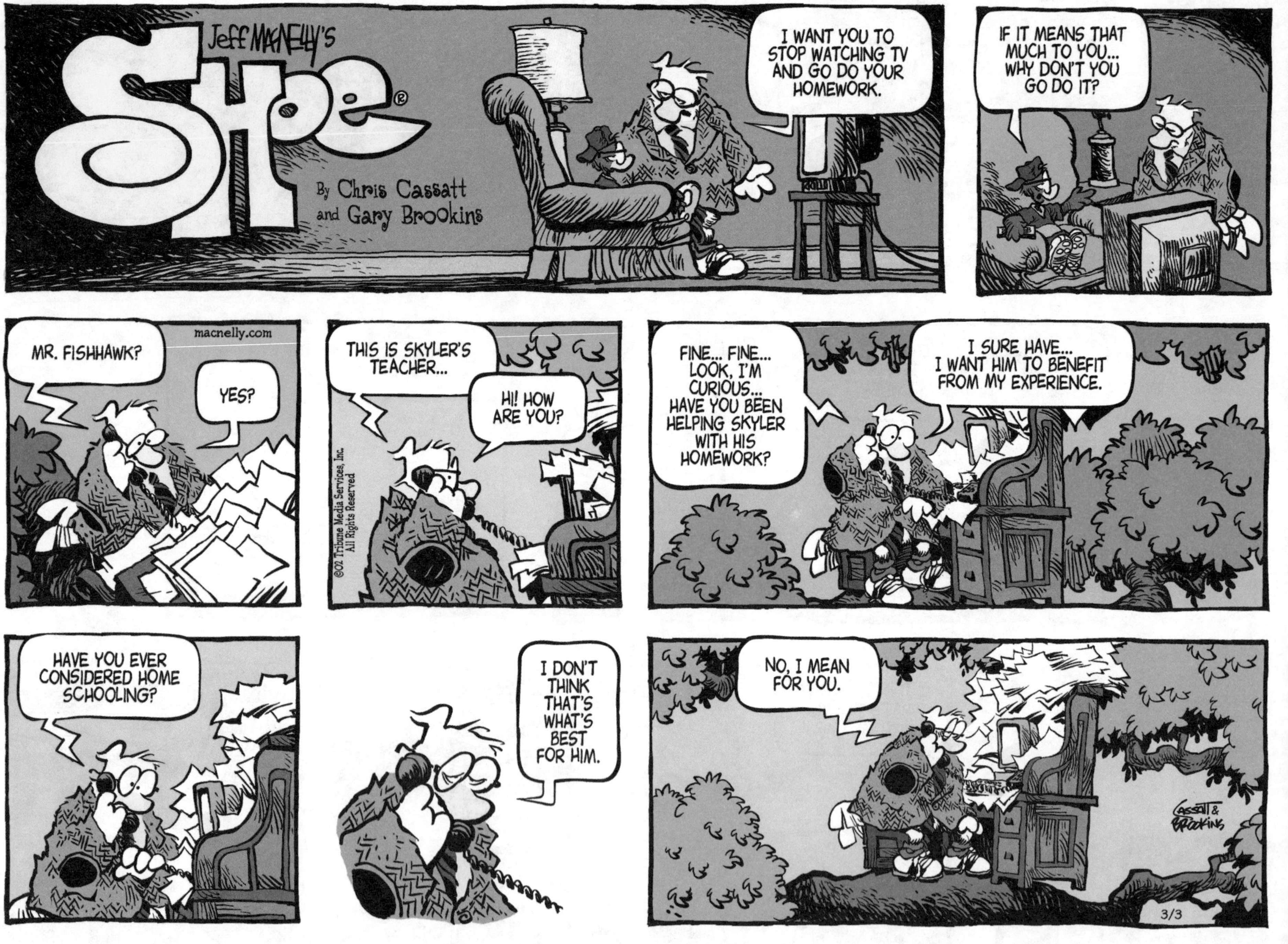
JEFF MACNELLY'S
SHOE®
By Chris Cassatt
and Gary Brookins
I WANT YOU TO STOP WATCHING TV AND GO DO YOUR HOMEWORK.
IF IT MEANS THAT MUCH TO YOU... WHY DON'T YOU GO DO IT?
macnelly.com
MR. FISHHAWK?
YES?
©02 Tribune Media Services, Inc.
All Rights Reserved
THIS IS SKYLER'S TEACHER...
HI! HOW ARE YOU?
FINE... FINE... LOOK, I'M CURIOUS... HAVE YOU BEEN HELPING SKYLER WITH HIS HOMEWORK?
I SURE HAVE... I WANT HIM TO BENEFIT FROM MY EXPERIENCE.
HAVE YOU EVER CONSIDERED HOME SCHOOLING?
I DON'T THINK THAT'S WHAT'S BEST FOR HIM.
NO, I MEAN FOR YOU.
CASSATT & BROOKINS
3/3

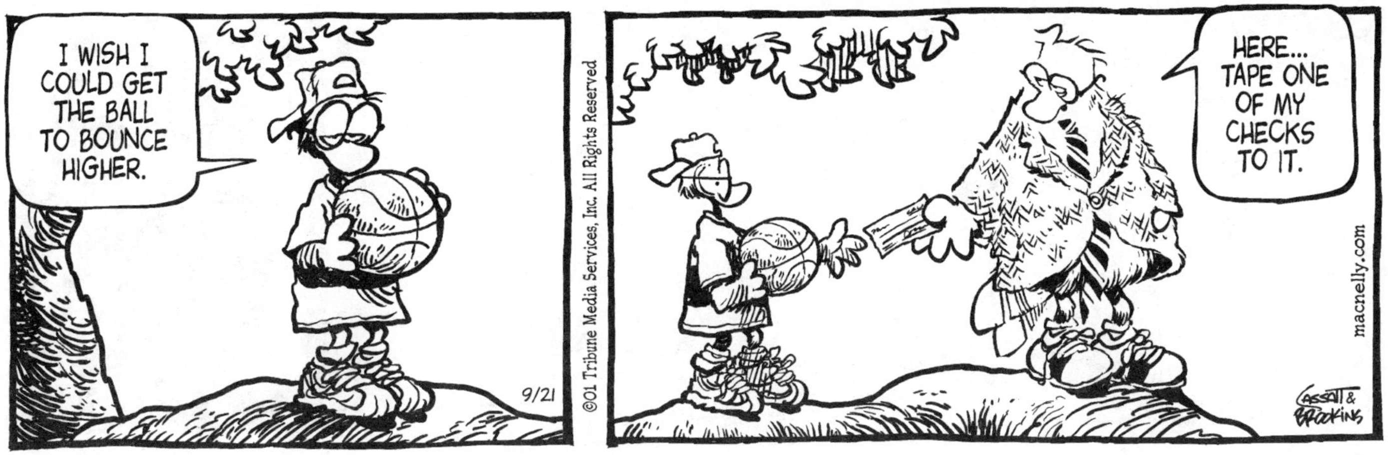
I WISH I COULD GET THE BALL TO BOUNCE HIGHER.
9/21
©01 Tribune Media Services, Inc. All Rights Reserved
HERE... TAPE ONE OF MY CHECKS TO IT.
macnelly.com
CASSATT & BROOKINS

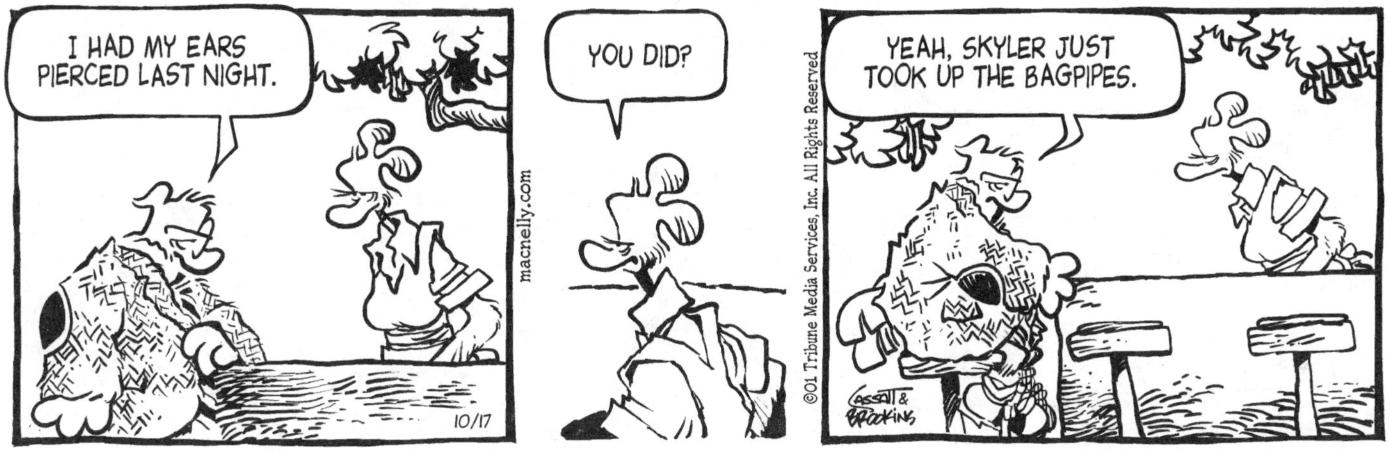
I HAD MY EARS PIERCED LAST NIGHT.
10/17
macnelly.com
YOU DID?
©01 Tribune Media Services, Inc. All Rights Reserved
YEAH, SKYLER JUST TOOK UP THE BAGPIPES.
CASSATT & BROOKINS

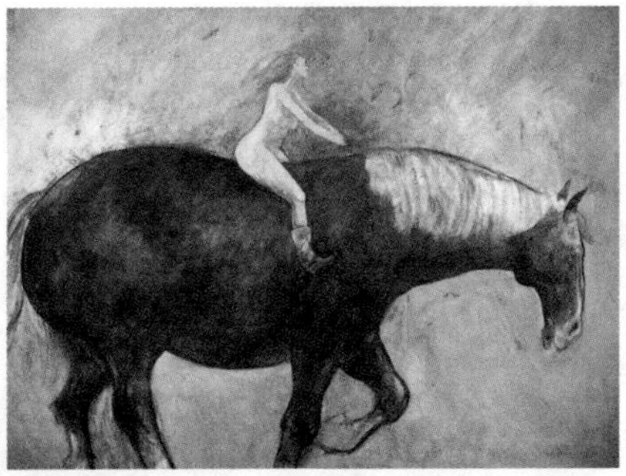

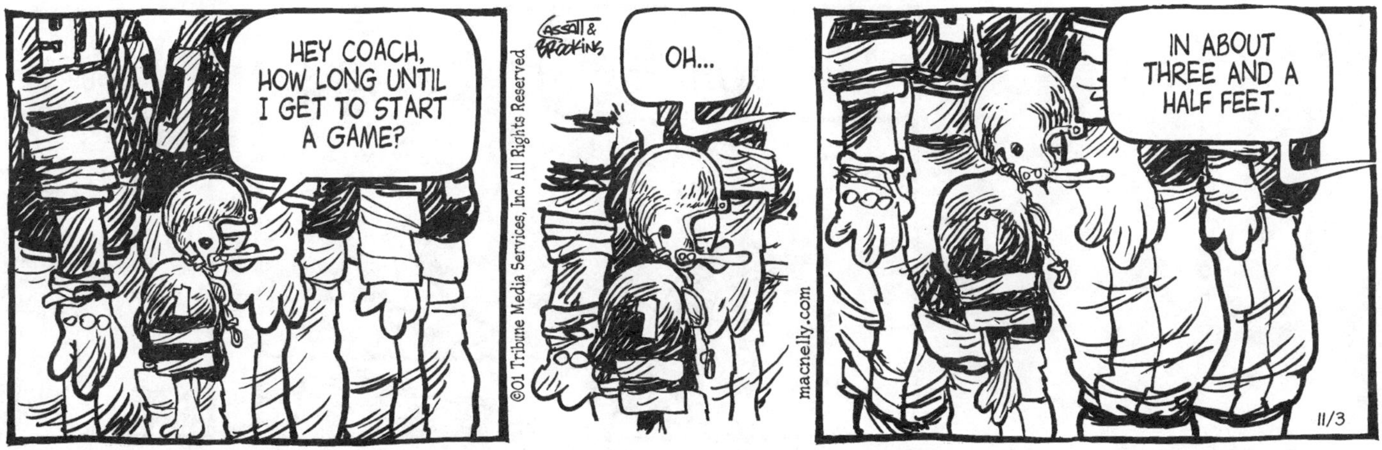
HEY COACH, HOW LONG UNTIL I GET TO START A GAME?
©01 Tribune Media Services, Inc. All Rights Reserved
CASSATT & BROOKINS
OH...
macnelly.com
IN ABOUT THREE AND A HALF FEET.
11/3

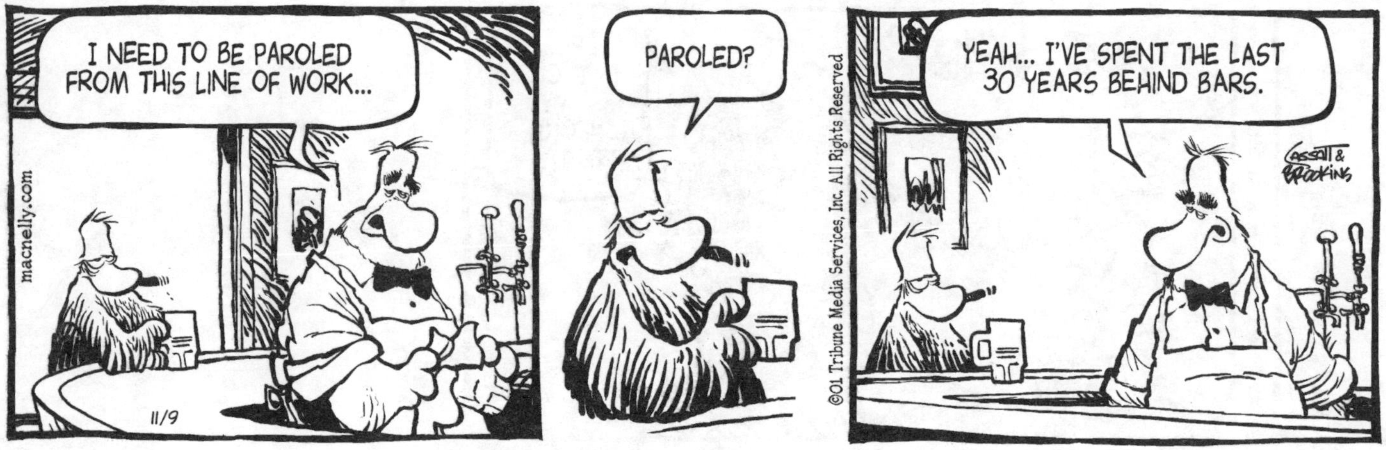
I NEED TO BE PAROLED FROM THIS LINE OF WORK...
PAROLED?
YEAH... I'VE SPENT THE LAST 30 YEARS BEHIND BARS.
macnelly.com
11/9
©01 Tribune Media Services, Inc. All Rights Reserved

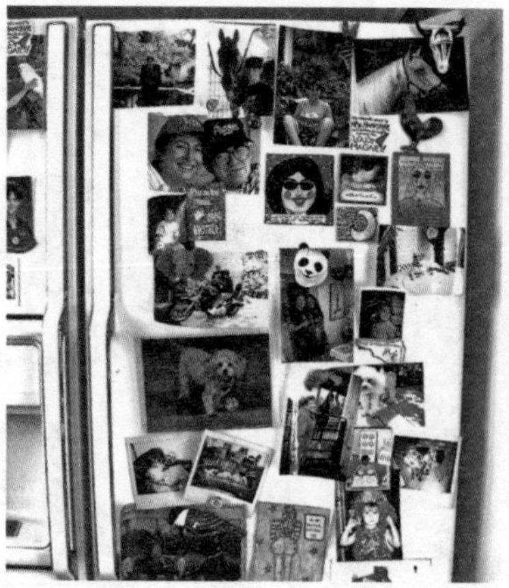

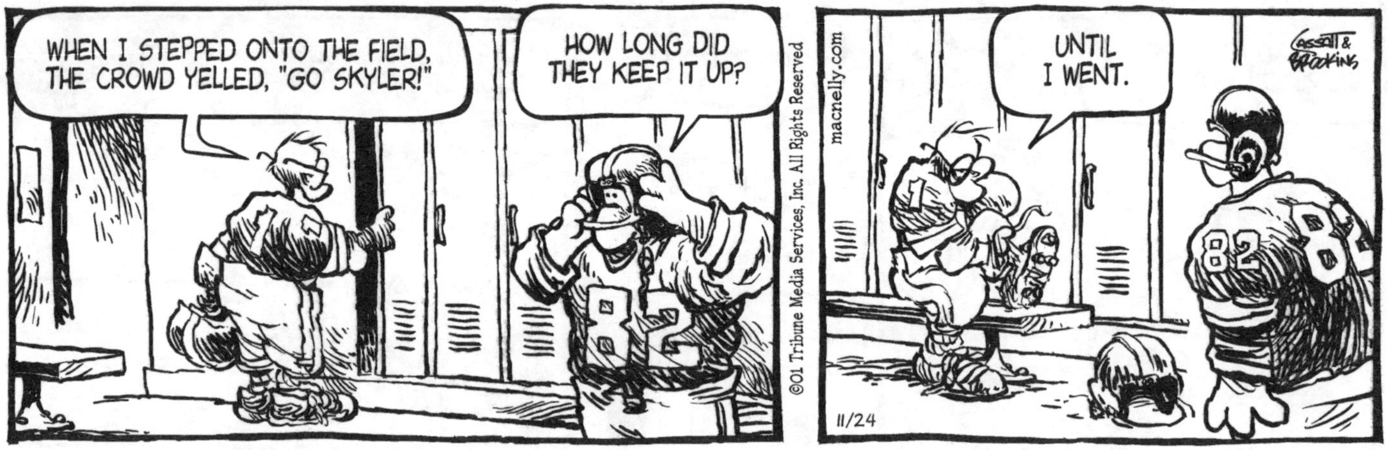
WHEN I STEPPED ONTO THE FIELD, THE CROWD YELLED, "GO SKYLER!"
HOW LONG DID THEY KEEP IT UP?
UNTIL I WENT.
©01 Tribune Media Services, Inc. All Rights Reserved
macnelly.com
11/24

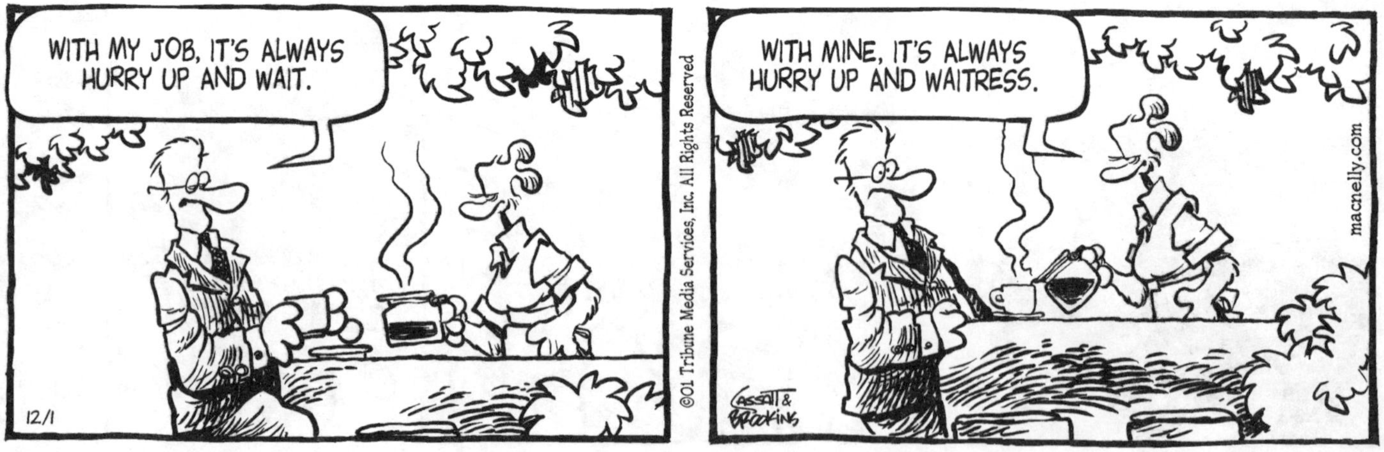
WITH MY JOB, IT'S ALWAYS HURRY UP AND WAIT.
WITH MINE, IT'S ALWAYS HURRY UP AND WAITRESS.
12/1
©01 Tribune Media Services, Inc. All Rights Reserved
macnelly.com

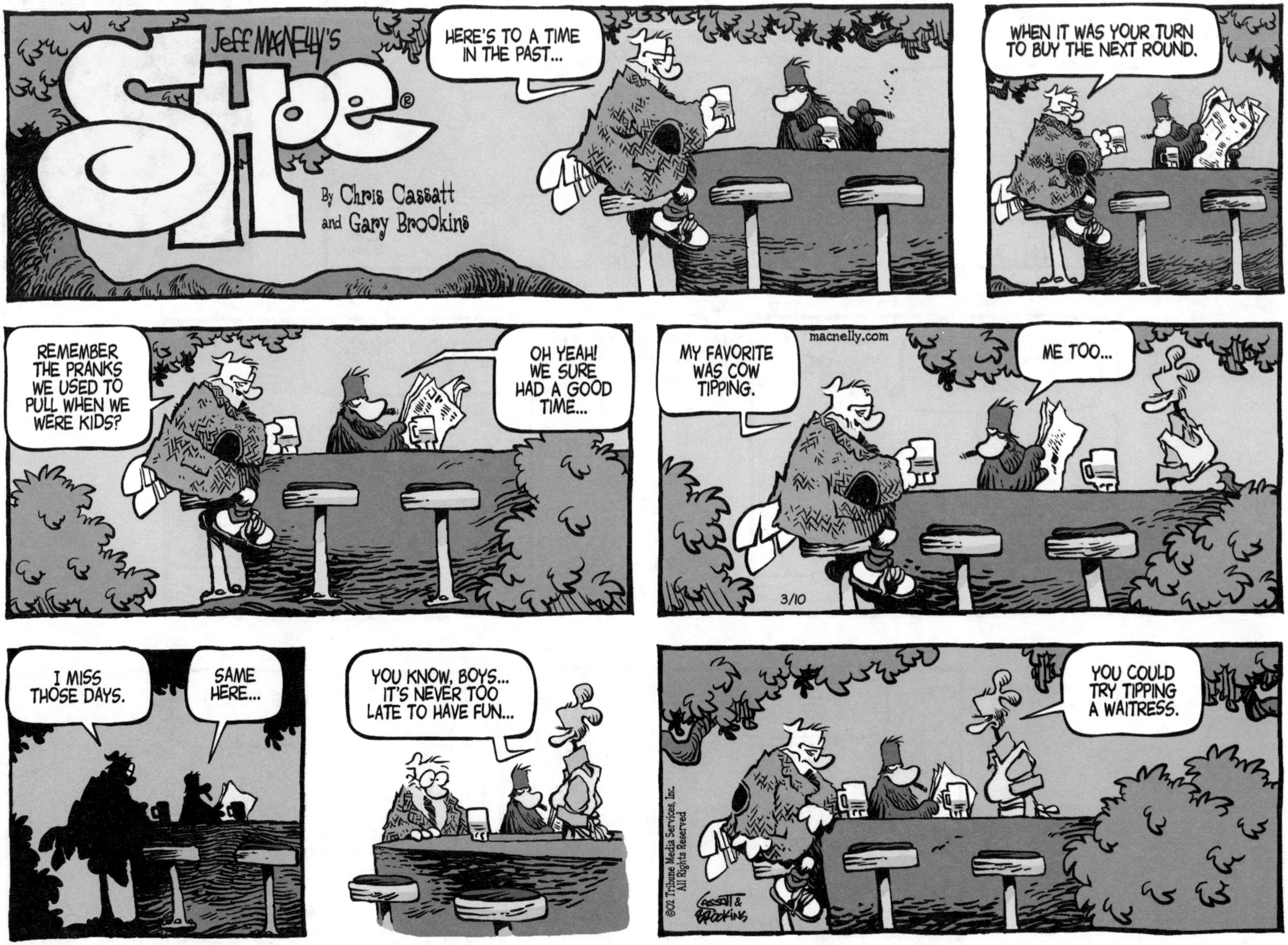
JEFF MACNELLY'S
SHOE®
By Chris Cassatt and Gary Brookins
HERE'S TO A TIME IN THE PAST...
WHEN IT WAS YOUR TURN TO BUY THE NEXT ROUND.
REMEMBER THE PRANKS WE USED TO PULL WHEN WE WERE KIDS?
OH YEAH! WE SURE HAD A GOOD TIME...
macnelly.com
MY FAVORITE WAS COW TIPPING.
ME TOO...
3/10
I MISS THOSE DAYS.
SAME HERE...
YOU KNOW, BOYS... IT'S NEVER TOO LATE TO HAVE FUN...
YOU COULD TRY TIPPING A WAITRESS.
©02 Tribune Media Services, Inc. All Rights Reserved
CASSATT & BROOKINS

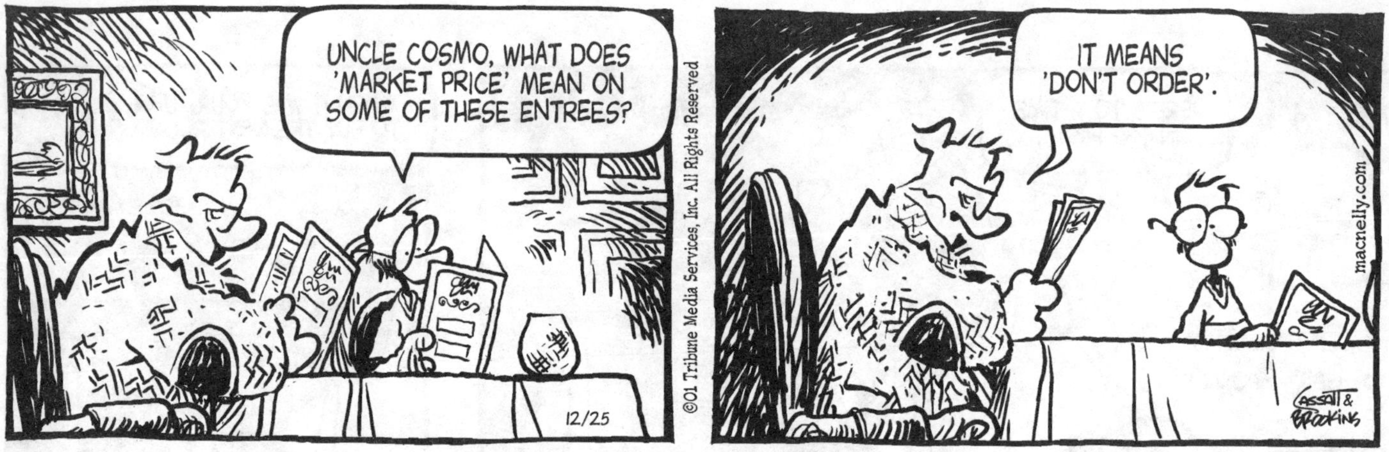
UNCLE COSMO, WHAT DOES 'MARKET PRICE' MEAN ON SOME OF THESE ENTREES?
12/25
©01 Tribune Media Services, Inc. All Rights Reserved
IT MEANS 'DON'T ORDER'.
macnelly.com
CASSATT & BROOKINS

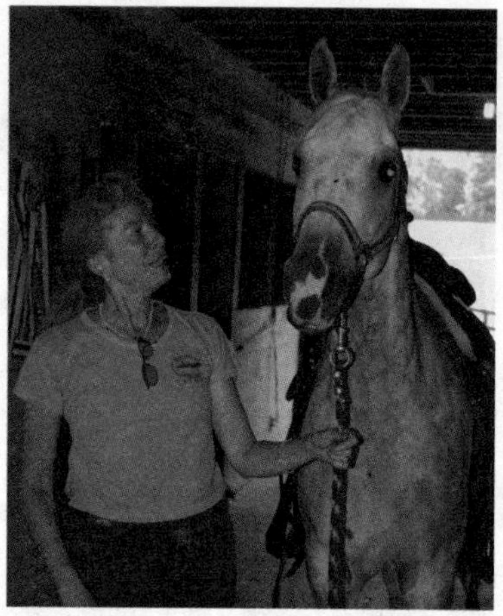

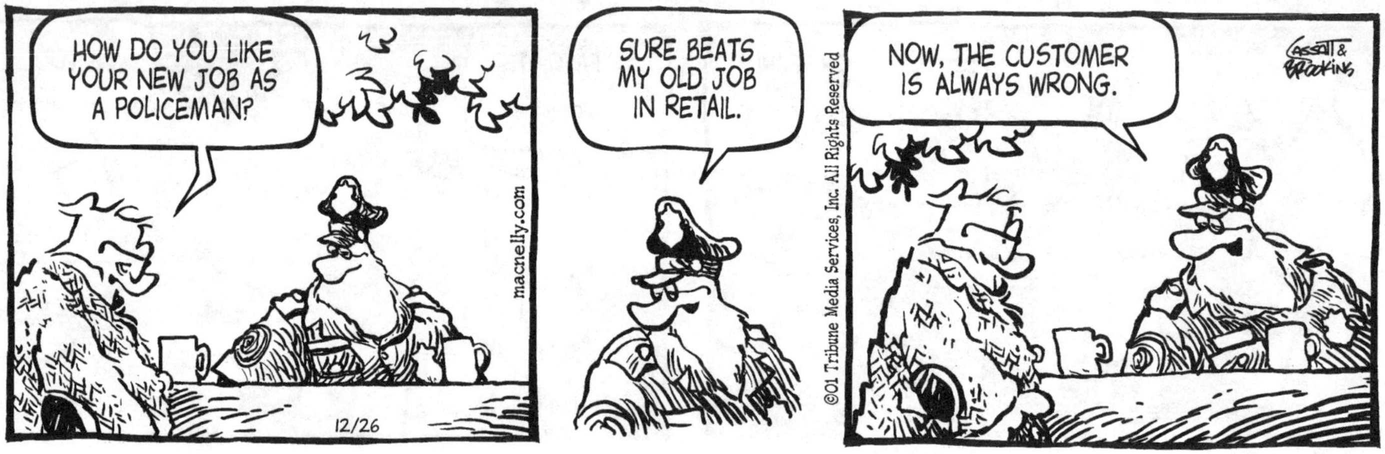
HOW DO YOU LIKE YOUR NEW JOB AS A POLICEMAN?
macnelly.com
12/26
SURE BEATS MY OLD JOB IN RETAIL.
©01 Tribune Media Services, Inc. All Rights Reserved
NOW, THE CUSTOMER IS ALWAYS WRONG.
CASSATT & BROOKINS

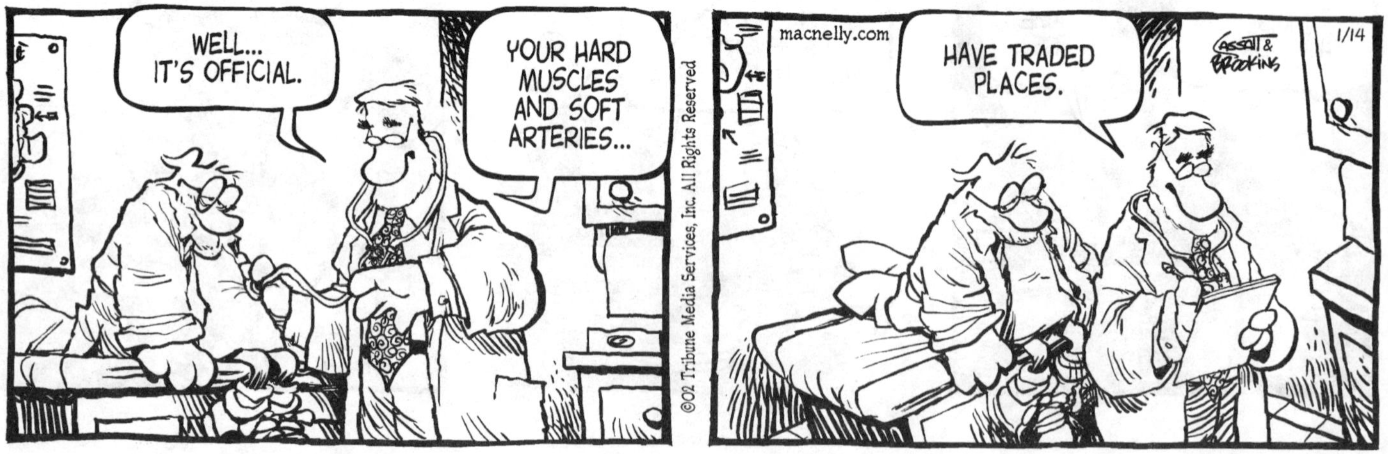
WELL... IT'S OFFICIAL.
YOUR HARD MUSCLES AND SOFT ARTERIES...
©02 Tribune Media Services, Inc. All Rights Reserved
macnelly.com
HAVE TRADED PLACES.
CASSATT & BROOKINS
1/14

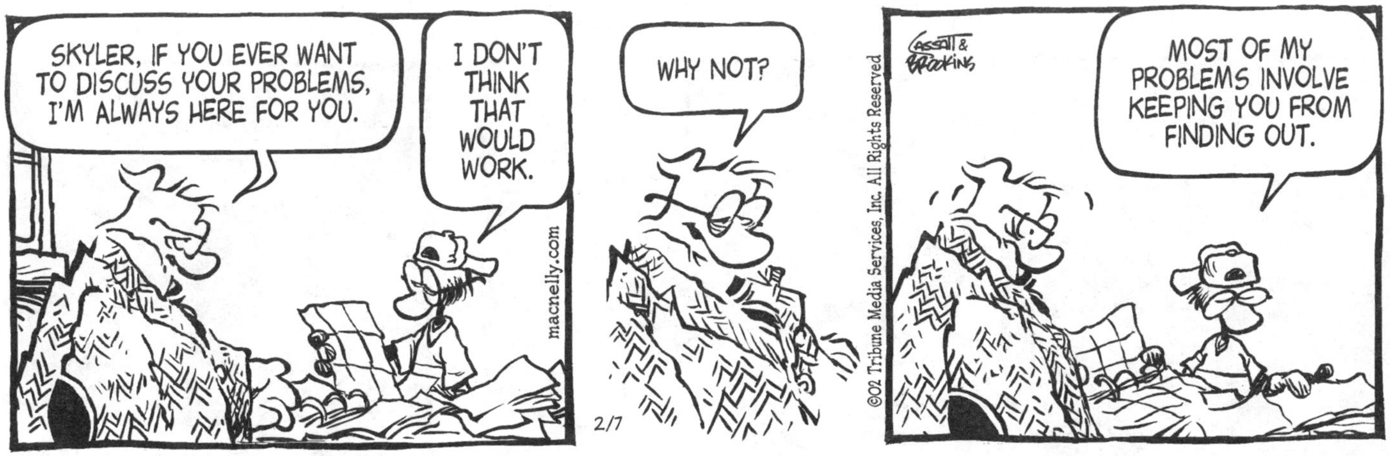
SKYLER, IF YOU EVER WANT TO DISCUSS YOUR PROBLEMS, I'M ALWAYS HERE FOR YOU.
I DON'T THINK THAT WOULD WORK.
macnelly.com
WHY NOT?
2/7
©02 Tribune Media Services, Inc. All Rights Reserved
CASSATT & BROOKINS
MOST OF MY PROBLEMS INVOLVE KEEPING YOU FROM FINDING OUT.

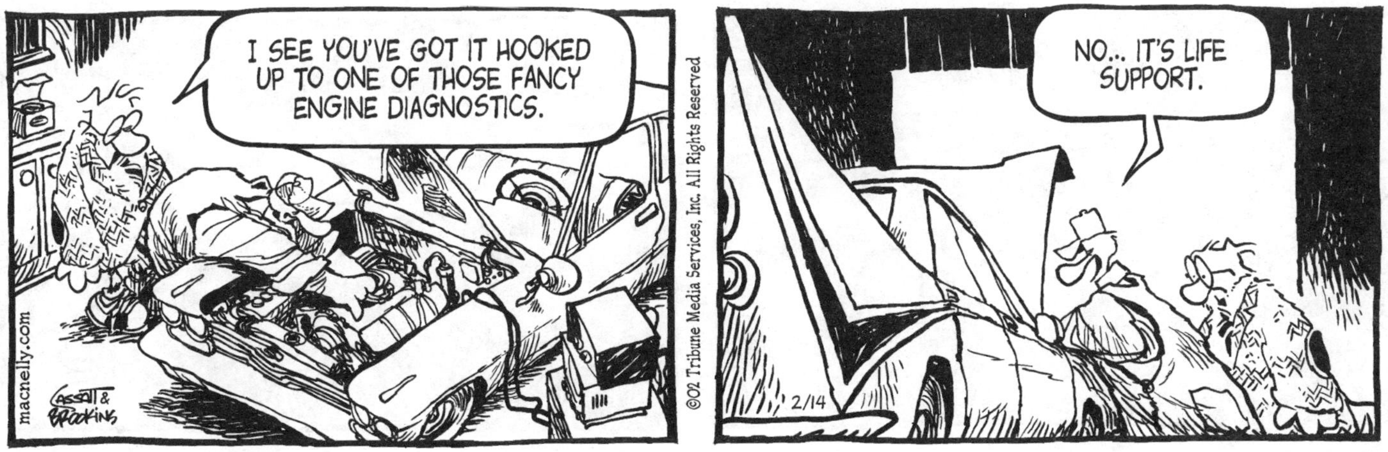
I SEE YOU'VE GOT IT HOOKED UP TO ONE OF THOSE FANCY ENGINE DIAGNOSTICS.
macnelly.com
CASSATT & BROOKINS
©02 Tribune Media Services, Inc. All Rights Reserved
NO... IT'S LIFE SUPPORT.
2/14

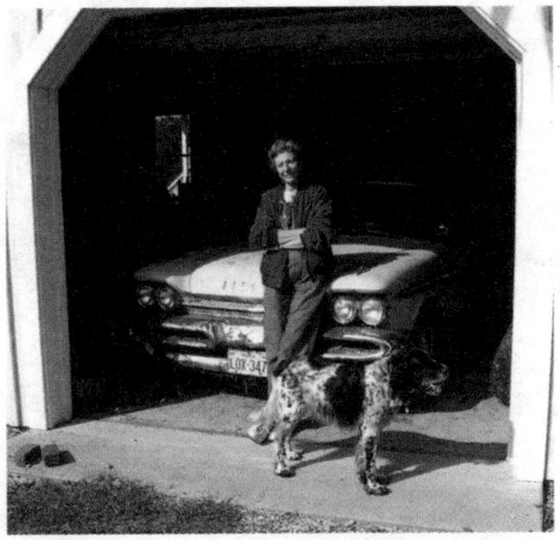

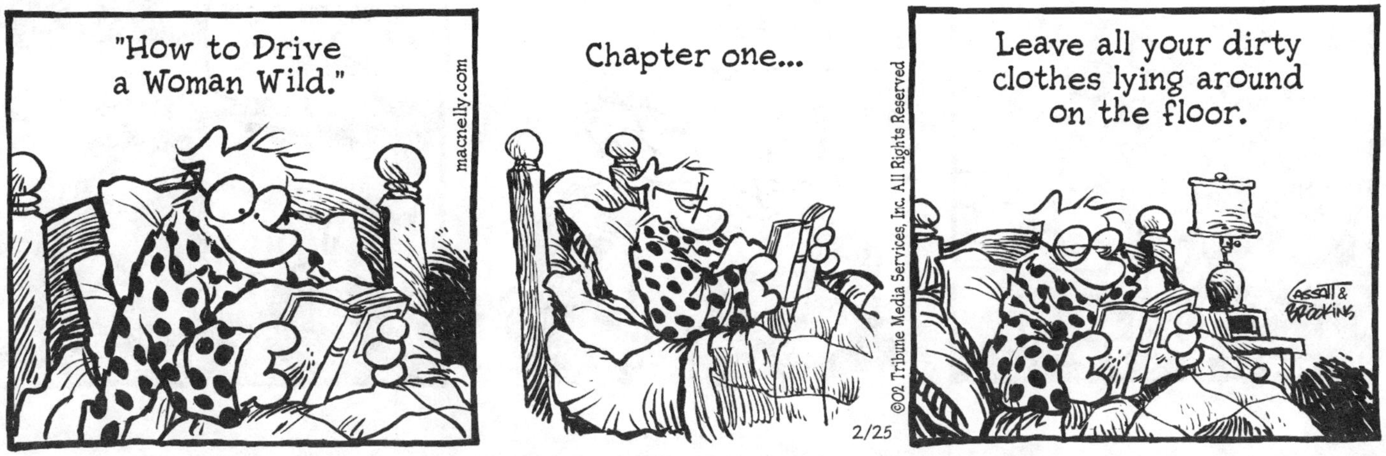
"How to Drive a Woman Wild."
macnelly.com
Chapter one...
2/25
©02 Tribune Media Services, Inc. All Rights Reserved
Leave all your dirty clothes lying around on the floor.
CASSATT & BROOKINS

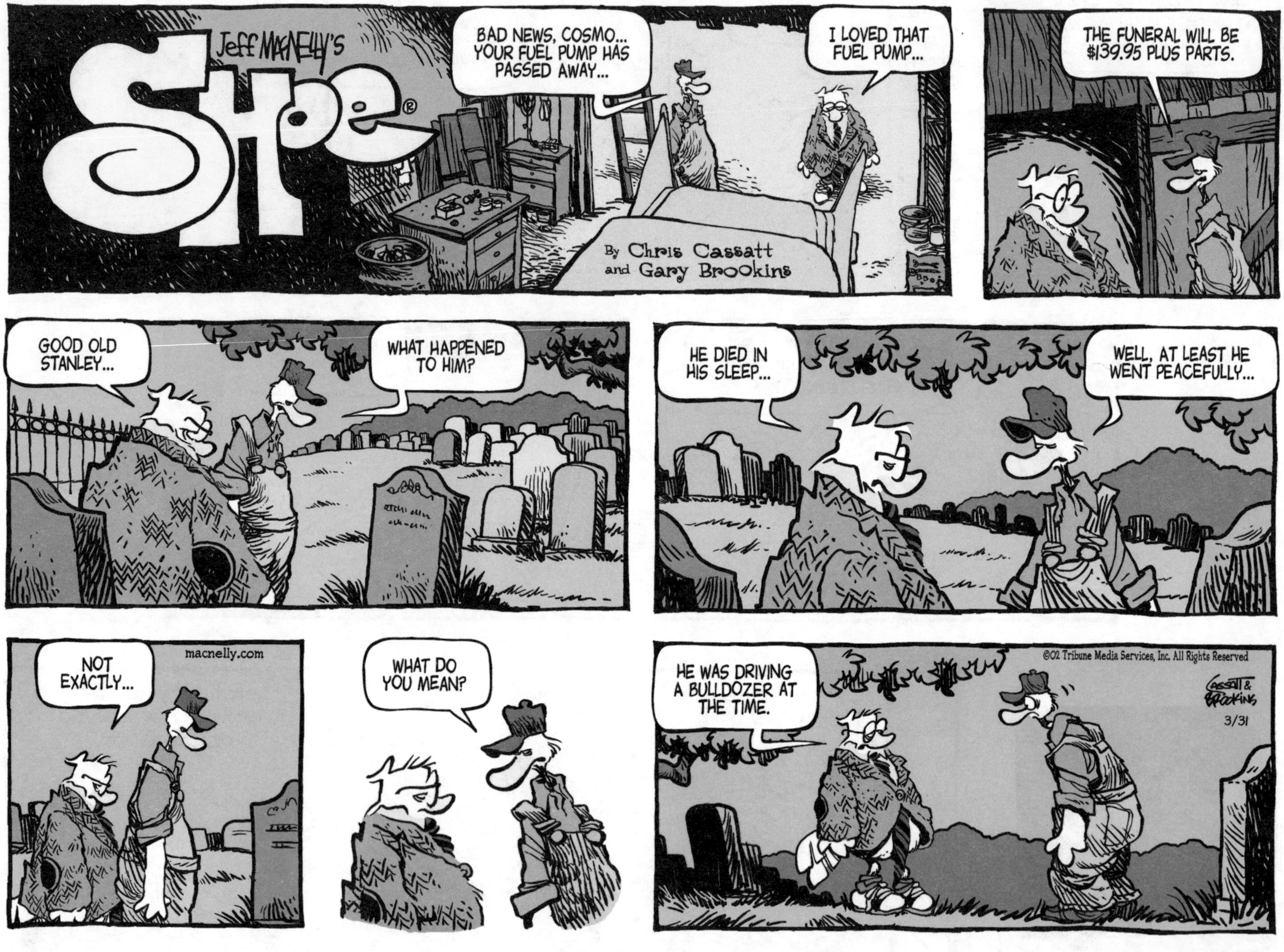

JEFF MACNELLY'S
SHOE
By Chris Cassatt and Gary Brookins
BAD NEWS, COSMO... YOUR FUEL PUMP HAS PASSED AWAY...
I LOVED THAT FUEL PUMP...
THE FUNERAL WILL BE $139.95 PLUS PARTS.
GOOD OLD STANLEY...
WHAT HAPPENED TO HIM?
HE DIED IN HIS SLEEP...
WELL, AT LEAST HE WENT PEACEFULLY...
NOT EXACTLY...
macnelly.com
WHAT DO YOU MEAN?
HE WAS DRIVING A BULLDOZER AT THE TIME.
©02 Tribune Media Services, Inc. All Rights Reserved
CASSATT & BROOKINS
3/31

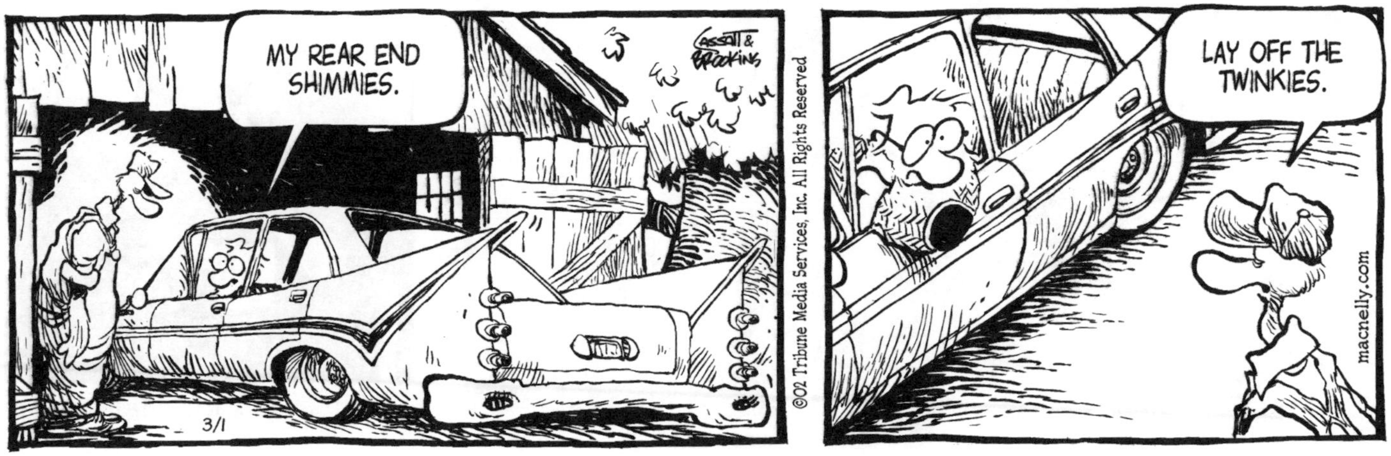
CASSATT & BROOKINS
MY REAR END SHIMMIES.
3/1
©02 Tribune Media Services, Inc. All Rights Reserved
LAY OFF THE TWINKIES.
macnelly.com

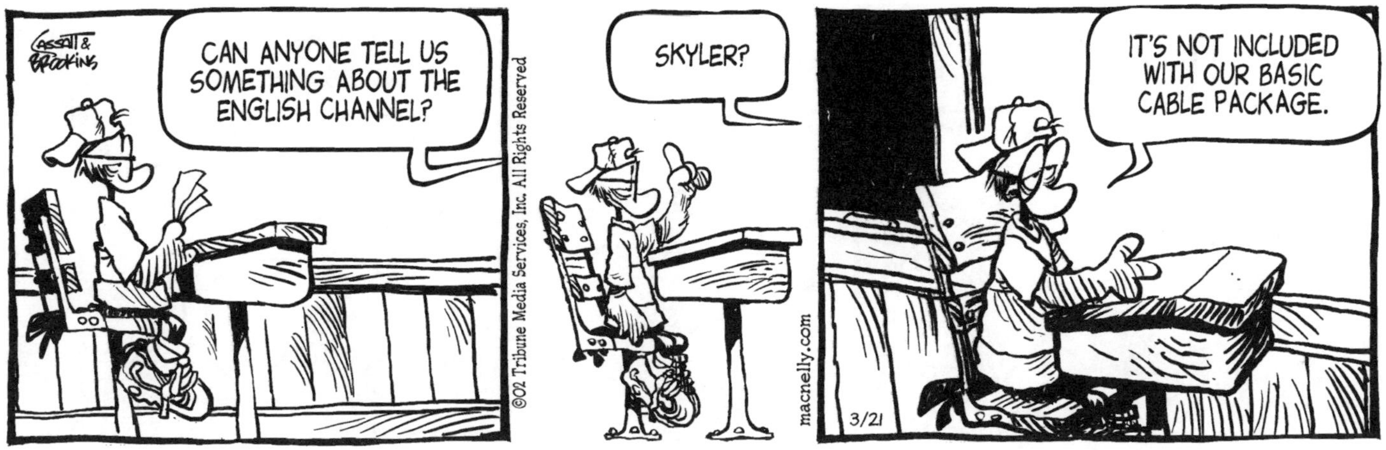
CASSATT & BROOKINS
CAN ANYONE TELL US SOMETHING ABOUT THE ENGLISH CHANNEL?
©02 Tribune Media Services, Inc. All Rights Reserved
SKYLER?
macnelly.com
IT'S NOT INCLUDED WITH OUR BASIC CABLE PACKAGE.
3/21

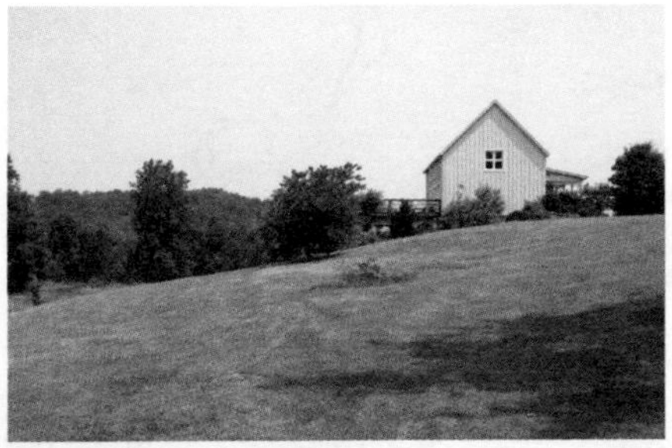
The farmhouse

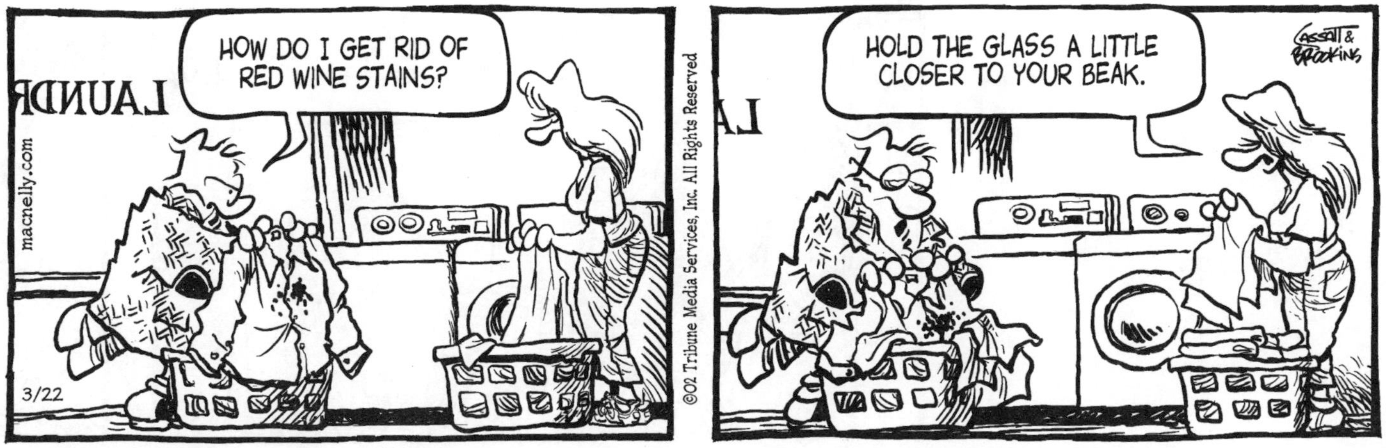
macnelly.com
HOW DO I GET RID OF RED WINE STAINS?
3/22
©02 Tribune Media Services, Inc. All Rights Reserved
HOLD THE GLASS A LITTLE CLOSER TO YOUR BEAK.
CASSATT & BROOKINS

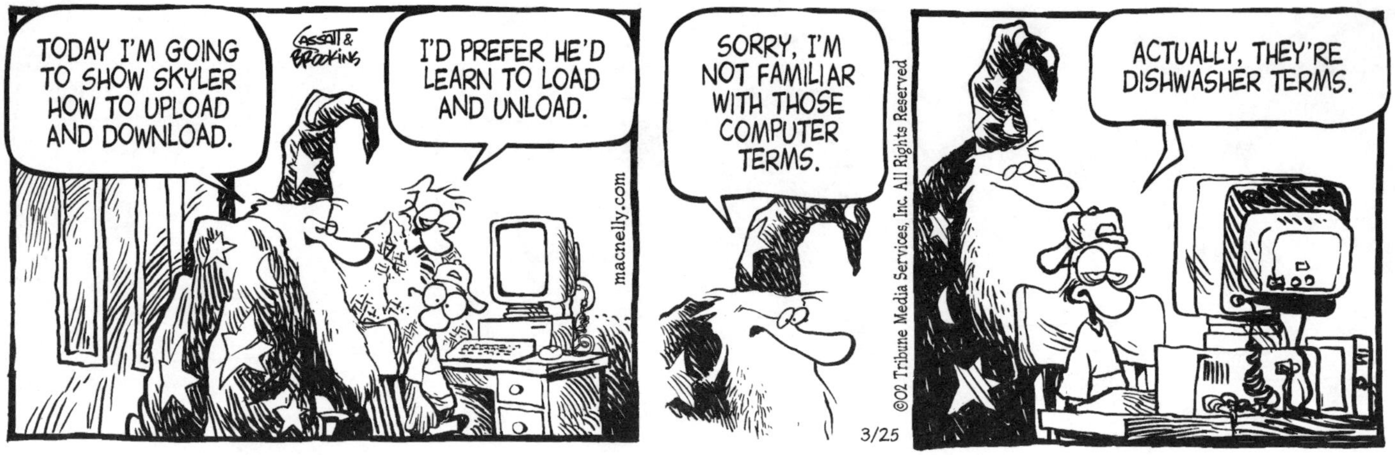
TODAY I'M GOING TO SHOW SKYLER HOW TO UPLOAD AND DOWNLOAD.
I'D PREFER HE'D LEARN TO LOAD AND UNLOAD.
SORRY, I'M NOT FAMILIAR WITH THOSE COMPUTER TERMS.
ACTUALLY, THEY'RE DISHWASHER TERMS.
CASSATT & BROOKINS
macnelly.com
©02 Tribune Media Services, Inc. All Rights Reserved
3/25

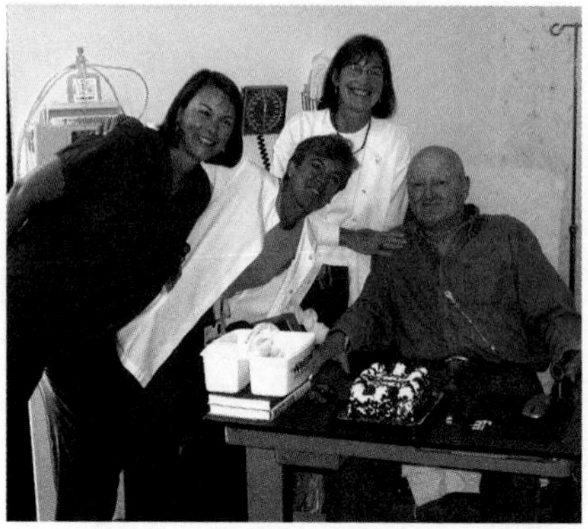

Chris and his chemosabes

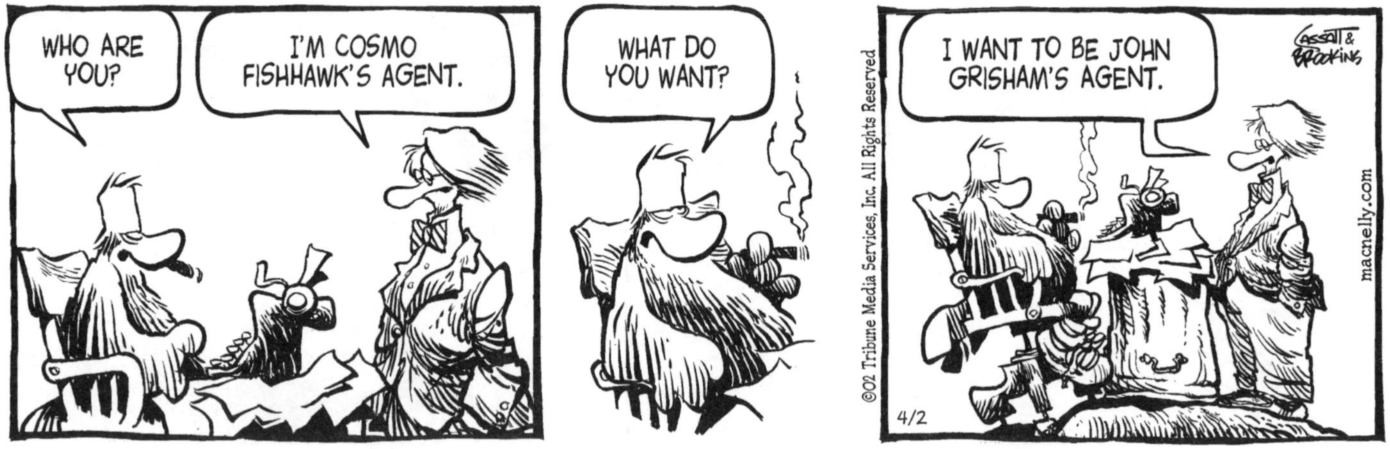
WHO ARE YOU?
I'M COSMO FISHHAWK'S AGENT.
WHAT DO YOU WANT?
I WANT TO BE JOHN GRISHAM'S AGENT.
CASSATT & BROOKINS
macnelly.com
©02 Tribune Media Services, Inc. All Rights Reserved
4/2

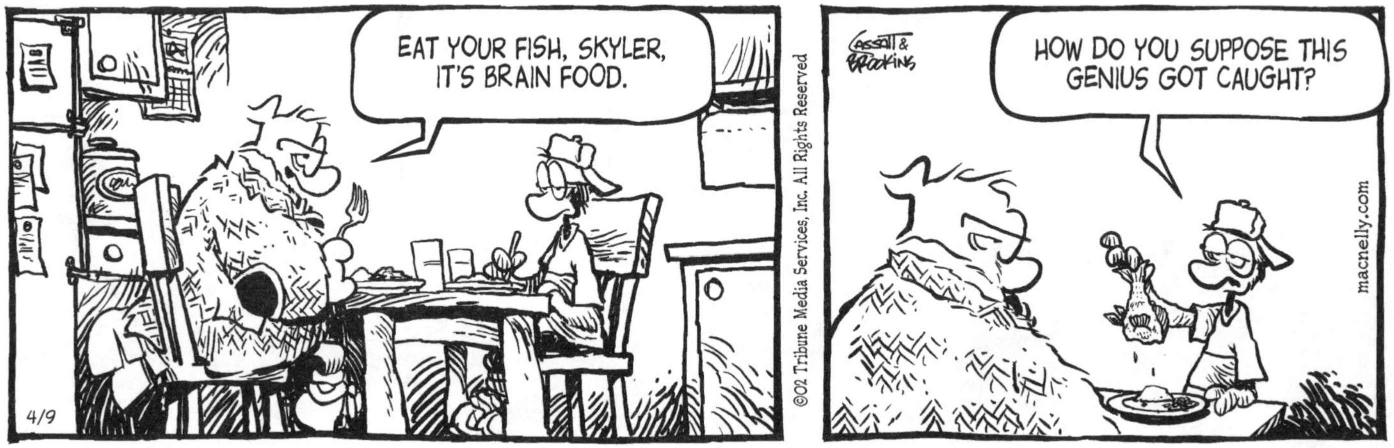
EAT YOUR FISH, SKYLER, IT'S BRAIN FOOD.
HOW DO YOU SUPPOSE THIS GENIUS GOT CAUGHT?
CASSATT & BROOKINS
macnelly.com
©02 Tribune Media Services, Inc. All Rights Reserved
4/9

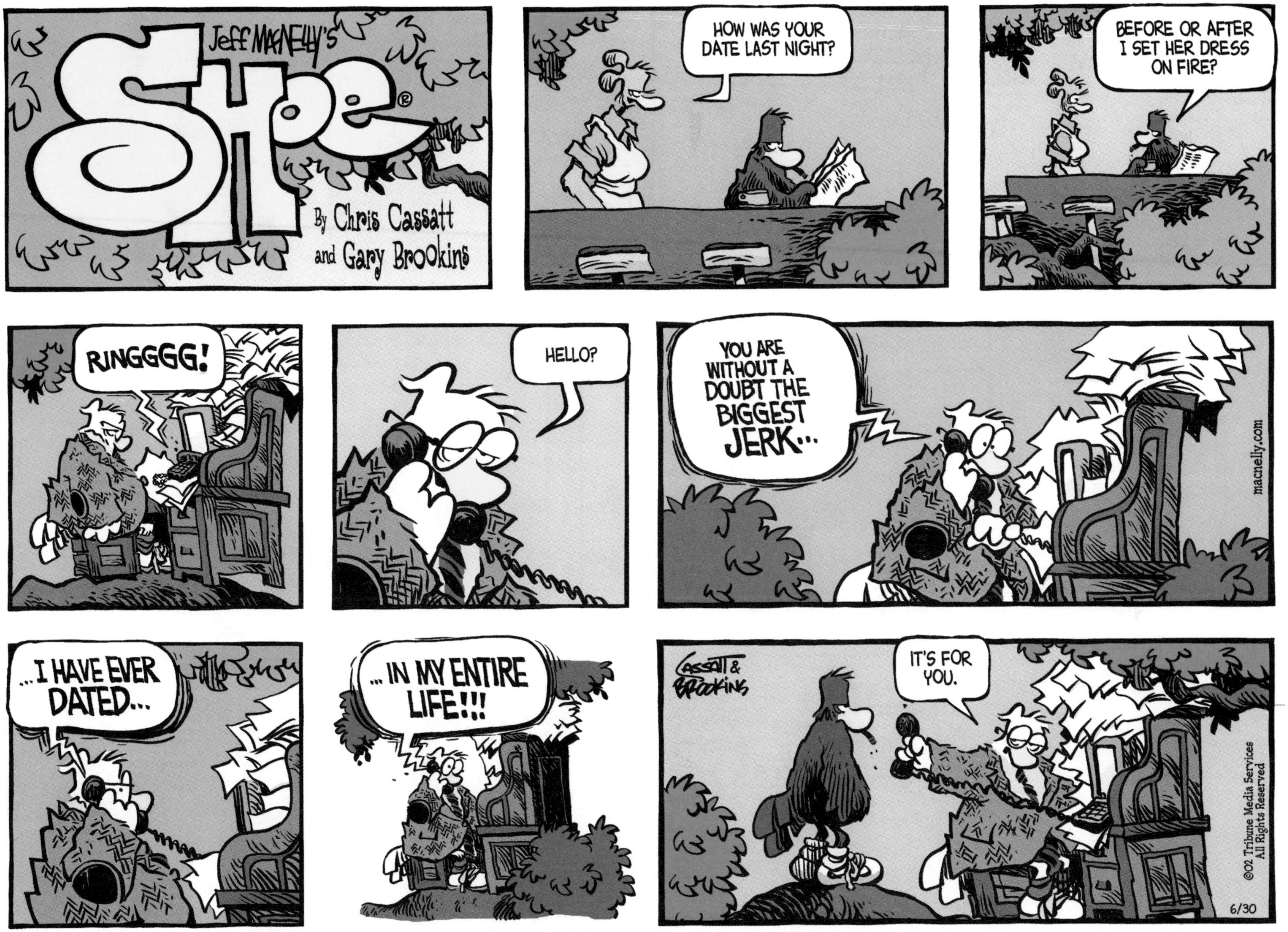
Jeff MacNelly's
Shoe®
By Chris Cassatt and Gary Brookins
HOW WAS YOUR DATE LAST NIGHT?
BEFORE OR AFTER I SET HER DRESS ON FIRE?
RINGGGG!
HELLO?
YOU ARE WITHOUT A DOUBT THE BIGGEST JERK...
macnelly.com
...I HAVE EVER DATED...
...IN MY ENTIRE LIFE!!!
CASSATT & BROOKINS
IT'S FOR YOU.
©02 Tribune Media Services All Rights Reserved
6/30

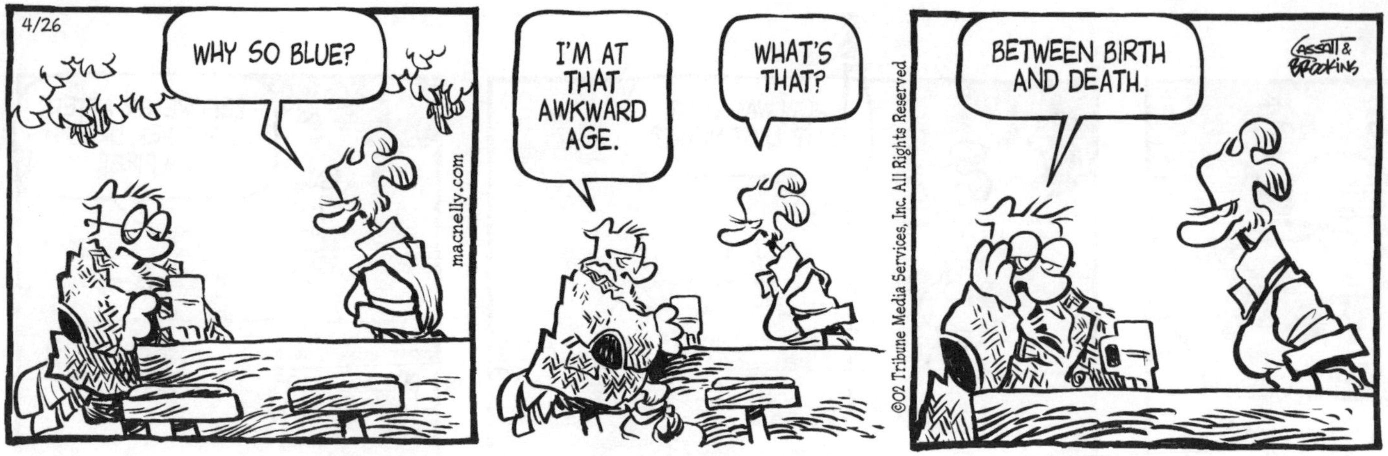
4/26
WHY SO BLUE?
macnelly.com
I'M AT THAT AWKWARD AGE.
WHAT'S THAT?
©02 Tribune Media Services, Inc. All Rights Reserved
BETWEEN BIRTH AND DEATH.
CASSATT & BROOKINS

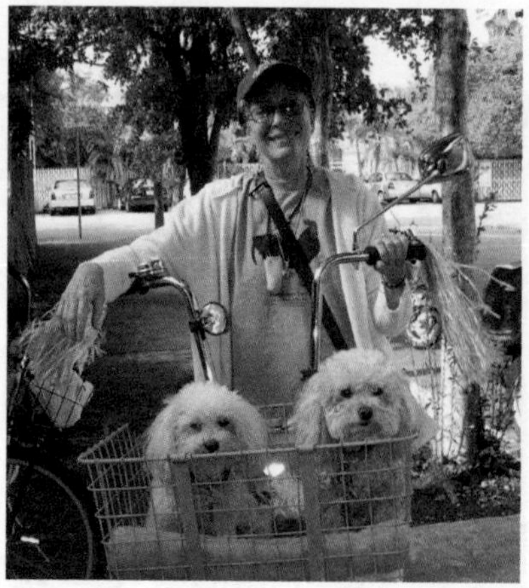

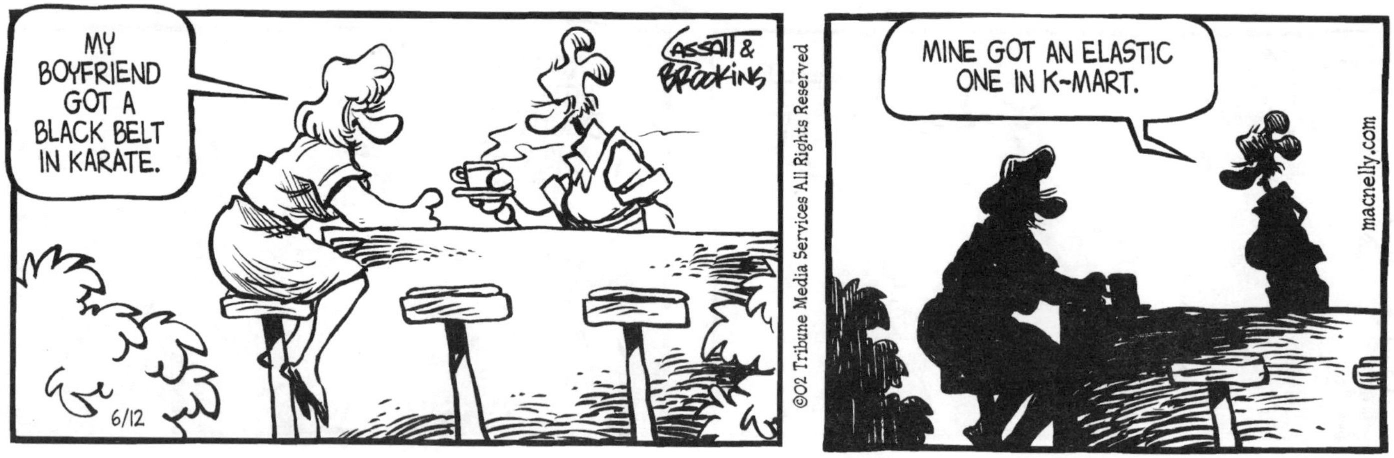
MY BOYFRIEND GOT A BLACK BELT IN KARATE.
CASSATT & BROOKINS
6/12
©02 Tribune Media Services All Rights Reserved
MINE GOT AN ELASTIC ONE IN K-MART.
macnelly.com

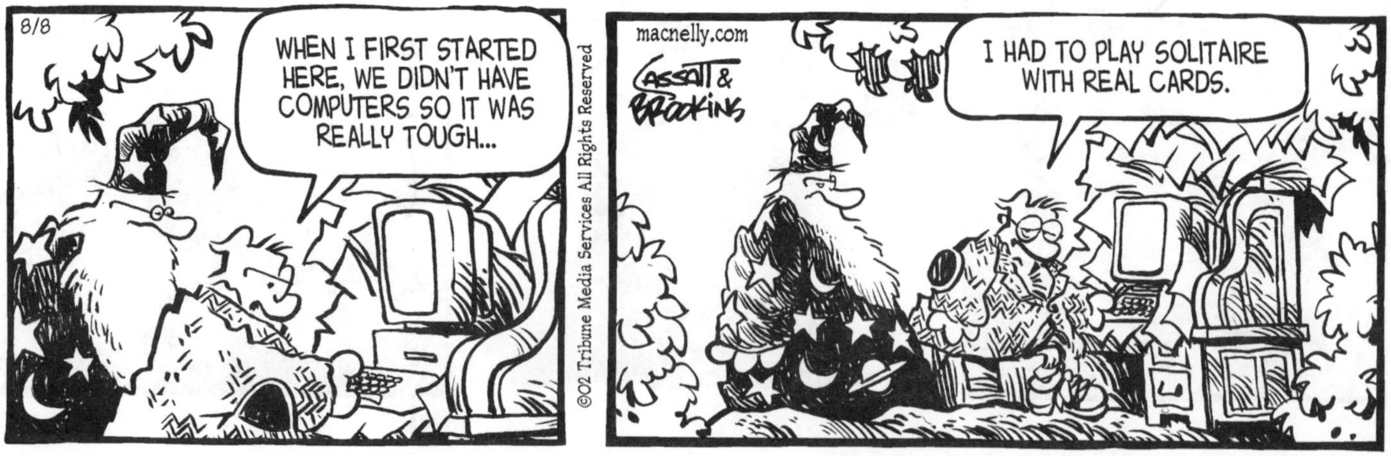
8/8
WHEN I FIRST STARTED HERE, WE DIDN'T HAVE COMPUTERS SO IT WAS REALLY TOUGH...
©02 Tribune Media Services All Rights Reserved
macnelly.com
CASSATT & BROOKINS
I HAD TO PLAY SOLITAIRE WITH REAL CARDS.

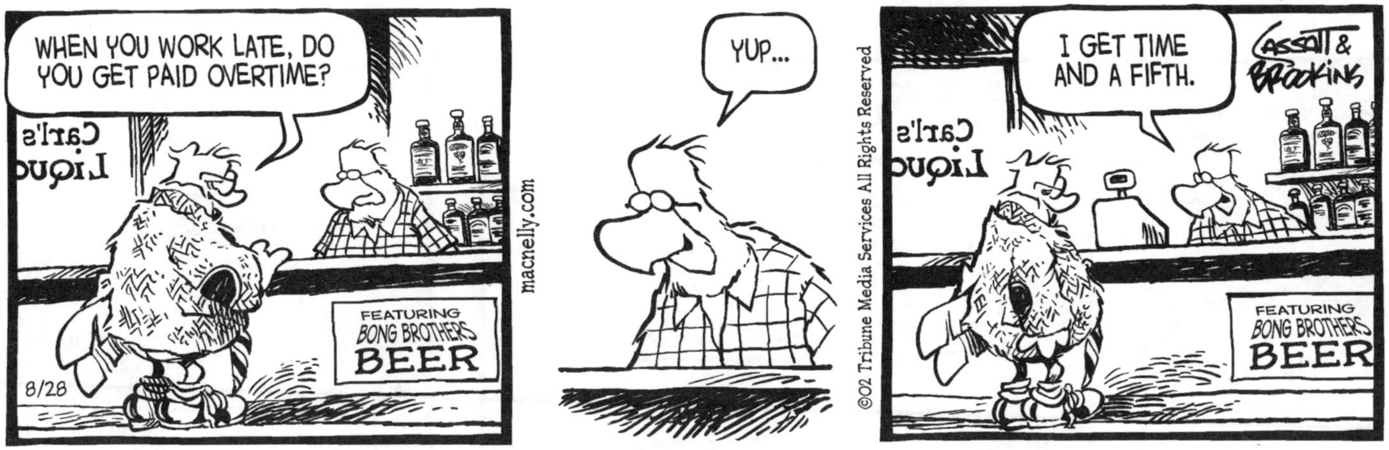
8/28
WHEN YOU WORK LATE, DO YOU GET PAID OVERTIME?
FEATURING BONG BROTHERS BEER
macnelly.com
YUP...
©02 Tribune Media Services All Rights Reserved
I GET TIME AND A FIFTH.
CASSATT & BROOKINS
FEATURING BONG BROTHERS BEER

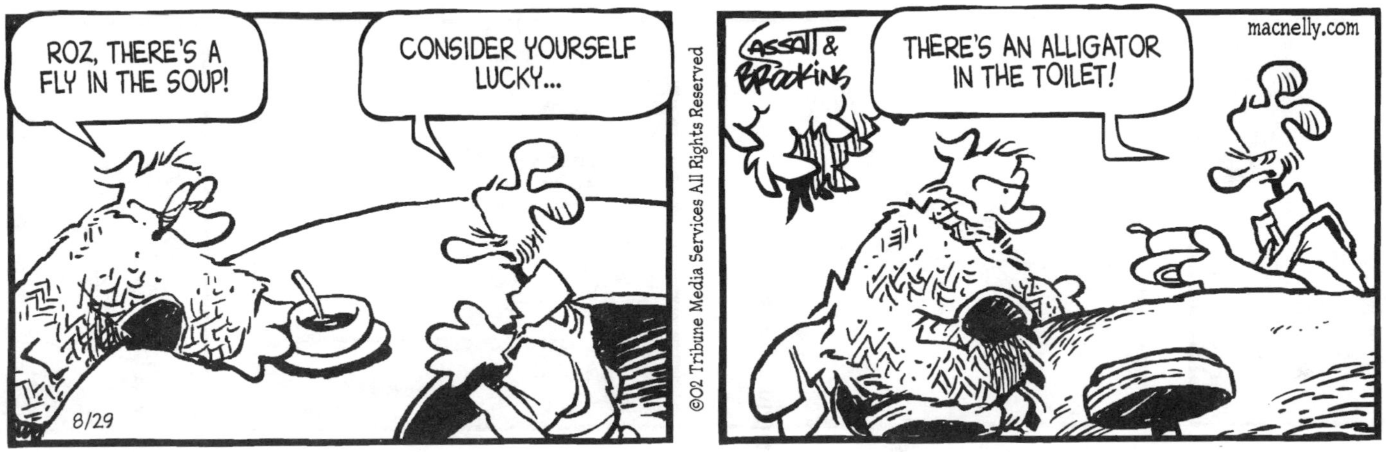
ROZ, THERE'S A FLY IN THE SOUP!
CONSIDER YOURSELF LUCKY...
8/29
©02 Tribune Media Services All Rights Reserved
CASSATT & BROOKINS
THERE'S AN ALLIGATOR IN THE TOILET!
macnelly.com

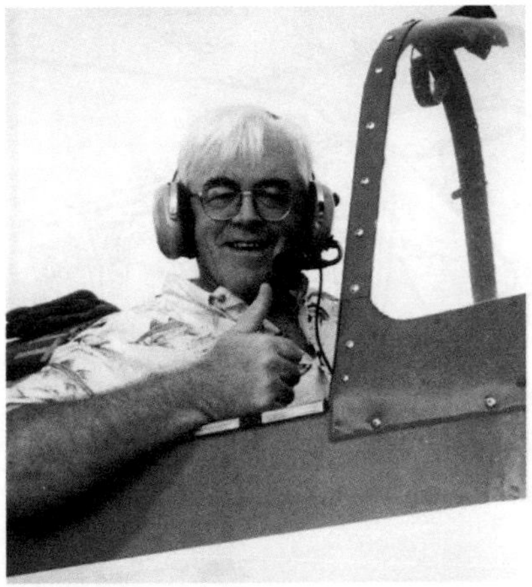

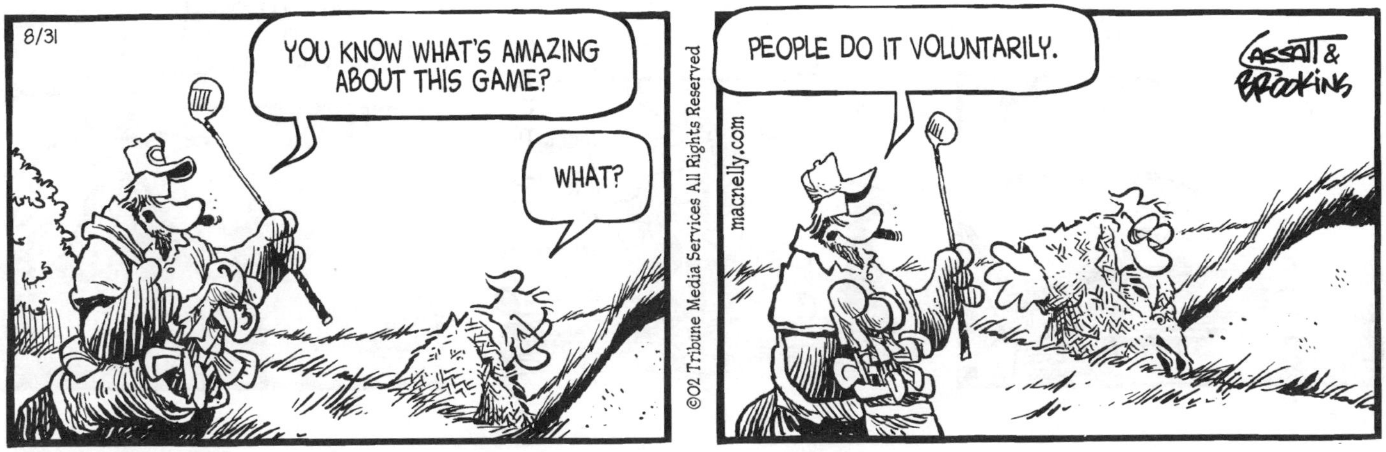
8/31
YOU KNOW WHAT'S AMAZING ABOUT THIS GAME?
WHAT?
©02 Tribune Media Services All Rights Reserved
macnelly.com
PEOPLE DO IT VOLUNTARILY.
CASSATT & BROOKINS

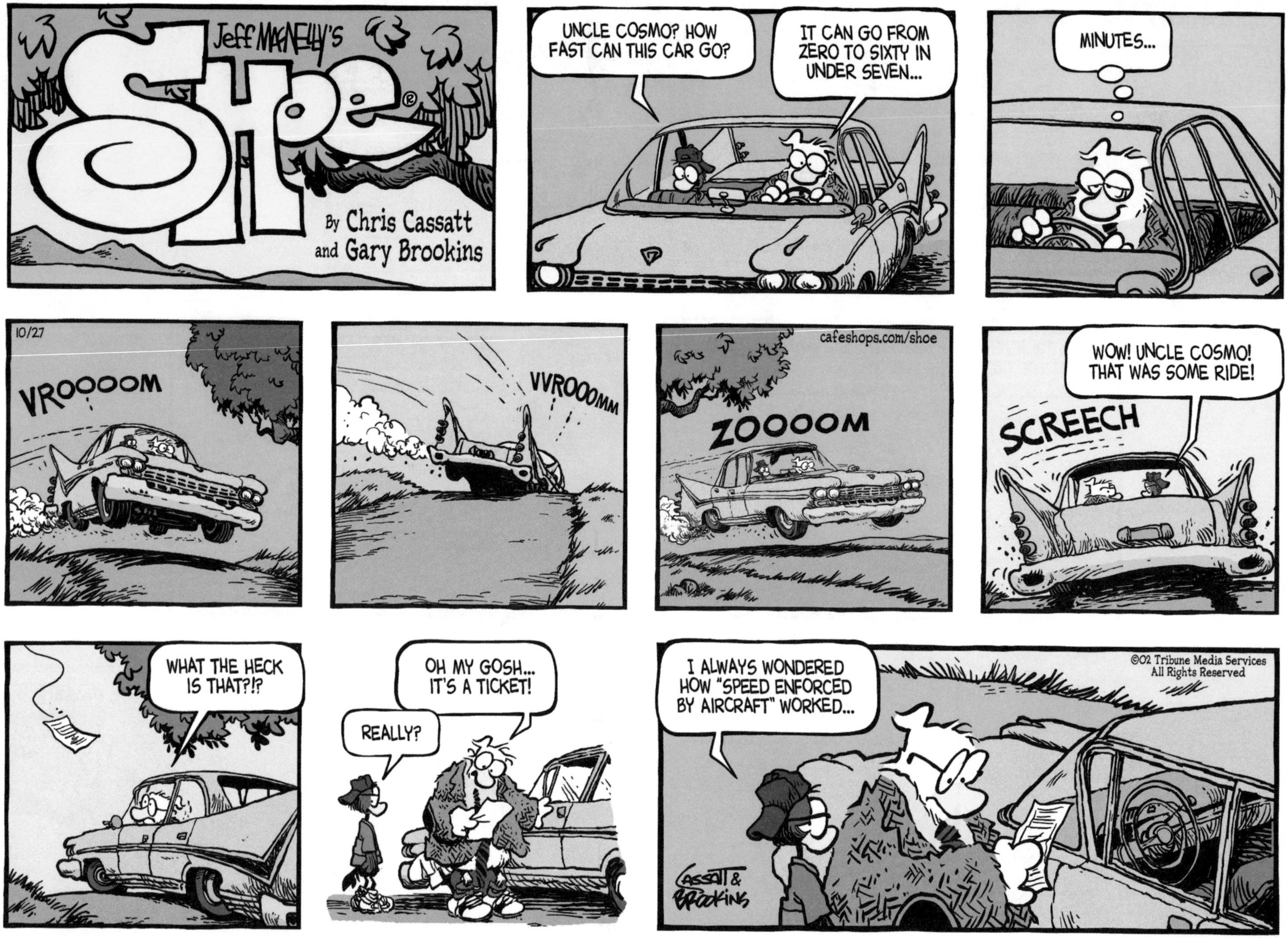
Jeff MacNelly's
Shoe®
By Chris Cassatt
and Gary Brookins
UNCLE COSMO? HOW FAST CAN THIS CAR GO?
IT CAN GO FROM ZERO TO SIXTY IN UNDER SEVEN...
MINUTES...
10/27
VROOOOM
VVROOOMM
cafeshops.com/shoe
ZOOOOM
SCREECH
WOW! UNCLE COSMO! THAT WAS SOME RIDE!
WHAT THE HECK IS THAT?!?
OH MY GOSH... IT'S A TICKET!
REALLY?
I ALWAYS WONDERED HOW "SPEED ENFORCED BY AIRCRAFT" WORKED...
©02 Tribune Media Services
All Rights Reserved
CASSATT & BROOKINS

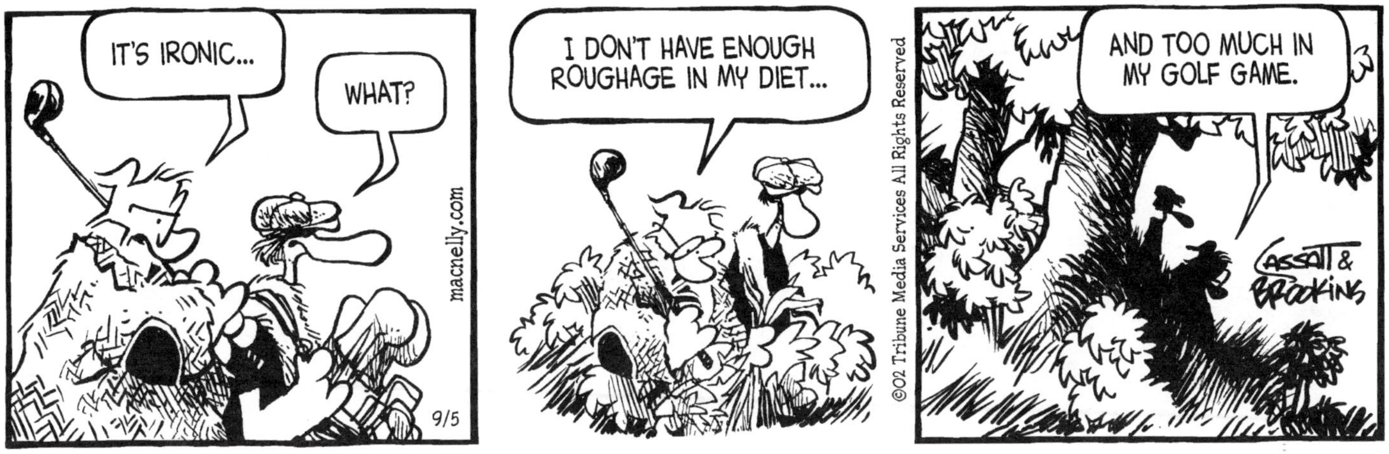
IT'S IRONIC...
WHAT?
macnelly.com
9/5
I DON'T HAVE ENOUGH ROUGHAGE IN MY DIET...
©02 Tribune Media Services All Rights Reserved
AND TOO MUCH IN MY GOLF GAME.
CASSATT & BROOKINS

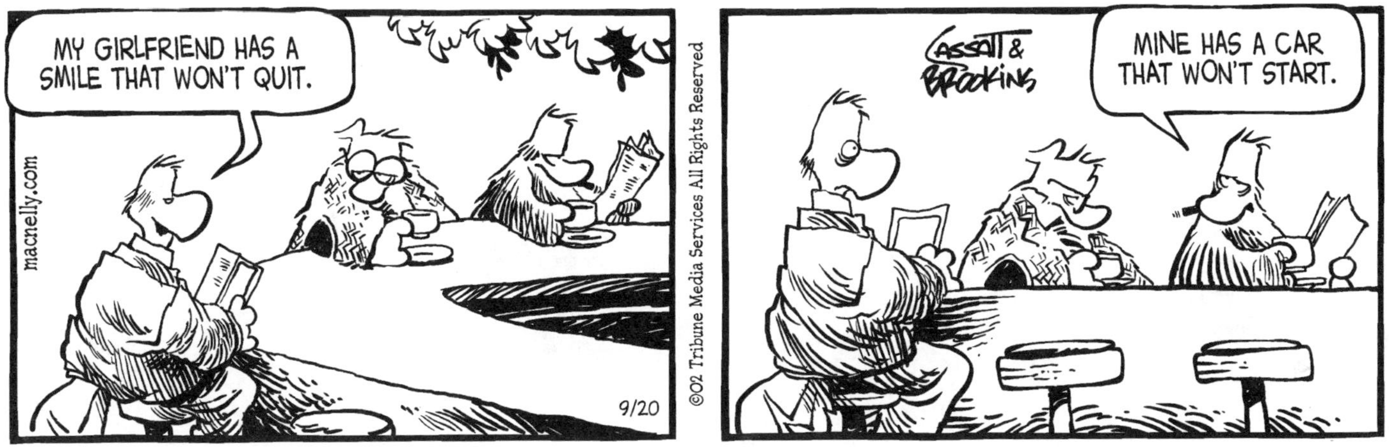
MY GIRLFRIEND HAS A SMILE THAT WON'T QUIT.
macnelly.com
9/20
©02 Tribune Media Services All Rights Reserved
CASSATT & BROOKINS
MINE HAS A CAR THAT WON'T START.

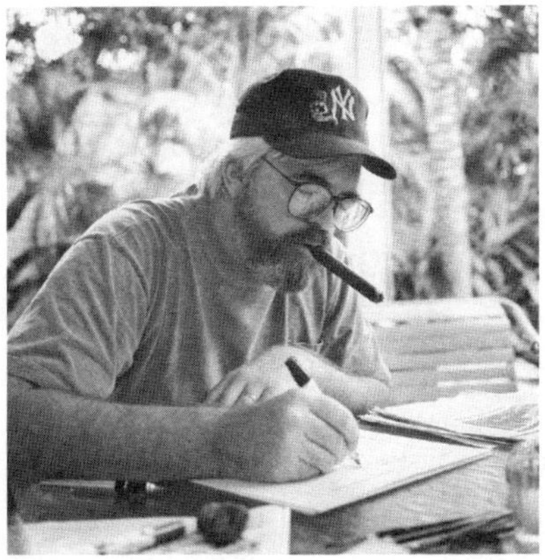

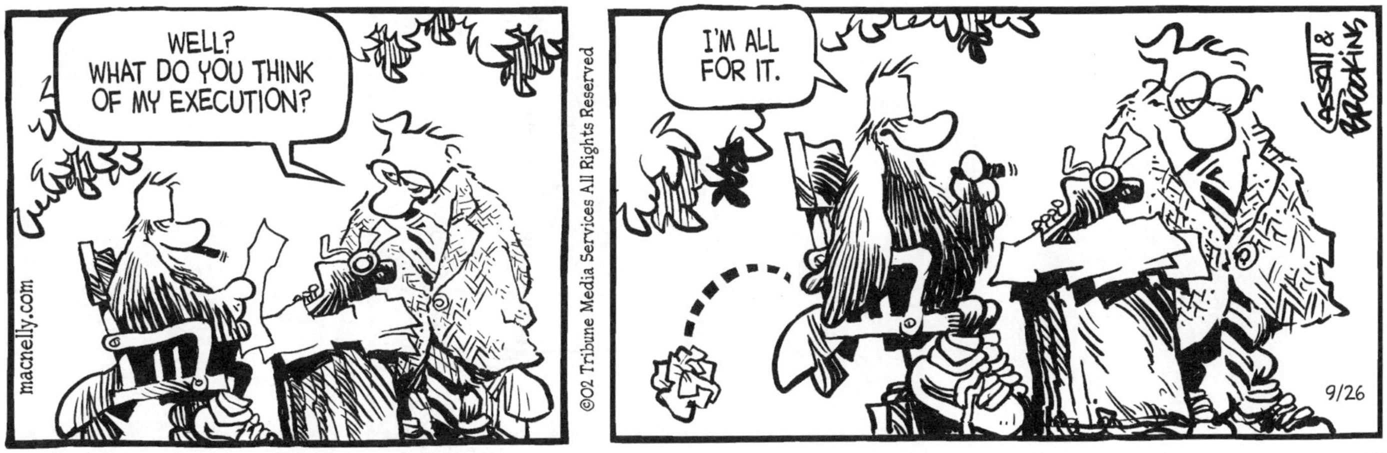
WELL? WHAT DO YOU THINK OF MY EXECUTION?
macnelly.com
©02 Tribune Media Services All Rights Reserved
I'M ALL FOR IT.
CASSATT & BROOKINS
9/26

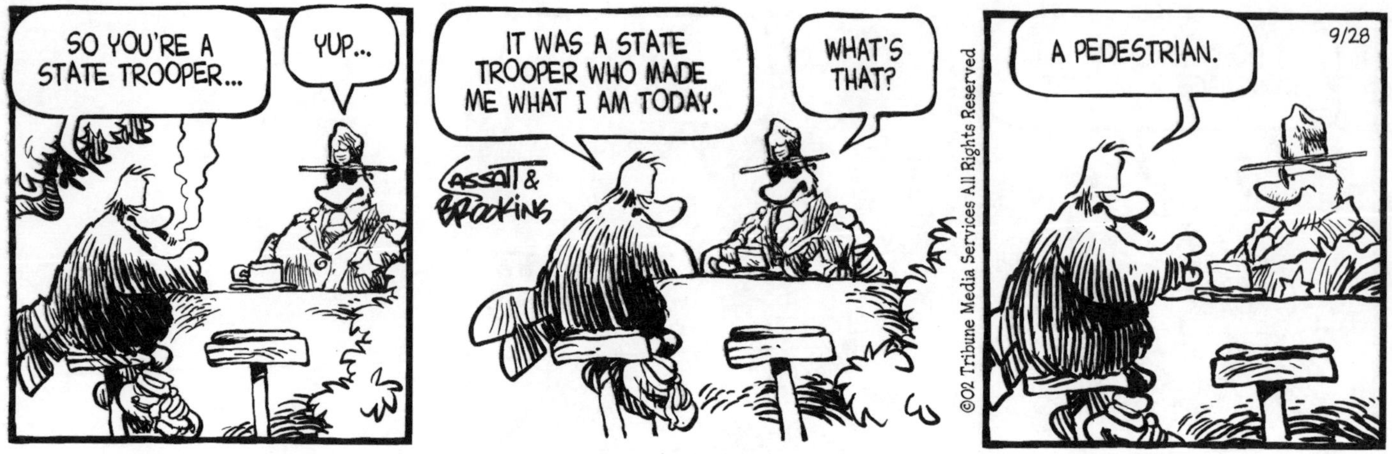
SO YOU'RE A STATE TROOPER...
YUP...
IT WAS A STATE TROOPER WHO MADE ME WHAT I AM TODAY.
CASSATT & BROOKINS
WHAT'S THAT?
©02 Tribune Media Services All Rights Reserved
9/28
A PEDESTRIAN.

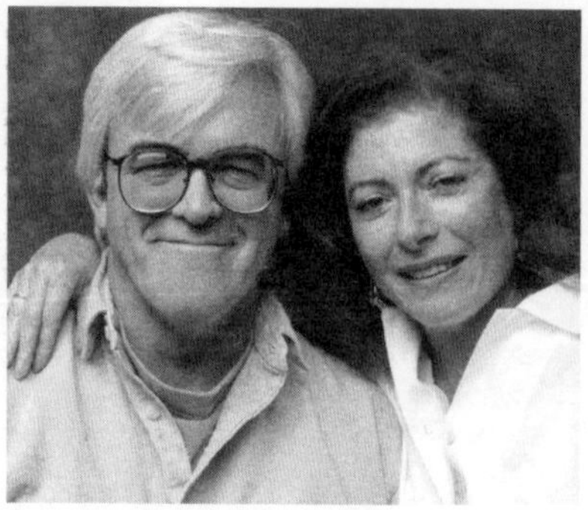

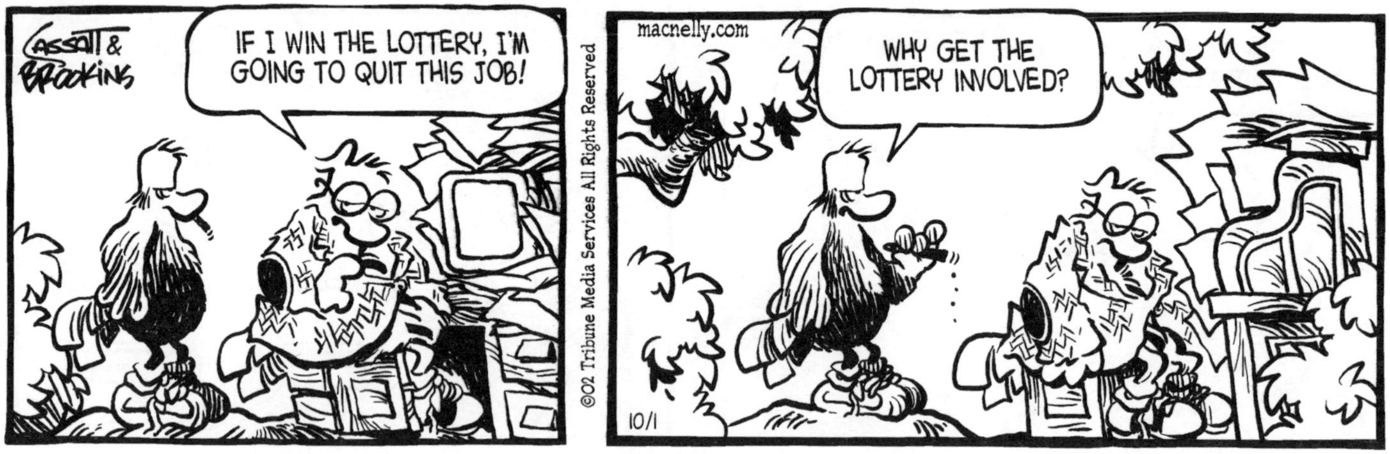
CASSATT & BROOKINS
IF I WIN THE LOTTERY, I'M GOING TO QUIT THIS JOB!
©02 Tribune Media Services All Rights Reserved
macnelly.com
WHY GET THE LOTTERY INVOLVED?
10/1

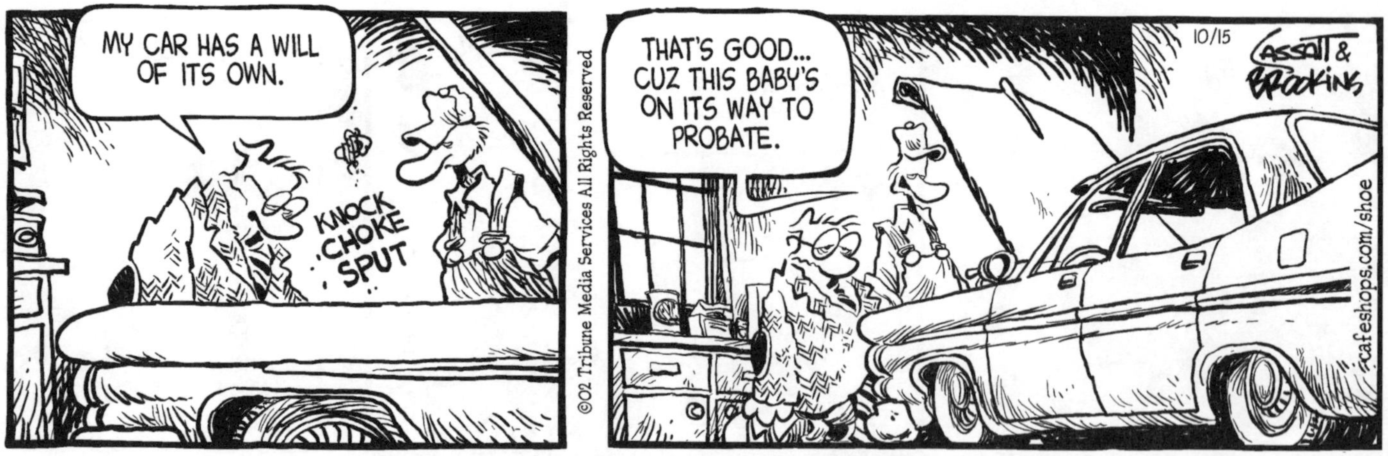
MY CAR HAS A WILL OF ITS OWN.
KNOCK CHOKE SPUT
©02 Tribune Media Services All Rights Reserved
THAT'S GOOD... CUZ THIS BABY'S ON ITS WAY TO PROBATE.
10/15
CASSATT & BROOKINS
cafeshops.com/shoe

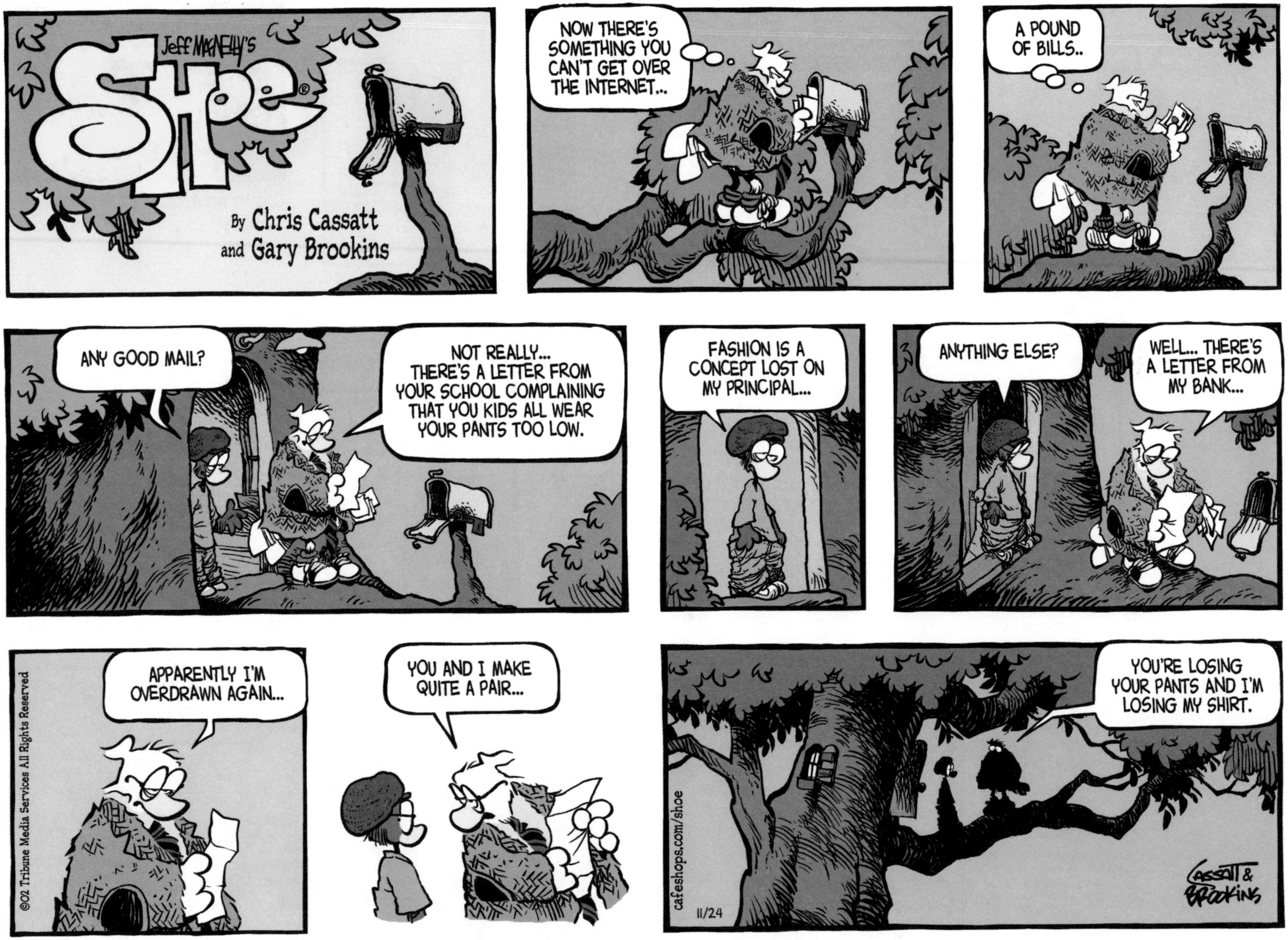

JEFF MACNELLY'S
SHOE®
By Chris Cassatt and Gary Brookins
NOW THERE'S SOMETHING YOU CAN'T GET OVER THE INTERNET...
A POUND OF BILLS..
ANY GOOD MAIL?
NOT REALLY... THERE'S A LETTER FROM YOUR SCHOOL COMPLAINING THAT YOU KIDS ALL WEAR YOUR PANTS TOO LOW.
FASHION IS A CONCEPT LOST ON MY PRINCIPAL...
ANYTHING ELSE?
WELL... THERE'S A LETTER FROM MY BANK...
APPARENTLY I'M OVERDRAWN AGAIN...
YOU AND I MAKE QUITE A PAIR...
YOU'RE LOSING YOUR PANTS AND I'M LOSING MY SHIRT.
CASSATT & BROOKINS
11/24
cafeshops.com/shoe

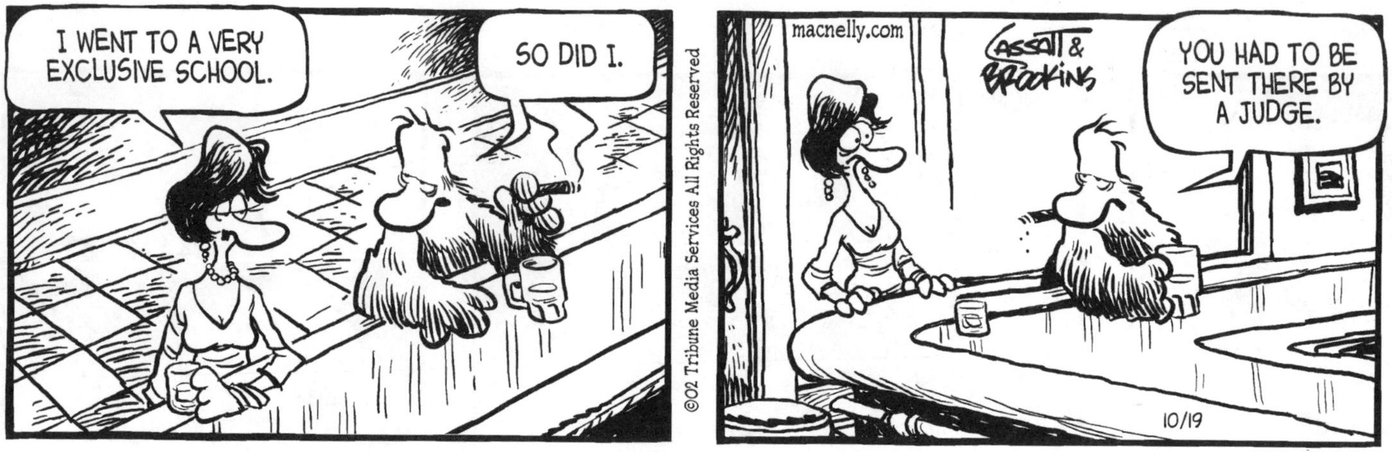
I WENT TO A VERY EXCLUSIVE SCHOOL.
SO DID I.
©02 Tribune Media Services All Rights Reserved
macnelly.com
CASSATT & BROOKINS
YOU HAD TO BE SENT THERE BY A JUDGE.
10/19

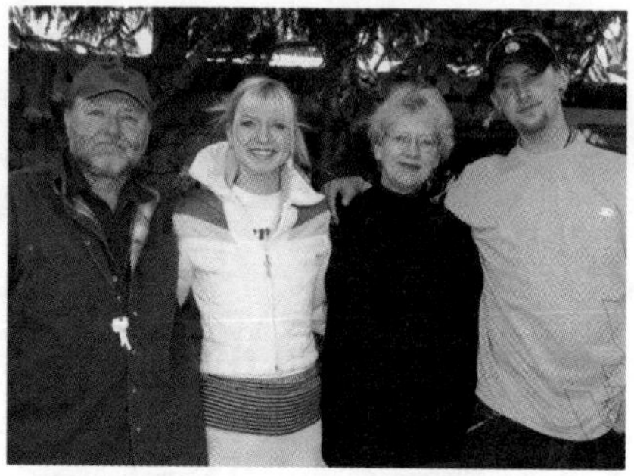

Chris and his family:
Hayley, Lauren, and Alex

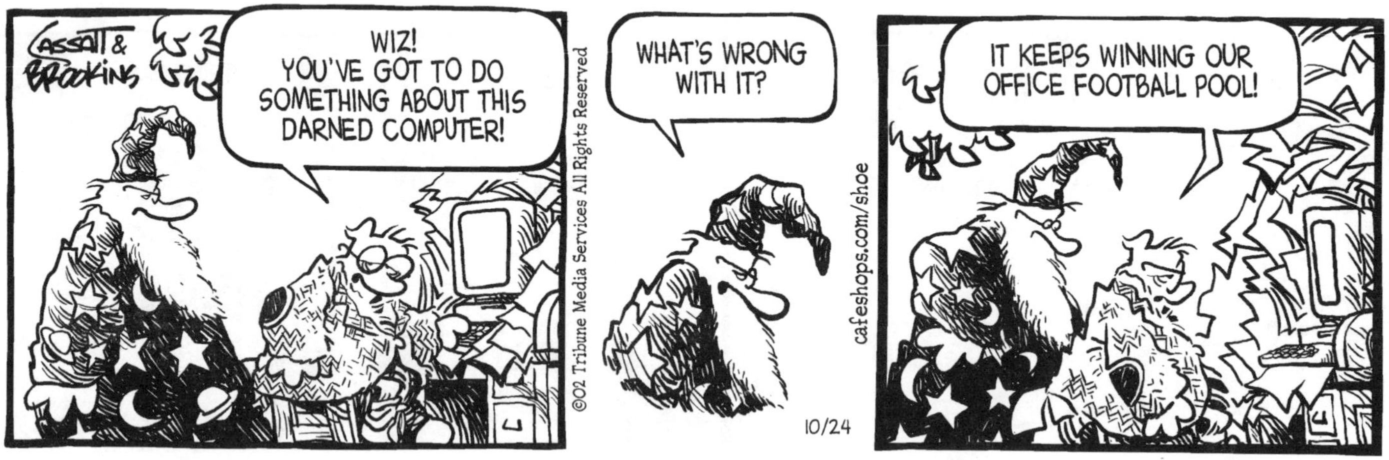
CASSATT & BROOKINS
WIZ!
YOU'VE GOT TO DO SOMETHING ABOUT THIS DARNED COMPUTER!
©02 Tribune Media Services All Rights Reserved
WHAT'S WRONG WITH IT?
cafeshops.com/shoe
10/24
IT KEEPS WINNING OUR OFFICE FOOTBALL POOL!

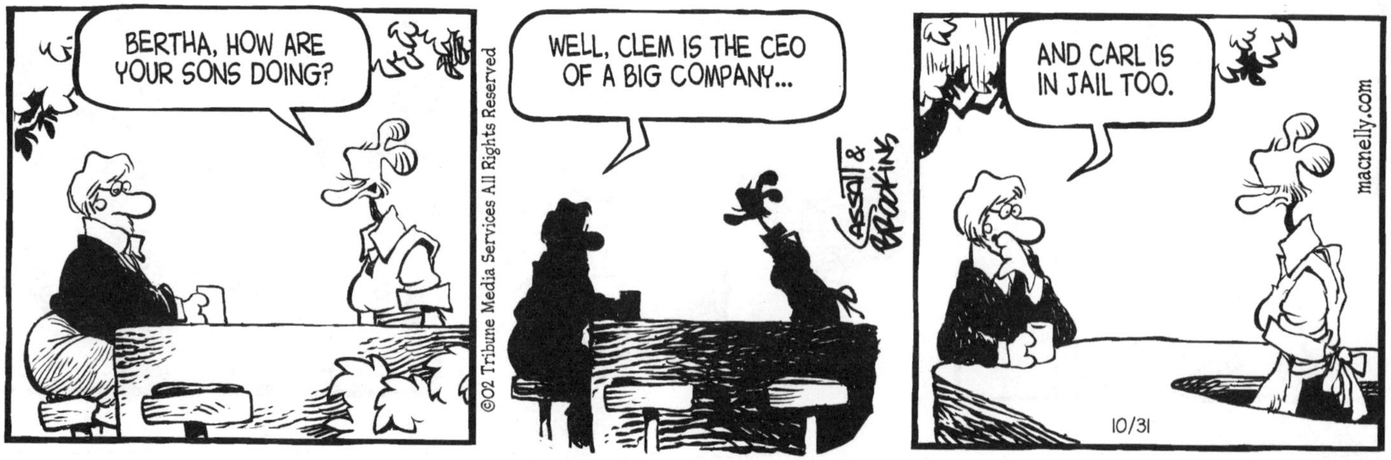
BERTHA, HOW ARE YOUR SONS DOING?
©02 Tribune Media Services All Rights Reserved
WELL, CLEM IS THE CEO OF A BIG COMPANY...
CASSATT & BROOKINS
AND CARL IS IN JAIL TOO.
macnelly.com
10/31

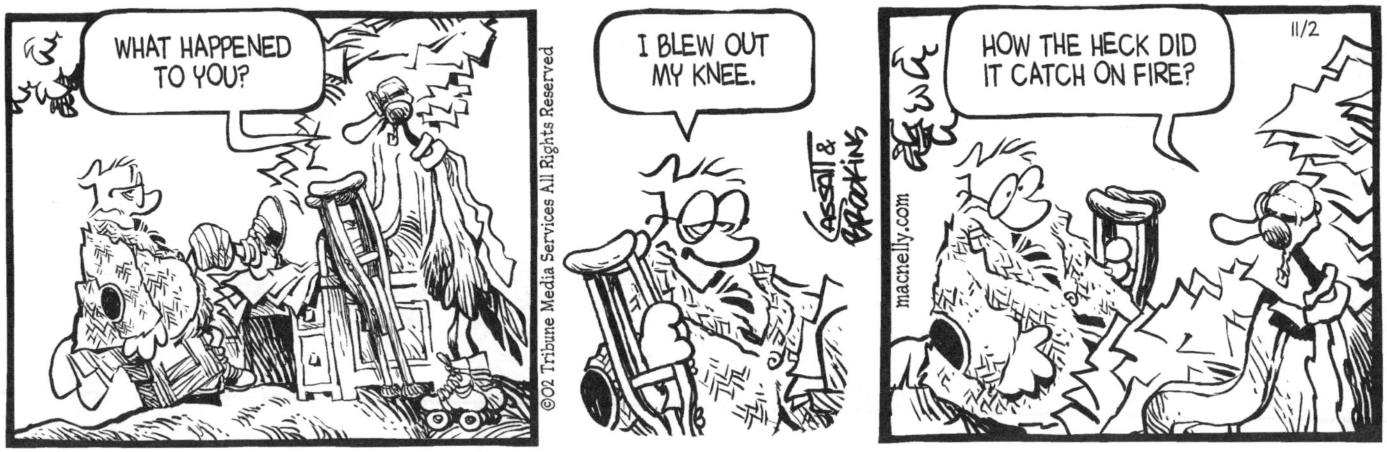
WHAT HAPPENED TO YOU?
©02 Tribune Media Services All Rights Reserved
I BLEW OUT MY KNEE.
CASSATT & BROOKINS
macnelly.com
HOW THE HECK DID IT CATCH ON FIRE?
11/2

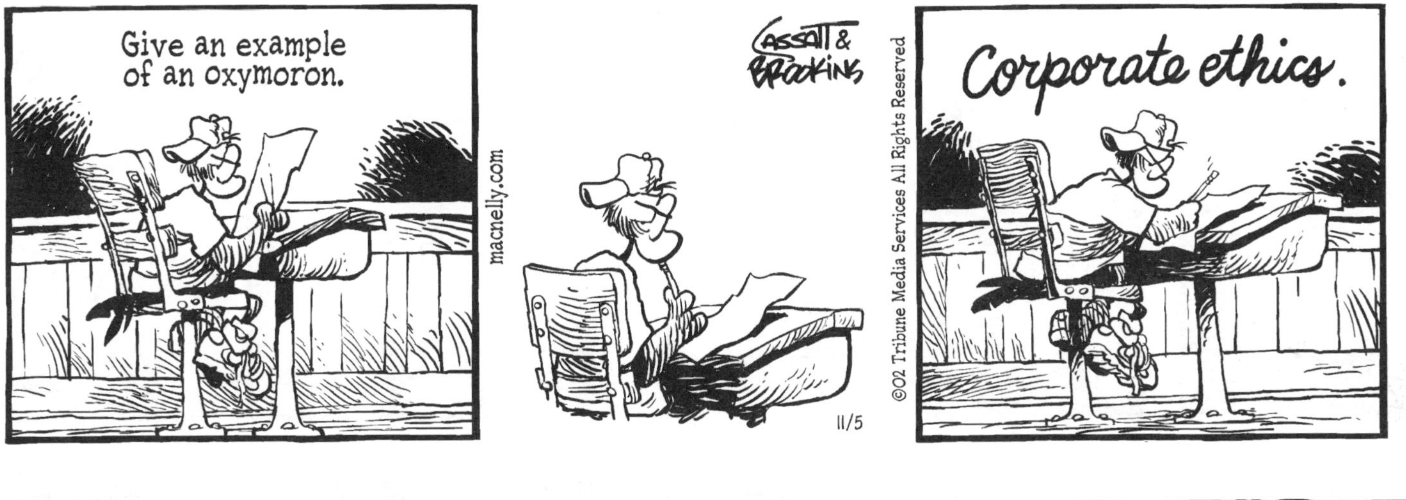
Give an example of an oxymoron.
macnelly.com
11/5
CASSATT & BROOKINS
©02 Tribune Media Services All Rights Reserved
Corporate ethics.

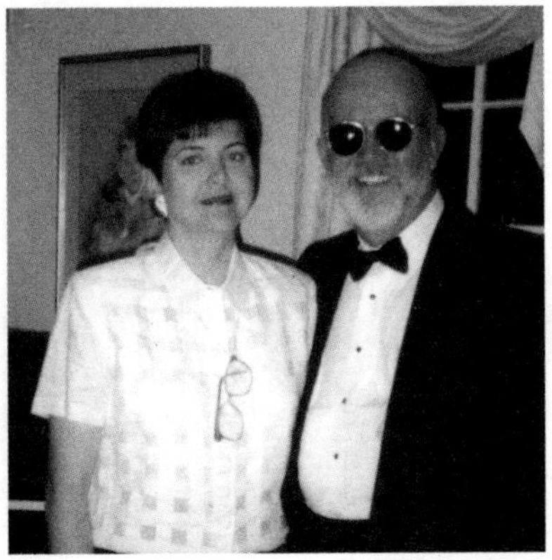

Janet and Gary Brookins

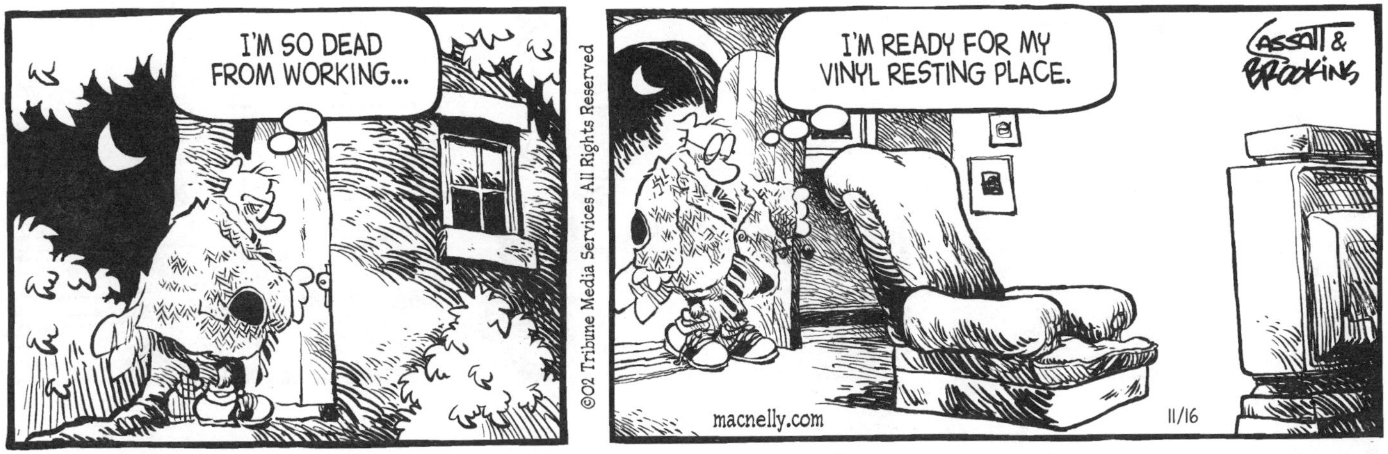
I'M SO DEAD FROM WORKING...
©02 Tribune Media Services All Rights Reserved
I'M READY FOR MY VINYL RESTING PLACE.
CASSATT & BROOKINS
macnelly.com
11/16

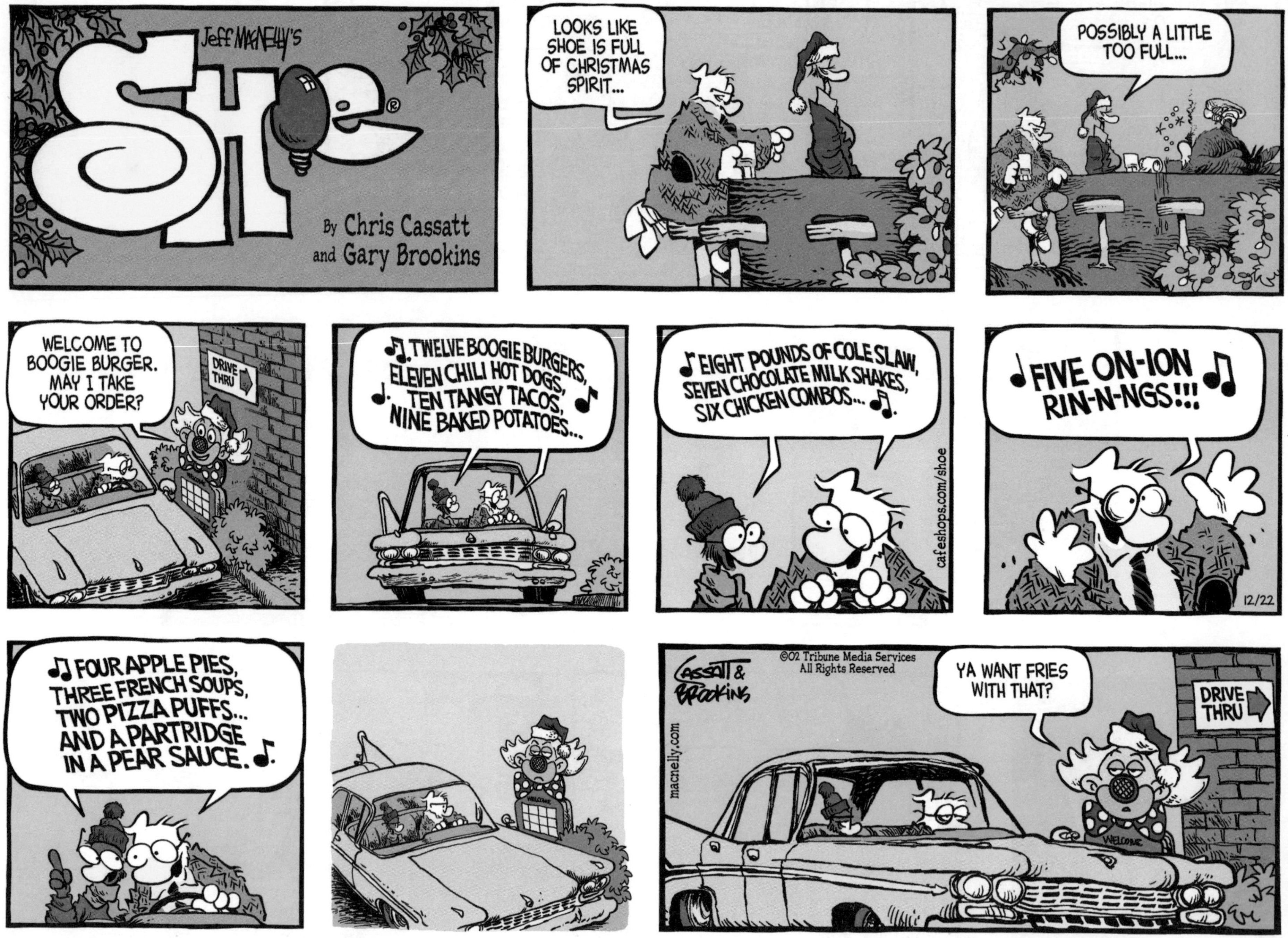

Jeff MacNelly's
Shoe
By Chris Cassatt and Gary Brookins
LOOKS LIKE SHOE IS FULL OF CHRISTMAS SPIRIT...
POSSIBLY A LITTLE TOO FULL...
WELCOME TO BOOGIE BURGER. MAY I TAKE YOUR ORDER?
DRIVE THRU
TWELVE BOOGIE BURGERS, ELEVEN CHILI HOT DOGS, TEN TANGY TACOS, NINE BAKED POTATOES...
EIGHT POUNDS OF COLE SLAW, SEVEN CHOCOLATE MILK SHAKES, SIX CHICKEN COMBOS...
cafeshops.com/shoe
FIVE ON-ION RIN-N-NGS!!!
12/22
FOUR APPLE PIES, THREE FRENCH SOUPS, TWO PIZZA PUFFS... AND A PARTRIDGE IN A PEAR SAUCE.
CASSATT & BROOKINS
©02 Tribune Media Services All Rights Reserved
macnelly.com
YA WANT FRIES WITH THAT?
DRIVE THRU

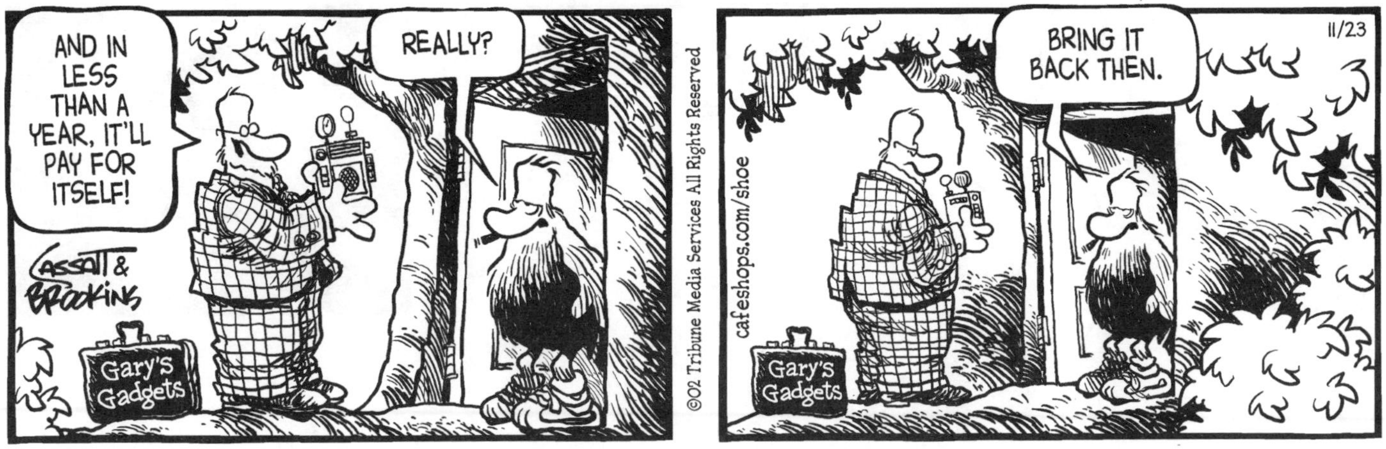
AND IN LESS THAN A YEAR, IT'LL PAY FOR ITSELF!
REALLY?
CASSATT & BROOKINS
Gary's Gadgets
©02 Tribune Media Services All Rights Reserved
cafeshops.com/shoe
BRING IT BACK THEN.
11/23
Gary's Gadgets

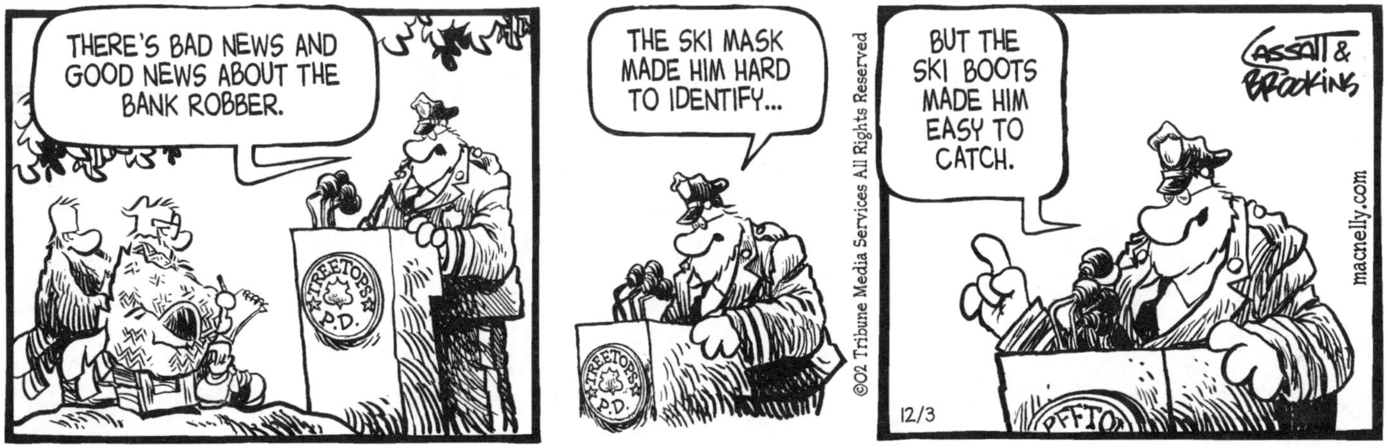
THERE'S BAD NEWS AND GOOD NEWS ABOUT THE BANK ROBBER.
TREETOPS P.D.
THE SKI MASK MADE HIM HARD TO IDENTIFY...
TREETOPS P.D.
©02 Tribune Media Services All Rights Reserved
BUT THE SKI BOOTS MADE HIM EASY TO CATCH.
CASSATT & BROOKINS
macnelly.com
12/3

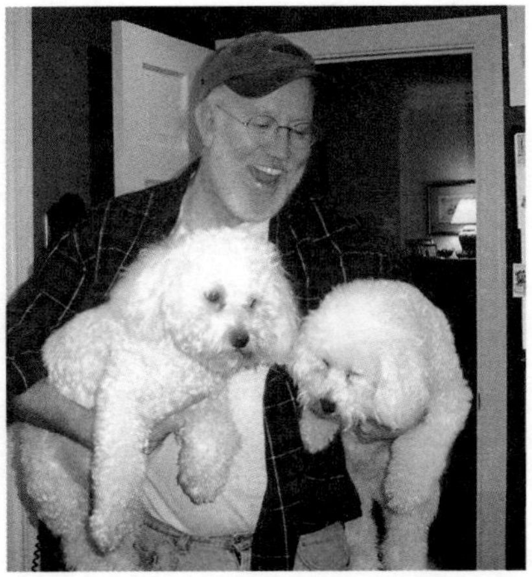

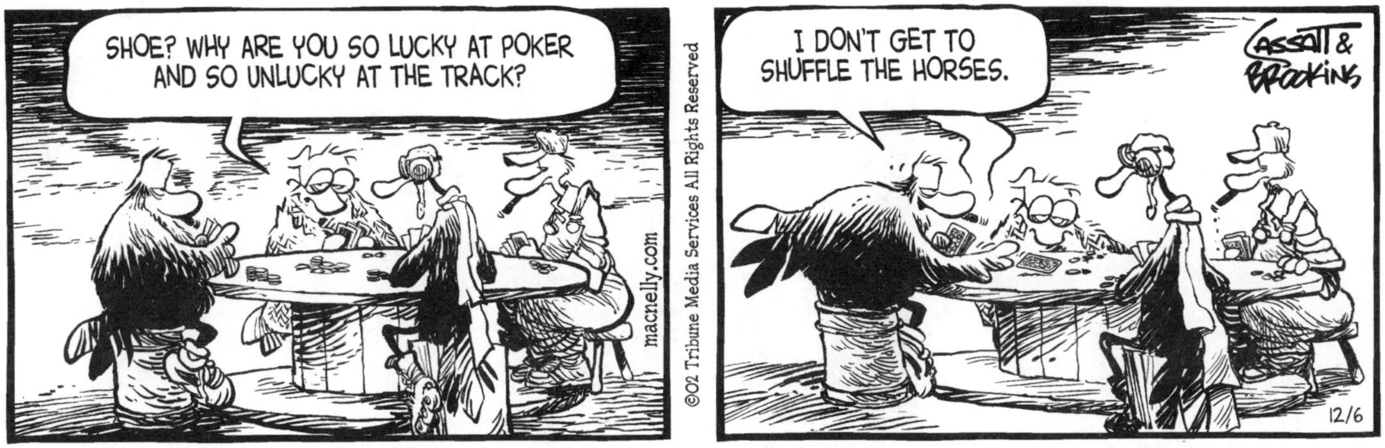
SHOE? WHY ARE YOU SO LUCKY AT POKER AND SO UNLUCKY AT THE TRACK?
macnelly.com
©02 Tribune Media Services All Rights Reserved
I DON'T GET TO SHUFFLE THE HORSES.
CASSATT & BROOKINS
12/6

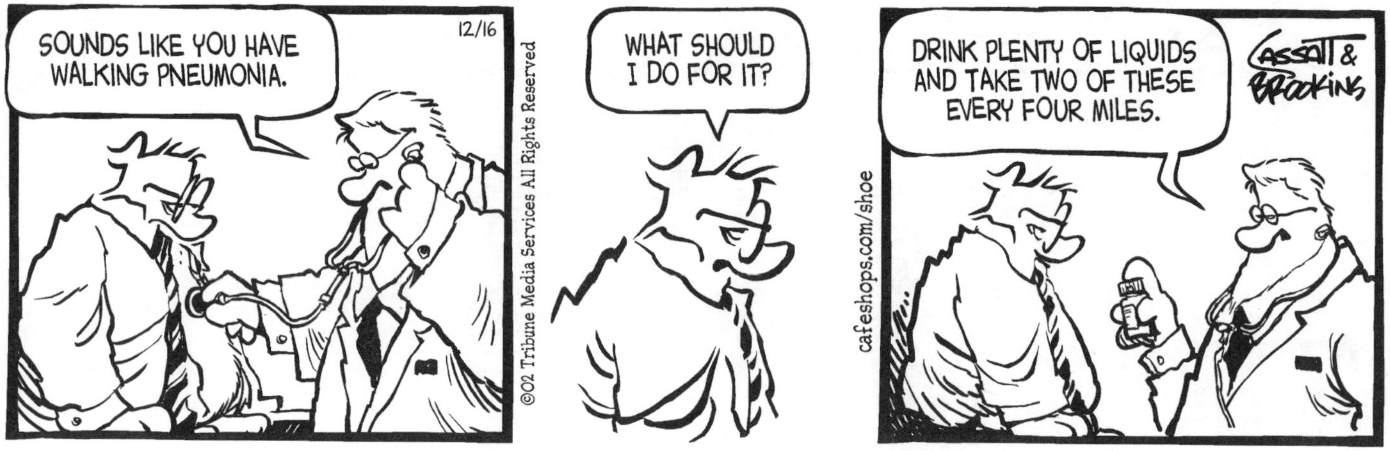
SOUNDS LIKE YOU HAVE WALKING PNEUMONIA.
12/16
©02 Tribune Media Services All Rights Reserved
WHAT SHOULD I DO FOR IT?
cafeshops.com/shoe
DRINK PLENTY OF LIQUIDS AND TAKE TWO OF THESE EVERY FOUR MILES.
CASSATT & BROOKINS

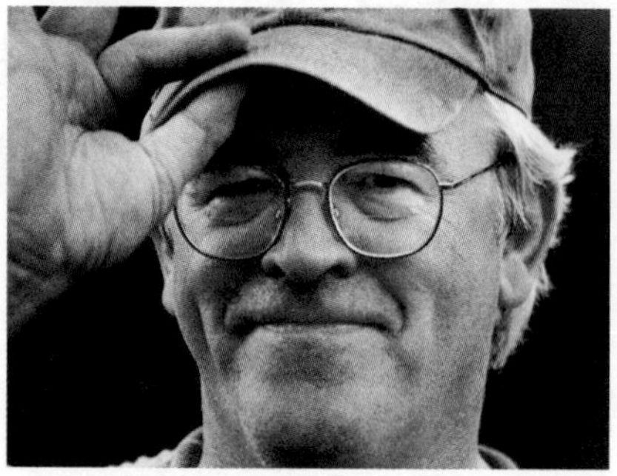

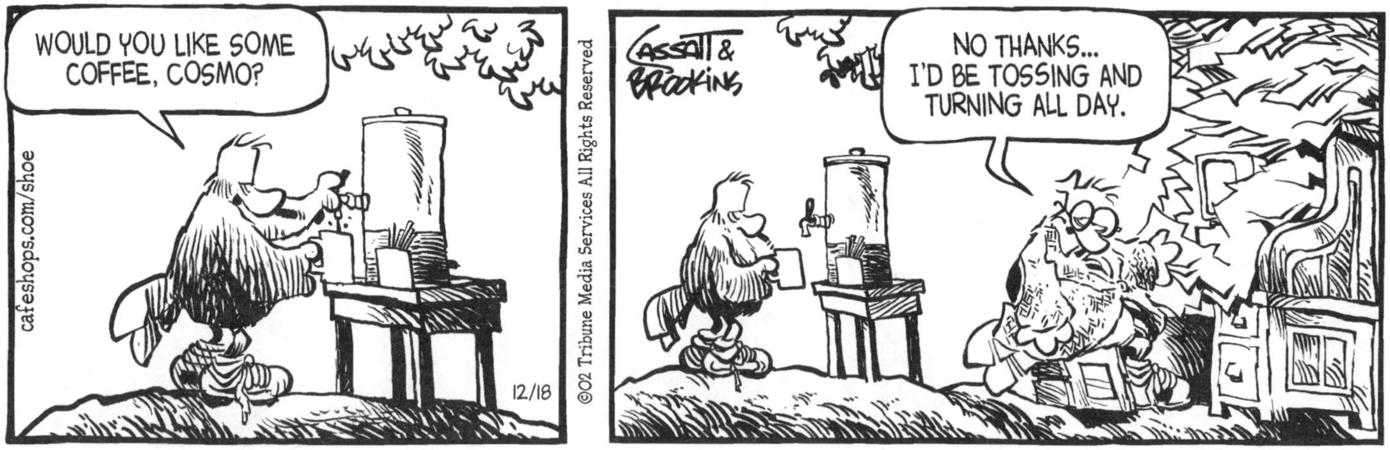
WOULD YOU LIKE SOME COFFEE, COSMO?
cafeshops.com/shoe
12/18
©02 Tribune Media Services All Rights Reserved
CASSATT & BROOKINS
NO THANKS... I'D BE TOSSING AND TURNING ALL DAY.

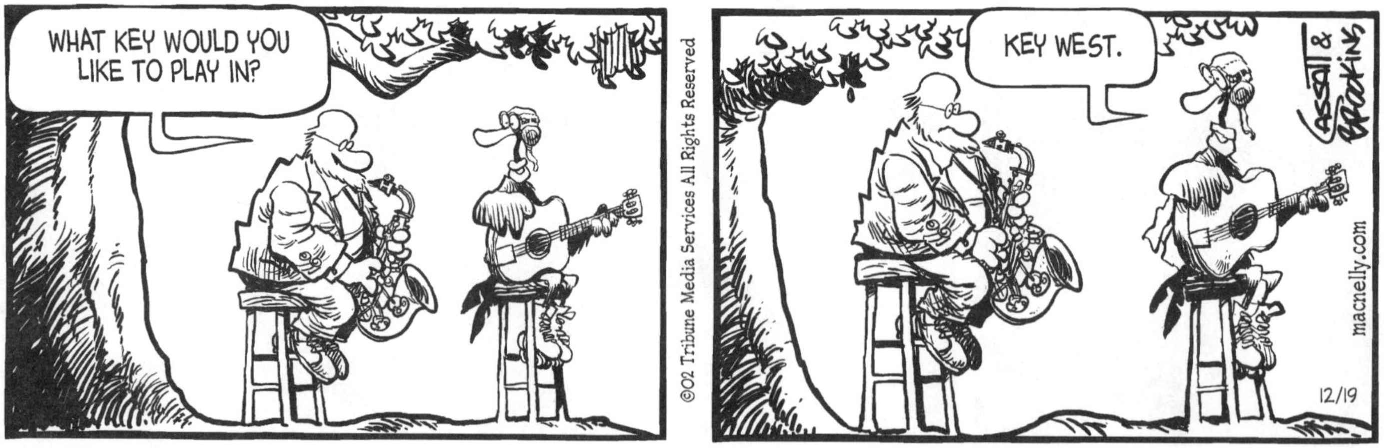
WHAT KEY WOULD YOU LIKE TO PLAY IN?
©02 Tribune Media Services All Rights Reserved
KEY WEST.
CASSATT & BROOKINS
macnelly.com
12/19

Then, now, and who knows when . . .

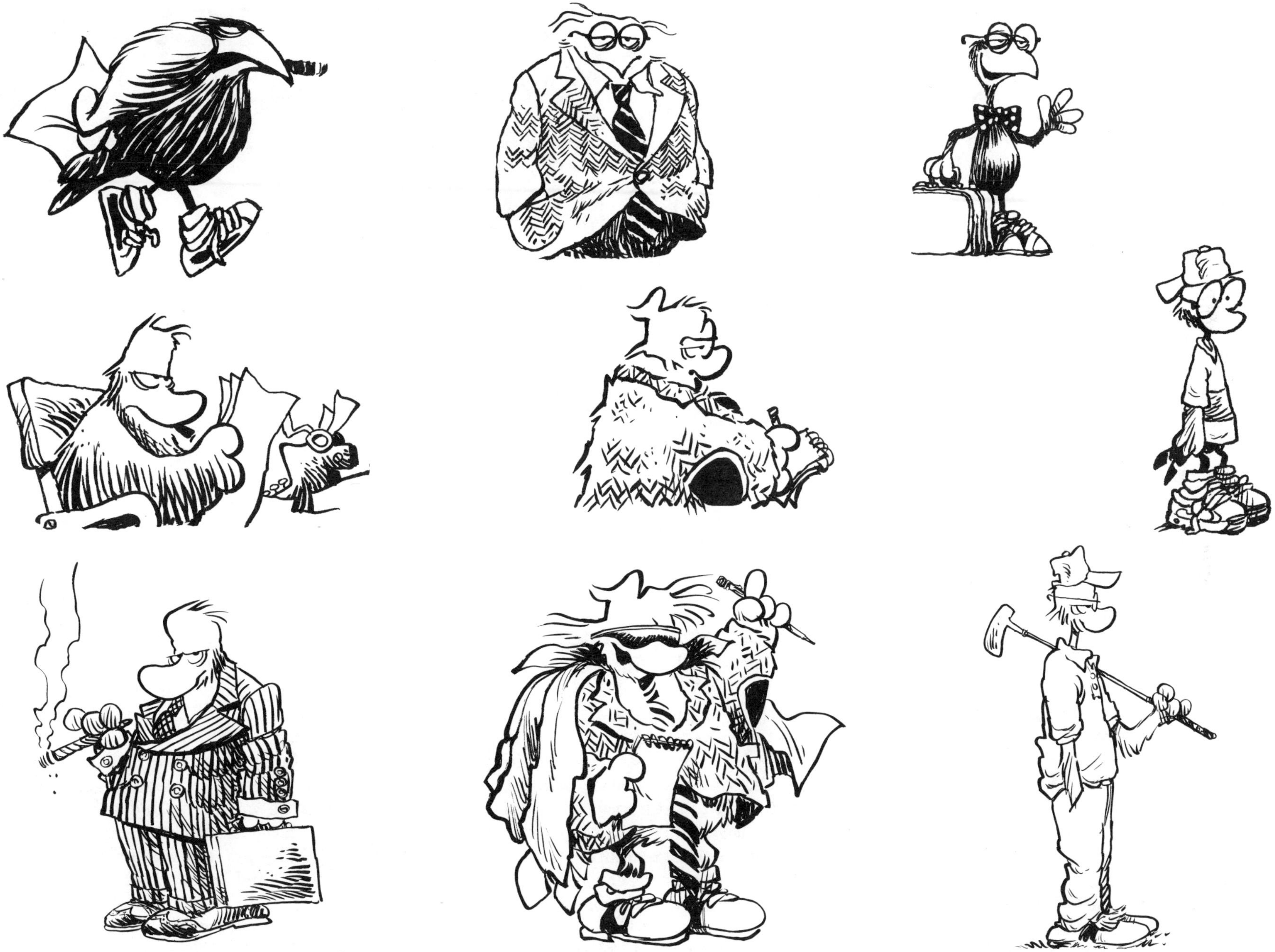

Backward by Mike Peters

Things I Learned from Jeff MacNelly

The first time that I met Jeff MacNelly was in San Antonio at an AAEC Meeting (Association of American Editorial Cartoonists; yes, they actually have conventions). Jeff and I were sitting together on a bus going to some event and he was telling me about how his newspaper was on strike. Because of this, he was helping out in the Engraving Department working on a linotype machine, a machine only Guttenburg or a teamster could run. This would foreshadow his lifelong fascination with machinery. I saw him draw on napkins, armrests, toilet paper, always constant and flowing. I left the convention early and when I got home, my wife asked what was wrong and I said I had just met this young guy who was brilliant and I had better start working harder.

During the Carter Democratic Convention (against Reagan) in New York, we went to Madison Square Garden. Along the way, the traffic was bedlam, people were yelling, there were flowers being put into policemen's lapels, there were street mimes, cab drivers screaming in all languages, people in chicken outfits, secret servicemen, and an Abe Lincoln on stilts. We walked across the street to go into the convention where we sat together taking notes of all the political nuances and machinations. Later that night we went to separate hotel rooms and I proceeded to draw an agonizing cartoon about Carter with his head in a basket and Ted Kennedy holding it or something. The next morning, I saw Jeff's cartoon and it wasn't about anything that went on at the convention. He saw that the real story was what went on outside: the cops, the cab drivers, the Abe Lincoln on stilts, everything we saw, he had

put into that cartoon! I had seen the same things but they passed right by me. Seeing and looking was what made Jeff so great. He trusted what he saw and if it interested him, he knew it would interest us.

You also never saw Jeff work. I don't know if it was intentional subterfuge on his part, but he always looked . . . dormant. He was always sitting drinking a coffee or a beer, watching some basketball game on TV, smoking a cigar or painting. But he was never working. He was like a mother salmon just sitting there for days on end not doing anything and then suddenly, THHHHPPTTT! she spits out 500 eggs. It was mystical. I would get up in the morning and he would have finished seven cartoon strips, five editorial cartoons, and an illustration for a book on golf or something.

I Was Jimmy Olsen to Jeff MacNelly's Superman

Somewhere around 1982, after two Pulitzers and two wives, Jeff dropped out of sight for a while. For some reason, even though he hated the phone to the point of phone-a-phobia, he continued to return my calls. I guess I always made him laugh while all of his other calls were either lawyers or accountants or just plain bad news. Anyway, people somehow found out that I had a connection with the Big Guy. Soon the syndicates started calling for deadlines and the Washington Post would call to find him for

Mike Peters and Jeff MacNelly in Tahiti

various social events. In fact, the Post would contact me in order to contact Jeff to attend a dinner for their syndicated cartoonists during which very famous Beltway folks did very crazy things. For twenty-five years this dinner weekend provided the chance for Jeff and I to enjoy the company of about eight other editorial cartoonists. We would hang out and tell stories and get the chance to meet the Washington elite.

Jeff and I traveled together, did speeches together and became great friends in the process. One of the great trips we took was to Tahiti. As always, I would cook up silly adventures and he would go along, rather embarrassed and bemused. These memories I will cherish always. There never was anyone quite like Jeff MacNelly and there never will be. He was the Best.

Jimmy misses Superman.